Books in the Game Design and Development Series

Introduction to the Game Industry
ISBN: 0-13-168743-3

Fundamentals of Game Design
ISBN: 0-13-168747-6

Fundamentals of Math and Physics for Game Programmers
ISBN: 0-13-168742-5

Introduction to the Game Industry

MICHAEL E. MOORE

with JENNIFER SWARD

Upper Saddle River, New Jersey 07458

Library of Congress Cataloging-in-Publication Data

Moore, Michael E.
   Introduction to the game industry / Michael E. Moore and Jennifer Sward.
     p. cm.
   Includes index.
   ISBN 0-13-168743-3 (alk. paper)
   1. Computer games—Programming. 2. Computer games—Marketing. 3. Electronic games industry.
I. Sward, Jennifer. II. Title.
   QA76.76.C672M622 2006
   794.8'1526—dc22

                        2006028567

Vice President and Publisher: Natalie E. Anderson
Associate VP/Executive Acquisitions Editor, Print:
  Stephanie Wall
Executive Acquisitions Editor, Media: Richard Keaveny
Executive Acquisitions Editor: Chris Katsaropoulos
Product Development Manager: Eileen Bien Calabro
Editorial Supervisor: Brian Hoehl
Editorial Assistants: Rebecca Knauer, Lora Cimiluca
Executive Producer: Lisa Strite
Content Development Manager: Cathi Profitko
Senior Media Project Manager: Steve Gagliostro
Project Manager, Media: Alana Meyers
Director of Marketing: Margaret Waples
Senior Marketing Manager: Jason Sakos

Marketing Assistant: Ann Baranov
Senior Sales Associate: Rebecca Knauer
Managing Editor: Lynda J. Castillo
Production Project Manager: Lynne Breitfeller
Manufacturing Buyer: Chip Poakeart
Production/Editorial Assistant: Sandra K. Bernales
Design Manager: Maria Lange
Art Director/Interior Design/Cover Design: Blair Brown
Cover Illustration/Photo: Gettyimages/Photodisc Blue
Composition: Integra
Project Management: BookMasters, Inc.
Cover Printer: RR Donnelley/Harrisonburg
Printer/Binder: RR Donnelley/Harrisonburg

Credits and acknowledgments borrowed from other sources and reproduced, with permission, in this textbook appear on appropriate page within text.

Pearson Education LTD.
Pearson Education Singapore, Pte. Ltd
Pearson Education, Canada, Ltd
Pearson Education–Japan

Pearson Education Australia PTY, Limited
Pearson Education North Asia Ltd
Pearson Educación de Mexico, S.A. de C.V.
Pearson Education Malaysia, Pte. Ltd

10 9 8 7 6 5 4 3
ISBN 0-13-168743-3

Contents in Brief

PART ONE Introduction to Games 1

1   An Introduction to Games 3
2   The Evolution of Games................................19
3   Game Genres 60
4   Overview of Game Platforms 118

PART TWO Game Development Cycle 157

5   The Production Cycle 159
6   The Production Team....................................186
7   Scheduling and Budgets 224

PART THREE Documenting the Idea 247

8   The Elements of Gameplay 249
9   Committing Ideas to Paper............................277
10   The Game Design Document 309
11   Technical Review 360

PART FOUR Implementing the Vision 391

12   Coding the Game 393
13   Visualizing the Game 428
14   Hearing the Game 468

PART FIVE Elements of Game Design Implementation..........493

15   Interface Design 495
16   Mathematics and Artificial Intelligence in Games 522
17   Storytelling in Games 548
18   Prototyping and Building Playfields.................568
19   Completing the Game.................................603

PART SIX The Business Side of Games 635

20   Marketing the Game...................................637
21   Economics of the Game Industry 662
22   Breaking into the Game Industry 692

Index 717

Contents

Game Design and Development Series Walk-Through x
Preface xii
About the Author..xvi
Acknowledgments xvi
Quality Assurance xvii

PART ONE Introduction to Games 1

Chapter 1 An Introduction to Games...................................3
    What Are Games? 6
    The Growth of the Game Industry 12
    The Game Development Process................................13
    Summary 17 | Test Your Skills 17

Chapter 2 The Evolution of Games 19
    The Beginning of Games 19
    The First Board Games 21
    The Rise of Commercial Board Games.........................26
    The Birth of Electronic Gaming 32
    Summary 53 | Test Your Skills 53

Chapter 3 Game Genres 60
    Game Genres 61
    Action Games 62
    Adventure Games 74
    Role-Playing Games 79
    Strategy Games 84
    Simulation Games 90
    Vehicle Games 93
    Puzzle Games..100
    Sports Games 106
    Summary 112 | Test Your Skills 113

Chapter 4 Overview of Game Platforms 118
    Game Platforms 119
    Evolution of Game Platforms 121
    Personal Computers 129
    Video Consoles...138
    Handheld Game Platforms 146
    Summary 151 | Test Your Skills 151

PART TWO Game Development Cycle 157
Chapter 5 The Production Cycle 159
    Phases of the Production Cycle................................160

Preproduction Phase 164
Production Phase 170

Summary 180 | Test Your Skills 181

Chapter 6 The Production Team 186
Management 187
Design 194
Programming 198
Art 206
Auxiliary Staff 213

Summary 219 | Test Your Skills 219

Chapter 7 Scheduling and Budgets 224
Management Tools 225
Building a Realistic Schedule 232
Budgeting 235

Summary 243 | Test Your Skills 243

PART THREE Documenting the Idea 247

Chapter 8 The Elements of Gameplay 249
The Fun Factor 250
Gameplay Elements 259
Design Goals 263
Dangers in Game Design 268

Summary 271 | Test Your Skills 272

Chapter 9 Committing Ideas to Paper 277
Coming Up with a Game Idea 278
Pitch Paper 283
Game Proposal 289

Summary 304 | Test Your Skills 305

Chapter 10 The Game Design Document 309
Purpose of the Game Design Document 310
The Concept Game Design Document 311
Structure of the Game Design Document 315
Section I: The Introduction 316
Section II: Gameplay Mechanics 322
Section III: Descriptions 344
Appendices 349
The Production Game Design Document 354

Summary 355 | Test Your Skills 355

Chapter 11 Technical Review 360
Technical Design Document 361
Structure of the Technical Design Document 363
Art Design Document 377

Structure of the Art Design Document 378

Summary 384 | Test Your Skills 384

PART FOUR Implementing the Vision 391

Chapter 12 Coding the Game 393
Coding Overview 394
Game Engine Modules 396
Other Programming Tasks 413
Nonprogramming Tasks 418

Summary 422 | Test Your Skills 423

Chapter 13 Visualizing the Game 428
Basics of Computer Graphics 429
2D Art Tasks 433
Art in a 2D Game 436
Character Art 437
Drawing 2D Art to the Screen 443
3D Art Tasks 446
Drawing 3D Art to the Screen 449
Additional Tasks for the Art Team...461

Summary 463 | Test Your Skills 463

Chapter 14 Hearing the Game...468
The Functions of Audio in Games 469
How Game Audio Works 470
Music in Games 475
Sound Effects in Games 479
Voices in Games 481

Summary 488 | Test Your Skills 489

PART FIVE Elements of Game Design Implementation 493

Chapter 15 Interface Design...495
User Interface Elements 496
Designing the Interface 497
Shell Interface...502
In-Game Interface 507
Ease of Use 515

Summary 518 | Test Your Skills 519

Chapter 16 Mathematics and Artificial Intelligence in Games 522
The Mathematics of Games...523
Charts and Tables (The Game Database) 530
Balancing the Game 535
Artificial Intelligence 537

Summary 543 | Test Your Skills 544

Chapter 17 Storytelling in Games 548
    Narrative Structure in Games..549
    Interactive Dialogue 560
    Summary 564 | Test Your Skills 564

Chapter 18 Prototyping and Building Playfields 568
    Prototypes 569
    Designing Playfields 578
    Map and Level Editors 590
    Summary 598 | Test Your Skills 598

Chapter 19 Completing the Game...603
    Balancing the Game 604
    Pushing Toward Completion 608
    Testing the Game 612
    Gold Release and Beyond 617
    Packaging the Game...621
    Conducting a Postmortem 626
    Summary 629 | Test Your Skills 629

PART SIX The Business Side of Games...635

Chapter 20 Marketing the Game..637
    Marketing Department Responsibilites 638
    Preselling a Game..639
    Marketing Campaign...641
    Advertising Games 647
    Other Marketing Tasks 653
    Summary 656 | Test Your Skills 657

Chapter 21 Economics of the Game Industry 662
    Game Industry Economics 101 663
    Mobile and Handheld Games 673
    Financial Drains 681
    Surviving as an Independent Developer 683
    Summary 687 | Test Your Skills 687

Chapter 22 Breaking into the Game Industry 692
    Getting a Testing Position 693
    Getting a Job 700
    Working at a Game Company 708
    Summary 711 | Test Your Skills 711

Index...717

Game Design and Development Series Walk-Through

The Prentice Hall Game Design and Development Series provides you with all the resources you need to set up your own game curriculum, combining theory and practical applications to help prepare students for careers in the game industry. All of the books in this series are filled with real-world examples to help you apply what you learn in the workplace. This walk-through highlights the key elements you'll find in this book, created to help you along the way.

Chapter Objectives. These objectives give you short-term, attainable goals. They mirror the titles of the step-by-step exercises.

Chapter Introduction. Introductory material at the beginning of each chapter explains why these topics are important and how the chapter fits into the overall organization of the book.

Chapter Objectives

After reading this chapter and doing the exercises, you will be able to do the following:

- Understand the differences between how computers and consoles work.
- Explain how computers developed into a major game platform.
- Understand the components of the computer as a game machine.
- Describe how consoles differ from computers for playing games.
- Understand the capabilities of different handheld game platforms.

Introduction

Electronic games are played on many different machines—or *platforms*. Most games today are created to play either on a computer or a console, but there is a growing market for handheld games played on the Game Boy Advance, cell phones, and new devices like the Nintendo DS and Sony PlayStation Portable. Indeed, it seems like whenever new electronic devices come out, they offer the ability to play games in addition to their primary uses.

IN THE TRENCHES: Warm-Up Exercises

Before diving into the session, it's worth the effort to take a few minutes to get everyone's mind working. A number of books offer warm-up exercises for brainstorming sessions and some improvisational theater techniques can be employed as well.

One simple word association exercise requires only a bouncing ball. Everyone in the session stands in a circle. The moderator has the ball at the start and says any word that pops to mind while bouncing the ball gently to another participant. The person receiving the ball

In the Trenches. These show you how to take concepts from the book and apply them on your own and in the workplace.

FYI. These boxes offer additional information on topics that go beyond the scope of the book.

Caution. These flag critical, not-to-be forgotten information that is directly relevant to the surrounding text.

summarizes the core of the
ears at the top of the paper
rsonal ad to sell the concept.
make them want to grab the
print ads, movie posters, or
style of the high concept. In
advertising blurb used by the

th the high concept, there's a
phs. If the idea is good, the
If the reader reads the entire

Caution
Writing Style

Keep to the active voice and use lots of action words when writing a pitch paper. Don't waste time with a lot of adjectives and adverbs. The

FYI · Online 3D Models

A number of Web sites offer 3D models either for sale or for free. Although a game developer might be tempted to use these models, the artists can discover some significant problems with them. They might use too many or too few polygons, the animation rigging might not match the company's game engine requirements, or the textures might have tears or holes. More important, the meshes can need considerable tweaking to make the models look like the characters dreamed up by the designers and artists. By the time the game company finishes making fixes to the model, it can spend as much time as it would have to build the models from scratch.

Test Your Skills

Each chapter ends with exercises designed to reinforce what you've just learned. There are four types of evaluation:

Multiple Choice Questions. Tests your understanding of the text.

Exercises. Brief, guided projects that help you apply individual concepts found in the chapter.

MULTIPLE CHOICE QUESTIONS

1. Play behavior is something that only children exhibit.
   A. True
   B. False

2. Play behavior is often the practice of skills one will need
   A. to survive.
   B. to fit in with society.
   C. to determine who is the best.
   D. to be better at game playing.

3. Which of the following best explains why there are few prehistoric finds of human games?
   A. Most early societies had no time to play.
   B. Adults never considered games important.
   C. The only finds have been images, not actual game pieces.
   D. The games were too simple for us to consider them to be "games."

EXERCISES

Exercise 2.1: Imagining a Game

Write a list of hunting skills that you would consider if you were designing a first-person shooter (FPS) game. (Fans of nonviolent games can consider instead the skills needed to use a camera for this exercise). Write down what the players would have to be able to use or do. How would they need to move? As you create the list, be explicit on whether players can only walk or if they can also run. Can they crouch and hide? While they are crouching, can they fire

DISCUSSION TOPICS

1. Compare the play behavior in the children of your society to that of the adults in your society. How do they differ? How are they similar? How does their daily life (work, school, or other) impact how and what they seem to play?

2. Scientists believe that the royal game of Ur could have been a game of religious significance or political meaning. Of what other kinds of human interaction might this simple board game have been an abstraction? Discuss other possible ways the royal game of Ur could have been used.

3. Discuss whether *Monopoly* should be considered an abstraction game. How is it different from a game such as *Sorry!*?

4. Discuss whether *Super Mario 3* should be considered an abstraction game. How is it different from an FPS?

5. Review the years of game history. What impacts do society, civilization, and industry have on gameplay, innovation, and creation?

6. Why is it important to understand the history of games for this book about video games? Discuss several ancient games that might be relevant in today's market. How would you have to change them to work on a computer?

Discussion Topics. Broader, topical questions that challenge students to think about what they learned in the chapter.

You'll also find code terms in `monospace type`, key terms in ***bold italics,*** and URLs in **boldface.**

Preface

In the past decade, the electronic game industry (computer, video, handheld, and mobile games) has become the 800-pound gorilla dominating the home entertainment industry, not just in the United States, but around the world. Games have grown from a specialist hobby appealing to a limited number of techno-savants to a multi-billion dollar industry with game platforms appearing in homes everywhere around the world. It seems that every electronic device that has a screen and controls has become a potential platform for games. The interest in games and the desire to create them permeates society and is intensely felt by young players who dream of creating their own game worlds in which others can play.

At first glance, the process of creating an electronic game appears to be relatively straightforward. Someone comes up with an idea for a game. The idea is expanded and described in various documents to the point where a production team feels comfortable that they can turn the concept into a finished product. The team then spends time building the assets for the game including the artwork, the playfields, the game data, and the various code modules. The product is subjected to thorough testing throughout production to remove inconsistencies and bugs, and the finished product is packaged and sent out to retailers so gamers can purchase and enjoy it. Of course, the process of creating a game is considerably more complex than this, and it takes a large team at least several years to make a modern computer or video game.

This book gives an overview of game creation and looks at what is involved in creating and marketing an electronic game. Because this book is aimed at a general audience, it focuses on game production primarily from the design and management viewpoint rather than from the technical side. It should give the reader enough information to appreciate what is involved in writing the code and creating the art assets without getting into too much detail. Additionally, the book examines the financial side of the game industry; how much it costs to make games today; and how much money companies can expect to make from sales.

By the end of the book, students should have an understanding of:

■ The history of electronic games and the platforms on which they are played

■ The steps involved in taking a game from initial concept to finished product

■ The functions and tasks of the various team members involved in building a game

■ How management develops game schedules and budgets

■ What is involved in marketing games to the public

■ How to prepare for a job in the game industry

Audience

This book is aimed at anyone who has ever wanted to design a game or work in the game industry. Its focus is the electronic game industry, particularly in the United States, and it provides an overview of the processes involved in turning an idea into a finished product.

Because it is an overview, it does not pretend to cover the many aspects involved in game creation in depth. Each chapter could be fleshed out into a book unto itself (or several).

Students should be familiar with current developments in video, computer, and mobile games, but they do not have to be programmers or 3D artists to understand the material. As an introductory textbook, *Introduction to the Game Industry* is intended to interest students in game production enough to undertake further study and perhaps to learn a programming language or develop the appropriate art skills to land a job in the industry. Of course, even if one does not develop such technical skills, there are still jobs available in the industry, although it is usually more difficult to get a foot in the door. More than anything, to succeed in the game industry, a person must have an overwhelming love of games, an ability to analyze them for their strengths and weaknesses, and a willingness to work long hours to turn dreams into reality.

This book is suitable for both introductory classes about the industry, as well as for technical classes that focus on the specific skill sets needed by the industry. It is also general enough to be informative to anyone who is interested in game design or product management.

Overview of the Book

Introduction to the Game Industry is organized in a way to lead a person through a complete game production cycle. Because this book is aimed at the general public, it does not include any code or mathematical formulas. Some chapters discuss the technical side of game creation but not beyond the scope of someone who has a rudimentary knowledge of computers and video games.

The following is a brief description of each chapter:

Chapter 1, "An Introduction to Games," defines the elements that make up a game and gives a brief rundown of the game production process.

Chapter 2, "The Evolution of Games," looks at the development of games from prehistoric times to the present, concentrating on the electronic game industry.

Chapter 3, "Game Genres," explains how games are classified into groups, or genres, and talks about the play elements common to each genre.

Chapter 4, "Overview of Game Platforms," examines the different devices on which electronic games are played.

Chapter 5, "The Production Cycle," summarizes the procedure involved in designing and developing a game from initial idea to final packaged product.

Chapter 6, "The Production Team," deals with the roles and responsibilities of the various members of a game development team.

Chapter 7, "Scheduling and Budgets," discusses the role of the producer in setting up a schedule for the team and developing a budget for the project.

Chapter 8, "The Elements of Gameplay," examines the actions a player performs in a game that are fun and shows how these elements are used in documenting the design.

Chapter 9, "Committing Ideas to Paper," looks at the first steps of documenting a game design, first in a high-concept pitch paper and then in a fleshed out game proposal.

Chapter 10, "The Game Design Document," presents an in-depth look at the structure and content of the game design document, which provides a blueprint for what the production team will build.

Chapter 11, "Technical Review," talks about how the programming and art teams determine what code and art assets they will need to create during technical review.

Chapter 12, "Coding the Game," gives an overview of the tasks and responsibilities of the programming team and looks at what goes into creating a game engine.

Chapter 13, "Visualizing the Game," looks at the tasks and responsibilities of the art team and explains how 2D and 3D art assets are used by a game engine.

Chapter 14, "Hearing the Game," discusses the audio requirements for a game and explains how the audio team incorporates the music, sound effects, and voiceovers into the finished game.

Chapter 15, "Interface Design," walks the student through the elements that make up a good graphical user interface.

Chapter 16, "Math and Logic and Artificial Intelligence," shows how charts and tables are used in games and looks at some of the approaches to artificial intelligence being used in games today.

Chapter 17, "Storytelling in Games," explores how stories are used in games and discusses interactive storytelling techniques.

Chapter 18, "Prototyping and Building Playfields," describes how prototypes are used to test design assumptions and speed up the creation of levels in a game.

Chapter 19, "Completing the Game," looks at the final steps involved in completing a game, including balancing the product, testing and debugging, and the product manufacturing process.

Chapter 20, "Marketing the Game," delves into the work of the marketing department at a game publisher and discusses how they promote and advertise games.

Chapter 21, "Economics of the Game Industry," is an overview of how the game industry makes and spends money and gives an overview of the role of the independent developer.

Chapter 22, "Breaking into the Game Industry," provides information about the skills needed by the game industry and gives suggestions on how to successfully apply for a job.

Conventions Used in This Book

To help you get the most from the text, we've used a few conventions throughout the book.

Snippets and blocks of code are boxed and numbered, and can be downloaded from the Companion Website (**www.prenhall.com/gamedev**).

New key terms appear in ***bold italics***.

IN THE TRENCHES: About In The Trenches

These show readers how to take concepts from the book and apply them in the workplace.

FYI | *About FYIs*

These boxes offer additional information on topics that go beyond the scope of the book.

Caution

About Cautions

Cautions appear in the margins of the text. They flag critical, not-to-be forgotten information that is directly relevant to the surrounding text.

Instructor and Student Resources

Instructor's Resource Center

The Instructor's Resource Center (IRC) is distributed to instructors only through the book's Companion Website and is an interactive library of assets and links. It includes:

- **Instructor's Manual.** Provides instructional tips, an introduction to each chapter, teaching objectives, teaching suggestions, and answers to end-of-chapter questions and problems.

- **PowerPoint Slide Presentations.** Provides a chapter-by-chapter review of the book content for use in the classroom.

- **Test Bank.** This TestGen-compatible test bank file can be used with Prentice Hall's TestGen software (available as a free download at **www.prenhall.com/ testgen**). TestGen is a test generator that lets you view and easily edit test bank questions, transfer them to tests, and print in a variety of formats suitable to your teaching situation. The program also offers many options for organizing and displaying test banks and tests. A built-in random number and text generator makes it ideal for creating multiple versions of tests that involve calculations and provides more possible test items than test bank questions. Powerful search and sort functions let you easily locate questions and arrange them in the order you prefer.

Companion Website (www.prenhall.com/gamedesdev)

The Companion Website **(www.prenhall.com/gamedesdev)** is a Pearson learning tool that provides students and instructors with online support. Here you will find:

- Online Study Guide, a Web-based interactive quiz designed to provide students with a convenient online mechanism for self-testing their comprehension of the book material.

- Additional Web projects and resources to put into practice the concepts taught in each chapter.

- A downloadable risk management evaluation tool, a gold master release checklist, a budget template, a risk management template, a budget example, and diagrams of production methods.

About the Author

Michael E. Moore has been creating various forms of entertainment since 1979. His first ten years were spent designing and developing board games; the next fourteen were spent producing interactive entertainment products; and the rest have been in teaching. Michael's extensive game design experience has afforded him the opportunity to design all types of content, from role-playing, to adventure, to mass market, to edutainment. Mr. Moore has worked for such companies as Simulations Publications, Inc., TSR Hobbies, Victory Games, Activision/Infocom, The 3DO Company, Ybarra Productions, and several start-up companies. He has held positions in product management, design, and writing. He was managing editor of three magazines at SPI for several years. Michael also has expertise in creative and technical writing. He has written numerous game manuals, creative briefs, and "in game" stories. For the last three years, he has been teaching game design and product management at DigiPen Institute of Technology in Redmond, Washington.

Acknowledgments

First and foremost, I would like to thank Jen Sward who generated the educational materials at the end of each chapter and also collaborated in editing the book. Her suggestions and contributions have been invaluable, and she helped me in areas where my own knowledge was sometimes thin. She has been a delight to work with and, as another instructor at DigiPen Institute of Technology, a ready resource I could tap at a moment's notice.

I would also like to thank Ben Ellinger and Paul Kohler for their extensive contributions to the book. Ben supplied indispensable technical advise about programming while Paul provided financial and marketing insights about the current state of the industry.

My thanks go to the management, faculty, and administrative staff at DigiPen Institute of Technology. They not only offered me constant support during the long writing process but also answered my many questions and pointed me to useful resources.

I deeply appreciate the expert development editing performed by Dave Fender who helped me improve my writing style and forced me to explain some technical issues more clearly.

On a personal note, I would like to thank Carolyn Lawrence for her patience and for providing me with an ear to bend during my rants and ravings. Likewise, I thank everyone in my family for offering constant encouragement and support. Finally, I would like to thank the many friends I've made in the game industry over the years. I have indeed been blessed because most of my adult life has been spent making games. I can think of nothing more enjoyable than gaming one's way through life.

Quality Assurance

We would like to thank our Quality Assurance team for their attention to detail and their efforts to make sure we got it right.

Technical Editors

Dan Leahy
Freelance Gaming Journalist

Bill Louden
Austin Community College

Reviewers

C. Dep-Wah Davis
Tomball College

Bruce W. Johnston
University of Wisconsin-Stout

Robert J. Smolenski
Delaware County Community College

Part | One

Introduction to Games

Games have existed in human societies since prehistory, and every modern culture plays games in one form or another. Most games throughout history were played either in specially created sports arenas (the first Olympics, chariot races, jousts, and so on) or on playing boards using playing pieces and dice. As the electronic age matured during the twentieth century, a new platform for games came into being. The development of the microprocessor has led to a proliferation of electronic devices upon which games are played today.

To understand the success of electronic games, it is important to know where they came from and how their technology developed. Games have always pushed the envelope of technology. One could argue that without games, 3D graphics and artificial intelligence would never have progressed as fast as they did. Games now look and sound realistic, and computer-controlled enemies behave almost as intelligently as human opponents. Games also have diversified into many types, or genres, that cater to the widely different interests of players. These genres offer many different challenges to players, allowing them to pick and choose which experiences they wish to recreate on a computer, video console, or handheld device.

Where playing a game once meant bringing a few friends together to throw dice and move tokens around a board, it can now mean joining friends from around the world in cyberspace and pretending to be space marines in a struggle to the death against realistic looking and sounding alien hordes. Games offer limitless horizons for the imagination. And they're fun!

- **Chapter 1:** An Introduction to Games
- **Chapter 2:** The Evolution of Games
- **Chapter 3:** Game Genres
- **Chapter 4:** Overview of Game Platforms

Chapter | 1

An Introduction to Games

Chapter Objectives

After reading this chapter and doing the exercises, you will be able to do the following:

- List the features that are common to all games.
- Explain why electronic games are so appealing.
- Explain why the game industry has grown in popularity.
- Describe the essential steps required to develop a game.

Introduction

In the past decade, the electronic game industry has grown from a hobby primarily for young males into a multibillion dollar industry that attracts players of all ages and both sexes. The growth of the industry has mirrored the explosive growth of computers, as electronic games both depend on and push the limits of computer technology. In the earliest days, computer games were relatively simple and were either text-based or used simple ASCII characters to represent characters and locations (see Figure 1.1). As game platforms grew in processing power and storage ability, the graphics improved and allowed animated sprites to move like cartoon characters against two-dimensional backgrounds (see Figure 1.2). Further advances have allowed for more realistic representations of highly detailed characters adventuring in three-dimensional spaces (see Figure 1.3).

The process of creating games has grown in complexity along with the technology. Where once it took a small group only months to complete a game, it now takes a large team of highly skilled designers, artists, and programmers several years to develop a major computer or console game from first concept to shipped product. The reason for the extra time and manpower is simple: We can now make larger and more complex games because faster computers and

FIGURE 1.1 A screenshot from *Castle Adventure* (1984), created by Kevin Bales. *Castle Adventure* was a text-based game that used ASCII character to create the castle map and roving creatures.

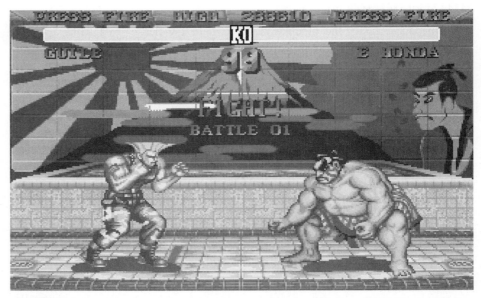

FIGURE 1.2 In the DOS version of Capcom's *Street Fighter II* (1991) shown here, the figures are 2D sprites that animate against a flat background.

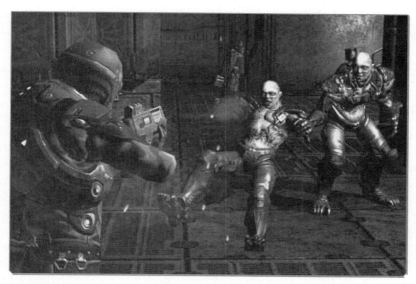

FIGURE 1.3 The 3D graphics of id Software's *Quake 4* (published by Activision in 2005) make the characters and game environments look alive and realistic compared to the flat 2D artwork in older games.

console machines with large amounts of memory and storage space enable the game engine to manipulate more data. These new machines can do many more things than the older machines they replaced, including:

- Manipulating 3D graphics

- Carrying out interesting artificial intelligence routines

- Processing complex mathematical formulas

- Streaming audio directly from storage

- Transmitting information over networks to other players around the world

The newest generation of games and machines allows users to play games alone or with friends online, and the games themselves continue to become more visually appealing and operationally sophisticated. But making these larger, more complex games obviously takes more time.

All signs indicate that games will continue to grow in popularity. A new generation of more powerful console machines is arriving, and the games for these machines will continue to look better and to offer new challenges. Meanwhile, other markets are developing: mobile games for cell phones and personal digital assistants (PDAs), online games played over the Internet, and handheld games played on the Game Boy Advance, the Sony PlayStation Portable

(PSP), the Nintendo DS, and other devices. Barring any catastrophes, the game industry will likely continue to expand and mature for the foreseeable future.

What Are Games?

Games are a pastime, something people do to amuse themselves when they have spare time. From the earliest games developed by prehistoric cultures to the present, playing games has always been based on the amount of spare time a person or group has. Mass-produced games came into their own in the late nineteenth and early twentieth centuries because the growing middle class in the United States and western Europe had more time and money to spend on nonessentials. Since World War II, the rise of television as a popular form of home entertainment has helped relegate board games mostly to youngsters. In the second half of the twentieth century, games took on a new form thanks to the appearance of computers that eventually moved from offices into homes. Because of the continuing advances in computer technology, electronic games have become one of the dominant forms of entertainment across the globe.

Features Common to All Games

The basic play elements of games have not changed significantly since the first ones were created sometime in prehistory. All games, regardless of the medium, share four basic features:

- First and foremost, a game has to be fun. If it's not, players will stop playing and move on to something else. Of course, what is fun for one person might not be fun for another. Some people think solving crossword puzzles is fun because they challenge the mind, whereas others think such games are frustrating and hard work. Some think piloting a plane in a flight simulation is fun, whereas others find it to be dull routine. Some think running around an area shooting everything in sight in a first-person shooter is fun, whereas others find such games simply too violent to enjoy. Some people think competing in a marathon is fun even though it is very hard work, and others can't imagine how something that causes so much pain could be fun. People consider many activities fun, and these all can become the topic of a game.

- Second, games offer a challenge to the player. The challenge can be physical, mental, or both. The challenge, however, is offered in a safe environment where no serious harm can normally occur to the loser. A physical challenge might test a person's strength (an arm wrestling contest), endurance (a triathlon), or dexterity (Konami's *Dance Dance Revolution*), whereas a mental challenge might test a person's spatial perception (jigsaw puzzle), memory (*Jeopardy!*), or counting ability and logic (bridge). A physical and mental challenge tests a person's ability to think as well as his physical prowess (for example, playing quarterback on a football team). If a game presents no challenge to a player, she will quickly tire of it and move on to something new because it is too easy to beat.

FYI   *The Challenge of Choice*

One hallmark of a challenge is that the person involved is continually faced with choices as to what to do next. Whether deciding to push oneself hard at the last possible moment to cross the finish line first or electing to use a knight to capture a bishop that threatens one's king, a player must choose between a number of options. Sid Meiers, one of the electronic game industry's best known designers, who created *Pirates*, *Railroad Tycoon,* and *Civilization* among others, expressed this idea as, "A game is a series of interesting choices."

- Third, games have rules and structure. The **rules** determine what the player must do to compete, and the **structure** determines the order in which actions take place. A game's rules and structure allow all players to compete equally at the start. The better (or luckier) players survive until the near the end, when the best one emerges. Most games have a defined goal that the player strives to achieve to finish the game. The goal often involves eliminating or outdoing opponents to determine a winner, such as being the last player with money in *Monopoly* or the first to cross the finish line in a marathon. A few games, such as *Tetris* and some arcade games, are more open ended and allow the player to continue the game until he is ultimately defeated. In such cases, the winner is considered the person who has the highest score or who lasts the longest. Cheating, or breaking the rules, is not allowed, and anyone who does so is usually kicked out of the game.

- Fourth, games are an abstraction. Games are not reality; they are an abstraction of reality. They are removed several degrees from reality. Some games are highly abstracted from reality; for example, card games that play with and manipulate numbers. Other games are not as greatly abstracted, although the part of the reality on which they are based is not intuitively obvious. Parcheesi, for example, is based on horse racing, and chess is an abstraction of war. Most games seem to reflect a part of reality, such as Milton Bradley's *Clue*, which imitates some but certainly not all of the steps involved in solving a crime. Simulation games come closest to holding a mirror up to reality, but they too are abstracted from reality because they have to leave out a considerable amount of detail. Players never confuse the fact that they are simply pretending and not actually living out a game situation.

Several other features are shared by many games but are not necessarily part of all games:

- Most games are interactive. A few simple puzzle games such as 20 questions and crossword puzzles involve little interaction between the player and the game world, but in most other games, the players' decisions significantly change the situation in the game world, and in some cases, the game world reacts to the players' actions. In a soccer game, if one player decides to pass the ball to a teammate, her action changes how all the rest of the players will act. In a game of *Risk*, one player might decide to use all his massed armies to take out the remaining players as he invades country after country, changing the world balance and possibly leading to world conquest. In both of these cases, the player's actions change the game world, but there is little reaction from that world itself. Electronic games, however, are highly interactive, and every gameplay action by the player changes how the game world looks and how it reacts to the player's actions. One gauge of a game's success (at least in games played solitaire) is how well the artificial intelligence (AI) reacts to the player's actions. If the AI is well designed, the player feels that she is actually playing another person who is reacting intelligently to each action she takes.

- Many games include a randomizing factor that changes the playing of the game. The randomizing factor can be a number generated by dice or, in electronic games, an algorithm or changes in the starting conditions of the game, such as shuffling a deck to change the order in which players receive their starting cards. Randomization not only allows a game to have new starting conditions to encourage replayability, but it also is one method used to help balance a game. When a game's starting conditions randomly change each time it is played, the better players make themselves known by their choices and reactions during play. Other games do not rely on randomization but instead depend on the player's innate mental or physical abilities; for example, a trivia game or crossword puzzle relies on a player's memory, whereas a 100-meter dash relies solely upon a contestant's physical strength and stamina.

> **FYI** | *Randomization and Balance*
>
> Randomization is discussed in some length in Chapter 16, "Mathematics and Artificial Intelligence in Games." Balancing a game is discussed in Chapter 19, "Completing the Game."

The Appeal of Electronic Games

If all games share the same basic features, what is it about computer games that makes them so popular? Though originally primitive in their ability to display graphics and offer much depth of play, the early electronic games—*Pong, Space Invaders, Centipede*, and others—became huge hits in arcades and later entered homes on the first video game consoles. Over time, the improvements in technology have led to better graphics and sound, more rigorous AI routines that make enemies behave almost intelligently, and an enhanced network capability that lets players around the world join in the same game without leaving the comfort of their own homes. In short, the games look better and behave more realistically than ever.

> **FYI** | *The Early Days of Electronic Games*
>
> A brief chronicle of games from their first appearance in prehistory to the present generation of computer and console games appears in Chapter 2, "The Evolution of Games." Likewise, a summary of the developments in game platforms is given in Chapter 4, "Overview of Game Platforms."

Because the monitors of the game platforms present a blank slate upon which anything might be shown, electronic game creators have capitalized on the ability of these machines to play any kind of game. Almost all games that exist in the physical world have been remade into some form of electronic game. Action-arcade games dominated the first game machines, but eventually other types of games (or game *genres*) appeared that offered new kinds of gameplay and, therefore, different challenges to players. Popular board/paper genres such as military simulations (war games) and role-playing games quickly made the transition into electronic versions, whereas other games such as racing and adventure games were born out of the unique powers and abilities of the new medium. Today, many different genres of games offer players many forms of wish fulfillment.

FYI *Game Genres*

A discussion of game genres appears in Chapter 3, "Game Genres."

In addition, electronic games have incorporated elements found in other media to enhance the basic gameplay. Traditional board games might have a theme, such as real estate in Parker Brothers' *Monopoly* or solving a crime in *Clue*, but there is no real narrative or story in these games. The first paper games to incorporate stories were role-playing games, starting with TSR Hobbies' *Dungeons & Dragons (D&D)*, where one player acting as storyteller leads the others through fantastic adventure stories. Early electronic games soon began mimicking these types of narrative games. Both adventure and role-playing games rely heavily on stories. They were relatively basic at first but have grown in complexity and depth as the graphics improved and the media for storing the game data grew larger.

Although stories in other forms of entertainment such as books and movies tend to be *linear* (the story is told in a fixed narrative structure that never changes from the author's original creation), stories in games are often *nonlinear*; that is, the players make decisions about what to do next or where to go, which in turn determine how events in the narrative will unfold, thus making each play-through different. Games with stories might include pregenerated animated sequences similar to short movies to give exposition or reveal a character's motives, but these narrative snippets are secondary to the player's actions and decisions that make up the gameplay.

FYI *Storytelling in Games*

Because games are interactive, the method by which stories are told in games is different from other linear media like movies, theater, and television. The use of stories in games is discussed in more detail in Chapter 17, "Storytelling in Games."

Games have also drawn upon advances in communication to enhance gameplay. The most obvious example is the Internet, which has become a prime conduit for playing games with other people from all over the world. Additionally, advances in mobile-phone technology now mean that the telephone has become a new platform on which to play games, either alone (or solitaire) or with other players. Although most electronic games use a form of artificial intelligence to control the actions of entities not directly controlled by the player (called nonplayer characters, or NPCs), nothing is as challenging as playing another human being who can do the unexpected and present challenges a computer-controlled opponent generally can't.

Electronic games offer players new ways to interact with and expand upon the game world. Traditional board games are usually not extensible, meaning that it is difficult to add new pieces, rules, or embellishments to the game. On the other hand, electronic games can be extended in a number of ways. The games themselves, if they sell well and prove popular, can be extended with sequels (complete games in themselves) and add-ons (software whose use requires the player to own the original product). The game platforms themselves can also be extended to provide new ways to play; gamers can purchase steering wheels to drive cars in racing games, joysticks that enhance the feeling of flying an airplane, and mats with sensors that detect a player's dance steps.

Games provide a diversity of experiences for players as well as an "in-your-face" immediacy that demands attentive concentration by players. This immediacy of experience in addition to the ability to interact in many ways with the game world gives players a sense of empowerment not found in other forms of entertainment. It's no wonder that games have become such a dominant form of entertainment in the early twenty-first century, earning billions of dollars each year worldwide and providing a growing market for employment.

Of course, this diversity has also made games the target of concerned parent groups and politicians who worry that the violence in many action games can negatively affect young players. Games do draw players into the world being depicted, and while surviving in a violent world may be cathartic for most players, it might prove overwhelming to younger players. A number of games published each year do depict violent and antisocial acts (especially first-person shooters); however, the majority of games (including games for handheld and mobile devices as well as Internet games) are not overtly violent and can actually teach players valuable lessons about handling resources, planning ahead, and experimenting with various combinations or tactics to see which ones work best without being as preachy or pedantic as schoolbooks.

FYI Game Rating System

The Electronics Software Ratings Board (or ESRB, at **www.esrb.org**) has set up a rating system to help parents determine the target ages for different games and thus help them determine which ones their children should play (and which ones they should not).

The Growth of the Game Industry

The first electronic games, though simple by today's standards, were at the cutting edge of technology in their day. That continues to be a hallmark of electronic games today; the game shows off the technology of the hardware, which in turn pushes the game and technology farther. Game development is now closely tied with the industry of hardware development, and the growth or decline of either one will certainly affect the other.

The electronic game industry is currently dominated by video consoles and computer games, although there are other devices on which such games are played (for example, handheld devices such as the Nintendo Game Boy Advance and cell phones). As the industry has matured, a definite split has emerged between whether computers or game consoles are the better platform for playing games. Computers offer customers the ability to play games in addition to performing other, more important functions such as paying taxes, managing household finances, writing letters, and going onto the Internet to shop or get information. Moreover, the technology continues to advance with better graphics cards—and now a new generation of physics cards—appearing. However, the continued improvements in technology have also harmed computer games because players don't want to spend a thousand dollars or more to upgrade their systems every couple of years just to keep up with the current state of games when the other software they use changes less radically. Thus, the audience for computer games has dwindled while the console game audience has exploded. This does not mean that games will no longer be created for computers, but the market has shrunk as video consoles increase in popularity.

Video consoles have gained dominance over computers for several reasons. Currently, they are cheaper than computers for the consumer; they require much less technical expertise to set up; and their technology changes more slowly, so there is no need to continually upgrade them with new video cards or memory chips. The console systems do change, of course, and so far, each new generation has offered much better graphics and gameplay than their predecessors. Now that they offer the capability to play games online, the last significant reason to use a computer instead of a console has been surmounted. On the other hand, the price of the new generation of video consoles has reached the price of low-end computer systems. In the not-too-distant future, the computer and video console might merge into one machine.

Ease of use also makes video consoles so popular. They are relatively simple to hook up to your home entertainment system, so you can begin playing games within a few minutes of unpacking the machine. Moreover, you only have to pop a game into the console to play it—unlike some computer games that require you to make significant changes to your system before they will play. Video game consoles are often set up in the main family room, which allows the whole family to join in the fun, whereas most computers are set up in special areas away from the family to keep them from being damaged. As high-definition televisions and home entertainment systems enter more homes, the graphics of new video games will seem even more vivid and the audio sound more realistic.

The market for handheld and mobile games is expanding as well. The best known series of handheld devices has been produced by Nintendo, with their Game Boys and more recently the Nintendo DS. However, Sony is challenging Nintendo's dominance with its PlayStation Portable (PSP), and other companies are competing, such as Nokia with their N-Gage, although they have been less successful to date. The cell phone platform is also gaining importance in gaming as the devices become more powerful and offer better graphics. Though the revenue from such games remains small compared to video games (see Chapter 21, "Economics of the Game Industry," for more details), their market share continues to grow as the technology used to create them advances. The newest generation of handheld devices offers 3D graphics and better sound, so the games designed for them can be as visually and aurally advanced as computer or video games.

As chronicled in Chapter 2, "The Evolution of Games," the electronic game industry has been through several cycles of growth and decline. One such cycle began in the 1960s and ended in the "crash" of 1983. We're currently in the second such growth cycle; it's difficult to accurately predict when the next peak or crash might occur.

It will be interesting to see whether the new generation of video consoles (Xbox 360, PlayStation 3, and Nintendo Wii.) will be perceived as offering the same kind of major advances in technology as earlier systems did or if they will be viewed merely as enhanced versions of the previous generation. The structure of the industry's finances makes it difficult to come out with original game ideas; instead of trying to develop new concepts, publishers put out sequels. But gamers eventually get tired of the sameness and want to do something new. If the new generation of consoles does not offer novelty, customers might migrate to a different form of entertainment. There is always the possibility that the game industry might suffer another downturn as happened in 1983.

The Game Development Process

The basic process of creating an electronic game remains the same even though the technology used to make the game platforms has changed considerably. First, someone comes up with an idea for the game; then someone creates the assets for the game (the code, art, dialogue, music, and other elements); and finally, the assembled product is debugged until it is ready to ship. Of course, the size and the scope of games have changed considerably as new technologies have become available, and the production team that builds the game has grown considerably in size, with team members taking on many different tasks. In the early days of electronic games, one person could create a game in a few months; it now takes teams of from forty to hundreds of people several years to complete all the assets in a blockbuster game, which is referred to in the industry as a *triple-A* (or *AAA*) game.

> ## FYI Game Production Cycle
>
> An overview of the production cycle for creating a game is given in Chapter 5, "The Production Cycle." The various roles needed to create a game are described in Chapter 6, "The Production Team."

There are no surefire methods for coming up with a good idea for a new game, although several techniques can help the creative process; for example, a production team can hold brainstorming sessions in hopes of crafting a good design. But interesting ideas often come from unexpected sources, so game companies usually encourage all employees to submit their suggestions. (They seldom accept suggestions from outsiders, however, because of legal and financial constraints.)

Most companies have a set process for turning an idea into a complete design. The first step in the process usually involves pitching the core design concept to management to see if they think it's worth developing. If so, a designer develops the idea into a *game proposal* that defines the gameplay elements in more detail and includes a marketing analysis to show that the product will sell well. Assuming the company management agrees, the next step is to create a full *game design document* that describes all the gameplay elements in detail to help the designers, programmers, artists, and audio staff understand everything that needs to be created for the final product.

> ## FYI Design Documentation
>
> For a description of the essentials of gameplay, see Chapter 8, "The Elements of Gameplay." The process of writing and pitching a game concept and a game proposal is described in Chapter 9, "Committing Ideas to Paper." Chapter 10, "The Game Design Document," examines what is included in the full design specification.

Before jumping into production, most companies have the production team perform a *technical review*. During this phase, the teams determine all the assets needed for the game, the order in which they will be created, and who will build them. This information is written up in a ***technical design document*** for the programming team and an ***art design document*** for the art staff. The producer, or project manager, works with the lead programmer, lead artist, and designer to create a timeline that lists all the tasks needed to complete the game. With this information, the producer and team leaders can develop a realistic schedule and determine what features will be available at the end of each major phase of production (otherwise known as ***milestones***). When the full production schedule is worked out, the producer can determine the overall budget for the project. The budget and production schedule are presented to the company management for approval. When they receive the green light, the team begins actual production on the game.

FYI *Technical Review*

During technical review, the programming and art teams document how they plan to implement the game. The elements included in the technical and art design documents are described in Chapter 11, "Technical Review." The steps involved in creating a full schedule and production budget for a game are examined in Chapter 7, "Scheduling and Budgets."

Early in production, part of the programming team might create tools that other teams will use to create the game assets (artwork, levels, database, and so on). Another group of programmers might create a working prototype of the game, using placeholder art and existing code modules to enable the designers to test their assumptions about gameplay and balance the gameplay before the final assets are created. The rest of the programming team starts working on the game engine, the artificial intelligence, the networking, and other code modules required to complete the game. The art team, meanwhile, starts creating the art assets for the game and figuring out how the graphic elements (the user interface) will be laid out on all the screens that players see when starting up the game and playing it. The audio team reviews their sound libraries for appropriate effects, records new audio samples, and begins adding the sound effects and music to the game.

FYI *Putting the Pieces Together*

The tasks assigned to the programmers, artists and audio staff during the production of a game are discussed in Chapter 12, "Coding the Game," Chapter 13, "Visualizing the Game," and Chapter 14,

▶▶ CONTINUED ON NEXT PAGE

▶▶ CONTINUED

"Hearing the Game." The elements that go into creating the user inter-face are discussed in Chapter 15, "Interface Design." Chapter 16, "Mathematics and Artificial Intelligence in Games," looks at how math and logic are applied toward the creation of the database or a scripting language for the designers of the game and also discusses artificial intelligence techniques used in games. The various proto-types used when making a game and playfield creation are examined in Chapter 18, "Prototyping and Building Playfields."

After all the tools are created and the main code modules are completed and integrated into the game engine, the final assets are incorporated into the game. The completed levels are balanced and tested to find any inconsisten-cies or bugs, and the problems are eliminated one by one. Finally, the game enters an intense testing phase where the most important remaining bugs are tracked down and removed. As the project nears completion, the marketing department, which has been developing a marketing campaign to promote the game throughout the production phase, provides sample versions to reviewers, prepares the packaging materials, and cranks up the advertising and other promotional efforts.

Finally, the game is finished, and the final version—*the gold master*—is delivered to a manufacturer that reproduces the game on CDs or DVDs, or in the case of video games, the developer sends the final copy to the video console manufacturer (Microsoft, Nintendo, Sony), who creates the CDs and DVDs for sale after approving the final submission. The components are then assembled into shrink-wrapped packages, put in cartons, and delivered to distributors or sent directly to retailers. At last, the game appears on retail shelves for eager customers to buy. Hopefully, the team has done a good job and the game will be a hit, selling hundreds of thousands of copies and allowing the company to make enough money to continue turning out new games.

FYI   *Completion and Delivery*

The final steps of balancing and testing the game and then assem-bling the game package for delivery are discussed in Chapter 19, "Completing the Game." The process and approaches for promoting a new game are examined in Chapter 20, "Marketing the Game."

▶▶ CONTINUED ON NEXT PAGE

▶▶ **CONTINUED**

How companies make money in the industry and where the money goes are considered in Chapter 21, "Economics of the Game Industry." Finally, Chapter 22, "Breaking into the Game Industry," talks about what skills game companies look for and explains how to apply for a job in the industry.

Summary

This book looks in some detail at the various aspects of creating computer, console, and handheld games. It does not try to be an exhaustive examination because each topic discussed could be the subject of an entire book. Creating games has become increasingly complex as the technologies involved in building them and displaying them have become more advanced. Teams have grown in size and responsibilities, and the process of preparing, testing, and balancing the assets that make up the game (art, design, code modules, music, sound effects, and so on) takes more time.

Because so much money is now at stake, creating a new video or computer game has become as risky as creating a new movie. Of the numerous titles that appear every year, many more games lose money than earn a profit for the publisher, but as in the movie industry, games can be very rewarding for those who create popular successes. In the end, those who work in the industry usually discover that the process of building a game, while often demanding and stressful, can be just as much fun as playing one.

Test Your Skills

EXERCISES

Exercise 1.1: Common Features of Games

The common features of games listed in this chapter are independent of the medium of the game. Consider five of your favorite games, regardless of the medium. List all the elements that made that game fun for you. Also include the challenge that you have to overcome when you play the game. Finally, try to quantify how difficult you think the rules are on a scale of 1 to 5. For example, fun or challenging aspects could be playing with friends, play acting, getting a high score, or improving on a skill. Ratings of rule difficulty might be tic-tac-toe, 0; chess, 3; *D&D,* 5. Compare the lists for each game. What common elements occur among the games that you like?

Exercise 1.2: Consoles versus Computers

List all the electronic games that you have owned and the type of computer or console used to play them. Explain if you think a particular game would have been better on a different hardware platform and why.

Exercise 1.3: Early Games

What early games have you played? List seven old games that you have played as well as the type of machine you played them on. Include games in arcades. State if you think or know if this is the game's original platform. Use online research, if possible, to verify whether the game was released on an earlier platform or if it was converted from a physical game to an electronic game.

Exercise 1.4: Common Features of Games

Physical games, for the most part, include an opponent. Basketball, for example, is just shooting hoops if you play by yourself. Name your favorite game and explain how it differs from just play. What elements could you remove from the game so that it would be a "sandbox" that you played alone in? Is the game now fun or challenging?

Chapter 2

The Evolution of Games

Chapter Objectives

**After reading this chapter and doing the exercises,
you will be able to do the following:**

- Know how the first games probably were derived from the survival skills needed by prehistoric hunters and warriors.
- Understand the origins of the first board games and how they extend from prehistory to today.
- Explain how board games developed in the nineteenth century as more people gained leisure time and a level of literacy.
- Understand how electronic games first developed in the computer age.
- Explain how games have driven the technological advances in computers.

Introduction

The history of games is long and complex. This chapter offers a brief overview of the development of games from prehistoric times to the present. It discusses some games that were progenitors of modern electronic games and puts them in the timeline of human history. If you want more details about the history—and prehistory—of games, refer to the works cited in the reference section at the end of the book.

The Beginning of Games

No one knows when humans first began playing games. No definitive artifacts from prehistory indicate that early humans played games. Certainly, no one culture is identified with being the first game maker. However, anthropologists might have already discovered artifacts that have not yet been identified as game pieces. In *The Oxford History of Board Games,* David Parlett mentions that anthropologist Richard Leakey found some boards in Kenya that date to the Neolithic Period. These boards of two rows with thirteen holes could possibly be an early version of the board game mancala.

Because early humans were primarily hunters as adults, they probably had little leisure time for play. Their main concerns were tracking down game and other food sources, making clothes, finding shelter, and keeping their children alive. Although the adults did not have much time for leisurely activity, their children might have.

Scientists have noticed that most mammals, both young and old, exhibit play behavior, in which they toss each other about, nip at each other, and otherwise behave in ways that we might interpret as having fun. This play behavior in young mammals echoes the physical skills they will need later to survive as adults, so a wolf pup wrestling with its siblings for a stick might mirror its later fighting over the choicest chunks of meat in a carcass as an adult. These youthful early contests are practice for improving the skills needed to survive in the wild. No doubt, young humans engaged in similar wrestling matches to determine who was strongest—and perhaps the next leader of the group.

Among early humans, several stimuli led to the creation of games as a leisure activity. First, hunting skills were important for keeping everyone in the group alive and healthy. It is easy to see how bragging about who could throw a spear the farthest or run the longest might lead to simple athletic contests. Drawing start and finish lines in the dirt would leave no recognizable artifacts for archeologists to find. Second, as groups grew larger, conflicts began to arise over resources, warfare developed, and hunting skills were turned against other humans. Honing their combat abilities—riding horses, commanding chariots, firing bows, and attacking with spears and swords—might well have encouraged soldiers to develop the first athletic contests. Again, such games would not leave any discernable evidence for archaeologists. The first recorded athletic games developed in Greece around 800 BCE, although their literature indicates that such contests were already well established.

FYI   *The Olympic Games*

The first Olympic Games in which most Greek city-states took part were held in Olympia, Greece, in 776 BCE. These contests were held regularly and survived almost one thousand years until they were halted in 393 CE by Emperor Theodosius, who banned all pagan cults from Christianized Rome. They were later revived in their modern form by Baron Pierre de Coubertin in 1896 in Athens, Greece.

2

The First Board Games

As early groups developed into nations, there arose ruling and priestly castes that did not have to spend all their time fighting or searching for food. They had time to play games. Our first examples of board games come from the early civilizations that developed around the Fertile Crescent, an area in the Middle East stretching from the Mediterranean Sea to the Persian Gulf and incorporating ancient Egypt, the Levant, and Mesopotamia. The earliest surviving games (at least, we assume they are games) were discovered by archaeologists in the royal tombs of ancient Egypt and Sumer. Sir Leonard Woolley, who excavated the Sumerian city of Ur from 1922 to 1934 and traced the city's history back to about 4000 BCE, described several artifacts from a royal cemetery of Ur as being a board game. The artifacts date to around 2600 BCE, and the game has come to be called the royal game of Ur.

Other excavations found similar boards with from 14 to 24 round tokens and 4 triangular "dice." Ancient documents mentioning such a game indicate it was a racing game in which two players tried to get their piece to the end of the board first. Figure 2.1 shows a copy of the game in the British Museum.

In Egypt, archaeologists have found many copies of another board and pieces that likely make up a game called senet (or senat—the game of thirty spaces). The earliest version dates at least to 3100 BCE. In 1922, Egyptologist Howard Carter found a copy of the game in the tomb of King Tutankhamen. Figure 2.2 shows several versions of the game of senet found in Tutankhamen's tomb that now reside in the Egyptian Museum in Cairo.

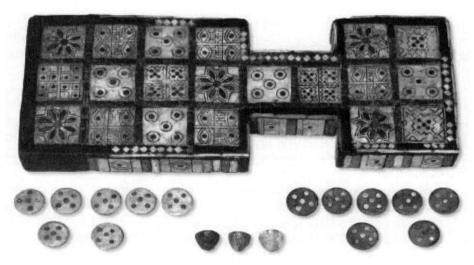

FIGURE 2.1 A copy of the royal game of Ur in the British Museum.

FIGURE 2.2 The game of senet in the Egyptian Museum.

The game of senet consists of a board, four to six playing pieces, and four throwing sticks. The board contains three rows of ten spaces with several of them bearing special markings that might have had special effects on gameplay. The throwing sticks were often white on one side and red on the other and were probably used to determine the movement of the playing pieces around the board. Although no rules for the game have been found, senet appears to be a simple racing game similar to the royal game of Ur. Each player throws the sticks to move one or more playing pieces around the board; landing on an opponent's piece probably forces it to start over. The winner is the first player to get all his playing pieces off the board. At least, that is one interpretation of how the game might play.

Equally as old as senet and the royal game of Ur, if not older, is mancala, which was played throughout Africa and the Middle East for thousands of years. There are many variations of this game, which consists of moving stones (or seeds) in and out of holes in parallel rows along a board. It might have arisen from a method for farmers to track where their livestock was grazing. Figure 2.3 shows a modern version of mancala.

These three games are pure *abstractions.* That is, they are several steps removed from realistic depictions of real-world events (such as hunting or fighting). One significant aspect of the earliest known games is that most of them tend to be abstractions, as opposed to "theme" games, such as Milton Bradley's *Monopoly* or *Operation,* that are connected to real-world situations.

FIGURE 2.3 Mancala.

Many of the popular games still being played today have their roots in ancient and medieval times, and a number of them can be played today in electronic form.

- Chess: The history of Chess is murky at best. Most likely, it was developed in India. One of its earliest ancestors might be a game developed in the sixth century CE called chaturanga (shaturanga), which appears to be an abstraction of combat with two players controlling playing pieces. In the early versions of this game the playing pieces represented infantry, cavalry, elephants, and even boatmen. The object of these early versions is to put the opponent's king in a stalemate position. Chess was introduced in Europe sometime before 1000 CE, when it is first mentioned in a Swiss manuscript. It became very popular in the courts of southern Europe near the end of the 1400s when changes made the queen the most dominant piece and extended the bishop's influence diagonally across the board.

- Checkers (or draughts): The earliest form of this game may be alquerque, an Egyptian game that dates from 600 BCE and possibly as far back as 1400 BCE. Alquerque is played on a board with five rows of five squares and 12 playing pieces per player. The objective is to capture all the opponent's pieces or trap her so she can't move anymore. The game was brought to Europe by the Moors when they invaded Spain. In the early Middle Ages, around 1100 CE, someone in France moved the game to a 64-square chess board and added more pieces. That version has come down to the present.

- Go: The game of Go (Wei-qi in China or I-go in Japan) is attributed to the ancient Chinese. The winner is the player who captures the most territory on the board. The Chinese *Book of Mencius* (or *Mengzi*) first mentions the game around 400 BCE, but its origins probably go back thousands of years earlier. According to Chinese history, Emperor Shun

FIGURE 2.4 Parcheesi.

(2255–2206 BCE) came up with the game as a tool to improve the brain of his oldest son, but this may simply be fiction. The game uses black and white stones on a square grid and is remarkably sophisticated; professional players spend years developing their skills. Players take turns placing stones on the board and trying to capture enemy pieces by surrounding them.

■ Parcheesi: This early board game is considered the national game of India. It likely developed from a more complex game called chaupar. Both games are known to have been in existence since the fourth century CE. Parcheesi is a simple racing game in which cowry shells (or dice) are thrown to move pieces around a track in the shape of a cross. Figure 2.4 shows a modern example of Parcheesi.

FYI *It's Good to Be King*

In the sixteenth century CE, the Mogul Emperor Akbar I played chaupur on a courtyard made of marble, using women from his harem as playing pieces. Several similar game-courtyards still exist in Agra and Allahabad.

■ Backgammon: The earliest version of this ancient game dates as far back as 3000 BCE in Egypt and Mesopotamia. The Romans played a game called the twelve-lined game (*Ludus Duodecim Scriptorum*),

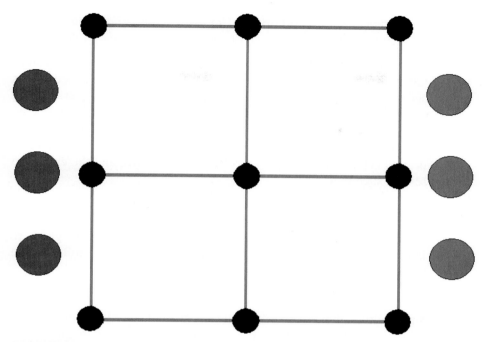

FIGURE 2.5 Layout for three men's morris.

which was much like the modern version. The earliest mention of the game in English appears in the *Codex Exoniensis* (1024 CE), where it is called tables. The game was a form of gambling and was prohibited by authorities until the reign of Queen Elizabeth I. The modern version was codified by English game expert Edmond Hoyle, who published *A Short Treatise on the Game of Back-Gammon* in 1743.

■ Morris: Carvings dating to around 1400 years BCE on Egyptian temples at Kurna show a game that may be three men's morris, a precursor to tic-tac-toe. Figure 2.5 shows the layout for three men's morris. The objective is to form a "mill" by placing three men in a row. Each time this happens, you can then steal the opponent's piece until he's down to just two pieces. There are several variants of the game using different numbers of pieces and allowing diagonal placement as well as horizontal and vertical.

■ Dice: The Greek tragedian Sophocles attributes the invention of dice to the Greek warrior Palamedes during the Trojan War. In his history of the Persian Wars, Herodotus gives credit to the Lydians. Both stories are erroneous because dice are known to have preceded the Trojans and Lydians by many centuries. Dice were used by a number of prehistoric societies for divination. Cubes with markings similar to dice have been found in Egyptian tombs from around 2000 BCE and at Chinese excavations dating to 600 BCE. The earliest dice were probably four-sided anklebones of sheep, and dice are still called bones today.

- Cards: The first card games were probably invented in the tenth century CE by the Chinese, who also created the first paper money. Their games seem to involve higher-value cards capturing lower-value ones. Playing cards using four suits and honor cards were introduced into Europe by the Muslims in the fourth century, although only the rich could afford the hand-painted cards. Many card games have evolved over the years despite occasional attempts by rulers, governments, and the church to restrict such play.

- Dominoes: These playing pieces also seem to be of Chinese origin. One form of the game was played in China around 1100 CE. Dominoes eventually made their way to Europe in the 1700s, although there is debate whether the Western version of the game is similar to the Chinese version.

All of these games that have been around for ages are relatively simple to learn and play, although they can take years to master. They have changed very little over hundreds of years. About the only interesting advance in game technology during that long time span is the use of dice for generating random numbers. These games do not rely on players' being able to read, except for determining the number of spots on a die. There is no text on any game board or on the playing pieces, so these games could be played by rich and poor, royalty and peasant alike. In addition to being easy to learn, the basic gameplay mechanics of these early games have been adopted over time and modified for use in later board and electronic games. The concepts of chasing things around a track, manipulating numbers, and engaging in combat are echoed in modern racing games, the Sudoku puzzle game found in newspapers, and paper and electronic war games.

The Rise of Commercial Board Games

The games discussed in the previous section grew in popularity over centuries and eventually reached every continent as Western and Eastern civilizations interacted with one another in war or in trade. All these games could be handcrafted, and making them did not require any specialized equipment. The people who played such games from ancient to modern times were primarily the wealthy and powerful who had time for such leisure activities. The vast majority of people worked long and hard just to survive and had little spare time for idle diversions.

Not until the Industrial Revolution in the eighteenth and nineteenth centuries did a leisured middle class arise. These nouveau riche not only had spare time for games; they also had extra money to buy manufactured games. Instead of handcrafted game pieces and boards, the improvements in printing and paper production in the nineteenth century meant that games could be printed on paper and glued to cardboard to make **board games,** and therefore they could be mass produced for public consumption. Moreover, the growth of literacy at this same time, as public schooling became the norm, meant that more complicated games could be created and played by more people. Thanks to the reform work by Charles Dickens and many others, children were released from the drudgery of working in mills and shops, and they could spend their extra time playing. It is no wonder that the end of the nineteenth century saw the rise of the first companies devoted to making games commercially.

Game Publishing Companies in the Nineteenth Century

One of the first successful board game companies in the United States was Milton Bradley, founded in 1860 by Mr. Bradley initially as a lithography business in Springfield, Massachusetts. Bradley needed a way to bring in more money and began manufacturing *The Checkered Game of Life,* a game he had previously patented. The game sold well, and in 1880, Bradley added jigsaw puzzles to his line. The company soon became the world's number one publisher of games and puzzles. Among the best known Milton Bradley games are *Chutes and Ladders* (published in 1943), *Candyland* (1949), *Yahtzee* (1956), and *The Game of Life* (1960).

Another important game company was founded soon after. A young boy named George S. Parker from Salem, Massachusetts, invented a game called *Banking* and used most of his life savings to publish it in 1883. The first edition, which George produced and distributed, sold well enough to merchants in Northeastern cities that he was encouraged to set up a game company in Salem in 1888 with his brother. They named the company Parker Brothers and continued creating new games that sold very well, including *The Railroad Game* and *Innocents Abroad,* which was based on the book by Mark Twain.

In 1934, Charles B. Darrow brought a game he had invented called *Monopoly* to Parker Brothers. Initially, the company rejected the game, saying it was too complicated and took too long to complete. Darrow began publishing the game himself and did quite well. The executives at Parker Brothers heard of the game's success and offered to buy publication rights in 1935. *Monopoly* was an immediate smash success and continues to be one of the company's best selling games, with many variations on the main theme now available. Parker Brothers went on to publish other classic board games—*Sorry!* (1934), *Clue* (1949), and *Risk* (1959)—that still sell today.

Meanwhile, another American game publisher, the Selchow and Righter company, had opened its doors for business in 1867 and brought the game of Parcheesi from India to the United States. Its two great hits were *Scrabble* (published in 1948) and *Trivial Pursuit* (1983 in the United States).

During this time, Fusajiro Yamauchi established the Marufuku Company in Japan in 1889. The company produced playing cards for a popular game called *Hanafuda* and then expanded into publishing Western playing cards in 1907. In 1951, the company changed its name to the Nintendo Playing Card Company (*Nintendo* meaning "Leave luck to heaven"). Eventually, the company became a leader in electronic games, as you'll read later in the chapter.

Board Games in the Twentieth Century

In the nineteenth century, the Prussian army developed the first realistic war games to train their leaders, using miniature figures to represent real military units. These games allowed the leaders to experiment with various tactics and strategies before engaging in combat. The practice was soon adopted by military leaders all around the world. Author H. G. Wells was intrigued by the subject and at the beginning of the twentieth century wrote a booklet called *Little Wars,* which gave some simple rules for playing such a game. Over time, many commercial games were developed using miniatures to represent military units of many different countries and different eras.

In 1953, Charles Roberts created a paperboard war game called *Tactics,* which had two hypothetical countries engaging in modern warfare with infantry, tanks, aircraft, and naval units. Instead of miniatures, *Tactics* used small cardboard playing pieces that moved across a map mounted on cardboard (see Figure 2.6). The game sold well enough that Roberts decided to found

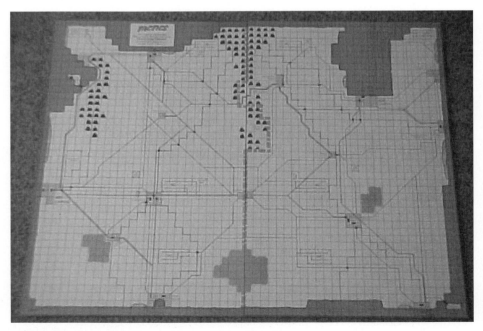

FIGURE 2.6 Cardboard map from *Tactics.*

a company called Avalon Hill in 1958 to publish the war games he created. Initially, the company did well, and the audience for such games increased, but by the early 1960s, a downswing in sales forced Roberts to sell his company to Monarch Publishing in Baltimore, Maryland. Even with this setback, war games continued to sell well enough to encourage a number of competing companies to appear during the 1970s and 1980s. But by the end of the 1980s, the paper war game hobby had almost died out as similar games were developed for personal computers, which had the advantages of taking no time to set up and requiring less space for a large map and hundreds of playing pieces.

In 1973, E. Gary Gygax and Dave Arneson of Lake Geneva, Wisconsin, jointly created a different kind of paper game—one that had no board, no cards, and no playing pieces. Their game was called *Dungeons & Dragons* (see Figure 2.7); it called on players to take on the roles of fantasy characters in a fantastic world. As one of the original *role-playing games,* it was based on rules for medieval combat using miniatures . . . but the game was not simply about combat. One player, called the dungeon master, leads the other players through a magical world in an ongoing epic story. The players resolve their actions—picking locks, springing traps, casting magic, and fighting battles—by rolling multisided dice and consulting various tables to determine the outcomes. Gygax and Arneson founded TSR Hobbies to manufacture and market the game. Role-playing games became immensely popular, especially with young males, and many of the war game companies brought out their own versions of role-playing games to rival *D&D*.

FYI   *"One Ring Rules Them All"*

J. R. R. Tolkien's epic fantasy *The Lord of the Rings* was originally published in the 1950s and became immensely popular in the United States in the 1960s and 70s. The popularity of the books helped contribute to the huge success of *Dungeons & Dragons* in the 1970s, because players could live out the adventures of epic heroes in game form. Many of the fans of these books and *D&D* eventually started working in the computer game industry making electronic versions of fantasy role-playing games.

A popular offshoot of the fantasy role-playing genre is the *Magic: The Gathering* (M:TG) card game. *M:TG* is published by Wizards of the Coast, which was founded in 1990 by Peter Adkison. In *M:TG,* players draw and play cards from decks they have carefully crafted to create creatures and cast magic to attack and defeat enemy wizards. The genre was so successful that it spawned many similar games, such as Wizards of the Coast's *Pokémon* (based on the popular Game Boy games) and Konami's *Yu-Gi-Oh!* (based on the popular Japanese manga-style comics).

FIGURE 2.7 The original *Dungeons & Dragons*.

Collapse and Consolidation

By the end of the twentieth century, the board game industry was suffering. One reason was the rise of video game consoles and personal computers that gave players a new outlet for different kinds of games. Families spent less time together, so social activities such as board games suffered. As earnings fell and industry pressures grew in the 1990s, many board game companies were sold to competitors.

The first merger came in 1984 when Hasbro, Inc., acquired Milton Bradley. Hasbro was founded in 1923 in Providence, Rhode Island, as a textile merchant. It eventually expanded into school supplies and then became a creator of toys and dolls. By the 1980s, it decided to get into games. Rather than trying to compete with the leaders, it bought the Milton Bradley Company. In 1989, Hasbro purchased the assets of Coleco Industries, which included *Scrabble* and *Trivial Pursuit,* both originally manufactured by Selchow and Righter. In 1991, Hasbro bought Parker Brothers. In 1998, Hasbro acquired war game publisher Avalon Hill; in 1999 it acquired Wizards of the Coast, which had previously acquired TSR in 1997.

As a result, at the turn of the twentieth century, the board game industry in the United States increasingly became dominated by Hasbro, except for one major competitor, Mattel. Although Mattel was founded in 1945 to produce picture frames and doll house accessories, it soon changed its focus primarily to toys and games. Its greatest success is the Barbie doll, created in 1959. The company publishes a number of games like *Uno* and *Othello*; however, it continues to be best known for its various toy lines.

FYI   *Hasbro Interactive*

In 1995, Hasbro tried to move into electronic games by creating a division called Hasbro Interactive. The company published electronic versions of some of the company's popular board games such as *Monopoly* and *Scrabble* and acquired several computer game developers (MicroProse and Spectrum Holobyte). However, despite becoming the number-three computer game publisher by 1998, Hasbro decided the division was not profitable enough and sold it to Infogrames in 2001 for $100 million. Interestingly enough, in June 2005, Hasbro regained many of the gaming rights for its toy lines from Infogrames for $65 million, and the two companies are now working together to produce games based on Hasbro properties such as *Dungeons & Dragons, Monopoly, Risk,* and other popular board games.

Many of the popular board games invented in the twentieth century are still available and selling well today. New board games are still being invented and marketed, although none has captured the public's imagination or matched the long-lasting success of classic games like *Monopoly* and *Scrabble*. Electronic games have become the dominant force in games today.

FYI   *Pinball*

The first coin-operated pinball game, *Ballyhoo,* was created in 1931 by Raymond Maloney, who later founded the Bally Corporation. The first pinball machines were wooden and relied on simple gravity (electricity was added in 1933). The machines became popular in the United States during the Great Depression as a cheap form of mass entertainment. The Golden Age of pinball came after World War II, from 1948 to 1958, following the flippers' invention in 1947. The introduction of solid-state electronics in the mid-1970s brought a resurgence of interest in the machines that lasted through the 1980s. However, the machine's popularity waned throughout the 1980s and 1990s due to the popularity of video games at home and in arcades. As of a 2004, only one designer and manufacturer was left—Stern Pinball.

The Birth of Electronic Gaming

The birth and success of electronic games follows the same path as the birth and success of computers in the twentieth century. In fact, the demand by game companies for better graphics, better audio, and more processing power has driven much of the improvement in personal computer technology. The history of electronic games is as much a story of the competition among game companies to develop ever more powerful game platforms as it is about the games themselves.

The following history of electronic games is chronological and gives a brief overview of the major innovations that affected electronic games. It does not pretend to be comprehensive.

1940s–1960s: Pioneers

Following the Second World War, several new companies appeared that, although not originally founded to create games, would grow to play a large role in the evolution of electronic games. In 1947, Akio Morita and Masaru Ibuka founded the Tokyo Engineering Company. In 1952, they acquired the rights to use Bell Labs' patented transistor to make small radios. The success of their transistor radio encouraged them to market it in America, and they decided to use a name that would be easier to say. They came up with Sony, from the Latin *sonus* meaning sound, which became their corporate name. The company soon became a giant seller of electronic goods from radios to appliances to televisions.

FIGURE 2.8 IBM 7090/94 computer installed at Goddard Spaceflight Center.

A few years later, in 1954, David Rosen, a Korean War veteran, founded Service Games to export coin-operated games from Japan to the United States. He soon decided to create his own games under the SEGA (SErvice GAmes) logo, which eventually became the name of Rosen's company.

International Business Machines (IBM) began in 1911 as the Computing-Tabulating-Recording Company. During World War II, it produced high-speed mechanical calculators that eventually evolved into the first electronic computers. In 1952, Thomas Watson, Jr., became president and the company invested heavily in computers. By the 1960s, they produced 70 percent of all the computers in the world. These early computers were huge, taking up entire rooms that required special climate controls. They were also expensive. The popular IBM 7090/94, shown in Figure 2.8, cost about $3 million to install.

The first electronic game, *OXO,* was a tic-tac-toe game created by A. S. Douglas in 1952 to run on the EDSAC computer as part of his doctoral thesis at the University of Cambridge. In 1958, *Tennis for Two,* was created by physicist Willy Higinbotham at the Brookhaven National Laboratories in New York to amuse visitors to the lab. It was a table-tennis game (a precursor to *Pong*) played on an oscilloscope; players could compete against each other using two controllers. However, Higinbotham did not bother to patent the device, thus allowing anyone to use this basic idea without having to pay to use it.

1961–1972: Spacewar and The Odyssey

The first true game designed to be played on a computer was created in 1961 by Steve Russell, a student at the Massachusetts Institute of Technology (MIT). *Spacewar* was played on a Digital PDP-1 computer with cathode-ray tube screens

FIGURE 2.9 Screenshot from *Spacewar.*

that displayed ASCII text characters for graphics (see Figure 2.9). *Spacewar* was the first interactive computer game, thanks to the development of the PDP's time-sharing ability, which allowed several people to use the computer at the same time.

These first games were played on computers that were too large and too expensive to be used outside a university, research center, or corporation. Such computers were intended to run "serious" programs such as databases and space programs, not games. Of course, people saw that games could be run on them, and as the 1960s drew to a close, several entrepreneurs became interested in creating electronic games on smaller computers for the home and for entertainment centers.

Ralph Baer was an early pioneer in electronic game development. Baer believed as early as 1951 that games could be played on television sets, although the company he worked for dismissed the idea. In 1966 he started researching such games, and by the following year he had produced two games and a toy gun that could distinguish different light spots on a TV screen. Baer patented his interactive television game in 1968 and in 1970 licensed his property to Magnavox, which spent several years developing the technology. The first video game system, Magnavox Odyssey, was initially marketed in 1972 with a street price of $100. The game system used 40 transistors and 40 diodes and included television screen overlays to make the graphics appear more intricate. The first games released were simple sports games and arcade shooters.

The Odyssey was not very successful at first because people thought it would work only with Magnavox televisions. It eventually sold 100,000 units and led to a successor, Odyssey2, in 1982.

1972–1976: The Rise of Arcade Games

Soon to be one of the forefathers of the video game industry, Nolan Bushnell first encountered *Spacewar* in the late 1960s at the University of Utah when he was an engineering student. He thought at the time that computer games might work well in arcades, but their manufacturing costs were too high. With programmer Ted Dabney's assistance, Bushnell set up a company, Syzygy Engineering, and created the first coin-operated arcade video game, *Computer Space,* which was similar to *Spacewar.* They sold the game machine to arcade manufacturer Nutting Associates, who released it in 1971. The game did not do well because arcade gamers (who were used to pinball and air hockey) found the controls too complex to grasp quickly.

The next year (1972), Bushnell and Dabney set up their own arcade video game company, which they named Atari (from the Japanese game of *Go*). They hired programmer Al Alcorn and asked him to create a simple tennis game, which became *Pong.* Bushnell originally tried to sell the game to pinball game manufacturer Bally. When they passed, he wound up building and distributing the game himself (see Figure 2.10). The game was an instant success. The controls were simple and the gameplay was easy to learn. In 1976, Bushnell sold Atari to Warner Communications for a hefty $28 million and was appointed Atari's chairman of the board.

The same year that *Pong* appeared, 1972, William Crowther, a student at Boston University, wrote *Colossal Cave* (also called *Adventure*) and posted it

FIGURE 2.10 The arcade version of *Pong.*

on the school's mainframe computer. This was the first text-based adventure game and established a new form of puzzle game.

In 1975, Bill Gates and Paul G. Allen converted BASIC, a mainframe programming language, for use on the Altair personal computer. They soon founded Microsoft and continued developing programming languages. This company would soon have a profound effect on electronic gaming.

By 1976, the era of electronic games had arrived. Games were being played on computers, on televisions via video game systems, and in arcades.

1977–1979: An Industry Matures

In 1977, Atari released the Video Computer System (VCS), a cartridge-based home game system. The VCS, which later was renamed the Atari 2600, had an 8-bit central processing unit (CPU), 16-color graphics, and two audio channels. It had a whopping 128 *bytes* of random access memory (RAM) and no video memory. Games were sold separately on cartridges, with the largest being 4 kilobytes. Hundreds of games were created for the system. It was one of the most popular video game systems ever and continued to sell until 1990.

Also in 1977, Steve Wozniak and Steve Jobs created the Apple II personal computer in Jobs' garage. One thing that made the computer so popular was its color display. The addition of Wozniak's low-cost hard disk drive to store and process information in 1978 and the appearance of the spreadsheet program *VisiCalc* increased the machine's popularity and made it a must-have. Of course, the Apple II's ability to play games also helped make it popular.

Atari recognized the potential market for personal home computers and created its 400 and 800 computer lines to compete. However, the company's success as a game machine confused the public, which perceived their computers to be little more than toys and stayed away in droves. The company decided to stick with arcade games.

Nineteen seventy-eight was a good year for arcade games. In March, Nintendo of Japan released an arcade version of the board game *Othello,* which they named *Computer Othello*. In addition, Midway brought the arcade game *Space Invaders* to America from Japan. *Space Invaders* was so popular in both countries that it caused truancy problems among American youth and a coin shortage in Japan.

In Boston, a group of MIT students formed Infocom in 1979 and published *Zork I,* a text-based adventure game for multiple home computer systems the next year. *Zork I* was a huge success even though it was only part of a larger one-megabyte game that wouldn't run on home computers because of those early machines' memory constraints. The success of *Zork I* led Infocom eventually to release the rest of the huge game as *Zork II* (1981) and *Zork III* (1982).

In 1979, Atari released the arcade game *Asteroids,* which became one of its best selling titles. That same year, Roy Trubshaw wrote the first **multiuser dungeon (MUD),** the forerunner of computer role-playing games, at Essex University in England. It ran on the university's DEC-10 minicomputer.

FIGURE 2.11 Box cover for *Code Name: Sector.*

By the late 1970s, board game companies had come to realize that video and computer games were a growing threat to their business, and they responded in kind by creating a number of stand-alone electronic games. In 1977, Parker Brothers released their first electronic game, *Code Name: Sector,* a submarine-hunting game (see Figure 2.11). Milton Bradley entered the electronic game market in 1978 with *Simon,* a handheld game that created increasingly lengthy and intricate patterns of lights and sound that the player had to copy in the correct order to win. In 1980, Parker Brothers responded with *Merlin,* a similar electronic game that became the best selling handheld game of the year.

1980–1982: High Water Mark

Another contender in the home market appeared in 1980 when Mattel Electronics released the Intellivision game console system (see Figure 2.12). Similar to the VCS, it connected to the television and played games that were sold as cartridges. At $299, the Intellivision was more expensive than its competitors, but it had better graphics, and Mattel hinted that they would release a peripheral that would upgrade the system into a personal computer (it never materialized).

Minoru Arakawa opened Nintendo of America in New York City in 1980 but moved to the Seattle, Washington, area shortly thereafter. Nintendo of America published a series of so-so "shoot-em-up" arcade games, and the future looked grim for the fledgling game division of the Japanese company.

FIGURE 2.12 Intellivision console with *Astromash*.

That same year, a number of Atari employees, unhappy that the company did not credit programmers in their games, left to form Activision, the first third-party game development company (***third-party developers*** are independents that are separate from publishers or console manufacturers). Unlike Atari, Activision credited the developers on the packaging and in their marketing campaigns. In 1992, Activision released *Pitfall,* which was the first platform game to allow the player to control a character that climbs up and down ladders, jumps from one platform to another, and fights creatures that are either attacking him or blocking his path.

In Los Angeles, Ken and Roberta Williams set up a home-based company, On-Line Systems, in 1980 and created *Mystery House,* a game that combined text and graphics for the Apple II. Eventually, after producing a number of successful games, the couple moved to Coarsegold, California, and changed the company name to Sierra On-Line.

The biggest arcade hit of 1980 was Namco's *Pac-Man,* which became the most famous and popular coin-operated game ever (see Figure 2.13). Within a year, the game appeared on home video systems as well.

FYI *Puck Man*

Originally, Namco's *Pac-Man* was going to be called Puck Man. However, when management realized what vandals could do to vulgarize the name, they changed the name to *Pac-Man*.

FIGURE 2.13 Arcade version of *Pac-Man*.

In 1980, IBM asked Microsoft to develop a new operating system for their personal computers. Rather than develop one from scratch, Microsoft bought the rights to QDOS (Quick and Dirty Operating System) from Seattle Computer Products, modified it, and published it as Microsoft Disk Operating System (MS-DOS).

Nineteen eighty-one saw the arrival of Shigeru Miyamoto's arcade game *Donkey Kong* (see Figure 2.14). The game was originally called "Monkey Kong" in Japan until the name was mysteriously changed for the American

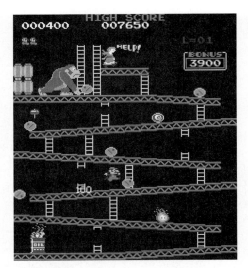

FIGURE 2.14 Screenshot from *Donkey Kong.*

version. The lead character, called Jumpman in the Japanese version, attempted to save his girlfriend Pauline from a barrel-throwing giant ape. Nintendo of America changed Jumpman's name to Mario to honor their landlord, Mario Segali. A franchise was born.

By 1981, arcade games ruled and had reached their pinnacle of success. According to "The History of Video Games" on GameSpot.com (**http://www. gamespot.com/gamespot/features/video/hov/**), arcade games netted $5 billion and accounted for over 75,000 hours of play in the United States alone.

1983–85: Crash and Recovery

Just as rapidly as the young electronic game industry had risen to prominence, it was devastated by a crash at the end of 1982. Atari, in particular, had a very bad year. They released a highly anticipated version of *Pac-Man* for the VCS, but it was not much like the arcade version and left consumers greatly disappointed. Even worse, the release of their *E.T.* game (based on the movie of the same name) was also received badly. Atari manufactured more cartridges of that game than there were VCS machines, expecting to sell more consoles with the title. Eventually, huge numbers of *E.T.* and other unsold game cartridges were buried in a landfill in New Mexico. On December 7, 1982, Atari released a press release that announced VCS sales would not meet their predictions for the year. The stock of Warner Communications, Atari's parent company, dropped 32 percent in one day.

The situation did not improve any time soon. By 1983, simply too many bad video games that all featured similar arcade gameplay from too many publishers were on the market. Third-party developers suffered the most, and many

went out of business. Those companies that had the financial resources to hang in and decided to continue operations suffered heavy losses because they were forced to lower their prices to compete or because they simply lost money on unsold inventory.

However, not all game industry news was bleak in 1983. Trip Hawkins had left Apple the year before and started a company initially called Amazin' Software, a name later changed to Electronic Arts. In May 1983, they shipped *Dr. J and Larry Bird Go One-on-One* for a number of home computer platforms (Commodore, Atari, Apple, Amiga, and PC). The game was a huge hit, and a giant of the game industry was born.

Still, the bad news for the video game industry continued through 1984, when Mattel announced it had lost $229.3 million dollars in its Mattel Electronics division in 1983 and had decided to shut it down. The division was acquired by a company executive and renamed Intellivision, Inc. Likewise, Warner Communications divested itself of Atari Incorporated's consumer division, selling it to Jack Tramiel, who had founded the Commodore Business Machines computer company in 1962. Warner Communications held onto the arcade division, renaming it Atari Games.

In 1985, most retailers thought that video games were a temporary craze whose time had come and gone. They were skeptical when Nintendo showed off the Nintendo Entertainment System (NES; see Figure 2.15), and having been burned once, they forced Nintendo to agree to buy back any unsold inventory.

FIGURE 2.15 Nintendo Entertainment System (NES).

Nintendo had already released the Famicom (Family Computer) system in Japan in 1983, which was immediately popular because it offered titles such as *Donkey Kong* and *Donkey Kong, Jr.* Nintendo test-marketed the NES in New York before deciding to release the system nationwide in 1986 featuring *Super Mario Bros.*

The NES featured an 8-bit CPU with 2 kilobytes of RAM. The system's graphics resolution of 256 × 224 pixels was capable of producing 16 colors simultaneously from a palette of 52 colors. It had 2 kilobytes of graphics RAM and could show up to 64 sprites simultaneously.

FYI | *8-Bit*

The term ***8-bit*** refers to the number of bits of data transferred during each read or write of computer memory. It is also the number of bits used by the CPU to process the data.

Sega had been an arcade developer for a number of years when they decided to enter the home video market and compete directly against Nintendo. They released their Sega Master System in the United States in 1986, but it did not have as many popular game titles as Nintendo and lagged behind in sales.

Atari Corporation also released its new game machine, the 7800 console, in 1986. Despite the increased competition, by the end of the year Nintendo outsold all rival systems by a 10-to-1 margin. This was largely due to the better games Nintendo offered, including the all-star lineup of *Super Mario Bros 2, Donkey Kong, The Legend of Zelda,* and *Metroid* that were all available that year.

Personal computers (PCs) were becoming a serious market for games as their graphics technology continued to improve. At the time, PCs were primarily used for text-mode business applications and did not require, nor did they offer, much in the way of graphics. The first improvement over monochrome graphic display was the Computer Graphics Adaptor (CGA), which was introduced by IBM in 1981. It could display 640 × 200 pixels in 2 colors or 320 × 200 pixels in 4 colors. In 1984, IBM introduced the 16-color Enhanced Graphics Adapter (EGA). It could display 640 × 350 pixels in 16 colors from a palette of 64 colors. Programmers began to capitalize on the improving graphics of the personal computer, including Alex Pajitnov, who designed the simple but addictive puzzle game *Tetris* in 1985.

1986–1991: The Console Wars Continue

Nintendo enjoyed continued success with the NES through the 1980s and dominated the video game market. In 1989, they introduced the handheld Game Boy to the United States. Each system shipped with a monochrome version of

Tetris and cost $109. The Game Boy showed that portable electronic games had a ready market among youngsters.

Nintendo encountered its first serious competitor that same year when Sega released the 16-bit Genesis in the United States for $249.95, which included a version of the arcade game *Altered Beast*. The Genesis ran at 7.6 megahertz, compared to the 1.79 megahertz of the NES. It also had 72 kilobytes of RAM and 64 kilobytes of video RAM. The system had a graphics resolution of 320 × 224 pixels and offered 61 colors simultaneously from a palette of 512 colors. It could show up to 80 sprites simultaneously and had 10 sound channels. Further competition came from NEC, which released the TurboGrafx-16 the same year for $189.

In 1990, Nintendo released their best-selling video game, *Super Mario 3* (see Figure 2.16). The NES had its most profitable year yet, despite the competition from Sega and NEC. Still, Nintendo knew they could not maintain their lead in the video game market with their old system, so they introduced the 16-bit Super Famicom in Japan in 1990 and renamed it Super NES (SNES) for the American market in 1991. The SNES system initially sold for $249.95. Sega countered by introducing *Sonic the Hedgehog* (see Figure 2.17) as their Genesis mascot, which went toe-to-toe against Nintendo's *Super Mario World* and helped Sega gain dominance over Nintendo in the 16-bit console market for the next several years.

FIGURE 2.16 *Super Mario 3.*

FIGURE 2.17 *Sonic the Hedgehog.*

1986–1991: Home Computers Gain Popularity

This same time period (1986–1991) saw major changes in the personal computer game industry. A number of contenders vied for leadership in the personal computer market—IBM, Commodore, Tandy, Amiga, and Apple II among others—and it was expensive for game companies to turn out games for all contenders. However, by the end of the decade, the IBM PC and its clones came to dominate the market. Other platforms, except for a few like the earlier Apple Macintosh, all but disappeared. One reason IBM succeeded while others failed was a huge marketing push to adopt their architecture as a standard, which allowed other companies to make hardware for the platform, thereby broadening the market. Of course, although its architecture became standard, IBM did not wind up the ultimate winner because other companies were able to turn out cheaper clones of the PC and eventually drove IBM out of the home computer market.

The graphics continued to improve as well. IBM introduced the Video Graphics Array (VGA) standard in 1987 with their PS/2 series of computers. VGA offered 256 colors at 300 × 240 pixel resolution, or a maximum resolution of 640 × 480 pixels in 16 colors from a palette of 262,144 colors. In 1989, a new Super VGA (SVGA) standard was introduced offering many resolutions—800 × 600, 1024 × 768, 1280 × 1024, and 1600 ×1200 pixels—using a palette of 16 million colors. In addition, audio for the personal computer advanced from the beeps and boops of the early machines to become much more sophisticated and lifelike. However, the standards for audio and video changed so rapidly that developers had a difficult time testing all the possible configurations for conflicts.

In addition to audio and video problems, a third major snag with personal computer systems was the operating system. MS-DOS users had to type in complex commands to get programs to load, and the system constrained programs to run within 640 kilobytes. In November 1985, Microsoft introduced Windows 1.0, their first graphic user interface (GUI) operating system. It wasn't very popular. Windows 2.0 soon followed in 1986, but it wasn't until Windows 3.0 arrived in 1989 that the operating system was widely accepted. Games could become more complex and intricately structured because they were no longer restricted to the 640k limit of MS-DOS. They could now use Window's *virtual memory* to handle the more complex graphics, audio, artificial intelligence, and other game features that had been limited by MS-DOS.

On the software front, dominance among publishers of computer games seemed to boil down to two contenders—Electronic Arts and Activision. By the end of the decade, EA emerged triumphant as the leader of the computer game industry. After losing money for several years, Activision, which had acquired Infocom in 1985, decided to close down that division in 1989 and filed for Chapter 11 bankruptcy in 1992. Under the leadership of Robert Kotick, however, it managed to become solvent again and has continued publishing games to the present.

1992–1994: The Arrival of 32-Bit Consoles

In 1992, Trip Hawkins, founder of Electronic Arts, announced that he was creating the 3DO Company to produce the next-generation game console—the 32-bit 3DO Multiplayer (called Opera internally). Major companies such as Panasonic and Time-Warner invested in 3DO, and Panasonic was the first to market the new machine in 1993 (see Figure 2.18). Its hefty $699 price tag kept many customers from buying the new console, and it never dominated the console market, but the 3DO Company survived and eventually began work on designing a 64-bit game console in 1994.

The year the 3DO appeared, Atari announced that they planned to skip a 32-bit machine in favor of the 64-bit Jaguar (which actually used two 32-bit coprocessors). Both Nintendo and Sega responded by saying they would develop next-generation machines as well.

During this period, the level of violence in some video games, particularly *Mortal Kombat* and *Night Trap,* led U.S. Senators Joseph Lieberman and Herbert Kohl to lead an investigation into violence in video games in 1993. During the investigation, they threatened to ban the sales of graphically violent games to children. The next year, the Entertainment Software Rating Board (ESRB) was set up to create a rating system for video games.

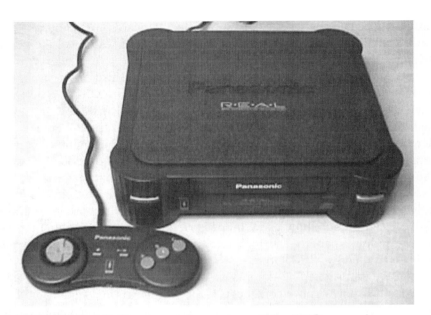

FIGURE 2.18 Panasonic's version of the 3DO console.

While the console wars were proceeding apace, id Software quietly released version 1.0 of their computer game, *Doom,* as shareware via the University of Wisconsin file transfer protocol (FTP) server in late 1993. Players could download the first third of the game and play it for free, but they had to pay to get the rest of the game. Not only did this represent a milestone in marketing games; it established the popularity of the first-person shooter genre as well as online player-versus-player gaming (called deathmatches). A revolution had been started, and soon almost all games would follow *Doom's* lead in using 3D graphics (see Figure 2.19).

In 1994, Nintendo nearly recaptured the 16-bit video game market from Sega with the release of *Super Metroid* and the visually stunning *Donkey Kong Country* for the Super NES. Sega responded by shipping a 32X peripheral for $179; it played new 32-bit game cartridges on its Genesis console. This device offered a hint of what was to come with the release of their Saturn 32-bit game console in Japan that year.

In addition, a new contender joined the console wars and dared to challenge the dominance of Nintendo and Sega. Sony had been developing the 32-bit PlayStation console since 1992 and finally released it in Japan in 1994 to compete with the Sega Saturn. Most consumers thought the PlayStation was superior to the Saturn, and the PlayStation had sold over 100 million units by June 2005, whereas the Saturn sold only 2 million units in the United States and was discontinued in 1998.

FIGURE 2.19 Screenshot from id Software's *Doom.*

1995–1997: 64-Bit and the Birth of Online Gaming

Nineteen ninety-five was a watershed year in the console wars. Sega initially planned to release the Saturn in the United States in September but advanced the release date to May. The Saturn, which was the first home console system to offer an optional module for connecting to the Internet, sold for $399.99. However, few titles were available because independent developers were not ready for the earlier ship date. Sony released the PlayStation in America for $299. In addition to being $100 cheaper than the Saturn, the PlayStation had a number of strong titles available when it debuted, and therefore, quickly outpaced its rival. Not to be outdone, Nintendo released its N64 in Japan, but it could not keep up with initial demands and soon ran out of stock of both hardware and software.

Both the Saturn and PlayStation included a CD-ROM drive, whereas the N64 retained the old-fashioned cartridge as the game medium. Still, when the N64 was released to the American market in 1996 at a sales price of $299.99, sales of the new console hit 1.7 million within three months. In terms of raw power, the new generation of console machines had come a long way since their humble 8-bit beginnings. As a Nintendo press release said of that company's new machine, "Nintendo64 can perform 3.5 times as many adds per second as the original Cray-1 (supercomputer), which cost $8,000,000 in 1976. The Cray 1 also consumed 60,000 watts of power, compared to the Nintendo64 machine's 5 watts." The 3DO Company developed their own 64-bit technology, M2, which they sold to Panasonic in 1995 for over $100 million. However, because competition in the console game arena was so fierce, the M2 never appeared on the market. The 3DO company decided to abandon the hardware wars and focus on game software only. The company declared chapter 11 bankruptcy in 2003 and finally shut down completely. Throughout this period, the Atari Jaguar was available but never fully caught on with the public. Production was discontinued in 1996 due to continuing sluggish sales.

A major milestone in computer games occurred in 1995, when Microsoft released Windows 95 and Internet Explorer 1.0. Although Windows 95 still supported MS-DOS, it improved the memory limitations of Windows 3.1 and sported a new, easier-to-use graphical user interface. The new operating system received a huge marketing push, and more than 7 million copies sold in a month. Late in 1995, Microsoft released the first version of the DirectX APIs (*application programming interfaces,* which make it easier to program graphics and sound) to encourage developers to use the Windows environment for playing games.

The Internet was becoming a potential platform for gaming. The first online massively multiplayer role-playing game that allowed many players to exist and play together in the same "persistent world" was *Meridian59,* published by the 3DO Company in 1996. Electronic Arts released *Ultima Online* shortly thereafter (1997), although to poor reviews.

In 1995. Hasbro decided to enter the computer game industry by creating a new division, Hasbro Interactive. Their idea was to transform their many lines of board games into computer/video games. They developed and released a computer version of their *Monopoly* game in 1995. The rest of the computer games they published were developed by independents.

In 1996, Electronic Arts released *Command & Conquer* by Westwood Studios. Building on the ideas developed in *Dune II, Command & Conquer* established the real-time strategy game genre (a form of war game where action is continuous instead of turn-based and players might focus as much on resource management as sending troops into battle).

1998–1999: Towards the Twenty-First Century

In 1998, Sega released their 64-bit Dreamcast in Japan. The system sold well, along with the street fighter game *Virtual Fighter 3.* The initial order of 150,000 units sold out quickly. To maintain its position in the console wars, Sony announced in 1998 that they were developing the PlayStation 2, but gave no indication of when it would ship. Nintendo shipped *The Legend of Zelda: Ocarina of Time* for the N64, selling 2.5 million copies of the game in just over a month. In September 1998, Sega released the Dreamcast in the United States. The company reported earnings of almost $100 million within the first day of the launch.

Yet another major player entered the video game market in 1999, when Microsoft announced it was working on a video game console using Windows CE as the operating system. The console would be called Xbox. Not to be outdone,

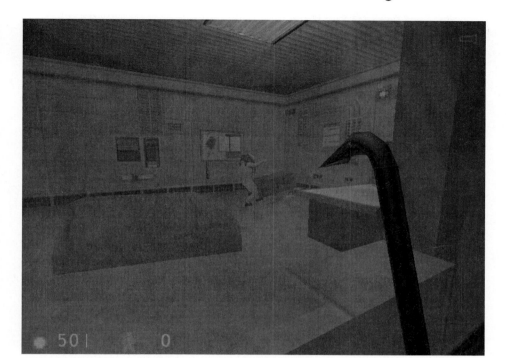

FIGURE 2.20 Screenshot from Valve's *Half-Life*.

Nintendo also announced that its new console, initially called Dolphin, would ship in 2000, although delays were to force the company to push the launch into the next year.

The late 1990s witnessed other interesting events in the industry. In 1998, Hasbro Interactive bought MicroProse, one of the leading strategy game developers for the personal computer. That same year, Sierra Entertainment shipped *Half-Life* by Valve (see Figure 2.20) and gave a boost to the sagging first-person shooter game genre. In 1999, the craze for massively multiplayer online games received a huge boost when Sony Online Entertainment released *EverQuest* (soon nicknamed "EverCrack" because it was so addictive).

2000: Sony, Sega, and Sims

As the twentieth century came to a close, Sony got the jump on its rivals by releasing the PlayStation 2 in October 2000. Unfortunately, due to component shortages, they were able to ship only half of the units they promised for the U.S. launch. Still, the launch of the PlayStation 2 was largely successful, with about 1.3 million games being sold by the end of the year (as opposed to the 3 million originally planned). This success was due partly to Sony's designing the PlayStation 2 to be compatible with most PlayStation 1 games, which kept customers who owned games for both platforms happy. Moreover, the console included a DVD player, allowing customers to play movies on the machine as well as games.

Not everything was rosy for everyone. One of the main console manufacturers, Sega, more or less threw in the towel on hardware development when it announced that it would start developing games for other platforms. It was rumored that Nintendo was looking to purchase Sega, although both companies denied the rumors. Electronic Arts' decision not to support the Dreamcast was one major reason the console failed. On January 31, 2001, Sega officially announced it would cease production of the Dreamcast and become a software publisher only.

2001: Xbox and GameCube Arrive

November 2001 saw the release of two new consoles in the United States. Microsoft released the Xbox with *Halo* (see Figure 2.21) as its main launch title on November 15, and Nintendo launched the GameCube (previously called Dolphin) with *Luigi's Mansion* on November 18. The Xbox allowed customers to play DVDs as well as games and had a built-in Ethernet port for Internet play. The GameCube, on the other hand, used proprietary minidisks, so customers

FIGURE 2.21 Screenshot from Bungie's *Halo* for the Xbox.

could not play DVDs on it. Nintendo hoped to compete by offering the Game-Cube for $199, $100 less than either the PlayStation 2 or the Xbox. However, neither the Xbox nor the GameCube could shake Sony's domination of the video console market. As of June 2005 (as reported on Wikipedia), over 103 million PlayStation 2 machines were sold worldwide, compared to 24 million Xbox consoles and 21 million GameCubes.

In addition to the GameCube, Nintendo also released the Game Boy Advance in the United States in 2001. The successor to Game Boy Color sold one million units in six weeks. It offered much better graphics and a serial port, so that players could hook up their devices for multiplayer games.

One of the most popular—and controversial—PlayStation 2 games debuted in 2001, Rockstar's *Grand Theft Auto 3*. Though the game used cartoonlike graphics, many people were upset at its violence toward police and women. Other games soon followed *GTA3*'s lead, which led to more calls for stricter controls on sales of violent video games to minors.

In October 2001, Microsoft released Windows XP, a new PC operating system that was no longer based on DOS. As a result, many older computer games (especially those using the old MS-DOS system) were no longer playable on home computers. Of course, the new operating system was much more multimedia friendly and supported better graphics and sound cards.

After six years of trying to become a major game publisher, Hasbro decided to get out of electronic games and sold Hasbro Interactive (including Atari and MicroProse) to Infogrames for $100 million. (In 2005, it reacquired many of those rights from Infogrames.) Hasbro remains the major publisher of board games, and Infogrames, after changing its name to Atari in 2003, continues to publish electronic versions of such popular Hasbro games as *Monopoly* and *Risk*.

2005: New Platforms

The next generation of game consoles began to arrive in 2005, with Microsoft's Xbox 360 leading the pack (see Figure 2.22). There are several configurations of the console, with the simplest being a faster and better video game machine, and the most elaborate expected to be the equivalent of a personal computer with hard drive, keyboard, and mouse that allows the user the functionality of a home entertainment system. Microsoft was unable to meet its initial shipment orders for the new console, angering some customers. However, by the end of 2006, Microsoft reported it had shipped 5 million units worldwide.

At the time this book was published, Sony's PlayStation 3 was in development and expected to ship in 2006, as was Nintendo's successor to the GameCube, named Wii.

The long dominance of the handheld game market by Nintendo's Game Boy Advance has also been challenged recently. First to appear was Nokia's N-Gage, which combines a telephone with a game machine. However, it

FIGURE 2.22 The Microsoft's Xbox 360 shipped in two versions: The Xbox 360 Core System (right) contains the console, wired controller, and composite AV cable, whereas the full Xbox 360 (left) includes a hard drive (upgradable to 20 GB), wireless controller, headset, and Ethernet cable.

received scathing reviews because of the clumsiness of the controls and the lack of interesting games. The Nintendo DS (double screen) system shipped in 2004 and was much better received. Three competing handheld systems also shipped in 2004–2005. Tiger's Gizmondo shipped in the UK in October 2004 but never was released worldwide, because of its poor reception and was eventually discontinued. Likewise, Tapwave's Zodiac was shipped in the UK in October 2004 but it was not well received either. Sony's PSP (PlayStation Portable) shipped in March 2005 and has sold 17 million units as reported at the 2006 E3 (Electronic Entertainment Expor). As of June 2006, Nintendo has reported similar sales of 17 million units for its Nintendo DS. Only time will tell which system will prove dominant.

As for game titles, the industry has adopted the Hollywood standard of producing multiple sequels to hits rather than trying to come up with innovative game designs. Two thousand four saw a plethora of sequels including *Halo 2, Half-Life 2, Doom 3, Grand Theft Auto: San Andreas,* and *EverQuest 2,* among others. The ten top-selling video games of 2005 included five sports titles, a racing title, three *Star Wars* tie-ins and a *Pokémon* title. As for computer game sales in 2005, Blizzard Entertainment's *World of Warcraft* (published by Vivendi International in 2004) was the best-selling title, followed by many sequels (four titles in Electronic Arts' *The Sims* series, Activision's *Call of Duty 2,* Atari's *Roller Coaster Tycoon 3,* and Electronic Arts' *Battlefield 2* and *Age of Empires III*). The only original title in the top ten sellers was Ncsoft's *Guild Wars.*

Summary

The first games appeared during prehistoric times, probably as abstractions of skills needed to be a successful hunter or fighter. Because they are several steps removed from actual danger, games also serve a social function, allowing people to compete in a safe environment. Games were initially reserved for society members who had leisure time—the royalty and upper classes. Eventually, as leisure time and literacy became available to the middle class in the nineteenth century, commercial games began to develop, and they became very popular in the twentieth century. Many of the game mechanics from these older games form the basis of gameplay in modern electronic games as well, and some ancient games such as chess and *Go,* as well as modern games such as *Monopoly* and *Scrabble,* have been transferred directly from boards to computers.

In addition to the more serious work they perform, the rise of computers in the mid-twentieth century offered a new platform for games. In addition to computers, companies developed special game-only machines—video game consoles. Despite some occasional setbacks, electronic games have become increasingly popular and might become the dominant form of entertainment in the twenty-first century and beyond.

Test Your Skills

MULTIPLE CHOICE QUESTIONS

1. Play behavior is something that only children exhibit.

    A. True

    B. False

2. Play behavior is often the practice of skills one will need

    A. to survive.

    B. to fit in with society.

    C. to determine who is the best.

    D. to be better at game playing.

3. Which of the following best explains why there are few prehistoric finds of human games?

    A. Most early societies had no time to play.

    B. Adults never considered games important.

    C. The only finds have been images, not actual game pieces.

    D. The games were too simple for us to consider them to be "games."

4. Most ancient games were which of the following?

    A. Abstractions of survival skills.

    B. Realistic representations.

    C. Abstractions of societal skills.

    D. Developed by the religious leaders of the society.

5. The earliest board games discovered to date were most likely played by which of the following?

    A. Peasants in their spare time.

    B. Nobles and religious leaders.

    C. Warriors as an offering before battle.

    D. Captured slaves with nothing else to do.

6. Dice were developed by which of the following societies?

    A. The Greeks during the Trojan War.

    B. Many ancient societies for use in divination or religious ceremonies.

    C. The Chinese around 600 BCE.

    D. The French.

7. Milton Bradley, the creator of *The Game of Life,* started off in which of the following careers?

    A. A newspaperman.

    B. A New York Stock broker.

    C. A dairy farmer.

    D. A lithographer.

8. Which of the following games is said to have been created by Charles B. Darrow?

    A. *Monopoly.*

    B. *Sorry!*

    C. *Clue.*

    D. *Risk.*

    E. All of the above.

9. Why was *Dungeons & Dragons* considered a new kind of game?

    A. It didn't require a board to play.

    B. It relied on a dungeon master to create events in real time.

    C. It included magical elements.

    D. It used dice.

10. Who bought Hasbro Interactive in 2001?

    A. Mattel.

    B. Parker Brothers.

    C. Infrogrames.

    D. Coleco.

11. What was the first true computer game?

    A. *Pong.*

    B. *Spacewar.*

    C. *Pac-Man.*

    D. *Adventure.*

12. Nolan Bushnell is famous for starting/creating which of the following?

    A. *Sim City*

    B. *ColecoVision*

    C. *Nintendo*

    D. *Atari*

13. Sega started out as a company that did which of the following?

    A. Made coin-operated arcade machines.

    B. Shipped software.

    C. Imported coin-operated arcade machines to the United States.

    D. Made video games.

14. Nintendo selected their name, "Leave luck to heaven," because they made which of the following?

    A. Playing cards.

    B. Lucky dice.

    C. Roulette machines.

    D. Dart boards.

15. The Odyssey worked with which of the following?

    A. Semitransparent overlays on the TV monitor for added detail.

    B. The first game pad.

    C. Magnavox TVs only.

    D. A PDP main-frame.

16. Which of the following best describes Atari's VCS?

    A. A home computer released in 1979.

    B. A home game system released in 1977.

    C. A home computer released in 1977.

    D. A home game system released in 1979.

17. *Asteroids* was published by Atari

    A. in 1979 for the VCS.

    B. in 1979 in arcades.

    C. in 16-bit color.

    D. with four add-on packs.

18. Nintendo released

    A. *Monkey Kong* in Japan and *Donkey Kong* in the United States.

    B. *Donkey Kong* in Japan and the United States.

    C. *Monkey Kong vs. Mario* in Japan.

    D. *Donkey Kong* and *Monkey Kong* at the same time.

19. Which of the following best describes third-party developers?

    A. They code the design made by a secondary company.

    B. They make games for another company's hardware platform.

    C. They write designs that are then programmed by a second company.

    D. They act as a legal entity for two other companies.

20. Why were text adventures popular?

    A. They were played on computers that used punch cards.

    B. Gamers liked figuring out solutions to the puzzles.

    C. Part of the game was guessing the correct word to type.

    D. It was considered typing practice essential to getting a job.

21. Infocom is best known for which of the following?

    A. *Zork*.

    B. Graphic adventures.

    C. *Mario*.

    D. Purchasing Hasbro Interactive.

22. What great advance in 1995 changed the game industry?

    A. Online gaming started.

    B. 3D games became popular.

    C. First FPS was sold.

    D. Microsoft released Windows 95.

23. Which of the following games established the RTS genre?

    A. *Command & Conquer,* Westwood Studios.

    B. *Dune Heretic,* Westwood Studios.

    C. *Red Alert,* Westwood Studios.

    D. *Ultima Online,* Origin Systems.

24. Which of the following systems can you *not* purchase in a traditional retail outlet today? (Select all that apply)

    A. ColecoVision

    B. Dreamcast

    C. PlayStation 2

    D. Xbox

    E. SNES

    F. Genesis

    G. Nintendo 64

    H. GameCube

    I. Odyssey

    J. Atari Jaguar

    K. 3DO

    L. Atari VCS

EXERCISES

Exercise 2.1: Imagining a Game

Write a list of hunting skills that you would consider if you were designing a first-person shooter (FPS) game. (Fans of nonviolent games can consider instead the skills needed to use a camera for this exercise). Write down what the players would have to be able to use or do. How would they need to move? As you create the list, be explicit on whether players can only walk or if they can also run. Can they crouch and hide? While they are crouching, can they fire their gun or take a photo? Write down all the mechanics of how the players would move in the world.

Exercise 2.2: Abstracting a Board Game

Having completed the first exercise, take the skills listed above and develop a board game for three or four players. Use a board similar to a chess board but with ten rows of ten spaces. How many play pieces do you need? Would there be different moves for different kinds of pieces, as in chess? Write a paragraph summary of the hunting (or photo shoot) board game idea. Write another list of mechanics for how all the pieces would move in the game. Is this abstraction of the game easier or more difficult to conceptualize than an FPS?

Exercise 2.3: Create Your Own Royal Game of Ur

Devise a two-player game using a board that has four rows of six squares, as shown in Figure 2.23. You have ten white and ten black tokens, along with four triangular tokens of gold. Given these pieces, what type of game could you make? Create your own rules for a game of capturing squares on the board and ultimately capturing all the triangular gold tokens. You may use (or not use) dice, cards, spinners, or any other tools to determine how the pieces move. You must determine a way to use all ten black and white tokens, though you can vary their attributes or movement abilities.

You can determine the number of players, the location of the players, objectives, and other rules. Make the game and play it. What works? When people played your game, how quickly did they apply your rules, or did they try to change them?

Exercise 2.4: Game Company Research

Research the history of Nintendo and list all game systems they created and released in Japan, the United States, and Europe. Include the number of units sold for each.

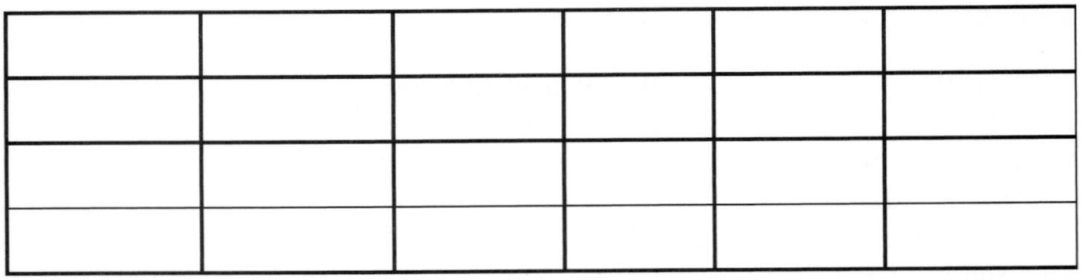

FIGURE 2.23 Layout of the board for the game created in Exercise 2.3.

Exercise 2.5: History of Games

Create a timeline for the history of games, showing your selection of the six most critical points. Start from the prehistoric and continue until the present. When complete, match your critical points in game history with the contemporaneous world is political, technological, and societal issues at each point.

DISCUSSION TOPICS

1. Compare the play behavior in the children of your society to that of the adults in your society. How do they differ? How are they similar? How does their daily life (work, school, or other) impact how and what they seem to play?

2. Scientists believe that the royal game of Ur could have been a game of religious significance or political meaning. Of what other kinds of human interaction might this simple board game have been an abstraction? Discuss other possible ways the royal game of Ur could have been used.

3. Discuss whether *Monopoly* should be considered an abstraction game. How is it different from a game such as *Sorry!*?

4. Discuss whether *Super Mario 3* should be considered an abstraction game. How is it different from an FPS?

5. Review the years of game history. What impacts do society, civilization, and industry have on gameplay, innovation, and creation?

6. Why is it important to understand the history of games for this book about video games? Discuss several ancient games that might be relevant in today's market. How would you have to change them to work on a computer?

Chapter | 3

Game Genres

Chapter Objectives

After reading this chapter and completing the exercises, you will be able to do the following:

- Understand that electronic games fall into two major categories—action games and strategy games.
- List the features of the eight major game genres.
- Understand that each major game genre has several subgenres.
- Understand which game genres are found on computers, consoles, or both.
- Examine gameplay for each game genre.

Introduction

Overall, games fall into two broad categories—games of action and games of strategy. Action games focus on developing keen pattern recognition and quick response to changes in the patterns. Strategy games focus on thinking things through and making deliberate choices. Action games are about speed—the more frenetic the better—whereas strategy games are about analysis and careful manipulation.

This duality appeared in the first games created by people. Athletic competitions were action games. The fastest, strongest, or best-coordinated player prevailed in running, throwing, and wrestling contests. The first board games, on the other hand, were all strategy games, usually turn based, in which players would take turns one at a time at whatever pace they wanted.

The arrival of electronic games continued to mirror the dualism. Early arcade games were all about action, whereas text-based adventures tested players' abilities to solve clever puzzles. Still, most electronic games tend toward action rather than strategy. As personal computer and game consoles became more powerful and were able to manipulate graphics more quickly, there was a natural trend toward visual action games. As the hardware continues to improve, however, more processing time is being devoted to making the artificial intelligence that controls computer-controlled enemies feel more realistic. As a result, games of strategy such as war games, real-time strategy games, and real-world simulations have gained in popularity. Of course, nothing compares—yet—to playing human opponents, and the rising popularity of games played over the Internet allows players from around the world to challenge one another directly.

Game Genres

Over the years, a number of standard game groupings—or **genres,** to borrow a term from literature and the movies—have developed. A game genre is a category that is used to group games that share the same kind of content, visual style, and gameplay actions. Electronic games have generally been divided into eight major genres that span all the different game platforms: action, adventure, role-playing, strategy, simulation, vehicle, sports, and puzzle. Each genre usually has several subgenres, with each subgenre providing a slightly different play experience. For example, the vehicle genre is sometimes divided into two separate categories: driving and flying.

To display games for customers, retailers could simply stack them alphabetically or group them by publishers. But these methods would give little information to consumers. Some buyers might be interested only in sports games, but others might like fast action games, so they would have to pick through a huge number of titles until they found the ones they wanted to buy. Retailers find it easier to group games by basic subjects and gameplay; for example, putting all sports games by all publishers in a sport games section.

Game genres are not absolute, and a game can overlap several genres. For example, *Crazy Taxi* is a game that combines action and car driving. The player drives a taxi around a cartoon town trying to pick up as many fares as possible in a limited amount of time and thus violating every traffic law in a manic attempt to find shortcuts between pickups and deliveries. It might be found in the driving section of a game store, but more than likely, it would be found in the action section because the emphasis is less on realistic driving than on nonstop, helter-skelter, knockabout action.

A given game genre can include games in both the action and strategy categories. The puzzle genre, for example, includes fast-paced games such as *Tetris* and *Lemmings,* as well as slow-paced games such as *Shanghai* and *You Don't Know Jack.*

Action Games

Action games are marked by exuberant activity and quickness of reflex. The player becomes fully immersed in the game world and must continually scan the area for new enemies or other dangers. The primary enjoyment for players is the adrenaline rush of responding as quickly as possible to whatever the game throws at them. The reward for having the quickest eye and the even-quicker reflexes is the highest score. The action game genre includes a number of different subgenres including arcade games, scrolling games, action-adventure games, first-person shooters, and third-person shooters.

Arcade Games

Most of the early electronic games, such as *Pong* (Atari, 1972), *Pac-Man* (Bally/Midway, 1980), *Asteroids* (Atari, 1979), and *Centipede* (Atari, 1981), were created for the arcades in the 1970s and 1980s. Arcade owners wanted players to keep pumping quarters into the machines, so games were designed to be of limited duration, at least initially, because when skilled players got the hang of the game, they were able to play for hours on a single quarter. Meanwhile, other players who watched these "pinball wizards" at work were sure they could be just as good and pumped quarters into the machine until they learned to survive.

Arcade games started out being played on dedicated machines at malls, convenience stores, arcades, or other public places where the specialized machines could be set up. The games eventually moved into homes as companies brought out home/console versions. Thus, the term *arcade* refers to the genre of games that were *originally* designed to play in arcades.

The primary actions in arcade games are usually moving and shooting. Movement might be restricted to back-and-forth along a horizontal axis as in *Space Invaders*, along predetermined pathways as in *Pac-Man,* or unrestricted in all directions as in *Asteroids*. In some more recent games (sometimes called *on-rails gun shooters*), such as *The House of the Dead* (Sega, 1996; see Figure 3.1) and *Time Crisis* (Namco, 1995), the player does not worry about moving, but the game itself automatically moves to a new spot after all enemies in a location have been eliminated.

FYI   Pac-Man *High Score*

The perfect score on a coin-operated version of *Pac-Man* is 3,333,360. The machine won't tally a score higher than that. The first person to reach a perfect score was Billy Mitchell of Florida in 1999.

FIGURE 3.1 Arcade version of Sega's *The House of the Dead,* an on-rail gun shooter.

The controls for arcade games are simple and might consist of a joystick or trackball for moving and a button or two for firing. For home game platforms, the controls have been kept equally simple. The first video consoles had only a few buttons and a direction pad that controlled the action. The learning curve for understanding the controls is kept to a minimum so players do not feel they are wasting quarters to learn complex commands. This simplicity of interface design continues in home video consoles with their thumbsticks/control pad to control movement and a limited number of buttons to control actions.

The artificial intelligence (AI) that controls the enemy in arcade games is extremely limited and usually follows a very basic pattern of movement and attack. Sometimes a bit of randomness is added to an enemy's pattern to keep players on their toes. The enemy seldom reacts to what the player does but keeps repeating its set patterns until either it or the player is destroyed. Obviously, if the enemy AI were the only challenge to the game, it wouldn't be much of a challenge and players would quickly lose interest. There are two ways to make such a game more difficult. First, several different enemies might appear on the screen at the same time, making it much more difficult for the player to respond quickly and correctly to the varied patterns. Second, the enemies might slowly speed up over time until the player is literally overwhelmed by their onslaught.

In a way, the arcade game industry's success was its undoing. People wanted to play the games at home, and manufacturers soon created video game consoles for home versions of arcade hits. Game publishers realized that more profit was available in the home market for arcade games and stopped creating new dedicated arcade machines. The success of the home video game market led to the waning of the arcade business, and many small arcades disappeared in the 1990s. However, arcade games have not disappeared altogether. A new generation of dance arcade games, such as *Dance Dance Revolution* (Konami, 1998; Figure 3.2), combine pattern recognition

FIGURE 3.2 Konami's *Dance Dance Revolution* arcade game.

and dance steps, and its success has drawn players back to the arcades. Arcade games are still being made for the home market as well; for example, simple games for handheld devices such as the Game Boy Advance and PlayStation Portable (PSP) by companies such as Handheld Games and Garage Games, as well as downloadable games from many game Web sites such as Pogo.com and MSN Games. As long as players enjoy a fast-paced, easy-to-play challenge, arcade games will continue to be popular both at home and at the surviving arcades.

Scrolling Games

For many years, the most popular game genre for video game consoles was the *scrolling game.* In these games, the player moves a character who is seen from the side back and forth across the screen. When the character reaches a certain point near the edge of the screen, the game scrolls over to the next area of the playfield, keeping the character near the center of the action. Such games are called *side-scrollers.* Many times, the central action of the game is hand-to-hand fighting or fighting using martial arts weapons. These games are referred to as *fighting games* or *beat-em-ups.* Examples include *Mortal Kombat* (Midway, 1992), *Virtua Fighter* (Sega, 1993; Figure 3.3), and *Double Dragon* (Tradewest et al., 1987).

FIGURE 3.3 Sega's *Virtua Fighter 3 Team Battle,* an action fighting game.

FYI Mortal Kombat *and the Senators*

Senators Joseph Lieberman and Herb Kohl denounced the violence and gore in *Mortal Kombat* in 1993. One result of the brouhaha was the creation of the Entertainment Software Rating Board (ESRB) in 1994, which led to game publishers' adding ratings to their games to help parents determine which ones were suitable for their children.

Other games in this genre, called **platform games,** allow the player's character to explore the upper reaches of a playfield through such actions as jumping on moving platforms, climbing ladders, and using ropes. Usually, the character attempts to elude the many enemies that occupy the playfield by jumping over them or atop them to knock them away. Some of the best known platform scrolling games include *Pitfall!* (Activision, 1982), *Sonic the Hedgehog* (Sega, 1991), *Mega Man* (Capcom, 1987), *Castlevania* (Konami, 1986), *Prince of Persia* (Brøderbund, 1989; Figure 3.4), and *Super Mario Bros*. (Nintendo, 1985).

FIGURE 3.4 Brøderbund's *Prince of Persia,* a platform scrolling game.

FYI *Super* Super Mario Bros.

Nintendo's *Super Mario Bros.* is the best-selling video game of all time, according to *The Guinness Book of Records*. As of 1999, the game has sold 40.23 million copies. Mario is quite a superstar. Since first appearing in *Donkey Kong* in 1982, the games in which Mario has appeared have sold over 152 million copies.

There are two other types of scrolling games. The first, sometimes called a **vertical** or **overhead** scroller, looks down at the map or space from above. The player usually controls a vehicle of some kind, moving in all directions while fighting off waves of attackers that appear from the top of the screen. *Xevious* (Namco, 1982; Figure 3.5), *Raiden* (Acer, 1991), and *1942* (Capcom,

FIGURE 3.5 Arcade version of Namco's *Xevious,* an overhead scroller.

1984) are examples of overhead scrolling games. The second type is a *diagonal* scroller, where the game scrolls from the lower left side of the screen to the upper right side; *Zaxxon* (Sega, 1982) is probably the best-known example of this type of game.

Scrolling games are usually **shooters** of one kind or another; that is, they are games in which the characters are equipped with weapons. The view moves persistently onward, forcing the player forward. Occasionally, the screen will lock and force the player to deal with all the enemies on the screen before unlocking and scrolling on.

Most scrollers have play levels made of multiple screens that the player visits one after another. The typical pattern of each level is to have some number of enemies on the screen attack the player, who must manipulate a character or vehicle around the enemies and/or blast them away without getting killed. Frequently **power-ups** are scattered throughout the playing area; the player can pick them up along the way to gain healing, extra lives, special weapons, or extra abilities such as a turbo boost or force field. The power-ups might also be targets the player must gather to gain points.

The enemies in scrolling games usually follow simple movement and combat patterns. The player's skill is tested by facing several different enemies on the screen at the same time. Often the player must defeat a **boss** at the end of a level before she can move to the next level. The boss is an opponent that is often larger than other enemies and is particularly difficult to defeat. The boss usually has a more complex movement/combat pattern, and the newer, more sophisticated AI for such characters has even enabled some more recent games to track the player's location. The player might have to attack the boss many times to understand how to defeat it.

Some scrolling games for video consoles, called **mascot** games, feature a cute or appealing character that can become a trademark representative that the company can use in promoting its products. Indeed, the Genesis was only moderately successful until Sega introduced the first Sonic game in 1991. A mascot can serve not only as the center of a series of fun games but as the mouthpiece for the company, appearing in advertisements and other promotional materials. Some of the best-known mascots include Nintendo's Mario, Sega's Sonic the Hedgehog, Sony's Crash Bandicoot, Eidos' Laura Croft (*Tomb Raider* series), and Microsoft's Master Chief (*Halo* series).

Although scrolling games were popular on home computers and video consoles, new scrolling game titles are rare today. The popularity of first-person shooters (discussed later in this chapter) beginning with the release of *Doom* marked the end of scrolling games on computers, although they continued to be popular on video consoles. As three-dimensional (3D) computer graphics improved in the newer generations of game consoles, scrolling games morphed into **third-person shooter** games. However, two-dimensional (2D) scrolling games are still around and being played on handheld game systems such as the Game Boy Advance and wireless game systems.

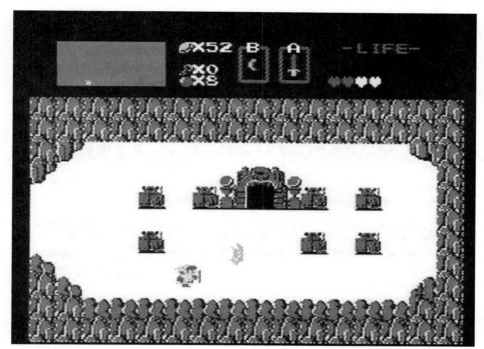

FIGURE 3.6 Nintendo's NES version of *The Legend of Zelda,* an action-adventure game.

Action-Adventure Games

As explained later in the chapter, most adventure games are associated primarily with storytelling and puzzle-solving. However, a subgenre of adventure games includes action-adventure games that incorporate arcade action elements while simplifying the puzzle-solving elements. Nintendo's *The Legend of Zelda* (1985; Figure 3.6) was one of the first games in this subgenre. These games usually incorporate combat as an action element, but the player is also involved in exploring the playfield, gathering items (especially quest items), and solving puzzles.

See the "Adventure Games" section later in the chapter for more details about the play elements of the adventure game genre.

First-Person Shooter Games

In a first-person shooter (FPS) game, the 3D playfield is viewed through the eyes of the main character. There are usually few information displays on the screen: health, armor, remaining ammo, and the barrel of the weapon being held. Thus, the focus is on maximizing the view of the playfield because detecting enemies at a distance is an important requirement for staying alive.

The player is encouraged to explore the world and search for hidden places that might contain special weapons and equipment. At the end of the game, the player usually encounters a particularly tough boss monster that can take quite a while to defeat.

The earliest first-person shooter (FPS) games showed the playfield and units in **wire-frame** (that is, all of the images were meshes of straight lines and had no surfaces). The first such game, *Spasim*, was created in 1974 and allowed up to 32 players to join together over the PLATO Network at the University of Illinois in a 3D space simulation. The first commercial FPS was Atari's *Battlezone* (1980; Figure 3.7), where the player commanded a tank taking on wire-frame enemy tanks and UFOs. In 1992, id Software released the first FPS PC game, *Wolfenstein 3D* (Figure 3.8); however, it was id Software's release of *Doom* in 1993 that redefined the genre. Using a first-person point-of-view in a more fully developed 3D setting suddenly made combat very personal. Many excellent FPS games were developed for the computer and eventually, when the game consoles became powerful enough to use 3D graphics, they appeared on video consoles as well.

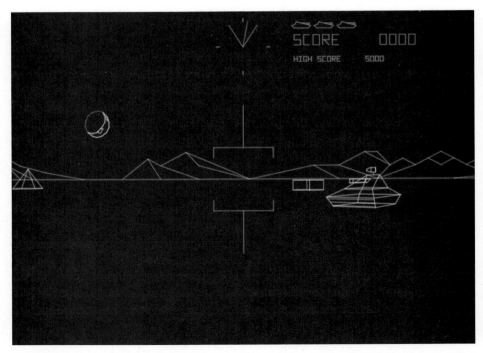

FIGURE 3.7 Atari's *Battlezone,* one of the earliest first-person shooter games using wire-frames to portray tanks and the battlefield.

FIGURE 3.8 id Software's *Wolfenstein 3D,* an early FPS game.

FYI *Omnipresent* Doom

id Software's *Doom* has probably been released on more operating systems than any other game, including the PC, Macintosh, UNIX, Sony PlayStation, Sega Genesis, Nintendo Game Boy Advance, and Nintendo 64, among others. It has spawned a series of books as well as a 2005 movie starring Dwayne "The Rock" Johnson and a television biopic about creators John Romero and John Carmack that is based on David Kushner's book *The Masters of Doom.*

An FPS game might include a story that gives the game a sense of purpose, but the story is generally secondary to running around and killing anything that moves. Recent FPS games—*Half-Life* (Sierra On-Line, 1999), *Star Trek Voyager: Elite Force* (Activision, 2000), *Halo* (Microsoft, 2001), and *Metroid Prime* (Nintendo, 2002)—have tried to make the story narrative more important, but the player's main desire and goal is still to kill everything on the playfield.

Some games, such as *Deus Ex* (Eidos, 2000) and *System Shock II* (Electronic Arts, 1999), include role-playing elements such as an inventory for holding items found during exploration, improved character statistics, and new abilities and skills over time. Other FPS games allow the player to control several characters either by having them tag along (*Half-Life*) or switching between characters (*Ghost Recon,* Ubisoft, 2001). There might also be some puzzle-solving involved. In *Doom,* the player must find keys on the playfield to exit a level, whereas *Half-Life* has several levels with no enemies, and the play is focused on figuring out how to get through the playfield. Adding these extra gameplay elements can give more depth to play and keep the player from getting bored with constant target practice.

Almost every FPS game includes a multiplayer version, in which players can join together over a local area network (LAN) or via the Internet for player-versus-player **deathmatches** or team games such as **capture the flag.** Multiplayer maps are usually included separately from the main game and can differ significantly. They are usually much more open, have few hidden areas, and have no monsters; on the other hand, they have many places where armor, weapons, and ammunition continuously **spawn** (appear repeatedly at the same place in a level), providing endless hardware as players dash around the map in search of each other. Some games, such as *Unreal Tournament* (GT Interactive, 1999; Figure 3.9) and *Quake III Arena* (Activision, 1999), are essentially multiplayer only, although they might include solitaire training maps populated by computer-controlled **bots** (enemy units whose actions are determine by the AI).

A subset of games in the FPS genre is sometimes called **first-person sneaker** games. Although the world is viewed through the standard first-person point-of-view, the player is encouraged to move quietly and stealthily through

FIGURE 3.9 Epic Game's *Unreal Tournament* (published by GT Interactive), primarily a multiplayer FPS game.

the world so as not to get involved in combat. The *Thief* (Eidos, 1998) series of games is a good example of this subset.

Third-Person Shooters

This subgenre of games can be viewed as a marriage of 3D scrolling games with first-person shooters. In this type of game, the player manipulates a character as though observing over the character's shoulder from a distance (see Figure 3.10). The player sees the character in the world, as opposed to seeing the world through the character's eyes. An advantage of this point-of-view is that the player can better judge distances and comprehend the relationship of objects around the character. Thus, actions such as jumping from one level to another or grabbing a swinging rope are easier to perform.

One drawback of these games is that coordinating the character's actions to perform a required motion quickly can be somewhat difficult. Finding the last pixel of a platform from which the character must leap to jump over a pit successfully can be frustrating and can pull players out of their immersion in the game world.

Some of the better-known third-person shooters include *Tomb Raider* (Eidos, 1996), *Prince of Persia: Sands of Time* (Ubisoft, 2003), *MDK* (Interplay, 1997), and *Devil May Cry* (Capcom, 2001).

FIGURE 3.10 Volition's *The Punisher* (THQ, 2005) is a third-person shooter that looks at the game action from over the main character's shoulder.

Adventure Games

Adventure games traditionally combine puzzle-solving with storytelling. The structure holding the game together is an extended narrative that calls for the player to visit different locations and encounter many different characters. Frequently, the path is blocked, requiring the player to gather and manipulate items needed to solve some puzzle that unblocks the path so the story can continue. Some of the first and most popular computer games were *text-based adventures,* but as computer graphics improved over time, *graphic adventure games* eventually eclipsed text-based games.

The main delight for players in such games is in figuring out how to solve the various puzzles in the game. Usually, such puzzles require *combinatorial solutions,* where the player must gather items by exploring the playfield or interacting with characters and then using those items in different ways until the correct combination gives the requisite solution.

The characters in adventure games do not "grow" (or *level up*) or improve over time as they do in role-playing games (see the later "Role-Playing Games," for more details). However, the lead character might change over time as the story unfolds, just like in a book or a movie. In traditional adventure games, combat is usually not a gameplay element; if it does appear, it is minimal and simple compared to the combat in action and role-playing games. As a result, the main character might not have any game statistics such as health, attack value, defense value, and so on because there is no need for them. This contrasts with the combination action-adventure games discussed in the chapter introduction, which do include combat as a major gameplay element.

The character usually has an inventory for holding items found in a game, although there are usually no health items, extra weapons, ammunition reloads, and such to worry about. Nor does the player have to worry about moving items around in the inventory to maximize storage space as in most role-playing games. The items are used to solve puzzles within the game, combined to form new items, or given to and taken by other characters. Often, items can be used only once; as they are used to solve puzzles, they are automatically removed from the inventory.

The best adventure games provide the player with enough clues in the game itself, along with the player's own insights, to figure out how to solve the puzzles. In those cases where no clues are given, the player might be forced to test every combination of items until the solution presents itself. Unfortunately, some solutions are so eccentric and nonintuitive that the player finally gives up in disgust and shelves the game for good.

Text-Based Adventure Games

One of the earliest types of computer games made (because it required no graphics), a *text-based adventure* presents a series of puzzles in story form for the player to solve. In a typical text-based adventure, the player moves from location to location by typing commands into a parser system. If the player enters the correct information (for example, "n" to move north, assuming that direction is allowed), a description of the new location appears. The game might include items the player can try to take or use to solve the many puzzles found in the game.

The first parsers were very simple and could interpret only one or two typed commands at a time. Eventually, parser systems became more sophisticated, and the player could input complex commands (such as "Take cat and put it on the bed"). The complexity of the command structure eventually led to the problem of *fighting the parser,* where a player might be forced to enter a large number of commands in different combinations before finding the right one. Or the location description might make the player think that some command was allowed, but no combination of inputs had any effect. For these reasons, text-based adventures, on the one hand, could be very annoying. On the other hand, coming up with the correct syntax for a command and having the game progress could be very gratifying.

In 1972, William Crowther created the first adventure game, a text-based game called *Colossal Cave* that was designed to run on a mainframe computer. One of the first companies to take advantage of home computers was Infocom, which was founded in 1977 by David Lebling and Mark Blank, originally to create a spreadsheet program called *Cornerstone*. They also dabbled with their own text-based adventure game and decided to release it publicly in 1980 as *Zork I* (Figure 3.11*)*. It was an enormous success and encouraged the company to keep producing games such as *Planetfall* (1983), *The Hitchhiker's Guide to the Galaxy* (1984, based on the Douglas Adam novel of the same name), *A Mind Forever Voyaging* (1985*),* and *Leather Goddesses of Phobos* (1986).

Several other companies published text-based adventures as well. In 1978, Scott and Alexis Adams started Adventure International and published a number of respected games like *Adventureland* (1978), *Voodoo Castle* (1980), and *The Golden Voyage* (1982). After the closure of Infocom in 1989, Bob Bates and Mike Verdu started Legend Entertainment and produced a number of games, including *Spellcasting 101: Sorcerors Get All the Girls* (1990, designed by Steve Meretzky), *Gateway* (1992, based on the Frederik Pohl science fiction novel), and *Eric the Unready* (1993).

Graphical Adventure Games

As the Apple II grew in popularity during the 1970s, its graphics capability fueled a demand for more graphics in games. One of the first adventure games to answer the call was Ken and Roberta Williams' *Mystery House,* which was published in 1980 by their company Sierra On-Line (the company later changed its name to Sierra Interactive). They soon created a number of *Quest* games—including *King's Quest* (1984*), Space Quest* (1986), and *Police Quest* (1987)—as well as the *Leisure Suit Larry* (1987) and *Gabriel Knight* (1993) series.

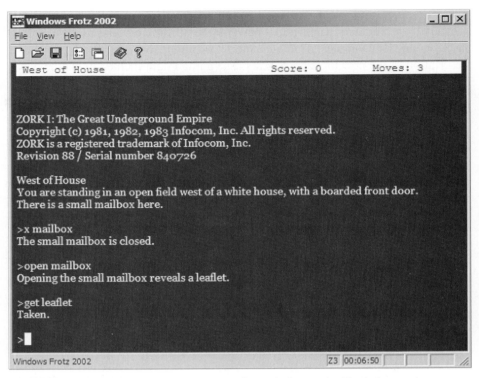

FIGURE 3.11 The opening scene from Infocom's *Zork I,* running on an updated interpreter for Windows.

The early Sierra games were similar to the text-based adventures in that players had to type the commands from a set list to make anything happen. The early graphics were primarily for show, but eventually the graphics became more important, for example, as the player directed the movement of the main character around the screen by mouse click.

Sierra's dominance in graphical adventures was finally challenged by Lucasfilm Games in 1987, when programmers Ron Gilbert and Aric Wilmunder created the Script Creation Utility for Maniac Mansion (SCUMM) script-writing system for the development of *Maniac Mansion*. SCUMM was a high-level language that allowed a designer to use the SCUMM tool to create locations, place items in the locations, and generate the dialogue without having to hard-code the information in the game's source code.

In addition to making it easier for programmers and designers to develop new games, SCUMM-based games also eliminated the need for the player to type commands. The new system allowed players to click on a menu of action words (for example, *Use*, *Take*, or *Talk*) and then on an object. If the combination was correct, an action would occur. Among the more popular Lucasfilm Games (later LucasArts) offerings were *Loom* (1990), *The Secret of Monkey*

FIGURE 3.12 LucasArt's *The Secret of Monkey Island,* a graphic adventure game using the SCUMM engine.

Island (1990, Figure 3.12), *Day of the Tentacle* (1993), and *Grim Fandango* (1998). *Loom* completely removed commands from the interface, and later games continued to minimize the interface in an attempt to free the player from having to guess or figure out how the programmer intended an item to be used.

FYI *Writing Help*

The insults during sword fights in Lucasfilm's *The Secret of Monkey Island* were written by science fiction writer Orson Scott Card, who wrote the *Ender's Game* trilogy. He also contributed to Lucasfilms' *The Dig* and *Loom*.

Another popular graphical adventure game was *Myst* (see Figure 3.13). Created by Cyan Worlds, Inc., in 1991 and published by Brøderbund in 1993, the game had a first person point-of-view with few animations, no characters to interact with, and no inventory for holding items. Its gameplay was extremely simple. Players were confronted with simple mixed-picture puzzles to sort out or scavenger hunts to find specific objects. The beautifully rendered graphics and intricate puzzles captivated a wide audience and showed that computer games could be targeted to adult audiences who were uninterested in combat or action-centered games.

Myst was the last adventure game to reach best-seller status. Each year, several new adventure games are published, but none has achieved the same success

FIGURE 3.13 One of the clues from Cyan's *Myst.*

of the early text-based and graphical adventure games. Sales trends seem to indicate that today's gaming audience wants more action and less contemplation.

Action-Adventure Games

As mentioned elsewhere in this chapter, a number of games include elements from both action and adventure games. These hybrid games have more action—usually combat—than standard adventure games, but they also rely on more puzzle-solving to get through the story than most first-person or third-person shooters. They are similar to role-playing games but without the leveling up or experience level increases that are granted to characters over time through combat or practice. Both tell stories, both have lots of character interaction, and both have puzzles (although in role-playing games, the puzzles can take the form of quests). However, characters in adventure games tend to be static in terms of game statistics while changing over time as the story progresses, whereas role-playing characters continually improve their game attributes and learn new skills and abilities without necessarily changing their personality.

Examples of action-adventure games include Interplay's *Alone in the Dark* (1992), Westwood Studio's *Blade Runner* (1997), and LucasArts' *Indiana Jones and the Infernal Machine* (1999).

This subgenre has not yet been fully explored or developed by designers. The difficulty in creating such a game is that players have a natural desire to focus only on any action (such as combat) that might be involved, to the exclusion of puzzle solving. The trick is to make the puzzles easy enough to decipher in a relatively short time (or to eventually bypass), yet challenging enough to keep the player intrigued for an extended period.

Role-Playing Games

Electronic role-playing games (RPGs) are all descendants of TSR Hobbies' *Dungeons & Dragons* (1973) and feature many of the same game elements:

- An overall story arc gives purpose to the events in the game and drives the main character toward achieving a goal (the central quest). The villain of the game usually desires the same goal, thus resulting in the tension that underlies the conflict in the story.

- The character(s) controlled by the player usually have a number of different game statistics that are used to resolve game actions. These statistics include the character's health (expressed as *hit points*), physical attack strength (expressed as *strength*), physical defense ability (based on the character's constitution and whatever armor is being worn), and many others (such as *intelligence, beauty, dexterity,* and so on).

- Characters usually start out very weak and improve their statistics over time. This usually occurs when the character wins in combat and/or reaches a new ***experience level.***

- In addition to improving their game statistics, characters can learn new abilities (such as magic spells) or skills when they go up a level.

- The player makes new discoveries during the game, such as weapons, armor, magic spells, potions, and so on. Some of these items improve the character's game statistics or provide new abilities and others are used toward achieving the central quest.

- As the story progresses, the character continually encounters new fantastic creatures and dangerous enemies as well as allies who assist in the main quest.

RPGs are story driven. Some classical epic RPGs feature an extended saga in which the player's character is the central protagonist. The main character travels to many locations and meets many ***nonplayer characters*** (NPCs), who might have small quests for the hero. The primary quest is the defeat of the master villain, who usually kicks off the story with some nasty act. These role-playing games are vast and can take a hundred or more hours to complete.

Some role-playing games (such as *Baldur's Gate*) are ***open-ended*** and allow players to roam anywhere within the world as long as they can survive. The main character might encounter many different NPCs who each want the hero to perform different tasks and reward him upon the task's completion. The player might wander all over the world, trying to complete these tasks (subquests) to gather the materials needed to defeat the main villain. Other games, particularly console RPGs, are much more linear and force the player to follow a narrative *track.* In these games, the world is not open for exploration until late in the game, when the hero has already visited the most important locations as part of the narrative. Track RPGs are easier to design than open-ended RPGs because the story and experience levels are delivered in a more precisely controlled manner and, therefore, are easier to playtest and balance.

Vast Worlds and Many Gameplay Elements

A role-playing game comprises many gameplay elements. Because so many parts must be carefully balanced, it is considered the most difficult genre to design. The designers need to come up with systems to generate and improve characters, resolve weapon and magic combat, handle inventory, buy/sell goods, and interact with other characters. In addition to basic gameplay, the designers must also create the world that players will explore, including the races that inhabit the many different lands.

A successful, original role-playing game frequently results in many sequels not only because players enjoy revisiting the world they've spent so many hours exploring but also because it's easier for the designers to expand upon a world that has already been created than to create a brand new world for each game. Successful role-playing game series have been developed for both computers and video consoles. Fantasy is the most popular literary genre for RPGs, followed distantly by science fiction and even more remotely by other genres.

Among the most popular traditional computer fantasy role-playing game series are *Ultima* (California Pacific Computer, 1981), *Wizardry* (Sir-Tech Software, 1981), *Might & Magic* (New World Computing, 1986), *The Elder Scrolls* (US Gold, 1993), and *Baldur's Gate* (Black Isle Studios, 1998; Figure 3.14). Some of the popular console-based fantasy role-playing game series include *Dragon Quest* (Enix, 1986), *Phantasy Star* (Sega, 1987), *Final Fantasy* (Square Co., Ltd., 1987; Figure 3.15), and *Suikoden* (Konami, 1996).

Popular science fiction role-playing games include *Wasteland* (Electronic Arts, 1987), *Fallout* (Interplay, 1997), *Planescape: Torment* (Interplay, 1999), *Star Wars: Knights of the Old Republic* (LucasArts, 2004), and the MMORPG *Star Wars Galaxies* (LucasArts, 2003). There have been a few RPGS in other genres:

- Horror: *Vampire: The Masquerade—Bloodline* (Activision, 2004)

- Super heroes: the MMORPG *City of Heroes* (MCsoft, 2004)

- Pirates: *Sea Dogs* (Bethesda Softworks, 2000)

Several first-person shooters have included role-playing elements. In both *Deus Ex* (Eidos Interactive, 2000) and S*ystem Shock II* (Electronic Arts, 1999),

FIGURE 3.14 Black Isle Studio's *Baldur's Gate,* a computer role-playing game.

FIGURE 3.15 Scene from *Final Fantasy X,* a role-playing game developed by Square Co., Ltd., for the PlayStation 2.

the main character gets stronger over time and learns new skills (as well as meeting NPCs that give them information or assign them quests) as in a traditional RPG, although the main activity is still shooting everything that moves from a first-person point-of-view.

Dungeon Crawls and Online Games

In addition to standard epic computer role-playing games, there are several subgenres:

■ Action Role-Playing Games: Often called **dungeon crawls,** these games are set at a smaller scale with less extended storytelling. Storytelling is secondary to hack-and-slash action. The focus is on the player's exploring various locations and killing every monster in sight. Some of the popular action role-playing games include *The Bard's Tale* (Electronic Arts, 1985), *Ultima Underworld* (ORIGIN Systems, 1992), *Diablo* (Blizzard Entertainment, 1996 Figure 3.16) and *Dungeon Siege* (Microsoft, 2002).

■ Multiuser Dungeons (MUDs): These are text-based role-playing games that are played over the Internet. In these games, players have the opportunity to create their own dungeons and then add them to a game

FIGURE 3.16 Blizzard Entertainment's *Diablo,* an action role-playing game.

for other players to explore. Some examples of MUDs include *Mirrorworld* (1985) and *Avalon, the Legend Lives* (1989).

■ Massively multiplayer online role-playing games (MMORPGs): Arguably, these are the most popular pay-to-play games on the Internet. Players pay a monthly fee to play the game, which is available only online. These games have the same main play elements as stand-alone RPGs including exploration, combat, puzzle-solving, inventory control, and the like, but they often lack a central overarching story. They are set in ***persistent worlds;*** that is, they do not change significantly over time because of narrative events. New players are always signing up to join the game and they want the same experience of exploring the world afresh as the seasoned veterans with whom they can interact have had. Expansion packs often open new lands for players to explore, making sure that those who know the game well still have many places to explore, experience levels to gain, and new skills and abilities to learn. Current popular MMORPGs include *Ultima Online* (Electronic Arts, 1997), *EverQuest* (989 Studios, 1999), *Asheron's Call* (Microsoft, 1999), *Dark Age of Camelot* (Vivendi, 2001) and *World of Warcraft* (Blizzard Entertainment, 2004; Figure 3.17).

3

FIGURE 3.17 Blizzard Entertainment's *World of Warcraft,* a massively multiplayer online role-playing game.

Strategy Games

This genre is often confused with simulation games because they both demand the player to think through problems, manipulate resources and make strategic and tactical decisions. For the purposes of this book, the *strategy game* genre is defined as games that deal with military, economic, and political conflict. We focus on three subgenres: war games, real-time strategy (RTS) games, and economic/political games. Abstract strategy games such as chess or Go are covered under the puzzle game genre later in the chapter.

It should be noted that a number of sources lump all combat-aircraft and vehicle (such as tanks) games that include combat into the strategy game genre. This book makes a distinction, grouping games in which the player is primarily flying the combat aircraft or driving a tank in the vehicle game genre. If a game focuses primarily on the player's commanding air units or tank units and making strategic plans that involve multiple NPC units during a battle, it is considered part of the strategy game genre.

War games

War games (often called *military simulation* games) are recreations of military conflicts. They can cover any time period of human history from the ancient conquests of Alexander to the present. Some games are set in fantastic times and worlds; for example, pitting humans against aliens, elves against orcs, or Caesar against Hitler. A player acts as the leader of one force or country and makes decisions about how his side will engage in the conflict. The units involved can range from the few men of a squad or platoon to entire corps and armies. The focus is on realistic military strategies and tactics, and the point is to let the player prove himself a capable leader of troops, given the initial starting conditions of the battle or war.

These games examine the strategies and tactics of warfare. *Strategy* can be defined as looking at the big picture and determining how a military campaign will be waged; for example, how a general might seek to roll up the enemy's line by maneuvering the brunt of his tank and infantry forces into position to attack the enemy's exposed flank. *Tactics* deals with the actual handling of forces in combat; for example, holding a tank force behind the line in reserve to deal with any breakthrough of enemy armored forces.

Computer war games trace directly back to paper war games, which were started in 1953 by Charles Roberts (see Chapter 2, "The Evolution of Games," for more information). Ironically, the success of computer games led to the decline of paper war games. Considering that a paper game might have several maps, each about 2×3 feet in size, and hundreds of cardboard playing pieces to represent the military units, it might take hours to set up such a game and tens of hours more to play it through to completion. With a computer, it's simply a matter of booting up the program, restoring the last saved position, and completing the game at one's leisure. However, there is a loss of the overall picture of the battle with computer war games. In a paper war game, the player can see the entire battlefield at a glance and check the locations of all units before deciding which ones to move in a turn. The computer monitor can show only so much detail, so controlling units in computer war games often feels like checking a series of snapshots of the battle and not the picture in toto.

There are three levels of scale for war games:

- **Tactical-level** games focus on a small portion of a battle, usually dealing with squads and platoons. Examples of tactical-level war games include *Squad Battles: Vietnam* (HPS Simulations, 1991), *Jagged Alliance* (Sir-tech Software, 1994; Figure 3.18), and *X-Com UFO Defense* (MicroProse, 1994).

- **Operational-level** games focus on a single battle (the Battle of the Bulge) or campaign (Waterloo) and usually deal with regiments and battalions. Examples of operational-level war games include Larry Bonds's *Harpoon* (Three-Sixty Pacific, 1988), *Panzer General* (Strategic Simulations, Inc., 1994) and *Sid Meier's Gettysburg!* (Firaxis, 1997; Figure 3.19).

- **Strategic-level** games deal with whole wars (World War II) or theaters of operation (the Russian Front in WWII) and usually deal with corps or armies. Examples include Sid Meier's *Crusade in Europe* and *Civilization* (MicroProse, 1985 and 1991, respectively) and *Master of Orion* and *Master of Magic* (MicroProse, 1994 and 1995, respectively).

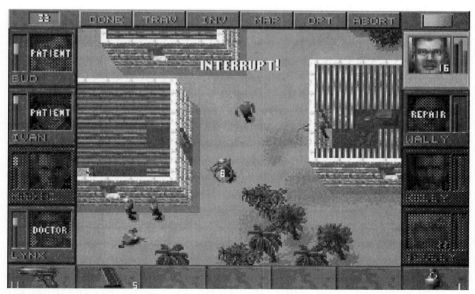

FIGURE 3.18 Sir-tech Software's *Jagged Alliance,* a tactical-level war games.

FIGURE 3.19 Firaxis's *Sid Meier's Gettysburg!* (published by Electronic Arts), an operational-level war game.

If a game recreates a historical battle, the developers generally try to do so as accurately as possible. The playfield recreates the battlefield as closely as possible, and game pieces are limited to the same routes taken by the units in the real battle. The military units that actually took part in the battle are represented by the playing pieces, and the rules are often tailored to match the military tactics of the time. For example, in games about battles in Virginia and the Eastern Theater of the American Civil War (1861–65), there is often a "stupid Union general" rule because the Union had such poor generalship until Ulysses S. Grant arrived to take over command. The rules for such games can be very complex, especially for battles from World War II to the present (and the future) in which mechanized armies' movement ability and firepower greatly outperform earlier weaponry. There might be special rules for leadership, lines of supply, the *fog of war* (uncertainty as to the enemy's location and actions), communications, artillery support, air missions, and the like.

The units controlled by the player are real military units of the time being portrayed. Each unit usually has a *movement rate* (how fast it can move across the battlefield), an *attack value* (its strength when attacking) and a *defense value* (its ability to defend itself when attacked). Other values can apply as well, based on the unit type. An air unit might have a ***range***—the maximum distance it can fly to perform a combat mission. An artillery unit might also have a range—how far it can propel a projectile. Other values might represent how far a unit can be from a leader and still be effective, how long a line it can trace (in movement points) to a supply depot, and how strong its morale is in combat.

In a paper war game, all these values would be printed directly on each cardboard playing piece, sometimes leading to eyestrain. An advantage of computer war games is that they don't have to show the player all the numbers associated with a cardboard playing piece. For example, in a game where players alternate between moving their units and attacking, the computer can determine the maximum distance a unit can travel in all directions and graphically inform the player of this information as a shaded area near the unit. The player does not have to count out every movement of each unit in computer games, and the complex combat resolution is handled easily by the computer, allowing the player to focus on strategy and tactics.

FYI | *Real War Games*

In his article, "History of War games" (**www.strategypage.com**), historian Matthew Caffrey writes: "The Japanese war game in preparation for the Battle of Midway was easily the most notorious war game ever played. During the game, the American side's airpower sank two Japanese carriers. Rear Admiral Ukagi Matome, Yamamoto's chief of staff and commander of their carrier force for the operation, unilaterally reversed the umpires' ruling on the loss of the carriers. The carriers were restored to the game, and the Japanese side went on to capture Midway. Weeks later, during the actual battle, the Americans sank the same two carriers, plus two more. This time Admiral Ukagi was not able to reach into the 'dead pile' and replace his ships."

Real-Time Strategy Games

The term ***real-time*** indicates that the action for all players in real-time strategy (RTS) games is constant and simultaneous. The structure of turn-based war games allows players plenty of time to consider where to attack the enemy and what units to maneuver into the desired offensive position. On the other hand, in RTS games, all sides act at the same time, so conditions on the battlefield are fluid, changing rapidly and forcing players to react to threats as they develop. Paper war games such as Simulation Publications, Inc.'s, *The Battles of Bull Run* (1973) and *StarForce: Alpha Centauri* (1974) experimented with simultaneous movement, but they were clumsy and not very successful. When the computer became a platform for gaming, war games could become real time because even the older, slower computers had the computational power to keep track of unit movement and actions that proved difficult for human players to remember.

RTS games tend to feel less realistic than war games, not only because the settings are often fantastic (science fiction or fantasy landscapes), but also because getting combat units into battle involves little strategy or tactics. The winner tends to be the one who "gits thar fustest with the mostest men" (a misquote attributed to Confederate General Nathan Bedford Forrest).

Whereas war games focus on maneuvering military units in combat, real-time strategy games are more about gathering enough resources to create the units and then pointing them to the battlefield where they are left to fend for themselves. The player of an RTS game feels more like a quartermaster than a battlefield general. The player spends about half her time in resource management and half her time exploring the map for enemy units.

In most RTS games, the player initially worries about gathering resources. The typical formula is to start off with a number of idle workers. The player assigns the workers to gather enough materials to erect buildings (housing, smiths, training centers, and so on) that in turn provide weaponry and train the workers to become warriors. The warriors are then sent out to scout for enemy units and engage in combat. The winner is the side that manages to destroy the other's combat units and/or settlements. Although these games might have as many combat values per unit as a war game, the values are usually hidden from the player. The values of most concern to the player are how many different resources are needed to build something and how long it will take until the object—building or combat unit—is finished.

Several of the first popular RTS games were developed by Dani Bunten. *Command HQ* (Microplay, 1990) dealt with war at a global level, whereas *M.U.L.E.* (Electronic Arts, 1983) was an economic contest for control of resources on an alien planet. Westwood Studio's *Dune II* (Virgin Interactive, 1992) is sometimes cited as the first "true" RTS, but it was the success of their *Command & Conquer* in 1995 that defined the subgenre's gameplay elements (see Figure 3.20 for a screenshot from the sequel, *Tiberian Sun*). A number of other classic games solidified the RTS subgenre as a leading seller for computers including Blizzard Entertainment's *Warcraft* (1994) and *StarCraft* (1997), *Total Annihilation* (Cavedog Entertainment, 1998), and Ensemble Studios' *Age of Empires* (Microsoft, 1998).

The prime platform for both war games and real-time strategy games is the personal computer. The mouse is the easiest way to select one or more units and click on a destination, and the keyboard offers many shortcut keys that cut down on the clutter of menus a video console would require.

Economic/Political Strategy Games

A number of strategy games don't deal directly with warfare, although they do center on conflict between "powers." These games might deal with economic

FIGURE 3.20 Westwood Studio's *Command & Conquer: Tiberian Sun* (Electronic Arts), a real-time strategy game.

conflict between moguls or political struggles between parties or nations. What separates these games from simulation games (discussed in the next section) is that they have a goal—to defeat the enemy—whereas simulations tend to be more like playthings that have no ultimate goal and, therefore, can go on until the player tires of them.

Such a game might deal with a subject on many levels. For example, a railroad game might deal with acquiring the right-of-way to build the railroad, buying equipment, funding research on better engines, selling stock to the public, and handling passenger and cargo shipments economically. A political game might deal with finding the right candidate for an election, giving speeches, drumming up support from various political blocs, raising funds, and setting up a political agenda to attract the greatest number of voters. These games are enjoyable because they offer intellectual challenges at many levels.

Some of the economic strategy games include Sid Meier's *Railroad Tycoon* (MicroProse, 1990) and *The Corporate Machine* (Stardock, 2001; Figure 3.21). Political strategy games include *Balance of Power* (Mindscape, 1985), *Hidden Agenda* (Springboard, 1988), *Gangsters: Organized Crime* (Eidos Interactive, 1998) and *The Political Machine* (Ubisoft, 2004).

FIGURE 3.21 Stardock's *The Corporate Machine* (Take-Two Interactive), an economic strategy game.

Simulation Games

For purposes of this book, ***simulation games*** are specifically those products that try to recreate at a reduced scale some aspect of the real world in a noncompetitive way. It excludes games that recreate flight and racing, which are discussed later in the section on vehicle games. In a way, *simulation game* is an oxymoron because most products that simulate the real world in miniature are open-ended, whereas games have a set goal or finish line and are thus goal-oriented. For purposes of this book, if the product has a definite goal that is achieved through conflict with other players (human or computer-controlled), it is a strategy game. Sid Meier's *Railroad Tycoon,* for example, is considered a strategy game because the goal is to beat other competitors and become the richest railroad magnate. Will Wright's *The Sims,* on the other hand, is a simulation game because it has no final goal toward which the player strives, no end point where the game concludes and a victor is determined, and no payoff for controlling peoples' lives better than anyone else. However, some simulations have real goals—for example, reaching a certain contentment level for the citizenry within a fixed timeframe—whereas

others are more open-ended, allowing the player to experiment freely with the game world and acting like a "god."

Simulation games are all about management of resources and making decisions on how the resources will be expended. The player becomes a god, deciding what to build or buy or otherwise lording it over the world being depicted. The game might be about building something—a city, for example—or about controlling lives. It's akin to having a chemistry lab where you can experiment with different combinations to see how one element affects others and which combinations are most effective. To handle the many problems that arise over time can be daunting, but the satisfaction for the player comes in doing the best job possible of meeting the changing demands of the citizens of the game world. Most simulation games are designed for computers rather than consoles. Consoles have a limited number of buttons compared to a keyboard, so controlling things in the complex world of the simulation would likely require a large number of menus. It is also easier to select and manipulate items and options with a mouse than to scroll through them with thumbsticks or a direction pad (D-pad). Thus, a player has a much easier time playing the simulation on a computer than on a console.

The first popular simulation game was Will Wright's *SimCity* (Brøderbund, 1989), which set the model for future products in the same category. In *SimCity,* the player acts as the mayor of a city, collecting taxes, building roads, erecting buildings, zoning areas of the city for different purposes, and trying to keep the populace as content as possible. The game immediately gained a vast audience and was even used by some city planners to study real-world conditions, although it had been rejected by fifteen publishers before Brøderbund agreed to publish it. Figure 3.22 shows a screenshot from *SimCity 3000.*

FYI **SimCity** *Original Cover*

The original front cover of *SimCity* includes a representation of Godzilla running amok. It eventually had to be removed because of copyright infringements.

In 2000, Wright struck gold again when *The Sims* was released by Electronic Arts. Instead of controlling something abstract like a city or anthill, the player controlled the lives of everyday people in miniature. The game inspired many ***add-ons*** (modules to be played with the original game) to the product line as well as *The Sims 2* in 2004. There are even simulations for younger gamers. Nintendo released *Animal Crossing* for the GameCube in the United States in 2002 (Figure 3.23), in which the player can live out his or her life as desired in a fantastic village.

FIGURE 3.22 Maxi's *SimCity 3000* (Electronic Arts), a simulation of city planning.

FIGURE 3.23 Nintendo's *Animal Crossing,* a simulation game set in a fantasy world.

Vehicle Games

Many simulation games include vehicles. This book breaks such games into their own genre for several reasons. First, not all games involving vehicles are pure simulations. Some racing games are simulations in that they try make the experience as realistic as possible for the player, but many are action games that do not try to imitate real life in the least and even involve combat against opponents. Second, vehicles other than cars and aircraft, such as boats, submarines, and futuristic vehicles, can involve racing, or games might try to simulate what it is like to command such vehicles.

To immerse players in a more realistic experience of flying a plane or driving a car, several peripherals have been created specifically for computer vehicle games. Steering wheels can be hooked up to the computer to let players maneuver racing cars on the screen, and joysticks let players feel that they are in the cockpit, controlling the aircraft as real pilots do. It should be noted that these peripherals are used more often for driving and flight simulations than for action vehicle games.

Land Vehicle Games

Driving games fall into three broads categories: arcade games, action games, and simulations. *Arcade games* are simplistic racing games, *action games* involve racing and combat, and *simulations* try to recreate driving a vehicle realistically.

Arcade Racing Games   Arcade racing games are located in physical arcades and run the gamut from simple stand-alone cabinets to minicars in which the player sits while playing. They usually have very simple controls— a steering wheel, an accelerator, and brakes. The usual idea is to be the first driver across the finish line, although some arcade games have slightly different goals. These games use more cartoon physics than real-world physics in the sense that when vehicles move in the game world they have more bounciness and can take much more damage than real cars could stand. Arcade racing games attempt to give players the sense of exhilaration of racing without all the humdrum details of pit stops and rules. These games often include power-ups that drivers can aim for to make the vehicle perform better, if less realistically. Some power-ups include turbo boosts to super-speed the vehicle, force fields to shield the vehicle, and occasional traps to slow down other racers.

Examples of arcade racing games include *Cruis'n USA* (Midway, 1994), *Super Mario Kart* (Nintendo, 1992), *Pole Position* (Namco, 1982), *Out Run* (Sega, 1986), *The Need for Speed* (Electronic Arts, 1994), and *Crazy Taxi* (Sega, 2000; Figure 3.24).

FIGURE 3.24 Screenshot from the Dreamcast version of Sega's *Crazy Taxi,* an arcade racing game.

Action-Combat Racing Games   Action-combat racing games are similar to arcade racing games in many ways, but they also include a lot of mayhem. In addition to racing vehicles, these games usually include some form of combat, even if the only weapon is the vehicle itself. In some cases, as in the *Grand Theft Auto* series, only part of the game has to do with driving vehicles. Some action games featuring tanks also fall in this category.

Examples of action racing games include *Carmageddon* (Stainless Software, 1997), *Interstate '76* (Activision, 1997), *Grand Theft Auto* (BMG Interactive, 1997), *World Destruction League: Thunder Tanks* (3DO, 2000), *The Simpsons Road Rage* (Electronic Arts, 2002) and *Twisted Metal: Black* (SCEA, 2001). One might consider adding Activision's *MechWarrior* (1989) to this class even though the game is about piloting giant robots in futuristic wars.

FYI *Role Reversal*

In the original *Grand Theft Auto*, the player was supposed to be a policeman trying to capture looters, thugs, and gang members. As the game neared completion, however, the production team decided to reverse the roles and have the player be a gangster.

Simulation Racing Games   Most people eventually get a driver's license, so there is little escapism involved in driving an everyday car in a mundane setting. However, there are some vehicles that most people never get to drive, and these might be the topic of simulation games. *Microsoft Train Simulator* (2001) lets the user experience being a railroad engineer in charge of a large train, and *Hard Truck: Road to Victory* (Valusoft, 1998) puts players in the driver's seat of a big rig traveling across the country.

In most simulation games, however, the vehicle is a high-performance sports car, racing car, or motorcycle, and the game tries to imitate as closely as possible the experience of drivers in such races. The physics are as close to the real world as possible, so players get a sense of traction of the tires, bounces from the suspension system, and violence of collisions. The player can enhance the experience by using a unique driving wheel peripheral that simulates the bumps and jerks during the race through the vibrations of the wheel (this is called *force-feedback*). In many instances, the racetracks are taken from real life, and the production team might try to recreate the track environment in photorealistic style. In other cases, players are allowed to build and modify their own tracks.

Some racing games are fairly intricate. Although they usually allow a player to just jump in and play-through a quick race, these games can include season-long campaigns where players have to worry about maintaining and upgrading their cars. Players use their winnings to replace worn out parts or invest in better technology, and if they run out of money, they have to scrape by with what they have on hand. This combination of racing, resource management, and strategy is all part of the vehicle racing simulation and can provide an even more fulfilling experience because players compete with their purchases as well as their driving skills.

Examples of simulation racing games include *Indianapolis 500: The Simulation* (Electronic Arts, 1989), *Motocross* (Gamestar, 1989), *NASCAR Racing* (Sierra On-Line, 1994; Figure 3.25) and *Gran Prix 2* (Microsoft, 1995). Some non-car vehicle simulations include *Tank: The M1A1 Abrams Battle Tank Simulator* (Spectrum Holobyte, 1989), *Motocross* (Gamestar, 1989), *Superbike World Championship* (Electronic Arts, 1999), and *ATV Offroad Fury* (SCEA, 2001).

Air Vehicle Games

This subgenre consists of two broad categories: combat simulations and civilian flight simulations. **Combat simulations** involve the player as a pilot during war from the first airplanes in World I to the present. **Civilian flight simulations** deal only with piloting regular airplanes. Some sources might lump spaceships into this category as well, but there are some differences, as noted later.

Combat Simulations   Combat simulations are as complex as the aircraft they simulate. World War I aircraft have far fewer controls than modern planes, so games of that period require fewer keyboard inputs than games that simulate the

FIGURE 3.25 Sierra On-Line's *NASCAR Racing,* a simulation racing game.

F-14 or A-10. When MicroProse released *F-15 Strike Eagle II* in 1989, it included a plastic overlay for the keyboard because so many commands were needed to play the game. It should be noted, however, that even the most complex combat simulation has simplistic controls compared to real combat aircraft.

The complexity for the player in these games is not only flying the aircraft, but also using the weapons aboard. There might be bombs to drop, machine guns to fire, and rockets to launch.

Examples of airplane combat simulations from WWI to the present include *Air Warrior* (Kesmai, 1986, which covered both World Wars and featured massive multiplayer air combat via the Genie online service), *Knights of the Sky* (MicroProse, 1990), *Red Baron* (Sierra On-Line, 1990), *Secret Weapons of the Luftwaffe* (LucasArts, 1991), *B-17 Flying Fortress* (MicroProse, 1992), *F-16 Combat Pilot* (Electronic Arts, 1989) and *A-10 Tank Killer* (Dynamix, 1989). Helicopter combat simulations include *Gunship* (MicroProse, 1986), *LHX: Attack Chopper* (Electronic Arts, 1990), *Apache* (Digital Integration, 1995), and *HIND: The Russian Combat Helicopter Simulation* (Interactive Magic, 1996; Figure 3.26).

Civilian Flight Simulations Civilian flight simulations try to present as realistically as possible the feeling of flying a plane that might range from small aircraft to a large jet. Many include add-on packs recreating the real terrain in different areas of the world to make the game even more realistic. A typical "mission" might involve taking off, flying to the destination, and landing.

FIGURE 3.26 Interactive Magic's *HIND: The Russian Combat Helicopter Simulation,* an air combat simulation game.

The controls are usually very complex and the learning curve for mastering them very steep. But the reward is watching the world below slide by and truly feeling that you are "king of the hill."

Examples of civilian flight simulators include *Microsoft Flight Simulator* (1982), *Flight Unlimited* (Looking Glass Studios, 1995), and *SimCopter* (Electronic Arts, 1996).

Water Vehicle Games

Water vehicle games are not as popular as land, air, or even space vehicle games. A number of games simulate naval combat, but most of these are better categorized under war games in the strategy games genre. Still, there are several examples of arcade racing games and ship simulations.

Water-Vehicle Arcade Racing Games These games are similar to other vehicle arcade games. The controls tend to be very simplistic—accelerate, decelerate, and steer left and right. Racing vehicles include speedboats and jet skis. Examples of water-vehicle arcade racing games include *Pro Powerboat Simulator* (Codemaster, 1989; Figure 3.27), W*ave Race* (Nintendo, 1990), *VR Powerboat Racing* (Interplay, 1998), *Hydro Thunder* (Midway, 1998), *H2Overdrive* (Crave Entertainment, 2001), and *Splashdown* (jet skis; Infogrames, 2001).

FIGURE 3.27 Codemaster's *Pro Powerboat Simulator,* a water-vehicle arcade racing game.

Water Vehicle Simulations   There are only a few sailing simulations, possibly because sailing does not pique players' imaginations as something unusual. There are some combat simulations, too, but most naval combat games tend to fall into the war games category because naval engagements usually have multiple participants on each side and the players become commanders of fleets and not just a single ship's captain. On the other hand, submarine simulators are quite popular, no doubt because each submarine normally acts on its own and, therefore, a player can become the boat's commander.

Examples of sailing simulations include *The American Challenge: A Sailing Simulation* (Mindscape, 1986) and *Virtual Sailor* (Quality Simulations, 2002). Examples of combat ship simulations include *Destroyer Command* (Ubisoft, 1993), *Age of Sail* (Talonsoft, 1996), and *Fighting Steel* (Strategic Simulation, Inc., 1999). Submarine simulations include *Sub Battle Simulator* (Epyx, 1987), *Silent Service* (Microsoft, 1985), *Das Boot: German U-Boat Simulation* (Three-Sixty Pacific, 1990), and *Command: Aces of the Deep* (Sierra On-Line, 1995; Figure 3.28).

Spaceship Simulations

George Lucas's 1977 smash hit movie, *Star Wars,* suddenly made spaceships an obvious subject for games, although it took time for computer technology reach the point where games could do justice to space combat. Spaceship simulations are almost all about combat, usually as seen from the cockpit of a small fighter. It is interesting to note that most space combat games use the same physics as

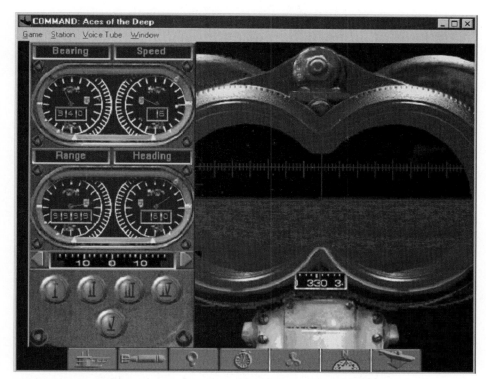

FIGURE 3.28 Sierra On-Line's *Command: Aces of the Deep,*
a submarine simulation game.

twentieth century aircraft. Never mind that there is no air in space to allow
spacecraft to quickly bank (tilt laterally during a turn) in one direction or
another. Lucas used dogfights from WWII as the models for space combat, and
most science fiction combat games have followed this model ever since. Aside
from *Microsoft Space Simulator* (1994), most space combat games are seen
from the vantage of a space fighter pilot, as in *Lightspeed* (MicroProse, 1990),
Wing Commander (Origin System, 1990; a screenshot from one of the sequels
is shown in Figure 3.29), and *Star Wars: X-Wing* (LucasArts, 1992). A few
games let the player command a large spaceship, as in *Independence War: The
Starship Simulator* (Infogrames, 1997) and *Star Trek: Bridge Commander*
(Activision, 2002). However, most games involving large-scale space battles fit
better inside the war game category.

Several games have centered on landing modules on the moon's surface,
the first being *Lunar Lander* (also known as *Moonlander*), which was commissioned by Digital Equipment Corporation to demonstrate the abilities of their
DEC GT40 graphics display terminal. In 1978, Atari released *Lunar Lander,*
a game that relied on Newtonian physics instead of a quick draw, in arcades.
Commodore released a similar game, *Jupiter Lander,* in 1982 for the Atari 400,
and Psygnosis published *Lander,* a 3D version of the Atari classic, in 1999.

FIGURE 3.29 Origin System's *Wing Command IV: The Price of Freedom* (Electronic Arts), a spaceship simulation game.

FYI | Wing Commander *and Mark Hamill*

Actor Mark Hamill, who played the role of Luke Skywalker in the *Star Wars* movies, was cast as protagonist Colonel Christopher Blair for the full-motion video scenes in *Wing Commander III: Heart of the Tiger, Wing Commander IV: The Price of Freedom*, and *Wing Commander: Prophecy*. However, in the *Wing Commander* movie (1999), Freddie Prinze, Jr., played Colonel Blair.

Puzzle Games

The puzzle game genre is something of a catchall because so many different kinds of games fall under it. Some authors do not consider most puzzles to be games at all because they are solitary exercises with no competition except against oneself and because player interaction with the game is sometimes minimal. Still, puzzles usually have a goal—finding the solution—and they have rules by which the player must abide. In addition to standard puzzles such as jigsaw puzzles and crossword puzzles, this book lumps traditional board and card games into this group, although those games could just as well make up their own genre.

Many puzzle games tend to appeal to one's mental acuity as opposed to one's physical dexterity, although there are "action" puzzle games as well. Some games test players' visual perception, others test their memory, and still others test their verbal skills. Most puzzle games set up an initial problem for the player to solve; some randomness might be involved in the initial setup (for example, as in how a card layout is dealt). After the game starts, the player usually competes against him- or herself with no opponent involved. The player ponders the impenetrable problem for a while until an insight suddenly strikes and the puzzle's solution becomes obvious. The *Eureka effect* is one of the main delights of such games.

Of course, after a player has solved most of these games, there is no need to replay them because the answer does not vary from play to play. However, solving one puzzle does not mean the player will become more adept at solving the next one. The "Aha! I solved it" moment may elude the player.

FYI *Games as Mental Exercise*

Evidence suggests that playing games that challenge one mentally might help prevent problems with the mind later in life. Just as physical exercise keeps the body fit, mental exercise keeps the mind fit. According to an article on the Medical World Search Web site (**www.mwsearch.com/Games4elderly.html**), games may help the elderly with such problems as the "impairment of cognitive function, loss of short-term memory and inability to learn new information."

Traditional games employ randomness, either in a random setup of the game (as in card games) or by using a random number generator (such as dice), to make each play-through a different experience. These games range from fairly simplistic (*Battleship*) to highly complex (chess or bridge). There is no solution to these games, but the player must achieve a goal in order to win. One advantage of playing these games on a computer or console is that they often include variations to the standard rules and let players determine the complexity of the game they wish to play. Many such games provide AI-controlled opponents of varying degrees of difficulty, so players can experiment with their strategies.

This book divides puzzle games into three subgenres: logic puzzle games, action puzzle games, and traditional games. *Logic puzzles* challenge a player's verbal ability, abstract reasoning, or visual perceptivity. *Action puzzle* games require some physical dexterity from the player in addition to mental discernment. *Traditional games* adapt games from other media for play on a computer or console.

Logic Puzzle Games

Logic puzzle games are among the most popular Internet games. Many of these games take only a short time to complete and are sometimes called *time wasters* for that reason. Such games usually have no time limits, and players can complete them at their leisure. Most popular television quiz shows including *Jeopardy!, Family Feud, Wheel of Fortune,* and *Who Wants to be a Millionaire?,* among others, are logic puzzle games. These games fall into three categories: word games, logic games, and image games.

Word Games Word games force the player to recognize words one letter at a time. They include crossword puzzles, acrostics, anagrams, word jumbles, and *Scrabble* imitators. The player might be presented with blank spaces to fill in by using clues provided by the editor to build the correct words one letter at a time. Starting off by filling in a few blanks, the player soon starts seeing patterns in the letters and finally deciphers the missing words that satisfy the clues. At other times, the player is provided with jumbled letters from which to make words. The player manipulates and places letters using the keyboard, mouse, or direction pad. Examples of electronic word games include *Boggle* (Hasbro Interactive, 1999), *Word Search Mania* (RomTech, 1999), and *Lexicon Word Challenge* (Nature Boy Software, 1998). Online game Web sites such as Pogo.com and WorldWinner.com usually have a section devoted to word games.

Logic Games Logic games are mental exercises that stretch the player's abstract reasoning ability and memory. They include mathematical puzzles; for example, a magic square where the player places numbers in a grid so that all horizontal, vertical, and diagonal rows add up to predetermined numbers. They can be simple "brainbusters" that present a series of verbal and visual clues that the player must interpret correctly to come up with an answer, like Sherlock Holmes using his deductive powers to pick the correct suspect. Examples of logic games include *Brainburst!* (XDGames, 2002) and *Minesweeper* (created by Robert Donner in 1989 for Microsoft Windows), as well as the incredibly popular Sudoku that was first created for a puzzle magazine and has gained such a following that it now appears daily in newspapers around the world. As with word games, logic games can be found on many online game sites.

Memory Games Memory games test a player's knowledge of the outside world. In electronic versions of these games, the player is given a question and then selects answers using the keyboard, mouse, or direction pad. In some games such as *Trivial Pursuit,* the questions are selected randomly from a large pool (frequently divided in categories like sports, culture, technology, and so on), whereas in other games such as *Who Wants to Be a Millionaire?,* the questions start off relatively easy and get progressively tougher over time. Electronic versions of such games include *You Don't Know Jack* (Sierra On-Line, 1995), *Trivial Pursuit* (Domark, 1986; based on the board game), and *Jeopardy!* (Share-Data, 1987; based on the television show). Memory games are a major category of online game sites.

Image Puzzles   Image puzzles appeal to players who enjoy the challenge of pattern recognition. They include jigsaw puzzles, although on the computer the proportions of the puzzle and the number of pieces are usually kept small so the player sees the gestalt of the picture as it comes together one piece at a time. Another image game that has sparked many imitators is *Shanghai* (Activision, 1986; Figure 3.30), where the player uses the mouse or direction page to pick off mahjong tiles one matching pair at a time until the board is empty.

Action Puzzle Games

Whereas logic puzzle games tend to be static (that is, nothing happens unless the player moves or selects something), action puzzle games have moving objects and require the player to deal with continuously, changing conditions,

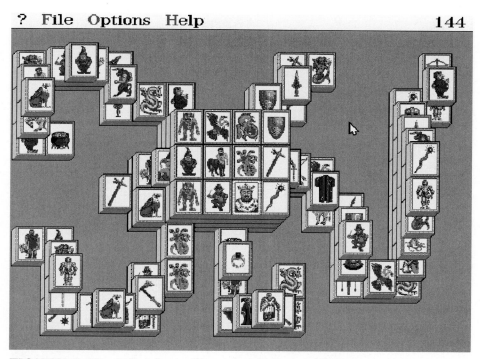

FIGURE 3.30 Activision's *Shanghai II: Dragon's Eye,* an image puzzle game where pieces are removed two at a time from the board.

either by moving the objects directly or dealing with them as they move. These games might start as a simple challenge, but they often pick up speed and force the player to deal with more and more moving objects or with faster moving objects as they test the player's ability to react quickly to changing patterns. Arguably, the most popular electronic game of all time—*Tetris* (Spectrum Holobyte, 1987)—is an action puzzle game. The player rotates falling tiles of different shapes and tries to fit them onto a grid in order to remove filled rows; this is a simple task, but the game becomes very challenging as the pace of the falling pieces picks up.

Some action puzzle games require the player to manipulate objects on the playfield, either directly or indirectly. In some games, such as *Katamari Damacy* (Namco, 2004; Figure 3.31), *Oddworld: Abe's Oddyssey* (GT Interactive, 1997), *The Lost Vikings* (Interplay, 1992), and *The Incredible Machine* (Sierra On-Line, 1993), the player directly moves the puzzle-solving objects. In other games, as in *Frogger* (Hasbro Interactive, 1997), *Galapagos: Mendel's Escape* (Electronic Arts, 1997), and *Lemmings* (Psygnosis, 1991), the player attempts to direct the movement of mobile objects to specific objectives while not actually controlling the moving objects themselves.

Pinball game simulations can be added to this category because, as in the real game, players control the flippers to keep the ball moving or to trap it so

FIGURE 3.31 Namco's *Katamari Damacy,* an action puzzle game.

they can rest their tired fingers. Likewise, dominoes belongs in this category because the pips on the domino blocks are matched adjacent to each other.

Traditional Games

As mentioned previously, the traditional games category is a catchall for many popular games that have migrated to the computer. It includes board games, card games, and games using dice (or similar game pieces). Not all such products are puzzle games, for they often allow a player to compete against other players.

Board Games   Many classic board games have been translated into computer and console games. Some of the oldest known board games—including chess, checkers, Parcheesi, and *Go*, among others—can now be played on computers and consoles. There are, of course, computer versions of the most popular commercial board games, such as *Monopoly*, *Risk*, *Scrabble*, and *Battleship*. Steve Meretzky's *Hodj 'n' Podj* (Boffo Games, 1995; Figure 3.32) is a computer game that includes many minigames and mimics the movement around a map similar to traditional board games.

FIGURE 3.32 Boffo Game's *Hodj 'n' Podj* (Avalon Interactive), a computer puzzle game that plays like a board game.

FYI *What's in a Name?*

The name of Boffo Game's *Hodj 'n' Podj* comes from the English word *hodgepodge*, which means a "mixture of dissimilar items," or a jumble. The game is a collection of unrelated traditional games.

Card Games   Card games fall into two subcategories: solitaire and multiplayer. Everyone who uses Windows has access to several solitaire games such as spider, solitaire, and freecell. Multiplayer games include gambling games, such as stud poker, draw poker, Texas hold'em, and blackjack. There are also nongambling games, of which bridge may be the best known. As with chess, many different bridge games are available because the game is so rich and complex in both bidding strategy and card-play strategy. There are many other card games that use the standard 52-card deck, ranging from children's games such as war and old maid to games for adults such as canasta, hearts, and gin rummy. One might add the ancient game of mahjong to this group because it is very much like gin rummy, although it uses etched tiles instead of cards. (Note that the original mahjong is completely different from the electronic game of the same name, which focuses on removing matching tiles from a board.)

Dice Games   Throwing dice is a familiar exercise for most gamers because dice are used in so many traditional board games. Of course, dice can also be used in gambling games, with craps being the most famous. Dice are also used in nongambling games such as *Yahtzee* and *Devil Dice* (THQ, 1998).

Sports Games

Sports games can range from arcade style games such as *Snoopy's Silly Sports Spectacular* (Kemco, 1989) and *Arcade Volleyball* (Compute Publications, 1988) to pure simulations such as *Championship Manager* (Domark, 1992). How do you tell the difference? In a baseball game, if the player is concerned only with swinging wildly at pitches, the game is arcade-like. If the player deals only with the management side of things such as handling trades, setting up rosters, and negotiating contracts, then the game is almost pure simulation. Most sports games fall somewhere in between, with the player acting sometimes as a coach or owner and sometimes as the players engaged on the field. The design for any sports game is limited by the rules of the sport being simulated. Serious sports games try to recreate as closely as possible the rules of the real game and, depending on licenses obtained, the look and feel of the players, uniforms, and sports arenas.

Sports games fall into two broad subgenres: team sports and individual sports. These subgenres can further divided into professional or amateur. *Professional* sports are those where the players are paid to play and can usually make enough money to live on. Getting into professional sports is difficult and demanding, and only the most talented athletes achieve a long-lasting career in their sport. *Amateur* sports are those where the players usually are not paid anything or are not paid enough to live on but engage in the sport "for the love of it." The majority of computer and console games recreate professional team sports (football, baseball, and the like) because they have the largest fan following, and most gamers are very familiar with the rules of the sports they love.

The amateur sports are often subject to rule changes from the real games. There are "street" versions of one-on-one basketball and scaled-down football games with fewer players on a team. There are even a few fantasy sports games that are completely fabricated and have little or no real-world counterpart, such as Disney/Pixar's *Monster Inc.: Wreck Room Arcade: Bowling for Screams* (Buena Vista Games, 2002) and *Blood Bowl* ("monster" football; Microleague, 1995).

It should be noted that although auto and motorcycle racing are considered sports, they are included in the vehicle games genre. The sports games discussed in this section deal with the recreation of individuals and their own natural athletic abilities, not the abilities of maxed-out machines.

Team Sports Games

Team sports, obviously, are those that have more than one person playing on a side at the same time. They usually require a special playfield and specialized equipment, and each team member generally focuses on a specific position on the team. The rules to these games can be complex and difficult to program completely in a computer or video game. Even more challenging is adapting a user interface to allow players to switch quickly and intuitively between players as the game proceeds.

Professional Team Sports   Team sports that are popular in one country might not be popular elsewhere. Whereas the best-selling electronic sports games in America are football, baseball, basketball, and hockey, they are not the most popular in other countries. Soccer is popular around the world and probably sells the most of any electronic sports game. Other team sports that have made electronic game appearances include cricket, rugby, and curling.

In many cases, team sports games turn into franchises such as Electronic Arts' *Madden NFL* football games that release updated versions year after year. Because the composition of most teams changes each year, it makes sense to keep updating the electronic version of a game, as long as it sells.

FIGURE 3.33 Electronic Art's *Madden 2006,* the latest in the popular line of football games.

Each new version might have slightly better graphics and AI, more refined user interface, and additional commentary and voiceovers.

Some of the more memorable team sports game series include John Madden Football (Electronic Arts, 1988, which changed the series' name to Madden NFL in 1993; the screenshot in Figure 3.33 is from *Madden NFL 2006*), MVP Baseball (Electronic Arts, 2003), *ESPN NBA Basketball* (Sega, 2003), and *NHL Hockey 1994* (Electronic Arts, 1993). Other team sports games from around the world include *FIFA Soccer 95* (Electronic Arts, 1994), *Cricket 2000* (Electronic Arts, 1999), and *Take-Out Weight Curling* (Global Star Software, 2002).

FYI *Electronic Arts Dominates Sports*

In December 2004, Electronic Arts signed a five-year exclusive licensing deal with the National Football League and the NFL Players Association to produce football games for video consoles and computers. In January 2005, EA announced a fifteen-year agreement with sports channel ESPN to use their personalities in games. Because sports games account for about 20 percent of video game sales, EA has assumed an even more dominant position in video games.

3

FIGURE 3.34 Electronic Art's *NBA Street,* a street version of three-on-three basketball.

Amateur Team Sports Amateur team sports include junior versions of major sports games—for example, Little League baseball and street basketball, some games of the winter and summer Olympics, and other games that usually have small teams of unpaid players with minimal equipment (such as volleyball). These games are not nearly as popular as professional sports, and few electronic games turn into long-lasting franchises.

Examples of games in this category include *NBA Street* (Electronic Arts, 2001; Figure 3.34), *Backyard Hockey* (Infogrames, 2002), and *Summer Heat Beach Volleyball* (Acclaim, 2003).

Individual Sports Games

Individual sports involve one person playing against other individuals. The games pit each player's skills against the others', and the rules are usually simpler and less restrictive than in professional sports. They might require special playing areas such as golf courses or bowling alleys, but the equipment generally is not as expensive, and there are no team colors, jerseys, mascots, or similar paraphernalia. Creating an electronic game based on such a sport is much easier because the user interface is much simpler, the demands on AI are less arduous, and the graphics are less demanding. However, aside from golf, most individual games have limited appeal to electronic gamers.

Professional Individual Sports   In the United States, individual sports usually make less money overall than team sports. However, some individual sports, especially golf and tennis, draw a lot of television coverage and earn healthy advertisement revenues. The most popular individual professional sports in the United States are golf, tennis, boxing, and bowling. Wrestling is also included as a professional sport, even if it tends to be more an entertainment than an athletic contest; one could easily reassign wrestling to the street fighter or beat-em-up category of action games. (Likewise, tag-team wrestling can be considered a professional team sport.)

Electronic golf games are very popular worldwide, both in the arcade and as computer or video console games. Golf, frustrating as it may be for the average player, continues to grow in popularity, and even those gamers who might be averse to waking before dawn are willing to play electronic versions of the game. Other individual sports games have not done nearly as well in electronic formats, although publishers continue to turn out new titles regularly. One problem with individual sports is that turning them into franchises with new versions to ship each year is difficult, primarily because there are so few yearly changes in each sport. Also, there are fewer "name" stars in these sports, so using someone's name in the title is not as big a draw as in professional team sports.

Games in this category include *Tiger Wood's PGA Tour 2000* (Electronic Arts, 2000; Figure 3.35 shows a screenshot from the 2006 version), *Smash Court Tennis Pro Tournament* (Namco, 2002), *Fast Lanes Bowling* (Enlight Software, 2004), *Knockout Kings* (Electronic Arts, 1998), and *WCW Nitro* (THQ, 1998). *Dr. J and Larry Bird Go One on One* (Electronic Arts, 1983), one of the earlier sports games, as well as other "dueling athletes" games also fit into this category.

Amateur Individual Sports   Amateur sports receive little media attention, although they might be the most widely played of all. They usually require minimal specialized equipment and they frequently are played at a leisurely pace compared to the time restrictions of many other sports.

There are many amateur individual sports, but participants make little or no money. The market for such electronic versions of these games is more limited than other sports. In addition to games of pool, ice skating, and skateboarding, there is a huge market for hunting and fishing games. There have been attempts to make these games—particularly the X-Games—more popular, which means that sports channels are willing to spend the money required to

FIGURE 3.35 Electronic Arts' *Tiger Wood's PGA Tour 2006,* a golf sports game.

create "new" games to fill up the empty hours when no professional games are available. However, no recently invented sport has yet caught the general public's attention. The closest thing to a star is skateboarder Tony Hawks, whose games have become popular, although recent releases are closer to action arcade games than to real sports.

Most electronic games dealing with the Olympics focus on individual sports. Even the Olympics, which certainly are well known enough to support a franchise, do not work exclusively with one game publisher, although the problem might come more from publishers going out of business than from lack of interest in the Olympics themselves.

One of the most popular console game series in history, *Tony Hawk's Pro Skater* (Activision, 1999), can be included in this category (if one considers extreme sports amateur). Other examples of this category include *Sharkey's 3D Pool* (Microplay, 1990), *Galactic Pinball* (Nintendo, 1995), *The Games: Summer Challenge* (Accolade, 1992), *Athens 2004* (SCEE, 2004; Figure 3.36), *Winter Olympics: Lillehammer '94* (U.S. Gold, 1993), *Deer Hunter* (WizardWorks Software, 1997), and *Top Angler: Real Bass Fishing* (Xicat Interactive, 2002).

FIGURE 3.36 Archery competition from SCEE 2004's *Athens 2004,* a sports game based on the Summer Olympics.

Summary

There are many different game genres, with each one offering different play experiences. In addition, each major genre has several subgenres, all of which are variations on a theme. Games are available for every type of player at every level of skill.

One reason people play games is that they want to experience the thrill of something dangerous or exotic without necessarily putting themselves in jeopardy. Games cover almost every conceivable human activity. Whereas some might find the idea of managing the growth of a city to be boring, others delight in acting as the mayor of a thriving metropolis and handling the diverse problems that arise while expanding the city's boundaries and improving the standard of living. Other players enjoy running around and shooting everything that moves on the map. Still others enjoy pretending to be race car drivers and winning the Indy 500. If players can't find the thrill they want in one genre, they can always try another.

Given this bounty of genres and multiplicity of opportunities to play, it's no wonder that electronic games have become the premier form of entertainment in the twenty-first century.

Test Your Skills

MULTIPLE CHOICE QUESTIONS

1. Which of the following are types of game genres?
   A. Action, vehicle, chess, fighting.
   B. Vehicle, strategy, fighting, puzzle.
   C. Strategy, puzzle, simulation, role-playing.
   D. Simulation, sports, fighting, racing.

2. What was the earliest genre identified for electronic/video games?
   A. Arcade.
   B. Action.
   C. Racing.
   D. Strategy.

3. What genre does the game *Pac-Man* belong to?
   A. Strategy.
   B. Puzzle.
   C. Arcade.
   D. Scrolling.

4. Scrolling refers to which of the following?
   A. The "scrolling" effect of the background.
   B. All games that have a background that moves vertically as you play.
   C. A magic effect when the player casts a spell from a scroll.
   D. The long movie sequences that tell the game's story.

5. If action games in ancient societies helped determine the most skilled athlete, strategy games helped determine which of the following?
   A. The strongest warrior.
   B. The smartest player.
   C. The shaman.
   D. The most skilled player.

6. In electronic games, the player's ability to cleverly solve puzzles is best tested in which of the following?

   A. An RPG.

   B. An adventure game.

   C. An FPS.

   D. A sports game.

7. Inventory management plays a significant role in which of the following games? (Select all that apply.)

   A. An RPG.

   B. An FPS.

   C. A vehicle racing game.

   D. An arcade game.

8. Graphic adventure games have always been popular, but what was the driving force behind their success?

   A. Improvements in art design.

   B. Better story-telling skills.

   C. Improvements in video cards and video memory.

   D. Windows.

9. How did FPS games broaden the consumer base of video games?

   A. Made it fun to shoot things.

   B. Made games easier to use.

   C. Broadened the consumer base from puzzle solvers to include active hunters.

   D. Sold more units than other games.

10. Which of the following is a distinct aspect of an RPG? (Select all that apply.)

    A. The inventory a player must manage.

    B. The player's statistics.

    C. Using combat to improve the character's skills and to level up.

    D. The scrolling graphics.

11. Strategy games are typified by which of the following?

    A. Fast paced action.

    B. Slow, deliberate choices.

    C. The formation and implementation of many levels of strategy.

    D. Guessing what the opponent will do next.

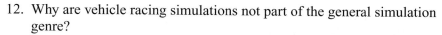

12. Why are vehicle racing simulations not part of the general simulation genre?

   A. The term *vehicle* might include imaginary vehicles, and simulations are always abstractions of real things.

   B. A defining feature of simulation games is resource management, and most vehicle games do not include this feature.

   C. Simulations only encompass games in which the player can create worlds.

   D. Most people have drivers' licenses and a simulation of driving would be dull and boring.

13. Where did war games come from?

   A. A desire from military strategists to reenact their greatest moments.

   B. A need of historians to reenact great battles.

   C. How fun it was to play with miniatures.

   D. A need for military strategists to study battles and plan alternative strategies.

14. Why do we break games into genres? (Select all that apply.)

   A. Similar to books, music or movies, we use genres so it's easier for stores to stock the shelves.

   B. Similar to books, music or movies, genres help the consumer select a game for purchase.

   C. Unique to this industry, genres are the best way for us to track sales.

   D. Genres are a shorthand way for a consumer to learn about a game based on her own personal experiences with similar games.

15. What is the most popular story genre for RPG?

   A. Fantasy.

   B. Science fiction.

   C. Paranormal.

   D. World history.

16. What is the most popular story genre (or setting) for RTS?

   A. Fantasy.

   B. Science fiction.

   C. Space exploration.

   D. World history.

3

17. Which of the following are examples of economic and political strategy games? (Select all that apply.)

    A. *Railroad Tycoon.*

    B. *Age of Empires.*

    C. *Balance of Power.*

    D. *Dune II.*

18. Of the professional team sports games series, which is the most popular worldwide?

    A. *Madden NFL.*

    B. *FIFA Soccer.*

    C. *NASCAR Racing.*

    D. *Cricket 2000.*

19. Upon what does the success of an electronic sports game solely rely?

    A. The licensing of real player images.

    B. The accurate representation of rules.

    C. The accurate representation of historic games.

    D. The resources the player must manage.

20. Individual sports games include which of the following? (Select all that apply.)

    A. Volleyball.

    B. Golf.

    C. Curling.

    D. Pool.

EXERCISES

Exercise 3.1: Gameplay Elements

Take a simple arcade game such as *Pac-Man*. Add a component from a strategy game (inventory, resource management, or equipment costs, for example) and some sort of puzzle element. Design two levels on paper and describe the new gameplay and any new required game pieces (enemies, interactive objects such as buttons or food, and so forth).

Exercise 3.2: Sports Game Review

Consider the differences between amateur sport games and professional sports games. Name three critical attributes that the consumer requires of one subgenre but not of the other. Consider how this might constrain the game designer. Explore an idea that you might suggest to get around the contraints.

Exercise 3.3: Design a Sports Game

Select an individual sports game that might not currently have a video game counterpart. Consider all the rules of play, all the equipment required, all of the tournament or other rules that allow a player to advance in some form of league. Create a simple abstraction of this game that does not require graphics, in other words that could be played as a text adventure or as a board or card game.

Exercise 3.4: Design a Card Game

Develop a card game based on basketball (or the sport of your choice). Either create your own deck of 52 cards with any number of suits or use a standard card deck. What would you discard from the original game of basketball to make a competitive card game? What would you keep?

Exercise 3.5: Team Balancing

Explore the possibility of an RPG based on your school that has two opposing factions vying for resources and dominance: for example, the science nerds and the athletic jocks. What attributes, skills, or tools would each team have that the other doesn't? How would you balance the teams so that they each have a fair chance of winning? What school resource would be considered valuable: the cafeteria, the water fountains, or others?

DISCUSSION TOPICS

1. What do you consider to be one of the "turning-point" genres in video game evolution?

2. Mascots have been common throughout the video game industry. Name three of your favorite past or present company mascots. Discuss how these mascots were used to promote the sales of game hardware. Discuss what age group the mascot appealed to and why.

3. *Baldur's Gate* is an open-ended RPG that allows players to freely roam and interact. Name another game that allows this sort of behavior as well and discuss the issues that a game designer might have to deal with when players are given an open world.

4. Genres are fairly well defined in the industry, though there are always games that cross boundaries and could fit into multiple categories. Discuss whether this is good or bad for the industry. Include how it impacts the development team, the marketing team, the stores that will stock the game, and the consumer.

Chapter | 4

Overview of Game Platforms

Chapter Objectives

After reading this chapter and doing the exercises, you will be able to do the following:

- Understand the differences between how computers and consoles work.
- Explain how computers developed into a major game platform.
- Understand the components of the computer as a game machine.
- Describe how consoles differ from computers for playing games.
- Understand the capabilities of different handheld game platforms.

Introduction

Electronic games are played on many different machines—or *platforms.* Most games today are created to play either on a computer or a console, but there is a growing market for handheld games played on the Game Boy Advance, cell phones, and new devices like the Nintendo DS and Sony PlayStation Portable. Indeed, it seems like whenever new electronic devices come out, they offer the ability to play games in addition to their primary uses.

The first game machines were primitive compared to those available today. The graphics have evolved from flat sprites running around a flat landscape to highly detailed, three-dimensional worlds filled with wonderful characters and objects. Likewise, the audio has vastly improved from the tinny beeps of computer speakers to modern Dolby 5.1 surround-sound standards. Most games nowadays include a multiplayer mode, unheard of just a decade ago, that lets players from all over the world join in the same game.

As new computer technologies are developed and become available to the public, they will certainly be incorporated into games. New game platforms will appear; existing ones will continue to improve; and older ones will disappear.

There is no predicting where things will go, but it appears gamers will always have a "brave new world" of gaming opportunities to explore.

Game Platforms

The game *platform* is the device on which a game is played. For most of the history of games, if there was a "platform" for playing a game, it was the game board—a flat piece of wood or cardboard with a design printed on it. Playing pieces, or tokens, were moved around the board according to the rules of the game. Aside from chess and checkers, which can both be played on the same board design, each board game has its own unique design. Therefore, in board games, there is an almost one-to-one relationship between the platform and the game played upon it. A player would be hard pressed to play *Monopoly* upon a *Risk* game board (although designing a game using *Monopoly* playing pieces on a *Risk* game board or vice versa would be an interesting exercise).

Many different kinds of games can be played with cards and dice, but most of them usually don't employ a platform or board in addition to the cards or dice. One attraction of card and dice games is that, because they don't require other game equipment, they can be played almost anywhere. Board games can be considered *platform dependent* (because the game plays only on the appropriate board), whereas card games are *platform independent* (because they can be played anywhere).

In electronic games, platform dependency has a different meaning. *Electronic game platforms* are the hardware upon which games are played. They include the personal computer (PC), video game consoles (such as the GameCube, PlayStation, and Xbox), and handheld devices (such as the Game Boy Advance, Nintendo DS, Nokia N-Gage, cell phones, and personal digital assistants). Each game platform features a monitor of some kind, input controls, a central processing unit (CPU), and a storage device on which the game itself resides.

Many different games—from racing games, to shoot-em-ups, to role-playing games, to card and dice games—can be played on each electronic game platform. The advantage of electronic game platforms is that they can be used repeatedly for different games as long as they can decipher the data on the storage medium. Consumers don't have to buy a new computer or console whenever they want to play a different kind of game. Nor does any game company have a monopoly on any genre, forcing players to buy their device to play such games. A player can enjoy a sports game on a computer, PlayStation, Nintendo DS, or personal digital assistant (PDA). Different versions of the same game often can run on several different game machines; for example, consumers can buy *Madden NFL 2005* for the personal computer, PlayStation 2, and Xbox. Publishers often make changes in games that are created for multiple platforms in hopes of interesting players who own the different platforms. Games that run on multiple machines are called *cross-platform.*

Each electronic game platform uses its own unique operating system to decipher information on the storage device, so a game that can be played on one game machine might not necessarily work on another even if the machines use the same type of storage device. For example, a game stored on a DVD that is designed for the PlayStation 2 will not run on an Xbox even though both console machines use DVDs for storage devices. A game developer must get a license from Nintendo, Sony, or Microsoft to create games that run on the GameCube, PlayStation 2, or Xbox respectively.

FYI *Console Development Kits*

Anyone with the right skills can create a game for the computer. There is nothing proprietary about writing the code or creating the art for a computer game. However, there are restrictions to creating console

FIGURE 4.1 Development station for the Xbox.

CONTINUED ON NEXT PAGE

▶▶ CONTINUED

games. Although the code and assets for a console game are created on computers, the developer must have a license from the console manufacturer to develop a game for that console. (Most developers prefer to grant licenses to developers who have proven themselves by shipping products.) In addition, the developer must pay $5,000 to $10,000 for a development station (Figure 4.1) that lets the code written on the computer run on the target platform. When the game is complete, the developer pays the console manufacturer to produce the final shippable version (on CD, or DVD).

4

One might think that game developers would want to create games only for personal computers because they don't have to pay any licensing fees. Moreover, computer users can run many other programs in addition to games, whereas video consoles can only run games. However, as it turns out, games developed for video consoles far outsell computer games, so game developers are willing to bear the extra licensing expenses and lower royalties payments for developing console games instead of computer games. The reasons for this discrepancy are detailed in Chapter 21, "Economics of the Game Industry."

Evolution of Game Platforms

The first electronic games were primitive by today's standards. Graphics were minimal—usually ASCII characters or small, blocky sprites moving around on a flat plane. The processing power of the machines was miniscule, so animations were limited and artificial intelligence (AI) routines were simplistic. The game controls were also simple—a few buttons and maybe a couple of levers, a steering wheel, a trackball, or a joystick to direct the action.

As discussed in Chapter 2, "The Evolution of Games," the first commercial electronic game platforms appeared in 1972 when *Pong* materialized in arcades and Magnavox began selling its Odyssey console for home use. *Pong,* of course, was a huge hit, but the Odyssey was less successful commercially, selling only 100,000 units. Still, the Odyssey proved there was a market for home versions of popular arcade games, inspiring other manufacturers to create their own machines—the ColecoVision, Atari VCS (later renamed Atari 2600), Bali Professional Arcade, and Mattel Electronics' Intellivision, among others—to compete. Unfortunately, the glut of consoles eventually led to a glut of bad games, and the market for home consoles collapsed in 1982.

The first console machines were primitive compared to modern machines. In 1982, the top-of-the-line ColecoVision had an 8-bit, 3.56 MHz CPU with only

48 kilobytes of RAM and no special memory or processing for graphics. The Xbox 360, released in 2005, offers a triple processor core clocked at 3.2 GHz, with 512 megabytes of unified memory architecture RAM (shared with the graphics processing unit). The advances in processing power, memory, and graphics capabilities for video consoles have been remarkable. But they have been a long time in arriving.

FYI *The Rise and Fall of Arcades*

The first video games appeared in arcades, starting with *Pong* in 1972. The classic age for arcades lasted until the mid-1990s. Arcades lost their audience for several reasons. First, arcade games initially had better graphics than home versions of the same games, although this advantage began to disappear with improvements in graphics cards and chips. Second, each arcade game was relatively expensive to produce because of its electronic components and cabinet, so manufacturers were forced to raise the cost per play of a game. Third, the rising rents for business space cut down on the profits to the owners of large arcades. Finally, the major game manufacturers, such as Midway and Atari, found that there was more money in publishing home video game software than in manufacturing arcade hardware and software. Arcades still survive in some places, such as the Dave & Buster's chain, but these places typically offer other activities and/or serve meals in addition to offering arcade games.

The Rise of Home Computers

While video consoles were making inroads into people's homes, so were personal computers. The first home computers, such as the MITS Altair (1974), were kits that customers were expected to put together. A customer needed a solid sense of electronics to assemble the machines and get them running. These computers also used their own individual machine operating languages, so little commercial software was available for them.

The Apple II (Figure 4.2), introduced in 1977, was the first computer to make computer games popular, perhaps because of its color graphics. It had the 6502 CPU, 4 kilobytes of RAM, and 16 kilobytes of ROM, plus a keyboard, game paddles, color monitor, and preinstalled BASIC language. The Atari Video Game System (VGS) featured an 8-bit, 1.19 MHz CPU, 128 bytes of RAM memory, and no video memory. However, the Apple II was expensive at $1,300.00 compared to the Atari Video Game System at $199.95. Both machines were quaint by modern standards.

FIGURE 4.2 The Apple II personal computer.

Whereas the video game industry collapsed and almost disappeared from 1982 to 1984, personal computers became more popular. A number of systems vied for dominance in the home market including the IBM Personal Computer (PC, introduced in 1981), Commodore 64 (1982), Compaq Portable PC (1982), Atari 1200 XLLL (1983), RadioShack TRS-80 (1983), Apple Macintosh (1984), and Commodore Amiga 1000. Because of the steep price for the ever more powerful microchips, personal computers remained very expensive compared to game consoles. Of course, many different software programs, not just games, were created specifically for computers. There were word processing programs, spreadsheet programs, 2D and 3D graphics programs, and much more. Whereas the consoles could only run games, personal computers could do many more tasks, making them worth owning no matter the cost.

The large number of competing personal computer systems was both a benefit and bane for game developers. The more systems there were, the more customers were available to buy a game. But each system had its own operating system and machine language, which required game developers to rework considerable portions of the code and graphics to make their games work on the different platforms. In addition, publishers had to maintain stockpiles of games for all the platforms. If one version of a game didn't sell, the publisher would be stuck with useless inventory.

One development tipped the computer market in favor of the IBM machine architecture. In 1952, IBM was accused of monopolistic business tactics in its computer business and became involved in a 30-year confrontation with the U.S. government. The lawsuit distracted IBM from the personal computer market and led the company to modify its business practices. When Compaq Computer Corporation successfully started mimicking IBM's method of using off-the-shelf components to create IBM-compatible computers in 1982, it sparked other companies to start building *PC clones.* The number of PC clones increased over the next few years to the point where competing computer systems were having trouble gaining traction in the market.

The introduction of Intel's 25 MHz 486 microprocessor (Figure 4.3) in 1989 and Microsoft Windows 3.1 in 1992 established the dominance of IBM-compatible PCs as the home computer of choice. Until the introduction of Windows 3.0 in 1990, PC users had to launch applications by typing somewhat clunky instructions at the DOS prompt. First Windows 3.0 and then Windows 3.1 offered a graphical user interface (GUI) that allowed a user to simply use a mouse to double-click the icon of a program to launch it. Home computers were becoming much more user friendly.

FIGURE 4.3 The Intel 486 microprocessor (also called i486 and 80486) helped establish IBM-compatible PCs as the home computer standard.

One factor driving the improvements in PC hardware in the 1990s was consumers' desire for better games to play on these machines. Computer programs such as word processors and spreadsheets don't need fancy graphics or sound effects, but games do. Gamers demanded higher graphic resolutions and more colors to make their games look more realistic. The success of id Software's *Doom* led to a revolution in 3D graphics, forcing video cards to handle more and more polygons on the screen to make the game world look more *real*. Players wanted their games to sound fantastic too, so developers looked at standardizing audio requirements while adding more instruments and channels to make the games sound as beautiful as they looked.

Of course, the early PCs still had many problems, especially when it came to graphics and audio standards. Even though the IBM PC standard had won the home battle, as it were, it was still difficult for game developers to deal with all the different audio and graphics standards. Compatibility testing to make sure the product worked on all platform configurations became very important. Another drawback to early home computers, which was based on their very success, was that the continuing advances in technology made PCs obsolete within a few years, but the hardware remained very expensive to upgrade or replace. Meanwhile, software publishers continued to enhance their products to take advantage of improvements in graphics, and cheaper processors, and storage mediums such as CDs and DVDs, and the enhanced programs eventually would not work on older equipment. The process of producing silicon chips and graphics cards was expensive in the 1990s, so the components inside computers were expensive. Consumers did not expect to have to replace other large ticket items such as cars or televisions every two years, so they were irritated at having to shell out a good deal of money for an up-to-date computer every few years.

FYI *Moore's Law*

In 1965, Gordon E. Moore, head of research and development for Fairchild Semiconductor, wrote an article for the journal *Electronics* in which he predicted that the number of transistors per silicon chip would double every year for the next ten years. This prediction was revised in 1975 to doubling every 18 months and has become known as **Moore's law.** So far, Moore's law has held true and will likely continue to hold true for the next decade or so.

More specifically for our purposes, computers, as flexible as they were, were not necessarily the best game platforms. There were enormous problems with compatibility issues that could make installing games and then playing them on a PC daunting. In those earlier days, anyone installing new software might accidentally erase some important data on the machine. The new software itself might not even work on the computer, not necessarily due to any negligence on the part of the programmers but rather to the multitudes of hardware and software options a computer could have.

In addition, parents were nervous about letting children play games on the computer. As the Internet gained popularity in the 1990s, new concerns arose about children being exposed to inappropriate content or, worse, to inappropriate behavior by others. It wasn't clear whether the home computer was going to ever be a successful game platform.

FYI | *Apple II and* Breakout

Steve Wozniak developed the *Breakout* arcade game for Atari in 1976. It had color, sound, and paddles—all of which made the machine popular with gamers. His work on that game greatly influenced him when he designed the Apple II home computer.

Revenge of the Video Consoles

The collapse of the first wave of the video game market from 1982 to 1984 left a vacuum that Nintendo was soon to fill. They released their 8-bit Famicom system in Japan in 1983 and eventually released it in the United States in 1986 as the Nintendo Entertainment System (NES). The console was a great success, no doubt in part because the first systems were bundled with a conversion of the arcade hit *Super Mario Bros*. Nintendo developed a number of popular intellectual franchises for the NES, including Donkey Kong and his son, Donkey Kong, Jr.; Mario and Luigi; and Link (of *The Legend of Zelda*). The machine's $199 price was reasonable, and the games were aimed at a younger market.

Nintendo dominated the video game market unchallenged for a number of years until the Sega Genesis console was introduced in 1989. The 16-bit Genesis (Figure 4.4) was more expensive ($249.95), but it had better graphics. Nintendo recognized the danger of losing its audience and responded by creating it own 16-bit machine, the Super NES (Super Famicom in Japan) in 1991. Sega soon retaliated and the console wars began.

The 1990s were a time of constant turmoil in the video industry as each console manufacturer tried to turn out a more powerful machine before its competitors. In addition, new competitors including the 3DO Company, Sony, Atari, and finally Microsoft all introduced game consoles—some successfully, such as Sony's PlayStation and Microsoft's Xbox, and others unsuccessfully, such as the 3DO and Atari's Jaguar. Those companies that previously had developed strong games with recognizable characters or situations (for example Nintendo with the Mario Brothers and Donkey Kong and Sega with Sonic the Hedgehog) did

FIGURE 4.4 Sega Genesis, the 16-bit console that challenged Nintendo's domination of the video game market.

better because customers knew what to expect and were willing to try out new systems. Moreover, some manufacturers were better than others at developing strong interest among independent developers in supporting their new consoles. Having a strong lineup of good games available when a new console shipped was one key to its success.

This intense competition among manufacturers has kept the price of new consoles relatively low because it has forced companies to lower their prices on hardware and software to match competitors. This price war has been good for consumers, but it has been harder on game developers and publishers. Developers and publishers have to pay a number of fees to console manufacturers, so they receive less money per copy for a video game than for a computer game. Developers working with publishers receive royalties, which are usually lower for video games than computer games. Thus, many more copies of a video game must be sold to pay off a developer's advances. As the costs of creating games continue to rise, it gets more and more difficult for developers to make a profit on games. See Chapter 21, "Economics of the Game Industry" for further details.

Finally, the expense of making a game that runs only on one type of platform can be terrifying for a developer who must invest several million dollars to bring a game to market. This has led to a hesitancy within the development community to support a new platform until they are certain it will succeed above and beyond other platforms. They prefer stability and security as they go forward in creating entertainment.

Handheld Games

Handheld games are a relatively new market that appeared in the late 1990s (after several earlier unsuccessful attempts by Milton Bradley and Epoch). Electronic toys, which are hard-wired toys that can play one and only one game, have been around since the 1970s. However, a platform that plays multiple kinds of games and that a child can carry around in the car or on the bus to school was an entirely new idea.

Nintendo helped establish the handheld game market with the Game Boy (Figure 4.5), which was released in 1989 and sold for $109. Several companies, such as Atari with their Lynx, tried to challenge Nintendo's dominance in the 1990s, but none were able to compete successfully. As with the console platforms, Nintendo's strong line of intellectual properties were adapted to handheld games and contributed to the Game Boy's success.

Recently, companies have again attempted to challenge Nintendo by releasing more powerful handheld machines; the first was Nokia's N-Gage followed by

FIGURE 4.5 Nintendo Game Boy.

Sony's PlayStation Portable (PSP), Tapwave's Zodiac, and Tiger's Gizmondo. Nintendo has responded in kind by releasing the Nintendo DS (Double Screen) system in 2004 and the Game Boy Micro in 2005. Time will tell if these higher-powered handheld challengers will overcome Nintendo's lead.

In addition to dedicated handheld game machines, cell phones, and PDAs (personal digital assistants) are emerging as major game platforms. Cell phone technology is primitive compared to the current generation of handheld game machines. However, their graphics capability and increased memory capacity could soon make them viable platforms. In South Korea, cell phone games are extremely popular, but they do not have the same level of popularity in the United States, primarily because there are multiple incompatible cell phone technologies competing with each other. Until a single technological standard arises, cell phones will not be as popular for games in the United States as in other countries.

For a time it looked like PDAs might be serious contenders against Nintendo's Game Boy and Game Boy Advance. A number of companies, such as Midway, brought back some of their classic arcade games in versions that could be downloaded and played on a PDA. However, PDAs were never as successful as the Game Boy, and the latest generation of cell phones can handle many of the functions of a PDA. Additionally, the cost of laptop computers, and now tablet computers, has continued to fall, and they are much more powerful machines than PDAs. Although PDAs and PDA games will no doubt continue to be manufactured, they are not likely to become a serious contender for the market share of computers, game consoles, or other handheld platforms.

4

Personal Computers

As soon as computers started showing up in homes, so too did games to run on them. Though there are a number of competitors for the title of "first home computer," the MITS Altair, released in 1974, certainly qualifies. Several text-based games such as *King, Bomber,* and *Startrek,* were designed for that system.

Home computers were expensive when they first appeared and continued to be so for many years, especially compared to game consoles. But computers were also more flexible in terms of the various kinds of programs they could run.

The personal computer was as important a game platform as the video console through the mid-1990s but finally fell behind as the current generation of consoles—PlayStation 2, GameCube and Xbox—was released and gained popularity. Computers always maintained the lead in better processing power, graphics, variability of input devices and Internet connectivity than consoles, yet despite these advantages, they have continued to lose their position as a primary gaming system for the home. Even the rise of massively multiplayer online games in the late 1990s could not help reestablish the computer as the foremost home gaming platform.

FYI *Decline of Computer Games*

Over the past several years, income from computer games has slowly fallen. In 2002, computer games earned about $1.4 billion dollars. In 2003, they earned $1.2 billion; in 2004, they earned $1.1 billion; and in 2005, they earned $.95 billion. Over the same period, video games (both hardware and software) had revenues of $11.4 billion in 2003, $9.9 billion in 2004, and $10.5 billion in 2005. A number of significant computer games were released in 2004 including *Doom 3*, *Half-Life 2*, and *World of Warcraft* to name a few. *Guild War*, *Battlefield 2*, and several *The Sims* expansions were important releases in 2005. Despite these major releases, the home computer market has continued to shrink year by year as video consoles have became the primary platform for games. One reason for the shrinking PC game market is that consumers are buying fewer new computers with the high-end graphics cards required by many new games, and older PCs can no longer run these new games.

The Microprocessor (Central Processing Unit)

The central processing unit (CPU) is the brains of a computer; it does most of the data processing, and in home computers it is usually housed on one chip, the microprocessor. In addition to performing mathematical and logical operations, the CPU reads the instructions from a software program stored in memory and then decodes and executes them. The more powerful the computer, the more calculations it can make per second. Early machines ran at 2 MHz (2 *million* cycles per second), whereas modern computers now run at 3.7 GHz (3.7 *billion* cycles per second) and higher.

To understand the real power behind these two seemingly vast numbers, we have to look at what the numbers really mean. With each cycle, the computer can perform one or more operations; for example, adding two numbers or transferring a value between two processors registers (a small amount of memory used to increase the speed of a computer program). The greater the number of cycles that can be processed per second, the more the computer can do.

The computer uses some of these cycles to maintain itself by performing such tasks as drawing the visual you see as a window, releasing unused memory, or doing other housekeeping chores. The rest of these billions of cycles are free for software applications. The primary CPU deals with the game's operating instructions, artificial intelligence, graphics, audio, and networking. Most computers and game consoles have a ***graphics processing unit (GPU)*** that assists in performing the calculations for the game graphics, especially 3D graphics (see Chapter 13, "Visualizing the Game," for more details). As computers become more powerful, even more demands are put upon them. Games continue to push the envelope in terms of using as many of these cycles as they can, especially for 3D art. Present-day computer games make games only a decade old look primitive and dull but will look primitive themselves a decade from now when computers will be almost eight times as powerful as today's machines.

Operating System

As important as the computer's speed is the operating system (OS), which determines how the cycles will be used. For many years, MS-DOS (Microsoft Disk Operating System) was the only system for IBM-compatible clones. MS-DOS had restricted multitasking capacities, as well as a 640 kilobyte memory limit. In this tiny amount of memory, the computer had to run its basic operations, as well as applications. Games quickly hit the wall because the narrow pipeline stymied the demands for improved graphics. The situation improved with the release of Windows 3.0 in 1990, which allowed applications to use more memory.

Memory and Hard Drives

The simplest way to define *memory* is to compare it to a brain, whereas the computer's *storage devices,* such as the hard drive, CD, and DVD, are like a library. Although you could take the time to read everything in the library, you probably wouldn't remember the information if you didn't actually use it. Instead, when you need that information again, you go to the library and get the information. Memory works in a similar way.

Early computers had very limited memory, which is where the currently executing applications are stored on the computer. The problem with having only a little memory is that it can hold a limited amount of information at any one time. Certain assets of games, such as art, graphics, sound, and music, can take up lots of space. So one of the biggest advances for computers in the 1990s was the creation of larger memory chips, which led to the availability of cheap memory.

Random access memory (RAM) is where program data and code are temporarily stored so the application can make changes to it. The memory contents can be accessed in any order. The storage is only temporary, and the stored data is lost when the power is shut off (that is, RAM is *volatile*).

Computers are now getting some of the specialized hardware that used to be reserved for consoles. Memory is also being used in other parts of a computer. For example, video cards have graphics processing units (GPUs) with their own memory, which is called *video RAM* (VRAM). VRAM is separate from the main RAM and is dedicated to displaying the graphics. Together with the GPU, it takes the burden of graphics processing away from the CPU, which can then deal with other processes. There is also the dedicated physics chip, PhysX (created by AGEIA), which is a *physics processing unit* (PPU) with 128 MB of memory designed to speed up such game physics processes as collision detection, fluid dynamics, and rigid body dynamics.

Graphics

Early computers, such as the IBM PC (released in 1981), frequently had monochrome monitors (green or white text on a black background) with very low resolutions. Graphics were blocky, so text-based adventures were popular in those early days. Some early games, such as *Rogue: The Adventure* (Epyx, 1986; Figure 4.6) and *Submarine* (Softdisk Publishing, 1989), used ASCII characters for graphics. The standards for computer graphics advanced in the 1980s and 1990s, progressing from 4-color **color graphics array** (CGA) to 16-color **extended graphics array** (EGA) to 256-color **video graphics array** (VGA) to modern 24-bit (Truecolor) and 32-bit standards allowing millions of colors. Additionally, the screen resolution increased as more pixels (picture elements) could be painted on the screen. Higher resolutions made graphics much sharper and more realistic. The current Windows environment allows resolutions of up to 1,600 × 1,200 pixels (depending on the monitor). In addition, games can often run in an expandable window as well as in full-screen.

Most of the early graphic computer games used flat, two-dimensional sprites that were animated like cartoons. In other words, the image of an object on the screen is shown briefly in one pose and then is replaced by the same image in a slightly different pose, then by another changed pose, and so on—all blending together to give the illusion of movement. Early video cards translated the image made by the CPU into electrical impulses shown on the monitor, but the CPU did most of the work in addition to handling the player's input, AI,

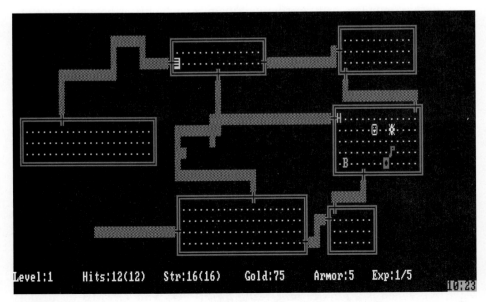

FIGURE 4.6 Screenshot from *Rogue: The Adventure Game,* an early computer game that used ASCII characters to create graphics.

audio, and system updates. As graphics cards improved, they took a considerable amount of graphics processing work away from the CPU. In fact, the highly detailed 3D graphics of current games would not be possible without continuing improvements to video cards.

The images on the screen are refreshed (that is, redrawn on the screen) at a rate of around 60 frames per second (fps). The illusion of motion comes from the optical phenomenon called *persistence of vision*—the brain retains an image for split second after the image disappears and merges the multiple images into a steadily moving picture. Games can run as slow as 16 fps and maintain the illusion, but 60 fps is the desired rate because it syncs with a monitor's standard refresh rate. See Chapter 13, "Visualizing the Game," for more information about frame rates.

New updates to video technology have improved and pushed the graphics of computer games. The CPU delegates considerable graphics work to the GPU and just checks in on occasion (about once a second) to verify that things are going right. The GPU can therefore focus on what it does best—making the graphics look as good as possible with higher resolutions that have reduced *jaggies* (the sharp, jagged edges of rounded images seen at lower resolutions); this makes the graphics look more lifelike, while still operating at 60 fps or faster. This kind of specialization means the computer operates faster and can do more with the graphics than ever before. Meanwhile, the CPU, which is much faster as well, is freed up to process more information from other parts of the game such as AI, combat data, or networking information.

Input Devices

The computer offers a number of different devices that enable the user to interact with the applications. The most common devices are the keyboard and the mouse. A keyboard has many keys, and it is possible to use them all to control a game. Many games can be played using the keyboard only, and some players prefer this approach to the mouse-and-keyboard approach used in many games. Of course, one drawback of using so many controls is that it can be difficult for the player to remember them all. Some simulation games have so many commands that they include cardboard overlays that fit over the keyboard to help the player remember which key controls each action (for example, *F-15 Strike Eagle* and *Red Storm Rising* by Microsoft). The keyboard does allow great flexibility in assigning tasks to certain keys and controlling game actions.

In the early days, players had to type in commands at the C prompt to make a computer do something. Learning all the different commands and their quirks was daunting. For example, when launching a game, players sometimes had to type in a series of extra commands to get the correct graphics or initiate a sound card, as shown in the following example (in this case, launching the game on a system with a Sound Blaster sound card):

C:\PUBLISHER\GAMENAME\strtgame.exe–sndblst

One typo in the command line was enough to keep the game from starting. The eventual emergence of the Windows GUI environment made launching a game much simpler. It also expanded the game audience to include people without this specialized knowledge.

A mouse is a simple device, consisting of a ball that controls the movement of a cursor on the screen, one to three buttons to select or manipulate the item on the screen, and perhaps a small wheel to scroll up and down a page. Modern mice often use optical sensors to detect movement instead of a ball. The mouse offers precise control in a game because the player can move the mouse cursor around the screen and select things quickly.

The main drawback to a mouse is that it can perform only a few functions. For that reason, more recent games often combine keyboard commands with the mouse's point-and-click capability. For example, most first-person shooters require the player to use the keyboard to move the character around the world while using the mouse to look around and fire weapons.

In addition to the keyboard and mouse, several other computer input devices have been developed for specialty games. Many driving games can be controlled by a steering wheel affixed to the table where the monitor sits. Most of these wheels have a feedback device that makes them vibrate so the player "feels the road" while playing the game. Likewise, many flight simulators work best with a joystick, a device that has been used with many other types of games as well. A typical *joystick* consists of a stick attached by pivot to a base (Figure 4.7); the

FIGURE 4.7 The PointMaster, an early joystick for the Atari 2600, manufactured by Discwasher in 1982. The device had only one button.

player moves the stick around in a circular motion, and the changes in coordinates are translated by the computer as changes in the direction of movement. The device usually has several buttons that allow the player to shoot weapons, turbo boost, throttle up and down, and perform other game activities. Joysticks also use force-feedback to give the player a sense of fighting the controls.

Other examples of input devices that have been used with computer games include light pistols to "shoot" at targets on the screen, dance mats, fishing rods, and motorcycle handlebars. Most of these peripherals are designed for a specific game. Perhaps sometime in the future when *virtual reality* devices become commercially available, players will don 3D glasses and control gloves to interact with the game world.

Storage

Over time, the storage mediums for games have increased greatly in capacity while shrinking in physical size. The first computer games for the Atari 2600 and Coleco Gemini appeared on cartridges, which were more expensive to manufacture than floppy diskettes. To reduce production costs, a number of computer game publishers switched to 5 1/4-inch floppy disks even though each disk could hold only 128 kilobytes of information.

Floppy disks improved to the point where they could hold up to 360 kilobytes. These disks really were floppy and were easy to damage. In the mid-1980s, smaller 3 1/2-inch floppy disks appeared that could hold 800 kilobytes of information. Shortly thereafter, *high density* 1.44 megabyte floppies appeared. These smaller floppies not only held more data but were encased in rigid plastic that better protected the magnetic medium.

For a time, games shipped with both large and small floppy disks in the same package, even though the cost of including all the disks was steep, because it took time for users to upgrade their equipment and change from the 5 1/4-inch to the 3 1/2-inch drives. Using higher-density disks meant that players did not have to switch disks as often while playing games. Most games during this time tried to stay within the storage limits of four floppies, which equated to about 4 to 5 megabytes of compressed data. Currently, many games' demos are 100 megabytes in size, and the games themselves run from around 300 megabytes to over 1 gigabyte in size.

The floppy disk was a standard for a number of years because it was so cost-effective—costing only pennies per disk. Eventually, the compact disc (CD) replaced the floppy disk as the cost of its production came down dramatically. The advantage of a CD is that it can hold hundreds of times more data than a floppy disk—up to 783 megabytes. Because the 3D graphics in modern games are massive, the CD is the current storage medium of choice. However, it will soon be replaced by the DVD (*digital versatile disc*), which can hold up to seven times as much data.

A great advantage that computer games have over video games is the hard drive, where data can be stored until needed. This wasn't always the case. The first storage media were cartridges, tapes, and floppies—in other words, each program was loaded onto the computer temporarily while being used, and data was then saved onto a storage medium when the game was shut down. The first hard drives were very expensive. The cost for a 5 megabyte Apple Computer hard drive in 1981 was $3,500, or $700 per megabyte. By the end of the 1990s, the cost of a hard drive was pennies per megabyte. A Seagate 200 gigabyte hard drive is available for around $140. Several gigabytes of game assets (art, music, code modules, and so on) can now be completely loaded onto hard drives, allowing customers to play a game without having to swap disks.

Future alternatives in storage might include online network repositories, where players pay for and download the game directly from the company. The success of this development remains to be seen, but several companies are exploring the option of delivering content as needed to a user and retaining the rest of the content on their server. In effect, consumers never have the full game on their computer but only the part they are currently playing. Whether gamers will be satisfied knowing they don't actually "own" the complete game remains to be seen. They might resent having to be constantly online to play their game even if it is a single-player, stand-alone game.

Audio

Audio in early computers consisted of "beeps and boops." Sounds were generated by the computer itself, and because the machine was initially viewed as a business machine, not a game machine, little consideration was given to its ability to produce or play back music, sound effects, or human voices. One way around the computer's limitations was to use a plug-in card for the audio. In this case, the program sends instructions to the audio card, which in turn sends the correct tones to speakers plugged into the card. Figure 4.8 shows the Sound Blaster Live! sound card by Creative. As with other PC technology in the late 1980s and early 1990s, the abilities of audio cards increased while the cost of the cards themselves decreased. Nowadays, all computers come either with a

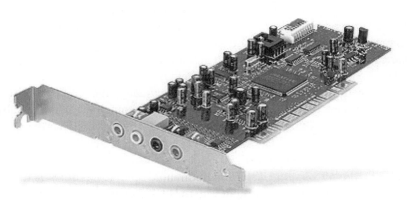

FIGURE 4.8 Creative's Sound Blaster Live! sound card for the PC.

sound card that allows them to do sophisticated audio effects or a sound card incorporated directly into the computer system motherboard.

Early on, the sound effects and music for computer games required considerable space on floppy disks, so developers put much effort into compressing the audio to make the files as small as possible and then uncompressing it during runtime. With the switch to CDs and DVDs, the need to compress files has vanished, and the increased storage available on hard drives allows most games to load the sound files directly onto the hard drive. File compression techniques continued to improve as the audio standards moved from .WAV and Redbook audio to .MP3 and .MP4 in the year 2005. See Chapter 14, "Hearing the Game," for more details about audio in games.

Internet Capability

Even when the Internet was in its infancy, people were looking at it as a way to facilitate player-versus-player games instead of only player-versus-machine. Multiuser dungeons (MUDs) were first introduced in 1978, and a few early computer games, such as *Bolo* (1987) for the Macintosh, featured multiplayer capability over the Internet. One of the first companies to offer online gaming was the GEnie network, created by General Electric in 1985, which featured a massively multiplayer online air combat game, *Air Warrior* (developed by Kesmai in 1987), among other games. Later, Sierra On-Line created a proprietary network devoted to Internet gaming in 1991. It was originally called the Sierra Network (eventually becoming the ImagiNation Network) and featured card games and board games, *Red Baron, Shadow of Yserbius,* and a Leisure Suit Larry area for adult chat. Neither of these online gaming services lasted.

The release of *Doom* in 1994 by id Software showed the way toward multiplayer gaming over the Internet, and id Software soon followed up by creating QuakeWorld, a free program to support their game *Quake*. That same year, the first graphical massively multiplayer online role-playing game, *Meridian 59,* was released by the 3DO Company, although it was not terribly successful. The success of *Ultima Online* in 1997 and *EverQuest* in 1999 showed that to play games online gamers were willing to pay monthly fees over and above the cost of buying the product in stores.

Until recently, the computer was the only platform on which games could be played over the Internet, and computers continue to be the platform of choice for online gaming. People can go to Web sites devoted to games, usually puzzle games, to play for free; they can go to sites that host multiplayer versions of popular boxed computer games; or they can pay monthly fees to play Internet-only games, the most popular of which are massively multiplayer online role-playing games. However, computers' dominance in online gaming has recently been challenged by video consoles, all of which offer online gaming.

Two of the most popular types of Internet computer gaming are gambling and "time-waster" puzzle games. Even though online gambling is illegal in the

United States, that hasn't stopped it from continuing to grow. An article from *The Economist Global Agenda* (June 27, 2005) forecasts that online gambling revenues will exceed $18 billion by 2008. Puzzle games have gained popularity because most people feel they can play a five-minute game of *Solitaire* or *Bedazzled* at work and not feel they are taking advantage of the office. Because computers are prevalent in the workplace, this sort of gaming experience is bound to continue.

Video Consoles

Nowadays, advancements in computer technology follow a relatively smooth slope, thanks to their open architecture—an improvement in processing speed here, an advance in hard drive technology there, a better video or sound card now-and-again. The owner can update a video card or add more memory without having to rework the entire computer. This is not the case with video game consoles. There is no such thing as adding a better video card or more memory to a console because all components are integrated as a unit. Console manufacturers are slower to advance their designs and might be likened to the characters in the platform action games that are so popular on these machines—they jump up a big level in technology and stay at that level until they are overwhelmed by "enemies" that force them to jump to the next level.

Whereas new computers have lots of RAM to work with and hard disk space on which to store game data, video consoles have much less RAM and are forced to regularly stream information off a cartridge, CD, or DVD. They may have lots of memory dedicated to dealing with graphics, but they rarely load huge levels containing many monsters into the graphics memory at the start of play as computer games do. Speed is the name of the game with video games, so they must quickly load the game for play. Video games have traditionally been associated with a fast pace and lots of action, thanks to their arcade game heritage. They are not generally associated with games that take lots of planning or require delicate manipulation of onscreen resources.

Video games vastly outsell computer games. According to a report by the NPD Group, video games and hardware sold almost $10.5 billion in 2005, a 6 percent increase over the $9.9 billion in 2004, where computer games sold only $953 million, a 14 percent decrease from the $1.1 billion in 2004. (The figure for computer games does not include sales from rentals, downloads and Internet gaming, or downloads.) One reason for this vast disparity in revenue is that the gaming audience is much more comfortable with video games than computer games because consoles are so much easier to deal with than computers. The components of a game console are much simpler than a computer, thus contributing to their lower cost. The main components are the central processing unit and game pad for inputting controls. There is no monitor; instead, the console plugs into a television set and uses

FIGURE 4.9 Nintendo's GameCube.

the set's speakers or auxiliary speakers for audio. The storage medium for all current consoles is the compact disc, although the Nintendo disc is smaller and differs from that used with the PlayStation 2 or Xbox. Figure 4.9 shows the Nintendo GameCube, which differs considerably in size and shape from the PlayStation 2 and Xbox.

Another reason for video games' dominance concerns ergonomics. Computers are often put someplace safe—that is, away from areas where boisterous children might damage the expensive equipment. Video consoles, on the other hand, are relatively cheap and, therefore, are seen as more expendable than computers. Consoles hook up directly to the television and, therefore, live in family rooms, whereas computers tend to live in dens or offices. Playing games in the family room is much more user friendly than playing them in out-of-the-way private places.

Yet another reason consoles are so popular is that they were targeted at a younger audience for many years. The 8-bit Nintendo Entertainment System and its immediate successors—up to the Sony PlayStation—were all seen as toys for children, and the games on them were generally considered safer than computer games. As the Nintendo generation has matured, however, video console games have likewise shifted toward more mature themes. For example, in 2004, the best selling video games were *Grand Theft Auto: San Andreas* (4.4 million copies sold), *Halo 2* (4.2 million copies), and *Madden NFL 2004* (3 million copies). The video game audience has come of age and wants edgier, more adult products, which game publishers are eager to provide.

As a result, many adults are increasingly concerned that electronic games in general have become too violent. Although the advances in graphics certainly can make the violence look more realistic—and perhaps more questionable—they have not necessarily affected the violence level in games. Games have always been violent (see Chapter 1, "An Introduction to Games," for more details about violence in games).

Central Processing Unit

A game console is, at heart, a small computer. The CPU for a game console is very much like that of a computer, but the operating system for each is unique. A buyer cannot play PS2 games on an Xbox or GameCube because each machine has a unique proprietary method of reading the storage medium and handling the game data. The Xbox, in fact, is at its core a Windows NT unit with much of the functionality stripped out.

Similar to computers, consoles do not play games directly from the storage medium but rather temporarily load parts of it into random access memory (RAM) during play. As the processing power of each generation has grown, so too has its RAM; this evolution is evident in the following list of systems and specifications:

- Nintendo Entertainment System (NES, 1986): 8-bit CPU operating at 1.79 MHz with 2 kilobytes of RAM

- Sega Genesis (1989): 16-bit CPU operating at 7.6 MHz with 72 kilobytes of RAM

- Sony PlayStation (1994): 32-bit CPU operating at 33 MHz with 2 megabytes of RAM

- Nintendo 64 (1996): 64-bit CPU operating at 93.75 MHz with 4.5 megabytes of RAM

- Sony PlayStation 2 (2000): 128-bit CPU ("Emotion Engine") operating at 300 MHz with 32 megabytes of RAM

- Nintendo GameCube (2001): IBM Power PC microprocessor ("Gekko") operating at 485 MHz with 40 megabytes of RAM

- Microsoft's Xbox (2001): modified Intel Pentium III processor operating at 733 MHz with 64 megabytes of RAM

The next generation of game consoles is beginning to appear, with the Xbox 360 shipping first in the fall of 2005:

- Xbox 360 (2005): three 3.2 GHz CPUs with 512 MB of 700 MHz GDDR3 RAM

- PlayStation 3 (2006–2007): 3.2 GHz Cell processor with seven synchronized processing units and 256 MB of 700 MHz VRAM (Figure 4.10)

FIGURE 4.10 Sony's PlayStation 3.

Nintendo has not yet released the complete specifications for its new console, Wii but they promise it will be at least two to three times as powerful as the GameCube. Of particular interest is the new Wii controller, which is shaped like a television remote control and has sensors to detect its position in three-dimensional space—the idea is that when engaging in a swordfight, for example, the player can wield the controller just as she would the weapon.

The new generation of consoles will match computers in power, at least for a while. The next wave of console machines will likely appear sometime in 2009–2010, and whatever processing power computers have at that time will be the new standard for the next next-generation consoles.

FYI *Bit Wars*

Game console manufacturers used to tout their new machines as being 16-bit, 32-bit, or 64-bit. Most consumers might assume that doubling the bit rate means the new machine is twice as good as the old. The bits refer to how much data is processed by the CPU. Modern computers use data groups of 16, 32, and 64 bits (referred to as the **word size**). But nowadays, word size is less a factor in defining machine performance than processor clock speed, size of memory, and bandwidth. The use of bit ratings is a marketing ploy that no longer carries much weight.

Graphics

As with computers, the desire for better graphics is one of the driving forces for making better and faster game consoles. More games are using 3D graphics, so consoles have continued to increase their processing power to manipulate the thousands of polygons used in 3D models and have expanded the amount of RAM storage space to temporarily hold the graphics. In addition to rendering graphics to the television, the graphics processor also deals with special functions such as mapping, textures, and geometry.

There are drawbacks to using the television as the medium for displaying graphics. The user can adjust the resolution of a computer monitor as desired from a low resolution of 640 × 480 to 1280 × 1024 (or higher), but a standard television has a constant low resolution of 640 × 480. The picture on a television is produced by an electron gun that shoots a beam at the screen; a phosphor coating on the screen is illuminated when hit by the electrons. Television uses an *interlace* method, painting every other line per sweep of the gun. Computers, on the other hand, use a *progressive* method of painting every line per sweep. Moreover, the visible area seen on the screen varies, depending on the brand and model of a television. To compensate, standard televisions over-scan the picture tube, meaning that the area shown on the tube is smaller than the actual picture. When designing video games, developers faced a usable resolution as small as 544 × 372; thus, they had to pull text and HUD (heads-up display) elements closer to the center of the screen so they could be seen. Finally, computers are meant to be viewed close up, and information on the monitor is easy to read, whereas televisions are usually viewed from a distance and, therefore, are fuzzier and less distinct. Old games always had a problem with jaggies and with the color red, which tended to "bleed" into other objects, making things look even fuzzier.

HDTV Resolution

HDTV screens have a **native resolution** (also called **addressable resolution**), which is the built-in maximum number of pixels that can be displayed on the screen; this defines the clarity of the image. The resolution is defined by the total number of pixels across a scan line times the total number of scan lines. An HDTV with a resolution of 1080i (the *i* stands for interlaced) has a standard 1,920 pixels per scan line, so the screen can show 2,073,600 pixels.

Televisions for many years used an aspect ratio of 4:3 (the width versus the height), which is the same standard as computer monitors. An HDTV has an aspect ratio of 16:9, which is the same as the 35mm film used in most modern movies. Thus, an HDTV can show widescreen formats without resorting to **letterboxing** (masking off the top and bottom of the screen with black bars to maintain the original aspect ratio).

As a result of these differences, the menu systems and any game text in video games are usually pushed away from the edges and displayed as large as possible. Likewise, the action on the screen is more centered so important information doesn't get lost in the over-scanned areas of the picture. Most console manufacturers have strict guidelines about how much screen real estate can be used in the game for their platforms. These restrictions are likely to change because the standards for HDTV are different than for standard televisions; however, as long as there is a significant distance between the television screen and the customer, video games will face restrictions on how they handle game graphics. Still, as high definition televisions become the norm, the 3D graphics in console games will look even more realistic. Microsoft has already led the way in supporting HDTV with the Xbox.

Input Devices

The main input device used to play games on a console is a *controller* or *game-pad*. Compared to the keyboard and mouse, there are far fewer inputs on a controller. Over time, however, the device has gotten more complex as additional buttons and features were added. The controller for the original NES was rectangular, with a *D-pad* (cross-shaped levers controlled by the thumb to control direction), select/start buttons and A/B buttons for game actions. The current generation of game controllers is molded to fit in the player's hands more comfortably and retain the D-pad, start/select buttons, four (or more) actions buttons, two thumb-joysticks, and shoulder buttons on the front of the controller.

Because they use fewer inputs, video games are often easier to learn than computer games. Some complex games have been designed for consoles, particularly role-playing games, but they often require the player to page through a number of menus to perform actions in the game. These games can be as daunting to learn as computer-based games. There is no simple way to type in information—a player's name, for example. The player is forced to scroll through letters and numbers to select each desired character and then approve the text. As a result, it is difficult to communicate with other players when playing a multiplayer game over the Internet, although some consoles like the Sega Dreamcast and Sony PlayStation 2 offer keyboards to offset this drawback.

Storage

All current game consoles use CDs or DVDs as the primary storage medium for games and cartridge or memory cards for storing gameplay data. The Xbox and PlayStation 2 both have proprietary 4.7 gigabyte DVDs. Both the Xbox and PlayStation 2 can play DVD movies, an extra selling point for those machines. The GameCube uses a proprietary 1.5 gigabyte optical disc. Not only does the Nintendo disc carry less game data, but the customer can use the console only for games, not for watching movies. Fewer GameCubes have been sold compared to its competitors; the use of the small disc might be a major factor in its lower popularity.

When a player starts up a game in any of the consoles, the data is loaded from the disc into RAM. None of the current generation of consoles have harddrive storage. Instead, game information is saved in memory cards. One advantage is that a gamer can easily carry the card to a friend's house and pick up play of a game they both own.

FYI *Why PlayStation 2 Sold So Well*

When Sony released the PlayStation 2 in 2000, the console sold slowly for the first year because there were few good titles available at the launch. However, Sony made three wise decisions that helped make the PS2 popular. First, the console was able to play DVD movies, so it was no longer seen as a games-only machine. Second, it was backward compatible, meaning that most of the original PlayStation games also played on the PS2. Third, it included an expansion bay where a Network Adaptor could be plugged in to enable multiplayer games over the Internet. In addition, Sony had already developed a reputation for publishing excellent titles for the original PlayStation (EA Sports titles, the *Final Fantasy* RPG series, and Tony Hawk's skateboarding series, among others), and this goodwill carried over to the next generation, even when there were not many titles available at launch. These factors helped make the PS2 the most popular console ever, with over 100 million units sold worldwide as of November 2005.

Audio

All three current video consoles use microchips to control the audio output. A player can hook up the machine to use either television speakers or other audio equipment. The consoles themselves have no direct audio output and rely on the amplification of the home audio system. This approach is partly a cost saving measure, but it also offers a savings in size, so the console itself takes up less space.

Internet Capability

Until recently, console gamers could not play games with each other over the Internet. Instead, to play multiplayer games, they had to hook up their controllers to one console. For example, the GameCube and Xbox each have four game controller ports, allowing four players to hook up to the same game and play it at the same time. The PlayStation 2 has only two game controller ports, but it does feature a "Dual Shock 2" force-feedback controller that vibrates in the player's hands in response to actions occurring during play. Sega was the first console manufacturer to set up a system, SegaNet, that allowed Dreamcast players to play each other over the Internet.

All current consoles have online capability. A player must buy an online adaptor to connect the PlayStation 2 to the Internet. The adaptor allows both modem and broadband hookups and is hooked to the back of the console. In 2003, Sony started their online service for playing *EverQuest Online Adventures* (Figure 4.11) on the PS2, but they also heavily rely on developers to support their own games online. For the GameCube, a player must also buy a broadband or modem adaptor that connects to the console. Only a few Nintendo games are available for online play. The Xbox contains a Nvidia media communications processor for a broadband connection and has a built-in Ethernet connection for online play. Microsoft started the Xbox Live gaming service in 2002 for subscribing players. This service features online voice support.

FYI — *Emulators*

Emulation lets a computer run software—including games—from another kind of platform, say, a video console. It bypasses the proprietary code of the original system. Software companies use emulators (called **simulators**) that are licensed from the console manufacturers to develop console games on the computer. Trying to use an emulator for other purposes for profit (that is, without the manufacturer's permission) is illegal. These emulators are typically very slow as well.

FIGURE 4.11 Screenshot from Sony's *EverQuest Online Adventures* for the PlayStation2.

Handheld Game Platforms

Games can be played on a number of different handheld devices, including the Game Boy Advance SP, personal digital assistants, cell phones, and a new generation of devices, such as the Nokia N-Gage, Nintendo DS, and Sony PSP (PlayStation Portable). Although the market for these games is significantly less than for computer and video games, it is healthy and took in $1.2 billion in 2004 (compared to $1.1 billion for computer games). A number of development studios have honed their skills in game production by starting out making handheld games and progressing to computer or console games.

Game Boy

Nintendo has dominated the handheld game market ever since the release of the Game Boy in 1989. Over 60 million Game Boys have sold since it was introduced. Its popularity led Nintendo to create the Game Boy Color in 1998, the Game Boy Advance in 2001, and finally the Game Boy Advance SP in 2003. Other companies have tried to compete with Nintendo for the handheld market—the Atari Lynx in 1989 and Bandai's WonderSwan in 2000 among others—but none has come near Nintendo's success.

The Game Boy Advance has very simple controls, much like the original NES. There is a D-pad for movement in eight directions, start/select buttons, A/B action buttons, and right/left shoulder buttons. It uses the Sharp ARM7TDMI processor, which runs at 16.78 MHz and has 32 kilobytes of main memory and 256 kilobytes of external memory. The SP features a front-lit LCD display with a screen resolution of 240 × 160 that can simultaneously display more than 32,000 colors. It comes with a rechargeable lithium battery that offers up to 10 hours of continuous play.

There are many games available for the Game Boy Advance SP. They are offered on small cartridges that contain the program and assets. The game cartridge is inserted into a slot on the machine, and it contains room to save the current game.

Additionally, an available communications cable enables a player to hook up the Game Boy Advance SP to a GameCube. An optional mobile phone adaptor enables players to hook up via the Internet to exchange game data and download games. One peripheral that parents are particularly thankful for is the headphone plug, which allows the player to hear the game without disturbing others.

Other Handheld Game Devices

Nintendo's dominance was challenged in July 2004 when Nokia released the N-Gage handheld game device, beating Nintendo's release of the Nintendo DS (double screen) system by four months. Sony released their PSP (PlayStation Portable) system in 2005. Other contenders in the wings include devices such as the Tiger Telematics' Gizmondo (Figure 4.12) and Tapwave's Zodiac. These new devices are more powerful than the Game Boy Advance SP, offering a faster processor, higher resolution graphics and more colors. Each has unique features as well. The N-Gage, for example, is also a mobile phone, and the Gizmondo will offer an integrated camera as well as MP3 and MPEG-4 media players. All will offer wireless Internet connectivity.

FIGURE 4.12 Tiger Telematics' Gizmondo, a handheld game platform.

The success of these new devices will depend on the games that will be available when they ship. It will be difficult for any company to dethrone Nintendo as leader of the handheld pack because Nintendo has the advantage of its popular intellectual properties such as Mario, Link, and other favorite video characters that they have translated into games designed specifically for their device. However, there have been complaints that the release titles for the Nintendo DS were weak, including a remake of *Mario 64,* a *Madden* football game, *Spider-Man 2,* and several others. Nintendo plans to deliver a number of stronger titles to solidify its position as leader of the pack. The N-Gage was slammed for its lack of decent release titles and has not been able to follow up with a "killer app." The success of the Sony PSP and other handheld platforms will depend not only on their initial releases but also on the desirability of the features they offer consumers.

FYI   *Microvision*

The first handheld game console that used interchangeable cartridges was Microvision by Milton Bradley (Figure 4.13), which was released in

FIGURE 4.13 Milton Bradley's Microvision.

CONTINUED ON NEXT PAGE

▶▶ CONTINUED

1979. The liquid crystal display (LCD) screen, microprocessor, and keypad controls were all integrated into the device. The handheld device appeared in the movie *Friday the 13th, Part II*. However, it had several technical problems. First, the extreme heat could destroy the primitive LCD screen. Second, a good jolt of electricity could fry the microprocessor. Third, the controls were difficult to use because they were under a thick plastic layer. Microvision went out of production in 1981.

Personal Digital Assistants

Personal digital assistants (PDAs) are devices that are smaller than laptop computers; they were originally designed to have only a limited range of abilities, but they still are microcomputers with excellent abilities. Figure 4.14 shows an Axim X50v PocketPC by Dell.

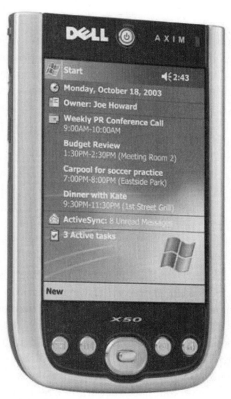

FIGURE 4.14 Dell's Axim X50v PocketPC.

Though PDAs never were designed to be game platforms, many customers who owned them wanted to play games on them. These devices have adequate capabilities. For example, the PocketPC has a screen resolution of 240×320, and the Palm handhelds have processors of over 100 MHz. One drawback of the PDA as a game platform is that the technology has advanced quickly and has not settled on a single standard, making it difficult to support all the different configurations.

Other drawbacks are that PDA manufacturers have given little support to the game community and the testing emulators are relatively expensive (compared to the average sales of a title). Finally, the PDA is seen primarily as an electric notepad for businesses and not a dedicated game device.

The PDA seems to be losing out to the laptop, a complete computer that can run both business applications and games, as well as to multifunction cell phones, such as the BlackBerry, that offer many of the same features as a PDA. As computer prices continue to fall and cell phones become more adaptable, the pressure will be on PDA manufacturers to make their devices more user friendly and, as far as games are concerned, more profitable.

Cell Phones

Cell phones share many of the advantages of PDAs. Both are excellent devices for storing and retrieving phone numbers, addresses, and other information, and both have been adding new features continually. For example, many cell phones now let users take and send digital photos. Customers can purchase games for cell phones either at retail outlets or by downloading the game directly onto the phone.

Cell phones have distinct disadvantages as game platforms, however. First, in the United States, there are a number of different incompatible formats that a developer must support. Second, cell phones are just not as powerful as PDAs—they have a smaller display, and they have serious latency issues (delays caused by sending network messages to remote computers, and getting responses back). Third, the phone companies have not supported game development. In fact, they force developers to bear the production costs and usually make customers pay extra to play games. Finally, the game applications and their presentation to the player are small because of the cell phone's limited memory. It should be noted, however, that the cell phone is a very popular game platform in Asia and Europe. There are fewer formats to support outside the United States, and in those continents, people tend to take public transportation, allowing them time to use the cell phone for something besides talking.

It remains to be seen whether cell phones can become viable game platforms. Certainly, they have a potential audience of tens of millions of customers, but no one has yet developed a realistic business model to make money via cell-phone games. Given that users generally expect to use a cell phone only to talk to people, it's not surprising that in the United States few companies make a living providing cell phone games.

FYI   *Motion-Sensing Cell Phones*

The next trend in cell phones might be handsets that have motion-sensing capabilities. Such models have been released in Japan and South Korea by Vodafone KK. The handsets can detect linear motion along the X and Y axes as well as twisting along the X, Y, and Z axes (detecting yaw, pitch, and roll). The *Full Swing! Golf* game by Taito, for example, lets the player use the handset like a golf club to swing at the ball (and comes with a warning not to hit nearby pedestrians when swinging).

4

Summary

Games have long driven the technological advances in computers and, of course, consoles. It seems that whenever a new form of electronic communications becomes available, one of the things that enhances its popularity is the ability to play games on it. Alexander Graham Bell never foresaw games being played on and over the telephone he invented, but nowadays they are. The scientists who developed the Internet did so to exchange information, but the technology has been used to play games and might become the primary outlet for downloading new game releases in the not too distant future.

In ten years time, people might look back at the current generation of game platforms as being primitive and "low end" and wonder how gamers could possibly play games that had such rough graphics and limited audio. Maybe in the not too distant future, the holodecks envisioned for the *Star Trek* universe will be real, and players will actually step into their games and not just stare at them through flat screens.

Test Your Skills

MULTIPLE CHOICE QUESTIONS

1. The cost for a 5 megabyte Apple Computer hard drive in 1981 was $3,500, or $700 per megabyte. In 2005, a 200 GB hard drive is available for around $140. How much is that per megabyte?

   A. $140.00 per megabyte.

   B. $20.00 per megabyte.

   C. $1.40 per megabyte.

   D. $.07 per megabyte.

2. A personal computer (PC) always contains which of the following types of hardware? (Select all that apply.)

   A. A CPU.

   B. A DVD burner.

   C. A graphics chip.

   D. An HD.

3. RAM stands for:

   A. Radium archived memory.

   B. Random access memory.

   C. Ridiculously assertive memory.

   D. Rapid access memory.

4. Home console units do not contain which of the following? (Select all that apply.)

   A. A CPU.

   B. A graphics card.

   C. A printer.

   D. A monitor.

5. What does it mean to be platform independent?

   A. The game does not need a platform to be played.

   B. The player can select any platform and play the game.

   C. The game is made so that it can be played on any platform, with certain modifications.

   D. The platform operates independently and does not need a computer to run.

6. Why were some of the most popular home PC games originally text-based adventures? (Select all that apply.)

   A. The writing of the stories was exquisite.

   B. The graphics capabilities of early PCs were too blocky and supported only two colors.

   C. DOS would not allow applications larger than 640 kilobytes to be run, so only small games could be made.

   D. Audio was just beeps and bloops, so text was the only alternative.

7. Which of the following is a handheld game platform? (Select all that apply.)

   A. Nintendo GameCube.

   B. Microsoft Gizmondo.

   C. Sony PSP.

   D. Nokia N-Gage.

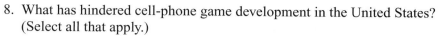

8. What has hindered cell-phone game development in the United States? (Select all that apply.)

   A. Too many competing technologies interfere with the games.

   B. The number of competing technologies makes it too expensive for a game to be cell-phone independent.

   C. Not enough people have cell-phones.

   D. Cell-phones do not have color screens, and no one wants to play black and white games.

9. How did IBM's business tactics positively impact the PC market?

   A. By having an open architecture, multiple manufacturers could make hardware, and PC-clones soon dominated the market,

   B. IBM forced out all other manufacturers, leaving only PCs.

   C. IBM created a machine so powerful that no other computers could compete.

   D. The operating system allowed for games, whereas other systems did not.

10. Why do new console platforms have a difficult time succeeding? (Select all that apply.)

    A. Consumers do not want to purchase new machines every year.

    B. Developers are not willing to commit time to make games for untried hardware.

    C. The cost of royalties to the hardware manufacturers makes it too expensive to make games for new platforms.

    D. Technology changes too fast, and it is too expensive to make new machines every year.

11. Which of the following statements is true? (Select all that apply.)

    A. The Nintendo GameCube has the largest number of Internet games of any console.

    B. Sega will release the Wii console in 2006.

    C. The Dual Shock 2 force-feedback controller is used by Sony.

    D. The internal components for a computer are two to three times as expensive as those used in consoles.

12. What is the CPU, and does a Nintendo DS have one?

    A. Computer processing unit, and no.

    B. Central processing unit, and yes.

    C. Computer processing unit, and yes.

    D. Central processing unit, and no.

13. What is VRAM?

    A. Virtual random accessed memory.

    B. Video random accessed memory.

    C. Very random accessed memory.

    D. Visually random accessed memory.

14. Why is it important to have a system with separate RAM and VRAM?

    A. It enables the computer to delegate graphics processing to the video card, which frees memory for other processes.

    B. It allows the computer to draw pretty pictures when the system is in standby mode.

    C. VRAM allows a video console machine to use a TV screen instead of a monitor.

    D. RAM is only for storing game data and cannot be used for graphics information.

EXERCISES

Exercise 4.1: Design a Cell Phone Game Concept

Write the concept for an interactive game for a cell phone that takes advantage of the communication power of the platform.

Exercise 4.2: Design Console System Requirements

Write the system requirements for a new console that you think would be fun to play. First, list all the technical needs that the console would have to support. Second, list the target price you'd want to purchase this console at. Third, compare your feature list with that of existing consoles and see where they have made tradeoffs.

Exercise 4.3: Research the History of Game Machines

Create a table listing all the game machines listed in this chapter from 1970 on. Break down each machine into at least seven different categories, including CPU, RAM, storage, and input. What are the tradeoffs for each machine? How would you, as a developer, evaluate these machines or a new one to determine if you wanted to develop games for it?

Exercise 4.4: Research Current Game Machines

To the list you created in Exercise 4.3, add the retail (purchase) price of each machine when it was new. Research the current price of all the machines if you bought them new today, if available. Include the current price of all machines if you bought them used. See if you can track how quickly the prices dropped. Is there a trend in the prices' dropping that you can relate to technology changes, introduction of new software or hardware, the global economy, and so on?

Exercise 4.5: Design a Game Console for the Consumer

Write the physical requirements for the console you designed in Exercise 4.2. What does it need to look like? Where do you envision someone using it? How easy would it be for a consumer to buy and set up? Write all the steps consumers would have to follow when they first opened the box and took out this device.

DISCUSSION TOPICS

1. How important is it to have a "killer app" when a new platform is launched, and why?

2. Why do Asia and Europe have much larger populations of cell-phone gamers?

3. Given the current trends in the launch of new consoles, when do you expect another new group of consoles to be launched? What sorts of technology improvements might you anticipate?

4. Consider what you would like to see in a new handheld game platform. What trade-offs would you be willing to accept?

5. Select two game machines from consoles, handhelds, or computers. How critical are the input devices to the console? What impact does the type of input have on the types of games made for those machines?

Part Two

Game Development Cycle

In the not too distant past, a small team of programmers and artists could design a game and complete it in nine to fifteen months. The graphics in such games were relatively simple, and the game program itself was fairly small because it had to run within the constraints of early processors and memory. In spite of these limitations, games were relatively easier to produce and could make a reasonable profit by selling a few tens of thousands of copies.

As the technology of computers and consoles continued to evolve at a steady but inexorable rate, new opportunities in game production arose, and the process of creating a game grew more complex. Highly detailed and realistic graphics, multiplayer, and networking components, and larger storage mediums all require more design, programming, and art efforts from skilled and specialized artisans, who can draw hefty salaries. Thus, a publisher today must sell hundreds of thousands of copies of a game to turn a profit.

Turning out a first-class game requires the entire process to be well thought out; as a result, the game industry has become more professional over the years. Some may bemoan the loss of innocence of those days when games were primarily a hobby for the hyperintelligent, but the investment in time and money required to turn out a best-selling computer or console game today demands that a company follow better business practices, such as those outlined throughout these chapters and throughout this book.

- **Chapter 5:** The Production Cycle
- **Chapter 6:** The Production Team
- **Chapter 7:** Scheduling and Budgets

Chapter | 5

The Production Cycle

Chapter Objectives

After reading this chapter and doing the exercises, you will be able to do the following:

- Understand the production cycle of electronic games.
- Know what is done during the preproduction phase and who does it.
- Understand how important a technical review is to planning what will happen in the production phase.
- Know what is done during the production phase and who does it.
- Know what is done during the postproduction phase and who does it.

Introduction

Computer and video games do not just miraculously appear on retail shelves. Many people put considerable time and effort into making an electronic game. Just as computer technology has advanced and become more complex over time, so has the process of making games become more daunting. Whereas computer games were once limited to low-resolution, two-dimensional (2D) graphics, imperfect artificial intelligence (AI), and minimal multiplayer interactions, most current games offer high-resolution, three-dimensional (3D) graphics, advanced AI routines, and robust online gameplay. Producing such complex games requires larger teams and longer schedules. The game industry has had to change and improve its business model side by side with changes in development methods. The game industry is still relatively young and still developing its corporate methods and models, but it is starting to act more like a business and less like a hobby.

The production cycle for a game has grown to be as long as, and sometimes even longer than, the production cycle of a movie. Both share the same basic procedures. In both cases, someone has to come up with an idea for the film or game, put the idea on paper, convince someone to finance the project, develop a budget and schedule, hire skilled employees, and transform the idea into a finished project. Meanwhile, another group of people work on promoting the product and delivering it to the consumer. But the movie industry is over 100 years old, and its practices are well established. Those who work on films know what they are supposed to do and go about their work professionally. The games business, on the other hand, has only recently become a multibillion dollar industry and is still developing its methodologies. Many people working on games are new to the industry and are still learning all of the steps required to produce a finished game.

This chapter gives those who are new to the industry an overview of the process of producing a computer or video game from scratch. No doubt the processes described here will change over time as a growing core of seasoned professionals learn more efficient ways of making games.

Phases of the Production Cycle

Although the development process for a computer or video game is similar to the production cycle of a movie, there are significant differences. Many people might be familiar with the development process of a movie, having seen television shows or movies that depict movies being made, but they might not realize that games have a similar development process.

Production Cycle for a Film

A film production typically goes through five phases:

- **Development:** The idea for the film is fleshed out in a series of screen treatments until the final screenplay is prepared. This phase concludes when a director and cast are signed and financial backing is complete.

- **Preproduction:** The production staff is assembled, equipment and filming locations are secured, and a storyboard is created to begin the process of visualizing the script (Figure 5.1). The shooting schedule and the budget are finalized.

- **Production:** The actors go through their paces before the camera. Sets are created, scenes are filmed and refilmed until the director is satisfied, and then the sets are torn down (Figure 5.2). Meanwhile, technical experts begin working on the visual effects if computer graphics or other special effects are needed.

FIGURE 5.1 Director Peter Jackson reviewing production sketches for the trailer with the crew of *King Kong* (Universal).

■ **Postproduction:** The raw film footage is assembled into a coherent story by the editor in consultation with the director. When the sequence of shots and scenes are finalized, special visual effects and audio components are added (Figure 5.3). The objective is to create a complete cut of the entire movie, which is then shown to test

FIGURE 5.2 Setting up a scene with a miniature King Kong for Peter Jackson's remake of *King Kong* (Universal).

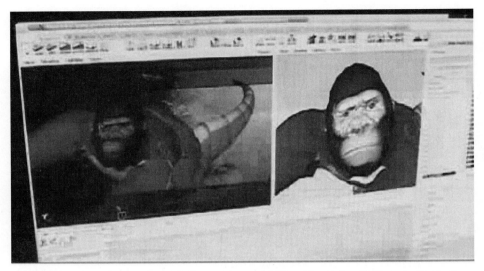

FIGURE 5.3 Refining a CG version of King Kong for Peter Jackson's remake of *King Kong* (Universal).

audiences to judge their responses. Based on the test audiences' feedback, additional editing might be required, and materials might have to be added until the final cut of the picture is ready to be released.

- **Distribution:** Copies of the final cut are made and sent to theaters. The marketing of the film goes into high gear as press kits and launch parties are prepared and ad campaigns are launched to let the audience know the film is in theaters.

Production Cycle for a Game

One major difference between film production and game production is that games do not normally use live actors, at least not as in-game characters controlled by the player. However, live actors might be used in full-motion video sequences that the player does not control, and of course, actors may provide the voices of characters the player does control.

Instead, game players control 2D sprites or 3D models built from scratch by the art staff. Actors might be used in a process called *motion capture* to make the human models move more realistically, but their image is not used directly in the final version of the game. Instead, the movements of characters as well as all the special effects are handcrafted by the artists and then brought to life by the programmers through the graphics engine. In other words, in games, the production and postproduction phases are one and the same.

FYI *Motion Capture*

Motion capture is a method of digitally tracking and recording a moving body, particularly the joints. It can be used by animation artists to generate realistic character movement. Sensors are attached to key locations on a performer's or athlete's body, and then the performer does the actions required in a game—running, throwing a ball, jumping, attacking with samurai swords, and so on. The performer's movements are recorded on a computer, and the game artists use the information when creating the 2D sprites or 3D models to make their animations as lifelike as possible. The two main technologies are electromagnetic (using magnetic sensors in EM fields) and optical (using reflective markers to reflect infrared light).

5

The production cycle for a game goes through three major phases:

- **Preproduction:** This phase combines the activities that make up the development and preproduction phases of a film. Someone comes up with the idea for a game and presents it to publishers. After the idea is accepted, the design is refined and then described in detail in a game design document. As the design takes final shape, the programming staff analyzes the design document to determine how the technical aspects will be implemented in code, while the art staff determines what the characters and environments will look like as well as the overall visual style of the product. Management, meanwhile, determines the product development schedule and the budget. The final step of this phase might be a simple interactive prototype to test the design assumptions. All this work is done before any real coding or art asset creation is started.

- **Production:** After the team knows what they will build and how they will build it, they start the actual process of writing the code and creating the art assets for the game. *Designers* create the map levels, develop the charts and tables that drive gameplay, generate dialogue, and keep the design documentation up-to-date. *Artists* create models of characters and the playfield, rig them for animation, and create the textures that will be applied to the models. The *audio staff* creates the music, sound effects, and voiceovers for the game. *Programmers* build the tools that the teams will need to make the game, generate the code for the various modules making up the game engine, and incorporate the final graphics into the game. As the game comes together, *testers* hunt down bugs and check to see if the game is fun and balanced. At the end of this phase, the master version of the final game is created and sent to the publisher.

- **Postproduction:** As far as the development team is concerned, this is the shortest phase of the cycle. After they complete the game, the team might hold a postmortem meeting to determine what went right and what went wrong during production (see Chapter 19, "Completing the Game"). They might also prepare for future game add-ons or a sequel if the game sells well enough. The programming staff might need to create a patch (or patches) if the game is for a PC platform and problems are discovered after the product ships. Some staff might also be involved in promoting the game or assisting customers. For the publisher, this phase involves duplicating the product discs, assembling the packaging, and shipping the finished product to distributors and retailers. It can also involve continued promotion for the game if management determines that the product needs more support.

For both films and games, the production cycle can be very long. It's not unusual for a film to take three years or longer to go from the initial idea to the final cut. Games can take just as long and even longer.

Now that we have looked at the game development process in brief, let's look at each phase in more detail.

Preproduction Phase

The preproduction phase of a game development cycle begins when someone comes up with an initial idea for a game. The rest of this section lays out this process and the documents produced during this phase.

Design Specification: Pitch Paper and Design Proposal

If you asked people on the street, many would be able to suggest a topic for a game. Coming up with an idea for a game is simple; turning it into a shippable product is hard work. The real work begins when someone documents the idea so that others can understand what the game will be.

The initial idea for a game is spelled out in a *pitch paper,* which presents the concept of the game without going into too much detail. Creating a one- or two-page paper takes little time and does not eat up much of a company's resources. Many companies encourage anyone on staff who has a good idea to put it in writing so that management can review it. The management at a publisher or larger developer might meet several times per year to review the accumulated pitch papers and decide which, if any, ideas are worth pursuing. Of the many ideas pitched, only a very few are chosen for further development.

If management finds an idea of interest, it might then be willing to pay a designer to spend some more time to further develop the idea in a *game proposal.* In addition to expanding the discussion of game mechanics, this proposal also

FIGURE 5.4 Creating concept art sketches for Ubisoft's *Myst V: End of Ages.*

includes a financial analysis of how well the proposed game is expected to sell. Creating a proposal can take a month or longer and involves not only the designer's time but also the time of other staff members such as an artist to create some simple 2D sketches (Figure 5.4), someone in finance to make a projection of sales, and someone in marketing to determine which existing or pending products compete with the proposed game. See Chapter 9, "Committing Ideas to Paper," for more information about brainstorming, pitch papers, and game proposals.

IN THE TRENCHES: Trying to Sell a Game Idea

In response to a question about selling a game idea to a company, Jay Powell of Octagon Entertainment posted this on GIGNews (**www.gignews.com**):

> Unfortunately there is very little you can do without the backing of a publisher, developer, or finance group. Publishers

CONTINUED ON NEXT PAGE

▶▶ **CONTINUED**

and developers very rarely pick up ideas that are not their own. Many larger publishers even have NDAs (non-disclosure agreements) that say they will not guarantee that they do not have a similar idea in the works. Your best bet is to find the financing to pay for the game. Many smaller developers exist that are avidly seeking contract deals. If you have the money, they will be happy to help your dream come to life. The other option would be to use your spare time to create a demo of the game. You could use the advances from a publisher to finish out your team and complete the game. There is very little chance at all of simply selling an idea by itself though.

Design Specification: Game Design Document

When the basics of the design are spelled out and the marketing analysis is complete, management reviews the information and determines whether to pursue the possibility of developing the game. If they give it the go-ahead, a *game design document* (also called a *game design specification*) is created. To create such a document, management must commit a goodly amount of time, resources, and money to put together a production team of one or more designers, several 2D artists, and a programming lead. This team expands on the proposal and writes up a *concept game document* that describes gameplay in detail and expands the backstory of the game (if necessary). The artists draw more detailed concept art for the characters and locations in the game, and the programming lead gives advice as to what can and can't be done in coding. It can take three to six months to complete this document, depending on the game's genre. A role-playing game, for example, takes a very long time to document because there are so many different game mechanics to explain—movement, combat, inventory, experience levels, and so on—plus the game's plot to develop. On the other hand, a puzzle game might take only a few months to document because it might have no characters, no locations, few items, and no backstory to explain.

FYI *Backstory*

The backstory includes all the events leading up to the moment the game begins. It is the history of the game's story. For example, id Software's *Doom 3* begins with the arrival of a marine (the player's

▶▶ CONTINUED ON NEXT PAGE

> ▶▶ CONTINUED
>
> character) at the main Martian facility of the Union Aerospace Corporation. His backstory includes the reasons why he became a marine and why he has been transferred to Mars, as well as what his family life is like. More important, the backstory explains the facility's interdimensional experiments, which have unleashed monsters from hell. All of this information is not provided upfront. As the game progresses, the player occasionally finds PDAs from dead staff members with information that fills in this backstory.

The concept design document might be reviewed and rewritten several times before management finally approves it. See Chapter 10, "The Game Design Document," for a closer examination of this process.

Technical Review Stage

When the production team receives the official okay (sometimes called the ***green light***), they proceed to the ***technical review*** stage. At this point, the company commits itself to turning the idea into a finished product and must invest the money and resources required to bring it to completion. During this stage, the various departments analyze the design to determine the best approach to building the game.

The programming staff determines what code modules must be written and the order in which they will be created. In addition, they must decide whether to build a game engine from scratch or license an engine from another company. Building an engine from scratch usually requires several senior programmers working for a number of years because of all the components the engine must support. As a result, licensing another company's game engine might be more economical. It might also be possible to reuse an entire internal engine or components from a previous game. However, even a licensed or reused engine usually requires additional programming to meet the requirements of the new game. In addition, the team determines what tools need to be created for the designers, artists, and testing staff.

The programming staff usually creates a ***technical design document*** (or ***technical specification***) to record their thoughts on paper for approval by the company's chief technical officer. After all the programming modules have been identified, the programming lead and the producer develop a timeline as to when the modules will be coded and who will write each one.

Meanwhile, the art staff does its own technical review to settle on a unified graphic style for the game and identify the tools needed to complete their work. They might need to update their graphics software during development and/or they might request some special plug-ins for their 3D modeling programs (such as Maya or 3ds Max) to create unusual animations, manipulate textures, add special visual effects, and the like. They define how these plug-in tools will work so the programming staff can write them. They start creating 2D characters, item, and location sketches that the 3D artists will later use to build the models. They also work out how the animations will work for the characters. The team might create an *art design document* (or *art specification*) to nail down their decisions. When they have everything figured out, the art lead works with the producer to add the art tasks to the project timeline.

The design staff also determines what they will do to help complete the game. They work with the programmers to determine what tools they will need to build the game (such as a level editor or scripting language). They might also create a paper prototype of the game to test their design decisions, especially where complex game mechanics are involved. When the various design tasks are determined, they decide which team members will do which tasks and when they will do them. The lead designer then works with the producer to plug the design tasks into the project timeline. The producing staff works with team leaders to build the project timeline. They determine the overall schedule for the product and set up a series of milestones that define when major components of the game will be completed, merged, and tested. They also determine the manpower requirements for each task on the timeline and decide when it might be necessary to hire additional staff and buy new equipment for the team. The end result is the *budget* for the product.

The team might spend several months in the technical review stage. When their analysis is complete, they present their technical findings, along with the proposed schedule and budget to management for final approval. Assuming the team has done its preparations thoroughly, management gives the final approval to begin production on the game. See Chapter 11, "Technical Review" for more details about this phase.

Selecting a Game Engine

The *game engine* is the core software component of the game. It includes the graphics rendering system and might also include the modules for artificial intelligence, physics, a scripting language, and other features. It does not include the art, audio, or design assets.

The team makes one of the most important decisions about the game during the technical review: whether to build the game engine from scratch, to use or modify an engine they have already created, to use another company's completed game engine, or to use a commercial development environment (called *middleware*). Each approach has benefits and drawbacks.

Building a game engine from scratch can take several years and usually requires the skills of senior engineers. An advantage of building a game engine from scratch is that the team does not have to create workarounds, which are sections of code that make someone else's engine do exactly what your team needs it to do. In addition, if the new engine amazes game players with its expanded capabilities, other companies might very well want to license it, thus increasing the developer's revenue stream. However, one problem with building an engine is that no useful work can be done on a game until the engine is close to completion; thus, the design and art staff might have little to do until they have the tools they need to build resources that the engine can use.

Using another company's game engine—for example, Epic Games' Unreal Engine—has the advantage of saving time and, therefore, money. It can take the programming staff some time to really understand how the engine works, but they can start turning out tools for the engine and modifying code modules as the new design necessitates more quickly than when building the engine from the ground up. There are drawbacks, of course. It can be very expensive to license a game engine and then, perhaps, get a separate license for each game platform. In addition, the company that produced the engine is probably busy on the next version of their engine and often won't be willing to invest a lot of their time or resources in customer support. Finally, the engine ultimately might not be able to do exactly what the production team needs it to do, forcing them to either extensively rewrite the code or make changes to the game design.

A possible solution is to use middleware, such as Criterion's RenderWare or NDL's Gamebryo. ***Middleware*** is software that provides some pregenerated code modules, particularly the code for rendering the graphics onto the screen, but not the whole game engine. It can also contain other modules that make the programming tasks much simpler. The code modules of the middleware are flexible enough that they can be modified as needed based on a game's requirements and are complete enough that the programmers can enhance the engine's abilities instead of creating them from scratch. A drawback to middleware is that it can be too generic and require the programming staff to rework many of the modules. Also, it might not allow the game to be implemented as designed. Using middleware can also be expensive because each game platform usually requires a separate licensing fee and a yearly service fee.

FYI | *Middleware Wars*

One of the most popular middleware programs, RenderWare by Criterion, has been used in such games as Rockstar's *Grand Theft Auto: San Andreas,* Activision's *Call of Duty: Finest Hour,* and Sega's *Sonic Heroes.* However, this might soon change because Criterion was acquired by Electronic Arts in July 2004. Although EA says it will continue to let other game companies use RenderWare, many rival game company executives might be skeptical of the offer because licensing the application will force them to give away the subject of the game they plan to build with RenderWare. It remains to be seen whether EA will continue to offer RenderWare as promised or will turn it into a proprietary tool to be used only by its developers.

As you can see, deciding how the game engine should be built is a major undertaking. The demands of the genre and the game platform should influence the developer as she makes the final decision about whether to start from scratch or use someone else's code. In either case, it still takes many months to make the game engine do everything it needs to do as outlined and defined in the game design document.

Production Phase

The production phase is the longest portion of the game development cycle and can last several years, depending on the complexity of the technology and the extent of the design. Producing a game requires a team of highly skilled experts. The artists build the 3D models polygon by polygon, rig them for animation, and generate the texture for a model's "skin" (Figure 5.5). Likewise, the environments are hand-crafted as the designers work in conjunction with level artists/designers to determine the gameplay in each map area. The programmers must write thousands upon thousands of lines of code while the designers continually tweak the charts and tables that define gameplay and refine the logic for triggering game events. The audio staff works with musicians and sound designers to add music and sound effects to the game. Meanwhile, testers offer suggestions on gameplay and balance and help hunt down bugs.

Interactive Prototype

The paper prototype created during the preproduction phase can tell the designers only so much about how the game plays, so one of the first steps in the production phase is often a simple *interactive prototype* of the main gameplay elements in the game. (Some companies consider this to be the last step of the technical review stage.) The prototype is a test bed for the designers to check

FIGURE 5.5 Model of a tiger showing progression from wireframe mesh to solid polygon model to final skinned model in Microsoft's *Zoo Tycoon 2*.

their design decisions before the programmers start real coding. An artist or two might be asked to provide simple *placeholder art* so the designers can also check the scale of objects as they appear on the screen. The game might suddenly play much differently than anticipated in the interactive prototype, requiring some elements of the design to be modified so that the game works the way the designers wish. It is much easier and much cheaper to make changes to the design early in production than to discover problems that must be addressed halfway through.

The purpose of the interactive prototype is to test design decisions such as how fast things move across the screen, how much real estate they take up on the screen, how combat plays out in real time, and so on. The code and art used to create the interactive prototype should be considered placeholder work only and should not be used in the final product. The code is normally cobbled together quickly and, therefore, is usually poorly structured and commented (if at all). If computer-controlled enemies are used, their AI routines should handle movement and combat as simply as possible. Likewise, placeholder art is used primarily to determine scale, so minimal effort should be made to generate it. Chapter 18, "Prototyping and Building Playfields," discusses prototypes in detail.

Designer Tools

In addition to the prototype, the designers generally need several other tools to make the design come to life. These include a map/level editor, a scripting language, a database, and others.

Map/Level Editor   Depending on the type of game and the desired dimensionality (2D or 3D), the design staff may be able to create the game maps themselves with a 2D map editor (Figure 5.6). A 2D map editor usually has sets of tiles that are used to build maps, somewhat like assembling the pieces of a jigsaw puzzle into its final shape. The tile sets might be organized by the types of terrain in the game, and the tiles are often designed so that they can be combined in many different combinations. The editor might also use invisible overlay maps to place items on the playfield and to trigger events.

If the game is 3D, the designers usually work with level designers or environment artists who are proficient in a 3D graphics program, such as 3ds Max (formerly 3D Studio Max) or Maya, to create the levels. A 3D map editor is much more complex and can be too difficult for the designers to use. It is much easier to think up a playfield on a flat map than to consider all the nooks and crannies and ups and downs involved in creating a three-dimensional map. The levels for 3D games are built with special graphics programs that show models from all perspectives (Figure 5.7). The finished levels are then imported into the game engine and tested. See Chapter 18, "Prototyping and Building Playfields," for more information about building playfields.

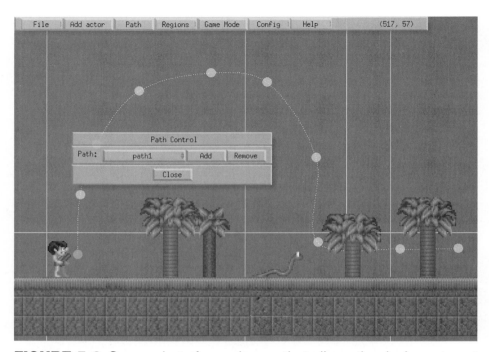

FIGURE 5.6 Screenshot of a work area that allows the designer to set a movement path in the commercial 2D map editor Game Editor (**www.game-editor.com**).

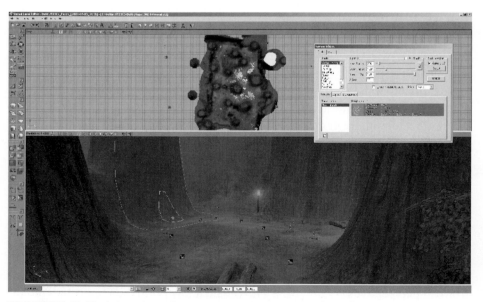

FIGURE 5.7 A level under construction using Epic Game's Unreal Engine 2.

Scripting Language A *scripting language* is a specialized collection of a number of prebuilt commands that a designer can use to trigger events in a game. Several common programming languages, such as Perl and Lua, that are called scripting languages might be used for just this purpose in a game. However, a developer might wish to create a simpler, proprietary scripting language that does not force a designer to know the intricacies of programming. Even so, such a language does demand that a designer have a strong grasp of Boolean logic—especially "if–then" statements. For example, the scripting language might use a logic that says "if the player enters this tile space, then trigger a scripted combat with the King Ogre." This script might be coded as follows:

Code Exhibit 5.1

```
if (CURRENT_SPACE(HERE,FACING_TEMPLE_DOOR) AND
    (GET_FLAG(OGRE_KING_FIGHT = 0)))
            {
            SET_COMBAT(OGRE_KING)
            SET_FLAG(OGRE_KING_FIGHT = 1)
            SET_BOOTY(OGRE_KING_RING)
            SHOW_TEXT("The King of the Ogres
                charges out of the temple to attack
                you."
            }
else
            {
            SHOW_TEXT("The Ogre King's ring gives
                you access to the temple.")
            PLAY_ANIMATION(TEMPLE_DOOR,OPEN)
            }
```

In this example, when the player enters the space in front of the temple door, the King of the Ogres charges out to engage in combat. Assuming the player wins the combat, he receives the king's ring, which opens the temple door from now on, and a flag is set to indicate that the combat has occurred to keep it from happening again.

Although a scripting language can be used to create interesting events in a game, it should not be used to generate AI for enemies because it takes longer to read and implement a script file than to trigger responses hard-coded into the game engine. Chapter 16, "Mathematics and Artificial Intelligence in Games," discusses scripting languages in more detail.

Database A game can contain many different kinds of charts and tables listing key values assigned to game objects that are used to resolve game actions. Together, these charts and tables form the game *database.* For example, a role-playing game might include the following charts and tables in the game's database:

- Charts:
  - Character Chart: Includes all values assigned to characters controlled by players, number of inventory slots, allowable weapons/armor, and skills and magic spells that can be learned. Used throughout the game.
  - Weaponry Chart: Contains values for all weapons and armor. Used during combat to resolve attacks with weapons.
  - Item Chart: Contains values for all items that are found or purchased during play. Includes restoring health and mana, durations of debilitating states (poison, stone, paralysis, and so on), costs to buy and sell in shops, and other values. Used in combat and other locations.
  - Magic Chart: Contains values for all magic spells in the game and target types per spell type. Used during combat to resolve magic attacks and outside combat to heat and restore characters.
  - Monster Chart: Contains values associated with enemy characters such as combat values, magic spells, number of experience points and gold received when defeated, and name and associated graphics representation.
  - Movement Chart: Indicates costs to enter type of terrain during movement, effect on inventory capacity, and modifiers to combat calculations.
  - Experience Level Chart: Lists the number of experience points needed to rise to the next level (based on race and career), how many points are given to the player to assign to a character's attributes and magic spells and skills at each level, and new spells/skills learned.
- Tables:
  - Character Generation Table: Used in generating a new character. Based on random results player receives a number of points to assign to a character's starting attributes.
  - Weapon Combat Table: Used to resolve combat with weapons. After calculating the modified attack and defense values, a random number is generated, and the appropriate column is referenced to determine how much damage was inflicted on the target.
  - Magic Combat Table: Used to resolve combat with magic. After determining how much damage a magic spell inflicts, a random number is generated to see if the target's luck attribute modifies the damage number.

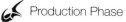

- Treasure Table: Used in random combat encounters with creatures to determine how much gold and experience points the player receives for defeating enemies.

- Random Combat Encounter Table: If a random combat encounter is triggered, a random die roll determines which enemy types are involved and the number per group.

The designers and tool programmers work together to determine all the different values that must appear on each chart or table. The design staff will probably want to create these materials as spreadsheets so they can view the information on each sheet as a whole and ensure that the values are correct relative to each other. The programmers create a simple application to strip the appropriate information out of the spreadsheet and put it into a data file for the game engine to read. The database is kept separate from the game engine so that the designers can continually tweak the figures during testing without having to ask the program staff to rebuild the game to test the changes. Database creation is covered in more detail in Chapter 16, "Mathematics and Artificial Intelligence in Games."

Other Tools In addition to the previously mentioned design tools, the programmers might need to create art tools such as a model exporter, material exporter, or the special visual effects exporter that loads artwork from the 3D graphics program into the game engine. Also, the map or level editor might require additional plug-ins to handle the artwork. The audio team might need tools to meet the music, sound effects, and voiceover requirements for a game. Finally, the testing staff might need tools to make sure that bug tracking works smoothly.

User Interface

One make-it-or-break-it facet of a game is its user interface. If the game feels almost like second nature to players as soon as they boot it up, its chances of becoming a success increase. If players have to continually refer to an explanation of how the interface works or if they find the controls hard to use, it is difficult for them to become fully immersed in the product; they might put aside the game completely if this becomes too irritating. Designing an interface that is intuitive and easy to learn is the ultimate goal of the production team. In fact, some companies hire specialists in interface design to make it as good as possible.

Of course, the more complex the game, the more complicated the interface. For action games, it is best to have as simple an interface as possible so that players can get the hang of play quickly and become fully engrossed in the game experience. Very young gamers usually have short attention spans and want immediate results, so a simple interface is desired in games designed for that age group. Older players might be willing to make the effort to learn a convoluted interface if they feel the reward is great enough, which is why complex games such as flight simulations and war games can maintain their audiences. User interface design is covered in more detail in Chapter 15, "Interface Design."

Balancing Gameplay

One of the more difficult aspects of creating a game is making sure that is balanced. The most important balancing consideration is that no one unit or strategy should win all the time, for when players discover this *flaw,* they will not try anything else. The designers are responsible for making sure that the data driving gameplay are evenly balanced so that a good player can brag of winning the game through skill and not just from dumb luck or an imbalance in a unit's values. However, it requires a lot of people's testing the game with "fresh eyes" to track down such imbalances in the game mechanics.

It's also important for the production team to remember the audience for the game and try to balance it accordingly. Action games are traditionally aimed at younger audiences, and making the controls easy to learn is the key to success. Young players are much better at learning complex hand-eye coordination routines than older players. They are also more willing to invest the time required to learn intricate patterns to perform game actions. Trying to slow down the action to draw an older audience might result in the game's becoming too easy for the target audience yet too difficult or repetitive for an older audience. On the other hand, a complex strategy game can require more foresight and planning than a young audience can, or is willing to, invest, whereas simplifying the strategies to appeal to them might make the decisions too one-dimensional for the intended older audience. Finding a happy medium for the difficulty level is quite challenging. Many games solve the problem by including user-selectable difficulty levels so players can determine the challenge level themselves.

Balancing a game is discussed in Chapter 19, "Completing the Game."

Debugging

Eventually, the code modules are finished, the artwork is complete, and the levels are built. When the game components begin coming together and can be tested, the first bugs will appear. The *quality assurance* (QA) department is responsible for finding the bugs and reporting them to the appropriate team. During tools development, one or more programmers might work with the head of QA to develop or modify a database for bug tracking. As the game nears completion, many more bugs will be reported, and it is up to the producer and QA to make sure that the most serious bugs are removed in a timely manner. Figure 5.8 shows the path node debugging tool used in Electronic Arts' *Medal of Honor: Allied Assault.*

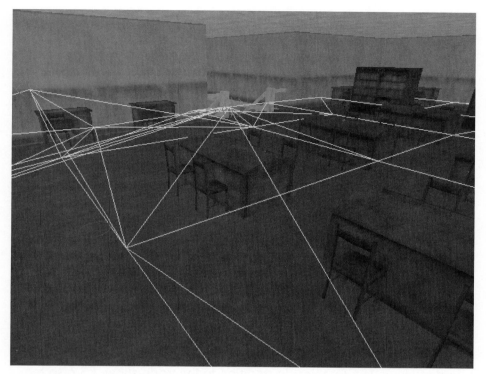

FIGURE 5.8 Debugging tool for movement nodes in Electronic Arts'
Medal of Honor: Allied Assault.

The last milestone in a production schedule is ***beta*** (see Chapter 7,
"Scheduling and Budgets," for more about milestones), during which the team's
effort is one-hundred-percent focused on debugging the game and making final
tweaks to gameplay. This step can last for many months while many people test
the game for unexpected problems. All bug reports during this stage have to be
tracked and resolved. Chapter 19, "Completing the Game," goes into more
detail about the process of completing a project.

Marketing

The production team can sometimes forget that it's not enough to simply turn out
the product at some point in the future; it also has to be sold to an audience. This
is the job of the marketing department. The process of marketing a game (which
is described in more detail in Chapter 20, "Marketing the Game") doesn't begin
when the game is complete; it begins as soon as the game has something concrete to show off, and it continues until after the product is shipped. Marketing
personnel frequently request screenshots during the game's development, and it
takes time to get the right pictures. Likewise, the marketing staff will demand
working demos of the product for reviewers, for interested gamers who want to

download them from a favorite game site, and for some of the important game conferences and trade shows, such as the Game Developers Conference (GDC) and the Electronic Entertainment Expo (E3Expo).

FYI | *Game Conferences*

The Game Developers Conference (GDC) is a gathering of game industry professionals held in March of every year in California. The first conference was organized by Chris Crawford in 1987 and was held in his living room. It has since grown along with the industry and regularly has well over 10,000 attendees each year. In addition to numerous lectures and roundtable discussions, the conference includes a job fair, an exposition where companies show off their tools for developing games, the Independent Games Festival, and GDC Mobile (a miniconference focusing on games for cell phones, PDAs, and other mobile platforms). For more information, see the GDC Web site at **http://www.gdconf.com.**

The Electronic Entertainment Expo E3 or E3Expo is a yearly trade show where game companies show off their upcoming releases to the press and retailers. It is held in May at the Convention Center in downtown Los Angeles. In addition to the trade show, E3 also features a three-day conference for industry professionals. Over 60,000 attendees visited the 2005 expo. For more information, see the E3 Web site at **http://www.e3expo.com.**

While the production team works to complete the game, the marketing staff works to promote and advertise it. The marketing staff sends out press releases, creates print and television advertisements, and shows off the product at industry shows. Their goals are to keep the product before the customers' eyes and to let the retailers know when the product will finally ship. When the product hits the shelves, the marketing department will keep promoting it as long as it continues to sell.

As well as advertising and promoting the product, the marketing department is often responsible for holding focus groups to test the game and give their feedback. This can often be another source of friction between marketing and production, with production feeling that such groups are a waste of time and marketing feeling that their vital input is being ignored. In fact, focus groups are very important to the success of modern games. The time, effort, and tens of millions of dollars that go into creating a triple-A title demand that a responsible publisher get as much feedback about the gameplay and user interface as possible throughout the production phase. Incorporating this feedback while there is still time to do it cheaply will make the game better and more intuitive.

A good producer will anticipate marketing's requirements, work with them to understand what they will need to promote the game, and build time into the project timeline for demos, screenshots, and other materials.

Postproduction Phase

The *postproduction phase* of a game deals primarily with marketing and distribution of the game. After the *gold master* is completed and tested, it is sent to the CD duplicator to be reproduced. The publisher might package the final game internally or send it to a company that specializes in assembly and distribution. The final assembled packages are shrink-wrapped, boxed, and sent to distribution centers, where they are delivered to eager customers. Some games can be purchased from publishers directly over the Internet and downloaded onto the target game platform. The customer may be given the chance to receive a boxed version of the product as well.

FYI *Gold Master*

The gold master (also called the release candidate) is the final version of the game with all the bugs removed (hopefully). The term probably derives from the music industry and refers to the master disks that were sent to the manufacturer. These disks had to be of excellent and more permanent quality because they were actually used as the source for the mass-produced retail copies, so they were made of gold. Therefore, the process of creating the master is often called "going gold."

At this point, the team that worked on the product can relax and catch up on missing sleep and personal relationships. There might be a few minor tasks left for them to do. If the game was designed for the computer platform, some remaining bugs might need to be fixed and released as patches available by download over the Internet. The team might decide to conduct a postmortem on the product to determine what went right and what went wrong during the whole cycle (see Chapter 19, "Completing the Game," for more information on postmortems). Depending on the needs of the publisher, some of the team might be assigned to help promote the game. For example, they might discuss their work in online chat rooms or make personal appearances at trade shows or conferences. Somewhere along the line, the team might clean up the design documentation in case the publisher is interested in developing add-ons or a sequel. Most likely, the team that spent years creating the product will be happy to hand off their documents to a new, fresh team to carry on the work.

The publisher will continue to promote the game as long as it continues to sell. Extended advertising campaigns might be planned to include televisions ads or other promotional materials to be distributed to the media, retailers, and customers. Publishers often have an internal (or external) customer service department to deal with customer complaints and problems.

Despite all these efforts, the shelf life of an electronic game, unless it is a smash success, tends to be limited. It might survive for a year or so before becoming "old hat" and disappearing into the remainder bin. The march of technology inevitably means that even the most popular games will become obsolete and will disappear from retail outlets. They might reappear in discounted versions or become part of a package deal with a hardware manufacturer (called an *OEM,* for original equipment manufacturer). Finally, the game will disappear forever, only to live in the memories of the people who worked on it and the gamers who once loved it.

FYI | *Shelf Life of Games*

Most large retail outlets, such as Target and Wal-Mart, devote only a limited amount of shelf space to games, generally stocking 200 to 300 titles at a time. In a typical year, some 1,500 game titles might be released, so the retailer is pressured to get rid of titles that do not sell. As a result, the shelf-life of a typical game can be anywhere from 2 weeks to 6 months. Most games make the greatest amount of money in the first 60 to 90 days after their release, but they may quickly wind up in the remainder bin if the strong sales don't continue. Some games continue to sell for years, but these are rare. Creating add-ons and sequels is one technique publishers use keep their popular games on retail shelves for the long run.

Summary

Video game production is similar to film production in that the more time and effort that goes into preproduction, the smoother the production phase will be. Game production begins when someone pitches an idea that management likes. During the preproduction phase, the idea is expanded upon in various documents. After a complete design is presented to management and accepted, the programmers and artists determine the tasks they must perform to turn the design into a finished product. When this initial preparation is completed, the teams begin the hard work of creating the game assets and writing the code during the production phase.

As the game begins to come together, testers give feedback on what works and what needs to be changed, and marketing starts its efforts to promote the game and get gamers interested enough to buy it. When the code is finalized and the assets are all in the game, the product goes through a debugging process until it is approved for shipping. The postproduction phase begins when the product is distributed to retailers, and the production team ties up any loose ends and gets some rest before diving headlong into the next project and starting the process all over again.

Test Your Skills

MULTIPLE CHOICE QUESTIONS

1. The film industry has been making movies for over 100 years. Approximately how long has the video game industry been around?

   A. 50 years.

   B. 10 years.

   C. 35 years.

   D. 70 years.

2. What are the three phases of video game development?

   A. Concept, postproduction, and sales.

   B. Pitch, production, and distribution.

   C. Preproduction, production, and postproduction.

   D. Development, production, and distribution.

3. What is a pitch paper used for?

   A. To get management to approve the production.

   B. To determine if the concept can be copyrighted.

   C. To get the team to understand the game idea.

   D. To quickly express the game idea to a variety of people.

4. What tools are commonly used in making a 3D game? (Select all that apply.)

   A. 3D level editor.

   B. 3D animation program.

   C. Script editor.

   D. Database.

5. Why are prototypes used during production?

   A. To test technology.

   B. To demonstrate gameplay.

   C. To demonstrate art and animation.

   D. To make cut-scenes.

6. When is customer service involved in the production cycle?

   A. During preproduction, to ensure the customers get what they want.

   B. During postproduction, to help customers and answer questions.

   C. During production, to evaluate how well the customer likes the product.

   D. During postproduction, to sell the product to the customer.

7. Which of the following tasks does marketing perform during the production phase? (Select all that apply.)

   A. Create advertising.

   B. Review game submissions.

   C. Run focus groups.

   D. Supply test plans to customer service.

8. Which of the following tasks are performed during the preproduction for a video game? (Select all that apply.)

   A. Design all the schedules.

   B. Record voices to be used in animated sequences.

   C. Pitch the game to publishers.

   D. Scout locations for video shoots.

9. Which of the following tasks are performed during the technical review stage? (Select all that apply.)

   A. Determine the technical tasks to be completed.

   B. Decide what form of game engine to use or write.

   C. Design the tools to be made during production.

   D. Write the production schedule.

10. What does the marketing department do during post production?

    A. Sell and distribute the game.

    B. Make demos and trailers.

    C. Continue the marketing campaign started during production.

    D. Clean up the design documents for any upcoming sequels.

11. The QA team is _____.

    A. Responsible for finding and reporting bugs to be fixed.

    B. Making gameplay suggestions before they start playing the game.

    C. Responsible for making sure the game meets the required specifications.

    D. Formed during postproduction.

12. What does the game engine do? (Select all that apply.)

    A. Draw the background.

    B. Install the game.

    C. Make levels.

    D. Automatically make updates to the game.

13. What choices must the technical team make about the game engine? (Select all that apply.)

    A. Whether or not to use middleware.

    B. Whether or not to use an existing engine.

    C. Whether or not to write their own game engine.

    D. Whether or not to have 3D sound in the game.

14. When is the user interface designed?

    A. Preproduction.

    B. Production.

    C. Development.

    D. Distribution.

15. Which of the following tools does the design team require?

    A. A database of charts and tables used to drive game actions.

    B. A 3D animation tool to make models.

    C. A scheduling program to keep track of tasks.

    D. Middleware to make the game engine.

16. Who makes the packaging for the game?

    A. The same group that makes the CDs.

    B. The publisher does it internally or hires a company.

    C. The developer.

    D. The marketing team.

5

EXERCISES

Exercise 5.1: Write a Pitch Paper

Pick a current game and write the concept of the game as a pitch paper. Summarize everything you think is important for a business to know about this game to decide whether or not to fund the production.

Exercise 5.2: Develop a Department Timeline

Select one department involved in game production, such as programming or art. Draw a timeline that represents the entire cycle of a game, from preproduction through postproduction. In each section, list the high-level tasks that department should be doing. When your lists are done, review them and reorganize them so that the order of the tasks makes sense. Discuss how critical you think preproduction is when making a game.

Exercise 5.3: Market Your Game

Write down the types of places where you think a video game should be advertised. What materials would each of these outlets need for advertising? Create a chart and show how the materials for any outlet could be supplied to other marketing outlets. Think as broadly as you can and push the boundaries of where games have been advertised in the past.

Exercise 5.4: Choose a Game Engine

Consider creating a new FPS game. Write an essay defending your pro or con stance on using an existing game engine for making the game.

Exercise 5.5: Create a Concept Document for a Cell Phone Game

Consider creating a game for a cell phone. Write a list of the features you think would be important to your game. What requirements would you have for a phone that would play the game, for example, a camera, a color display, a gamepad–like mouse? Explain, in a concept document, why you think this game would be fun to play.

Exercise 5.6: Test Gameplay

Make a paper version of a game with simple gameplay, such as Pac-Man or a turn-based strategy game. Play through several times; then make a small change to the gameplay such as the number of dice used or the movement patterns of enemies. Discuss the importance of playing the game like this before actually committing programming time to development.

DISCUSSION TOPICS

1. If making a game engine is like building a camera every time someone makes a movie, why doesn't everyone use existing game engines? As you consider this, also consider why there is little need to build a new camera with every film. Finally, what films can you list from the previous 20 years that required the creation of new filming technology?

2. The movie industry has been around for 100 years, the video game industry for significantly less time. What production techniques do you think are worthwhile for the game industry to incorporate into their own production cycle?

3. How early in the development cycle do you feel marketing should get involved? Production? Postproduction? Preproduction? Why that particular phase? What benefits could there be to their later or earlier involvement?

4. It often seems to people new to the industry that a lot of time is spent writing documents and not making games. Discuss what you think can happen to a game if you spend too much time writing or if you don't spend enough time writing.

5. When production cycles lengthen, it's easy for the development team to get bored. What are some ways to maintain the interest of the core team? What would you consider doing with play testing to help the development team regain focus?

Chapter 6

The Production Team

Chapter Objectives

After reading this chapter and doing the exercises, you will be able to do the following:

- Understand the roles of executive, operational, and functional management in a game company.
- Appreciate the tasks and responsibilities of the design team.
- Appreciate the tasks and responsibilities of the programming team.
- Appreciate the tasks and responsibilities of the art team.
- Learn how auxiliary staff contribute to game creation.

Introduction

As the technology used in games continues to improve, the products have expanded in size and scope. In the early days when computer games were trapped within the 640K memory constraints of MS-DOS, there was no Internet play; graphics were mostly low-resolution, 256-color sprites animating against two dimensional (2D) backgrounds; music was flat and repetitive; and computer-controlled enemies used easily predictable finite-state machine artificial intelligence (AI) routines. Nowadays, most computer games—and many console games—offer an online multiplayer version and feature high-color, highly detailed, three dimensional (3D) graphics; multichannel, multi-instrument music, sound effects, and voiceovers; and enemy AI routines that are more intricate and responsive to the player's actions. All these new and improved features in games depend on one thing: highly skilled individuals. The programmers, artists, and designers who create games are all highly-skilled artisans, and artisans are expensive.

Game teams have grown in size over time. Only a decade ago, a team of 6 to 10 individuals could complete a triple-A game in about 15 to 18 months.

It now takes teams of at least 20 to 40 (and often many more) professionals from 2 to 4 years to complete projects. As a result, the budgets for games have ballooned (as discussed in the next chapter) along with the manpower requirements, meaning that a game now has to sell many more copies to make a profit. It is still possible to create smaller games with smaller teams—for example, games for cell phones or PDAs—but the trend is toward larger teams working many months to handcraft the final game product.

FYI   *AAA Titles*

The game industry used to classify game titles as being A, B, or C. **A titles** were the major releases that had very high production values and were worthy of major marketing campaigns. These games were expected to make big profits for the company. **B titles** were less glamorous and received less fanfare, but were still expected to earn back the costs. **C titles** were cheapies with low production values that might be used to hold shelf space until a better title was ready. Nowadays, publishers are primarily interested in the very best products that have the highest production values and that obviously look like large teams worked on them. These games are referred to as **AAA (or triple-A)** titles and receive almost all the marketing efforts and fanfare. B titles are still published, but they often stay on retail shelves for a only limited time. Publishers are no longer interested in C titles.

This chapter looks at the various team members who work on a game and examines what they do during the production cycle. The exact composition of a team differs from company to company, but the primary tasks needed to bring the product to completion are the same in all companies. The terminology used by the game industry to define job positions is open-ended. Job titles can, and do, differ among game companies, and the same title, such as creative director, can be used to define very different responsibilities across different companies. Therefore, you should focus on the responsibilities of each position instead of its title as you read this chapter.

Management

Game companies usually have three levels of management: executive, functional, and operational (Figure 6.1). *Executive management* is responsible for setting up the strategy and defining the vision for the company in terms of what they plan to

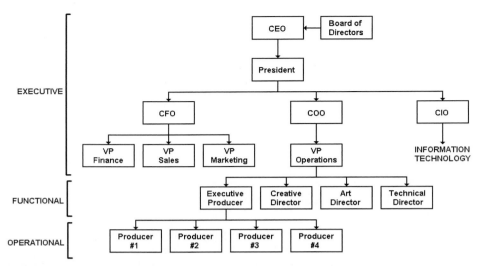

FIGURE 6.1 Sample organization chart for a large game company, showing the executive and functional management levels.

make and how. ***Functional management*** makes up a secondary layer whose duty it is to support the decisions made by the executive staff and turn the strategy and vision into a reality. The third level, ***operational management,*** comprises the people responsible for the day-to-day specifics of getting the work done. The following sections discuss each layer of management in more detail.

FYI | *Starting Up a Company*

It is much more difficult to start up a new game company these days than it used to be. To create a full-blown computer or console game requires a large team that will likely spend several years working on the project. In addition, the team needs top-of-the-line equipment and software. To start such a company requires an investment of at least $5 to $10 million. Of course, there are other ways for small groups to start a game company. By concentrating on initially doing smaller games for handheld platforms such as PDAs or cell phones or shareware games that allow players to download and try the product before buying it, a small group of passionate gamers can make enough money to cover their expenses. As they develop a reputation for creating good games, they can take on more projects and hire more people until they have a staff that can produce the triple-A titles the major publishers are looking for.

Executive Management

The executives who actually run a company are often referred to as the "suits." The larger the company, the more suits there are because there are more departments, with each department having its own corporate structure. A small third-party developer might have only one or two executives (for example, a president and finance officer) who might be as directly involved in actually working on a game as handling the larger aspects of running the company. Larger developers and publishers have many more executives. Electronic Arts, for example, lists thirteen executives on its top management staff plus a board of directors that offers guidance to the company. Each of these top executives is responsible for a portion of EA and has a large staff to handle its operations.

The executive staff of a large company usually has the following positions:

- **Chief Executive Officer (CEO):** The CEO carries the overall responsibility for the company's operations. In publicly held companies that issue stock and have stockholders, this person meets with the board of directors to set up long-term strategic plans and policies for the company and then oversees their implementation by the executive staff. If the company is privately held, the CEO is responsible for setting the strategies for the company. The CEO might hire a president to handle some of these duties.

- **Board of Directors:** The board is a group of individuals who are elected by the stockholders in a publicly held company to help make corporate policy and to appoint officers. These individuals are often executives from other game companies or companies closely associated with the industry (such as Microsoft, Adobe, or Intel). The company CEO is usually a member of the board. The board acts as advisors to the company's executive staff, makes suggestions about what new directions the company might consider taking, and represents the shareholders' interests.

- **President:** This person is a leader of the company and helps make the most important decisions about its strategy. This person might report to the CEO or be the top executive in a smaller company that does not have a CEO. If the company is publicly traded, the president makes sure the shareholders feel they are being rewarded for their investment. In a large game company, this person often has little or no direct involvement in the production of games because most of his or her time is taken up with meetings with other executives to discuss organization structure, goals, strategies, and company rules. In midsize and smaller game companies, the president often becomes involved in approving which game designs receive the green light for development.

- **Chief Financial Officer (CFO):** This person is responsible for the financial operations of the company. The CFO makes sure that there is enough money available to start new projects and bring them to conclusion, makes appropriations and authorizes expenditures for the company, develops economic strategies, and makes financial forecasts. When a game is pitched to the executive staff, the CFO or other designated member of the finance department analyzes the financial risks and rewards associated with doing the project and prepares a projection (called a ***return on investment*** or ***ROI***) outlining expected sales and profits.

- **Chief Operating Officer (COO):** In a large company, this person is responsible for overseeing the day-to-day operations of the company and reports back to the CEO on how things are going. The COO generally has little say on what games are chosen to produce but is instead concerned with making sure that after the decision has been made the teams have the staffing and equipment they need and that they stay on schedule.

- **Chief Information Officer (CIO):** Some companies have an executive in charge of the company's ***intranet*** operations (the company's internal network). This person also oversees the company's connection to the Internet and other external networks, manages hardware and software installations, and is in charge of in-house technical support. In addition to ensuring that an adequate hardware and software infrastructure is in place and maintained, this person might also assist in the creation of a Web site to promote the company's products and corporate image.

- **Vice Presidents:** A large company usually has a number of executives who oversee the work of specific departments or company locations. For example, a publishing company might have vice presidents to handle sales, marketing, finances, operations, and production. If the company makes its own packaging, it might also have vice presidents of creative services and public relations. These executives often give input into the project selection process. Whereas the daily operations are usually handled by managers and directors who report to the vice presidents, departmental and corporate decision making is handled by the vice presidents themselves.

FYI   *Small Development Companies*

Privately held companies sometimes use different titles than those listed above and often have variations as to specific corporate responsibilities. For example, they might not have a board of directors at all but only a president who wears all the corporate hats. Instead of having a chief financial officer, a small company might just have a financial director or an accountant who reports to the president. In a truly

▶▶ CONTINUED ON NEXT PAGE

▶▶ CONTINUED

small company, the president, who is often a sole proprietor, usually holds many responsibilities that have not been delegated to others. For the purposes of completeness, the rest of this section discusses the roles of management in a large company.

Functional Management

This level of management includes the managers and supervisors who turn the corporate vision into reality. In large game companies this level can include specialists who have risen through the ranks and amassed a huge knowledge base that the company wants to draw upon to make their games better. These specialists include:

- **Executive Producer:** A large game company such as Electronic Arts that produces many different kinds of games often appoints people who fully understand the game production process to the positions of executive, managing, or senior producer. The person might run a studio (that is, a subsidiary developer not directly incorporated into the company headquarters) or be in charge of a specific line of products (for example, the company's sports games). Executive producers are usually the people who listen to game pitches and then determine which specific games the company will develop.

- **Creative Director:** A company that produces multiple titles often has a senior designer in this management position. Its main responsibilities are to help the design teams complete and update their documentation and to offer suggestions about gameplay during the production phase. The creative director might also be responsible for handling the performance reviews of the design staff. This position is more advisory than participatory and is seldom hands-on for any project.

- **Art Director:** Companies sometimes appoint a senior artist as art director to help define the overall graphic look of their products. This person supervises the work of the art leads and might help develop the art design document for each game. An art director seldom works directly on a game but instead oversees the art schedules for the teams. She might review new graphics hardware and software and be responsible for ordering equipment for new art hires. Many companies call the person in this position the creative director.

- **Technical Director:** The technical director is a senior engineer who knows the ins and outs of programming and can help the program leads design the architecture of the code for their games, develop the coding standards, and set up the programming budgets and schedules.

The technical director also investigates new technology that can be used to create games and often is responsible for ordering equipment for new programming hires.

The executive and functional management leads in each group are sometimes referred to as the *stakeholders* because each of these groups has a stake in making the game. All stakeholders are usually required to sign off before starting a project, making changes to a project, accepting milestone deliveries, and of course, approving the final project.

Operational Management (Producers)

The day-to-day operations of game teams are handled by *producers.* The term is borrowed from the film industry—a producer is really just a project manager. Being a game producer has a certain cachet and does point out some of the similarities between making games and movies. A good game producer not only has to be able to crunch numbers to come up with a reasonable budget and timetable but also has to learn how to deal with the differing personalities of programmers and artists. As with the film industry, the game producer position requires a delicate balance between artistic sensibilities and business sense. It can be difficult for the game artisans to learn to handle the business end of the industry and deal with the needs of disparate teams. On the other hand, it can be just as difficult for people with management experience outside the game industry to jump in and successfully lead a game team.

At one time, the producer was the person who came up with the idea for a game and sold it to management. However, the process of documenting the design takes so much time and effort that it is better left to the design staff. More realistically, producers act like stationmasters in that they make sure that all the trains run on time and deal with crises as they pop up. It is rare for a producer in a large company to be able to work directly on a project, although producers in a smaller independent companies often wear several hats as an executive as well as a designer or coder.

A producer at a large company often becomes the patron of a game idea and puts together the team that will develop it. He normally ushers the design through the approval process and can spend a considerable amount of time reviewing the game in various stages of completion:

■ During the documentation stage, the producer offers suggestions on how the design should work and begins developing an initial schedule and budget for the product.

■ After the game is approved for production and enters the technical review phase, the producer sits down with the programming, art, and design team leads to develop a timeline (often using Microsoft Project) that shows all the tasks that must be completed during production. In addition, he meets with the marketing department early in the development process to determine their needs so they can be worked into the overall schedule.

- When the game enters full production, the producer holds regular meetings with the team and with the leads to determine if the project is on track, to check on potential bottlenecks that have developed, and to determine when new equipment and software need to be acquired. Meanwhile, he often sends weekly reports to top management so they know exactly when the product will ship.

A producer often works with ***third-party development teams*** (independent companies that create games but do not publish them) and is responsible for setting up their contracts and tracking their work to make sure they meet their milestones. Most publishers conduct regular quarterly or semiannual reviews to check the progress of products; the producer is responsible for preparing and delivering a presentation for each project under development.

A producer might have one or two assistants helping with the day-to-day tracking of the product. The many tasks assigned to these assistants include the following:

- Dealing with paperwork involved in new hires and their hardware and software needs

- Meeting with each team member regularly to update the project timeline

- Working with quality assurance staff to make sure that bugs are tracked and disposed of correctly

- Overseeing the builds at each milestone

- Presenting the projects to management in regular reviews

- Dealing with the producer's correspondence

Each company defines these roles differently, but the people who fill them are generally given the title of ***assistant producer*** or ***associate producer.*** In some companies, these assistants are little more than glorified gofers or administrative assistants, whereas in other companies they may be given the responsibility of managing a product on their own.

Depending on the company, there may be several levels of producer. Some companies use ***line-producers,*** who deal with all team members on a daily basis. Other companies assign this role to the assistant or associate producer. Still other companies create the role of ***production coordinator*** to help keep the asset and resource pipeline flowing properly.

The producer does not manage every person on the production team individually. Instead, the programmers, artists, and designers have leads who manage the teams and report to the producer (Figure 6.2). These positions are usually considered part of the team and not operational management. The rest of this chapter discusses the other members of the teams in more detail.

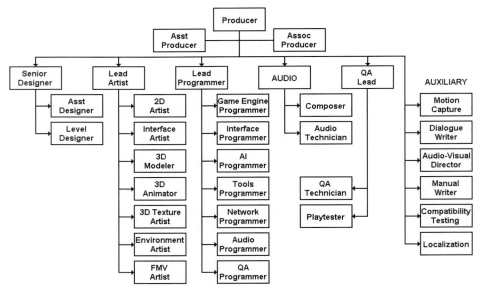

FIGURE 6.2 Sample organization chart for a game team. Note that multiple people on a team can have the same title.

FYI *Titles for Managers*

The titles given to operational managers in the game industry vary widely. **Project manager** is an engineering term to designate the person who is responsible for managing the project and completing the product as close to on-time, on-budget, and on-design as possible. **Product manager** is a marketing term to designate the person who is responsible for managing a product or a product line and for the sales and presence of the product in stores. Producer is somewhere in the middle, depending on the company. Electronic Arts now calls these people **directors;** other companies reserve the title of director for a high mid-management position as described previously in this chapter.

Design

The design staff is responsible for developing a game idea, documenting it, presenting it to management for approval and then implementing, testing, and debugging it. Given the wide scope of tasks for which the design staff is responsible, it is interesting to note that the role of designer is relatively new to the industry.

In the early days when teams were small, a programmer or artist might double as the team's designer. This worked out well when only a few people were needed to complete a game. Most early electronic games were action or arcade games that had no story and featured only a few simple playfields. The trick was to make the games as compelling as possible with limited graphics and audio. The major design consideration was to squeeze every last drop of fun from each line of code. But by the early 1990s, as games grew in complexity and the budgets and timelines for producing them increased progressively, the need for a real designer became apparent because companies came to realize that it was best to work out the details of the design and document them before starting to build the product.

Some games require more design work than others. Role-playing, adventure, strategy, and simulation games are very complex and require considerable planning and structuring of the game mechanics. Sports games, on the other hand, might not need a designer because the rules are already known, and the team may simply have to decide which aspects of the sport they wish to include because they do not have to design the rules from scratch. Likewise, highly realistic driving and flying games might require less design work, whereas arcade driving and flying games need lots of designer input. Puzzle games fall somewhere in between, depending on their complexity and structure. A simple game such as *Tetris* needs little design assistance, whereas a game such as *Oddworld: Abe's Oddyssey* (Figure 6.3) needs someone to figure out all the puzzles and describe the characters and settings for the artists.

Senior Designer

The ***senior designer*** is in overall charge of the game design. Each game team usually has one person in this position. It generally takes many years to gain the skills and vision to achieve this position. The senior designer must have the vision to see all parts of the design as a whole and the communication skills to explain the many details of the design to many different people with different mindsets:

- Management must be presented with convincing arguments as to why the game should be made at all.

- Marketing must be provided with a simple, high concept so they can sell the game to the public.

- Programmers must agree on the tools needed to create the product as well as on a detailed analysis of game mechanics so the coders can determine what modules to create.

- Artists must have enough description of characters, locations, and items in the game to spark their imaginations.

- The composer and audio staff must have an indication of the desired mood that should be provided by the music during each portion of the game, as well as a complete list of all possible sound effects and dialogue for voiceovers.

FIGURE 6.3 Screenshot from Oddworld Inhabitants' *Oddworld: Abe's Oddyssey* (published by Atari in 1997). The game contains many fiendish puzzles and secret areas and involves Abe's rescuing fellow Mudokon slaves.

Each of these groups must, in turn, sign off on the final design because they are stakeholders in the project as well.

The senior designer is responsible for fleshing out gameplay during the design documentation process, working with the art staff to develop the concept art and storyboards, and helping the producer present the materials to management for approval. During the technical review phase, the senior designer and lead programmer decide whether to create an interactive prototype and determine whether any special design tools need to be created such as a map/level editor, scripting language, or database manager. After the design tools are ready, the senior designer oversees the implementation of the design by the associate and level designers and may actually be involved in creating parts of the game. Early in the production phase, the senior designer works with a programmer and artist to define the user interface (UI) for the game; the designer concentrates on ensuring that the UI is easy to comprehend and use, whereas the artist focuses on its graphic style, and the programmer decides how it will be coded.

As the game takes shape, the entire design staff tests it to make sure it plays as it should and to help hunt down bugs. Meanwhile, the senior designer makes sure that the game design document is updated whenever any major changes are made during development. The senior designer often writes the first draft of the manual, being as familiar with the design as anyone on the team, and might conduct a postmortem after the game ships to determine what went right and wrong during production.

In addition to all these responsibilities, the senior designer has the most important task of being the "keeper of the flame." Nowadays, when it can take many years to complete a game, someone has to keep the team on track. Familiarity with the game can lead to contempt and a desire to make changes. It is up to the senior designer, in conjunction with the producer, to keep everyone on the same page about what the final product will be and to keep reminding the team that the published game will indeed be fun to play.

Assistant Designer

A production team can include several assistant designers; the size and complexity of the game design determines how many assistant designers are needed. As with assistant producers, these individuals are often promoted from within—usually from artists and programmers who have shown some design ability and occasionally from the playtesters. Their primary duty is to assist the senior designer in documenting the design and then implementing it using the tools created by the programming staff. They might be brought onto the team while the game design document is being written (if it is a complex design) or later when the design tools are ready to be used. They remain on the team until all the game design elements are in the game and have been fully tested. Assistant designers must have great patience because they are intimately involved in the detailed process of building the game, including creating a map or level, testing it and tweaking the values and layout, and then retesting it over and over until everything works as planned. Persistence is the greatest asset for assistant designers.

Level Designer

This position is relatively new but has become important in games created with 3D graphics programs such as 3ds Max (also called 3D Studio Max), Maya, and Lightwave. As you have probably guessed, the level designer is responsible for building three-dimensional playing fields and, therefore, has to combine design and art skills. In addition to knowing how to use 3D graphics programs, which can require years of training, a level designer has to have a good eye for architecture and environments and a well-developed sense of gameplay, including an understanding of what is fun about exploring a level.

Frequently, the level designer works with the senior designer and, perhaps, a programmer to build an visually interesting play area with well-placed encounters whose appearances are triggered by the scripting language. Level designers might also work with the artists who create the textures for the environment if they do not create the textures themselves.

> ## FYI | *Titles for Designers*
>
> As with the titles for operational managers, the titles for game designers can also vary widely. Some companies use *scripter* as the title for designers because the primary work in the early stages of the game centers around producing the various documents to sell the game to management and then describe what will be in it. Other companies use the title *director,* similar to the meaning of the title as used in the movie industry—that is, the person responsible for overseeing the work of programming, art, and audio staffs in bringing the vision to life. Still other companies reserve the title *creative director* for the senior designer, who might simply oversee the work of the other designers.

Programming

The programming team is generally second in size to the art team. Many different tasks face the programmers during production. Programming on many games for PCs and the current generation of consoles is done using the C/C++ language, although a good programmer probably knows several other languages such as Assembly or a scripting language such as Python, Perl, or Lua. Other platforms, such as handheld units, PDAs, or online games, use different languages including Java, BREW, or J2ME. In all cases, the programmers hired to work on games must be experienced in the development language used by the company, and the C/C++ family is a good knowledge foundation.

> ## FYI | *Java, BREW, and J2ME*
>
> Java is an object-oriented programming language that was originally developed by James Gosling at Sun Microsystems to replace C++. Java code can be used on many different platforms (write it once, run it anywhere), but it is bulkier than C++ and runs more slowly, so it has not replaced C++ in major computer and console games. BREW (**B**inary **R**untime **E**nvironment for **W**ireless) was developed by Qualcomm as a platform for developing software for mobile phones. It offers a set of application programming interfaces (APIs) that enables the software download and play small programs such as games, messaging, and photo sharing. The programs themselves are actually
>
> ▶▶ CONTINUED ON NEXT PAGE

▶▶ CONTINUED

written in C/C++ or Java. J2ME (Java 2 Platform, Micro Edition) is a set of Java APIs specifically developed for cell phones, PDAs, and other appliances. The advantage of J2ME is that it allows games to be emulated on a computer before being uploaded and does not require the expensive system-specific software development kits and accompanying hardware of other systems.

Until the mid-1990s, games were smaller, and a programmer might be involved in many aspects of coding, including game design. But as games have grown in size and complexity, most programmers eventually focus on one or two major coding tasks and only assist in others. This section examines programming tasks by functionality instead of by title because titles and actual responsibilities vary from company to company. Whatever their title, and whichever part of the code they work on, each programmer helps breathe life into the game world and has an enormous impact on making the game fun to play.

Lead Programmer

This position is at the same level as a senior designer and is usually given to a seasoned professional who understands all parts of the code in a game. The person who fills this position is usually identified early in the design process, perhaps as early as the game proposal phase, although he might not actually do any work until later.

It is important for the lead programmer to understand what will go into the design and to provide early input as to what can actually be coded within the proposed schedule and budget. During the technical review phase, the lead programmer works with the technical director to determine the architecture of the game and helps the rest of the programmers prepare the technical design document that identifies all the coding tasks and sets the coding standards for the project (see Chapter 11, "Technical Review," for more details).

After the tasks are known, the lead programmer joins the producer, senior designer, and lead artist to create the master timeline, define the milestones, and determine hiring needs. This team also determines if the programming team will need to create any special tools for the project. The lead programmer has experience with flow-charting, understands the overall architecture of the game engine, and makes recommendations on the technical issues that the programming team needs to resolve.

In the production phase, the lead programmer's prime responsibility is to make sure the code tasks are completed on time. Managing the team can be a full-time responsibility, which means the lead programmer can spend considerable time in meetings with management and with the programmers. The producer might demand frequent written production reports that summarize the programming team's weekly progress. If new programmers must be hired, the lead programmer is involved with interviewing the top candidates both over the telephone and in person. After a hire is made, the lead must make sure that the new staff member is properly equipped with hardware, software, and office space by the first day on the job. Because the production phase lasts so long, the lead often has to consider updating equipment and software applications over time and must make sure that such upgrades don't seriously affect the schedule or budget. In fact, the lead programmer often learns that dealing with management issues takes up so much of the workweek that little or no time is left for programming, so she should expect to do more advisory work than hands-on coding.

Game Engine Programmer

Until relatively recently, each game was coded individually and, therefore, each had a unique game engine that handled all the components of playing the game. To build a game engine from scratch, the programming team has to write the code modules to handle graphics rendering, gameplay, physics, artificial intelligence (AI), audio, and networking. Moreover, the engine has to support whatever tool sets the other teams will need—such as a scripting language for the designers or a plug-in for artists to test animations—and these tools cannot be started until the engine is nearly finished. As games grew more complex, especially 3D games, it began to make sense for companies to license existing game engines rather than build their own. Because it did so many things so well, *Doom* by id Software was built on one of the first game engines that other developers wanted to license to use in their own games. Nowadays, many game engines are available, and one of the most important decisions developers make is whether to create their own game engine from scratch or adapt an engine someone else has created.

Using a preexisting game engine is not always the best solution, so the team has to decide early on whether to create its own game engine or to license an existing engine. With game engines needing to do so much—graphics rendering, physics, artificial intelligence, audio, scripting language, networking, and more—it can take years to build an engine from the ground up. The team building the engine should look at making their code scalable, so that it can be reused and expanded upon and they will not have to build an engine for the next game from scratch as well. A 2D game engine is simpler to build than a 3D engine because rendering 2D graphics is not as involved as rendering 3D graphics. The physics and the AI are simpler to compute because objects move in a flat, two-dimensional world. Therefore, most companies build their own 2D engines; nonetheless, because few major game releases are 2D, 3D engines are more critical.

Designing a 3D game engine from scratch is not a trivial matter, however. If a company decides to build their own 3D engine, they usually assign their most experienced programmers to the task. Programmers who work on the engine should have experience with low-level assembly language, a good knowledge of graphics and graphic cards, and a solid understanding of the operating system for the target platform. Making an engine is expensive. Because these programmers are usually senior, they tend to have the highest salaries. Moreover, the rest of the team might have to sit idly by while the engine is under construction, eating up money without producing anything worthwhile.

As a result, many developers license an existing game engine (for example, Epic Games' Unreal Tournament engine) rather than create one from the ground up. Another option is to use middleware such as Renderware (EA/Criterion) or Gamebryo (NDL), which are applications in which the graphics renderer and some programming routines are already implemented. However, using these solutions does not mean that the licensed software will work straight out of the box. The game engine programmers need a solid understanding of how the existing engine or middleware works because they might need to make significant modifications to it in order to make the game behave the way they want. To change how the AI module works, for example, a programmer needs a solid understanding of how the existing AI code is written and what needs to be changed in the code to get the desired behavior into the game. Whether building a new engine from scratch, modifying an engine they have previously coded, or using a licensed game engine or middleware, working on the game engine is probably the most challenging and enjoyable task for programmers.

6

Tools Programmer

Several teams of programmers might work in conjunction with the game engine programming team to develop a set of proprietary tools for other team members to build the game. For example, the design staff might need a map or level editor, a scripting language to set up event-handling triggers, or a method for loading the game database into the game without having to recompile the game engine. The artists might request special tools to import their models from a 3D graphics program into the game for rigging, animating, and texturing. The audio staff might need special tools to make the game's music, sound effects, and voiceovers work correctly. The testing group might need a special database to track bugs and assign the right team member to fix them. The tools developed for one project may or may not be useful in other projects. The programming team creates all of the needed tools.

Some programmers see tool creation as a thankless task, primarily because tools do not have the consumer recognition of other programming tasks. Players can see how well the artificial intelligence works or how well the game engine handles the graphics and special visual effects, but they doesn't necessarily appreciate the tools used to build the game. Thus, many developers make the mistake of foisting off tools onto junior programmers, which can lead to significant problems. Junior programmers make more mistakes than seasoned veterans

Caution

Bad Attitudes

Veteran programmers might consider their time to be worth more than designers and artists because they draw higher salaries. This attitude can lead them to churn out buggy tools with poor interface designs. If the other teams then have difficulty using these tools, they can wind up creating substandard assets or missing their milestones.

and do not have the knowledge base that experience brings. As a result, they might make the tools difficult to use, frustrating other team members and slowing implementation of the design.

It is up to the lead programmer, senior designer, and technical director to make sure that the tools created for a game have workable interfaces and are easy enough for nonprogrammers to use. Programming tools may not be the most glorious job, but it is an absolutely vital part of making sure that a game is good and that it ships on time. To provide the best possible user interface, a tools programmer should have a good understanding of the person or team who will be using the tool.

AI Programmer

Artificial intelligence is becoming increasingly more important in games, not only in those played against the computer but also in those played online against human opponents. Recent computer and console games have emphasized realistic and stunning 3D graphics while AI has lagged behind. As game machines continue to get more powerful, more cycles are becoming available to use for smarter AI routines. Most production teams include at least one AI programmer who is responsible for making creatures or bots appear "smart." This position is usually held by a senior programmer with previous AI experience. Occasionally, a specialist is hired temporarily to help design the AI routines.

The AI programmer determines what routines will be needed in the game. The AI code can be simple to write or very complex, depending on the desired behaviors for the AI-controlled entities. In an action game, the AI-controlled entities move around and engage in combat, so the programmer determines what pathfinding and target selection routines to implement. In a sports game, the AI-controlled opponent might have to select which football play or baseball pitch to use next, so the programmer might decide to use fuzzy logic to give a range of possible choices. However, when the AI programmer structures her code, she has to make sure that the decision-making process ultimately enhances the gameplay while not being so complex as to affect the overall frame rate or other processes.

Interface Programmer

The interface programmer deals with all of the screens, pop-up windows, and menus that the player interacts with in the game and determines how to set up the input devices that activate their functions on the screens. This is a difficult task and is often given to a senior programmer who has considerable experience in making interfaces work as desired. In smaller companies, the programmer who works on the interface is likely to work on other parts of the game was well.

FYI *Graphical User Interface Elements*

The **graphical user interface (GUI)** in a game includes all the visual displays with which the player interacts during a game. A **screen** is a graphic display that takes up the entire monitor or television screen (such as a combat screen, playfield movement screen, or inventory screen). A **window** is a pop-up display with several options that take up only a portion of the monitor or screen. A **menu** is a list of options that the player scrolls through to make a selection. It usually takes up only a portion of the monitor or screen.

The interface programmer and senior designer work together with an artist to determine how to combine the needed functionality of each screen with the best and most visually appealing presentation of the information. After the initial interface design is determined, the interface programmer begins writing the code to make it work. Depending on the game genre, the interface design can be very complex and require extensive testing to make sure that players find it easy to understand the controls and all the functional elements on each screen. A well-implemented interface is key to a game's success, so the interface programmer must spend many months building and restructuring the screens as the game design changes during development based on testers' feedback. The elements that go into making a good user interface are described in Chapter 15, "Interface Design."

Networking Programmer

Electronic games have a long history of allowing multiple players to join in the same game on a competitive or cooperative basis. Coding the modules for multiplayer mode has long been a major task for game teams. With the continued success of massively multiplayer online games, many computer games no longer support a single-player version. Most computer games offer some sort of Internet play, and the ability to play games over the Internet has become important to the success of many games. Console game manufacturers have just started to offer online game services, which usually require players to have a broadband connection. Some of the new handheld platforms—cell phones, the N-Gage, and others—also feature Internet play. Online gaming is here to stay and will continue to grow in popularity, so teams need to make sure they include this capability when working on a new design.

Getting a game to run over the Internet is challenging and usually requires the efforts of several Internet programmers. The Internet was not designed for playing games, so these programmers often have to use clever tricks to get around its technical limitations and keep players happy. The programmers have to decide which Internet protocol to use (TCP/IP or UDP), worry about message packet size and transmission rate, iron out the server–client side problems, implement security to keep hackers out, and deal with many other issues specific to Internet play. It takes special training and a lot of experience to become a top-notch Internet programmer, but the role is vital to the success of games.

Companies that provide online services for gamers also hire network programmers to configure, deploy, and maintain the networking hardware and supporting infrastructure. They have to deal with the routers and switching devices, and therefore, they need a strong understanding of the various Internet protocols (TCP/IP and UDP; see Chapter 12, "Coding the Game," for more details). If the company hosts a massively multiplayer online game (MMOG), it also hires programmers to provide database administration, server support, network security, and Web design.

IN THE TRENCHES: Overtime Abuse in the Game Industry

Anyone who has worked in the game industry for any length of time can tell you about having to put in long hours during crunch time—when a version of a game just *has* to be done on a certain date to meet a milestone. In fact, the game industry is notorious for demanding unpaid overtime from its workers to meet deadlines. In November 2004, the wife of an Electronic Arts programmer wrote an article castigating the company for its policies (**http://www.livejournal.com/users/ea_spouse/274.html**). A lawsuit also has been filed against EA for this practice. However, the game industry continues to be perceived as a glamour industry, and many people continue to want to get into it, so competition for jobs can be tough. Publishers take advantage of that competition to demand incredibly long hours from their employees. As long as people who love their work are willing to suffer for it, the problem with overtime abuse is likely to remain.

Audio Programmer

Players have come to expect music and audio effects in their games, but it's taken a while to get games to sound good. The early game platforms could not handle complex music and sound effects due to the simplistic audio technology in computers and the limited storage space for audio files. Creating realistic sound required too much space and ate up too many cycles. As computer sound cards became more sophisticated and game platforms could handle more data, audio became much more important. Nowadays, a programming team usually has at least one person dedicated to the game's audio requirements.

Although an audio programmer's primary concern is creating the tools to store and play back sound files, coding might also be involved in making the sound match the mood of the game or in creating special audio effects. Many games try to make audio more organic and interactive to gameplay so that as the mood changes—for example, when combat is initiated—the audio changes as well, perhaps heralding the martial themes of combat when the enemy springs an ambush. To make the music interactive, the audio programmer works with the composer to determine how the music will be structured, what themes will be needed, where and how looping music will end so a new theme can be started, and what will trigger these changes. Likewise, the audio programmer works with a sound designer if the sound effects have complex requirements, such as when setting up the ambient sound effects for a level. The audio programmer might also work with the designers to determine how sound and music might be triggered via a scripting language. Even without trying to be too innovative, an audio programmer still has many tasks, so most production teams have at least one person handling them.

Quality Assurance Programmer

Many large companies have junior-level programmers working with the quality assurance (QA) department to make sure that bugs are tracked and removed from the game correctly. The QA programmer might help the QA department set up a bug-tracking database and tailor it to the development team's specific needs. As games grow larger, many testers can be involved in bug-hunting, not only those working inside the company but also outsiders involved in blind-testing the product. Massively multiplayer online games, in particular, need extensive testing to prove that the server farm's backbone can hold up under the onslaught of new users.

QA programmers might feel their contributions to the team are minimal because they are not writing "real code." But even grunt-level programming work is absolutely vital for making sure that a game ships on time with a minimal number of bugs. Some companies (such as Microsoft) require their QA staff to have a bachelor of science degree in computer science because they actually go into the code to fix bugs rather than just reporting them to other team members.

IN THE TRENCHES: World of WarCraft *Launch*

Blizzard Entertainment suffered through a bout of "be careful what you wish for" when they launched their MMORPG *World of WarCraft* on November 23, 2004. The game quickly sold about 240,000 copies worldwide, creating a vast pool of players just itching to start playing. The server system quickly became unstable, and Blizzard Entertainment was forced to rush to get more servers up and running. They even stopped selling the game in retail outlets until they could sort out the problem. They finally fixed most of the problems and have sold over 3.5 million copies of the game. The company says they have an average of 500,000 subscribers playing the game 24/7.

Art

Completing all the art assets for a major release takes considerable time, and the art staff is usually the largest team on a game. In addition to the art that appears in the game, the art staff also creates storyboard and concept art, animated sequences, and the artwork for the graphical user interface. Some large companies are developing an assembly line model where artists work at the same art task (creating the 3D meshes, rigging the models, creating the textures, and so on) on many games as opposed to doing multiple tasks on just one product for an extended time.

All art in a game, both 2D and 3D, is first generated by hand by trained artists—the best computer graphic artists also have the best traditional art skills in addition to the ability to use complex computer art programs. Like the preceding section on programmers, this section examines each task by function instead of by title.

Lead Artist

This position is at the same level as a senior designer and lead programmer. As with those positions, it is held by a seasoned professional who understands all the art needs for a game. The lead artist is usually assigned early in the production process, possibly beginning with the design proposal. This person may have little direct work until management approves the game design document. In fact, there's a good chance she might be finishing an earlier project during the documentation stage. Two-dimension artists might work on concept or character sketches during the documentation stage, and the lead artist might offer suggestions and supervise their work without becoming directly involved.

During the technical review phase, the lead artist actually joins the team and helps them settle on the overall graphic look for the product and generate a list of all art tasks to be done. The art team might create an art design document (see Chapter 11, "Technical Review," for details) for the team to use as a reference throughout the production phase. When the tasks are known, the lead artist joins the producer, senior designer, and lead programmer to create the master timeline, define the milestones, and determine manpower loading and then assigns the art team for the project. The lead artist also helps decide if the programming team needs to create special tools for the project. This usually involves plug-ins for 3ds Max or Maya.

In the production phase, the lead artist (like the lead programmer) is responsible for seeing that the art is completed on time. As with the lead programmer, the lead artist has so many management issues to deal with each week that little time remains for hands-on artwork. Managing an art team is a full-time job, and the lead artist's workweek is usually filled with meetings and art reviews. He might have to compile weekly production reports to inform the producer of which tasks have been completed and which will be tackled next.

The lead artist is also responsible for conducting phone and in-person interviews for new hires and must be able to talk knowledgeably with a wide range of candidates about all aspects of the art process. New employees have to be set up with equipment and trained in the company's work methods. The lead artist must also keep abreast of changes to art tools and be ready to switch the team to updated versions of art programs so that the transition has a minimal impact on the production schedule.

A lead artist should be a highly skilled technical artist who understands the process of making artwork for games and delivering it to the programming team. This person also needs to be a skilled manager who is able to work with both artists and programmers as well as designers and the production team.

2D Artist

At one time, all art in electronic games consisted of two-dimensional animated sprites moving against flat backgrounds. Even games with an isometric projection (sometimes referred to as 2–1/2D) used 2D animated sprites. When 3D graphics programs became popular—and relatively cheap to produce—most games switched to 3D graphics and some thought that 2D artists would go back to the fine arts. However, 2D games continue to be produced, so game companies still employ these artists. Moreover, 2D artists have certain skills that are just as important in a 3D game environment as in a 2D one.

One of the most important skills a 2D artist brings is the ability to draw things in perspective on a flat surface using traditional art tools such as pens, pencils, and paint. In addition, 2D artists have to be familiar with computer art programs such as Macromedia Freehand, Adobe Photoshop, and Adobe Illustrator. Many 3D artists are proficient in 3ds Max or Maya but are completely unable to draw anything.

IN THE TRENCHES: The Cost of Early 3D Graphics

For a time in the early 1990s, Silicon Graphics, Inc., (SGI) was the source of all things 3D—at least for the game industry. SGI developed a series of workstations for creating 3D graphics that could be used in games (as well as in movies and television). These systems were expensive, however. One SGI system could cost between $10,000 and $100,000. In 1993, Namco produced the *Namco Flight Simulator*, an arcade game that used SGI's Onyx system to control six play units. A single simulator setup cost $750,000 with a $100,000

▶▶ CONTINUED ON NEXT PAGE

>> CONTINUED

yearly service contract. Although the 3D graphics look primitive by today's standards, it took eight years for others to reach the same level. When 3D graphic programs such as 3ds Max, Maya, and Lightwave that could be used on a PC appeared, game developers quickly switched to them because they cost much less—only a few thousand dollars.

Traditional art skills come in very handy throughout the production cycle (Figure 6.4). First, a 2D artist might be assigned to work with a designer on a game proposal. The artist contributes sketches and drawings that show what the characters, items, and locations will look like and how they might move in their environments. It is infinitely easier and cheaper to have a 2D artist create hundreds of sketches offering a multitude of ideas than to have 3D artists labor for months over models that might never be used. Determining the right look and actions for a character takes time. When the final versions are approved, they go into the art design document so that the 3D artists can refer to them while building the models.

As the game is fleshed out, 2D artists might be asked to create storyboards that step through important sections of gameplay or are used for creating animated

FIGURE 6.4 Concept artist Robb Waters uses Steve Kimura as a model for a new superhero character for *Freedom Force* in Irrational Studios' Boston office.

sequences. The storyboards help the animators and 3D artists visualize the action and understand the desired mood.

Often, the 2D artists who work on a 3D game switch from their preproduction work on sketches and storyboards to helping work out the graphical user interface during the production phase (see the next section).

In 2D games, which are still popular on most PC, online, cell phone, PDA, and handheld platforms, such as the Game Boy Advance, all of the art is done by 2D artists. After a character is created and approved, the 2D artist animates it, usually using a digital program such as Adobe Photoshop. She can also use traditional cell-animation and then scan the completed frames into the computer, though this approach is used less frequently.

Within the 2D art world, but usually distinct from 2D animators, are 2D background artists. This position creates the backdrops against which the 2D characters animate. The scenery is often created in a program such as Adobe Photoshop or generated by hand and then scanned into the computer to be touched up.

Interface Artist

Many large companies have one or two artists devoted to creating the artwork for the game interface. The artwork can be two- or three-dimensional, depending on the overall look the team decides on. The interface includes the head-up display (HUD) on the main in-game screen, other screens and windows that pop up during play, and the shell screens for setting options. It often includes developing a unique font to be used for all text within the game, from menus to dialogue boxes. Depending on the complexity of the design, there can be dozens of screens to lay out and change. The interface artist continues to work with the senior designer and interface programmer throughout the production phase, trying out new control combinations and generating new artwork for icons and backgrounds until everyone agrees on the final configuration. A good interface artist understands not only the value of background art in setting and maintaining the mood of the game but also how important the iconography is in helping the player to comprehend the game's controls as quickly as possible.

3D Modeler

If the game is set in a three-dimensional world, then the characters, vehicles, and objects in that world are all created by 3D modelers. These artists use special graphics programs such as 3ds Max (Figure 6.5), Maya, and Lightwave to create meshes from polygons. *Meshes* are open framework structures upon which textures are applied like a skin. A 2D artist might create a *character sketch* showing the front, back, and side of the character. Modelers then import this sketch directly into the 3D program and shape the polygons to match the sketch. The modelers might then rig the meshes for animation and apply the textures themselves or hand off these tasks to specialists.

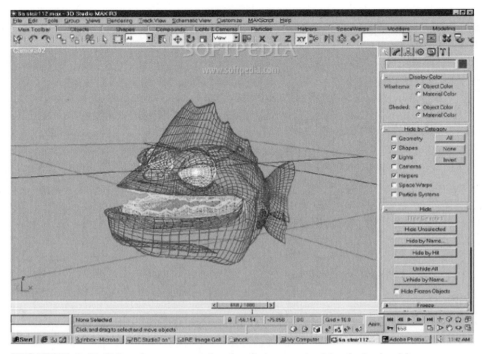

FIGURE 6.5 Wire-frame mesh of a fish created in Autodesk's 3ds Max.

Building 3D models is time-consuming and challenging. Not only must the modeler have an excellent eye for art, but he must also understand the intricacies of the graphics program and be able to make every polygon count. Until the time that 3D graphic programs become simple and inexpensive enough for nontechnical artists to use, the game industry will rely on hiring skilled 3D modelers. Of course, these same skills are in great demand by movie animation studios, so anyone with 3D experience has many career paths available.

3D Animator

Depending on the company, an art department might divide 3D graphics among specialists. One group, mentioned previously, are the modelers who build meshes in a 3D graphic program. In large companies, these meshes might then be handed over to 3D animators, whose job involves rigging the models for animations. Whereas the modelers are concerned with the shape of the models, the animators are concerned with the innards—especially the skeleton—and how best to make the bodies and objects twist and turn and move realistically. The animators might break the model into sections and link them programmatically so that they flow as a piece. Moving a finger forward, for example, draws the wrist forward and straightens the arm. Some programs such as *Biped,* a plug-in for 3ds Max, are available to help animators rig and animate the models.

Making characters and objects move so that the player accepts them as real is a major challenge for 3D animators. Real does not simply mean emulating the "real world." For example, because games are often set in fantastic worlds, a 3D animator might be expected to make three-legged creatures move as realistically as bipeds and four-legged animals. Having previous experience and skills in 2D animation using traditional tools is an asset for this role.

3D Texture Artist

Just as important as the framework mesh and the skeleton for animation is the *skin* that is applied to the exterior of the model (Figure 6.6). Large companies might have artists who specialize only in creating the textures that are applied to meshes. These artists apply the textures to the models until they are satisfied with the final appearance, and then they save the final texture as a 2D flat image. The image is then applied to the mesh surface during runtime.

The 3D texture artist also has to make sure that the texture retains its distinctive look as the model shrinks and grows based on the player's distance from it during play. There's nothing worse than a beautiful high-polygon creature turning into a muddy blur when reduced in size to appear at a distance. The graphics engine handles the task of enlarging and shrinking the model, which is called

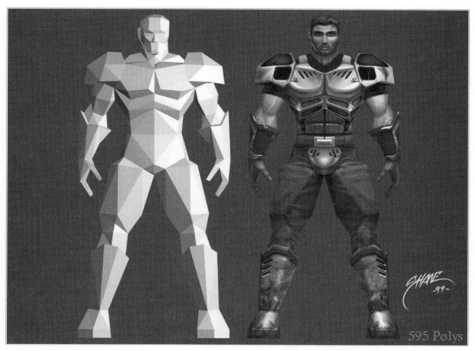

FIGURE 6.6 A soldier model created by artist Shane Caudle to be used in Epic Games Unreal Tournament.

continuous level of detail. The textures stretch and shrink to match the model, based on how the artist assigns the texture to the model. The artist must also check that the texture does not tear (have gaps appear) as the model animates and that the skin covering the joints also appears normal as it deforms during movement.

In addition to creating creature skins, the 3D texture artist might work with environment modelers to provide textures for the interiors and exteriors of buildings, as well as the ground features and flora. He might also contribute to 3D art in the user interface.

> ## **FYI** *Online 3D Models*
>
> A number of Web sites offer 3D models either for sale or for free. Although a game developer might be tempted to use these models, the artists can discover some significant problems with them. They might use too many or too few polygons, the animation rigging might not match the company's game engine requirements, or the textures might have tears or holes. More important, the meshes can need considerable tweaking to make the models look like the characters dreamed up by the designers and artists. By the time the game company finishes making fixes to the model, it can spend as much time as it would have to build the models from scratch.

3D Environment Modelers

Some companies hire 3D artists who have an excellent eye for architecture to build the interiors and exteriors of structures. Other artists might be hired to create terrain features as well as the trees and plants for exterior settings. These 3D environments are often static and appear either as structures constructed during play or as noninteractive playfield elements in strategy and simulation games. If a company does not hire level designers (as discussed previously), it might employ environment modelers to lay out the levels in conjunction with the design staff. These artists might create the textures for the structures or hand this task over to 3D texture artists.

Full-Motion Video (FMV) Artists

A game often opens with an animated sequence and/or has a storyline developed by the design team that requires animated sequences interspersed with gameplay. Each sequence follows a script, and the player does not interact with the game while the scene plays out. These are called *cut-scene sequences* because they cut into the gameplay "scene."

These materials are provided by a dedicated team of *full-motion video (FMV)* artists or filmmakers. They usually create these animated sequences in 3D,

but some games still use 2D artwork, so the group might contain either 3D artists or 2D artists (or both). Some sequences, called *run-time sequences* (or *in-game sequences*) are created to use the models already loaded into the engine. Other scenes are short films created in an art program or filmed with live actors. These *pre-rendered cut-scenes* are generally of higher quality. The FMV artists might work with motion capture technicians (discussed in a later section) to make the animated sequences look as realistic as possible.

Large companies often have their own motion capture studio so that they can create the animated sequences internally. The recorded data is handed off to the appropriate art team, who then create the animated sequence. Smaller development companies might ask to use the publisher's motion capture studio (assuming the publisher has one) or they might contract with a company that specializes in this work. As projects expand in scope, many companies prefer to use external art studios who specialize in creating animated sequences so that work on creating the animations can proceed without requiring extra work from the game team.

6

Auxiliary Staff

A number of other people might work on a game part-time and can be involved with several projects at once. The size of a company often determines whether these auxiliary staffers are employed full-time or hired as freelancers to work on one project at a time. The more projects under development, the more likely the person will be working for the company, although there are exceptions.

Audio

The audio staff consists of those people who work on the music, sound effects, and voiceovers in a game. As discussed previously, most companies have at least one audio programmer to oversee the merging of the sound files into the game. The other members of the audio team include the composer and the audio technician.

Composer   This person composes the music for the game. The composer works with the producer and senior designer to determine how many different themes or songs to create and where music will appear in the game. The actual music may be performed by the composer or by other trained musicians. Many games include music tracks featuring full symphony orchestras or rock bands. As game platforms have improved so has the technology for playing the music, which in-turn has become much more sophisticated and compelling. Composers are finally gaining recognition for their contributions to games, as discussed in Chapter 14, "Hearing the Game."

Composing music for a game differs considerably from doing so for theater, movies, or television. The player is immersed in a game for many hours, so the music must be varied and not draw too much attention to itself lest the player grow weary of it and shut it off. The composer usually has a good understanding of how computers work, and these technical skills can come in handy if the team desires special musical effects; for example, music that changes mood and tempo based on the player's actions or the current situation in the game. If the game has interactive audio, the composer must work closely with the programming team to create music that can segue seamlessly from theme to theme.

Audio Technician The audio technician is responsible for creating all the sound effects in the game. A game can include hundreds of sounds including everything from the roar of charging monsters and the rattle of machine guns to the soft tone of an option button being pressed and released. Available libraries of prerecorded sound effects are often mixed, combined, and otherwise modified by the audio technician to better reflect what the player sees on the screen. In addition to working with prerecorded effects, the technician often has to create sounds from scratch. The methods and tricks developed by Foley artists for movies are just as relevant to games. Finally, the audio technician may also be responsible for recording the voices of actors for voiceovers in the game.

IN THE TRENCHES: George A. Sanger (The Fat Man)

One of the best known composers in the game industry is George "The Fat Man" Sanger, who has composed music for about 200 games including Origin Systems' *Wing Commander* (1990), LucasArts' *Loom* (1990), Microprose's *Master of Orion* (1993), and Virgin Games' *The 7th Guest* (1993).

Sanger started working on games in 1983, back when music was mostly tinny beeps and weird sounds. His roommate at the time, Dave Warhol, asked him to write a tune for an Intellivision game, and he has been composing game music ever since. According to the biography posted on his web site (**www.fatman.com**), "He wrote the first General MIDI soundtrack for a game, the first direct-to-MIDI live recording of musicians, the first redbook soundtrack included with the game as a separate disk, the first music for a game that was considered a 'work of art,' and the first soundtrack that was considered a selling point for the game."

He lives in Austin, Texas, and can usually be identified at the GDC or E3 conferences by his Stetson hat and Nudie suit. He helps organize Project Bar-B-Q, a yearly conference on interactive music.

Quality Assurance (Testing) and Playtesting

Medium to large companies usually have a quality assurance (QA) group dedicated to testing products and reporting bugs. Smaller companies usually cannot afford to maintain a staff devoted to product testing because there is not enough work to keep them occupied full-time and they need resources such as computers and office space that might be needed by other staffers. Therefore, smaller companies generally rely on the publisher's QA department for testing and bug reports. Also, a large company usually has video recorders and other debugging equipment that a small company cannot afford (Figure 6.7). Quality assurance includes the following staff roles: the quality assurance lead, the quality assurance technician, and the playtester.

Quality Assurance Lead   The QA lead is primarily responsible for managing the QA department and making sure that bugs and problems are reported correctly and fixed. The person in this position has considerable experience testing and debugging games and might start looking at the project as early as the game design document phase.

The QA lead develops a test suite of all the player interactions with the game that must be tested. The test suite is then divided among the QA group, with people checking their part of the code as thoroughly as possible. The

FIGURE 6.7 The quality assurance lab for compatibility testing at Blizzard Entertainment.

Caution

Time Zones

If a developer relies on the publisher for bug reports, the producer should make sure that lag time is factored into the schedule to account for differences in time zones. A three-hour time difference between office locations can result in a bug report's being delayed 24 hours because the developer or publisher has left work for the day.

QA lead works with a QA programmer to set up a debugging database that sends bugs to the team members responsible for fixing them and then follows up to make sure the bugs have been eliminated without causing new bugs. The QA lead also works with the producer and team leads to make sure they are receiving the correct reports on which bugs are still open and which have been closed.

This job can be very demanding, especially if the company has a number of projects under development. In the case of an MMOG, quality assurance is an ongoing job, even after the game has shipped.

Quality Assurance Technician   The quality assurance technician has usually risen through the ranks of testing to a position of some responsibility. In addition to testing for bugs, a QA technician might give feedback to the team about gameplay and offer suggestions on changes to make the game better. This person usually has a good grasp of technology and might know some programming. In addition to testing games, the QA technician might help develop the debugging database and work with external testers to enter their reports into the tracking system. In some companies, QA technicians also give suggestions about the gameplay as soon as the game reaches the point of first playable version. They actually help determine what is fun about the game and what needs work.

Playtester   This position is at the bottom rung of the production ladder. Testers are often the last hired and the first fired when a project is done. Their job is, at best, temporary, but their assistance is essential for turning out polished products. A tester's primary responsibility is to take a portion of the QA lead's test suite and test it as thoroughly as possible, trying every conceivable combination of inputs in search of crash bugs. The work can become tedious and demanding. Whenever a bug is found, the tester fills out a report and sends it to the QA lead for assignment to a team member. When the bug is fixed, the tester checks to confirm that it has been smashed and to see if the fix caused any other problems.

Playtesters are often poorly paid (if at all) and seldom fully appreciated. However, this job is one of the few entry-level positions into the games industry that doesn't require programming or art skills. Many producers and designers started out as testers.

External Resources

During production, some tasks may be handed off to external specialists who have skills that are needed only occasionally. Large companies might fill these positions internally, but most small and medium companies use freelancers or outside production houses. These positions include:

- **Motion Capture Technicians:** Game (and film) companies use these specialists to assist with creating smooth animations. Technicians attach sensors to "performers" (including actors, athletes, animals, and other

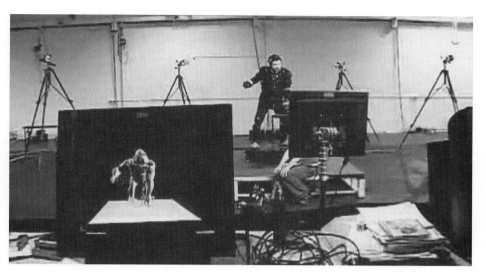

FIGURE 6.8 Actor Andy Serkis (who brought Gollum to life in the *Lord of the Rings* movies) uses motion capture to bring the CG version of King Kong to life in Peter Jackson's remake of *King Kong* (Universal).

trained individuals) and then have them perform the desired actions, which are captured as computer data. This data is then used by animators to position and polish their 3D models correctly, so that the resulting animations look very realistic (Figure 6.8).

- **Dialogue Writer:** Many companies use freelance screenwriters to polish characters' dialogue, especially if it will be spoken by actors. In these companies, the design staff develops the structure for the dialogue, including all the branches needed for interactive dialogue, and then hand the script over to the screenwriter for polishing. There is a great difference between dialogue shown as text and words spoken by actors. Therefore, it is useful to hire trained writers who understand the nuances of spoken conversations to create compelling dialogue.

- **Audio and Visual Director:** In games that incorporate spoken dialog or full-blown video playback using live actors, the company might hire a director with stage or film experience. Occasionally, this person works full-time for the company. More likely, a specialist is hired to run the external audio or video. If the game requires actual set building or extended filming, the role is expanded to accommodate the need.

- **Manual Writer:** Just as a professional screenwriter can improve a game's dialogue, so too can a freelance writer provide a polished manual. A skilled manual writer must have a good grasp of technical writing as well as an ability to create interesting, easy-to-understand prose. The size and scope of the manual determines if a freelancer is needed, but if it is to contain fictional materials to enhance the product's story, a publisher would be wise to spend the money to hire someone who can make the prose entertaining to read while still providing all the technical information needed to install the product and troubleshoot problems.

■   **Compatibility Tester:** Many different sound cards, graphics cards, and other components make up a computer. It would be wasteful for a game company to try to have every possible combination of hardware in-house, especially when it is not used for anything but checking for incompatibility issues. Fortunately, there are companies that specialize in testing various combinations of hardware and reporting bugs to the game company. These companies focus primarily on games for computers. Video consoles face few compatibility issues because their makers only rarely change the hardware inside the platform.

■   **Localization Staff:** If the product is to reach an international market, it must be translated into many different languages. In addition, some of the content and art might need to be altered to make the product palatable in other countries. Again, there are companies that specialize in the localization process. It is much quicker to have these companies prepare a game for different markets than to tie up in-house staff members in such tasks when they could be preparing for the next production cycle.

FYI   *Localization*

Some development companies readily agree to help with the localization of their games for foreign markets without realizing how complex the process is. In addition to changing all the text in the game on a per-market basis (for example, translations into German, French, Spanish, Japanese, Chinese, Korean, and so on), some of the game art itself may have to change. Germany, for example, doesn't allow red blood, so a company must change the art wherever blood appears. Before agreeing to handle the localization effort, a developer should discuss with the publisher what changes will be needed for each market and then research the best way to handle such changes. Keeping all the game's text in a separate file is one step, as is separating the text from the background art. Contracting with a company that specializes in localization might be the best choice.

Summary

The size of game teams has grown significantly in the past decade and will likely continue to grow with the next generation of game consoles. As long as technology continues to advance, there will be new skills for people to learn and new roles for them to play on a game team as they apply their new skills.

In many ways, games are becoming more like movies in terms of how they are produced. Each team now contains many specialists who focus on one portion of the game instead of several. It is difficult for any one person on the team to have all the skills required to create a game—much less be proficient in them all.

In the not too distant future, game companies are likely to split up and shrink as highly talented individuals form their own companies to service a number of developers. Games are currently cheaper to create than movies or television shows, but the cost of producing them is rising and will continue to rise. As a result, the game industry might become more like the movie industry in terms of how products are put together. In other words, a development company will consist of a small team of managers who contract with different groups to provide specific services and talents for a specific game.

Conversely, game teams might continue along the same lines as they are today, and the number of people working on a game team might continue to grow as the products themselves grow. As long as it is economically reasonable to keep large teams together to produce new products, it is likely that the current structure for game teams will continue to exist.

6

Test Your Skills

MULTIPLE CHOICE QUESTIONS

1. What role does the chief operating officer (COO) in a corporation perform?

   A. Balancing the checkbook.

   B. Making sure everyone has an office.

   C. Keeping the daily operation running smoothly.

   D. Attending long golf meetings.

2. In a small company that might not have a CEO, who would be responsible for making strategic decisions?

   A. Senior designer.

   B. Executive producer.

   C. Technical director.

   D. President.

3. Which of the following responsibilities does a technical director have?
   (Select all that apply.)

   A. Setting the code comment standards for the company.

   B. Determining the technical direction of all projects.

   C. Selecting third-party software for use in any specific project.

   D. Testing the software to see if it meets technical specifications.

4. Who writes the game design document?

   A. Senior designer.

   B. Producer.

   C. Technical director.

   D. Art director.

   E. All of the above.

5. Who assigns artists to work on a particular project?

   A. Art director.

   B. Producer.

   C. Art lead.

   D. Senior designer.

6. Which of the following are responsibilities of a level designer? (Select
   all that apply.)

   A. Create the concept art of the environment during the concept stage.

   B. Study the architecture of the world.

   C. Use a level editing tool to build and test levels.

   D. Design the enemy AI specific to a level.

7. Which of the following is an example of localization? (Select all
   that apply.)

   A. The company changes the box and manuals for a foreign country.

   B. The company translates all text/audio in the game for a foreign
      country.

   C. The company makes a local advertising campaign for a game.

   D. Playtesters evaluate the game for cultural significance.

8. Who makes the 3D models move?

   A. 3D modelers.

   B. 3D texture artists.

   C. 3D animators.

   D. 2D concept artists.

9. What tools do 3D artists commonly use? (Select all that apply.)

   A. 3ds Max.

   B. Lightwave.

   C. Maya.

   D. Photoshop.

10. The senior designer often has to maintain the executive staff's enthusiasm for a game. What tools do they use during production to do this?

    A. The game design document.

    B. The technical design document.

    C. Slide shows.

    D. Demos and milestone deliverables.

11. What is middleware?

    A. Software that is installed on the user's machine before installing the game.

    B. A completed software engine that can be licensed or purchased for development.

    C. A suite of software tools that can be licensed or purchased and used during development.

    D. "Average" software.

12. An assistant designer is usually

    A. Hired directly out of high school.

    B. Promoted from the ranks of playtesting or programming.

    C. An artist.

    D. A person who is organized and can do a lot of scheduling help for the producer.

13. Which of the following statements applies to the user interface (UI)?

    A. It is created at the beginning of a game so it can be fully tested.

    B. It is created at the end of the game, after the game engine is complete.

    C. It is created by artists.

    D. It is created by the producer.

14. The creative director is in charge of which of the following? (Select all that apply.)

    A. Making sure all the games made by the company are fun.

    B. Making sure all the games made by the company meet certain standards.

    C. How the game looks.

    D. The day-to-day management of the designers on a project.

6

15. Which of the following tasks is often performed by the lead programmer? (Select all that apply.)

A. Coding the most difficult or challenging tasks.

B. Leading the design portion of the production cycle.

C. Managing all programmers on the team.

D. Working on multiple projects at a time.

16. The lead artist on a team is often (Select all that apply.)

A. The best 3D modeler that works at the company.

B. Responsible for maintaining the art pipeline.

C. Responsible for writing concept proposals for new art tools.

D. Responsible for maintaining the artists on the team.

EXERCISES

Exercise 6.1: Run a Production Meeting

Divide into groups of 4 or 5 within the class. Have each person in your group take one of the following roles: producer, lead artist, lead designer, and lead programmer. Select one game that each of you has played recently, such as *World of Warcraft, Solitaire, Medal of Honor,* or a current FPS. You may select any game. Take 10 minutes and discuss the good, the bad, and the ugly. The producer should take notes. At the end of the 10 minutes, spend another 10 minutes deciding on 5 things you would improve in the game, 5 things you would remove completely from the game, and 5 new things you would add. Try to come to a consensus.

DISCUSSION TOPICS

1. Which games have you used in the past 3 years that have included level editors, map editors, or character editors? Discuss what was good or bad about them and whether you liked or didn't like the abilities the editors gave you. Share your initial reaction when you first started playing with the editor. Did your experience with the editor support that reaction? If so, how?

2. Assume you are the head of a large game publisher and you are looking at the direction of the industry for the next 5 years. With which individuals within your group would you discuss where the industry is heading? Which of the following focuses would you think the most likely to be

profitable for the next five years: technology, art, story, movie or other licensing, or other?

3. Consider why the role of a producer of a game might be more difficult than the role of a producer of a film. What are the major differences?

4. What skills do you think help make a good lead artist? A good lead programmer? A good lead designer?

6

Chapter | 7

Scheduling and Budgets

Chapter Objectives

After reading this chapter and doing the exercises, you will be able to do the following:

- Describe the management tools a producer uses to keep on schedule.
- List the milestones for a game.
- Demonstrate what it takes to build a realistic schedule for a game.
- Apply the basics of creating a budget for a game.
- Analyze a sample budget for a startup company developing a game.

Introduction

When games were small and not so technologically advanced, it was easy to set up a schedule and develop the budget. Until the early 1990s, a game could be completed by a staff of six to ten in a year or so, so management could quickly calculate the expenses required to keep the group together for a short time and determine the point at which the product would start making a profit. As games have become more complex, requiring larger staffs to complete the myriad tasks involved during production, the job of defining a realistic schedule—and therefore, a realistic budget—has become more complicated. Despite the increased complexity of the development process, management must set a reasonable schedule at the start of production to calculate the necessary budget for staff salaries and equipment. Without an accurate budget, management cannot determine the point at which the product will become profitable—or if it will make a profit at all.

Any game company that starts several projects without knowing when they will ship and start making a profit is asking for trouble. Such a company can easily overextend itself and find itself short on staff or money—or both. Game publishers have become much more competitive now that the business is no longer a simple hobby but a multibillion dollar industry. Predicting when products will ship so that they can be promoted and marketed properly is vital for a company's long-term survival. If they don't know when products will ship, company executives cannot know when they will receive money from game sales to keep the company going and fund new projects.

One of the biggest difficulties about accurately scheduling a game is that so many unknown factors are involved. If the company is creating its own game engine, for example, the rest of the staff must wait until the engine is nearly complete before they can produce any art or code to correctly integrate with the engine. If the company has to create new tools for the designers or artists, then the programmers have to complete work on the tools before the others can begin implementing the design and creating useful art.

Games have always been at the leading edge (or "bleeding" edge) of technology and have frequently driven the advances in computer audio and video standards. One problem with being on the leading edge is the difficulty of scheduling an exact date when a breakthrough will occur. A team might have to try several approaches before coming up with one that works. Still, even though there is much imprecision involved in developing a schedule, the job must be done. It is up to the producer and the team leads to draw upon their experience to come up with a workable timetable so that a budget can be agreed upon.

7

FYI | *Fast, Good, Cheap*

If companies had limitless money and endless time, they could take as long as necessary to turn out finished products. Such is not the case. Management types often refer to the *project triangle,* which balances the specific time, scope, and budget for a project. The project triangle can be a useful tool to consider tradeoffs when one of these factors has to change. The closer the project is to completion, the greater the tradeoff must be to keep it on track. Simply put, you get to keep only two of the three factors. If you want something fast and good, it won't be cheap. If you want it cheap and good, it won't be fast. And if you want it fast and cheap, it won't be good.

Management Tools

The producer has the responsibility of developing and maintaining the schedule for a game. Trying to keep all the information inside one's head is impossible, so a producer uses various management tools to develop an overall schedule, keep track of what tasks the team is working on, note what tasks have been completed, and predict when major milestones will occur. Whether using commercial software or custom-built applications, the tools used by the producer and team leads should provide the following information to show if the project is on schedule or starting to slip:

- Project Timeline: The timeline is created during the technical review stage from all the identified tasks needed to complete the project.

- Milestone Schedule: After the timeline is determined, the producer can determine when the major milestones will occur. A **milestone** is a significant point in the overall development of the game when management can gauge the progress of the product.

- Production Reports: When teams begin working on their tasks, they write weekly reports to indicate which tasks have been completed and which will be tackled next.

- Bug Reports: In the later stages of development, when the game is getting close to completion, the quality assurance lead provides the producer with updates on the number of bugs remaining to be resolved before the game can ship.

These tools are explained in more detail in the next four sections.

Project Timeline

After management approves the game design document, the producer and the team leads can begin working up the overall project schedule. During the technical review stage, the various teams identify all the work they must do to complete the game, and they break each item into component tasks, each of which lasts no more than a few days. The tasks are listed in the order in which they should be completed and all dependencies (where one task must be completed before another one can be started) are noted. The tasks are then assigned to team members, including future hires, and an estimate is made as to how long each task will take to complete. For example, one item on the timeline might be creating a character for the game, so the art team would list modeling, rigging, animating, and texturing as the component tasks. The programming team would then list their tasks (create the walk animation, the run animation, the death animation, and so on) to start when the animated model is complete.

After the individual tasks have been identified, the producer begins building the master timeline for the product. The most important information to track on the timeline includes when the task will start and when it will be completed, which team member is responsible for the task, and where the dependencies are. A producer might want to create two versions of the timeline, one that lists all the tasks chronologically by team from start to finish and another that lists the tasks by each individual on a team. Each team member can then look at the timeline and easily see what he or she is supposed to be working on that week, so any slips in the schedule can be detected early and acted upon.

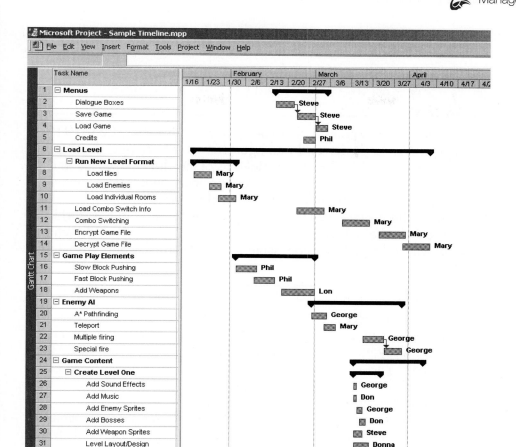

FIGURE 7.1 A small part of a sample timeline for a game as shown in Microsoft Project's Gantt chart view.

A commercial tool such as Microsoft Project (Figure 7.1) is commonly used to develop and keep track of schedules. Regardless of which tool is used, it needs to be able to define tasks, assign personnel (resources), assign duration (how long the task will take), show dependencies (which tasks must be done before others can either start or finish), and block in milestones.

Ideally, the program would also provide a means to see a ***critical path,*** which is the string of tasks that, if delayed, would impact the overall schedule for all tasks. The tool should also provide a means to see resource loading (how many hours a day, week, or month a particular person needs to work to accomplish all of her assigned tasks). This program should also be able to show a timeline schedule in the form of a ***Gantt chart.***

A team working on a project can also use a spreadsheet program such as Microsoft Excel to create a timeline. Although such programs usually do not offer the same features as a project management program, a spreadsheet is useful early on to define the major tasks facing each team before breaking them down into their individual components and determining the dependencies in project management software.

FYI *Gantt Charts*

The Gantt chart is named after Henry Laurence Gantt (1861–1919), a mechanical engineer and management consultant who developed the tool in the 1910s. The horizontal axis of the chart shows the entire time span for the project in convenient increments (days, weeks, months). The vertical axis contains a list of all tasks that must be completed on the project. When a manager sets the start and end dates for a task in the software, a bar for the task appears on the chart along with other information such as dependencies and resources allocated to the task.

It takes experience and training to learn how to estimate a timeline accurately. But even with a great deal of experience, the first pass at the project timeline is usually little more than an estimate (sometimes called a SWAG for "silly wild-a** guess") because there are so many unknowns. Therefore, it's always a good idea to add considerable padding to the first timeline until the most difficult tasks are well understood or completed.

As production gets underway, the producer and team leads should continually revisit the timeline and revise it, comparing their original estimates with the real results. If they find that they grossly under- or overestimated the time to complete tasks, they should adjust the remaining schedule to bring it back in line. If they are under a tight deadline, they might need to cut features or hire more staff to get back on schedule.

Milestones

Milestones are points during the development process when major portions of the game have been completed, reviewed, and approved by management. They create a sense of continuity to the whole project and give each team defined goals to be achieved by certain times. Milestones are a time for management to review a project and assess its progress. They are also often trigger points for payments to independent developers.

During the technical review stage or contract negotiation (for independent developers), the publisher and production team decide what will be delivered at each milestone. A typical milestone deliverable usually consists of the current build, source code, and game assets as well as a list of all the features implemented so far and those that are still to be done. The producer reviews the build and determines if the team has met its goals. If so, the milestone is passed and the team begins work on the next one. An independent developer often receives the next payment advance for completing a milestone.

If the team does not meet a milestone, they either have to consider what features to cut, how to rearrange the tasks on the timeline to get back on schedule, or ask for an extension to the overall schedule. Independent developers might not get their next advance until all requirements of a milestone have been met. If the team falls too far behind its schedule, management might decide to cancel the project altogether.

FYI | *Milestones and Independent Developers*

As discussed in Chapter 21, "Economics of the Game Industry," the economics of the game industry are harsh for most independent game developers because they survive on payments that are tied to successfully meeting milestone deadlines and they never collect royalties. Therefore, they generally live and die by their milestone schedules. If they do not define the milestones realistically and precisely at the start of a project, they might find themselves pulling resources from another project to work on the one whose milestone is coming up—thereby endangering the other project's timeline as well as their revenue stream.

7

A typical milestone schedule includes these steps:

1. **Game Design Document (GDD):** This first milestone occurs when the game design document is approved by management. The process can take from 3 to 6 months, depending on the complexity of the design and the number of revisions that must be made. The deliverables are the finished game design document, an art specification (art design document), and a complete list of all other assets required for the game's content. It also usually includes an updated estimate of the overall schedule and budget and a summary of marketing opportunities for expansion, international markets, and secondary products based on the design. At this point, management either signs off on the document or kills the project.

2. **Technical Review:** This milestone marks the end of the preproduction phase and generally occurs two to three months after management accepts the GDD. The deliverables are the technical design document, the production timeline, a formal milestone schedule and checklist, a list of resource needs, and the final development budget. Additionally, a developer might be asked to provide demonstration code to prove the

FIGURE 7.2 Engine proof for *Firmament: Chapter I of the Other World,* by Golan Trevise, playing on a PocketPC.

technology. This is another point where management will either green light the project for production or kill it.

3. Engine Proof: This is generally the first major milestone in the production phase of the game and is the point when the team must prove that the proposed technology is doable. This milestone occurs after the interactive prototype is up and running, which is generally a few months into the production phase. The deliverable of this milestone is always one or more demonstration programs of the technology (Figure 7.2), such as movement and combat. The deliverable often includes sample art for review by management, especially if the game is built on a licensed brand or character.

4. First Playable: At this milestone, the most important gameplay elements as described in the game design document are working. Depending on the complexity of the game, reaching this milestone can take from a few months to over a year. The deliverable is a working version of the game, the associated documentation to support the version, and an updated schedule and budget based on the current state of the project. Ideally, at least one entire level is working and includes all of the major game activities the player will deal with, such as movement, combat, item manipulation, and character interactions. A sample of the game art might appear on the screen, although the game engine might not yet be able to handle all the animations and special effects.

5. Interim Checkpoints: Between the first playable and alpha milestones are generally several "mini-milestones," or checkpoints, at which the

developer demonstrates continued progress on the game and, usually, targets some major technologies or gameplay to be completed and showable. These checkpoints generally occur once a month. At each checkpoint, the team needs to deliver a working version of the game along with documentation explaining the status of the game and all changes that have been made since the previous version.

6. **Alpha:** At this milestone, all major gameplay elements are coded to enable a player to play the game from start to finish. It might contain a considerable amount of placeholder art, and the shell interface will probably be missing, but the main gameplay is there. Most publishers refer to the alpha milestone as being "feature complete."

7. Interim Checkpoints: Between the alpha and beta milestones, a series of interim checkpoints are scheduled to make sure the missing assets of the game are finished as planned. All artwork is completed, the levels are completed, the audio is added, and the final code modules are completed. Playtesters begin checking the game for gameplay issues and reporting major bugs. The period between the alpha and beta milestones is the longest in the production phase.

8. Beta: When the project reaches the beta milestone, the game is finished and nearly ready to ship except for fine tuning and final testing—at least, this is the standard industry definition for beta. During this step, the publisher and developer prioritize the remaining bugs and attempt to remove as many as possible, especially those that cause crashes or violate software standards. This period between the beta and gold master milestones can take from two to six months (or more), depending on the complexity of the product.

9. Gold Master: This is the last milestone and consists of the production team's turning over the gold master of the final disk(s) to the publisher for final verification and approval. When the gold master is accepted, the production cycle ends.

Production Reports

To help keep track of which tasks have been completed, the producer might ask each team member to submit a weekly ***production report.*** This report consists of three sections:

- The *attainments* section indicates which tasks were started or completed during the previous week.

- The *objectives* section lists the tasks for the current week.

- The *problems* section deals with work-related problems such as missing equipment or software, waiting for someone else to complete a task, or conflicting objectives for the week.

The purpose of the weekly report is to identify potential delays in the schedule as early as possible so that the affected team members can switch their priorities or be assigned more resources to help complete problematic tasks.

The individual reports are submitted to the team leads, who then create a summary for each department. These summaries, in turn, are sent to the producer, who combines them into a master production report for management. Most producers have weekly meetings—if not with the whole team, then with the team leads—to go over the production report and discuss any problems that have cropped up.

The producer also has production meetings with management during the production phase to keep management updated on projects. These meetings provide an opportunity for producers to request assistance from other teams when extra resources are needed or offer assistance to other teams when they have resources to spare.

Bug Reports

When the project reaches the alpha milestone (or earlier, depending on the company), the quality assurance lead works with the producer and team leads to set up a bug-tracking system. Although commercial bug-tracking software is available, many companies prefer to create their own database system.

Bug-reporting and fixing (also known as *regression testing*) is an iterative process that goes on for months. When problems are detected, they are written up and sent to the correct team member to fix. The fix itself is then tested to make sure no other bugs have crept in.

The producer usually asks the QA lead for a weekly bug report that breaks down the remaining bugs by level of seriousness. The producer might include the weekly bug report as part of the production report to let management know what needs to be fixed before the game is finished. Most publishers insist that the worst bugs—those that cause crashes or other problems—be removed before the product can ship. However, less serious bugs can slip through, especially in computer games that can be fixed via patches downloaded from the Internet. After the product is shipped, a final composite bug report is turned over to the consumer support group. This report provides the service department with a listing of known problems as well as workarounds to provide to gamers who contact them.

Building a Realistic Schedule

When setting up the schedule, it is important for the team and the producer to define for management the features that will appear in the product at each milestone. The features list should read almost like a shopping list; for example, "Pre-Alpha Milestone #2: 2 forest levels complete (see attached sketches) with

terrain artwork, 3 animated/textured monsters, and tested scripts." The more precisely the producer defines what is due at each milestone, the better the team will know where they are slipping and be able to address problems early, before the project gets out of control.

Scheduling a game is not simply a matter of listing all the tasks needed to complete the project. Additional time must be added to the schedule for tasks that are not directly related to building the game but affect the ship date; for example, balancing the game and marketing it correctly. Every project has its own unique challenges when it comes to writing the code, creating the artwork, and building the playfields, so there is no one perfect way to build a realistic schedule.

Likewise, every production team has particular strengths and weaknesses that affect how efficiently tasks are completed. The more seasoned the team is, the more likely they will be able to complete their tasks on time, but there is never a guarantee that things will run smoothly over an extended schedule—people get sick, run into problems, and even change jobs. Still, it is important to create a schedule of some kind, or management will never approve the project.

The following suggestions will help you build a realistic schedule:

- Work with the team leads to make the schedule. They're the experts in their respective field and they're in the best position to understand the capabilities of their team. As such, they will have a good idea of the duration and difficulty of each task. Every team lead (art, production, design, programming, test) should break down each major task into smaller tasks and then break those down into even smaller tasks. The goal is to assign no task that will take longer than 5 days to complete. If any task is scheduled to take more than 5 days, it's probably made up of smaller component tasks. For example, if the programmer working on the AI module simply puts down "AI 20 days," the lead programmer might ask her to break the module into smaller tasks: "pathfinding 5 days, object avoidance 5 days, target acquisition 5 days, AI testing and debugging 5 days."

- Review the milestones and make sure the difficult tasks are tackled as early in the production phase as possible. You can put off the easier tasks if necessary, but definitely start the new technology as soon as possible.

- Add as much padding as possible to the schedule. Inevitably, when the team is running out of time and a build must be completed, Murphy's Law will take effect and things will fall apart. If the producer builds extra time into the schedule, the team has more time to fix problems without having to go into crunch mode before a major milestone is due.

- Just to be safe, the producer might consider using a multiple of the time estimates from each team rather than the given guesstimates. Time has different meanings for different teams: Some tasks on a game project are inherently more difficult than others and, therefore, harder to forecast. The hardest tasks fall to the programmers because they usually deal with the most unknowns when coding. The second hardest tasks belong to the artists, especially 3D artists who use complex graphics programs such as 3ds Max and Maya. The third hardest tasks fall to the designers if they use proprietary tools such as a scripting language or level editor. As a rough rule of thumb, multiply whatever time a programmer gives as an estimate by 5 (for example, if a programmer says it will take only a day to do something, assume it will take up to five days). Multiply an artist's estimate by 3.5 and a designer's by 2 (or by 3 if using proprietary tools). To be safe, multiply other teams' time estimates by 1.5.

■ Build in enough downtime: A person working full-time will not necessarily put in 52 full weeks of pure production. The producer should be aware that people have (and need) vacations, can get sick, and might have family or other personal problems to deal with. Many game companies in the United States shut down the week between Christmas and New Years. In addition, there are other times when production will slow down if not come to a standstill. Some of the staff might go to the Game Developers Conference (GDC) in March, and the team might be asked to demo the game for retailers at the Electronic Entertainment Expo (E3) in May. In addition, the producer should allow time for the team to get screenshots and make special builds for marketing. Therefore, it is a good idea to build at least four weeks of downtime per year for each staff member into the project timeline.

FYI *S&M Demands*

S&M is a derogatory term applied to the sales and marketing departments, who are sometimes seen as the enemies of the development team (and vice versa). A game team might feel put-upon when the sales and/or marketing departments make a sudden and unexpected demand for a working build or screenshots. Meanwhile, sales and marketing might think they are being perfectly reasonable about asking for demos and screenshots without realizing that the most current version of the game might be buggy and contain placeholder art. It is up to the producer to mediate between these camps and to make sure that the timeline includes sufficient time to prepare marketing materials. It is also a good idea always to have on hand a version of the most recent build that works, has final art (or close to it), and doesn't crash when demonstrated.

- By the same token, be prepared to make changes to the game based on feedback from management after a show like E3. Make sure you add some time after the conference to incorporate requested changes if necessary without impacting the overall schedule.

- Determine if stakeholders need time to review and approve builds. For example, if the game is based on a licensed product or is made for a console, make sure to build in time in the post-beta period for the license holder or console manufacturer to review and approve the game. Give them at least two weeks for their review, as well as one to two weeks to fix any outstanding issues after the review.

- Allow sufficient time to acquire new tools and hardware and have the teams become acclimated to them.

- Revisit all the staffing issues regularly to make sure enough manpower is available to get the work done or determine if staff members need to be reassigned to other projects when they finish their work.

Budgeting

As with scheduling, preparing the budget for a game has become more challenging as teams have grown in size and timelines have stretched out for years. When making games was not much more than a hobby, a small team could put together a game in a year or so for about $200,000 to $300,000. A publisher could make money by selling only from 6,000 to 10,000 copies of the game— a pittance by today's standards. Today, a company can spend millions of dollars over many years to create a game, so it must sell many more copies to make a profit. Even though the numbers have grown, the same basic financial precept still holds true today as in the early days of the industry—a company has to make enough money from a product to pay for its development and, ideally, to bootstrap the next product.

To establish the budget for a game, the publisher looks at the timeline developed by the producer to determine how much money will be spent on a monthly basis throughout the production cycle. This figure includes employee salaries, as well as hidden costs such as benefits, equipment, and corporate overhead. The sales and marketing departments determine how many copies of the game they think they will sell and whether that number will result in a profit for the company. They present their profit-and-loss (P&L) analysis to management, who determines if the game will be profitable enough to receive a green light to go forward.

A publisher receives around 65 percent of the retail price of a computer game. This percentage is the publisher's ***wholesale price.*** For a game with a retail price of $50.00, that works out to about $32.50 per copy. (The situation is different for console games, as explained in Chapter 21, "Economics of the Game Industry.") One could simply divide the total budget for a game by $32.50 to determine the number of copies that must be sold to break even. However, additional factors are involved because the publisher bears the cost of manufacturing and distributing the product as well as the overhead costs required to keep the company running. All these extra expenses are included in the P&L analysis. Generally, when a computer game costs several millions of dollars to produce and even more to market, the publisher must sell well over a hundred thousand copies to break even.

For an independent developer, the situation is slightly different. A developer usually gets a percentage of the publisher's retail sale percentage, or **net sales revenue,** as a royalty. For example, a royalty rate of 15 percent on the publisher's $32.50 comes out at just less than $5 per copy for the developer. However, to finance the production of a game, a developer usually receives advances against these royalties, which means that a publisher pays the developer a scheduled amount of money at each milestone until the product ships. The publisher then recoups this advanced money before distributing any royalty payments to the developer, so it can take a long time before the developer actually makes a profit. As you will see in the following section, it can be difficult for independent developers to survive unless they are able to turn out an occasional smash hit.

FYI | *Return on Investment*

Every game publisher uses a **return on investment (ROI)** formula that helps them determine the number of copies of a game they must sell to recoup the initial investment and start making a profit. This formula can be very complex and is usually done on a spreadsheet where values can be added and changed as information becomes available. The expenditures side of the formula includes the salaries of the production team, secondary expenses such as benefits and corporate overhead, and the expected cost of the marketing campaign. The income side of the formula includes the estimate provided by the sales department as to the expected number of retail sales plus secondary income from direct mail sales and special versions offered at reduced prices. The income side should far outweigh the expenditures side, or the product is not worth making.

Sample Budget

The best way to get an idea of the budgeting process is to consider an example of how it is done in the real world. The sample budget included here is meant to give a broad idea of the expenses involved in developing a game and should not be considered inclusive of every expenditure involved in starting a company.

Assume that several game industry professionals have decided to form their own company to develop games. The group consists of a producer, a designer, three programmers, and three artists. They plan to develop a triple-A product, and thanks to their connections in the industry, they have lined up a publisher. Before they can get the contract, however, they must come up with a design, generate a game design document and build a working prototype of one level. These tasks take them about six months. For the purposes of this sample budget, let us assume that they bankroll themselves until the contract is approved. They set up a milestone schedule to deliver the game in 18 months after signing the contract.

What would their budget look like? Figures 7.3 through 7.5 show an Excel spreadsheet with the new company's expenses for the 18 months of development divided into six-month increments. All numbers are shown in U.S. dollars. The rest of this section discusses each expense category in detail.

7

Game Team Budget: First 6 Months						
	PRE-ALPHA					
Staff Salaries	Apr-06	May-06	Jun-06	Jul-06	Aug-06	Sep-06
Producer	6,000	6,000	6,000	6,000	6,000	6,000
Designer	5,000	5,000	5,000	5,000	5,000	5,000
Asst Designer						3,500
Lead Programmer	7,000	7,000	7,000	7,000	7,000	7,000
2nd Program/Tools	6,000	6,000	6,000	6,000	6,000	6,000
3rd Program/Engine	6,000	6,000	6,000	6,000	6,000	6,000
4th Program/Engine		5,500	5,500	5,500	5,500	5,500
5th Program/Network						5,000
Lead Artist	6,000	6,000	6,000	6,000	6,000	6,000
2nd Artist/3D Model	5,500	5,500	5,500	5,500	5,500	5,500
3rd Artist/3D Animate	5,000	5,000	5,000	5,000	5,000	5,000
4th Artist/3D Texture		4,500	4,500	4,500	4,500	4,500
5th Artist/3D			4,500	4,500	4,500	4,500
6th Artist/3D					4,500	4,500
7th Artist/3D					4,500	4,500
8th Artist/Interface					4,000	4,000
Total Salaries	46,500.00	56,500.00	61,000.00	61,000.00	74,000.00	82,500.00
Benefits	11,625.00	14,125.00	15,250.00	15,250.00	18,500.00	20,625.00
Staff Expenses	58,125.00	70,625.00	76,250.00	76,250.00	92,500.00	103,125.00
Other Expenses						
Office rent/utilities	35,000.00	35,000.00	35,000.00	35,000.00	35,000.00	35,000.00
Furniture	4,000.00	1,000.00	500.00		1,500.00	1,000.00
Insurance, legal, etc.	2,000.00	2,000.00	2,000.00	2,000.00	2,000.00	2,000.00
Computers	21,000.00	6,000.00	3,000.00		9,000.00	3,000.00
Software	33,000.00	10,000.00	7,000.00		21,000.00	3,000.00
Game Engine	75,000.00					
Total	228,125.00	124,625.00	123,750.00	113,250.00	161,000.00	147,125.00
6 Month Total						897,875.00

FIGURE 7.3 Budget for the first six months of the new game company's existence.

Game Team Budget: Months 7-12						
	ALPHA					
Staff Salaries	**Oct-06**	**Nov-06**	**Dec-06**	**Jan-07**	**Feb-07**	**Mar-07**
Producer	6,000	6,000	6,000	6,000	6,000	6,000
Asst Producer		4,000	4,000	4,000	4,000	4,000
Designer	5,000	5,000	5,000	5,000	5,000	5,000
Asst Designer	3,500	3,500	3,500	3,500	3,500	3,500
Lead Programmer	7,000	7,000	7,000	7,000	7,000	7,000
2nd Program/Tools	6,000	6,000	6,000	6,000	6,000	6,000
3rd Program/Engine	6,000	6,000	6,000	6,000	6,000	6,000
4th Program/Engine	5,500	5,500	5,500	5,500	5,500	5,500
5th Program/Network	5,000	5,000	5,000	5,000	5,000	5,000
6th Program/Audio		4,500	4,500	4,500	4,500	4,500
7th Program				4,000	4,000	4,000
Lead Artist	6,000	6,000	6,000	6,000	6,000	6,000
2nd Artist/3D Model	5,500	5,500	5,500	5,500	5,500	5,500
3rd Artist/3D Animate	5,000	5,000	5,000	5,000	5,000	5,000
4th Artist/3D Texture	4,500	4,500	4,500	4,500	4,500	4,500
5th Artist/3D	4,500	4,500	4,500	4,500	4,500	4,500
6th Artist/3D	4,500	4,500	4,500	4,500	4,500	4,500
7th Artist/3D	4,500	4,500	4,500	4,500	4,500	4,500
8th Artist/Interface	4,000	4,000	4,000	4,000	4,000	4,000
9th Artist/3D	4,000	4,000	4,000	4,000	4,000	4,000
10th Artist/3D	4,000	4,000	4,000	4,000	4,000	4,000
11th Artist/3D				4,000	4,000	4,000
12th Artist/3D				4,000	4,000	4,000
13th Artist/3D				4,000	4,000	4,000
14th Artist/3D				4,000	4,000	4,000
15th Artist/3D						4,000
16th Artist/3D						4,000
Music/SFX					5,000	5,000
Lead Tester				4,000	4,000	4,000
Total Salaries	90,500.00	99,000.00	99,000.00	123,000.00	128,000.00	136,000.00
Benefits	22,625.00	24,750.00	24,750.00	30,750.00	30,750.00	32,750.00
Staff Expenses	113,125.00	123,750.00	123,750.00	153,750.00	158,750.00	168,750.00
Other Expenses						
Office rent/utilities	35,000.00	35,000.00	35,000.00	35,000.00	35,000.00	35,000.00
Furniture	2,000.00	500.00		3,000.00		1,000.00
Insurance, legal, etc.	2,000.00	2,000.00	2,000.00	2,000.00	2,000.00	2,000.00
Computers	6,000.00	3,000.00		15,000.00		6,000.00
Software	14,000.00	3,000.00		29,500.00		14,000.00
Game Engine						
Total	172,125.00	167,250.00	160,750.00	238,250.00	195,750.00	226,750.00
	172,125.00	167,250.00	160,750.00	238,250.00	195,750.00	226,750.00
12 Month Total						2,058,750.00

FIGURE 7.4 Budget for months 7 through 12 of the startup game company.

Salaries   Salaries and benefits are the largest expense for a company. The salaries shown in the figures reflect the seniority of the various team members. In a real startup, the leads often do not pay themselves, instead relying on their personal savings until the company starts making a profit. This example assumes the senior staff is paying themselves salaries starting in April 2006 (Figure 7.3), but at a lower level than they might get at an established company.

Game Team Budget: Months 13-18						
	ALPHA			BETA		GOLD
Staff Salaries	Apr-07	May-07	Jun-07	Jul-07	Aug-07	Sep-07
Producer	6,000	6,000	6,000	6,000	6,000	3,000
Asst Producer	4,000	4,000	4,000	4,000	4,000	4,000
Designer	5,000	5,000	5,000	5,000	5,000	2,500
Asst Designer	3,500	3,500	3,500	3,500	3,500	3,500
Lead Programmer	7,000	7,000	7,000	7,000	7,000	3,500
2nd Program/Tools	6,000	6,000	6,000	6,000	6,000	3,000
3rd Program/Engine	6,000	6,000	6,000	6,000	6,000	6,000
4th Program/Engine	5,500	5,500	5,500	5,500	5,500	5,500
5th Program/Network	5,000	5,000	5,000	5,000	5,000	5,000
6th Program/Audio	4,500	4,500	4,500	4,500	4,500	4,500
7th Program	4,000	4,000	4,000	4,000	4,000	4,000
Lead Artist	6,000	6,000	6,000	6,000	6,000	3,000
2nd Artist/3D Model	5,500	5,500	5,500	5,500	5,500	2,750
3rd Artist/3D Animate	5,000	5,000	5,000	5,000	5,000	2,500
4th Artist/3D Texture	4,500	4,500	4,500	4,500	4,500	4,500
5th Artist/3D	4,500	4,500	4,500	4,500	4,500	4,500
6th Artist/3D	4,500	4,500	4,500	4,500	4,500	4,500
7th Artist/3D	4,500	4,500	4,500	4,500	4,500	4,500
8th Artist/Interface	4,000	4,000	4,000	4,000	4,000	4,000
9th Artist/3D	4,000	4,000	4,000	4,000	4,000	4,000
10th Artist/3D	4,000	4,000	4,000	4,000	4,000	4,000
11th Artist/3D	4,000	4,000	4,000	4,000	4,000	4,000
12th Artist/3D	4,000	4,000	4,000	4,000	4,000	4,000
13th Artist/3D	4,000	4,000	4,000	4,000	4,000	4,000
14th Artist/3D	4,000	4,000	4,000	4,000	4,000	4,000
15th Artist/3D	4,000	4,000	4,000	4,000	4,000	4,000
16th Artist/3D	4,000	4,000	4,000	4,000	4,000	4,000
Music/SFX	5,000	5,000	5,000	5,000	2,500	0
Lead Tester	4,000	4,000	4,000	4,000	4,000	4,000
In-house Tester (x3)		9,000	9,000	9,000	9,000	9,000
Temp Testers (x4)			4,800	6,400	6,400	3,200
Total Salaries	136,000.00	145,000.00	149,800.00	151,400.00	148,900.00	122,950.00
Benefits	32,750.00	32,750.00	32,750.00	32,750.00	32,750.00	32,750.00
Staff Expenses	168,750.00	177,750.00	182,550.00	184,150.00	181,650.00	155,700.00
Other Expenses						
Office rent/utilities	35,000.00	35,000.00	35,000.00	35,000.00	35,000.00	35,000.00
Furniture		900.00	900.00			
Insurance, legal, etc.	2,000.00	2,000.00	2,000.00	2,000.00	2,000.00	2,000.00
Computers		6,000.00	3,000.00	3,000.00		
Software		3,000.00	3,000.00	1,000.00		
Game Engine	25,000.00					
Total	230,750.00	224,650.00	226,450.00	225,150.00	218,650.00	192,700.00
18 Month Total						3,377,100.00

FIGURE 7.5 Budget for the last six months of the new game company's first project. Note that toward the end of the cycle some team members are reassigned to work on the next project, so their salaries are removed and added to the new project (not shown).

The salaries have also been rounded off to make calculations simpler. Here is how the salaries of the original group break down by position:

- Producer: Has worked in the industry for over a decade and has shipped multiple titles. Acts as the new company's management staff. Salary: $72,000 year/$6,000 month.

- Designer: Designed three shipped titles, one was a smash success and the other two were respectable hits. Salary: $60,000 year/$5,000 month.

- Lead Programmer: Has worked in the game industry for over eight years and has shipped multiple titles. Salary $84,000 year/$7,000 month.

- Senior Programmer/Tools: Has worked in the game industry for eight years on many different tools for designers and artists. Salary: $84,000 year/$7,000 month.

- Senior Programmer/Engine: Another veteran with seven years' experience building game engines and using middleware. Salary: $72,000 year/$6,000 month.

- Lead Artist: Worked her way up to creative director at the last company she worked for and has shipped six titles over eleven years. Salary: $72,000 year/$6,000 month.

- 3D Model Artist: Worked on three shipped titles over seven years and a whiz with 3D Studio Max. Salary: $66,000 year/$5,500 month.

- 3D Texture Artist: The most junior group member, having been in the industry five years and shipped two titles. Salary: $60,000 year /$5,000 month.

There are three major milestones for the team: alpha at month 7, beta at month 16, and code release at month 18. During the months leading up to alpha, the company adds two programmers, five artists, and a junior designer to the team. During alpha, they add two more programmers, eight more artists, an assistant producer, and a quality assurance lead as full-time employees. In addition, they hire several part-time employees including someone to write the music and create the sound effects. Several full-time and temporary testers are also hired. In the last month, just before the product is ready to be released and is down to debugging, some of the senior staff members leave the team to start work on the next project.

To cut expenses, they decide to hire newcomers and industry professionals with only a few years' experience. Their salaries work out as follows:

- Employees with some industry experience or good skills. Salary: $54,000 year/$4,500 month.

- Employees with minimal experience but good skills. Salary: $48,000 year/$4,000 month.

- The in-house testers, who are scheduled to be hired in May 2007 (Figure 7.5) are paid $16/hour for a 40-hour week, with extra money allotted for overtime, so each makes about $3,000/month.

- Starting in June 2007, the company plans to hire four temporary playtesters (Figure 7.5) at $10/hour, or $1,600/month at 40 hours per week.

FYI | *Hourly Wages for a Game Team*

Even though the members of a game team might seem to be paid well, most companies require their salaried team members to put in extra time at certain points during production (called **crunch time**). Crunches usually come just before major milestones and important trade shows such as E3. For an artist earning $60,000 per year, the hourly wage for a normal 40-hour workweek is about $28.85 an hour ($60,000/2080 hours per work-year). However, if the artist has to work 60 hours per week for half the year to keep up with the production schedule, the hourly wage drops to about $23.00 an hour. That works out to an equivalent salary of about $47,840 for someone who works a steady 40 hour workweek. In companies that abuse crunch time, for example, by typically requiring staff to work 60 hours or more per week, the hourly wage drops even more. Of course, the team is working on a game, and many will find deep satisfaction in turning out a top-notch product. As a result, salary considerations are often secondary to love of the product. (Some companies also have ways to compensate for crunch time, for example, by offering compensatory time or giving bonuses for meeting milestones.)

Other Expenses   Of course, many other expenses go into starting a company, and they must appear in the budget as well. Now that the company has found funding, it plans to give employees some benefits. As a rough rule of thumb, benefits can add up to 25 percent of an employee's salary, so this amount of money must be earmarked for each full-time employee. Standard company benefits include vacation time, sick time, medical coverage, and life insurance. Additional benefits include stock options, educational opportunities, dental coverage, employee parking places, and so on, but these extra benefits are usually available only at large companies.

The company must have an office now that it is a real business, so they find a 2,000-square-foot space that rents for $15.00 per square foot per month.

In addition to the $30,000 monthly rental, they budget an extra $5,000 per month for utilities and other bills. Of course, an empty office is useless, so they have to buy furniture every time they hire someone. They decide on two desks, a chair, a lamp, a telephone, a whiteboard, and a bookshelf for each new staff member and budget $500 per person (because they are a startup, they buy used materials and equipment whenever possible). For temporary employees, they budget $300 per person. They decide not to set up the office with cubicles at this point because the wall units are relatively expensive. The rental space includes small offices, which they decide to designate as conference rooms where small groups can get together to talk and the executives can meet with outsiders in a quiet area.

The company also includes a monthly stipend of $2,000 to cover lawyers, accountants, agents, and other external advisors as well as the corporate insurance policy.

The next major expenditures are for top-of-the-line computers and software packages for each employee. They decide to budget $3,000 per employee for new workstations that will be used for the duration of the project. Because each member of the group has worked in the industry for years, they know how important it is to secure licensed copies of all software for each employee. The producer, designer, and QA lead each receive $1,500 for software, which includes Microsoft Office, Adobe Photoshop and one or two other programs. Each programmer is budgeted $3,000 for software to cover the C++ programming environment with the various necessary tool add-ons in addition to Microsoft Office. The artists receive the largest budget—$7,000 each—because they each need a 3D graphic package such as 3ds Max or Maya and traditional art supplies in addition to Microsoft Office.

FYI *Capital Expenditures*

In our sample budget, the cash outlays for items such as office furniture, hardware and software, and the license for the Gamebryo middleware are examples of *capital expenditures.* Capital expenditures are one-time outlays for assets that will benefit the company for an extended time. They offer some relief from corporate taxes (a subject for another time) and are an important accounting distinction from day-to-day operating expenses.

Finally, the team decides that they will use Emergent Game Technology's Gamebryo middleware package (**http://www.emergent.net/**) to develop their game engine. The license fee is $50,000 plus a $25,000 yearly maintenance fee for updates and support.

As the spreadsheets show, the first month of operations costs almost a quarter of a million dollars, and the average monthly expenditures (also called the burn rate) are about $188,000. After 18 months, the company will have spent almost $3.4 million to ship the product. At a royalty rate of $5 per copy, the game must sell over 675,000 copies to pay off the advances! Only a very few computer games sell anywhere near this huge number of copies. The situation is even worse for console games because the profit margin for developers is even smaller.

The finances for the game industry are examined in more detail in Chapter 21, "Economics of the Game Industry." Needless to say, it is getting much harder for new game companies to start up and survive because they make such expensive products.

Summary

Creating a realistic schedule is vital to completing a game project on time and within the allotted budget. A producer works to build a production timeline with the team leads during the preproduction phase to determine the tasks each team member will perform throughout development. When the timeline is determined, the team can then establish when the major milestones will be due and what each will include. At that point, the producer can create a realistic budget that not only accounts for the man-hours spent on the project but also for benefits, general office expenses, and capital expenditures. All of this information is compiled and used by management to determine the break-even point—the number of copies the game must sell to pay off the initial investment. Ideally, the game will sell well beyond the break-even number and bring in considerable profits to the company, for without enough cash, the company is sure to shut down.

Test Your Skills

MULTIPLE CHOICE QUESTIONS

1. How often should a producer review tasks with the team?

   A. Once a day.

   B. Once a month.

   C. At the delivery of each milestone.

   D. Once a week in production reports.

2. What is the main purpose of a milestone schedule?

   A. To schedule when the program should be completed.

   B. To determine the number of programmers and artists to hire.

   C. To provide management with a tool to gauge the progress of the project.

   D. To give the publisher some way to determine a payment schedule.

3. What is the wholesale price?

   A. The cost of goods for the product.

   B. The cost of the product for the retailer.

   C. The cost of the product when someone purchases an entire lot.

   D. The cost to the developer.

4. How is the retail price generally determined?

   A. 154% of the wholesale price.

   B. Based on the number of units manufactured.

   C. $32.50.

   D. As a percentage of the development cost.

5. When building a schedule, what should a producer do with the estimates from programmers?

   A. Multiply them all by 5.

   B. Divide them all by 2.

   C. Spread all the tasks out equally to all team members.

   D. Pad each task with an additional day.

6. A timeline is most useful

   A. As a tool to keep management content.

   B. As a means to show progress.

   C. As a way to watch time fly.

   D. During preproduction.

7. At alpha, a game should be at which of the following stages of completion?

   A. Complete except for all bugs.

   B. Close to being ready to ship.

   C. Ready for the final tuning.

   D. Completely playable from start to finish, with some existing bugs and some gameplay left to complete.

8. True or False: First Playable is a prototype that is delivered during preproduction.

   A. True.

   B. False.

9. What deliverables should the development team turn in at engine proof?

   A. The modified game engine.

   B. All engines that will be in the game.

   C. A sample of the technology that is critical to the game.

   D. Concept art and walk animations for the lead character.

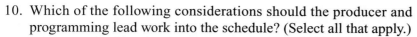

10. Which of the following considerations should the producer and programming lead work into the schedule? (Select all that apply.)

   A. Schedule easy tasks first, to get them done quickly.

   B. Schedule hard tasks first, to get them out of the way.

   C. Schedule tools before all game engine code.

   D. Schedule time for all marketing needs and for demos.

11. What is a QA lead responsible for? (Select all that apply.)

   A. Writing the game test plan.

   B. Maintaining the bug database.

   C. Verifying bug fixes.

   D. Keeping to the schedule.

12. Capital expenditures include which of the following? (Select all that apply.)

   A. Computers.

   B. Chairs, pens, and telephones.

   C. The producer's home theater system.

   D. Rent.

13. Payments by a publisher to a developer during the production cycle are

   A. Royalties.

   B. Advances against royalties.

   C. To be paid back by the developer, with interest.

   D. Bonuses.

EXERCISES

Exercise 7.1: Modify Your Budget

Note that the sample budget included in this chapter shows monthly totals for all personnel but doesn't show the totals for programmers only, artists only, or designers only. Using the spreadsheet from the example above, modify it to display this information.

Exercise 7.2: Identify the Critical Path

Look at the following schedule. What is the critical path for this short segment of a project?

Exercise 7.3: Identify the Milestones

Look at the schedule from Exercise 7.2. If the physics module slips, what else will slip?

Exercise 7.4: Assess the Impact

Refer to the budget from the scenario in the chapter. If the company decided not to use Gamebyro, which would save them 12 man-months of development by a senior lead programmer, what would the game costs be if they did the development themselves? What impact would this choice have on the overall schedule?

DISCUSSION TOPICS

1. Why is it so important to know all the tasks that must be done to make a video game? Do you think the importance varies depending on if the team is making a cell phone game that will take 4 months to develop versus an RPG that will take 18 months to finish?

2. Why do developers want to make games if the costs are so high and the challenges so great?

3. If you were a producer or a team lead, what means do you think you would you use with your team to keep them motivated for an upcoming milestone?

4. What factors would you consider when deciding whether or not to use a completed game engine such as Gamebryo instead of writing your own? What possible benefits and consequences can you see from this decision?

Part Three

Documenting the Idea

One of the most enjoyable parts of creating a game is coming up with an original concept and developing it into a complete game. Of course, anyone can come with an idea for a game, but few ideas ever end up as finished products on a retailer's shelf. Turning an idea into a shippable game involves a process, and the first step in that process is to put your ideas on paper so others can consider them and offer suggestions. The game design goes through several phases from a simple pitch paper to selling the central concept, to a game proposal that explains the gameplay in more detail, to a final design document that describes in great detail everything that will appear in the shipped product.

In a game company, the process of documenting an idea takes place during the preproduction phase. The designer works with artists to determine what the game world and characters will look like. When the gameplay elements are fully defined, the designer works with programmers to determine what code modules will be needed to bring the game to life. By the end of the preproduction phase, everyone on the team should share a common vision of the game and know the order in which the game assets will be created.

- **Chapter 8:** The Elements of Gameplay
- **Chapter 9:** Committing Ideas to Paper
- **Chapter 10:** The Game Design Document
- **Chapter 11:** Technical Review

Chapter | **8**

The Elements of Gameplay

Chapter Objectives

After reading this chapter and completing the exercises, you will be able to do the following:

- Identify what the "fun factors" are in a game.
- Describe what makes up the elements of gameplay.
- Identify the four goals of a designer.
- Describe the dangers of underdesigning a game.
- Explain why "feature creep" delays completion of a game.

Introduction

The idea of "fun" is subjective. What one player might consider fun—for example, running around a city and blowing away everything that moves—another player might consider boring or repetitive. Fortunately, electronic games are not restricted to one genre and one form of fun. Instead, each player can choose a genre (or genres) that allows him to perform certain activities he considers to be fun. These activities are what make up ***gameplay***.

Trying to determine what game concept will sell sometimes feels like roulette—you put down your money and hope you've selected a topic that a large audience will find enjoyable and that your team can do a good job of transforming it into a game that's fun to play. Of course, the stakes have risen over the years. As discussed in previous chapters, a game team now takes years to build a triple-A game and spends millions of dollars doing so. No wonder game publishers are reluctant to commit their money on a wild-eyed design concept. They would like to think they are investing in a product that will not only repay the initial investment but also make enough profit to fund new projects while making investors happy.

Similar to the movie business, the game industry has become hit driven—a few blockbusters make most of the money, leaving precious little for the smaller companies to survive on. Rather than gamble on something new and different, it is much easier for publishers to make sequel after sequel for a known product because the audience is already familiar with the topic. As a result, it can be difficult to get a big publisher interested in a revolutionary new concept. Despite the fact that most publishers seem to want to publish only sequels to previous hits, there is a market for new game concepts, but coming up with a new idea that management will be willing to bet on is difficult at best. A designer who understands the basic elements of gameplay—what makes a game fun to play—will have better luck pitching a new idea to management than someone who has little more than a basic concept for a game and no idea of what its basic gameplay will be.

The Fun Factor

The most important thing about an electronic game is that it must be enjoyable for an extended period so customers will be willing to invest anywhere from dozens to hundreds of hours playing it. Whereas a movie might be satisfying to a customer in its two hours of runtime, games are expected to offer much more entertainment over a longer time. Moreover, it takes the player time to become accustomed to the controls and to start understanding all the nuances of gameplay to really have the most fun. One of the standard mottos of the industry is that a game should be easy to learn and hard to master.

Interactive Fun

If you ask players what exactly they find fun about a game, chances are their responses will be widely varied. Does the fun come from simply pressing the computer keys or the controller buttons? Obviously not, or people could sit in front of a blank television or monitor and drive themselves into a frenzy with frantic key/button pressing. Of course, you also wouldn't need all the fancy 3D graphics, complex AI, networking capability, and levels of difficulty. The keyboard, mouse, and controller are tools the player must master to play a game, but manipulating the tools is not where the fun factor lies.

Does the fun in a game come from watching a story unfold? Many games include extensive cut-scenes and animated sequences that tell the background of the game or indicate what the player is to do next. But although sitting back passively and watching a story unfold can be enjoyable—after all, theater, opera, puppet shows, movies, and television have been offering such forms of entertainment for millennia—passive enjoyment is not the primary fun factor in a game.

Interactive Fun

A game is fun because the player gets to interact with the game-world environment and do things in, with, and to the environment. Playing a game is not a passive form of entertainment, but an active—indeed, an *interactive*—form. The keys and buttons let the player control things in the game environment, but a good user interface quickly becomes transparent to the player as he becomes completely immersed in the game world. Although the player has a considerable amount of direct control over the game environment, a bit of unpredictability can make a game even more fun. There is usually some randomization involved in the resolution of activities, so the player is never quite sure how things will turn out, thus building suspense and adding to the game's replayability.

Among the foremost fun factors in a game are such activities as exploration, combat, exploitation, physical dexterity, puzzle solving, construction, destruction, storytelling, and driving or piloting a vehicle.

Exploration   People are inquisitive beings who have been exploring the world since the first modern humans left Africa some 100,000 years ago. Most games present a world of some kind to be explored, whether a fantasy kingdom, a battlefield, or a racecar track. Players are compelled to look over the next hill to see what's there and enjoy discovering that which is new. Some unknown danger might await in the unknown territories, but finding and confronting the danger is part of the fun. Likewise, stumbling upon resources or other beneficial objects on the playfield can lead to great delight and an advantage over the other players (Figure 8.1). Often, the fun begins to fade when players realize

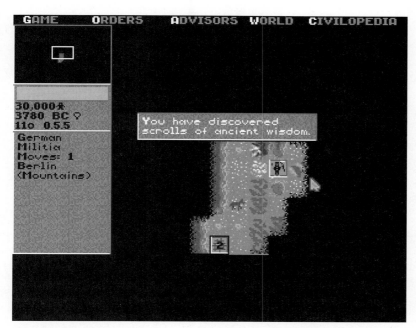

FIGURE 8.1 In *Sid Meier's Civilization* (MicroProse, 1991), the unexplored area of the map is dark. Players reveal the world and new resources as they send out explorers.

there is nothing new to explore. Other fun factors must then come into play to keep their attention.

Combat   Many game genres—adventure, action, role-playing, military simulations, real-time strategy, and combat simulations—involve some form of combat resolution. The fun, of course, comes in being the victor instead of the vanquished, and victory can depend on any number of reasons, from the martial prowess of one brave soldier, to the combined capabilities of a party, to the military genius of a general, to a lucky roll of the dice. Combat occurs at many levels in games, and players can find some levels more interesting than others. Someone interested in role-playing combat involving individuals or small parties might find tactical combat most interesting (Figure 8.2), whereas those who read about the great leaders in history might find operational or strategic level combat more to their taste. The fun factor comes from the player's testing various tactics during a game in an attempt to overcome even the most daunting enemy.

Exploitation   Most games let the player acquire objects during play such as power-ups offering short-term benefits, money to buy things, or resources with which to build assets (Figure 8.3). Learning to manipulate these resources is

FIGURE 8.2 A military unit in Sega's *Rome: Total War—Barbarian Invasion* (2005).

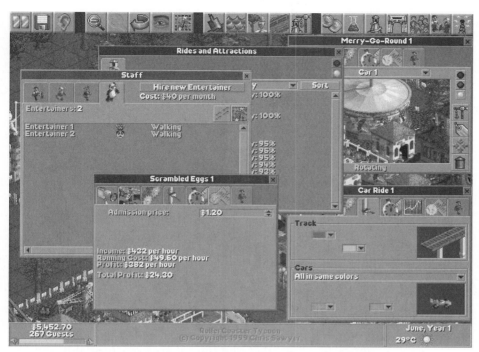

FIGURE 8.3 In Infograme's *RollerCoaster Tycoon* (1999), players earn money to build new park rides, hire staff, and expand their amusement parks.

8

often a matter of trial and error, and the player may have a moment of bliss when she discovers that a certain manipulation of items leads to something completely unexpected. Or the player might be thoroughly aware of what resources can do and be willing to use them boldly and with great precision at just the right moment.

Physical Dexterity In action games, players have the chance to control the physical actions of the central character (or characters) and make them perform outstanding feats of dexterity (Figure 8.4). The controlled character can bounce from platform to platform, jump over obstacles, or run across walls, all the while dodging or fighting enemies. Sports games offer the same kind of visceral excitement when players feel they control athletes' actions up and down the playing field. The actions can become increasingly difficult to master as new motion combinations become available or the game world becomes more challenging to transit.

Puzzle Solving Some games include purely abstract puzzles that offer players a series of problems to be resolved (Figure 8.5). These puzzles can be visual, such

FIGURE 8.4 Making a risk leap in Activision's *Pitfall: The Lost Expedition* (2004) requires dexterity from the player (and the character).

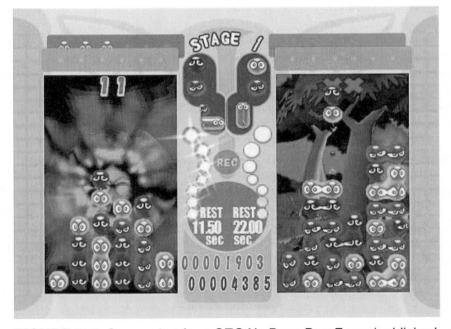

FIGURE 8.5 Screenshot from SEGA's *Puyo Pop Fever* (published by Nintendo in 2004), a puzzle game in the tradition of Tetris.

as jigsaw puzzles or rebuses; verbal, such as crossword puzzles and trivia games; or logical, such as magic squares and the Rubik's Cube. Other games include puzzles of a subtler sort; for example, in adventure games, the puzzles are obstructions that must be overcome to continue the story, and role-playing games present players with a series of miniquests (or minipuzzles) that are all part of a larger, overarching quest that drives the main character to action. Whether the puzzles are overt or subtle, the fun comes in that moment of discovery when the answer reveals itself and the player can shout "Eureka!" ("I have found it!").

Construction   Building things can be a lot of fun. Children enjoy building sand castles on the beach or creating buildings with blocks. Likewise, players enjoy the challenge of building things; for example, laying out the foundation and then building a city in Maxis' *SimCity* or setting up a nationwide railroad in MicroProse's *Sid Meier's Railroad Tycoon* (Figure 8.6). Many games include some kind of construction set or map editor to allow players to experiment with game assets and improve the world depicted in the game.

FIGURE 8.6 A nearly completed town as seen in Gathering of Developers' *Railroad Tycoon 3* (2003).

FIGURE 8.7 The Monster is a useful and fun tool for flattening parts of a city in Maxis' *SimCity 2000* (1993).

Destruction   As much fun as building something up is the enjoyment of knocking something down. Although few games focus only on the negative aspects of annihilation, many games offer players the chance to smash things into pieces and knock things down (Figure 8.7). It can be very cathartic for players to blow things apart, just as it is to beat enemies up, without causing any damage in the real world.

Storytelling   Games provide players the chance to tell their own stories, whether it be creating the perfect simulation city, winning a basketball game, or living the life of the main character on an epic quest. Unlike stories in other art forms, storytelling in games ideally is interactive, with each decision the player makes having an effect upon the rest of the game world. Because randomization is often employed when determining the outcome of game actions, the players tell the central story in a slightly different way each time they replay the game (Figure 8.8). However, the story is not always determined entirely by the player. When a game includes an animated story segment, the player stops telling the story and sits back passively to listen to events occurring outside her control. When the scene ends, the player takes control again and continues telling her individual story.

FIGURE 8.8 In LucasArts' *Star Wars: Knights of the Old Republic* (2003), the player can engage in conversations with the many characters populating the game world in whatever order she likes.

8

FYI   *Story versus Gameplay*

Many novice game designers assume the story is the game. If you ask a beginning designer what is fun in his or her game design, the young hopeful will frequently launch into a spirited discussion of the important plot points of the game's story. New game designers often forget that players want to be active, not passive. They don't want to be told a story, they want to tell the story themselves. Listening to exposition, watching animated sequences, and even interacting with characters is always secondary to exploration, combat, item manipulation, and puzzle solving. The story is incidental to gameplay and serves only as a framework for moving the player from place to place in the world.

Driving/Piloting a Vehicle   Racing and flight games let players experience the thrills and excitement of controlling a high-power vehicle that they would never be allowed to command in the real world (Figure 8.9). Even though a player simply sits in front of a television or computer monitor, the sensation can be very real—if the

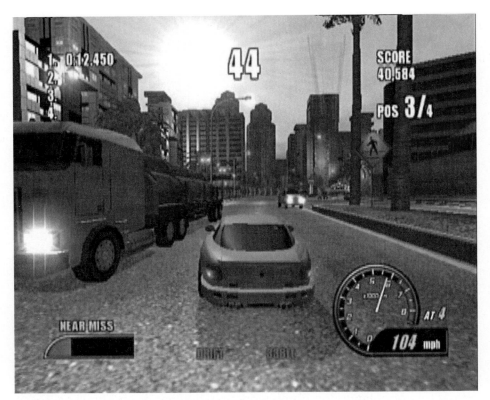

FIGURE 8.9 Something players normally don't do in real life—driving against traffic in Criterion Games' *Burnout 2: Point of Impact* (published by Acclaim Entertainment in 2002).

game team has done its job correctly and totally immerses the player in the artificial world it has created. Joysticks and steering wheels are peripheral input devices that can be used with such games to make the games feel even more realistic.

Percentages of Fun

One way to determine what is important to the game is to break out the gameplay elements and assign a percentage of time the player will spend doing each activity. Obviously, the percentages have to add up to 100, but young designers often try to cram an extra ten to twenty percent into the mix because they feel all game actions are equally important. When determining the percentage for activities, the designer should leave out all animated sequences and focus only on what the player is actively doing during play.

A first-person shooter game might break down as follows:

- Exploration: 65 percent

- Combat: 25 percent

- Puzzle solving: 6 percent

- Inventory: 2 percent

- Character interaction: 2 percent

Notice the percentage of exploration versus combat. One might expect there to be more combat than exploration, but if you look closely at most FPS games, you realize that the players spend a lot of time going back and forth through each level, searching for item and solving puzzles (where they look for items, keys, or even characters to progress to the next area of the game). You can certainly increase the combat percentage and reduce the percentage devoted to exploring the level, but then the size of the levels would need to shrink and more enemies would need to be added.

The pitch paper is a perfect place to describe the fun factors in a game at a somewhat abstract level (that is, when talking about the game's "high concept") without attempting to go into detail about exactly what the player does that's so much "fun." See Chapter 9, "Committing Ideas to Paper," for more details on pitch papers.

FYI   *Games and Learning*

Games, of course, offer children (and adults) the opportunity to learn new subjects in a fun and interactive way as they try different ideas and approaches for winning. Games do not have to be designed specifically for children, for they will usually learn how to play a game their parents play no matter how difficult it is—if they want to learn it. Children can learn from these games as well. Certainly, Will Wright's Sim games have valuable lessons to teach, such as managing resources, dealing with money, planning for the future, and dealing with the unexpected, as do such games as *Sid Meier's Civilization*, *Microsoft Flight Simulator*, and even *Madden NFL 2006*.

8

Gameplay Elements

When the approximate percentages for the various fun elements in a game have been decided, the designer can start determining what the real elements of gameplay will be. It's all well and good for a designer to say, "the player will be involved in combat 25 percent of the time in this first-person shooter," but what does the percentage translate into in terms of how the player interacts with the game environment? Ideally, the designer works out the basics of how combat will occur while creating the game proposal before going into elaborate detail on the actual game mechanics in the game design document.

The fun factors discussed previously are used to identify, in general, the enjoyable activities the player performs during a game. Each fun factor activity (for example, driving a vehicle) consists of a number of separate actions done by the player; for example, stepping on the gas, dodging oncoming traffic, slamming on the brake, and so on. The designer's job is to identify and describe these actions, which are the *gameplay elements,* in terms that management and team members can comprehend. To make comprehension easier, the designer usually organizes actions by functionality; for example, all forms of combat involving ranged weapons would be grouped together.

The following gameplay elements would fall into the various fun factors described above. Note that these lists are certainly *not* all-inclusive.

- Exploration:
  - Moving across the playfield
  - Seeking out hidden areas
  - Trying out new modes of transportation
  - Scouting for enemy positions
  - Searching for resources
  - Testing the terrain to find shortcuts
  - Dealing with the *fog of war* when an explored area is no longer in sight

- Combat:
  - Engaging in hand-to-hand fighting
  - Selecting weapons to use against an enemy
  - Trying to flee or retreat from an enemy
  - Throwing ninja stars at an attacking dragon
  - Maneuvering forces to outflank the enemy
  - Advancing after combat
  - Healing oneself instead of attacking

- Exploitation:
  - Picking up items dropped by a retreating/defeated enemy
  - Buying and selling items in stores
  - Improving the quality of weapons and armor
  - Spending hard-earned money to buy something powerful
  - Gathering resources revealed during exploration
  - Manipulating the inventory to maximize carrying capacity
  - Outbidding an opponent for an item

- Physical Dexterity:
  - Jumping from moving platform to platform
  - Running along walls
  - Combining moves at the right moment to gain a special power
  - Double-jumping to reach a high ledge
  - Hitting an inside-the-park home run
  - Throwing a touchdown pass in the Super Bowl
  - Knocking out an opponent during a championship fight

- Puzzle Solving:
  - Solving a crossword puzzle
  - Putting the last piece of a jigsaw puzzle in place
  - Using inventory objects to overcome an obstacle
  - Fulfilling a quest and receiving a special item in reward
  - Inputting the right code to open a cabinet of weapons
  - Playing the last card to win a game of solitaire
  - Putting the pieces of an incredible machine together in the right order to accomplish a task

- Construction/Destruction:
  - Building a castle from blocks
  - Blowing up a building and watching it collapse into rubble
  - Upgrading a smithy into an armory
  - Laying out the ground plan for a new city
  - Smashing gophers on the head with a mallet
  - Bulldozing a rundown area of town for a new sports center
  - Adding a better engine to a racecar

- Storytelling:
  - Talking with townspeople to find out who has attacked them
  - Giving the correct answer to the oracle to learn the character's destiny
  - Hearing the story of a character's true past from an old man who has recovered his memory
  - Reading a message from a spouse who's been kidnapped
  - Dickering with a merchant over his merchandise
  - Gloating as a desperado admits he's been bested in combat
  - Showing off the award for being most valuable player in the championship game

8

- Driving/piloting a vehicle:
  - Completing a death-defying loop-the-loop
  - Edging out a rival's racecar to take the lead in the Indy 500
  - Driving a tank through the wall of an enemy fortification
  - Commanding a spaceship as it enters an unknown star system
  - Jumping over a long row of barrels on a supercharged motorcycle
  - Spreading chaff to deflect incoming heat-seeking missiles and then making a death-defying midair turn
  - Safely delivering a package to its destination by taking side streets to elude mob pursuers

Note that the gameplay elements are accomplishments that the player achieves, not passive situations the player endures (for example, an extended scene of exposition). Gameplay is all about what the player does, not what he experiences. Many novice designers make the mistake of explaining in the game documentation only what happens to the player and not what the player *does*. Games are inter-*active,* with an emphasis on the *active.*

After the team agrees on which gameplay elements will be incorporated into the game, the designer describes how the actual game mechanics should work so that the programmers can create the code. Each gameplay element should be described in as much detail as possible in the game design document. For example, if the gameplay element under discussion is "stepping on the gas," the designer might write the following to describe the input that causes the action as well as what events occur as a response to that input:

> *The player presses the B button to accelerate the vehicle, which goes from a dead stop to 60 miles an hour in 6 seconds. When the B button is first pushed, there is the sound of screeching tires and the controller vibrates for a few seconds to simulate the sudden acceleration as the car fishtails. After two seconds, the shaking stops as the tires grip the road. The screech turns into a powerful, constant roar of the engine and four seconds later the car reaches its top cruising speed. Meanwhile, the speedometer on the dashboard indicates the vehicle's current speed in miles per hour.*

Defining the gameplay mechanisms can be somewhat tedious because there is so much repetition in the process, but explaining the details of gameplay in complete detail makes it is easier for the programming team to implement the mechanisms correctly as envisioned by the designer. Chapter 10, "The Game Design Document," discusses how to describe the gameplay mechanisms in the game design document.

Design Goals

When setting out to create a new game, the designer should keep a number of simple goals in mind. These goals include making the game challenging, making it enjoyable, making it balanced, and making it easy to "get into" (become immersed in). Although these goals might be simple to state, actually achieving them can become quite a challenge over the long period of development. Still, a designer should never shirk from the responsibility of keeping the game enjoyable, no matter how long it takes to bring the original idea to fruition. The secret is to keep looking at the design with fresh eyes to continually find new and interesting aspects of something that has the potential to grow stale from such long acquaintance.

Making It Challenging

One of the hardest goals of game design is keeping players challenged for hours on end. Throughout the game, players must feel there are new worlds to explore, new enemies to encounter, and new wonders to experience. All too often, a game reveals everything too early—giving players all the weapons, introducing all the different types of enemies, visiting all the areas in the game world—with nothing new to offer from midgame on. After a time, players realize there is nothing new to find and their interest in the game wanes. Many games remain half-completed because players feel that gameplay has simply become repetitive. Familiarity breeds contempt.

In many ways, designing a game is similar to composing a piece of music. A composer doesn't just throw a lot on notes on a page and hope the musicians will be able to make sense of them. A musical piece, whether classical, jazz, or popular, is carefully constructed to keep the audience attuned for an extended time through methods such as counterpoint, changing motifs, and variations on a theme. Even though the main theme might be heard repeatedly, it is often altered slightly each time it appears so listeners feel they are hearing it fresh for the first time. The music often builds to a thrilling crescendo at the end, which gives the audience a sense that the musical story has reached its peak and has ended. Likewise, a game should feel fresh all the way through as new elements are revealed or variations are introduced to make gameplay continue to feel challenging. And, of course, there should be a satisfactory resolution to the game so players walk away feeling they have been fulfilled. A designer-to-be is well advised to study the structure of music, as well as the structure of stories, to use as guidelines when they create new worlds and game experiences.

One way a designer might approach the problem of keeping things challenging is to list the possible variations of the previously defined gameplay elements. For example, suppose that the designer is creating a new sidescrolling platform-jumping game. She could list all the variations of a basic platform-to-platform jump and then try to rate them by complexity. The list might look something like this:

- Two stationary platforms with a small gap (tutorial, complexity rating of 1)

- Two stationary platforms with a large gap (introductory, complexity rating of 2)

- Two stationary platforms with gap and sharp object thrusting up from gap (intermediate, complexity rating of 4)

- Starting platform stationary, target platform moving a small horizontal distance with a small gap (tutorial, complexity rating of 1)

- Starting platform stationary, target platform moving a large horizontal distance with a medium gap (introductory, complexity rating of 3)

- Starting platform stationary, target platform moving a medium vertical distance with a medium gap (intermediate, complexity rating of 4)

- Starting platform stationary, target platform moving randomly with a large gap (advanced, complexity rating of 8)

- Starting platform moving, target platform stationary with a small gap (tutorial, complexity rating of 1)

The designer is unlikely to come up with every possible variation during the process of documenting the design. Many ideas won't become evident until after the tools for building levels are available. When the map building tool is ready, the designer should experiment with it to find even more variations that will keep the play fresh and challenging.

The designer will find it useful to create a paper layout of each level as he plots the placement of the gameplay elements. Then, the designer should look at the gameplay actions of each level individually and compare all the levels to make sure there is a steady progression of challenges to the player throughout the game. The player should always have a goal that compels her to keep going, and the game should give continual feedback on how well she is doing to achieve that goal. All elements of gameplay, no matter how challenging, should point the player toward the next step of fulfilling the goal.

A designer can end up with a huge list of gameplay variations, but many won't make it into the game because they are simply not enjoyable. Some might be too hard, some too easy, and some so bizarre that they break the player's immersion in the game. It is difficult to predict ahead of time which gameplay variations will work and which must be tossed aside. Still, it is useful to keep the list of variations on hand during production as a reference the designer can consult whenever a change is needed.

When the elements have been put into the game, the production team can test them in the context of the game as the first step in determining how enjoyable each one is. The team can then tweak gameplay until they are satisfied the game is enjoyable. However, it's a good idea to get different groups of play testers to check each level and give feedback as to what is enjoyable and what isn't. New groups of play testers are needed throughout the process to look at a level with "new eyes" after each revision. The process of refining gameplay continues until the game finally ships.

The player's enjoyment comes not only from mastering the gameplay, but also from the overall ambience and feel of the game. *Ambience* refers to the mood engendered by the game's visual and audio elements and, if appropriate, the storytelling (Figure 8.10). *Feel* refers to how the controls work as well as the feedback the player receives from interacting with the game world. Ambience and feel should not be afterthoughts to be created only after the gameplay elements have been worked out. While the production team is tweaking the gameplay, they should also be tweaking all other constituents of the game including the physical elements of the graphics, the audio, and the player inputs, as well as the aesthetics of the storytelling and the overall experience (or gestalt).

FIGURE 8.10 Westwood Studio's adventure game *Blade Runner* (1997) captures the ambience of Ridley Scott's classic science-fiction movie and gives players a sense of foreboding for this film noire detective story set in a decaying, cyberpunk future.

IN THE TRENCHES: Great Ideas

In his article, "So you Wanna Be A: Game Designer" on GameSpot.com, Bob Colayco quotes designer Ken Levine *(System Shock 2, Freedom Force, Tribes: Vengeance)* as follows: "A great idea is meaningless. A great idea that leverages your existing technology, gets the team excited, is feasible to do on time and budget, is commercially competitive, and, last but not least, floats the boat of a major publisher . . . Now you have something."

Making It Balanced

As well as making the game challenging and enjoyable, the production team has to make sure it is *balanced.* A solitaire version of a game is balanced if the player has a choice of equally weighted approaches to resolving gameplay situations. The game becomes unbalanced if it offers one or two overpowering strategies or playing pieces that the player will use almost exclusively during play. If such powerful items are a part of the game, they should be counterbalanced with some drawback or weakness (Figure 8.11). For example, if the

FIGURE 8.11 The power of the BFG in id Software's *Doom3* (1997) is offset by its being slow to fire and difficult to control.

player can wield a weapon of incredible destruction, there should be some penalties for using it—limiting the amount of ammunition, setting a very slow firing rate, doing damage to the player as well as to the enemies, restricting its use to certain environments, and so on.

This caveat also applies to level design. The team should watch testers to see if they are gaining unfair advantages from the way the level has been created. If so, they should make necessary changes to keep the game challenging yet enjoyable.

In a multiplayer game, balance comes from a number of factors. Some players will naturally be better than others, either because of better hand-eye coordination or better familiarity with the game systems and their limitations. The production team can offset such inequities in playability by including a handicapping system to level the playing field for all players— whether novice or veteran. For example, in a deathmatch FPS game, a novice player might play the game at the easy level (which might give the player more powerful weaponry) while veterans play at difficult (which might make the player easier to kill). Additionally, the team should pay attention to the overall balance of units available to players to make sure than no one group is too powerful. Again, by using compensating factors, it is possible to allow one group to be very powerful in one way (for example, in overall attack capability) but weak in another (for example, having a slow movement rate). Gameplay balance is discussed in more detail in Chapter 19, "Completing the Game."

Making It Easy to Get Into

Electronic games are a complex form of entertainment when compared to most other forms of leisure. They demand interactivity from players, and they often include several different play modes (such as solitaire and online) and many gameplay options. Computer games often have the most complex controls because the standard 104-key keyboard and mouse offer the player so many different inputs. But even video games have become more complex over time by adding more buttons to enable players to perform more actions in games. Players can quickly become overwhelmed by the amount of information they must absorb before they can play a game with ease. To keep players immersed in a game, its interface and controls must quickly become second nature so players don't have to look away from the screen to determine what input to use next.

One of the best ways to familiarize players with the control setup is a tutorial. Some games put the tutorial outside the main game in the main options screen, but players might bypass it to dive headlong into the game. In a growing number of games, the tutorial is included in the main game itself, either as a training exercise at the beginning of play (as in Looking Glass Studio's *System Shock 2,* which has an excellent tutorial for training players in the three military branches the main character can enlist in) or as an ongoing series of instructions as new gameplay elements become available (as in Square's *Final Fantasy X,* which features an extended tutorial that covers the many different aspects of the complex role-playing game).

The designers should differentiate between the primary and secondary controls and make the player comfortable with the primary controls as quickly as possible. *Primary controls* are the ones that are used most often and that have the greatest effect on gameplay. They should be the easiest to access during play. *Secondary controls* are used less frequently and have less direct impact on gameplay. They can be assigned to harder-to-reach keys or buttons. For example, when driving a real car, the primary controls are steering, accelerating, and braking, whereas secondary controls include lights, horns, turn indicators, and so on. In a first-person shooter game, the primary controls are usually the keyboard commands for moving and using items as well as the mouse for looking around and shooting weapons, whereas the secondary controls include the keyboard commands for special moves (leaning, crouching, jumping), manipulating weapons and items in inventory, chatting, and so on.

Fortunately, as with automobiles, the primary controls for most game genres have become standardized so players need less time to understand the basics. Instead, they can focus on familiarizing themselves with secondary controls as needed. It's a poor design choice to try to break the mold by imposing unusual command layouts on players (unless the game has an option to allow players to reconfigure controls as they wish).

However, just because a designer should keep a game easy to learn does not mean that it has to be easy to master. A good designer is as familiar with the KISS principle (Keep It Simple, Stupid) as with the saying "less is more." Rather than adding complexity to complexity, a good design takes a few basic elements and uses them in many different combinations and variations. The player can learn to control these elements easily, but mastering them can take many, many hours of play—and that is where the fun is.

Dangers in Game Design

There are many reasons why a game might fail commercially. Some of them are outside the production team's control. For example, the team might not anticipate or adopt a new technology in time, the audience's taste might change, or a publisher might go out of business. However, other reasons are within the team's control and offer bleak lessons on why projects die before shipping or don't do well when they do ship. The Gamasutra Web site (**www.gamasutra.com**) offers many postmortem discussions about what went right and what went wrong during the production of many different kinds of games.

Many problems arise from poorly thought out design decisions made during preproduction. When the game is implemented during the production phase,

these problems rear their ugly heads and make life difficult for the team. In addition to poor design decisions, other problems can arise during implementation, either due to inefficient implementation of code and art or the crunch of tight deadlines. With all that can go wrong during the creation of a game, sometimes it's a wonder that so many things go right.

Preproduction Problems

The number one offense—whether in the design or the implementation of the design—is breaking the player's immersion in the game. A novice designer might try to overdesign the game and cram it full of gameplay elements, which will eventually make the interface difficult for the player to learn. Although it is certainly easier to cut back on play elements during production, any change makes it likely that the schedule will slip. By assigning priority levels to the gameplay elements in the documentation stage (as discussed previously), the team will know which elements *must* be implemented to make the game work before layering in other, less essential elements if time and budget allow (which they seldom do).

Underdesigning the game is another preproduction problem. Unfortunately, many beginning designers think that merely explaining the story of the game and describing the characters and locations is all that's necessary for the documentation. This approach tells the programmers nothing about the actual game mechanisms they will be expected to code. As a result, during production the team might find themselves running out of ideas and begin repeating ideas over and over again in each new level.

Production Problems

Even if the design is thoroughly worked out and tested before development begins, obstacles continue to face the team—some of their own making and others from outside influences. One of the greatest obstacles facing the team is making a good interface for the game. If the elements of the heads-up display (HUD) are poorly laid out, the controls are difficult to learn and use, or the audio and visual feedback are inconsistent, there is a good chance that players will be distanced from the game and lose their sense of immersion. Therefore, work on the interface should begin early, with the designer discussing the functionality of each element in the game design document. The team should get a version of the in-game interface working as early as possible in the production phase to get feedback from quality control testers and focus groups.

More often than not, the team will find themselves adding features in mid-alpha or later, with each addition demanding more production time (called *feature creep*). Making changes based on player feedback should be expected, but adding more features late in production is asking for trouble. Feature creep is a major cause of schedule slippage and budget overruns. Prototyping the game is one way around this problem (see Chapter 18, "Prototyping and Building

Playfields," for more discussion about prototypes). It is better to overdesign the game during preproduction, knowing that things will be removed during production, than to underdesign and try to add fun elements later. These added features often stand out as hurriedly jammed-in ideas in stark juxtaposition to those gameplay elements that were thought through from the beginning.

Another common problem for the team is utter exhaustion with the game. There might come a point where the team is bored with the project, and someone on the team may suggest making some changes to the basic gameplay to make it "more interesting." If this suggestion is accepted, the project schedule is likely to slip. Or a new technology may become available, tempting the team to employ it somehow in the game, again leading to slippage and delay. Changing the basics of gameplay is, of course, more problematic than merely adding extra features because every asset so far completed will likely need to be modified or tossed aside.

There are many reasons why teams might need to make changes, such as dull and repetitive gameplay, unsolvable puzzles, inconsistencies in the storytelling, poor AI, or poor interface design, but changes such as these during the later part of the production should be limited to fixes to existing code—not completely new code modules. In "You Got Game!: Part 4, Development," an article on GameDev.net, Drew Sikora points out that "hard data shows that a change can cost up to 50 times more towards the end of a project than at the beginning." If a change is so important that it makes or breaks the game, it should be implemented, but if the change is merely cosmetic or adds minimal play value, it should be dropped. People promoting the changes usually offer the excuse that the change will take only a "few hours" to implement. But inevitably, it will take days for the new code and art to be created and then inserted into the existing program. More likely than not, the change will then cause one or more bugs or inconsistencies that will have to be tracked down and fixed.

A number of outside issues also can cause problems during production. There is a good chance that someone on the team will leave during the long production phase. Someone will then have to be hired or moved into the open position and brought up to speed on the work. The work of the entire team might be suspended until the new person reaches full productivity, and this delay can cripple the schedule. Therefore, it's a good idea to have a backup assigned to each team member so in the event that someone has to leave the team unexpectedly, the accumulated knowledge won't leave with him. In addition, the team should continuously comment their code to explain how it is structured and what it does in case someone has to take over or otherwise help finish a module.

Small development houses usually live and die by their milestone payments, so it is important that they stay on schedule. The longer a developer has been around, the more likely the owners or management can make a reasonable estimate of how long a project will take to finish. Still, whether due to forces in or out of their control, it is quite possible for the developer to fall behind and be forced to shift resources from one project to another to play catch-up, perhaps creating a domino effect that causes slippages in several schedules. Because a small developer can take many years to become profitable, there is a natural tendency to underestimate how long it will take to complete a project in an effort to get paid as quickly as possible to meet their financial obligations. This creates extra pressure to meet the milestone schedule and any small burp along the way leads to disaster.

Another problem for small developers occurs when there is a change in management at the publisher. Producers come and go, get promoted or fired, and take on additional projects that result in new producers being assigned to outside projects. The new producers might want to add or cut features that could threaten to extend the production cycle beyond the original deadlines. Although developers should be willing to listen to any suggestions offered by their publisher, they should also be ready to show the publisher how expensive proposed changes would be.

Another factor outside a developer's control is the power politics that often go on within the management of publishing companies. No matter how good the developer is doing on a project, the pressures of making a profit can lead to unexpected changes in the publisher's management or in how they plan to meet their financial goals—even leading to the complete cancellation of the project in midstream. A small developer should always be prepared to react quickly to such a financial emergency and should include a **_kill fee_** in their contract; this provides the developer with some money if the publisher cancels the project. It is also a good idea, if possible, to work with several publishers in case one of them runs into trouble.

> **Caution**
>
> **Be Realistic about Changes**
>
> No matter how unrealistic the request for changes, a good developer should be realistic about schedules and budgets and not promise anything they know they won't be able to deliver. If they act against their better judgment and fail on one project, they might not get the chance to work on another.

8

Summary

Designing and making a game requires a great deal of time and effort on the part of all team members. The designer has to be concerned with what is fun in a game and should spend enough time to work out all the gameplay elements.

The documentation process is the means by which the designer translates her vision into a description of the mechanics of gameplay. By the end of the process, the final game design document needs to explain all game elements as thoroughly as possible so that the programmers can figure out how best to implement them. It is a good idea to overdesign the game initially to help stave off feature creep later in production. To prevent feature creep, the designer should establish the priorities for the game elements and make sure the core elements are tackled first. Additional elements should be added only if there is a real need to improve gameplay and there is time and money left in the budget to accommodate the changes.

No matter how well you plan, problems will inevitably come up during production. Many of these problems will be outside of the developer's control. Although even the best-designed preproduction phase cannot prevent every problem that might arise, it will enable the developer to effectively manage those that do.

Test Your Skills

MULTIPLE CHOICE QUESTIONS

1. What is feature creep?
   A. Slowly adding new features to the game during the design phase.
   B. Adding more gameplay elements to the game during balancing.
   C. Making minor changes to gameplay late in the production.
   D. Changing the game features in production.

2. When should the HUD be designed and by whom?
   A. During production, by the programmer.
   B. During preproduction, by the producer.
   C. During production, by the producer.
   D. During preproduction, by the designer.

3. What are some of the common pitfalls that can occur during production? (Select all that apply.)
   A. Change in management.
   B. New employees.
   C. Feature creep.
   D. Balancing.
   E. Game elements.

4. Which of the following are common gameplay elements? (Select all that apply.)
   A. Exploration.
   B. Combat.
   C. Innovation.
   D. Physical dexterity.
   E. Music.

5. Which of the following are the primary controls for a role-playing game (RPG) on a PC? (Select all that apply.)
   A. Keyboard input for movement.
   B. Keyboard input for combat.
   C. Keyboard input for inventory control.
   D. Mouse input for movement or direction.
   E. Mouse input for main menu.

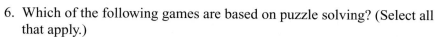

6. Which of the following games are based on puzzle solving? (Select all that apply.)

A. Chess.

B. Basketball.

C. NASCAR racing.

D. *Tetris.*

E. *Solitaire.*

F. *Dungeons & Dragons.*

7. What are the important aspects to consider when making a game? (Select all that apply.)

A. Make it challenging.

B. Make it grueling.

C. Make it multiplayer.

D. Make it balanced.

E. Make it easy to get into.

F. Make it enjoyable.

8. When designing each level, what should the designer consider?

A. Making the first levels the most impressive.

B. Making it easy for the new player to learn.

C. Putting in at least five variations of the same game elements.

D. Building on the existing player experience within the game.

9. What is the complexity rating?

A. The rating on the exterior of the box.

B. How the programmer knows where to put a puzzle.

C. An attribute of all puzzle elements within a game.

D. A factor of the balancing and making the game challenging.

10. When is a tutorial best?

A. When it has a lot of printed material to read.

B. When it repeats the same topic until the player perfectly understands all of its aspects.

C. When it is subtly integrated within the early levels of gameplay.

D. When it can be played only the first time the game is installed.

8

11. Why is game balancing important?

    A. It keeps players from having too much fun.

    B. It can extend the production cycle and the developer can charge more money.

    C. It ensures the game stays interesting from start to finish.

    D. It ensures that each level takes the same amount of time to complete.

12. When playing a real-time strategy (RTS) game, which of the following would distract the player from the main gameplay and break her immersion in the overall game?

    A. Building armories.

    B. Exploration.

    C. Training musicians.

    D. Combat.

13. Which of the following gameplay elements could be included in an RPG? (Select all that apply.)

    A. Inventory management.

    B. Keyboard.

    C. Exploration.

    D. Building armories.

    E. Combat.

    F. Leveling up.

    G. Balance.

    H. Bargaining with merchants.

14. Which of the following game elements should be included in a graphic adventure game? (Select all that apply.)

    A. Leveling up.

    B. Exploration.

    C. Driving a boat.

    D. Conversing with other characters.

    E. Combat.

    F. Solving puzzles.

    G. Combo moves.

15. Which of the following game elements in a first-person shooter (FPS) video game might affect the player's immersion in the game? (Select all that apply.)

    A. Leveling up.

    B. Building an armory.

    C. Exploring.

    D. Talking with other characters.

    E. Solving puzzles.

    F. Combo moves.

    G. Accuracy scoring.

EXERCISES

Exercise 8.1: Control Characteristics of a Puzzle Game

Select a puzzle game such as *Pac-Man*. Write down all the primary and secondary controls within the game.

Exercise 8.2: Control Characteristics of an FPS

Select an FPS game. Make a chart of all the primary and secondary controls within the game.

Exercise 8.3: Balance of Fun Factors

Use the list of play elements within the chapter to create a game with the following balance of fun factors:

- Exploration: 65 percent

- Combat: 25 percent

- Puzzle solving: 6 percent

- Inventory: 2 percent

- Character interaction: 2 percent

Ideally, you should have a minimum of 10 different items spread across the selection.

Exercise 8.4: Board Game Analysis

Take any board game and break it down into its gameplay elements. Then analyze the game for fun factors (exploration, combat, puzzle solving, inventory, and character interaction) and estimate the percentage of the game that is involved in each.

Exercise 8.5: Variations on an Enemy Theme

Start with a simple enemy, such as a turret that fires a gun at time intervals. Create at least 10 variations of this enemy for either an FPS or side-scrolling game.

DISCUSSION TOPICS

1. Select one of your favorite games and then select a nonvideo game form of play that you enjoy. What is the difference in the fun factor? Do the two have any common elements of gameplay?

2. Think back to your favorite game 5 years ago—either video game, board game, sport, or other game. How has your taste in games changed? What do you recall enjoying about that game that you would not find as much fun now? Why?

3. What do you recall from the game in Question 2 that you would still find fun? Would you have to update the play or the game elements in some way to make it as enjoyable as your current favorites? What would you change and how?

4. Of the games that you are currently playing, which one(s) do you think you might recall as being a great game 10 years from now? Why? What aspects of the game(s) do you think will last?

5. Most children enjoy construction with some form of building blocks. Discuss the element of construction (or deconstruction) and how it was fun. How did the play change when you and your playmates tired of the basic play?

6. How many of the five fun factors discussed in the chapter do you feel should be equally included in a game? Why? What do you think of a game that would have game elements equally distributed among these fun factors?

Chapter 9

Committing Ideas to Paper

Chapter Objectives

**After reading this chapter and doing the exercises,
you will be able to do the following:**

- List the first steps in turning an idea for a new game into a product.
- Conduct brainstorming sessions to come up with ideas for new games.
- Write a pitch paper and design proposal and present them to management.
- Explain how the sales and marketing departments can help promote a game idea to management.
- Describe the approval process involved in making a game.

Introduction

The process of generating the documents needed to explain a game idea fully can be daunting. A game idea might start as part of a story, an interesting or unusual gameplay mechanism, or a striking visual image. But that is simply a beginning. Although it's easy to dream up a general idea for a game, the real challenge comes in sitting down and working out how the elements will all work together as a whole. As discussed in the previous chapter, a game contains many gameplay elements that must be thought out in detail and then committed to paper so the whole team can read them over and discuss them. When the team reaches an agreement on what to build, management will be more inclined to agree to their design document and give permission to proceed.

Because games are so expensive to fund and take such a long time to complete, it is important for the team to have a blueprint of what they will build. The design process allows a designer the opportunity to refine her ideas over time as the game slowly takes shape during the documentation phase. Generally, the process involves presenting various concept pitches to management in order to get their reaction to the game and to determine if the game will be financially successful. The documentation should not be viewed as a straightjacket that limits the team's creativity during the production phase but more as a skeleton that provides the structure the team needs over the many months and years needed to bring the game to life.

Coming Up with a Game Idea

Obviously, a designer's background and life experiences will have a significant effect on his ability to come up with new and different concepts. This is because ideas tend to be iterations of existing products rather than the interlinking of original and unexpected associations. If the designer has lived a limited, sheltered life, he will have fewer data points to link together by imagination. A designer's brain should be like a maelstrom, continually taking in new data from many sources and letting ideas swirl together and clash against each other. A designer should be a voracious absorber of information from many different sources including books, movies, television, games, travel, work, overheard conversations, and so on. Additionally, a designer should know how to do research in libraries and bookstores as well as through the Internet to find other sources of relevant data.

Simply absorbing information is of limited use if a designer doesn't know how to process it, which means putting ideas down in words. A designer should be comfortable with writing—indeed, a significant portion of a designer's life revolves around writing the documents that explain how a design works. For those who have trouble writing, some simple exercises can help with getting into the habit:

- Keep a notepad for jotting down ideas.

- Scribble your activities and observations in a diary every day, no matter how mundane life has been.

- Force yourself to type at least one page of something each day (a story, an essay, some poetry, lines of dialogue, or whatever).

Eventually, the process of writing will become second nature—even if it still feels like a grind.

First Steps

The first step of the design process is coming up with an idea for a game. The idea can come from anything—an article, a television program, another game, or just a random thought. It can usually be worded as a "What if . . . ?" statement. For example, "What if pigs could fly?" or "What if humans started acting like lemmings?" or "What if the hero of a role-playing game turns out to be the clone of the major villain?" From this starting point, the designer lets his mind

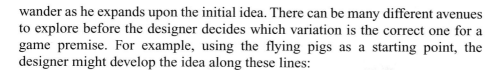

wander as he expands upon the initial idea. There can be many different avenues to explore before the designer decides which variation is the correct one for a game premise. For example, using the flying pigs as a starting point, the designer might develop the idea along these lines:

- What if the pigs were outfitted with weapons and took part in dogfights during World War I?

- What if Pegasus was really "Pigasus" and all mythological creatures were based on farm animals?

- What if a special substance distilled from pork rinds made things levitate or fly?

- What if knights in medieval times rode giant flying pigs and took part in jousts?

- What if farms existed in the clouds and farmers had to deal with livestock in a 3D environment?

This list is not exhaustive, of course, and a designer could concoct many other scenarios that involve flying pigs.

When the designer comes up with a premise, she then thinks of what gameplay elements would be required to bring it to life. What game genre would the variant fit into? What actions would the player perform that are fun? How easy would these actions be to learn and perform? Some premises will be very promising, others not so workable. Many variants will be tossed aside before the designer comes up with a viable concept for a game design.

9

FYI   *Sources for Ideas*

If you find yourself running dry of ideas, you should develop some mental exercises to spark your creativity. One approach is to regularly read magazines that have some tangential connection to games such as science digests, science fiction/fantasy magazines, archeological journals, and so on. While reading, stop occasionally to ask yourself: "Can I make a game out of the events discussed this article or story?" Every once in a while, an idea will occur with great gaming potential.

Brainstorming Ideas

Sometimes a designer just draws a blank when trying to think up new concepts or gameplay elements for a game. At such times, it's often useful to hold a brainstorming session to get the creative juices flowing. Anyone on the team who wants to participate should be encouraged to join in. Although management might be interested in participating, no one in authority should be allowed to control the session. A brainstorming session is a creative, not a business, meeting.

FYI *Improvisational Theater Exercises*

Improvisational theater acting is similar to brainstorming, and some of the theatrical warm-up exercises can be used to get a team ready to brainstorm. The Spolin Center (**www.spolin.com**) is dedicated to Viola Spolin, one of the great promoters of improvisational theater. She helped devise a number of "Theatre Games" that have been used by Chicago's famous Second City and other improvisational theater groups. The site has a number of games that can help loosen up a stodgy group of designers, programmers, and artists to get their minds ready to brainstorm.

Ideally, the brainstorming session should be held in an environment where there are fewer chances for interruption. Everyone involved should turn off their pagers and cell phones. Make sure the group has plenty of pens and paper available. It's useful to have a whiteboard or other large surface on which to write ideas as they are offered so that everyone can see them (Figure 9.1). Someone on the team should be assigned the role of scribe to jot down the ideas that arise and put them in writing after the session is over, so they can be distributed to the participants.

There are a few simple guidelines for brainstorming sessions:

■   Avoid criticism—No idea is bad. The idea is to let people's minds range freely, so no one should be judgmental about the ideas that others come up with.

■   Avoid the temptation to steal existing ideas—The idea is to come up with something new, not to regurgitate what already exists.

■   Assign someone to act as moderator—It can quickly become chaotic if everyone throws out ideas randomly, and one or two individuals might hog the spotlight. Someone, generally the producer or senior designer, should act as the moderator to make sure everyone gets a chance to speak. The moderator should not be the one taking notes.

The brainstorming session might wind up with something new, or it might wind up with nothing. Even when it seems that nothing useful comes from the meeting, it will still be useful because it gives the designers the chance to stretch their creative muscles and puts them in a better mindset to be creative.

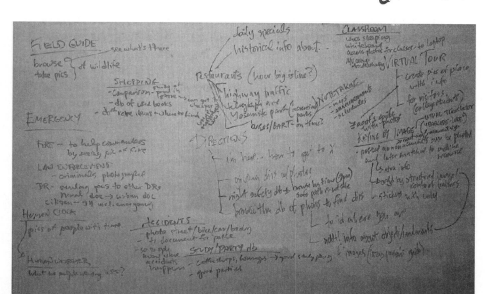

FIGURE 9.1 This whiteboard shows the results of a brainstorming session at the University of California, Berkeley.

IN THE TRENCHES: Warm-Up Exercises

Before diving into the session, it's worth the effort to take a few minutes to get everyone's mind working. A number of books offer warm-up exercises for brainstorming sessions and some improvisational theater techniques can be employed as well.

One simple word association exercise requires only a bouncing ball. Everyone in the session stands in a circle. The moderator has the ball at the start and says any word that pops to mind while bouncing the ball gently to another participant. The person receiving the ball tries to come up with another word that is somehow associated with the first. For example, if the moderator started with "orange," the second person might say "juice." The second person then bounces the ball randomly to someone else, repeating the word he or she just spoke, and the third person tries to come up with another associative word (for example, "squeeze").

The exercise can go on for 5 to 10 minutes until everyone is warmed up. It's important that the ball be thrown randomly so that everyone stays on their toes throughout the exercise; it's also important to encourage people to always say the first thing that pops into

▶▶ CONTINUED ON NEXT PAGE

▶▶ CONTINUED

their mind rather than try to think of an answer. There are no right or wrong answers in this exercise and it should not be considered a competition. It's simply a way to stretch the mind and improve the way people make connections between ideas.

In another exercise to get the team thinking about games in particular, the moderator asks the members to shout out game genres and writes them on the whiteboard. (There are a limited number, so this shouldn't take long.) When the genres are exhausted, the scribe writes the genres' names on paper and then cuts up the paper so that one genre name appears on each piece. Then the moderator asks for fiction genres (horror, science fiction, romance, detective, and so on), again writing them on the whiteboard as the team shouts out their names. Meanwhile, the scribe writes down the fiction genres on a paper and cuts them into individual strips. The game genres are put into one container and the fiction genres are put into another. The moderator mixes the papers and draws one scrap from each container. The team then spends 15 to 20 minutes trying to design a game that matches the combination. This approach can lead to some very interesting ideas—the wilder the combination, the more fun it is to come up with gameplay elements.

Research and Notes

After a game idea has been selected, the designer should do extensive research on the topic. If the subject matter is "real"—say, for example, a historical subject or simulation topic—the designer can use the Internet to look up references on the topic. It can take a while to sift through the many Web sites that might be devoted to a given subject, but the effort can pay off handsomely if several Web sites are devoted to the subject matter. In addition, the designer should acquire books and articles on the subject either by purchasing them or borrowing them from a library. There might also be movies and documentaries about the subject, although you should be wary of any fictional depiction of historical events.

For fictional subjects, the matter can be a bit trickier. There can be a number of novels on a given genre (such as science fiction, horror, or fantasy), so a designer can get lost in reading and spend time that should be devoted to design on more and more "research" instead. In addition, there will likely be films and television shows and perhaps comics and graphic novels that cover the same subject. These are all rich sources for helping to visualize the final design. Most likely, there will be games based on the given theme to check out as well.

A company should be willing to offset a designer's research expenses because it can be expensive to find and collect materials, especially source

Caution

Plagiarism

When doing research for a game, the designer should take care to keep from plagiarizing published materials. Not only is it reprehensible to steal the work of others and claim it as one's own, it can lead to lawsuits.

materials. The company should consider building its own library of source materials and make sure that the materials it acquires are protected. The team can find itself continually referring to these materials during the production process, and there might be add-ons and sequels to design as well.

A designer should keep meticulous notes during research, although this is, as Hamlet says, "a custom more honour'd in the breach than the observance." If nothing else, the designer should make the effort to note where materials came from. She might need to refer back to the notes frequently during production, and it is a waste of time if she has to retrace her steps to find a source. At the end of a project, the designer should put all her notes into a research folder (making several backup copies) so they can be referred to whenever the need arises, and you can be sure the need will always arise after the designer tosses old notes away.

Pitch Paper

When the designer has an idea worked out, he writes it in a pitch paper to present to management. The *pitch paper*—also called a *high concept paper*—encapsulates the central gameplay of the design in a few paragraphs. It is not an exhaustive description of the game; the idea is to get management hooked on the central premise of the game and green light further development of the idea.

The pitch paper is one way a company can separate good ideas from copycat and uninteresting concepts. Companies often encourage all staff members to submit ideas for games because no one knows where the next great idea might come from. Some companies host open brainstorming sessions where anyone can attend—again with the idea that a good idea can come from an unexpected source.

The design staff is expected to come up with ideas as part of their job, of course, but there's no guarantee that their ideas will nose out other suggestions just because they are designers. Someone who has a good idea but has difficulty expressing it should try to find a champion among the design staff to write up her ideas and present them. Anyone who comes up with a good idea should be well rewarded by the company—although the reward might take the form of praise and credit for the idea in the final product instead of cash or a bonus.

Once upon a time, an independent developer could get a contract for a game just by doing a good pitch to a publisher. Faced with the current soaring production costs and extended milestone schedules, however, few (if any) publishers are willing to fund a developer just for an idea. It is not worth the effort for a small developer—or an individual—to send a pitch paper to a publisher in hopes of getting money to develop the idea into a game. Many companies will not even look at unsolicited game ideas for fear of being sued and will return such materials unread. Most companies require a designer, either a staff member or an independent, to sign a ***nondisclosure agreement*** (known as an NDA) that protects them from legal hassles. Then they *might* be willing to look at a game idea. Because it is easy to come up with ideas; however, there is a good chance that a game company will already have some similar idea in-house.

> ## FYI — *Nondisclosure Agreements*
>
> A ***nondisclosure agreement*** (NDA, also called ***confidential disclosure agreement***) is a legal contract between two parties that allows them to share information with restrictions. Most game companies require outsiders to sign NDAs as a matter of course to protect their intellectual properties and trade secrets. As a legal contract, the game company can sue the outsider if they disclose any secrets learned during negations or conversations with company employees. It also generally includes language to protect the game company in the event they decide not to pursue a working relationship with the outsider but later publish a game that is similar to the idea the outsider submitted. Essentially, an NDA protects the game company more than it protects the outsider. Anyone who is asked to sign an NDA would be well advised to show it to a lawyer first to make sure he doesn't give up anything important.

The person who actually writes up the pitch should show the idea to other people in the company for feedback—especially the marketing department and producer corps. A marketing executive or producer who likes the idea can become an evangelist and promote the idea to the rest of management. The writer might also learn a thing or two about the market for such an idea and be able to revise the pitch so it has a better chance of acceptance by the management.

A designer never throws away a pitch that doesn't sell immediately. The idea might be ahead of its time, or it might be seen as too expensive to build. Eventually, the idea might come back to life if it really is good, or the person proposing the idea might mull over the concept and rework it in a more interesting way. Good ideas never have to die if their owners believe in them firmly enough.

Structure of the Pitch Paper

A pitch paper is a short document that should be no longer than one to two pages. The idea is to encapsulate the idea of the game and give a sense of what is new and exciting about the idea. The focus of the paper is on the high concept—the heart and soul of the game—so an extended discussion of the game mechanics or the backstory is out of place. The pitch should be short and sweet and to the point.

The following sections outline one method for structuring a pitch paper.

High Concept (Header)   This brief statement summarizes the core of the game in ten to twenty words or less. It often appears at the top of the paper instead of a title. Think of the high concept as a personal ad to sell the concept. It should evoke strong emotions in the reader and make them want to grab the game and play it. Advertising headlines—whether print ads, movie posters, or comic books—are a good reference for the writing style of the high concept. In fact, a really good high concept might become the advertising blurb used by the marketing department to promote the game.

If the writer can grab the reader's attention with the high concept, there's a good chance the person will read several paragraphs. If the idea is good, the reader will then continue reading the whole paper. If the reader reads the entire paper, there is a better chance that the game will get the go ahead for further development. Because there is so much riding on it, it can be difficult to come up with the high concept, so this might be the last thing written after the designer determines what is "hottest" about the game idea. The high concept should not refer to other games ("An action game like *Legend of Zelda* meets *Half-Life*, but set in sewers.") but should stand alone ("Only you and your Bow of Cleanliness can destroy the mutant King Rat in his underground lair.").

First Paragraph   There's a good chance that the person reading the pitch paper, busy as he or she may be, will only pay attention to the first paragraph, so it must convey the essence of gameplay. The first sentence is the most important. It should tell the reader the game genre, the fictional genre, the central gameplay element, and the goal of the game. It also should be short—20 words or less. The information does not have to be rote ("This is a science fiction shooter where the player kills monsters on a moon of Jupiter."), but can be conveyed within the context of the game setting ("A Space Marine trapped on Callisto Space Station must destroy hordes of mutant were-rabbits before they reach Earth!").

The second sentence can give a very short summary of the overall story, if one exists, so the reader will understand the basic game situation and its overall tone (serious, comic, adrenaline-pumping, and so on). For a game without a story, the second sentence can describe the main gameplay element, especially if it is new or different. Likewise, the third sentence can highlight another important selling point; for example, the game might have multiplayer features, come with a world editor, or debut an exciting new technology. Another sentence might point to a successful product similar to the new game.

The first paragraph can conclude with three basic targets:

- Target audience (such as young males, age 18–35)
- Target game platform (game console, PC, Game Boy Advance)

Caution

Writing Style

Keep to the active voice and use lots of action words when writing a pitch paper. Don't waste time with a lot of adjectives and adverbs. The tone should be like a sales pitch, although not shrill or screaming. Each paragraph should be short—three to five sentences.

- Target Entertainment Software Ratings Board (ESRB) rating (EC for early childhood, E for everyone, E10+ for everyone 10 and older, T for teen, M for mature, and AO for adults only)

This first paragraph is packed with information, but even the most harried executive should be able to stop reading at this point and still have a good sense of what the game is about.

Second Paragraph In the second paragraph, the writer should give enough background information for the reader to understand the world of the game. If it's a storytelling game, for example, the writer could describe the events leading up to the start of the game as well as the background information of what is really happening similar to the following:

> *The evil vizier Oglard has tricked the young prince into thinking Princess Moonflower has betrayed him, when in fact, the evil wizard has concocted her kidnapping so he can marry her in secret. Unbeknownst to the vizier, the cosmic demon Ak-dah-mer has switched places with the princess and will be unleashed upon the unsuspecting world when the rite of marriage temporarily opens a rift between the demon dimension and Earth.*

For a strategy or simulation game, the second paragraph can include information that is central to the situation being depicted in the game. For example, a war game might include a short history of a battle, the participants, and its importance to world history. A simulation could discuss the factors that drive the simulation such as the importance of managing money as the mayor of a city. A puzzle game could detail the central problem, give the rules of play, and explain how to win. A racing game could talk about the tracks where the races will take place and discuss the technology of the vehicles.

Third/Fourth Paragraphs (or More) Now that the background has been explained, the designer can turn to gameplay and other important elements that will make the game profitable. It's time to summarize the most important gameplay elements—what the player does that's fun. The dull, repetitive parts such as inventory management, resource allocation, and other bookkeeping tasks should be skipped unless they are central to the player's enjoyment of the game (although it's hard to imagine they would be). Each gameplay element should be given its own paragraph and explained in enough detail so that the reader will understand not only what the player does but why the activity is fun.

Fifth Paragraph (or More) The last third of the paper can discuss any secondary points of interest that may apply. For example, if the design will include an emerging technology (lighting, AI, physics, and so on) that is gaining attention, the writer should discuss how it will affect gameplay and the player's

FIGURE 9.2 3D Realm's Max Payne (2001) has a film noir look that gives it a unique graphic style. When pitching the idea for such a game, the designer should discuss how important the art style is for setting the dark mood of the game.

9

immersion in the game world. The writer might also discuss the graphics style envisaged if it is different or unusual (such as the film noir look of 3D Realm's *Max Payne* [2001], shown in Figure 9.2). The writer might also discuss what licenses might need to be acquired for the game, perhaps a popular cartoon character or a movie tie-in or the music of a rock band.

Penultimate Paragraph The writer can discuss marketing concerns near the end of the paper. For a story-based game, there might be a discussion of why the characters and story in the game can become important intellectual property for the company that might appear in sequels and add-ons. The writer might show that the property could be used in other game genres (for example, Nintendo's Mario as an adventurer *and* a kart-racing driver) or even cross over to other media (such as Laura Croft or *Doom*). The writer can also compare the suggested game to similar games in the genre that have done particularly well and show why the idea will also succeed.

This paragraph can also be used to discuss any outside technology the company will need to create the game, such as an existing game engine or set of development tools. The writer should explain how using outside technology will either make the game better or speed up its development.

Final Paragraph   The pitch paper should conclude with a short recap of the game concept and a final sales pitch to emphasize why it will succeed. It is well worth the time to come up with a brilliant *capper* for the pitch that will stick in the readers' minds and point them toward approving the next step of development.

Bullet Points   The pitch paper might include some points that need to be mentioned yet do not merit a full paragraph. These can be included as bullet points at the end of the paper. They should be interesting to read and treated as selling points for the idea. For example, the writer might want to talk about special combination moves, interesting missions, unusual weapons, or the many hidden areas on the playfield. Other points might discuss special visual effects, commissioned music, and other technical issues. The key point to remember is that the bullet points should not be just simple lists of things. For example, instead of saying, "Six main characters," the writer could say, "Six heroic characters from all points of the galaxy, each having unique skills that range from underwater wrestling to moon walking somersaults to intergalactic cattle rustling."

Pitching the Idea

Some companies offer the opportunity to pitch ideas with presentations in addition to the pitch paper, so the writer (who could be a designer, an artist, a programmer or any other company employee) might want to create a presentation using PowerPoint or similar software. One advantage of such a presentation is that the writer can include visual references to help the audience understand what other products are similar to the proposed game. For example, if one of the main selling points is the visual look of the world or the characters, the writer should try to include sketch artwork by staff artists as a major selling point in the presentation.

The presentation should be structured similar to the pitch paper itself and designed to reinforce the writer's concept. A clever writer should be able to use the program's graphics capabilities to present dynamic visualizations of the gameplay. Again, the writer should think of the presentation as a sales pitch and try to make it as dynamic and interesting as possible.

FYI   *Toastmasters International*

Presentations to management occur frequently in the game industry, whether pitching an idea, discussing a game proposal or design document, or updating the product's status at a quarterly review. Being

CONTINUED ON NEXT PAGE

>> CONTINUED

able to communicate clearly and effectively at such times is vitally important. If you feel nervous about speaking in public, you should consider joining Toastmasters International (**www.toastmasters.org**), an organization dedicated to helping people speak effectively and improve their communication skills.

After the paper and presentation have been submitted, the writer might have to defend the concept in a company meeting. If the writer truly believes the concept is interesting and commercially promising, she should be able to convince any doubters that it is worth pursuing. When preparing for the meeting, the writer should make copies of her pitch paper and PowerPoint presentation for everyone who will attend. If time allows, the writer might ask someone to help create a demonstration of the game using a prototyping tool such as Macromedia Director. Also, the writer may want to compile sales data from other successful games to demonstrate the financial reasons that the company should select the idea.

If the company's management likes the idea, they may approve the next step of the process—the game proposal. However, a writer should not be discouraged if the company turns down the idea. There can be many reasons why the company can't or won't support the efforts needed to create a game proposal, including the following:

- The idea isn't strong enough.

- There are too many similar products on the market.

- It will be too expensive.

- It will take too much time to create.

For every ten pitches, a company might select only one or two to develop into a full game proposal.

9

Game Proposal

The next step in fleshing out a game design is to write a ***game proposal,*** which is a halfway step between the pitch paper and the game design document. It allows the designer to flesh out the play in the game while marketing does some research on the topic. Some companies might skip this step and proceed directly to the game design document, but doing so can result in a designer's being tied up on the project for many months without knowing whether the game will sell.

In the game proposal, the designer discusses the gameplay elements in some detail, although not exhaustively. Where the pitch paper tries to crystallize the game idea in a few paragraphs, the game proposal is more leisurely and discusses the main gameplay elements in greater detail. The document also tries to capture the emotional response the designer wants players to get from the real game. Thus, if the game is comic in nature, the proposal should be written in a way to make the reader smile and laugh. If the game is about uncovering a mystery, the proposal can be set up as a standard mystery with clues scattered throughout and the answer to the mystery appearing on the last page.

A full-blown game proposal requires at least one designer working full time on the project and might require the assistance of several 2D artists for the concept work. A senior programmer might also be called on in an advisory capacity to help the designer determine what can and can't be done in code. The writer of the game proposal is usually an experienced game designer who not only understands the mechanics of gameplay but is also able to explain how things will interact and work.

It can take several months to complete the proposal, depending on the complexity of the game. It can be relatively easy to explain a puzzle game in 8 to 10 pages, whereas a role-playing or real-time strategy game might require 30 pages or more to adequately discuss its many game elements. Whatever the complexity of the game, it is essential for the designer to talk about the most important gameplay elements in some detail so the audience will clearly understand where the fun is.

One of the most important goals of the game proposal is to get the marketing and sales staff interested in the project. The designer should talk to the decision makers in these departments to get their feedback on the idea. Many companies require a ***marketing analysis*** as part of the final game proposal, so the designer should try to find someone in the marketing department who shares the same passion for the proposed game idea to help sell it. The marketing department should be asked to research competing games. They can look for games that are similar to the proposed design to see how well they have sold and to help determine if there is a hole in the marketplace that the new game can fill. Because it can take years to complete the production on the game, trying to predict the success of the new game can be iffy at best. Many things can happen between the proposal and the final delivery: buyers might grow tired of the genre, the target game platform might disappear, or the company might run out of money. Still, marketing research is an important step in determining the likelihood of the new game's succeeding.

It is also important for the sales department to give their opinion of the game idea based on their knowledge of the current game market and the sales estimates for competitive products. If they project good sales numbers for the project, management might be more willing to approve the creation of the game design document.

Game proposals are usually evaluated by management (including marketing, sales, and finance) to determine if a project is strong enough to merit further development. A proposal might have to be rewritten several times before it is finally approved or rejected. Because the next step—writing the game design document—requires a considerable investment by the company, only a limited number of game proposals are generally approved and funded.

Structure of the Game Proposal

The size and structure of a game proposal will vary depending on the subject and how much the designer has to explain to the reader. Generally, the focus is not on the nitty-gritty of how the game mechanics actually work but rather on an overview of gameplay and what the player does that is fun. The reader should walk away with a good sense of how the game will actually play.

The following sections outline one method for structuring the sections of a game proposal.

Introduction   The first few paragraphs should encapsulate the basic concept of the game. In fact, the designer can reword the pitch paper as the first part of the introduction. The introduction should refresh the memory of readers who are familiar with the game and explain the basic concept of the game for those who aren't familiar with the original pitch.

As with the pitch paper, the opening paragraph should contain:

- The basic concept of the game (including game and fictional genres) in 20 words or less

- A one- or two-sentence background or history (if necessary)

- The main gameplay elements

- The target platform, audience, and ESRB rating

The rest of the introduction should expand on the information from the pitch paper about gameplay elements. The designer might then complete the section by comparing the game to similar products in the genre and referring the reader to the marketing section.

Background Fiction/History   If the game has a story or historical basis of some kind, the next section can give a capsule summary of the situation at the start of play and of what the player will discover during the course of play. The designer might break this material into two parts: backstory and game plot. *Backstory* refers to the events that lead up to the start of the game, which are often shown as an introductory animated sequence. Usually, the main villain (*antagonist*) sets up the basic conflict that the player's character (*protagonist*) must resolve by the end of the game. In addition, depending on the complexity of the story, there might be information that neither the protagonist nor the antagonist is aware of but that is central to the game plot, and this information should be shared with the reader. The *game plot* is a summary of what the player discovers as he travels around the world and interacts with other characters.

For a reality-based product such as a war-game or a real-time strategy game, this section can give the history of the situation or explain what parts of reality the simulation is trying to imitate. The designer has to give only enough information for the reader to understand what is happening in the game, including why the opponents are fighting or what everyday activities are being simulated.

These background materials should convince management that the designer knows the topic sufficiently to design a game about it, but they should be kept to a page or so. The proposal should focus primarily on the fun elements of the game and not on its fiction or history.

Objective/Goal The next section should explain the game's goal. How does the player win the game (or lose it)? If the objective is something as simple as "score as many points as possible," then it can be stated in a sentence. If the goal is more vague, such as build the best railroad possible, the designer might need to go into more explanation about what standards would determine the "best" railroad.

Gameplay Elements Now that the reader knows the goal of the game, the designer can discuss the gameplay elements and how they help the player reach that goal. As explained in the preceding chapter, the designer needs to discuss several gameplay elements in detail, so this section of the proposal is usually the longest. However, the discussion of gameplay does not have to include every variation of a theme; for example, the proposal does not need to discuss every weapon or nonplayer character in the game. At this point, the design is still being worked out, so the explanation of the details will be tentative at best. Still, the designer should think out which major gameplay elements will appear in the game and how much time the player will devote to each one.

This section of the proposal should be structured to present the most interesting gameplay features first, with less interesting play elements receiving secondary emphasis. Remember, the purpose of the game proposal is to sell the basic concept to management, so emphasizing the fun elements is important. A few points the designer might wish to talk about in this section are:

- Is there something new and different about the combat system?

- Does the product include both multiplayer and solitaire versions, and if so, what is most interesting about each version?

- How difficult is the game? Can players select their preferred difficulty level?

- How much replay value does the game have, and what would make players want to replay it a number of times?

- If the game is based on licensed material (for example, a movie or television show), what gameplay elements in particular will capture the popular features of the character or situation? Also, how will the game differ from the licensed property so players will feel they are getting something new and different (Figures 9.3 and 9.4)?

FIGURE 9.3 The Sand People posed a major threat to Luke Skywalker in *Star Wars IV: A New Hope*.

9

FIGURE 9.4 In LucasArts' *Star Wars: Knights of the Old Republic* (2003), the player gets to fight the Sand People on the planet Tatooine. The game extends the Star Wars universe and lets players interact with creatures from the original movies.

FYI | *Licenses and Games*

Movie studios realize that games can be very profitable, and therefore, they charge hefty licensing fees for their properties. Unfortunately, game companies sometimes spend so much time and money acquiring a license to develop a game based on a movie that they don't have enough time or money remaining to make as good a game as they might like. In addition, there is usually only a small window of opportunity to get the game out in time to capitalize on the movie's publicity. A game that ships months after the movie disappears from theaters might have no audience. Fortunately, more game companies realize the importance of having tie-in products appear at the same time as the movies do, as witnessed by the success of Activision's *Spider-Man 2* (2004) and Electronic Arts' *Harry Potter and the Goblet of Fire* (2005) and *The Lord of the Rings: The Return of the King* games.

▶▶ CONTINUED ON NEXT PAGE

>> **CONTINUED**

Movie studios are always looking for interesting characters and stories to turn into films, and games have become a source for such properties over the past decade. The improvements in graphics have resulted in much more realistic-looking characters who have unique appearances and distinctive personality traits, as well as more highly detailed game world backgrounds. Still, most movies based on games, from *Super Mario Bros.: The Movie* (1993) to *Doom* (2005), have not done particularly well at the box office. The game characters don't currently have the same depth of characterization as comic book characters such as Spider-Man and Batman who have successfully appeared in films.

Game Controls   After the gameplay elements have been discussed, the proposal should cover the first approximation of how the controls will work and what will appear on the major interface screens. The controls can be presented in a simple diagram or chart, with each key or button corresponding to a game action (Figure 9.5). If the plan is to release the product on multiple platforms,

DOOM 3 CONTROLS

Movement	1st Control	2nd Control		Attack/Look	1st Control	2nd Control
Forward	W	Up arrow		Attack	Control	Mouse 1
Back	S	Down arrow		Previous Weapon	[	Mouse wheel up
Move left	A			Next weapon	]	Mouse wheel down
Move right	D			Reload	R	
Jump	Spacebar	Mouse 2		Look up	Page Down	
Crouch	C			Look down	Delete	
Turn left	Left arrow			Mouse look	J	
Turn right	Right arrow			Center view	End	
Strafe	Alt			Zoom view	Mouse 3	
Run	Shift			PDA/Score	Tab	
Weapons	1st Control	2nd Control		Other Controls	1st Control	2nd Control
Fists	1			Drop weapon	Backspace	
Pistol	2			Chat	T	
Shotgun	3			Team chat	Y	
Machine gun	4			Vote yes	F1	
Chaingun	5			Vote no	F2	
Grenades	6			Ready	F3	
Plasma gun	7			Quick save	F5	
Rocket launcher	8			Toggle team	F6	
BFG-9000	9			Spectate	F7	
Chainsaw	0			Quick load	F9	
Soulcube	Q			Screenshot	F12	
Flashlight	F					

FIGURE 9.5 The game proposal should include a simple diagram or chart that indicates how the controls work in a game, in this case id Software's *Doom 3* (2004).

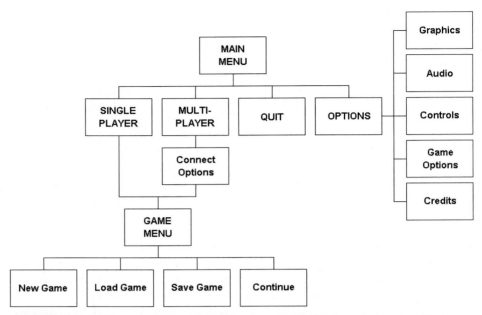

FIGURE 9.6 This schematic shows the interrelationships of various interface screens the player encounters between starting up the product and entering the main game playfield screen.

the designer might want to include all control pad/keyboard/joystick configurations to show that the game will work as envisaged on all platforms.

The designer can also include a simple schematic of the most important playfield interface screens (movement, combat, inventory, and so on) to explain the main functions for each screen. In addition, a simple flowchart or diagram can indicate how the various screens will interrelate to one other during play (Figure 9.6). The game proposal does not have to go into excruciating detail at this point because the interface mechanics will be worked out in the game design document.

Art Specification   This section should discuss the general style of the graphics envisioned for the game. The first topic to discuss is the overall look and feel of the game environment. For example, is it cartoonish, grittily realistic, cyberpunk, or horrific? Is the environment dark and dangerous, light and airy, or psychedelic and eye-popping (Figures 9.7 and 9.8)? It's a good idea to include 2D concept art in the proposal to give readers a sense of the desired art style. A staff artist can create the concept materials, or the designer might find examples of similar graphics. Materials from outside the company can be included in the document as long as they are credited to the original source and not distributed externally; otherwise, the company should set up a licensing agreement with the material's copyright owner.

FIGURE 9.7 The art style in Atari's *Taz: Wanted* (2002) is light, airy, and cartoony, as befits a Warner Brothers cartoon character.

FIGURE 9.8 The style in Atari's *The Matrix: Path of Neo* (2005) is psychedelic, dark and dangerous, matching the mood of the movie series.

The designer should include descriptions of the major characters appearing in the game as well as the major locations. There should be one or more pieces of art per description. Some of the more interesting villains and monsters should also be included. In addition, any exciting and unusual items that will appear in the game (weird weaponry, fantastic vehicles, mystical armor, and so on) can also be described and pictured. However, the designer should be selective about the materials appearing in this section because it is very likely that these objects will change considerably before the product finally ships. The idea is to whet the reader's appetite for the product's exciting graphics.

Audio Specifications   Similar to the art specification, this section discusses the general style of the music and sound in the game. Where will the music be light and bright, dark and mysterious, military and blaring, or ominous and threatening? What type of musical instruments (heavy rock guitars, symphonic tympani, country music banjos, and so on) would sound best? The designer can refer the reader to other well-known music of a similar style, either in games or by composer. It also helps to include links to Internet sites that allow people to sample such music.

The sound specification covers both audio special effects and voiceovers. Audio is very important for a product, and the designer should make the effort to describe how the sound effects reinforce the mood of the game. The designer might want to set up an internal Web site where audio samples are located to help the reader understand the mood and style of the audio effects. Likewise, when discussing voiceovers, the designer can point to well-known actors who perfectly define what the characters should sound like. After all, the game proposal is just a wish list at this point, so the designer can cast anyone he wants for the voice talent.

Ports to Multiple Platforms   If the game is intended for several game platforms, the designer should discuss how each version is different. Some gameplay elements will have to be left out of certain platforms or new ones might be added. The changes in inputs could also be discussed in the section on game controls (as mentioned previously). This section might also include a discussion of how the technological limitations of each platform will likely affect gameplay. The designer might want to stress her familiarity with how the different platforms work to show that she knows what challenges each one offers.

Estimated Schedule   The designer should work with a producer, a senior programmer, and an artist to come up with a semirealistic schedule for the product. The schedule should consist of three sections:

1. The rest of the preproduction phase, during which the game design document will be written

2. The technical review phase, during which the art and programming teams will analyze the product and work out their schedules

3. The production phase, during which the game is developed and implemented according to a milestone schedule

In addition, this section should include a rough first budget for the game based on estimated manpower and equipment requirements. A designer would be wise to pad the schedule and budget as much as possible so there will be room to negotiate with management. A designer does not want to commit a team that has not yet been selected to an impossible schedule and unreasonable budget. At this point, the schedule is mostly a guesstimate, but it does indicate to management how many resources will likely be needed to complete the game.

Marketing Analysis

Before a publisher's management will be willing to invest millions of dollars in a product that will take years to build, they have to believe that the game is commercially practical. A designer might be able to gather some information about the marketplace and determine how well similar games have fared, but it will be difficult for him to make an accurate sales forecast or predict how retailers will respond to the title. There are marketing information companies that gather sales figures for the game industry and sell it to publishers (for example, NPD Funworld), but the sales data is expensive and might be more than an independent developer can afford. The designer can also check various Web sites (such as Gamasutra and Gamestats, which are devoted to the game industry) to learn what games are selling well on a weekly basis, but these sites usually don't publish actual sales figures.

Therefore, the publisher relies on those departments that deal with marketing and sales to help determine if the game idea will sell. Marketing can help determine if the topic is popular, and sales can estimate the number of copies the game will sell, assuming it is executed professionally and ships when scheduled. The designer will find that marketing and sales can be valuable allies when selling the game idea—if they know what the game is about and why the designer thinks it will sell. Note that although the marketing and sales staff will provide the information, it is usually up to the designer to incorporate it into the proposal.

> **Caution**
>
> ### Don't Go Overboard
>
> It is important for the designer to remember while working on a proposal that it can be shot down at any time. The design proposal is just that: a pitch for a new game idea. It is not a design specification for a complete game.

9

FYI   *Research Companies*

Gathering information about the sales of various game titles and determining the number of copies each game has sold are time-consuming activities, so most game publishers subscribe to one or more research companies to obtain regular reports about the financial health of the

▶▶ CONTINUED ON NEXT PAGE

>> **CONTINUED**

industry. IDC (**www.idc.com**) and DFC Intelligence (**www.dfcint.com**) are two such companies. The reports themselves can cost thousands of dollars, but large game companies use this information to help decide what projects to approve for full production.

When writing the marketing analysis section of the game proposal, the designer should consider discussing these topics:

- **Target Market:** The target market is defined by the game genre, the platform, and the intended audience. The designer should define each of these components of the market in some detail and point out similar titles that have sold well. The game's genre should be appropriate to the platform and the intended age range. For example, complex simulations do not sell well on video consoles because the interfaces are so involved and the intended audience is limited to adults who are not willing to invest time to learn a complex game. An action game might sell better on video consoles than personal computers because the intended audience is preteens, who are more likely to play their games on consoles. The designer can rely on the expertise of the marketing and sales departments to help determine the best market for the new game.

- **Top Performers:** The designer should list the top performers in the market that have target audiences similar to those for the new design. Actual sales numbers will help to emphasize their success. Also, the designer should consider listing the sequels and add-ons to an original product that extend the life of the intellectual property (such as Nintendo's Mario, who has appeared in many different guises, as shown in Figures 9.9 through 9.12). If similar products have successfully crossed into other media such as movies, comics, and toys, the new concept might also do the same, thus offering other sources of revenue to offset production costs.

- **Feature Comparison:** The designer should break down the selling features of the top sellers and compare them to those in the new design. What made the other games popular, and how does the current design compare to them? What were the weaknesses of the other games, and how does the current design eliminate them? The end result, of course, is that the designer's new game should address the problems of competitor products and result in a much stronger product.

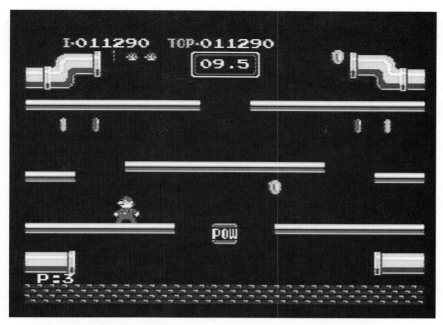

FIGURE 9.9 Nintendo's *Mario Bros.* for the NES (1983).

FIGURE 9.10 Mario as he appeared in *The Super Mario Bros. Super Show* syndicated cartoon show (developed by DiC Entertainment, 1989).

9

FIGURE 9.11 Mario appeared in the Game Boy #3 comic book.

- **Competitors:** The designer should describe upcoming releases by other publishers that could compete with the new design, either in gameplay or in release dates. Many game sites discuss upcoming releases by other companies, and the designer should be aware of these products and how they may compete for the consumers' cash. However, as project schedules get longer and longer, it becomes increasingly more difficult to predict what games will be competitive two or three years down the line. Still, the more a designer knows about the potential competing products that are under development, the better she will be able to make changes to the design to differentiate her product from others.

A designer should realize that a brilliant idea for a game in and of itself will not guarantee approval by management. Many companies come up with brilliant game ideas, but the products never make it to the shelves, either

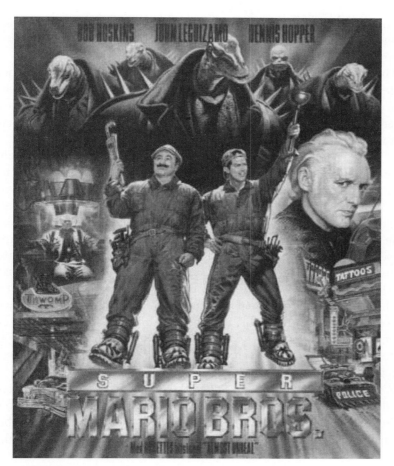

FIGURE 9.12 Bob Hoskins portrayed Mario in the 1993 movie, *Super Mario Bros.*

because sales projections aren't good enough or because the game winds up trying to compete against other blockbusters released at the same time.

The Approval Process

By the time the game proposal is finished and accepted for further development, the designer will probably have presented the concept to management a number of times and revised the document repeatedly along the way. The process can feel burdensome, but a designer should look at each review as a chance to polish the concept and clear up any misinterpretations about how the game will play and why it will sell.

Most large companies have special committees that meet regularly to review game proposals. These groups usually consist of staff members who understand the game production process in detail (producers, designers, technical director, art director, and an executive or two) as well as someone from marketing and sales. The panel grills the proposal writer on the ideas presented, offers suggestions and criticisms, and usually asks for another revision.

The review process can take several months, but the designer should not view the review process as some kind of Spanish Inquisition trying to suck the life out of the game idea. Instead, he should see it as a chance to clearly and repeatedly explain why the game idea works and why it should be funded for further development.

A wise designer anticipates problems in the design such as competitive proposals, financing concerns, budget and scheduling expectations, prejudices of committee members, and historical misfires. These concerns should be addressed proactively to disarm criticisms or negative reactions by the panel. One of the worst faults for a designer is being inflexible to changes. No one has all the answers about a project as complex as a video game, and the designer should be ready to listen to advice from others who are willing to share insights gleaned from years of successes and failures in the industry.

Although a designer should be fond of his proposal, he shouldn't tie his ego to it. There is a very good chance that a given game proposal will be turned down—no matter how good it is. For every ten game proposals that are considered, only one or two will be approved for the next step. The designer should never take it as a personal affront that a proposal is denied. The next one might be exactly what management wants.

When a game proposal is accepted, the designer can expect to take the game idea to the next step: the game design document (GDD). At this point, the company is committing itself to a hefty outlay of money and resources because a designer and several other team members will be required to work on the document. The company is betting that the team will be able to refine the design over several months and present it in precise detail for approval. After defining the overall scope of the game in the proposal, the designer and the team should know exactly what they plan to build and should be ready to detail their final vision in the game design document.

Summary

Coming up with ideas for new games is easy; implementing those ideas is hard. Today's games take a long time to build and require many resources, so publishers want to make sure that their products are likely to succeed and make a profit. Therefore, they normally require that a new game concept be thoroughly thought out before agreeing to fund its production.

Many game ideas are pitched, but few are chosen. A designer might have to pitch several ideas to management before receiving a nod of approval to expand one into a game proposal. The process of pitching an idea and then creating a more detailed proposal takes time, but it allows the designer and some of the team that might work on the project to think through what will be involved in bringing the idea to life. It is well worth the time to "sell" the concept to the marketing and sales staff because if they like an idea they can be powerful allies in convincing management that the concept is worth getting the green light for further production.

A designer should put as much effort as possible into creating a professional and compelling game proposal that will convince the company managers the idea is worthwhile and merits funding for further development. However, the designer should keep in mind that many proposals will be submitted and only a few will be selected. The game proposal allows the designer and the team the opportunity to define their vision in detail and understand the essence of what they plan to build. By the time they start work on the game design document, they should be prepared to explain in great detail exactly what the finished product will look like.

Test Your Skills

MULTIPLE CHOICE QUESTIONS

1. What are some of the key things a designer should do to inspire new game ideas? (Select all that apply.)

    A. Continuously learn about things.

    B. Look for interesting information from every available resource.

    C. Spend spare time playing only other video games.

    D. Keep a notepad to write down ideas.

    E. Create interesting and unusual combinations.

    F. Throw out all notes as soon as the are written into a GDD.

2. Which of the following applies to a pitch paper?

    A. It distills the idea of a game.

    B. It is an exhaustive description of the game.

    C. It is reviewed by playtesting teams.

    D. It includes all of the game elements.

3. What are pitch papers are used for?

    A. To pitch ideas to publishers.

    B. To help internal pitching of game concepts to find team leads.

    C. To get marketing to approve the game.

    D. To get a signed NDA.

4. Where can game ideas come from? (Select all that apply.)

   A. Designers on a team.

   B. A movie.

   C. Playing other games.

   D. Internal brainstorming sessions.

   E. Anyone in the company.

5. Why should you show your idea to other people in the company? (Select all that apply.)

   A. You might get good suggestions to improve the pitch.

   B. No company will accept a pitch that hasn't been approved by marketing.

   C. A manager might like the idea and help promote it.

   D. You might learn something that could improve the idea.

6. Who evaluates game proposals? (Select all that apply.)

   A. Internal management.

   B. Publishers.

   C. Playtesters.

   D. Producers and designers.

7. What is the difference between a game proposal and a game design document?

   A. A proposal summarizes all the game elements and the GDD fully defines all the elements.

   B. A proposal is used to sell the idea, and a GDD is used to conceptualize the idea to the team.

   C. A GDD is a sales tool taken around by marketing to see if the design is complete and the proposal is used to see if the idea will sell.

   D. A game proposal defines the team and resources, and the GDD defines all the technical requirements.

8. Who should control a brainstorming session?

   A. The company management.

   B. The marketing team.

   C. The design team.

   D. The programming team.

9. What should be the outcome of a brainstorming session?

   A. Eliminate useless or unprofitable ideas.

   B. Determine if an idea is technically feasible.

   C. Take existing ideas and finalize them.

   D. Come up with as many unique ideas as possible.

10. What are the important techniques of a brainstorming session? (Select all that apply.)

    A. Remember that there is no such thing as a bad idea.

    B. Write down everything, whether or not it seems reasonable.

    C. Write down only the things that the group as a whole agrees with.

    D. Make sure there is plenty of paper and pencils for all involved.

11. What should a game proposal include? (Select all that apply.)

    A. A summary of the game design.

    B. A discussion of the ports of the game.

    C. A lengthy and in-depth backstory that explains the game setup.

    D. A sample of the dialogue.

    E. Concept art and sketches.

    F. A summary of market competitors.

EXERCISES

Exercise 9.1: Genre Brainstorming

Select a game genre and a literary fiction genre combination that is as unique as possible. Write a description of how you would overcome the difficulties of combining their elements. For example, how could you get the brooding characters from an Emily Bronte story into a real-time strategy game, which doesn't usually have any characterizations.

Exercise 9.2: Brainstorming Practice

In teams of three or four, run your own brainstorming session. Identify who will lead the meeting and select one person to take notes of the session. Make sure everyone has plenty of paper and writing materials. Use the ideas given in this chapter for relaxing, then create a game concept based on a genre drawn from a hat. Set a target ESRB rating for the game.

Exercise 9.3: Competition Review for Exercise 9.2

Based on the theme selected in Exercise 9.2, find three or four games that might be considered competitors. Select games that have had some sales success. Research the key features of each game; then summarize how your game idea would be the same, differ from, or improve upon each of the key features.

9

Exercise 9.4: Practice Writing a Backstory

For the theme created in Exercise 9.2, write a short (two-paragraph) backstory and a one- to three-paragraph summary of the gameplay for both solitaire and multiplayer play.

Exercise 9.5: Create a Pitch Package

Imagine that you are making a pitch proposal for a tropical action/arcade game on a console. Create the package that you would hand to your company executives. What other things might you consider doing to set the tone or convince the executives to fund the proposal?

DISCUSSION TOPICS

1. What are some techniques or exercises (other than those listed in this chapter) that you might try to relax the team at the beginning of a brainstorming session?

2. One of the basic premises of a brainstorming session is that no idea is bad. How do you, as the session moderator, deal with an idea that you know is not appropriate for the game? How would you deal with a team member who insisted on arguing about ideas?

3. Why is it important for marketing and sales to support your game idea? What can you, as the designer of a concept, do to promote the game to the sales and marketing teams?

4. Discuss the differences in the way horror is used in books, movies, and games. How is it the same? What story elements typical of the genre could be used as a game element?

5. Discuss different avenues of inspiration and research for a game design. How would you research a WWII military combat RTS? What research would you do for a fantasy romance RPG?

Chapter 10

The Game Design Document

Chapter Objectives

After reading this section and completing the exercises, you will be able to do the following:

- Explain what goes into a game design document.
- Structure and write a game design document.
- Explain what materials management is most interested in reading.
- Explain the gameplay mechanics for the programmers.
- Discuss the descriptive elements that interest the art team.

Introduction

After management approves the game proposal, the designer is ready to tackle the first generation of the *game design document* (GDD; also called the *game specification*). This document explains the design in enough detail that the other members of the team can figure out how to build the game. The actual size and complexity of the GDD depends on the game's genre and the number of features that must be included. A simple puzzle game usually requires a smaller document explaining the basic rules of the puzzle and a description of the interface. A sports game might include a quick summary of the sport itself and then focus on other important features unique to the product; for example, the team logos, venues, special sound effects and voiceovers, and special AI routines. A role-playing game is often the most complex game to document because there are so many gameplay elements to describe, an entire world to depict, and an epic story to lay out. As a result, a GDD for such a game can run to hundreds of pages.

For the designer, writing the GDD is one of the loneliest—and most exhilarating—steps of the design process. The designer still has considerable

Caution

Stay Focused

At brainstorming sessions, there is a natural desire for the programmers to get into technical details about the actual implementation of the game and for the artists to jump into character design. No matter how enthusiastic they are about their work, they must remember that the point of such meetings is to discuss the gameplay elements in general.

work to do before the rest of the team is ready to begin their efforts. For the next few months, she will work mostly alone fleshing out the design and filling in the details. At this point, the staff members who will be the team leaders should be identified, although they should not actively begin creating code or artwork yet. Throughout this period, the designer should meet regularly in brainstorming sessions with the team leads and anyone else who might join the team. Everyone involved should be encouraged to offer suggestions about the design, especially regarding trouble areas that the designer has identified. This is a great opportunity to build consensus within the team as to what they will eventually develop.

Purpose of the Game Design Document

The GDD explains the features and function of the product. It continues the process of fleshing out the vision expressed in the pitch paper and game proposal and serves as the culmination of the ideas, criticisms, and discussions to this point. The target audience of the GDD is the team that will build the product, as well as those responsible for approving the game design. It is the foundation upon which the technical and art specifications, as well as the budget and schedule, will be built.

Why all the paperwork? Why spend so much time defining the product when the team could just go ahead and start building something? The simple answer is: to prevent wasted time and effort. Everyone involved in the creation of a video game is an artisan who has developed special skills unique to game creation. Nothing is more frustrating to such people than wasting their time and skills generating assets that are thrown away or repeatedly changed because no one knows exactly what is being created. The GDD helps prevent this wasted effort by providing a blueprint that gives everyone on the team a vision to follow.

The design team should try to encompass as much of the design as possible in the GDD so that the tasks needed to complete the project can be decided upon and put into a reasonable schedule. However, the GDD should never become a straightjacket that prevents future flexibility. Many companies try to design everything in a game during this step, but such an approach allows no leeway for modification. It is likely that some features will change during the actual development based on what the team learns about the game engine's capabilities and player feedback. The technology used in making games changes so fast that being inflexible can make a product dated before it even ships. Assumptions about how the gameplay will turn out can be proven false, and changes might have to be made to get the project back on track. On the other hand, something unexpected and wonderful might appear during production, and the team would be foolish not to capitalize on such serendipity.

FYI *Preventing Feature Creep*

Sometimes it is better to overdesign the product up front, knowing that materials will be cut as shipping time approaches. It's far easier to cut materials than to add them later because adding new materials tends to have a cascading effect where one change forces another to be made, and then another, and so on. Adding extra gameplay elements is called **feature creep,** and it is something the design staff should try to avoid at all costs.

The GDD also serves as an anchor for the team during development. Over time, new employees will be hired or brought onto the project and will have to be brought up to speed on what the project is about. If the GDD is made available on the company's intranet, the new team members can refer to it to see how all the parts will fit together.

Of course, it does no good if only the original GDD is available to review because the design is likely to change over time. Therefore, it is important for the design staff to regularly update the GDD whenever a major change is made to the game. The game design document should be viewed as a living, organic entity that evolves over time. Thus, there are really two versions of the GDD. The first is the *concept* document, which fleshes out the design in as much detail as possible before production begins; this is the version that management agrees to fund to completion. The second is the *production* document, which is continually updated during the production phase to reflect changes in the design. This is the version that should be posted on the intranet as a reference for the team members.

10

The Concept Game Design Document

Before starting the first draft of the GDD, the designer should ask himself "Who will be reading this?" The primary readers will be management— executives, marketing, sales, producers, and senior designers—and the team that will finally build the product. The designer should be aware of the audience and structure the GDD accordingly. Management must learn enough about the game to feel comfortable that it can truly be created as envisaged in the GDD, and the team wants to know what they are expected to build. Unlike the pitch paper and the game proposal, the concept game design document is not a *selling* document. Instead, it breaks the overall game design into bite-size, easily digestible chunks that every reader can understand. As a result, the document can wind up being a bit dry and monotonous because there are so many small details to work out. Nonetheless, it is important to detail every-thing that will go into the game, so it is in turn important for the GDD to be as complete as possible.

Researching the Subject

Before putting words on paper, a designer should know exactly what it is she plans to design, which can require extensive research. Some games require more research than others. A war game set in the real world, for example, might require the designer to spend many hours online or in a library doing research to make sure that the historical facts are accurate. A fantasy game, on the other hand, can be made up whole cloth from the designer's imagination, although she might still need to make extensive notes on the creatures of the world or how the magic works.

Whether real or a fantasy, for a game to work, its world has to be self-consistent. A designer can fill many notepads with ideas or data collected from outside sources. Something such as a flight simulator or sports game might require the designer to walk away from her computer and get out into the real world to take a spin in a jet aircraft (Figures 10.1 and 10.2) or stand in the batter's box during batting practice. One of the joys of being a designer is that you get to learn something different with each new project, and some-times that means experiencing the real thing, "in the flesh."

FIGURE 10.1 The real cockpit of an Su-27 Russian fighter jet.

FIGURE 10.2 The cockpit of an Su-27 jet as it appears in Eagle Dynamics' *Lock-On: Modern Air Combat* (published by Ubisoft in 2003).

Three types of sources of information are useful to the whole team:

- Written information including history and biographies, science fiction and fantasy novels, scientific research papers and theses, sociology and psychology textbooks, and Internet sites devoted to the subject. The designer should have these resources available to show to the team members who have questions about the game topic.

- Visual sources including books, comics, magazines, movies, Web sites, posters, ads, or other artwork. These help the art staff come up with a unified vision for the game.

- Other games, both paper and electronic, that have explored the subject in one way or another. The design staff should be willing to see what topics these games have emphasized and ignored.

What the Concept Game Design Document Is Not . . .

The concept GDD is *not* a novel. Some novice writers get carried away with the background story of the game (especially role-playing games) and create a massive document with elaborate plots that include many incidents and

10

crises. Although the game might have a story that acts as the backbone supporting the gameplay, the story itself is not the game. Management might be interested in the story at first but will soon grow tired of getting nothing but background. The descriptive passages in the GDD can help the art staff create concept sketches for the characters, locations, and items in the game, but if the story is presented in a novelistic format, the artists will soon tire of mining the story for the relevant details. The programmers, on the other hand, will likely skip over the story completely. If the GDD doesn't provide them with the game mechanics, they will create their own—which might be nothing like the designer had in mind. Nobody wants to wade through a GDD the size of *War and Peace*. Ideally, the writer should consider limiting the backstory to an appendix in the GDD.

The concept GDD is *not* a screenplay. Many budding game designers have the itch to make the movie based on their game and skip the game part to go right into the movie script. Likewise, Hollywood writers who understand movies are more likely to write a script treatment for a game instead of an analysis of gameplay. One problem with this approach is that games, of course, are interactive. Therefore, the dialogue branches, with each character having multiple responses arising from different interactions with the player. A screenplay is linear and cannot handle branching storylines and dialogue. Moreover, it's difficult to describe how the gameplay mechanics work in a movie script format. A good GDD might contain a script for voiceovers or a movie sequence, but it should not be the major part of the GDD—only a part of the overall content.

The concept GDD is *not* a technical analysis. This approach is the direct opposite of the mistakes discussed previously; here, the designer spends all his time talking about gameplay and ignoring the look and feel of the game. A designer's job is to describe how the game should play, not to tell the programmers how to do their jobs. Besides, most designers are nowhere near as technically knowledgeable as programmers about the many code modules that will have to be created to make the game work. The technical discussion should be left for the technical design document (TDD). Even if the designer has programming experience, it's not a good idea to make the concept GDD too technical, for it will make the artists' and management's eyes glaze over when they try to plow through it. A good way to view the difference is that the GDD should talk about what the game will be (all the elements of play) and the TDD should talk about how the programmers will make it happen.

Finally, the concept GDD is *not* a "suit of armor." The designer should not fall in love with the GDD and think that what is described in the document will be exactly what the final game will be. The purpose of the concept GDD is to convince management to invest a considerable amount of money in developing a product that has been thoroughly thought out by the team. When the production phase starts, changes will inevitably occur as the team discovers what actually works and what doesn't in the original GDD. Nor should a designer feel that criticism of the contents of the GDD is a criticism of her as a human. These changes benefit the original idea, and she should be open to suggested changes as long as they don't lead to feature creep in later stages of development.

Structure of the Game Design Document

This section presents one method for structuring the game design document. Most companies have their own preferred ways of doing things, but for our purposes, the specific structure of the GDD is less critical than the content. The method presented here has been used successfully a number of times by the author when creating GDDs for various publishers.

Because the document is aimed both at management who must bless the final design and at the various teams who must construct it, the GDD can be broken into four major sections, with each section targeted to a specific audience:

- Introduction: This section is aimed at management. It gives an overview of the project and perhaps an example of play so that the nongaming managers can visualize what is happening in the game. It contains the initial schedule and budget, as well as the marketing analysis developed for the game proposal. This section is relatively short and easy to read. Whoever reads it should walk away with a good idea of what the game is about, how much it will cost, and where it fits in the market.

- Gameplay Mechanics: This section is aimed at the programming team and discusses the rules of the game and how things interact. It should include all the activities the player performs in the game as well as an idea of the overall game structure and user interface. After reading this section, the programmers should be able to figure out the architecture of the game and what code modules will be needed.

- Descriptions: This section is aimed at the art staff and describes what the characters, locations, and items in the game look like and what they do. The art staff should find enough information here to start creating some sketches to show the whole team.

- Appendices: This section contains everything that doesn't fit in other sections. It includes a significant amount of information that the other teams don't have to worry about, such as an extended history of the world, the assembled charts and tables comprising the database, a flowchart of the interface screens, and perhaps, a first pass at some dialogue.

No one in management or on the team will read the entire GDD, but they will read the sections containing the information of most interest to them. This structure for writing the GDD allows the audience to pick and choose which materials to read and in how much detail. Most readers will read the introductory material. Management might scan the rest of the document for completeness but not read the materials attentively. The programmers, meanwhile, will focus on the game mechanics section and skip the descriptive "fluff," whereas the artists will skip the gameplay to find out what the world and characters are like. Everyone can skip the dull minutia in the appendices that the designers worry about. Interestingly enough, the material in the appendices will continue to expand throughout the production phase as page after page of completed level maps and interactive dialogue are slipped into this section.

Section I: The Introduction

This section is the shortest in the GDD—for good reason. Its primary audience is management, who are the people who will decide whether or not the product will be developed. They are busy people and don't usually have time to read the entire document in detail, so the designer should put the most important material for them right at the front of the document; the decision-makers can read the introductory material and walk away with a good sense of what the game is about, how long it will take to build, and how well it will sell.

Front Matter

A good designer is also a good organizer and a reasonably good writer. Formatting the GDD correctly might seem pedestrian, but it's what separates the beginner from the veteran. As boring as it might seem, it is important to add page numbers, section headers, a table of contents, copyright information, team member names, and other minutia because it demonstrates the writer's professionalism and expertise.

IN THE TRENCHES: The Disaster

A designer (who shall remain nameless) at a major publisher was running behind in getting his GDD prepared for a review committee. His GDD of some 150 pages lacked chapter headers, page numbers, and a table of contents. He printed out 10 copies of the GDD, but did not have the time to bind them. On his way into the meeting with the executives, senior producers, and sales and marketing representatives, he tripped on the doorstep. The paper went flying everywhere, and he spent the rest of the meeting trying to put the pages back together. He never got the chance to present the GDD to the committee. At the next meeting, however, the GDD had a TOC, page numbers, headers, and was bound into a folder. It was finally approved.

The *front matter* includes the title page and the table of contents. These elements contain important information that is often overlooked and make the document more accessible to the reader:

- Title Page: By this time, the game should have a good working title, whether suggested by the team, marketing, or management. The game title should stand out prominently. The rest of the title page can include the following information:

  — Contact Information: Names and e-mail addresses of the designer, producer, and/or manager who can answer questions about the document.

  — Version Number: The document will go through many changes, so using a version number lets everyone know which one is most current.

  — Copyright Information: The correct copyright information should appear on the title page. It's also a good idea to have the copyright appear on every page of the document, either in the header or the footer.

  — Team Members (optional): The people who will be on the team, as well as those who have contributed to the game so far, will enjoy seeing their names prominently appear on the title page. More importantly, the designer should insist that each team member who worked on the document sign his or her name to the document (often on the last page). In any event, having the team names on the front cover reinforces their commitment to creating the game described inside.

- Table of Contents (TOC): The table of contents is an important reference tool for the reader, especially in a large document. Whenever a change is made to the document, the TOC should be updated and checked for accuracy. The TOC should have at least three levels of headers that match the headers in the actual text in case the reader needs to refer to a specific topic. The automatic TOC function in Microsoft Word and most other modern word processing programs is excellent for creating a multilayered table of contents.

High Concept/Overview

These items can be culled from the pitch paper or game proposal. As discussed in the preceding chapter, the *high concept* is a statement that sums up the core of the game in 20 words or less. It can be presented in bold type on page one above the section heading so it is the very first thing the reader sees. It's the sales pitch that captures the essence of the game in a few words. A great, succinct high concept is essential for getting a new reader to understand the game immediately.

The *overview* (also called the *executive summary*) is a precise description of the product and should be short, no more than a page or two. It should give the basic theme of the game, the genre, a little background, and the most important gameplay elements. Many busy executives won't have time to read anything else but this portion of the GDD; thus, although it should be only a few paragraphs long, it should give the reader all the essential information needed to understand what the game is about, as well as its intended audience so that management will know everything it needs to make a decision about the project.

Background Story

If the game contains a story (including the history), the designer should give a *short* (limited to a few paragraphs) synopsis of the main game plot without going into too much detail. If there is no story, this portion of the introduction can be ignored. For a game with an elaborate story (role-playing or adventure), the extended plot can be fully described in an appendix.

At this point, the reader is primarily interested in two things: the situation at the start of the game (the *prologue*) and the main thread of the story. The first paragraph should give the background information that sets up the situation at the start of the game and usually introduces the main characters. The focus should be on the seed of contention between the main characters that will drive the action of the plot. The second paragraph can give a brief summary of the main plot, including how the story concludes. Management doesn't want to be teased or left hanging, so the designer should also explain in this section how the main conflict will be resolved.

The story is not the critical focus of the product, but it does set up the plot and the point at which the game starts. It should be brief enough to make the reader want to play the game to see how the story is resolved.

FYI *Backstory and Exposition*

The larger the backstory for a game, the more the characters will have to stop to give exposition as to why things are happening the way they are. It can be really boring for players to hit several spots in an action game where things just halt while someone describes what the villain's master plot is all about or explains that the protagonist behaves a certain way because of the way he was treated as a child. Game designers should take lessons from scriptwriters about telegraphing information in a few words and letting the players' imaginations fill in the details.

Core Gameplay

Again, materials from the pitch paper and game proposal can be used in this section, which describes the important and/or new gameplay mechanics in enough detail for the reader to walk away understanding what the player does during the game that's fun. The section can be several pages long, depending on what needs to be described. However, it should not go into the gameplay mechanics in much detail, for that is the focus of the next part of the GDD. If the gameplay elements are unusual or need extended explanation, the designer might want to follow the core gameplay section with an example-of-play section (see the Optional Materials section later in this chapter) that verbally walks the reader through the game's actions.

For a game whose gameplay elements are well known, such as a sports or racing game, the designer might wish to describe the elements that differentiate this product from its competitors. For example, if discussing a baseball game, the designer might focus on the improved AI, the inclusion of minor rules, or other audio/visual enhancements to the product. For a puzzle game, the designer should give an overview of play without going into details. An extended example-of-play section with visuals can do more to explain how the game plays than a description of the play mechanics themselves.

Marketing

In this part of the GDD, the designer can deal directly with how well the game should sell when released. Again, this material can be drawn from the game proposal marketing information. It's a good idea to include data from three or more products that are similar to the proposed design either in visual style or in gameplay. Sales figures for competitors will help management determine the proposed game's likelihood for success. The designer can point out the proposed design's similarities, as well as show where it is better. Even though most of this material has already appeared in the game proposal, it's a good idea to include it again to remind management of what they liked about the game to begin with.

In addition, this section should include the target audience, game platform, and desired Entertainment Software Ratings Board (ESRB) rating. The three targets should be complementary. For example, if the product is a simple action game with cute characters, its intended audience might be children ages 6 and up; the game platform might be the Nintendo GameCube; and the desired ESRB rating would be E (everyone). If the product is suitable for several game platforms, the designer should point this out and suggest what changes might be needed to make the game work on platforms other than the one targeted.

This part of the section should also point out significant marketing points such as cross-marketing opportunities, strong intellectual properties and/or proprietary technology, and licensee/licensor issues. Management will pay particular attention to this portion, so it should not be given short shrift.

Estimated Budget and Schedule

Management needs to know how many resources will be needed to complete the project and, therefore, how big the budget needs to be. As the initial design nears completion, the designer, producer, and project leads should sit down and start working out the first timeline. At this point, the schedule will be a guesstimate because the full timeline won't be completed until the technical review phase. However, an experienced team should be able to make a good educated guess of the tasks facing the team, the manpower and equipment needed, and the likely time needed for development. If employees have been earmarked to join the team, their names can be plugged into the schedule and their current salaries can be used to estimate salaries of future hires.

The team can then determine the major milestones and suggest dates when they will be met. It is important for the document to emphasize that the information is a first guess at the final budget and schedule, which will be created in detail during the technical review. If management desires a "realistic" budget and schedule at this point, the team should pad both items as much as possible because the figures will likely fall far short of the actual dates and expenditures.

Optional Materials

Some companies might also require an example of play, a team mission statement, or hardware requirements. If so, these elements can be added to the introduction. Again, the idea is to keep the discussions in this part short and to the point.

Example of Play

If the game has unusual gameplay elements or is difficult to explain simply (such as a puzzle game), the designer might want to include an example of how the game plays. The example should focus on the main gameplay elements, not on secondary matters (such as a multiplayer version or character generation in a role-playing game). This section should be written so the reader can visualize what is happening in the game world, and it might include a simple sketch or two to capture the mood or style. This part is a blatant attempt to sell the "sizzle"—the elements that make the game so fun to play. If necessary, the materials can be *storyboarded* if the game has lots of action that is hard to describe in words (Figure 10.3).

FYI *The "Sizzle" in Games*

There's an old marketing saying: "Don't sell the steak, sell the sizzle." The idea is to sell the customer on how good the steak will taste when cooked, not on the piece of cold meat bought at a grocery store. So, when trying to sell management (especially marketing) on

▶▶ CONTINUED ON NEXT PAGE

▶▶ CONTINUED

a new game idea, they will usually be less interested in the game genre than in the game's setting, characters, and special features. They want to know what will separate your first-person shooter from all the other FPS games on the market. Don't be afraid to sell them the "sizzle."

FIGURE 10.3 One of the storyboards for Bungie's *Halo II* (published by Microsoft 2004).

10

Team Mission Statement   The team might wish to include a statement about their goals for the game. The goals can be technical, artistic, or both. The team mission statement sets a stake in the ground for the team and can be reviewed later to see how close they came to meeting their stated objectives. If the team (and company) approaches the product as a learning experience, they will inevitably discover new approaches and methods for completing the game. Their hard-gained experiences should then be encapsulated in a postmortem that is eventually added to the final production GDD.

Hardware Requirements   For a computer game, it's important to determine the minimum requirements for the hardware the game will play on. Obviously, the lower the hardware requirements, the wider the potential audience. However, if the product uses cutting-edge technology, the game might not run on older systems or video cards. So it is wise to include the minimum requirements (the game will play on such a system but not very well) as well as the recommended requirements (for best play experience). Also, if the game includes any special hardware (dance mat, laser pistol, and so on), the team should discuss how it works, how much it costs, and how the peripheral is central to gameplay. Management will want a good idea of the expense involved in making the peripheral to determine how it will affect the final retail sale of the product.

Section II: Gameplay Mechanics

This section of the GDD is aimed at the programming team and discusses the mechanics of gameplay. The general reader (management and artists) might read a bit of this section, but most will likely skim over it because much of the material is mechanistic and dry. On the other hand, by the time they finish this section, the programmers should have a thorough understanding of how everything in the design is supposed to work, and they should be able to determine the code modules needed to bring it to life. The section is divided into the following parts:

1. The first part outlines the game flow and what the player does at different times during play.
2. The second part defines the attributes of the characters or objects.
3. The next parts discuss the actual gameplay mechanics—movement, combat, item manipulation, and so on—in the order in which they will be needed to create the trial prototype.
4. The next part discusses the multiplayer mode (assuming the game will have this mode).
5. Finally, the section concludes with a discussion of the audio requirements.

Depending on the game genre, the designer might generate a number of charts and tables to define attribute values. The appropriate charts and tables should appear in the areas where they are discussed. They should also be gathered as a group and included as the game database part of the appendix for easier reference. However, at this point, the values assigned to attributes and appearing on the charts and tables are little more than placeholders because they are likely to change during implementation.

The remainder of this section discusses different gameplay mechanics. Of course, not every game uses all the mechanics described in this section. When structuring a concept GDD, the designer should describe only those mechanics that appear in the game and ignore the rest. Also, the designer should indicate in the introduction to this section which primary gameplay features must go into the product (the *A* features), which secondary features should go in (the *B* features), and which would be nice additions to add if time allows (the *C* features).

Game Flow

The interface will change significantly during the production process, but it is a good idea for the designer to offer a starting point. This part of the GDD can present a flowchart of the interface screens that the game is expected to have. It can start at a very high level: the player's launching of the application, working through the major shell interface screens and in-game interface screens, and eventually leaving the game. The *shell interface* consists of all screens and windows, including installation, title screen, main menu and various options' submenus, and everything preceding the first in-game screen (Figure 10.4).

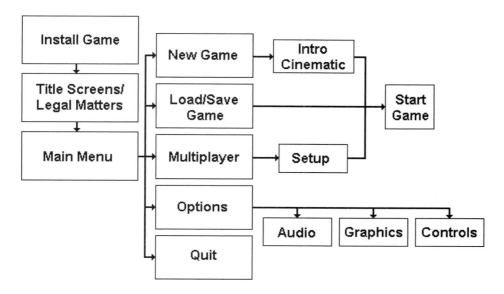

FIGURE 10.4 A simple flowchart can be used to show the relationship of the shell interface screens.

The in-game interface consists of all screens and windows the player uses while playing the game.

After the high-level screens have been defined, the flowchart can indicate how the shell and in-game interface screens will link together. The most important thing to discuss is the functionality of each screen, as opposed to the layout, which will probably change as the game is implemented.

Because the list of player interactions can get very complex, the designer might want to keep the discussion of the interface simple at this point and save the details for later (in an appendix). However, a highly detailed interface analysis helps the quality assurance lead create a thorough test plan for the product. See Chapter 15, "Interface Design," for a discussion of the game interface.

Game Object Attributes and Abilities

This part of the gameplay mechanics section explains the functionality of the game characters and objects (vehicles, puzzle pieces, machinery, and so on) that are controlled by the player or the artificial intelligence (AI). The focus is on the functionality of the objects as opposed to their physical appearance, which is described in the next section of the GDD.

This part defines the various attributes assigned to the objects. An *attribute* is a quantifiable property of an object that defines one or more actions it can perform. It often takes the form of a numeric value that is used in calculating some gameplay mechanic. An attribute can be universal to all objects (such as movement rate, hit points, defense strength, and so on), unique to a class of objects (such as patrol range for air objects, bombardment radius for mortars, and so on), or specific to an individual object (such as skill with a crossbow, ability to speak, and so on). An object that can do many different things in a game has many attributes, whereas an object that does only one or two things usually has a limited set of attributes.

This part deals less with an object's story or history than with the actions it performs in the game and how the numeric values associated with each attribute affect these actions. The values assigned to attributes can be on a *relative scale* (for example, 1 = very slow to 8 = very fast) initially because they will likely change during development. It helps to put the information in spreadsheet charts so the relative values can be considered as a whole and can be shown to be balanced. If the designer is able to create a paper prototype of the game (see Chapter 18, "Prototyping and Building Playfields"), these first values might wind up being close to the final values.

In addition to giving their relative values, this section should also explain how the various attributes are used in play (Figure 10.5). For example, strength might be associated with resolving combat as well as with the ability to move heavy items and carry extra equipment. This information can help the programmers decide whether to use *lookup tables* (that is, data files that list all values

FIGURE 10.5 The attributes for the Union infantry in Cat Daddy Games' *American Civil War: Gettysburg* (published by Global Star in 2005) include starting hit points, current hit points, damage, range, and accuracy.

separately) or ***algorithms*** (that is, values determined by a mathematical formula) when coding the mechanics.

A sampling of attributes commonly seen in games includes:

- Attack Strength: Value when attacking an opponent

- Defense Strength: Value when defending against an attack

- Armor Strength: Amount of damage that can be absorbed by armor during an attack

- Hit Points: How much damage an object can take during combat before it is destroyed or knocked out of action

- Combat Range: Maximum distance that an attacker can be from a target during combat and still do damage

- Reload Rate: How much time it takes to reload ammo before the weapon can launch another attack

- Batting Average: Cumulative value of the batter's ability to hit a ball (in baseball)

10

- Face Value: Numeric value of a playing card from 1 (ace) to 10 (ten and face cards)

- Turning Radius: Ability of a car to turn quickly

- Build Time: Length of time required to build an object when the resources are available

As you might guess, there are many attributes that could be used. It is up to the designer to select those that are most important in terms of gameplay. The designer should also discuss any dependencies between attributes, such as when a new attribute is not available until an existing attribute reaches a certain value. For example, an RTS game might require that the player build a smithy before being able to build mounted knights because their horses need metal horseshoes.

FYI *Game Object Attributes*

In computer and video games, the actual game mechanics for resolving gameplay actions are usually hidden from the player. For example, you don't see the mathematical formula used to resolve a combat directly, although you usually see the values involved (for example, the attack and defense strengths used by the formula) and the amount of damage inflicted on a target. Thus, a game object might need only a few attributes to resolve every game action. In a role-playing game, a character can have a half dozen attributes or more, but because players don't see how all these numbers are used in the game, they don't mean much. The players are happy to increase strength and defense values and magic points when their characters go up a level because changes to these values are obvious. But they might not see much reason to bump up luck, or agility, language skills, or other attributes because they don't appear to do anything. The designer should indicate which values are seen by the player and which aren't and explain how all values are used to resolve different game actions.

In addition to attributes, this part describes the special abilities of objects. A *special ability* is a talent, skill, or enhancement that is unique to an object type. For example, flight is a special ability that airplane or dragon objects have but artillery or knight objects do not. An ability can serve many functions in a game, such as defining what actions the objects can and cannot perform (for example, fly), modifying the normal values of attributes (for example, an archery ability for ranger objects adds a positive die-roll modifier when those objects fire any kind of bow), or giving special actions to

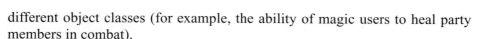

different object classes (for example, the ability of magic users to heal party members in combat).

Leadership is an important ability in many war games and real-time strategy games, as well as in some role-playing games and military vehicle simulations. A number of attributes can be associated with an object's ability to lead troops in battle (command radius, supply chain, morale, and so on). It can be considered the same as management ability in a sports or racing game. However it is used, the designer should explain all the different actions that leadership abilities affect.

The designer should discuss the AI requirements, if any, for allied and enemy objects in this part, although there is no need to get too technical. The AI demands are better addressed in the technical design document, but this is a good place to discuss the desired behavior of objects. The information can be relatively descriptive (for example "The aliens move in a predetermined pattern, traveling horizontally until the first ship collides with the right wall, then moving down en masse one level and moving horizontally to the left until they hit that wall, and so on for eight levels, at which point they might collide with the player's ship, ending the game") or more specific (for example, "The fixed turret tracks the player at all times and fires every 8 seconds, but its accuracy is only 60 to 70%. The accuracy drops 5% each time it takes damage until it is destroyed"). Finally, if the player can interact directly with other characters in the world, the designer can discuss how these interactions occur and what the interface is like.

Character Generation, Selection, and Improvement

Role-playing games often let the player modify a preexisting character or create a character from scratch before play begins. In this portion, the process the player follows to generate a character is explained. A number of different interface screens can be involved including one for defining the character's physical appearance, one for assigning points to the character's attributes and abilities (Figure 10.6), and one for the character's inventory including the items currently being worn. The designer should explain the purpose and functionality of each screen, as well as how the player interacts with the game (for example, "The player drags a shield from an inventory slot directly onto the character to arm her with that shield"). Generating a character can be very complex process, with the player making most of the decisions about the character's race, sex, appearance, profession, magical abilities, and armament, or it can be relatively simple, with the player simply selecting from a number of pregenerated characters or, in many console games, using only the main character provided.

In addition, one of the standard features of a role-playing game is that the character gets better over time with experience. The character might go up an experience level after a number of battles in which the player gathers *experience points.* At this point, the player might receive points to assign to the

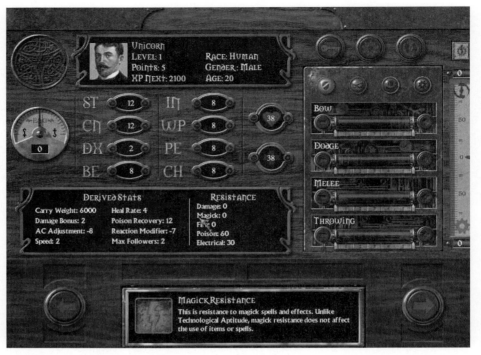

FIGURE 10.6 One of the character generation screens from Troika Games' role-playing game, *Arcanum: Of Steamworks & Magick Obscura* (published by Sierra On-Line in 2001).

character's attributes and abilities in a character-generation interface screen. On the other hand, the attributes and abilities might improve automatically without the player's doing anything. However the game uses experience points and levels, the mechanics have to be explained so the programmers will know how to make them work.

Other game genres might involve a similar mechanic for generating or selecting objects and then improving them. For example, in a racing game, the player might be able to select a car from several available models and use the money he earns by winning to improve his car. In the game of *Monopoly*, the players select their playing piece at the start of the game, and as they purchase properties they can upgrade them by building houses or hotels on them. Even in a game as simple as this, the designer still has to explain the mechanics of how the player selects a playing piece at the beginning of the game and then improves properties during play. A number of different interface screens can be involved in the selection and improvement processes, each requiring an explanation of its functionality in the GDD.

As with game object attributes, all charts and tables associated with object generation, selection, or improvement should appear in this area, with explanations about how they work. They should also be included in the game database section of the appendix.

Playfield and Movement

This part describes the movement of objects on the playfield and their scale relative to the overall play area. One of the most important decisions a designer must make is the scale of objects as they appear on the screen during play. If a lot of important activity is going on at great distances from objects, the object's scale will likely be small so the player can get a better overview of what is happening. If it is important to see the area immediately around the object clearly—for example, to judge the distance to a ledge—the object's scale will be larger. For guidance on the desired scale of the game, the designer can review games of the same genre to see how large their objects are on the playfield.

The main in-game interface usually has objects moving on the playfield. The designer should explain the functionality of everything on the screen as well as what inputs are used to move objects. For example, does the player mouse-click on objects on the playfield to select them and then click on a space to move them there? Is there a click-and-drag function to select large groups of objects? Does the object controlled by the player move whenever the player pushes a thumbstick or arrow key?

In addition to the main interface, secondary interface screens or windows can be associated with movement (formations, maps, and so on). These should be described as well. It's a good idea to include a schematic of each screen and window, pointing out the various functions on each one (Figure 10.7).

In addition to the playfield, the designer needs to explain all of the game's different movement actions in this part. If a character can walk, run, jump, swim, duck, and perform other actions, the designer needs to include them all in the GDD and explain how each one works (including suggesting the input for making the action happen). The designer also has to determine the rate of movement for each action, as well as how the move affects the view of the playfield. For example, the designer might decide that a character walking through a hallway moves at 3 miles per hour and moves at double that speed when running. As a result, the hallway walls will appear to move half as fast when the character is walking than when he is running. Modifiers might apply to movement as well. For example, if an object is damaged or wounded, it might not be able to move as fast as a healthy object. Likewise, the weight of the items an object carries can slow its movement. Fuel or food is another point for discussion here if they affect the object's movement. Many games include some kind of *fog of war*, where objects can see enemies only within their line of sight and not beyond. If included, this effect should also be discussed in detail.

The game might include different modes of movement, and each one has to be explained. For example, in a first-person shooter, the main character might

> **Caution**
>
> **Determine Scale Early**
>
> The scale of objects versus the size of the playfield should be determined as early as possible in the production phase after a working prototype is up and running. The scale has many repercussions in the game, such as the level of detail for 3D models, and their textures, and the number of polygons appearing on the screen.

10

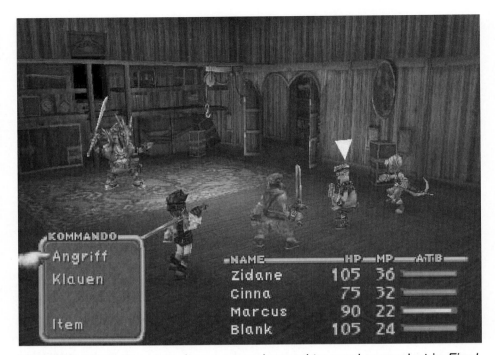

FIGURE 10.7 This interface screen is used to resolve combat in *Final Fantasy IX*. The size of the characters is different then their size in the movement screen, and the player does not actively move them during combat; instead, she selects an action and then the characters move independently.

be able to walk, run, drive a ground vehicle, and even fly an air vehicle. Some modes might be *abstracted*, such as when a character boards a train the scene switches to an animated sequence of the train moving to the next station. The designer should include the movement rate and the affect on the playfield view for each movement mode.

The designer should describe the different terrain features that appear on the playfield if they affect play. There should be a list of all the terrain features appearing in each major environment. For example, a forest can contain trees (obviously), thickets and bushes, boulders, open glades, entrances to towns, caves, and so on. Some types of terrain (such as walls, mountains, and rivers) might be impassable or block sight between objects on the playfield, whereas other terrain might slow movement (such as woods, steep hills, or creeks) or speed it up (such as highways, escalators, and teleports). Some terrain might kill an object that touches it (lava, for example). Any animations needed for terrain features should be included, along with the number of steps required per animation. The document should also discuss how enemies use terrain features to their advantage.

FYI *Game Genre Terrain Effects*

The game genre or the setting for the game might call for special terrain effects. In a science fiction setting, for example, heavy gravity may make characters move sluggishly, whereas low gravity would allow them to jump to great heights. In a racing game, the surface of the track and the weather may affect traction. In a football game, the weather—rain, snow, fog—may affect both vision and footing.

A game might include multiple versions of a map (Figure 10.8). The playfield map where objects appear most of the time might be at one scale, and one where combat occurs might be at another. Also, if the overall playfield is large, a strategic map of some kind (radar, inset map, or separate map screen) might appear either on the main in-game screen or when called up as a separate screen or window. The designer should discuss the scale and functionality of each map type in the game.

FIGURE 10.8 This World Map screen in Bioware's *Baldur's Gate II: Shadows of Amn* (published by Interplay in 2000) allows players to view both the entire world of the game as well as individual cities.

As a part of the discussion of the playfield, the designer might include maps of each level to indicate where various objects are to be found such as animating terrain features, quest items, nonplaying character (NPC) encounters, set-piece battles, entrance and exit points, and so on. In addition, the designer might also note whether players will visit a given map only once or as often as they wish. Do monsters respawn on a map? Do they become more powerful? The more details the designer can give about how the playfields work, the better the programmers can determine what code is needed to enable the gameplay mechanics.

A final topic of discussion is how the game camera will work in a 3D game. Does the player have any control over the camera, or is it handled automatically by the game engine? Can the player jump between first- and third-person points of view? In a racing or flight simulation game, will multiple cameras show the vehicle from many different views such as ahead, behind, cockpit, and overhead?

Combat

If the game contains any form of combat, the designer should explain in detail how it works and anything that affects its outcome. A logical way to approach the subject is to talk about the various categories of combat first. There are two basic combat categories:

- *Melee Combat:* The combatants use their hands (or other appendages), either bare-fisted or with handheld weapons (clubs, knives, axes, maces, nunchakus, and so on). This form of combat is also called ***close combat*** because the combatants have to be adjacent to each other to inflict damage (Figure 10.9). Generally, this type of combat is not as damaging as ranged combat. However, in some games, the damage increases as the player correctly performs combinations (combos) of multiple attacks.

- *Ranged Combat:* The combatants stay at a distance from one another and use weapons to attack each other (Figure 10.10). Although combat that involves attacking with weapons on long sticks such as a halberd or poleax might be considered ranged combat, the usual weapon is an item that is thrown (such as a knife, shuriken, or grenade) or that fires a damaging projectile (such as an arrow, bullet, cannonball, or mortar). Even artillery and air bombardments can be considered ranged attacks. Ranged-combat weapons frequently have a limited amount of ammo that needs to be replenished over time, and some weapons might require specified intervals between firing for reloads. Ranged combat weapons do not always have to be physical; in fantasy games, magic spells, energy launchers, or mental projectors can all damage enemies.

FIGURE 10.9 An example of melee combat in Square's *Final Fantasy X* (published by Square Electronic Arts in 2001). Note that close combat is frequently used in fantasy games.

In addition to offensive weaponry, this part of the GDD should also discuss any defensive *armament* that affects combat. The armament can be something that is worn (such as gauntlets, armor, shield, or a Kevlar vest) or something projected in front of the combatant to absorb damage (such as an energy field, mind shield, or magic spell). The armament might be permanent or temporary (for example, a defensive magic spell), or it might last until it takes a certain amount of damage and is destroyed. The weight of the armament can affect the object's other combat attributes, too.

The designer usually describes weapons and armaments by type, so the relative values can be compared against each other. It is more important at this point to discuss how weapons and armament function instead of how they look (they can be described in the next section of the GDD).

The designer should determine which attributes are most important in defining how combat will be resolved. A simple formula or algorithm is usually used to determine how combat is resolved. For example:

```
Attack Strength - Defense Strength = Damage Amount
(applied to defender's Hit Point total)
```

On the one hand, using such a straightforward formula makes each combat very predictable, which might be what the designer desires. On the other hand, many games use a combat result table (CRT) to vary the results of combat.

10

FIGURE 10.10 An example of ranged combat from Ubisoft's *Far Cry* (2004). Most modern weapons are ranged weapons that can hit enemies at great distances.

The CRT might be a single column with multiple results generated by a random dice roll (such as by rolling two 10-sided dice and reading the first die as the number in the tens' place and the second die as the one's place to give a result of 0–99). Or the CRT can also be a more complicated matrix that resolves combat involving multiple objects. See Chapter 16, "Mathematics and Artificial Intelligence in Games," for a discussion of how math is used in games.

Combat attributes and outcome can be subject to modification for any number of reasons. The combat values might be affected by realistic factors, such as combat exhaustion, lack of communication, poor morale, and battlefield terrain and by abstract factors, such as magic spells, curses, and the like. The designer should explain what modifiers affect the combat values, as well as how they are applied to the combat formula. The result can be relatively complex, so the designer might include examples to show how each kind of combat is resolved.

Some games, especially role-playing games, allow combatants to use items other than weapons during combat. These items might be physical (health potions) or immaterial (magic spells). The designer should discuss what these items are and how they work. The designer should also specify how and when they can be used.

Finally, the designer should discuss the outcome of combat. What happens when an object's hit points reach zero? Is it destroyed or simply knocked out of action? Can it be resuscitated? Will objects flee or retreat posthaste automatically if badly damaged or shaken, or is this a decision for the player to make? What happens when all of one side's objects are destroyed? Can the player save the game in the midst of combat? If a weapon runs out of ammunition, does the player have to reload it or does it do so automatically? These are just a few of the questions that need to be addressed.

In addition to discussing combat resolution in detail, the designer should include schematics of the combat interface (if it is different from the movement interface) as well as what inputs are used to manipulate objects during combat (Figure 10.11). Any secondary screens and windows that appear during combat (such as inventory, spell lists, and so on) should also be described in detail.

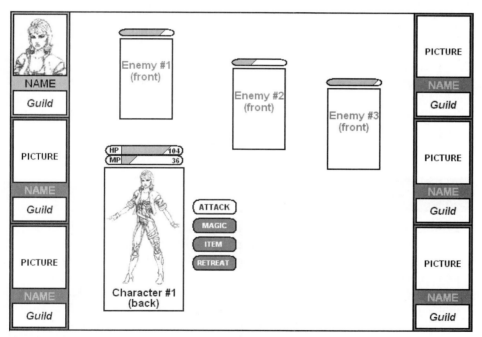

FIGURE 10.11 A combat interface schematic for a fantasy role-playing game, showing what appears on the screen when combat occurs. In this case, there are slots on the left and right edges for six characters. The active character is highlighted with the options available next to her picture. The meters above the character show her health points (HP) and magic points (MP); those above the enemies show only their HPs. Female figure by Ed Williamson.

Resources, Power-Ups, and Other Collectable Items

During the game, the player might find things while traveling across the playfield or might be allowed to build things from items already collected. The designer should group these items by functionality and explain how each group functions. The physical description of the items can wait until the next section, but programmers will want to know what the items do and how the player interacts with them.

Collectable items include such things as resources, power-ups, weapons and armor, ammo reloads, and inventory items. The designer should explain how these items are collected; that is, whether the player must actively select them or if they are picked up automatically when touched. The items might appear prominently on the playfield, or the player might be required to hunt for them. Some items automatically activate upon contact, whereas others go into an inventory for later use. Some items, such as those used to complete quests, might have no direct effect on gameplay and instead go into a special inventory. One or more interface screens might be dedicated to these items. The designer should indicate the functionality of the inventory interface and how the player uses collected items. Many games have an inventory system that shows the items the player has collected. The interface might be relatively simple or complex. A first-person shooter game, for example, usually has a limited number of items that might appear on the main interface screen as the player travels across the playfield. A role-playing game might include many different items and usually includes a special inventory screen for handling spare items. Some games let the player buy and sell things, either during play or between missions, races, or sessions. The designer can explain here how such sales work and what interface screens are needed.

FYI *Easter Eggs*

Easter eggs are features hidden in a game—such as a piece of art, an animation, a sound effect, and so on—that are not specified in the GDD but are sneaked in by a programmer or artist. The player often has to use some undocumented sequence of key or button pushes to access the hidden feature. They are usually intended to be funny, but the industry frowns on the practice not only because it is unprofessional but also because of the potential legal issues than can result from using unlicensed music or images, profanity that could affect the ESRB rating, libel, and so on. One example of an Easter egg appears in Sierra On-Line's *Conquests of Camelot: The Search for the Grail* (1990); the animated game knights break into the song "We're Knights of the Round Table" from the movie *Monty Python's Holy Grail* (1989) if you type "ham and jam and spam a lot" while in the treasure.

Magic and Technology

For a fantasy or science fiction game, the designer might find it useful to devote some space to magic or technology, especially if the system is complex and has its own interface screens and windows.

Magic

Magic in the form of magic spells or magic items has many uses in a fantasy game. Sometimes, the user must undergo special training or have an affinity toward an element (earth, air, fire, or water) or other mystic factor to use magic. At other times, the magic can be used by anyone without any preparation. Occasionally, the player gets to play with magic, rather like a chemistry set, testing various numinous ingredients in combination to see what spells result. However the designer approaches magic, she should define how it works in detail so the programmers can create their own magic as they bring the system to life in the game.

Magic can usually be grouped by functionality into three major categories:

- Combat: Many magic spells are equivalent to long-range weapons that attack the enemy at a distance. Other magic spells act as temporary armor that defends the user during battle. Attack spells are usually one-time shots at the enemy, although some (such as poison, petrifaction, confusion, and so on) might have lingering effects on the target. The player might be limited to the number of magic spells that can be cast in a given situation, or she might be allowed to cast spells as long as she has enough *mana* (or whatever is used to power the magic). The target of the attack might be a single enemy, a group of enemies, or all enemies. Some magic might be particularly powerful against a specific target type (for example, the undead), and sometimes the magic affects both the user and the enemy. In any event, the designer should define this type of magic in the same way as defining how weapons work.

10

FYI   *Mana*

In most fantasy games, the source of magic's power is a mystical substance called **_mana._** Mana is to magic what oil is to technology. When a character casts a spell, he uses a certain amount of mana, and he can only cast so many spells before the mana is exhausted. A quick shopping trip at the local apothecary often allows the character

▶▶ CONTINUED ON NEXT PAGE

▶▶ CONTINUED

to replenish his mana from a bottle of Wizard John's Magic Juice. This is all tripe, of course, but it is useful for the number juggling that is involved in creating and balancing magic charts in the game. The main thing is for the designer to be consistent about how magic works in the game, even if she relies upon the tried-and-true clichés of traditional paper role-playing games.

■ Modifiers: Many magic spells have a temporary effect that benefits the user or impairs an enemy. A spell can affect one or more of an object's attributes for a limited time or until counteracted. During combat, a beneficial modifier spell can make the attacker stronger, faster, or immune to damage (Figure 10.12), whereas a detrimental spell can slow or weaken an enemy, reduce its magic defense, impose a persistent state (poison, petrification, confusion, and so on), or otherwise cause havoc. Some modifier spells increase the target's health or remove persistent states. Although it can be a chore, the designer should make sure that these modifier spells are well balanced so that no one spell is too powerful and all spells are worth using one way or another.

FIGURE 10.12 Rikku casts a modifier spell, Pray, to protect the party in Square Co.'s *Final Fantasy X-2* (2003).

- Creatures: Some magic spells make creatures appear on the playfield. The creatures can then be used to attack enemies, carry items, or otherwise act as cannon fodder to deplete the enemy. The creatures might be allied with the caster or they might act independently and attack whatever crosses their paths. Their appearance might be permanent, or they might exist for a short time and then disappear.

Technology   Technology works much like magic in a game. It often works as a modifier that makes objects more powerful, faster, or somehow better than they were at the start of the game. One driving force in many strategy games is the race to improve objects faster than one's opponents. Usually, a game that allows technological advances uses some kind of *technology tree,* which is a branching system that evolves from simple to complex over time as the player funds research or otherwise makes technological breakthroughs (Figure 10.13).

The simpler technologies are usually prerequisites for the advanced technologies, and investment expenditures can serve to limit the number of technologies being researched at any one time. The player might also have to acquire raw resources (lumber, ore, gold, metals, and so on) to build

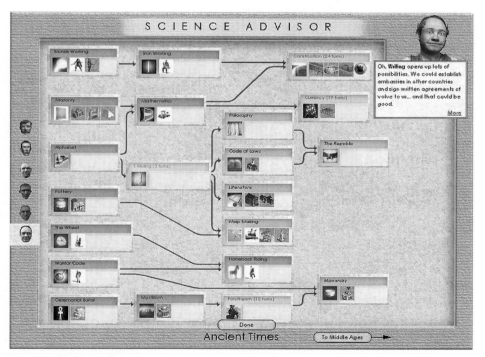

FIGURE 10.13 Part of the technology tree appearing in Firaxis Games' *Sid Meier's Civilization III* (published by Infogrames in 2001).

newly discovered items or to maintain existing structures. Resources often gradually dry up, forcing the player to keep exploring the playfield for new sources.

Whether the game has magic or technology, it might use special interface screens and menus for handling them. The designer should include schematics that describe the functionality of each of these screens as well as the inputs the player uses on it (Figure 10.14). These schematics should also appear in the game interface appendix.

Puzzles and Quests

If the concept is a puzzle game, most of the GDD materials discussed up to this point are often irrelevant. However, if the game includes characters of any kind, some of the previous sections might still be pertinent.

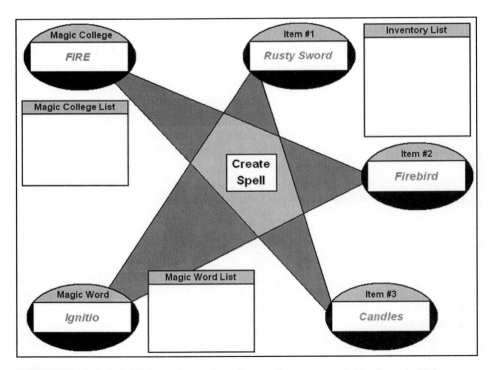

FIGURE 10.14 This schematic shows how magic spells might be created in a fantasy role-playing game. The player selects a college of magic, a magic word associated with the college, and up to three ingredients. Pushing the Create Spell button combines the ingredients; if the mixture is correct, a new spell is created. The designer describes each function of the interface screen and how a spell is created in this section of the GDD.

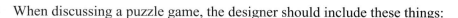

When discussing a puzzle game, the designer should include these things:

- Playfield: What does the main interface screen look like? What functions appear on this screen during play (a timer, score, and so on) and what inputs are used to control objects (or tokens) on the screen? Are there secondary screens and windows that also have to be discussed? What actions do the objects/tokens perform on the playfield?

- Rules: What are the basic rules of the game? Must the player perform activities in a certain order? How does the player win or lose the game, and what happens in each case? Are there variants to the basic game?

- AI: If there is a computer-controlled opponent, does it perform the same actions as the player? What logic does the computer AI use to make decisions about what to do next? This logic can be defined in a series of if–then statements that look at each possibility and make decisions based on the current game situation. Note that this is not a trivial matter and can take many pages to describe thoroughly.

- Construction Set: Does the product include a system to enable the player to generate her own playfields? If so, how will it work? What is the interface for the construction set and what controls are needed?

- Multiplayer: If the game includes a multiplayer version, does it involve any changes to the basic rules? Is the game **_turn-based_** (each player performs a series of actions one after the other) or **_simultaneous_** (all players perform actions at the same time)?

Many games in other genres—adventure and role-playing games in particular—include puzzle-like situations including quests. The designer can explain how they work in this section. The major puzzles/quests that must be solved to get through the game should be explained first. The designer might include such information as how the puzzle/quest is initiated, the steps the player must perform to resolve it, and the payoff for completing it.

Secondary puzzles and quests can be discussed later, when production is fully underway. They are not central to the main plot and are often added during level creation when the design team has learned how many different elements the tools and game engine will allow. These puzzles/quests should be fully documented and included in the final production GDD, however.

Multiplayer Mode

By this point in the document, all the major gameplay mechanics should be laid out. If the game includes a multiplayer mode, the designer should discuss how it works in this portion of the document. In particular, he should explain how it differs from the solitaire version. Do players compete head-to-head against each other, and if so, do they compete on teams or "every man for himself ?" Is there a cooperative play option, and are there restrictions on the players when using this version? How many players will be supported? Will the game use a server–client system where everyone who plays goes through a central hub to join, or will it be limited to a direct, player-to-player connection either through multiple input devices into the machine or over a local area network (LAN)? The designer should discuss how the players hook up to the game and how the input devices work.

> ### FYI | *Hot Seat*
>
> In a ***hot seat*** game, multiple players use the same computer and have to take turns using the keyboard and/or mouse. This differs from console games that link multiple controllers to let multiple players simultaneously play the same game. The term arises from the fact that players look like they're sitting on a "hot seat" as they bounce up and down, taking their turns.

Obviously, if the focus of the game is primarily on the multiplayer version or the game is exclusively multiplayer, the designer should discuss her vision of how the game will incorporate multiplayer elements throughout the GDD. The designer might have grand ideas about the game that the lead programmer will have to rein in because of technological limits the designer may not be aware of. Multiplayer-only games involve many technical issues that should be discussed thoroughly during the technical review phase to determine whether the game will work as envisioned.

Audio and Special Visuals

The final area to discuss in the gameplay mechanics section is the requirements for audio and visual effects. The audio requirements cover the music, sound effects, and voiceovers in the game.

- Music: The designer should discuss his ideas for the type of music for the game. If the game creates a lot of excitement, the music likely will be loud with a fast tempo. If the game mood is quiet and reserved, then the music can be slow and melodic. The designer might envision a big symphonic score that requires hiring professional musicians and a classical composer, or the game might feature a compilation of songs licensed from popular performers. In addition to the style of music, the designer should make a first guess at the amount of music needed for the game. More importantly, the designer should indicate any special requirements such as having the music continually change to match

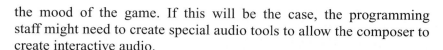

the mood of the game. If this will be the case, the programming staff might need to create special audio tools to allow the composer to create interactive audio.

- **Sound Effects:** The ambient sounds in a game are an important part of establishing the mood of the game. The designer should indicate the desired style of such sounds based on the game environment as well as events in the game world. Sound effects can run the gamut from comic to realistic to eerie, so it's important for the designer to discuss the desired mood in the concept GDD to guide the person responsible for providing the sound. Sound effects not only help establish the correct mood for the game world but also provide vital feedback to the player when interacting with the interface and the objects in the game. It's a good idea for the designer to include suggested sound effects either here or as a separate appendix when describing creatures (roars, stomps, growls), items (weapons fire, explosions, bullets hitting) and locations (throbbing engines, birds chirping, waterfalls). Also, the designer should note the sounds needed for the user interface (clicks, button press/release, beeps), as well as for special warnings (picking up items from playfield, warnings when doing something wrong, pop-up messages).

- **Voiceovers:** The designer might decide that storage capacity of CDs or DVDs provides enough room for voiceovers in addition to written dialogue. Although the finished dialogue will likely not be complete by the time the concept GDD is approved for production, the designer should try to estimate how much dialogue will require voiceovers. At this point, the designer should determine how many characters will speak, so that actors can be lined up to provide the voices. If possible, the designer should work with the producer to develop an estimate of the expenses involved in hiring artists, technicians, and recording studio sessions, which would then be reflected in the budget section. When the final dialogue is ready and written either by the designer or by a professional writer, it should go into an appendix.

It's a good idea to start thinking about these needs early rather than waiting until near the end and then rushing to complete them.

In addition to the audio requirements, the designer should also determine what animated sequences or special visual effects will be needed. Animated sequences include the opening introduction to the game, between-mission materials, special in-game sequences, and the final payoff cinematic that ends the game. The content of these sequences can be described in the next section, but the designer should point out here where they will occur in the game so the programmers will know when they are needed.

Section III: Descriptions

This section, which is written for the art team, gives detailed descriptions of the characters, objects, locations, items, and animated sequences in the game. Management might also be interested in the material, not only because the content is less daunting than the gameplay explanations but also because the characters might be interesting enough to become the focus of the marketing efforts. In addition to the written descriptions, the art staff creates 2D sketches to accompany the text in this section. When the design is finally approved for production, the 3D artists will use these samples to begin working on their models and textures.

Of course, if the game design doesn't call for any characters, objects, or locations (for example, in an abstract puzzle game), the designer can skip this section. In this case, item descriptions can be included in the previous section's discussion of objects. In a game where objects are neutral, such as a racing game, it can still be useful to create this section to describe to the artists what the objects look like and how they behave.

Characters/Objects

The characters or objects in the game can be lumped together in three basic groups: player characters/objects, enemies, and independent characters/objects. The player's objects are usually the heroes; the enemies are the villains, and the independents assist the player without becoming involved in the action themselves.

Player Characters/Objects   This group includes the main characters/ objects controlled by the player and those who are closely allied with the player. In a story-based game, the player usually controls the main protagonist. Because the protagonist is at the center of the plot, this character should be described in detail. The protagonist might have a love interest of some kind; in many stories, the protagonist embarks on a journey to find a lost love. Even if the love interest does not directly appear much in the game, he or she should be described in detail as well. The main characters can become a valuable intellectual property for the company, so the designer should spend plenty of time fleshing them out and making them as interesting as possible.

The second tier of lead characters are the allies who actively help the protagonist achieve the final goal. These characters might join a party with the main character or appear regularly to offer assistance of some kind. They, too, deserve detailed descriptions because they might later spin off into their own games.

The third level of allied characters are those who assist the protagonist without actively joining the quest. They can be friends and family who offer advice, give limited assistance, and propose quests, but they don't leave their posts to join the party. The designer can give these characters shorter descriptions.

If the player controls objects of some kind (such as race cars or military vehicles) instead of characters, the designer should still give a thorough description of what they look like and how they behave. As with characters, it's a good idea to include sketches to help management visualize their appearance.

Enemies This portion includes the characters/objects who oppose the player as well as those who independently clash with the player. In a story-based game, the main antagonist is in direct conflict with the protagonist, and they are usually pursuing a mutually exclusive goal (for example, battling to become the one whom the love interest will marry). Indeed, it is often the antagonist who kicks off the action by performing some action that upsets the peaceful balance of the world. The main antagonist, who is often called the *boss, major villain,* or *mastermind,* should be thoroughly described because he or she can become another valuable intellectual property of the company.

The antagonist often has several henchmen ready to assist in hindering the protagonist. These henchmen might work directly for the major villain or be independently hostile to the protagonist. These characters are often called *sub-bosses* or *minibosses* because they obstruct the protagonist's goal of finding the main boss. These characters should receive a thorough treatment by the designer because they will occupy a significant amount of screen time and one or more might wind up becoming the antagonist in a sequel or add-on product.

The lowest ranking enemies are the *minions;* these are the cannon fodder troops that work for the antagonist and his henchmen. They seldom act independently and strictly follow orders. Because they have little personality, they can be dealt with in a paragraph or two.

Similar to minions are the independent creatures and monsters that the player encounters during the story. They are not allied with the antagonist but instead act aggressively against the hero. In many cases, a successful encounter with these critters will provide money, experience points, and an occasional item or two. As with minions, they usually deserve only a paragraph or two of description.

Finally, a nonstory game might include objects controlled by an enemy to which the player has no access (for example, military vehicles that are unique to the enemy). These objects can also be listed in the enemy objects part and described in as much detail as needed.

10

FYI *Motivations for Villains*

Many novice designers don't give antagonists a sensible reason for their evil deeds. Instead, the villain simply does evil for evil's sake. These villains are cardboard figures who are uninteresting to players. If the goal the antagonist strives for is petty or meaningless, the player's efforts to thwart those plans feel like cheap melodrama instead of real drama. Therefore, spending the time to give antagonists concrete reasons for their misbehavior not only makes them more interesting but also makes the protagonist stronger.

Caution

Details Matter Too

The designer should make sure that the mechanics for all the moves discussed in the characters/objects section are explained in detail in the section on gameplay mechanics.

Independent Characters/Objects   This part of the GDD includes those individuals whom the player does not control directly but who do not aid and abet the enemy side. In storytelling games, these characters (called *nonplayer characters* or *NPCs*) often serve as window dressing to make towns look occupied. Some assign minor quests, offer advice, provide services such as buying and selling weaponry, and otherwise occupy their own world. The designer might lump such groups together by town or location and give a short description of how the individuals relate to their environment. These individuals do not necessarily have to appear in the concept GDD because they are so unimportant, but they should be added to the production GDD for the purpose of comprehensiveness.

In nonstory games, objects also serve as window dressing or provide minor services for the player (for example, a truck convoy providing supplies). Again, the designer can provide short descriptions of these objects, but they do not need to appear in the concept GDD.

When describing the most important characters, the designer can include a short history of the person (no longer than a page or two). However, the artists are more interested in the physical description of the character, how he or she moves, and any special talents or abilities. The designer should describe every action for every character in the game and specify the number of steps for each animation (see Chapter 13, "Visualizing the Game," for more about animations). The animators will use this information to create appropriate models or sprites for all the different actions a character/object can perform.

Locations

The *locations* are the places in the game world where action takes place. Depending on the scale of the game, locations can be relatively small (a soccer field) or quite large (a whole world; a country; or an environmental zone, like a desert). They can be real places, such as race tracks, battlefields, and football stadiums or imaginary countries and planets dreamed up entirely by the designer. Real places are easier to research and get accurate information about thanks to sources such as the Internet as well as the ability to go there and take direct measurements. Imaginary places can be more fun for the designer to create but require more work to find visual sources to help the artists create the correct graphic style.

Depending on the scope of the game, the first and largest-scale location that the designer needs to describe is an entire world. In fantasy or science fiction games, where the player might crisscross the world and even travel to different worlds, the designer should give an overview of each world, especially if the surfaces differ from one world to another. The designer does not need to go into too much detail at this point (detailed materials can be put in an appendix), but she should give enough information to enable the artists to create appropriate textures for planet surfaces and world maps. Of course, if the game is less vast in scope, this level of location can be ignored.

The next level of location is the country or ecosystem (desert, ocean, tundra). If a game includes many different countries and/or ecosystems, the designer should point out what is unique about each one and try to provide artists with some source materials that have a similar look. The designer should explain the terrain features in each location, the connections to other locations in the game world (roads, rivers, and so on), and the social and political aspects as they affect the location's appearance.

The next location level includes population centers (cities, towns, villages), outdoor settings (forests, plains, polar regions), and special sites (caves, ruins, mazes). These are the most important locations to describe in detail. It's a good idea for the designer to create a rough overhead sketch of each location, either hand-drawn and scanned into the computer or created in an art program, that shows the places where important events occur. In addition, the designer should include the following information about each of these locations:

- General description of the area and its topography and ecology

- Description (and examples) of the area's visual appearance

- Building exteriors and interiors with any game functionality (for example, a chapel for healing, a store to purchase/sell items, or a foundry to improve armor)

- Story characters (ally and enemy) found in the area and their function

- Nonplayer characters that affect the storyline in any way (for example, by offering minor quests)

- Minor monsters and enemies the player might encounter

- Items, treasures, power-ups, weaponry, and so on that the player might discover

- Cinematic sequences set in the area

- Music and sound effects specific to the area

10

As with the other game elements discussed in the GDD, locations can go through multiple changes during production, so the design staff should update the playfield maps regularly. The testers' job will be much easier if they have accurate maps of each location and know where to find the important trigger points.

Items

The length of this part depends on the number of items in the game. The items can be grouped by functionality, with each item given a short description and (if possible) some visual reference for the artists to work from. The same graphic might be used to represent an entire class of items (for example, a scroll might represent different magic spells appearing in the inventory). The items appearing in games can include, among others:

- Weapons (normal and magic)
- Armor (normal and magic)
- Clothing
- Inventory items (potions, magic spells, charms)
- Quest/puzzle items
- Power-ups
- Ammunition reloads
- Playfield icons (health, resources, clues)

For armor and weapons, it's a good idea to include a visual reference of how the item is worn or carried and wielded in battle. If the designer wants characters to carry every different weapon and wear every kind of armor or clothing, the demands on the artists can be overwhelming. For example, just four weapons and four kinds of armor/clothing require sixteen variations to cover every combination. The art staff might recommend ways to cut down on the number of art assets, such as arming characters with a generic sword to represent all normal swords and perhaps a sparkling sword to represent all magic swords.

Another problem is how to represent abstract items on the playfield. The game might include visual resources, clues, power-ups, and other items that are important to gameplay but are confusing to represent visually. The designer should work with the art staff to create appropriate icons to represent these abstract items. Some icons might be self-evident (for example, a red cross to represent a health item), whereas others are obscure (for example, a flashing red cube to represent a turbo boost power-up).

Finally, the designer and artists should attempt to represent these items consistently on the playfield and in the player's inventory. In other words, what an item (a magic sword, for example) looks like when the player sees it lying on the playfield should be similar to how it appears in her inventory.

Animated Sequences

The last part of the characters/objects section describes the animated sequences the designer would like to see included in the final product. These sequences can be divided into cut-scene animations and full-motion videos. A ***cut-scene animation*** temporarily interrupts the game to play out a prescripted scene using the characters and location models controlled by the game engine. ***Full-motion videos (FMVs)*** are prerendered animated sequences that usually include the opening and closing scenes plus other scenes that might play out between missions or levels. See Chapter 13, "Visualizing the Game," for more about animated sequences.

In either case, the designer should give a short synopsis of each animated sequence, including the location and characters involved. By the time the concept GDD is approved, the art staff should have a good idea of how many sequences are needed, so they can determine whether to create them in-house or farm them out to external groups.

Appendices

The appendices form the last major section of the concept GDD. This section can hold all the dull bits and pieces (such as lists of art and audio files) as well as the long-winded stuff (such as the complete history of the game world and/or an extended backstory). It is also a useful area for reference materials such as the complete interface flowchart and collected charts and tables that form the database. Although this material can be useful to the designers in particular, it can be tedious for management and the other teams.

Schedule and Budget

The management of some companies might want a detailed analysis of the schedule and budget in the introduction, whereas others want only a synopsis of this information. In the latter case, the designer might include as thorough an analysis of the schedule and budget as possible in this first appendix. The team will work out a more realistic schedule and budget during the technical review phase, and these materials can be included in the production GDD for purposes of comprehensiveness.

For the concept GDD, the schedule can define the major milestones for the project and their projected dates of completion. Of course, this information is subject to revision during the technical review phase, but it's a good idea to get it down in writing so everyone can start picking the schedule apart and suggesting changes. Likewise, the budget can only be guessed at this early in the development process, but some semirealistic number should be included to help sales and marketing determine the break-even point.

10

Full Interface Description

This appendix includes a full description of all interface screens, the functionality of each screen, and the game controls used in each screen. As mentioned previously, the designer should give an overview of the game interface at the beginning of the game mechanics section to let everyone know how involved the interface will be without getting bogged down in the details. The reader should then be directed to this appendix for a full analysis of the interface. One or more programmers will eventually be assigned to work on the interface, and a full description here will let them know how much work needs to be done.

The quality assurance group also needs the full analysis of the interface in order to develop a thorough test plan, so the designer should try to list every possible interface screen and window in addition to describing the functionality of each screen and window. *Functionality* refers both to those things the player interacts with directly (for example, clicking on the playfield to move an object) and to information displays (for example, remaining health points, laps remaining in the race, timer, or scores). When defining how the player interacts with each screen, the designer should describe every possible player input (control pad buttons, mouse clicks, thumbsticks, keyboard).

The material can be divided into two groups: shell screens and in-game screens. The *shell screens* are those that are not used directly when playing the game. They include the installation screens, introductory screens, main menu screen, game controls screen, and so on. The *in-game screens* include the main playfield as well as the secondary screens and windows that appear during play, such as the inventory, store screen for buying and selling items, strategic map, journal, and so on.

History/Backstory

A game is not a novel or history book, so the backstory or world history is of very limited interest to management and the rest of the team. However, it might be important for the designer to work up an extended history of the world and the characters as well as what goes on outside the realm of the game itself. If management likes the game concept and thinks it might make a good series, this material can be very useful when planning sequels and add-ons.

The art staff *might* look at some of the fictional or historical material in this section if they need more inspiration, but the programmers and other team members will never read it. Thus, putting it in an appendix reduces the amount of material management and other team members must read to comprehend the basic game.

Dialogue

Games with stories—adventure and role-playing games in particular—will likely have considerable dialogue. However, this information will probably not be needed for the concept GDD unless the story has been fully developed and the

---

Caution

Keep It Simple

If the designer can't reduce the essence of the plot to a short, one- or two-page summary in the introduction, there is a good chance that the customer who plays the game in fits and starts will be confused by the complex plot.

designer knows each character's dialogue. A game based on a movie, for example, might use some of the dialogue from the movie, and it's a good idea to include it at this time. It's also a good idea to indicate what else needs to be written.

Other games might give the player mission briefings or other background information to help him understand the next part of the game. Even if the dialogue has not been written yet, the designer might want to include a synopsis of what the narrator will talk about.

When the game enters production, the real dialogue will be written. The first pass might be written by the design team, with a professional writer brought in to polish it. It's a good idea for the design team to include the dialogue in its various incarnations in the production GDD. The team might be involved in localizing the game for other countries, so having the final text and dialogue available as a reference is extremely useful for making sure the translations are correct.

Story Flowchart/Schematic

For a storytelling game such as an adventure game or role-playing game, the designer should create a flowchart or schematic of the plot points or bottlenecks within the game. It should show what objects players need to collect or what information they must acquire to get through each point or bottleneck (Figures 10.15 and 10.16). If the story is linear, the designer can create a straight timeline of events that indicates where the player must go and what she must do to get an object or information. If the story is more open-ended, the task is more challenging; the designer might want to break the overall story into chapters and then create parallel or overlapping timelines per chapter.

Game Database

As mentioned previously, the charts and tables used to resolve game actions should appear throughout the second section, where they are first discussed. In addition, it's useful to gather them all together into an appendix as a reference tool. The charts and tables can go through several iterations before everyone is satisfied with their structure and how the pertinent information is defined and displayed.

Playfield Maps

The designer should have a good grasp of what tasks are needed to complete the game and what the playfields will look like. Although it helps to have the maps drawn on paper, their designs can change radically as the actual maps or levels are created. If nothing else, the designer should break down the elements that will appear on each map—NPCs, items, encounters, puzzles, and so on—in outline format. Grouping all the maps together in an appendix makes a handy reference.

When the game is in production, the design staff might include the playfield maps in the production GDD. This is easier if the game uses a two-dimensional playing surface because three-dimensional maps are more

10

CHAPTER 1						
Location	*Floors*	*Rooms*	*Items*	*Connects to*	*Enemies*	*Characters*
Ralph's Cottage	Top Floor	Parents' bedroom	King's letter	Castle Road to Newberry		
		Ralph's bedroom	Cloth coat			
			Boots			
		Hallway				
		Stairway (down)				
	Main Floor	Stairway (up)				
		Main room	5 gold ducats			
			Father's letter to Ralph			
		Library	Book w/ heal spell			
		Kitchen	Carving knife			
		Pantry	Burlap bag			
			Food			
		Front door				
	Cellar	Root cellar	Small Mana juice			
		Stairway up				
Castle Road				East to Newberry gates	Wolf	
				West to Ralph's Cottage	Bear	
				South to Forest	Bandit	
Town	*Maps*	*Locations*				
Newberry	Plaza West	Gate to Castle Road		West to Castle Road		Gate sentry
		Smithy				
		Herbalist				
		Church				
		Plaza	3 gold ducats			Tourist
						Young boy
						Sleeping man
		Bridge to east plaza				
	Plaza East	Bridge to west plaza				
		Duke's Castle				
		Lady's Cottage				
		Man's Cottage				
		Soldier's Hut				
		Well				
		Gate to Forest		East to Forest		Woman at gate

FIGURE 10.15 A designer might want to use a spreadsheet to help determine where the locations, items, characters, and enemies will be located in a role-playing game.

difficult to show on a flat page. However, any maps that can be included will make the lives of the playtesters easier because they will know where items, encounters, and other trigger points are located, which enables them to more easily test changes.

File Names

The production GDD can serve as the primary repository of information about the game. One type of information that can prove useful to the team is a list of all the files in the game, broken down into art, audio, design, and code. Whenever the team does a build of the game, they must make sure to merge all the latest versions of the files.

It can be a chore to keep the list updated, especially if it runs into thousands of files, but the design team can have the producer forward the list of files to include in the production GDD with each new version of the game. Such lists are often generated automatically by version control software, making the task simpler. A complete list of files can be a lifesaver, especially, if the team is involved in localizing the product for foreign markets.

RPG: Chapter 1

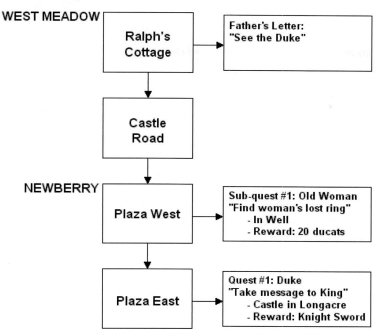

FIGURE 10.16 When creating the GDD, the designer might want to include a simple schematic showing the major plot points of the story to help the reader understand the flow of the action.

Multiple Versions

Management might plan to ship the game on multiple game platforms. This appendix focuses on the differences between the versions. Each platform has its own limitations and idiosyncrasies, and the designer can use this appendix to indicate how the game must change to meet each platform's technical requirements. In addition to the changes required by different hardware and operating systems, management might want each version also to have different content to lure customers into buying multiple versions.

The producer might write up a report for management on the scheduling and budget requirements for creating multiple versions. That document and other materials can be included in the production GDD.

In addition, this appendix can be useful for tracking assets that need to be changed or modified during localization (assuming the game will be sold in foreign markets). The names of the files that have to be changed (including files for the text, voiceovers, and artwork that includes text) can be grouped in this appendix.

Team Summary

This appendix contains a one-paragraph biography of each team member. It serves several purposes. First, it can be used to make sure that everyone whose name is to appear on the credit screen is noted. Second, it provides marketing with information they might want to include in press releases. Finally, it enforces the idea that this is the *right* team to make the game, which can help build support for management to green light the project.

Technical and Art Design Documents

After the concept GDD is approved by management, the product enters the technical review phase (see the next chapter for details). As part of this phase, the programming team might generate a technical design document (TDD) while the art team generates an art design document (ADD). Even if the design team is not directly involved in creating these documents, they might want to include the final versions in the production GDD for purposes of completeness.

Finishing Touches

The last step in completing the concept game design document is to have everyone on the team sign it—in effect saying that this is the project they will finish. It's important for the team to make this commitment because there will be strong temptation during the production phase to overhaul the design completely. Finally, the completed, signed concept GDD should be turned over to management and the corporate review committee (if applicable) for consideration.

The Production Game Design Document

The concept game design document describes in detail what the team plans to build so management will have the information they need to approve the concept (or not). The design can go through a number of revisions before management finally agrees to fund the project. Even when the project has been approved, the designer's work on the GDD should not stop. At this point, the GDD assumes its second identity as the *production GDD*, which is sometimes called the *bible*.

The GDD should be posted on the company's intranet at this point so the team will have ready access to it. Having the most up-to-date version of the production GDD available to the team is important for three reasons. First, as new hires join the team, they have the GDD available to explain what they're building. Second, if there is ever a disagreement among the team members or between management and the team about how the game is supposed to play, the designer can point to the updated GDD as the "source of all truth and knowledge." Finally, keeping the GDD updated throughout the production phase will help when it comes time to create a walkthrough or game guide for the product.

The production GDD will certainly grow over time. The final production GDD for a role-playing game can reach hundreds of pages. The production GDD still has to be a useful reference work for the team, however, and each team will be interested only in those sections that have information pertinent to their responsibilities. Most of the additional material can go into appendices rather than bloating the main body of the document. Keeping the main body of the document relatively short and to the point will make everyone more willing to use it during the production phase.

Finally, another important (if not selfish) reason to update and maintain the GDD is that by the end of production, when the game finally ships, the team will be exhausted and will likely hate the product and never want to see it again. Thus, when management drops by to congratulate the team and ask when they can start work on the sequel, they can proudly hand over the most recent version of the production GDD and tell the executives to find someone else—anyone else!—to create the follow-up. "Here," the designer can say as she hands over the massive production GDD, "is the blueprint they'll need to make the greatest sequel ever." Then the team can go home and catch up on their lives.

> ## Caution
>
> **Save Some Trees**
>
> Printing multiple copies of the GDD is generally a waste of paper because the team members should be familiar with it, having signed the management-approved version.

Summary

The GDD is a living, working document that should be completed during the pre-production phase and then revised, updated, and maintained by the producer and designer during the production phase. A game will always benefit from having a full and complete design. However, the development team should not feel constrained to this design. They should embrace new ideas as the game progresses, although the producer must closely watch and carefully balance the trade-off between improved gameplay and feature creep that might delay the release of the game.

The production GDD reflects what the team actually created and serves as a starting point for the sequel or follow-up games. Overall, the process of writing a solid, professional GDD involves a complete understanding of all the rules, pieces, elements, and interactions of elements within the game as well as the ability to write it down clearly so that others understand it as well.

10

Test Your Skills

MULTIPLE CHOICE QUESTIONS

1. True or False: The GDD is a blueprint of the game design that should be followed exactly.

   A. True.

   B. False.

2. What is feature creep? (Select all that apply.)

    A. Changing technology during the development.

    B. Adding new features.

    C. Designing additional levels.

    D. Redesigning game features after alpha.

3. Why should you keep a current version of the GDD updated during production? (Select all that apply.)

    A. So that sequels are easier to make.

    B. To make it easier to explain the game to new team members.

    C. To keep track of all the ideas that the team creates.

    D. To keep the producer busy.

4. What is evolutionary game design?

    A. A new method of making games that has evolved from the old.

    B. A method of design that relies on creating an idea, implementing it, testing it fully, and then creating the next new idea to incorporate.

    C. The best way to make a complex, new game such as an MMOG.

    D. Usually funded by the publisher.

5. What are good sources of information for game design? (Select all that apply.)

    A. Similar games.

    B. Books, including history, fiction, or others set in the genre or time period of the game.

    C. Movies.

    D. Magazines.

6. A GDD is many things. What is it not? (Select all that apply.)

    A. A script.

    B. A story.

    C. A summary of game elements.

    D. A concept.

7. What is an attribute?

    A. A unique characteristic that, combined with other attributes, makes an object or character distinctly different from other similar objects.

    B. A software term for programming levels.

    C. The way for a designer to describe a personality.

    D. A physical characteristic, such as the grey uniforms that all soldiers wear.

8. True or False: A GDD should contain an extensive and accurate budget.

   A. True.

   B. False.

9. True or False: Multiplayer mode should be left for the technical review to define.

   A. True.

   B. False.

10. Which of the following are important elements for the GDD to include? (Select all that apply.)

    A. Attributes of all enemies.

    B. Art requirements, such as file format.

    C. Music style.

    D. All objects the player can pick up.

    E. Objects the player cannot interact with.

11. What should the interface that is designed in the GDD include? (Select all that apply.)

    A. Main menu.

    B. HUD.

    C. Inventory screen.

    D. Installer.

12. True or False: The file formats to be used during development should be called out in the concept GDD.

    A. True.

    B. False.

13. True or False: The concept GDD should contain the final dialogue for the entire game.

    A. True.

    B. False.

14. True or False: All the assets required to make the game need to be called out in the GDD.

    A. True.

    B. False.

10

15. Which of the following are considered elements of a game? (Select all that apply.)

    A. Gameplay rules.

    B. Units.

    C. Characters.

    D. Weapons.

    E. Modifiers.

    F. File names.

    G. Localization issues.

    H. Enemies.

    I. Level maps.

    J. Inventory items.

16. True or False: The producer and designer should update the concept GDD into a production GDD immediately after the technical review phase.

    A. True.

    B. False.

EXERCISES

Exercise 10.1: Write a High-Concept Introduction

Select your favorite game and write a Section 1 introduction for that game. Use all the subsections described in the chapter.

Exercise 10.2: Game Element Creation

Imagine a new card game that does not include any form of gambling. List all the game elements that you can think of.

Exercise 10.3: Core Mechanics

Describe the core mechanics of *Half-Life*. (You may select another game if desired.)

Exercise 10.4: Game Mechanics by Platform

Play a game such as *Scrabble* that has been released on multiple platforms (computers, consoles, paper/board, cards, and so on). List the similarities and differences between the gameplay on the different platforms. Compare the limitations of each platform and the choices made by the development team to make the game work on each platform.

Exercise 10.5: Game Element Summary

Select an RPG or an RTS, and using the game's manual, write down all the gameplay elements you can think of. Include the interactions between the elements. Create a chart to help demonstrate the various attributes of each item.

DISCUSSION TOPICS

1. Discuss the merits of fully designing a game and writing a GDD versus using evolutionary design. What benefits could you take from both methods to use in your own production?

2. Story and backstory are not generally considered important in video game design. Discuss why you do or do not agree with this. Argue both sides. Use examples of games to support your reasoning.

3. Although much of the GDD is written by a designer or design team, a lot of ideas come from the development team as a whole. Discuss how you, as a designer, would involve the programmers and artists when coming up with gameplay elements. How would you deal with suggested game elements that you did not agree with?

4. It's very important that the GDD be thorough, complete, and definitive. Yet it's also critical that it not be a straightjacket that constrains the development team. Discuss what has to be done within the document and within the team to make this happen.

5. Discuss the research necessary to make an accurate WWII military strategy game. Where would you go for information? How would you evaluate the accuracy of your research? What portions of this research could you delegate and to whom?

10

Chapter 11

Technical Review

Chapter Objectives

After reading this chapter and completing the exercises, you will be able to do the following:

- Explain the structure and format of the technical design document.
- Outline the technical review process.
- Explain the importance of creating a solid milestone schedule based on the technical review.
- List the technical information that must be worked out before coding starts.
- Demonstrate how the art design document is structured and laid out.

Introduction

A carpenter doesn't just wake up one morning and decide to start building a house. He has to plan first because there are many issues to consider. What is the best overall design for the house? What kinds of tools will be needed? How will the rooms connect to one another? What is the order in which the tasks should be tackled? These and many other points must be worked out in detail before construction begins. Otherwise, the carpenter might run out of materials at a critical point or do considerable work on a part of the house before the owner decides to change plans and construct a cathedral or decides she no longer wants a building at all.

Similarly, the plans for building a game must be laid out in detail, just like the plans for a house. To rush in and start creating assets as soon as the concept game design document has been approved is as foolhardy as starting to erect walls before a building's foundation has been laid. The customer—that is, the publisher—will not be happy and might cancel the project even though the carpenter—that is, the development team—has invested considerable time and resources in the effort.

The technical review process should be the last stage of preproduction. The concept game design document describes *what* the team plans to build, whereas the two documents created during technical review, the technical design document created by the programming team and the art design document created by the art team, specify *how* the game will be built. A company that skips this stage puts itself in jeopardy; therefore, every publisher should make technical review one of the major milestones for the project.

Technical Design Document

The ***technical design document (TDD,*** also called the ***technical specification document)*** is created by the programming team as a roadmap that specifies how the game will be implemented in code. The technical director of the company should oversee the creation of the document, placing the lead programmer in charge and assigning programmers to write those parts of the document that they will eventually code. After the document is written, it should be thoroughly reviewed by the team, the technical director, and management. The document can be subject to revision, but it usually does not go through the rigorous iteration process of the concept game design document (GDD).

Although management will want to be involved in the approval process for the TDD, they will probably skim through the document—assuming they get beyond the first page. The TDD is a document created *by* the programming team *for* the programming team. It is not a literary work and is generally full of programmer jargon that will put a marketing director to sleep. Therefore, rather than present the full document to management, the lead programmer can create a short summary that outlines the team's technical findings along with the milestone schedule, budget, and project timeline for management's review and approval.

Purposes of the Technical Design Document

The TDD is an integral part of the technical review process and serves several purposes:

- It helps the programming team determine all the code modules they need to write to complete the game.

- It helps nail down the tools and software that will be developed in-house and those that will be purchased or leased externally.

- It helps the programmers establish coding standards that everyone on the team will be expected to follow.

11

- It allows management to determine when new programmers must be hired along with subsequent equipment and software requirements.

- It helps the producer determine a realistic project timeline and milestone schedule.

The first step of the TDD process is for the programming lead and technical director to analyze the game and break it down into major code modules: game engine, graphics renderer, audio, artificial intelligence, physics engine, networking, tools, and so on. The team can then list all the tasks associated with each code module, assign them to team members, and estimate how long it will take to complete each one. Obviously, the programmers responsible for each task should be consulted as to how long finishing it will take. When this information is gathered, it is given to the producer so she can create the master timeline for the project.

Another important decision for the programming team is which tools and applications they will develop internally. These tools include the software that will be needed by other teams to complete their work, such as a map editor or scripting language for the design team or an animation plug-in for 3D Studio Max for the art team. The tools also include the software needed by everyone on the team, such as the project pipeline or a bug-tracking database.

The team might decide to use commercial software for some of the code modules, such as the Tokamak or Havok physics engine, the Miles sound system, or middleware packages, such as Criterion's Renderware or NDL's Gamebryo's for the graphics rendering system. They might decide that another company's finished game engine, such as EpicGames' Unreal Engine 3, has all the features they need and will be cheaper to license than to build from scratch. In addition to considering outside software for various code modules, the program team should include a list of all the commercial software each team member will need—Microsoft Office, Borland Compiler, Microsoft Visual Studio, Microsoft Project, Adobe Photoshop, and so on.

FYI | *Licensing Software*

Each team member should use only licensed software; otherwise, the team is engaging in piracy. Buying individual licenses for software can be expensive, but many software publishers offer volume licenses for groups that reduce the individual cost for each person using the software. A new developer with limited funds might be tempted to cut corners and share software, but they can find themselves in legal trouble as a result. Software vendors can audit a developer to make sure they have the correct number of legal licenses, and a developer can pay a substantial penalty if they don't change their habits.

In the TDD, the program lead defines the coding standards that the team is to follow. Having a unified style for the code makes it easier for everyone on the team to understand the structure of each other's work and, more importantly, helps new hires quickly learn how to read the existing code. If someone leaves the team, production can grind to a halt until a replacement coder comes up to snuff on the existing code, so having strict coding standards makes it easier for that person to quickly become productive. Without guidelines, the code can dissolve into *spaghetti code* that no one but the original programmer can understand.

Breaking out the tasks for each code module helps the programming lead and producer determine when they will have to hire new team members. The team will have to interrupt their work to take part in the interview process, so knowing when this will happen helps the producer set up a more realistic timeline for everyone. In addition, the new hires will need office space, equipment, hardware, and software, so these purchases need to be factored into the budget.

When the TDD is complete, the programming lead hands off a complete list of code modules and their associated tasks to the producer. This list of tasks forms the backbone for determining the overall timeline for the product. The art, design, audio, and testing tasks are then merged into the programming tasks to form the final timeline that includes every task that must be completed in the game. With this knowledge in hand, the producer can determine the milestones for the project and what features will be available at each milestone. After the timeline and milestone schedule have been reviewed and approved by management, the team is ready to start actually building the game.

Structure of the Technical Design Document

Each company can have its own preferred structure for the TDD. The structure presented in this chapter is just one approach to the document. Again, the TDD is written by the programming team as a tool for determining what will be in the game, who will do it, and what they will need to complete their work—in other words, how everything in the game will be built. Without a thorough design, the programmers will waste a lot of time in trial and error, rewriting code or hacking around solutions that end up not working as well as had been hoped.

Introduction

The introduction to the TDD presents an overview of the project and the programming team's planned approach to implementing the code. It assesses the risks involved and defines the major milestones for the team. This section can also serve as the summary that is shown to top management at the culmination of the technical review process. Although it is the first section of the document, it is often the last to be written because it is easier to recap the major points after

---

"Freedom Force vs. The Third Reich" System Requirements

Minimum System Requirements:
733 MHz Intel Pentium III or AMD Athlon processor or equivalent
128 MB RAM
ATI Radeon 7000 or NVIDIA GeForce GTS or equivalent
DirectX 9.0c compliant 32 MB video card with hardware T&L (transform and lighting)
Microsoft Windows 98, Me, 2000, or XP operating system
4X CD-ROM
700 MB of free hard disk space
DirectX compatible sound card
56K modem or broadband Internet connection for online play
Keyboard, mouse

Recommended System Requirements:
1.8 GHz Intel Pentium 4 or AMD Athlon 1800+ or equivalent
256MB RAM
ATI Radeon 9600 or NVIDIA GeForce FX 5700 video card or equivalent
24X or faster CD-ROM
Broadband Internet connection

FIGURE 11.1 The minimum and recommended system requirements for Irrational Game's *Freedom Force vs. The Third Reich.* The game will barely play on a machine with the minimum requirements. The recommended system requirements (or better) allow the player to enjoy the game fully.

all the details have been worked out and explained in the body of the document. The introduction generally includes the following elements:

- Game Concept: This is a short (two pages or so) recap of the game design taken directly from the introductory material in the GDD. It lets the reader know the topic of the game, the basic gameplay elements, and the target platform, audience, and Entertainment Software Ratings Board (ESRB) rating.

- Platform Requirements: The capabilities of computer systems, including audio and graphics cards, vary widely, so it's a good idea for the team to list the minimum system requirements for a computer game as well as the recommended requirements (Figure 11.1) for optimal performance. The list should include the processor speed, memory size, operating system(s), audio and graphics cards, input and storage devices, and network/Internet requirements. Video console platforms are different because each manufacturer's machine has a set standard, so the team can simply list the machine and any special hardware requirements. The team should be aware that the requirements might change based on new developments in platform technology, but it's still a good idea to "put a stake in the ground" to serve as a starting point.

- Technical Goals: These are the programmers' goals for the game such as creating a new game engine, "pushing the envelope" on some cutting-edge technology, or experimenting with a new and improved production process. Other goals might focus on team-building or streamlining the way things have been done so far. After the game ships, the programming team should revisit these goals to see how successful they were in reaching their objectives.

- Risks: This section goes hand-in-hand with the technical goals. Because games tend to exist on the cutting-edge of technology, a wise team will point out those places where they plan to experiment and the potential pitfalls they might encounter as a result. More importantly, they should also indicate fallback positions if their experiments fail or take too long.

- Internal and External Tools: In this section, the team indicates which tools they plan to build internally and which they will buy or lease from other companies. This discussion should include every tool used by the team, whether it is purchased, built by the team specifically for the game, or built by external teams. Tools built for other teams (marketing, online support, customer service, audio, and so on) also need to be included in this section. Details about these proprietary tools can be included at the end of the document if necessary.

- Timeline and Milestones: The GDD sets forth an estimate of the timeline and milestone schedule. After all the teams have completed their task analyses and estimated each task's time requirements, the producer can produce a realistic timeline that shows every element needed to complete the game, along with the production time required for completion. As a result, the team can present a sensible milestone schedule to management. If the executives are not satisfied with the schedule, the producer can point out the features that can be cut to meet the desired deadline. Eventually, the team reaches an agreement with management about the scope of the project and when it will be finished.

Main Game Loop

This section of the TDD is an overview that describes how the code handles everything from the moment the player launches the game until she leaves it. The ***main game loop*** continually checks to see where the player is, whether starting the game, playing the game, or leaving the game, and supervises the various systems for that area of the game. When starting up the game, the main game loop runs the initialization system that prepares the screen display, loads the 2D and 3D graphics, prepares the audio, and initializes the variables used by the games (such as the high scores). Likewise, when leaving the game, the main game loop runs the systems that delete the game assets, restore the default audio, and reset the original screen display.

During the game, the main game loop is called once per animation frame to check player input, change the graphics, and update the state of the game. It checks to see if the player has pressed a button or key; executes sections of the game code to deal with AI, physics, game logic, audio, and other functions; and changes the art on the screen as necessary. The main game loop does not handle all these functions itself but instead tells other systems to run their part of the code. The main game loop is like a trains stationmaster who is in charge of all the station operations but actually performs only a few limited actions himself.

FYI | *Animation Frames*

As described in Chapter 13, "Visualizing the Game," each action performed by a character is broken into a number of discrete steps. Each step is shown for a specified number of milliseconds on the screen (the ***frame rate***) to become one frame of the entire animation sequence. If the frame rate is fast enough, the frames blend together to give a sense of smooth animation. While a frame appears on the screen, the player can decide to press a key or button to change the direction of movement. The change is detected by the game code, which carries out the transition to a different animation (for example, going from walking to jumping) as smoothly as possible.

The team might present the main game loop in a flowchart to help visualize how the various systems work together (Figure 11.2).

Game Application Modules

The next section of the TDD gives an overview of the various code systems that make up the heart of gameplay. Each of the following systems should be discussed in detail in its own section (we discuss each of these systems in detail later in this book):

- Game Objects: Every object in the game—characters, vehicles, projectiles, and so on—is controlled by a manager system. Each object has a list of properties that are continually updated, often on a frame-by-frame basis. These properties include model/sprite animations, physics, artificial intelligence (AI), and game script. Based on the current situation in the game, the object manager receives input from other systems to determine if a given object moves or performs some other action, then outputs the results to the graphics and audio systems as well as any other systems that are affected.

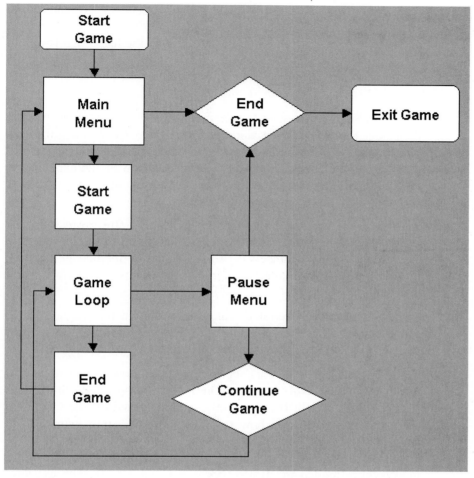

FIGURE 11.2 This diagram shows a simple game loop flowchart, from starting the game to exiting.

11

An ***object manager*** is a section of code that enables the programmer to manipulate all objects in a given class (characters, weapons, vehicles) the same way, rather than having to write individual code modules for each and every one. The object manager can handle such things as current location, movement direction and speed, collisions, and damage assessment the same way for all game entities in the object class.

- Characters/Units: This section focuses on the mechanics of controlling the main units in the game. It can include units controlled by the player as well as those controlled by the AI, although the team might want to defer the discussion of the behavior of AI-controlled units to the section on artificial intelligence. Topics of interest include animations, movement, collisions, AI, health, damage, and so on.

- Weapons: This section specifies the mechanics of how weapons work in the game. Topics include weapon and armor classes and the attributes, visual effects, and animations associated with the weapons (such as recoil by artillery), and any audio effects. The team should explain how the game engine uses the attributes, how the graphics will work, and how the special effects will be coded.

- Projectiles: If the game includes weapons that fire projectiles, the team might want to discuss how they are handled in a section separate from the weapons themselves. Topics to cover include generation, graphics, motion, collision, damage, visual effects, audio effects, and removal.

- Level Loading: This section discusses how and when levels are loaded into memory. Topics include streaming data off the CD/DVD, loading data during gameplay, and stopping play to load entire new levels.

- Terrain/Level Loading: This section discusses how the resources for the level will be loaded and how animations associated with terrain features are handled. If the resources are streamed off the CD/DVD, the team should discuss how the level is loaded into memory and when the loading occurs; for example, is it loaded piecemeal in the background while the game is being played or does play stop while a new level is loaded in? It also covers special effects such as snow, rain, sunrises/sunsets, shimmering water, and so on. If the terrain is automatically generated, the team should explain how this process will work. If the terrain is affected by weapons (or other game mechanics), the team should explain how it is deformed or otherwise shown visually.

- Physics: This section discusses how the game engine will handle such things as motion, gravity, and collisions. If the team plans to use a third-party physics engine, they should discuss any changes needed to make it fit the game design.

Artificial Intelligence Module

If the game has system-controlled units of some kind, the team can talk about how the artificial intelligence will work in this section. In a solitaire game, the AI controls the enemy and neutral units. In a multiplayer game, it controls the

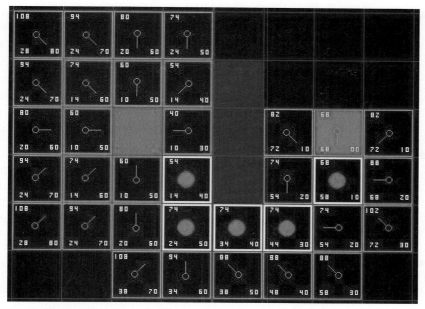

FIGURE 11.3 This diagram shows how a path is determined from the green space to the red space using the A* pathfinding method.

bots that might populate the game map. This discussion might touch upon the following topics:

- Pathfinding: The AI-controlled units must be able to make their way about the playfield. The team can discuss whether they plan to use a standard approach such as A* (called A-Star; Figure 11.3), modify an existing approach to make it more efficient, or create their own method for tracing movement paths.

IN THE TRENCHES: AI.Implant

BioGraphic Technologies' AI.Implant API (**www.biographictech. com**) is a plug-in for 3ds Max, Maya, or a company's proprietary level editor. It creates dynamic intelligent navigation that enables characters to perform such feats as staying on sidewalks, respecting stoplights, and avoiding bumping into walls. It also features real-time crowd simulations, which allows crowds to mill around nervously during a crisis or even break into rioting, looting, and hysterical panicking. This API speeds the process of defining movement paths not only for individual characters but also for large crowds, which greatly simplifies the life of the AI programmer.

11

- Tracking: The AI-controlled units have to be aware of the player's unit(s) to be able to react to them, so the team should explain how this will happen. The process can be as simple as checking to see if the player's unit is within a certain radius of the AI-controlled unit to create the effect of "seeing" the player's unit through a limited field of vision. Tracking can also be much more complicated; for example, when dealing with the *fog of war* (where enemy units that are not in direct sight are not tracked), avoiding obstacles, or tracking multiple units per side.

- Target Selection: If some kind of combat is involved, the team can explain how the AI-controlled units will select a target (and perhaps a weapon to fire). The team must answer questions such as whether the AI-controlled unit needs a line of sight to the target or just fires blindly in the direction of enemy units and how it will prioritize which target to select from player units and other AI-controlled units.

- Behaviors: Another important AI concern is the behavior of the AI-controlled objects. They can all have the same basic behavior (for example, kill everything within the line of sight) or each type can have its own quirks. The boss enemies, in particular, usually have unique behaviors. The behaviors might be handled by existing methods (flocking, finite state machines, fuzzy logic, neural networks, and so on), or the team might decide to experiment with their own system. In games where the AI controls a number of units (such as war games or real-time strategy games), the team might want to discuss group behaviors in addition to individual behaviors—in other words, how information and decisions are passed up and down the chain of command.

The team should be careful not to wed themselves to one AI methodology at this point. A number of factors, such as how processor intensive the AI routines turn out to be, can affect the way AI is finally implemented. The team might plan to implement unbelievably realistic AI routines, only to find that the processing time drags the frame rate down to an unacceptable point. Therefore, in addition to discussing the desired AI routines, the team should also discuss alternative methods to use if their original ideas do not pan out.

Graphics Engine

The *graphics engine* renders the 2D and 3D graphics elements on the screen. The engine contains a number of different managers to handle the different parts of the rendering process (see Chapter 13, "Visualizing the Game"). This section should detail how this system works. Some of the topics to be discussed include:

- Rendering System: The team can create their own rendering system from scratch or use an available Windows-based *application program interface (API)* such as OpenGL or DirectX. Building their own rendering system means more work, but they might have to if the game runs on a non-Windows-based platform such as Nintendo's GameCube. If the team builds their own system, they should explain in detail how it works (see Chapter 13, "Visualizing the Game," for more details). OpenGL and DirectX both allow the team to perform a number of important functions for rendering the graphics to the screen, but each has certain benefits the other lacks, so the team should explain why they want to use one API over the other (supporting both is recommended).

- Models: This system handles the 3D models in the game (both landscape and characters/units) by loading them into buffers to be displayed. The team should indicate what file format they plan to use in the game engine for model loading and animations.

- Animations: This system manages the animations of movable 3D models. The team might decide to use a tool that comes with a commercial software package such as the Character Studio (Biped) plug-in for 3D Studio Max (Figure 11.4), or they might build their own animation manager.

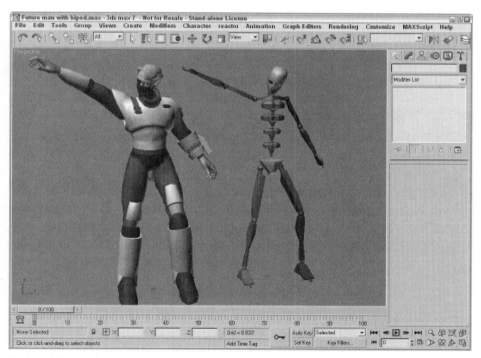

FIGURE 11.4 An animation for a human figure is created using the Biped skeleton on the right, and then a skin is attached to it (on the left) with Physique. Both modules are included in Discreet 3ds Max graphics program.

- Textures: This system deals with the way textures are applied to 3D models. It also deals with animations to make sure the textures do not tear as the models animate.

- 2D Graphics: Even a 3D game might use 2D graphics (for example, in the shell interface screens or the head-up display on the main game screen), so the team should discuss how they will show these graphics. If the game is strictly 2D, the team might expand this discussion to include such topics as sprite handling, font control, scaling, rotating, and special visual effects.

- Particles: The design might ask for blood splatter, sparks, snow, or other visual effects using *particles* (points appearing on the screen that represent natural phenomena, where each particle has independent motion and properties such as color and duration). This section discusses how the particles will be generated, updated, rendered on the screen, and removed.

- Text: This section discusses how fonts will be handled in the game and how text will be shown on the screen. The team can use a pregenerated font set or have the artists create a new one.

- Camera: In this section, the team examines how the camera will work in a 3D game in terms of its placement in the scene and how it moves through the world. They might also need to explain how the camera will shift between a first-person and third-person point of view.

FYI *Camera*

The *camera* is the point of view through which the game is viewed on the monitor or screen. In a first-person shooter, the view is through the eyes of the main character, whereas in a third-person shooter, the view is outside and some distance from the main character. There is no real camera per se in a game; instead, it is a set of rules that determines the visual representation of the game world.

- Renderer: The *rendering system* deals with the initialization, destruction, and rendering of graphic elements and text. The graphics can be rendered directly in software or through a video card. This section should focus on how the team plans to render the graphics on the screen.

- Display Manager: This system handles both the full-screen and windowed modes in PC games and deals with switching and restoring screen resolutions between the system default and the settings that the game requires. Of course, console games do not need such a system.

- Lighting, Shadows, and Other Special Effects: Other effects that the graphics engine might be required to create include weather, lasers, lighting, shadows, and darkness. The graphics might also require pixel and vertex shading as well as other hardware techniques. In this section of the TDD, the programming lead needs to discuss how these other effects will be handled within the game.

- Special Animations: Another topic to be discussed in this section of the TDD includes special animations, such as a reaction to a hit or a character's carrying or using different weapons. Though they are relatively simple to handle compared to other graphic engine issues, the engine has to accommodate these special events as much as possible.

Networking

If the game will include a multiplayer version that can be played over a LAN or via the Internet, the TDD should include a section that describes how the networked version of the game will work.

Playing a game over the Internet differs considerably from playing the game locally on the player's machine. Usually, the player connects to a server system that hosts the game and then hooks up with other players connected to that server to join in a game. As players perform actions on their machines, the software sends information packets to the host, which processes the actions and then transmits them to other players.

Several issues relating to networking need to be discussed in this section of the TDD, including client and server operation, protocol, packet structure, game specific information, online chat, and other servers.

Client and Server Operation   Networked games usually require a *server* to host the game as well as *clients,* which are the platforms that players actually play on. There are many ways that a networked system can work, so the TDD needs to discuss the team's approach in great detail.

A server can be a *dedicated server,* which means that it serves this purpose only and cannot also be used as a client, or it can be identical to the client machines and act only temporarily as a server. Most massively multiplayer online games (MMOGs) or games that require extensive computations or database look-ups utilize a dedicated server. The dedicated server is the only machine that knows everything about the entire game at any given time. All other machines connected to the server (the clients) know only about the portion of the game in which their player is currently involved.

Protocol   A *protocol* is a procedure that regulates the transmission of data between a server sending information packets and a host receiving them. The team must decide whether to use *UDP/IP (User Datagram Protocol/Internet Protocol)* or *TCP/IP (Transmission Control Protocol/Internet Protocol).*

> ## Caution
> **Cover Everything**
>
> It is critical that the lead programmer and lead artist go over the details of the graphics engine to make sure it can handle all of the special art, animation, and other effects described in the GDD. It is always painful when art is created that the engine cannot support because it wasn't discussed and designed to do so.

11

A turn-based game with limited player activity and, therefore, slower messaging and data transfer, might use TCP/IP because it offers more error-recovery services, whereas an action game might use UDP because it is faster, although less accurate. Technically, the team could create their own protocol, but that is highly unlikely.

Packet Structure A *packet* is a data structure that is transmitted as a unit between two or more computers. Packets have headers that identify their function as well as contain address information to ensure they arrive where they are supposed to. They are used to set up a game, transmit game actions (events), and allow communication between players. The team should indicate what information a packet will contain (for example, an update to a game action such as movement or firing a weapon).

Game Specific Information Multiplayer games' gameplay elements are often different from the solitaire version's, and these changes should be reflected in the GDD as well as the TDD. In addition, a number of different games can be included in the multiplayer version of the game. These include *cooperative* and *competitive* modes, where the players either work together against the game or compete with one another. Popular game modes include deathmatch (highest body count wins), capture the flag, king of the hill, and last man standing, among others.

Online Chat As it's name implies, *chat* is a mode of communication that enables players to send text messages to each other during the game. The team needs to design how the chat protocol will work by itself as well as in conjunction with the game network protocol. They also need to determine what limits or restraints to put on content, such as whether or not to allow swear words. If restrictions will be put on content, a server must usually be designated to check all incoming text messages against a database before allowing the message to continue. The TDD must fully specify how this will work and what will happen if a player tries to send an illegal text message.

Other Servers Some MMOGs games use separate sets of servers to handle different functions. An independent server that is separate from the game server usually handles customer purchases or subscriptions. The content database for the game is also usually kept separate from the server running the game, though it is obviously accessible to the game. A player database with information about players, their subscriptions, home addresses, and so on might be hosted on a third machine. All of these other servers, whether the host databases or other functions, should be described in the TDD.

FYI *Network Latency and Games*

In networking, ***latency*** is defined as the time required for a packet to go from its source to its destination. The less time it takes for the packet to arrive, the lower the latency. The components of the user's machine and the speed of his Internet service provider are two major factors in latency. Dealing with latency is a major issue in dial-up Internet service. In online games, older computers that use a modem to connect to the Internet can have serious latency issues depending on the type of game being played. Latency is less of an issue in turn-based games than in games with lots of action such as first-person shooter or racing games. On a slow system, the enemies can appear to jump in great gaps (called ***warping***) because the player's machine does not keep up with the server. Enemy positions are updated when the server sends the correct update, so if the information takes longer to make its way to the client, the enemy's positions appear to warp.

Audio

This section of the TDD discusses how the audio will be incorporated into the game, rather than the content of the audio. It also discusses what tools will be needed. The topics to discuss include:

- Audio Format: The team should give an overview of the audio recording parameters such as sampling rate, bit size, and number of channels. They should also indicate the file format they plan to use.

- Compression/Decompression: To save space, large audio files can be compressed and then decompressed before playing. Depending on the compression method, the audio quality can suffer, so the team should consider alternatives for storing, compressing, and decompressing the files.

- Sound Manager: This system handles the various audio functions and usually manages the sound card/chip, which handles a lot of the coding grunt work directly. The manager controls the buffering of the audio files so that the sound is consistent. It also pauses and restarts the audio, allows the music files to keep looping, and adds special effects such as echoes and tempo changes.

- Special Audio Effects: A number of audio effects might require special programming. One is surround sound, where the sound effects can appear to come from all around the player's location through the clever use of a high-end stereo system. Also, rather than simply recording a number of songs that play repeatedly through looping, the team might have the

11

composer create several music themes to match the mood of the game. Blending the various sound tracks together or using a synthesizer to create the music on the fly are two ways the team can make this approach possible.

User Interface and Inputs

The team should scrutinize the user interface as described in the GDD to make sure that the designer described all the interface screens and their functionality in sufficient detail. The interface screens are handled by the graphics engine, but the team should indicate in the TDD how they plan to handle both the 3D graphics of the playfield and the 2D graphics of the shell screens and the HUD.

The inputs include all the buttons, keys, thumbsticks, joysticks, and mouse buttons the player manipulates while interacting with the game. The team should define the commands for all inputs and indicate how the player can reassign the inputs if this functionality is included.

Coding Standards

This section of the TDD should specify the standards that all programmers are expected to follow. These standards should be made available to the current team, of course, as well as to new hires. A well-defined coding style guide makes it easier for everyone on the team to quickly find the files they need and to understand how the code works.

A section on file formats should also be included. It should specify the format for all text files that have game data, for the art files, and for the audio files. For a networked massively multiplayer game, it should explain how the files that are shared across the network should be interpreted by the server and the client.

Other topics for the team to discuss in the TDD include file structure, header files, the use of global constants, code document standards, modularity standards, identifier naming conventions, variable names, pointers and references, preferred and disallowed programming constraints, rules regarding commenting the code, authorship, and copyright notices. In addition, the team should define the directory structure to be used in whatever version control program they decide upon. They should also define the directory structure of the installed game (assuming a hard drive will be utilized).

Development Tools

This section of the document should discuss the functionality of the tools the programming team will build for the various teams working on the game. The programmer responsible for coding the tools should work with the leader of the appropriate team (art, design, audio, testing) to make sure not only that the functionality is agreed upon but also that the interface for each group is user friendly.

The TDD should include a complete list of all development tools including the level editor, map editor, graphics, animation, audio, scripting language, and so on. In addition to ensuring that everyone on every team has functional and user-friendly tools, this information may prove invaluable for other teams who plan to build similar tools.

Art Design Document

The *art design document (ADD)* is for the art team what the technical design document is for the programming team—an analysis of the game design to determine the art requirements *before* production begins. When game teams were small, it was common for a producer to come up with an idea for a game and grab some artists to build animated sprites without really knowing what the game would be. As production costs for development soared, game companies came to realize that they must try to keep down the wastage of resources to stay profitable. The time and expense required to build, texture, and animate 3D models prohibits the old cavalier approach. For artists, there is nothing worse than seeing assets they worked on so hard get permanently shelved.

Purposes of the Art Design Document

Similar to the TDD, the ADD helps the art director and lead artist break down the art requirements into a set of major components and then create a list of smaller tasks associated with each component. They can then determine how long each task will take to complete, as well as decide who will perform each task and when new hires must be made.

The second important purpose of the ADD is to serve as the central repository that the artists can consult whenever they have questions about the game's art style. The process of determining the game's style begins when the concept game design document is being written. At that point, the art director and the lead artist work with the designer and sketch artists to come up with the look for the characters and locations in the game (Figure 11.5). The concept art included with the GDD might show a portrait of each character with one or two action drawings as well as several views of each location. Management can look at the art and make suggestions about the style and the specific look of each character or location. A team usually turns out many concept drawings for each character and object in the game as changes are suggested, but by the time the concept GDD is approved, the art team should have a firm handle on the final style for the characters and locations. The lead artist should hang onto the sketches generated during the design process, in case someone needs to revisit earlier concepts at a later date. Ideally, the sketch art in the ADD will eventually be replaced by the finished sprites or models, so that by the end of the project, the ADD will be an accurate and complete reflection of all artwork in the game.

Another use for the ADD is to help the art team nail down the potential technical issues they might face during production. The document should identify

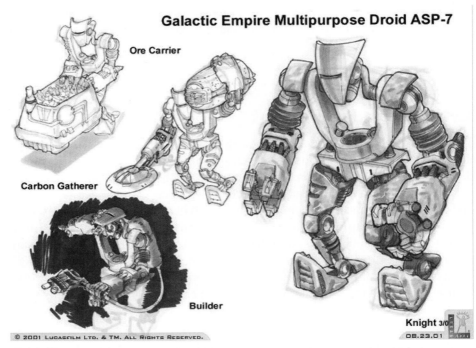

Galactic Empire Multipurpose Droid ASP-7

Ore Carrier

Carbon Gatherer

Builder

Knight 3/0

08.23.01

FIGURE 11.5 Concept art for a multipurpose droid created for LucasArts *Star Wars: Galactic Battlegrounds: Clone Campaigns*.

all the tools the art team will need from the programmers and specify the structure of the pipeline for creating and storing art files. External software requirements for the team should be identified at this point as well. The lead artist should try to anticipate if upgrades to important art tools will become available during the production phase and, if so, when they will be needed. In some cases, the team will need to spend some time learning how the upgrades work before being comfortable with them, resulting in a gap in asset production. The art director and lead artist should try to estimate a drop-dead date for updates.

Structure of the Art Design Document

Unlike the concept GDD, the ADD is created by the art team for their own purposes and is not meant to be shown to management. As such, it usually has a short introductory section before the bulk of the document focuses on the art and technology requirements without regard to whether anyone outside of the art team can understand it. The ADD should be kept up-to-date throughout the production process so new hires can use it to quickly understand the look and feel of the game.

Introduction

The introduction to the ADD is similar to that of the TDD and is often presented to management as a summary of the art team's goals. The introduction should include the following elements:

- Game Concept: This is a short recap of the game design taken directly from the introductory material in the GDD. It lets the reader know the topic of the game as well as the basic gameplay elements and the target platform, audience, and ESRB rating.

- Risks: If the art team plans to experiment, they should indicate potential problems and recommend fallback plans if their experiments fail or take too long.

- Internal and External Tools: The team should indicate the commercial software packages they will use to build the art, as well as the tools they need from the programming team.

- Timeline and Milestones: This section contains the art team's timeline for completing the art tasks. The art department should check with the marketing department so their requirements (screenshots, manual art, packaging art, and so on) can be taken into account when creating the schedule. The producer combines these estimates with those of the programmers, designers, audio team, and QA group to come up with a master timeline and milestone schedule for the entire project.

Character/Units

Descriptive material about the characters and/or units can be copied into this section from the GDD. Its purpose is to give artists reference to help them define the look of the characters/units and how they animate. This section should define the following elements for each character/item:

- Character/Unit Name: It is important to nail down the name of each character or unit as quickly as possible. The marketing department might want to run focus groups to determine which names are best, but it makes everyone's lives much easier if everyone is on the same page and knows the names of the characters early on.

- Description: This information is taken from the GDD's descriptions chapter. It specifies what the character/unit looks like as well as any special traits or abilities it might have. For example, if the character is very shy, its face might turn red the first time it talks with a character.

- Actions: This information is taken from the GDD's description and gameplay mechanics chapters. It is a list of all the different actions the character/unit performs in the game (with explanatory text if necessary).

For example, a character might perform an overhead attack when armed with a staff and a sideways attack when armed with any other weapon.

- **Physical Dimensions:** These include each character's/unit's dimensions (height, weight, width, depth, and so on).

- **Template (or Model Sheet):** A 2D template showing the front, back, and one side of each character/unit (called a **turnaround** in animation) is created from the final approved sketch of the character. The template includes the final texture and colors for the character/unit as well as the appropriate dimensions. When building 3D models, this template can be imported directly into the graphics program to help the artist create the wire-frame mesh and skin texture.

- **Animation Flowchart:** The flowchart shows how the animations all work together from the point when the character/unit starts at an idling state, to moving, to using weapons, to when they die. For example, to show a character being knocked unconscious to the ground in combat, the character would transition momentarily to the idling state, then to the falling prone state, and finally to the unconscious state.

- **Technical Information:** This includes the polygon count for a 3D model, the number of frames per animation, the rigging method, and all other procedural notes related to bringing the character/unit to life.

- **File Names:** This is a list of all art asset files associated with each character/unit. The naming conventions should be agreed upon as part of the technical review process.

Environment Locations

The scope of the game determines how much information goes into this section. For example, when creating a baseball game, the art team should include the layouts for the stadiums that will be included in the game as well as notes about what makes each one unique. For a role-playing game, however, the team might look at the whole world, continents, urban centers, and other places of interest (caves, ruins, and so on). Whatever the scope, the most important purpose of this section is to make sure the art style is consistent for all areas the player will see in the game. The elements to discuss in this section include:

- **Location Name:** Each location should be given a name.

- **Description:** This information is taken from the GDD Descriptions chapter. It includes what the location looks like as well as notes about its environmental factors, the ecology, geological features, and so on.

- **Animated Features:** This section describes animated terrain features (such as flowing lava or water spouts). The team determines if a feature needs to be modeled for animation (such as if characters interact with it)

or if it is background animation that can simply be projected on a polygon. The team might also include a section of notes directed to the programming team so the art lead and program lead can discuss how best to implement the animations.

- Special Terrain/Environment Objects: This section talks about terrain features or objects found in the playfield that have special gameplay significance, such as boxes that can be shoved around or lifted and placed on one another. The focus is on how these objects work in the game. If an object becomes part of a character's inventory, it can be described later in the items section; otherwise, it is an environment object and can be described here.

- Storyboards/Sketches: This section includes the most recent concept sketches for the location (Figure 11.6).

- File Names: This section consists of a list of all art asset files associated with the location.

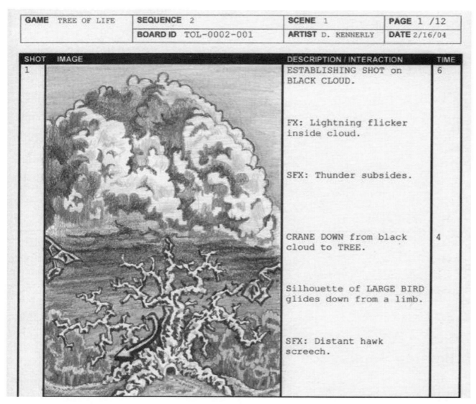

| GAME | TREE OF LIFE | SEQUENCE | 2 | | SCENE | 1 | | PAGE | 1 /12 |
| BOARD ID | TOL-0002-001 | | ARTIST | D. KENNERLY | | DATE | 2/16/04 |

SHOT	IMAGE	DESCRIPTION / INTERACTION	TIME
1		ESTABLISHING SHOT on BLACK CLOUD.	6
		FX: Lightning flicker inside cloud.	
		SFX: Thunder subsides.	
		CRANE DOWN from black cloud to TREE.	4
		Silhouette of LARGE BIRD glides down from a limb.	
		SFX: Distant hawk screech.	

FIGURE 11.6 Sample storyboard created by David Kennerly for a game called *Tree of Life*. Note that the team can add information about audio and visual effects in the column next to the illustration.

┌───┐
│ **FYI** *Using Contrast in Games* │
├───┤
│ It is important that game objects stand out from the backgrounds, │
│ especially in games with lots of action. Although a muted texture for a │
│ 3D character might look nice when viewed up close, it can be a mud- │
│ dle when viewed at various levels of detail. As a rule of thumb, the │
│ background is normally muted and game objects are more brightly │
│ colored to make them readable at all levels of detail. │
└───┘

Items

This section includes all the items found or used by the player during the game. It includes items that can be attached to a character (such as weapons and armor), items that go into the inventory, and power-ups. Elements to discuss in this section include:

- Item Name: Each item should be given a unique name.

- Description: This information is taken from the GDD's descriptions chapter and includes what the item looks like, as well as notes about any special effects (such as sparkles for a magic weapon). The section should also discuss how items will appear on characters, if they can be held. For example, will each sword have unique artwork associated with it, or will the character hold a generic sword to reduce art requirements?

- Item Appearances: This section talks about where the item appears in the game (on the playfield, carried on a character, in inventory). The team should determine what each item looks like when it appears and whether a generic icon will be used anywhere for multiple objects.

- Animations: If the item animates, this section describes what happens and the number of animation frames it takes to do it.

- Sketches: This section includes 2D sketches of the item. There can be one drawing for how it looks on the playfield and another for when it has been picked up.

- File Names: This is a list of all art asset files associated with the item.

Animated Sequences

This section includes a list of all animated sequences planned for the game including real-time animations using the game engine and prerendered sequences using full-motion video. The designer should describe what goes into each sequence in the description chapter of the GDD, so the art team can determine the best method for creating each sequence.

Each sequence should be storyboarded to show the key actions that occur and to indicate what dialogue is needed. Also, the team should try to estimate the running time of each sequence and the resources that will be required to create it.

User Interface

This section discusses the style for the user interface based on the interface flowchart in the GDD. The art director should work with the interface artist to determine a graphic style for all interface screens (both in-game and shell) that is consistent with the look of the playfield. The exact interface layout will likely change during the production phase, but at this point, the art director and interface artist should be able to determine which interface elements will be full-screen and which will be pop-up windows/boxes. The designer should provide a schematic of the HUD for the interface artist to use as a reference for deciding how the graphic elements will appear on the screen.

Title Screen and Company Logos

This section should discuss the requirements for the game title screen and company logos that appear when the game is first started. The title screen normally contains artwork and a specially designed font that will probably appear in marketing materials as well. It can take a while to finalize the artwork and fonts for these introductory materials, but the team should indicate from the beginning that they are aware these materials need to be created.

Licenses

If the game is based on a license, then all artwork needed from the licensee should be indicated. There might be special requirements for how the artwork for a licensed character or other brand appears in the game. The team should also discuss the approval process for signing off on the artwork so that it can be included in the overall schedule.

Fonts

This section discusses what fonts will be used in the game. As mentioned previously, the game title is frequently created in a font designed specifically for the game and might not appear anywhere else. But the team also needs to determine which fonts they will create themselves and which ones they need to license. Additionally, the section should discuss localization issues including how the fonts will be stored, whether text will appear on the artwork or be applied to it as a decal at runtime, and whether special visual effects (such as sparkles) will be applied to the fonts.

> ## FYI | *Licensing Fonts*
>
> A number of free fonts can be used in games, but many fonts have licenses that require payment to the creators for use in a game. Publishers usually create their own fonts for titles appearing in the game and on the packaging. They may license a font for use in a game, heavily modify the outlines of a true type font (built into the Mac and Windows operating systems), or look for an appropriate free font online. One source for free fonts is Acidfonts (**www.acidfonts.com**).

Miscellaneous Art

Time may be needed to create other art in the game, such as icons appearing on a computer desktop, art for the installer, and decorations for dialogue boxes. This section lists such artwork and talks about any special requirements (such as animations).

Summary

The technical review gives the production team the opportunity to explain the process they will use to turn the ideas outlined in the GDD into a final, shippable product. The programming and art teams face the greatest amount of work during the production phase and, therefore, theirs is the greatest challenge. To surmount that challenge, these teams have two management tools, the TDD and ADD, at their disposal to assist them in nailing down all the details of their work assignments and determining the order in which they will complete their tasks. These documents also address the methodologies the teams plan to use to create the art assets and code modules.

By the end of the technical review, management should feel confident that the team has thought through the problems involved in creating such a large-scale project and has agreed upon the solutions. Then—and only then—the *real* work can begin.

Test Your Skills

MULTIPLE CHOICE QUESTIONS

1. Who leads the creation of the TDD?

    A. A programmer.

    B. The technical director.

    C. The producer.

    D. The designer.

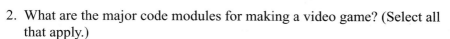

2. What are the major code modules for making a video game? (Select all that apply.)

   A. Game engine.

   B. Physics engine.

   C. 3D art.

   D. Sound effects.

   E. Artificial intelligence.

   F. Graphics renderer.

3. What kinds of tools are commonly needed for making a video game? (Select all that apply.)

   A. Level editor.

   B. Animation tool.

   C. 3D art tool.

   D. Physics engine.

   E. Game engine.

   F. Modeling tool.

   G. Paint tools.

   H. Hammer.

4. Why is it important to define a coding standard?

   A. It makes it easy to write code.

   B. It makes it easy to understand the gameplay.

   C. It makes it easy to read the code and understand the code components.

   D. It makes it easy to train a new producer on the team.

5. What do the programming lead and producer work together on during the technical review phase? (Select all that apply.)

   A. Breaking the code into manageable tasks.

   B. Determining when new programmers need to be hired.

   C. Creating a realistic timeline for the development.

   D. Determining what new hardware, software, or other purchases are required to make the game.

6. What is the technical design document?

   A. All the coding standards that should be followed.

   B. An explanation of the physics in the game.

   C. A list of all the game mechanics.

   D. The design of all technical elements within the game.

7. What does the main game loop do?

   A. Shows how the menu system works.

   B. Controls the order of gameplay actions within the game.

   C. Outlines the gameplay mechanics.

   D. Controls the processes within the game.

8. What is the frame rate?

   A. A single frame of an animation from a 3D model.

   B. A single frame that is rendered 24 times within a second.

   C. The concept art that is used to create textures.

   D. The rate at which the screen is redrawn, usually stated as number of times per second.

9. What are some different types of AI that the technical lead should consider while working on the TDD? (Select all that apply.)

   A. Neural nets.

   B. State machines.

   C. Pathfinding.

   D. Inventory management.

10. What elements does the graphics engine contain? (Select all that apply.)

    A. 3ds Max.

    B. Renderer.

    C. Level loader.

    D. Camera.

    E. Particles.

    F. Pathfinding.

11. What is a packet?

    A. A small amount of information about a game object.

    B. A network structure that contains information about the game.

    C. A protocol for communicating between computers.

    D. A method of input.

12. What is a client?

    A. A networked computer that runs a master version of the game.

    B. A computer that receives information about a game from online.

    C. A computer that the player actually plays the game on.

    D. A computer that hosts a game.

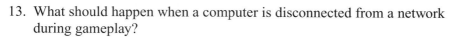

13. What should happen when a computer is disconnected from a network during gameplay?

    A. An error message should appear and the game should stop.

    B. The game should keep playing without informing the user of the disconnection.

    C. The game should play as well as it can without interruption.

    D. An error message should prompt the user and allow him to continue to play, stop the game, or restart the game.

14. What is in-game chat?

    A. Networking that uses a phone line.

    B. Text only networking.

    C. An independent communication mode that is available only before the game starts.

    D. A means of communication within the game between players that is independent of the gameplay, requires no validation, and doesn't require speed.

15. Why is it important to have an ADD?

    A. It is too expensive to make a game without using resources wisely.

    B. It's critical to know all the audio resources in a game.

    C. An ADD helps the programmer know all the animations in the game.

    D. The producer needs concept art for the first playable.

16. One reason to have an ADD is to set the art style for the game. What is another reason?

    A. To help schedule all the tools and hardware.

    B. To schedule the art personnel throughout the development cycle.

    C. To help management know how far along the art development is.

    D. To help in playtesting and debugging.

17. What should the ADD include? (Select all that apply.)

    A. Fonts.

    B. HUD.

    C. Concept art.

    D. Audio lists.

    E. Sign off from licensees.

11

18. Technical issues for the art design include which of the following? (Select all that apply.)
    A. Risks.
    B. Tools.
    C. Art pipeline.
    D. File formats.
    E. Box art.

19. What role does the producer have during the technical review phase?
    A. Writing the TDD.
    B. Writing the GDD.
    C. Working on the programming schedule and milestones.
    D. Working on the overall schedule and milestones.

EXERCISES

Exercise 11.1: Risks of Making a First-Person Shooter

The process of mitigating risks is usually broken into three components: name the risk, name a deadline by which the risk must be resolved, and list possible solutions or paths that might be taken. List a few risks for a new company that is making their very first FPS game and creating their own game engine. Specify when you think the risks must be resolved. Finally, list some possible solutions to each risk, including cutting the feature that the risky element supports or even canning the entire game production.

Exercise 11.2: User Interface Design on Paper

Select a development tool such as a level editor, and design its user interface.

Exercise 11.3: Art Pipeline Estimations

If it takes an artist 3 days to create a concept sketch, another 4 days to create the model, 4 more days to make the clothing and skin texture, and 2 weeks to animate it properly, how long should it take a team of 5 artists to make the art for an RPG with 100 characters (enemies and players)? Would it be any faster with a team of 10 artists?

Exercise 11.4: TDD Example—*Pac-Man*

Write the gameplay description of the AI behaviors of the ghosts in *Pac-Man*. Then write the technical descriptions of those behaviors. What is different?

What does the programmer have to think about to make the behavior (chase until Pac-Man is caught or until Pac-Man eats a power-up, then run for a certain length of time)? How are the four ghosts the same and how are they different? Now consider a first-person shooter where the computer-controlled characters need to "sneak" around until the player gets to the flag, and then the AI-controlled characters run and hide. How is this different from the Pac-Man example above? How are they the same? Write out the technical requirements you would add to the Pac-Man AIs to make them smart enough to be in an FPS.

Exercise 11.5: Art Design

Consider an online game that will have monthly updates of character content such as new weapons, new costumes, or new objects. How would you plan these updates in the ADD and in the schedule? Consider seasonal updates that might be made, such as a winter holiday scene or Halloween costumes.

Exercise 11.6: Error Messages in Networked Games

Write two error messages that a game will display to a player in the event that a network connection is lost. Write the first one to be as short as possible. Write the second to provide as much detail as possible. Create a compromise error message that is short but provides the player with enough information about what has happened and what she should do next.

DISCUSSION TOPICS

1. What risks can you think of that would face a new team making an FPS for the first time? Consider the gameplay, content, art, technical issues, tools, resources, staffing, and so on.

2. A good portion of preproduction is spent writing and maintaining documents and working with a team to design a game. Form a group of three or four students and select a game genre. Select one person to be the designer, one to be the producer, one to be the art director, and if there is a fourth person, one to be the programmer. Spend 10 minutes discussing what critical gameplay elements (puzzle, collecting items, flying in a race) the game should have. At the end of the 10 minutes, create a list of the gameplay elements that should be included. Now evaluate how your group was able to agree on these gameplay elements. If there was arguing, how was it resolved? If everyone was in agreement, were they enthusiastic? Given the opportunity, would you work together on the project?

11

3. Discuss whether or not it is beneficial to use a preexisting game engine in making an FPS. What are the pros and cons? Consider time, cost, and experience required.

4. Discuss how the producer works with all the different groups and coordinates the effort during the technical review phase. What is the producer's primary goal during this time?

5. Discuss how the technical director should write the TDD. What are the benefits of one person's writing the document and then providing it to the others? What are the drawbacks? What are the benefits and drawbacks of delegating sections of the document to other team members? What is the minimum experience level that a team member or technical director should have before writing any part of a TDD?

Part | Four

Implementing the Vision

The process of producing a game can be compared to how a body works. The game documentation acts as the skeleton that gives structure to the whole and is the basis upon which everything else is built. The code is the flesh and blood that gives life to the body and makes it move and act. The art is the skin that others see and that gives identity to the body. The audio is the voice. All these elements must work together as a unit for the body to exist.

The elements forming a game must work together, too. When the game design has been worked out and everyone knows what needs to be done, the teams start creating the assets for the game. The programming team is responsible of creating the code modules that make things happen in the game plus the tool sets used by other teams. The art team builds and animates the 2D sprites or 3D models, fashions the playfields, creates the graphics for the various menus and displays in the game, and constructs the animated sequences for a story-telling game. The audio team incorporates the music from the composer and the sound effects into the game. By the end of the production phase, all the assets have been created, tested, refined and, hopefully, the final product will prove to be a success.

- **Chapter 12:** Coding the Game
- **Chapter 13:** Visualizing the Game
- **Chapter 14:** Hearing the Game

Chapter | 12

Coding the Game

Chapter Objectives

After reading this chapter and doing the exercises, you will be able to do the following:

- List the tasks the programming team completes during production.
- Explain what goes into creating a game engine.
- Explain the difference between 2D and 3D game engines.
- List the tools that programming teams create for other team members.
- Appreciate the noncoding tasks for which programmers are responsible.

Introduction

A brilliant game design means nothing if the words on the page can't be translated into an application that runs on a computer or video console. The "translator" is the computer program written specifically to make the game run on the desired platform. To make a game operate, the game program must handle many functions including graphics, sound, artificial intelligence, networking, physics, user interface, and so on. The programming team is responsible for creating the code that brings the designer's vision to life and makes the game work.

After management approves the timeline and budget created in the technical review, the game enters the production phase, and everyone goes about their coding assignments. In addition, programmers must perform other duties that support the game's creation including building tools, supporting the playtesters, maintaining the version control system, and maintaining the company intranet.

Coding Overview

Going back several decades to the early days of computers, programmers had to tell a computer what to do by feeding it a series of encoded commands made up of *1*s and *0*s. Even today, all computers operate off these encoded commands (called **binary code** or **machine language**). However, programmers no longer have to enter the *0*s and *1*s by hand. **Assembly languages** have been developed that use recognizable names for all the encoded commands and thus enable a programmer to write code in human-understandable form. The **assembler** then converts the code into machine language. Although assembly language is considerably easier to use than machine language, it still has drawbacks; for example, every command still has to be entered individually, which makes it difficult to write extremely complex programs.

To handle the growing complexity of computer programs, **high-level languages** have been developed. These languages allow programmers to write code that is an abstraction of what the computer is actually doing. A single command in a high-level language might be turned into several or even dozens of machine language commands (this translation is handled automatically by a **compiler**). Thus, programmers can create much more complex programs in less time. There are many high-level languages, but the most common are FOR-TRAN, Pascal, BASIC, COBOL, and C.

FYI *Code*

The **code** is a set of instructions that is read by the machine, telling it to perform certain functions in a specific order. Code is arranged into **modules** that are each designed to handle a specific function.

Currently, most major games are programmed in an object-oriented version of the C language called C++. An **object-oriented programming (OOP)** language creates **objects** by combining **data structures** (a way of organizing related pieces of information such as files, lists, arrays, and so on) with **functions** (operations applied to the data structures). Programmers can then create reusable modules that contain one or more functions, and these modules can then be applied to new object types without having to reassign the functions to each module. This allows programs to be extremely complex while still being easy to modify. C++ is also very fast compared to most other languages, which is essential for handling the 3D graphics demands of modern games.

Two modern high-level languages have begun to challenge C++ as the primary language of games: Java (from Sun Microsystems) and C# (from Microsoft, pronounced "C-sharp"). Both are similar to C++, but they are simpler, safer, and easier to use for writing complex programs. However, it will be a while before they overtake C++ as the language of choice because C++ is faster and neither Java nor C# currently works on consoles.

Programmers might also use simplified, easy-to-use *scripting languages* to control various parts of the game, such as checking to see if game events have been triggered. Perl, Lua, and Python are the most common of these languages and are often used to create tools, but because of speed issues, they are not used to create the game code. In addition, a custom scripting language might occasionally be written for a given game. See Chapter 16, "Mathematics and Artificial Intelligence in Games," for more about custom scripting languages.

Most games are programmed on personal computers in the Windows environment, and therefore, the programming team needs a Windows *integrated development environment (IDE)*. The IDE enables a programmer to write the code, compile it, and debug it all in one place. Microsoft Visual C++ is probably the most popular environment.

Programming console games is in many ways similar to programming computer games, but a developer needs to obtain a license from the console manufacturer (Nintendo, Sony, or Microsoft) to get a *software development kit (SDK)*. The kit includes the company's proprietary *application programming interface (API)*, instructions on how to program for the console, development tools, and a special console, called an *emulator*, to run the code after it has been compiled.

FYI *Application Programming Interface (API)*

An API acts as an interface between an operating system and an application. It allows a programmer to communicate directly with a device or software without having to know exactly how the device or software works. For example, the OpenGL API enables programmers to generate three-dimensional effects using a graphics card without knowing exactly how the card is built. The programmer does not have to write the code from scratch each time to use device or software.

12

All games require the program to communicate directly with the graphics card. This communication covers everything from moving a character's arm one pixel up, to applying a skin or texture to a 3D model, to creating the effect of a light source on one side by lightening all the surfaces that are perpendicular to this light source and lighting all other surfaces based on their orientation toward this light. Of course, this communication is also written in code, not English, and writing this code is challenging. It is also highly repetitive because most games today require graphics on the screen to move. Fortunately, tools called *graphics APIs* that are able to do all this detailed, difficult, and convoluted communication with the graphics card are available, which frees the programming team to work on other issues.

If the game will have 3D graphics, the programming team must decide during technical review whether to use DirectX or OpenGL (Open Graphics Library). On the one hand, OpenGL was originally developed by Silicon Graphics as a platform-independent graphics API to provide direct access to the hardware. It gives programmers great control over how the graphics are rendered in real-time. On the other hand, DirectX was developed by Microsoft as a suite of APIs to move game companies away from the DOS environment to Windows. It includes not only the Direct3D graphics API but also Direct Draw (a memory manager for video memory), DirectInput (for inputs from joysticks), DirectPlay (network communications), and DirectSound (audio). There is considerable debate about which system is better, but most new graphics cards support both, so it is up to the team to decide which one(s) to support.

Game Engine Modules

When you look at the directory for a game project, you will find two different kinds of files: those that make up the game *assets* (art, music, sound effects, database) and those that make up the game engine modules' *source* (renderer, physics, networking) These code modules eventually get compiled into the executable file that is the game and manipulates the asset files.

A ***game engine*** contains the graphics renderer, the networking, the audio, the artificial intelligence, the physics, the animations, the lighting and special visual effects, the game camera, and more. The main difference between a 2D and 3D game engine is how it deals with the graphics; as you might expect, 2D graphics are not as processor intensive as 3D graphics.

2D Graphics Rendering

In a scrolling or platform 2D game, the animated objects (creatures, units and terrain features) move around in front of a flat background. The game might also include special visual effects such as ***parallax scrolling,*** where multiple layers of background art (clouds, mountains in the distance, trees in front of characters, and so on) move at different speeds, thereby giving a sense of depth to the scene. Also, it might include foreground art that momentarily blocks the animating object, such as a tree in the foreground that the character can hide behind. Meanwhile, the graphic elements of the head-up display (HUD), such as health bars and scores, remain in place on the screen as a framework for the player while the objects and the background move.

The background and foreground art on which the other objects move is often created from tiles using a special editing tool called a ***tile editor*** or

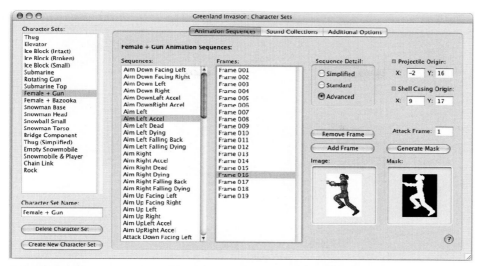

FIGURE 12.1 This window is used to set up character animation sequences in Sawblade Software's Power Game Factory, a software kit for developing side-scrolling games for the Macintosh.

map editor (see Chapter 18, "Prototyping and Building Playfields," for more about this tool). The animated objects are made of individual sprites that are displayed rapidly enough to give the illusion of movement. A technique called *page flipping* is used to quickly redraw the image on the screen. As the program displays one step of the animation onscreen, the next step is loaded into a nonvisible background page (or *buffer*). When a page is being loaded, the sprites are drawn over the background art, and then the foreground art and HUD are drawn as the top layer, closest to the player. After the designated amount of time has passed, the background page flips with the current image, which then becomes the new background page as the next step is loaded in and prepared. Figure 12.1 shows the Character Sets window in Sawblade Software's Power Game Factory, which is a tool used to set up and edit an animation sequence in a 2D side-scrolling game.

Certain special visual effects are handled either as sprites or as part of the background. For example, if something causes a spray of particles to appear, each particle can be handled as an individual object with several animation steps to change its color, size, and/or trajectory until it disappears. Shimmering water is created by assigning several shades of blue to the pixels forming the water art, and the program then cycles through the palette to give the impression of water moving.

Games that use an *isomorphic view,* where the map is tilted 45 degrees to the player to give a sense of perspective on the playfield, are sometimes called 2–1/2D or 3/4 perspective games (Figure 12.2). Instead of offering just four directions of movement (left, right, up, down) as in scrollers, these games usually offer 8 directions of movement (north, south, east, and west as well as northeast,

12

FIGURE 12.2 The map in Sirtech Canada's *Jagged Alliance 2* (1999) uses an isomorphic viewpoint that gives the playfield a sense of perspective missing from side-scrolling games.

northwest, southeast, and southwest) along with up and down for jumping. From a coding standpoint, the graphics are rendered the same way, with background drawn first, then the animating objects, then the foreground features and HUD.

The game engine for top-down view games is identical to that of scrolling games. The background, sprites, and foreground are all treated the same even though the player will view the image as being in an entirely different perspective.

FYI | *Rotating 2D Images*

One of the benefits of DirectX or other APIs is their ability to easily rotate an image on the screen. In the early days, every possible view of an item or character had to be drawn by the art team. The animating object itself was moved vertically or horizontally (or diagonally in a combination of the two) by the program when the game was running. But the program could not rotate an object to point in a new direction unless the artist already had created that image facing the new direction.

▶▶ CONTINUED ON NEXT PAGE

▶▶ CONTINUED

DirectX and other APIs solved this problem and others as well. Now, an artist needs to create only one set of animations for a 2D game, and the graphics renderer will rotate it from 1 to 360 degrees. Moreover, the image can automatically be scaled so it gets larger or smaller as the player appears to move closer to or farther from it. Another benefit of modern tools is their ability to scale or zoom in on the game playfield. In certain RTS games, for example, it is possible to zoom in and see the action up close or move back to see the entire playing field.

3D Graphics Renderer

The graphic elements that go into a 2D game are relatively simple compared to those required for a 3D game. Three-dimensional graphics are rendered in a completely different way than 2D. In a 2D game, all of the animating objects in the world are made up of sprite sets, with each step of an animation drawn and saved as a separate image. Animation happens when the images are displayed in rapid succession and, just as in a movie, they appear to blend together and are translated by our brains as smooth movement. In a 3D game, the models are saved as points in the 3D world (called *vertices*). The computer is programmed to understand how the vertices relate to one another, so it can draw lines between the points and form surfaces on which textures can be drawn. When the lines are drawn and the textures filled in, the player sees the 3D graphic on the screen.

When the vertices of a 3D model are joined together, polygons are formed. The smallest polygon that a 3D graphics card recognizes is a triangle. Its three vertices are called a *graphics primitive* because it is the lowest rendering unit possible. Of course, two triangles can be joined along a side and share two vertices to create a square. A cube (or box) is constructed on eight vertices, and when the lines are drawn between them, the cube shows six surface faces (Figure 12.3). All 3D models are formed from combinations of graphics primitives. As you might guess, it can be very challenging for an artist to make a realistic human being out of triangles.

A *model* in a 3D game is composed of a wire-frame mesh that contains thousands of polygons and the various textures that cover each polygon with the mesh. The more polygons it contains, the higher its level of detail. To animate the model, the program changes the positions of the vertices in the 3D world, thereby changing the locations of the surfaces. Other than the textures that clothe the mesh, no image files are involved. All animation is done mathematically.

A problem arises when too many polygons are on the screen at one time. In addition to the objects moving around the playfield, the environment itself

12

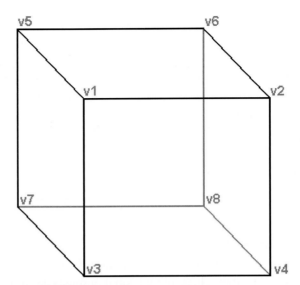

FIGURE 12.3 This model of a cube shows the eight vertices (marked v) of a cube. The lines drawn between the vertices form the six surface faces.

has to be modeled in 3D as well. If you have many objects on a complex play-field, the polygon count can become astronomical. With computers and the next generation of consoles scheduled to have 3+ GHz processors that will be able to perform over 3 billion operations per second, it would seem that polygon count would not be a problem. However, there are other limiting factors. Graphics are not the only thing the game engine has to handle. In the background, the game deals with physics, artificial intelligence, networking, audio, and other factors, and each one takes up processing time.

Furthermore, the game machine itself can have limitations such as limited memory or a slow CPU that hinder the transfer of the art to the graphic card for processing. Even though video card manufacturers might brag that their card can process millions of polygons per second, in reality the card must also deal with other instructions such as lighting, texturing, and manipulating the polygons that lower the actual number to several hundred thousand polygons per second.

To make everything blend together smoothly on the screen, the programmers try to maintain a rate of 60 frames per second (fps), even though it can drop as low as 16 fps before the eye notices jerkiness of movement. To keep the frame rate high, they try to limit the number of polygons the graphics card has to handle. One way to reduce the number of polygons is to not perform the calculations needed to display those things that cannot be seen, such as the backs of objects or things hidden behind other things.

Some form of ***hidden surface removal (HSR),*** which is the programming art of not spending time drawing things that are hidden behind other things, is always used before anything is drawn. The programmers use a ***culling*** process to determine which polygons to show and which to ignore. There are a number of ways to perform culling. One method is to use a portal system to divide the world model into sections and render only those sections that are currently viewed. When the player moves to another area where the next section can be viewed, that part of the model is rendered and everything that is no longer viewable is ignored. Another method for levels that are not divided into discrete physical sections is to use ***binary space partitioning (BSP),*** which is a method of dividing the world model into small sections (or partitions) and then showing only those sections that are currently visible (Figure 12.4). A purely graphical method is to use fog or some other visual obscuring condition to limit how far away objects can be seen; all objects in and beyond the fog do not have to be rendered.

In addition to showing the polygons that are visible, the renderer deals with other visual effects such as lighting, textures, shadows, fog, alpha blending, antialiasing, particles, and so on. Lighting can be as simple as figuring out the angle between a light source and a polygon surface and applying the right level of brightness, or it can be as involved as creating special light maps that are applied to the basic polygon texture. The graphics API might offer special

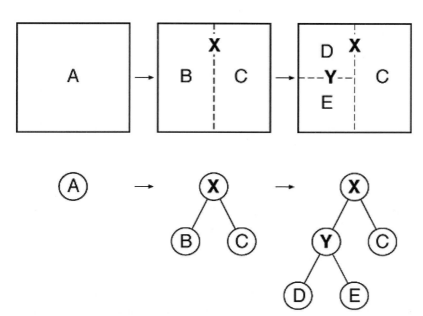

FIGURE 12.4 In this diagram, playfield A is divided along the axis X to create two smaller areas (B, C) that form branches of a BSP tree. The B area is subdivided into two smaller areas (D, E) in the third panel.

lighting techniques such as vertex lighting and even pixel lighting (that is, calculating the lighting value per vertex or pixel, with the latter method offering more control and nuance). See Chapter 13, "Visualizing the Game," for more information about these graphic effects.

Level of detail (LOD) is another graphics matter that can apply to both 2D and 3D art. This technique is used in games where objects that are farther away are drawn smaller to give the illusion of perspective. This is easily seen in first-person shooters, where enemies, buildings, and objects appear to be closer or farther away. Because objects that are farther away are smaller, less detail can be seen. Although video cards and computer systems are fully capable of scaling 2D sprites or 3D meshes and polygons down to size, it takes processing power, and much of the resulting graphic detail is wasted because it can't be seen. In short, it does not make sense to use the same sprite set or mesh model close to the front of the screen and far in the distance.

To get around this problem in a 2D game, when the view reaches a certain distance, the sprite set is swapped for one drawn at a smaller or larger scale, depending on whether the player is moving away from or toward the object. In a 3D game, there are two ways to approach this problem: first, the artists can build a number of models with different polygon counts (for example, a 3,000-polygon mesh for close up and a 300-polygon mesh for distant) and have the program swap the meshes similar to a sprite set based on distance. The second method is to dynamically reduce the number of polygons in the mesh based on distance, although this method can be processor intensive.

The texturing of models can be handled in a number of ways. A *texture* is a small image applied to the surface of a polygon. When all the polygons in a wire-frame model are covered with textures, the model appears to be wearing skin, clothes, paint, or windows. It can take a lot of memory to store all the textures that clothe even simple wire-frame meshes, so they are usually compressed to take up less space in video memory. Decompressing them can take time, but even with all the demands on a central processor, this is less critical than space.

Another method to save memory is for the programmer to apply several textures to the same polygon, overlaying them one atop the other. The overlay textures can have transparent or semitransparent patches through which the lower textures are seen. This method is one way to create shadows on an object (by laying a black texture with transparency over the base texture). It is also commonly used for such things as changing the color of a uniform based on which team the player is on.

Chapter 13, "Visualizing the Game," discusses how graphics cards render 3D models in more detail, but as you can see, the renderer for a 3D game performs many functions. As graphics cards get better, the demand for a more photo-realistic look to games will continue to increase. As complex as 3D engines are to build, it is no wonder that more game companies are using commercial game engines or middleware to assist in rendering the graphics.

Physics

Physics refers to the interaction, collision, and collision response of all objects within the game world and with each other. Depending on the game, the physics module can be relatively simple (such as a platform game that deals only with collision and gravity) or fairly complex (such as a racing simulation that deals with acceleration/deceleration, steering, skidding, the suspension, and collisions). For a simple game, the programmers usually write the physics algorithms themselves. For a complex game, the programmers might decide to use a commercial physics component rather than spend the time and effort to create it themselves.

IN THE TRENCHES: Physics SDKs

Examples of currently available physics SDK's include Havok (**www.havok.com**), NovodeX (**www.novodex.com**), and Tokamak (**www.tokamakphysics.com**). RenderWare also includes a physics SDK in addition to their graphics, audio, and AI modules.

No program is perfect, however, and a team can find itself having to make extensive changes to get the physics to work the way they want. If the program has to perform many computations to get the physics to work correctly, it can wind up stealing valuable cycles from other modules and bog down the frame rate. In the near future, AGEIA (**www.ageia.com**) plans to release a plug-in card for computers with a PhysX physics processing unit (PPU) that would perform these computations in much the same way that a video card is responsible for most of the graphics computations, so the slow-down problem might soon disappear.

One of the most important elements of the physics engine is *collision detection*, which determines when a collision occurs between a projectile and anything else on the screen. If a character shoots a projectile at an enemy, the graphic rendering component of the engine manages the bullet moving across the playfield. The physics engine deals with how fast the bullet travels, whether gravity has an effect on it, whether the projectile is moving through some viscous substance, and what happens when it reaches the target. Collision detection is also used to keep a character from falling through floors and walking through walls and other characters.

In a 2D game, the program checks for an intersection of the *bounding box* (or circle or other shape that encompasses an object's length and height) of a sprite with the bounding boxes of all other objects on the screen (Figure 12.5). When a moving projectile intersects a bounding box, a collision occurs, and the results are determined. For example, damage is assessed against the target; the projectile sprite is removed from the screen; a blood spurt animation appears in

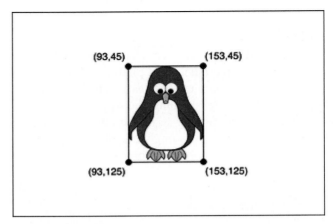

(93,45)   (153,45)

(93,125)   (153,125)

FIGURE 12.5 A bounding box encloses the 2D figure in this example. If something intersects with any part of the box, a collision occurs.

the appropriate spot on the target sprite; sound effects for the projectile hit and scream of pain are triggered; and so on.

In a 3D game, the programmer puts a 3D bounding box (or sphere) around a model and the physics engine checks to see if the projectile intersects that box. If precise collision detection is desired, the programmer might set the engine to check if the projectile collides with an individual triangle on a model, but this is much slower because there are many more bounding boxes to check.

Collision reaction or *response* occurs immediately after collision detection. It determines what happens to the objects that have collided. As everyone knows, a person swinging a bat or stick will feel a shock as the stick or bat connects with a ball. The ball will change direction depending on where it hit the bat, where the bat was during its swing, how fast the ball and bat were moving, and many other variables. It is the responsibility of the programmer to make sure that the resultant action in a game—in this case, the ball's moving on the correct trajectory toward (one hopes) the centerfield wall—looks and feels right to the player. Another example might be a character falling down stairs. If the figure falls stiffly, it might look like a store mannequin.

FYI *Rag-Doll Physics*

An unconscious figure falling down the stairs in a 3D game could be created as an animated sequence by an artist. In this case, every time the figure falls, the sequence looks the same. Another approach is to treat the figure as a series of rigid bodies (head, torso, arms, legs,

CONTINUED ON NEXT PAGE

>> CONTINUED

and so on) that are tied together and constrained in how they move relative to one another. When the figure goes unconscious, the constraints are loosened; the figure collapses like a rag doll, and the limbs bounce around and can end up in any configuration (hence, the name **rag-doll physics**). In this case, the figure can look different each time it bounces down a flight of stairs.

A programmer does not always try to accurately apply all the natural laws and equations of physics. Indeed, real physics may not be as much fun as cartoon physics or modified physics. It would be impossible for spaceships to perform dogfights à la *Star Wars* in the vacuum of space (much less to hear the roars of the engines and the explosions), but gamers expect spaceships to behave as if wings and tailfins influence their flight abilities in a vacuum. One of the delicate balancing acts for programmers is to make the physics of the game feel real, but not so real that the fun is taken away.

Artificial Intelligence (AI)

Due to the computational constraints of early computers and consoles, the enemies in early games were given simple behavior scripts (finite state machines) to follow. Players quickly learned the limitations of enemy actions and could easily defeat them. As machines grew faster and more powerful, additional computational cycles could be allocated to more advanced AI routines. But even those faster machines could get bogged down with the massive number of calculations needed to make computer-controlled enemies appear independent and humanlike, especially while also drawing advanced graphics, calculating physics and reactions, and interpreting user input. Now that the graphics constraints in 3D games have been mostly overcome, programmers can start devoting more time to improving the AI routines.

In most games, AI serves the primary functions of moving objects around the playfield and handling combat. Determining a course for an object to follow is called *pathfinding.* One component of pathfinding is *obstacle avoidance,* in which a character determines the best way to go around an obstacle in its path. In scroller games, the pathfinding can be as simple as arbitrarily determining whether to go left or right from the current position and selecting a direction to go to avoid an obstacle as it is encountered. More complicated obstacle avoidance can estimate the best path from a given point that avoids current obstacles before moving. AI-controlled movement in a 2D world is somewhat simpler than in a 3D world because there is one less dimension—height—to worry about.

12

FYI *Bots*

In FPS games with multiplayer online ability, the computer might control the actions of robotic (ro-BOT-ic, hence the term **bot**) entities that approximate the actions of other humans. They can help human players learn the rules of the game and practice their shooting skills before encountering real human opponents. Bots follow preprogrammed movement routines. **Static bots** follow paths that have been programmed into the map via waypoints or nodes (as in id Software's *Quake III: Arena* and Epic Game's *Unreal Tournament*), whereas **dynamic bots** learn their way around the maps as they play (as in the RealBot package by Stefan Hendricks and Tub for *Counter-Strike*, a *Half-Life* mod).

One of the most popular algorithms for handling pathfinding is called A* (pronounced "A star"). A* and its derivatives are used in both 2D and 3D games. At its heart, it determines the starting point for the object as well as the end point (usually wherever the player is located). It then tries to determine the shortest route between the two points, while factoring in impassable terrain features and selecting terrain through which the object can move most quickly. A* works well in slower-paced games such as turn-based strategy games, but it works less well in fast-moving action games, so the AI programmer usually has to tweak it to improve its performance. Alternatives to A* include **nodal pathing,** in which the programmer sets a series of waypoints throughout the level. The AI entity traverses the level from point A to D by going from point A to point B to point C to point D. This is a common means of pathfinding in simple games. See Chapter 16, "Mathematics and Artificial Intelligence in Games," for more on pathfinding.

In a computer-controlled world, it is easy for the computer to cheat because a computer-controlled enemy can "see" everything on the playfield at any level. The player, on the other hand, must have a clear line of sight to an enemy. AI that appears to take advantage of being a computer is unacceptable to most players. The player can feel cheated if the enemy automatically detects her and comes running in a beeline no matter how sneakily she tries to approach it or if the enemy seems to anticipate her moves much faster than a real human opponent would play.

One solution to this problem is for the programmer to restrict what information the computer enemy can act upon, or "know." For example, instead of a computer enemy's having the ability to know the player's location anywhere within the level, the AI code can enable the enemy to react only to things within a forward arc of vision. Ideally, this code will also account for terrain features or objects that lie between it and the player and thus limit the information the computer can use to determine further courses of action.

Other AI programming techniques include programming the enemy to respond to aural clues as well as visual ones; for example, no aural detection occurs while the player uses "tiptoe" movement, whereas a normal footstep, loud weapon, or noisy object (such as a cell phone) triggers a reaction from the patrol unit.

Changing environments is also a challenge. What does the enemy do if it comes to a hole that was blasted in a wall or a stack of crates that were knocked over? Not only does the AI have to figure out how to navigate around the field as it is originally configured, but it also has to control the animations so that the enemies select the right sequences to go over, around, or under the terrain as it is manipulated throughout the game.

As AI algorithms have become more refined, there is a push for ***emergent behavior,*** where the actions happen in ways even the programmer did not expect. In this method, the computer is given a set of rules that encompass how the game world works, and then it "plays" by those rules and tries different variations with them. Rather than having the programmer code every single instance of possible behavior, the hope is that the program will come up with unexpected answers to problems. A simple example of emergent behavior (which can also apply to the player's performing unanticipated actions) is a puzzle that requires a weight to be placed on a button that then opens a moat gate. Traditionally, a programmer would define that the player or enemy place a specific item such as a bag of sand on the button. Instead, to allow for unanticipated approaches to the problem, the programmer might instead determine how much weight it takes to depress the button and then assign weights to all objects in the game. The players or enemies can decide which items from their inventory to use to trigger the button, which leads to unexpected behaviors when a character selects which items to abandon in order to open the gate.

Because emergent behavior is the result of not knowing exactly how things will act within the game, this field will offer programmers many areas to investigate in the future. There is much to be learned in this area, but it will be interesting to play against a computer opponent that learns from its mistakes and successes as well as from the player's mistakes and successes.

Networking

Networking is a term used to describe a system where two or more computers are connected in some manner. Local area networks (LANs) are the kind of networks commonly seen in most offices. In a LAN, all the computers are always interconnected, usually with a networking card such as an Ethernet card. A LAN often includes a central server system that stores data and helps coordinate all the communication between the computers, printers, and other office peripherals. One of the key features of a LAN is that the computers in the network are almost constantly within the LAN, with the obvious exception of mobile computers and laptops.

On the other hand, the Internet is the network of computers that most people commonly think of when they discuss networking. In actuality, the Internet is not a single network, but a worldwide system of thousands of interconnected commercial, academic, domestic, and government computer networks that communicate with each other using standardized protocols. A computer on a LAN, of course, can often access the Internet as well, using the modem of the LAN servers rather than its own modems.

From a game programming standpoint, it is important to note that the Internet was never designed for playing games. It was started as a system for people at distant locations to transfer information to one another quickly. However, the usefulness of the Internet as a platform for playing games soon became apparent. Although it was not the first game to incorporate Internet play, id Software's *Doom* (1994) was the first to deliver such an exciting online experience that players began demanding more of the same.

There are two basic architectures for multiplayer games: peer-to-peer and client-server. In *peer-to-peer* architecture, multiple machines hook up to play the same game and information packets about player locations and actions are sent directly between the machines. Because all the machines are running the same game and sending information to all other machines, there is a chance that the game can get out of sync, especially if someone is playing on a slower machine or has a slower connection (a sluggish modem versus speedy broadband). In a *client-server* architecture, one machine acts as the host (server) that runs the game, and all other machines (clients) hook up to it. The host receives input from all the machines, processes the data, and sends out packets to update the client machines. This approach means that one machine does most of the work, and therefore, the host should be fast and powerful. A major advantage of a client-server architecture is that all players' information can be kept on the server and transferred back to the players when they start up a game, thus reducing cheating or code-hacking.

There are two protocols for sending messages across the Internet as well as within a LAN. In both protocols, the sender breaks up the data into *packets* that are reassembled by the receiver. *TCP/IP (Transmission Control Protocol/Internet Protocol),* relies on intercommunication between the sender and receiver to transmit the information packets. The sender will continue resending the data until it receives a notice that the receiver got the packet. This method can slow information transfer, but it guarantees delivery of packets, which was particularly important in the early days of the Internet when the system was used to send documents and other data between schools and laboratories. TCP/IP works well in slower games such as turn-based strategy games and role-playing games. However, action games with lots of simultaneous movement and combat have trouble using this protocol, so programmers usually opt for *UDP (User Datagram Protocol)* for these games. Unlike TCP/IP, UDP doesn't wait for an acknowledgement from the receiver before sending another information packet. Because packets might be lost or dropped, the host can either send multiple copies of packets, or the client machine can interpolate the missing data. For example, if the client sees an enemy moving along a path when a packet is dropped, it can be set up to continue to have the enemy move as calculated until another packet arrives with the correct location.

All networking engines perform some method of prediction and interpolation to allow the game to continue if there is a delay in the information exchange between the computers. The programming team has to ensure that any delays or glitches in the networking go unnoticed by the player. In addition, the networking programmers are responsible for making sure that the game gives the players as much information as possible in the event of a failure—*failing gracefully,* as the term goes. This means the programmers must write code that continuously tries to maintain or regain system integrity as well as write brief, intelligible error messages to cover all possible error scenarios.

There is a major difference between adding a multiplayer version to a game and running an online service for games. Because most games tend to use the client-server model, someone has to provide the central machine to process the game information. A number of online services let players set up their own small client-server systems where one player's machine acts as the host and the other players hook up to that machine. In this case, the online service just acts as a conduit for transferring messages, and this type of online play is free. The other method, where gamers pay a monthly fee to play the game, is used by a number of companies that create and host massively multiplayer online games *(*such as *EverQuest* and *World of Warcraft)*. The company sets up a server farm with many host computers that enable thousands of players to join in the same game. Maintaining the server farm and providing 24-hour customer service is expensive. In addition to running the games, the company also has to deal with handling the subscriptions and making sure the system is secure. It can be very expensive to host an MMOG, so the companies require users to pay monthly service fees.

A subcomponent of networking is the chat feature that is present in most games. This feature allows players to type or talk to each other while they are playing the game. Chat is considered a requirement for all team-based online games and most online games in general.

The additional programming required to create an online game includes setting up databases for customer information and login, programming Web site interfaces, writing tools for uploading new code or new content, and maintaining the server and client software with patches and bug fixes.

Audio

The sounds in games have come a long way from the electronic chirps of arcade games and early computer games. Most computers now come with a reasonably good sound card that handles audio functions, and video consoles have a sound chip that controls the player's audio setup, whether through a television set or a stereo system. The sound in a game has become more important as the technology has improved. Not only does it help set the mood for the game, it also provides clues to the player as to where the enemy is lurking.

There are several ways audio can be played in a game. DirectX provides two APIs, DirectSound and DirectMusic. OpenAL (Open Audio Library) is an API for sound, just as OpenGL is a graphical API. RenderWare includes an audio component, as do most commercial game engines. Separate programs also provide sound support, such as the Miles Sound System by RAD Game Tools (**www.radgametools.com**) and CakeWalk Pro by Twelve Tone Systems (**www.cakewalk.com**). See Chapter 14, "Hearing the Game," for more about audio.

One recent approach to game audio that is gaining popularity is ***interactive sound*** or ***dynamic sound.*** For many years, game music consisted of one musical theme looping over and over endlessly while a player explored a level. Then, as sound card technology improved, a song might fade out as another started playing, for example, when a combat encounter occurred. Now, music cues can be scripted to reflect the emotional impact of what is happening onscreen, just like the use of incidental music in movies and television shows. Additionally, games are starting to use surround sound to make players feel like are in the middle of the action instead of just being a spectator.

Sound cards function similarly to graphics cards: the computer CPU loads audio files to the sound card to process and play, thereby freeing the CPU for other computations. This processing includes surround sound, fading of sound effects or music for the perception of distance or speed, and shifting or modifying the music during actual gameplay.

As with the graphics engine, the audio engine uses a variety of techniques to ensure that the audio plays without interruption. Most of this work is now handled by the APIs listed previously; the audio engine often employs a double-buffering technique similar to the one that the graphics engine uses. Audio data is loaded into one buffer and playing begins. As the first buffer is played, the second buffer is loaded with the next section of music. When the first buffer is complete, the audio engine begins playing the second buffer, and the audio engine loads the first buffer.

Cinematics

Most games show an animated sequence when the game is first launched to get the player into the game world and then again at the conclusion as a reward for completing the game. There are two methods of handling the sequences:

- The first method involves creating a compressed video segment that is stored on the DVD or CD and then uncompressing and playing the video at the appropriate time. This technique is similar to playing back a movie.

■ The second method is to create the sequences in a 3D graphics program (3ds Max, Maya, and so on) and then use the game engine graphics renderer to construct and play them along with an audio file.

The advantage of the latter method is that the files are much smaller. In addition, the first method often creates lovely cinematics that look very different from the graphics in the game, which can be problematic because the player might lose immersion in the game when noticing this significant visual change. A number of APIs are available for creating streaming multimedia, including Microsoft's DirectShow and RAD Game Tools' Bink Video.

Tools

Depending on the teams' needs, the programmers might have to develop several tools, some of which are incorporated directly into the game engine. These tools can include a scripting language, an animation editor, a world geometry editor, and/or an outdoor terrain editor. Other tools are used only during the development of the game and do not ship with the product:

■ Scripting Language: To assist the designers, the programmers can create a proprietary scripting language that is used to trigger events in the game. This form of scripting language, which is akin to a natural language such as English, should not be confused (although it is confusing) with several programming languages that can be used for scripting, such as Perl, Lua, and JavaScript. A script often uses "if–then" statements to trigger events in the game, such as encounters, doors opening, and changes in NPC dialogue. (See Chapter 16, "Mathematics and Artificial Intelligence in Games," for more about scripting languages.) By incorporating the scripting language as part of the engine, the designers can make changes to a script and test it without having to leave the game environment.

■ Animation Editor: In a 3D game, this tool is often a plug-in to an existing graphics program such as 3D Studio Max or Maya. Although 3D graphics programs usually have some kind of animation editor, the team might decide to build their own tool, especially if they are trying some unusual approach to animation (for example, modified motion capture). This tool imports the model from the graphics program and enables either the artists or programmers (or both) to decide how the object will move. The team might enable the scripting language in this editor, allowing the designers to create special animations that are triggered by the player's actions during play.

There are two basic approaches to animating the mesh models. The first approach is to animate the mesh one step at a time, similar to a 2D

12

sprite. The program must define where every point is in each step of the animation, and all this data must be kept in memory. The second approach is to use a *skeletal animation system,* where a bone system is built inside the mesh and used to animate the model. The vertices are tied to specific bones, so that as the bone is moved the associated vertices move with it. Another advantage to using a skeleton is that each bone can influence the others, giving them weight. For example, a leg moving forward pulls on the hip, which twists and pulls on the spine and the other leg. One drawback to the skeletal system is in handling something like hair, each strand of which has to be given its own bones. See Chapter 13, "Visualizing the Game," for more details about animation.

- World Geometry Editor: As discussed previously, in a 3D game the team might decide to use a portal system to cut down on the number of polygons that must be shown. A geometry editor can be used to separate a large model into sectors or to combine smaller sectors as desired. The scripting language can be used with this editor to make sectors appear or disappear from the player's view. Also, if the model includes animated objects, this editor can let the artists see how they move in real-time as opposed to making the changes, importing the file, and then starting up the game again to view the changes.

- Outdoor Terrain Editor: The programmers might want to handle the outdoor terrain differently than interiors. With interiors, it is a simple matter of determining the total polygon count at any point in the model. Because the outdoor model might have an almost unlimited line of sight, the programmers might want to add terrain that blocks the view. This editor might run at real-time so that the artists and programmers can see how the open vista affects frame rate. It can also be used to create mist to reduce visibility or to import third-party terrain features such as realistic tree models where leaves move naturally, as in Digimation's SpeedTree 3 (**www.digimation.com**; Figure 12.6).

- Online Tools and Marketing Tools: In the realm of online gaming, several support tools need to be created including, but not limited to, tools for databases, content management, upload and download management, installed version control, payment, and credit checks. In addition, several research and marketing tools might be required to track game usage, download times, database access times, and impact on delivery systems. Marketing will also want reports on users, usage, and a variety of other information that will assist them in providing new versions or new games in the future.

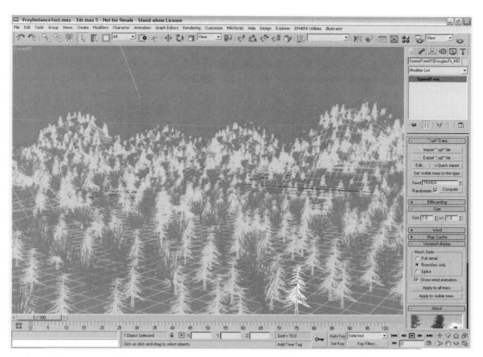

FIGURE 12.6 Example of a forest of 3,500 trees created in Digimation's SpeedTree 3. Its library includes 30 different trees at various resolutions.

Other Programming Tasks

Creating the game engine's various components is the programming team's primary objective, but several auxiliary tasks involved in producing a game are just as important as the engine.

Directory Structure

When the project is underway, people will be creating assets and writing code, and the team will set up a directory on the company's intranet so everyone has access to it. For port and localization purposes, there might be duplicates of some folders, but it's generally a good idea to keep the duplications to a minimum. Because games have grown so large, it is important that the directory structure be thought out and approved by everyone on the team beforehand as part of the technical review stage. The directory should include these folders:

- Doc (Documents): Contains the most recent versions of the game design document (GDD), technical design document (TDD), milestone schedule, and project timeline.

12

- Src (Source): Contains all the code files in the game.

- Obj (Objects): Contains the target files for the most recent builds of the game. It's wise to have separate directories for a debug version, a build version, and a release version. The debug version of the game has lots of cheats and shortcuts and should not be given to anyone outside the team. The build version contains the game in progress and might include files that are being tested and debugged. The release version should contain the most recent, complete version of the game. Materials from the build directory should never go into the release directory until the files are debugged.

- Bin (Binary): Contains the game assets including art, design, and audio materials. This is a good place to put marketing materials, including the most recent build, screenshots, and other materials.

- Test: Contains materials pertinent to testing the game. The testers might need special builds with cheats to let them jump to different places in the game out of order.

Version Control

There's nothing worse when creating a game than seeing a file you've worked on be accidentally overwritten by someone else. Not only do you lose the time spent in creating the file to begin with, but you have to spend more time recreating the lost material. *Version control* is a method of protecting files to keep them from being changed or deleted by accident. The idea is for only one person to work on a file at a time and, when her work is done, to release the file so someone else can work on it. Each change to a file is saved as a new version, so if a problem arises, a team member can go back through the older versions to find where the problem arose. One problem with version control is that it can quickly eat up a huge amount of disk space, especially when graphics are involved.

Some of the more popular version-control programs include Microsoft's Visual SourceSafe (**www.microsoft.com**), CVS (Concurrent Versions System, **www.nongnu.org/cvs/**), NXN Software's Alienbrain Studio (**www.nxn-software.com**), and Perforce Visual Client (**www.perforce.com**; Figure 12.7). Both SourceSafe and Alienbrain have licensing fees, whereas CVS is open-source.

In addition to using version control, the company should make daily backups of all their files in case a power outage or other problem forces a team to restore their work environment. It is a good idea to keep a weekly backup copy off the company's premises in the event of a catastrophic problem such as a fire, flood, or earthquake. There are companies that specialize in picking up and storing these materials securely. It is better to lose only a week of work than a whole project.

Caution

Don't Overwrite the Work of Others

Although a version control system can be set up to let multiple users work on the same file concurrently and then merge the work one user at a time into a new version, this approach is trickier and can lead to lost data.

Familiar folder hierarchy   File history with branching relationships

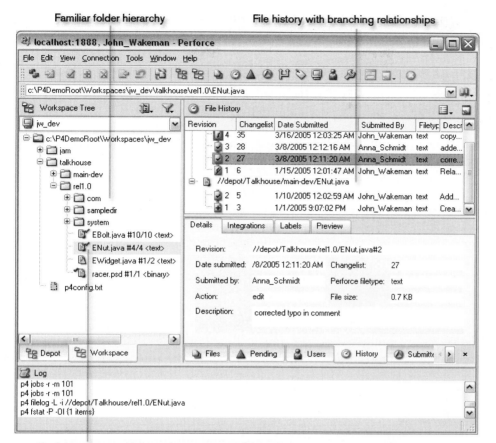

Real-time file status information supports collaboration

FIGURE 12.7 A screenshot from Perforce Visual Client, a popular commercial version control system that enables a team to get information about a file and its history.

IN THE TRENCHES: *Half-Life: Counter-Strike*

One of the most popular mods of all time is *Counter-Strike*, which is an adaptation of Valve's *Half-Life* into a multiplayer online stand-alone package that was released in 2000. When a mod differs so much from the original that it is almost a new game, it is called a **total conversion.** The gameplay is team-based and involves counterterrorists confronting terrorists. The project was spearheaded by Minh Le and Jess Cliffe and proved so popular that Valve acquired it and turned it into a commercial product.

12

Builds

As games grow ever larger, stretching to multiple CDs or DVDs, the process of putting all the assets and files in the right places on the disks also grows more complex. In a speech at GDC 2005 about asset management for Bungie's *Halo 2*, Matthew Noguchi said that they had 12 gigabytes of in-game assets spread across 39,000 files. This is an enormous amount of material to keep track of, and making sure that no files are left out or that the wrong files are not incorporated into a build can be daunting. The process of creating an installable version of a game is called *building the game.*

A game build is done by running one or more batch files, with each file launching a series of commands involved in creating the build. One batch file might gather all the resources—game engine, models, audio, game assets, and so on—from the appropriate game directory and put them in a temporary directory. Another batch file might compile the entire game to make sure there are no errors. A different file might run a program to check the localization builds (swapping out the text files in the game and making other changes for foreign markets). Yet another file might run all versions of the game to make sure each one initiates without a problem. Another might compress some files; another might run the files through a copy protection process; another might distribute the files over multiple disks. Finally, the build process produces a version that can be burned onto CDs or DVDs for distribution.

> **FYI** | *Batch Files*
>
> A ***batch file*** contains a series of commands that are executed in a specific order. It allows the automation of builds as well as other repetitive and/or tedious functions because you only have to launch the batch file instead of each individual command.

When the installable version is ready, someone should take it to a ***clean machine*** (that is, a computer on which the game has not been installed or has been correctly uninstalled) and make sure that the machine installs the game correctly. Fortunately, there are programs that assist in the process of build creation, such as Kinook Software's Visual Build Professional (**www.visualbuild.com**), as seen in Figure 12.8.

Testing and Debugging

One of the most tedious chores involved in making a game is the long process of testing and debugging it. The programmers who write the code obviously have to test it to make sure it works before committing it to the latest build directory. However, so many code modules are interdependent on one another

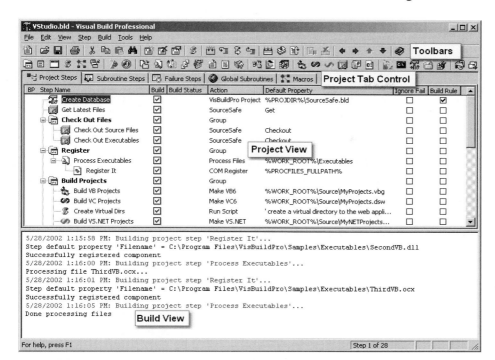

FIGURE 12.8 Visual Build Professional provides a graphical user interface to help simplify the process of creating a build of a game.

that each change has the potential to cause unexpected problems elsewhere. Of course, it is not just the code that must be tested. The art, the actual design work, and the audio all have to be checked and rechecked for problems as the game lumbers through the production phase.

The QA department has the somewhat thankless task of trying to make the final product as bug-free as possible. They might need help from the programming team setting up a bug-tracking database to route bugs to the right person on the team for resolution and to iterate the process until the bug is either corrected or left unfixed. See Chapter 19, "Completing the Game," for more about testing and debugging.

Several junior-level programmers might be assigned to the QA department to help determine to whom a bug will be sent and to test the fixes to make sure the repair didn't cause problems elsewhere. Programmers can be of particular help tracking down the bugs associated with the proprietary tools created for the project because these tools often do not have any debugging features. Helping to debug a game is not the most prestigious job for a programmer, but it is a vital task, and it is a good entry-level position for recent college graduates.

In some companies, such as Microsoft, the QA department is fully staffed with senior programmers. They not only have the task of finding the bugs but also that of tracking down the erroneous code or asset and fixing it. However,

12

this separation between the code creators and the code fixers is not common in the industry because it requires a large secondary staff of trained engineers.

A programmer might be assigned to build a tool that performs a statistical analysis of the debugging process to show how many new bugs are reported and how quickly they are dealt with. It can reveal to management that more programming help is needed to deal with the bugs, especially if a major milestone is approaching.

Installation, Patches, and Updates

When the game is close to completion and entering the final test phase, an installer must be written or incorporated to make the game easy for the consumer to install. Although some companies write their own software for this process, many use commercially available programs such as InstallShield (**www.installshield.com**), Inno (**www.inno.com**), or others.

A final task for the programming team is to provide patches or version updates for the consumers who have purchased and installed the game (this applies primarily to computer games). Ideally, the programmers will include a version number and some means to enable patches for fixes and upgrades in the final shipped version. They can change the version number for each new patch to make sure customers need to install only the most recent version.

Nonprogramming Tasks

Programmers do not spend their entire workweek sitting in front of their computers and writing code—as much as they would like to. They must perform other nonproject related responsibilities for the company that are as important as coding.

Meetings and Code Reviews

Meetings are a necessary evil for every company. The opportunity to share information face-to-face or over a phone cannot be overrated. E-mails and memos often are not read, but people will respond well to an organized meeting. A programmer's role in these meetings is to ensure that she hears all important information and to get her questions answered.

Programmers should keep track of their daily and weekly tasks. They need to update their schedules and inform their technical director or project leader of their progress. They also need to inform these people of all problems or issues that arise, especially if the issue can impact the schedule or the budget. By having these materials up-to-date, a programmer can help meetings run faster and more efficiently.

Caution

Avoid Meeting Hell

Meetings without agendas or without a leader can quickly degenerate into confusion or relax into a gabfest. Sharing details about weekend excursions can wait until employees have some free personal time.

Programmers should come prepared to demonstrate the current version of the game, which means that they should have one built, installed, and ready to go. They should bring all materials cogent to the meeting agenda and be prepared to discuss options. Although it's all right to use meetings as an opportunity to learn about possible solutions, a well-prepared programmer will come with several solutions ready to propose and support when management agrees.

One vital management tool that many companies ignore or misuse is the code review. Unlike other meetings, *code reviews* are specifically for programmers (as art reviews are for the art staff and design reviews are for the designers) because the topics discussed in a code review are technical and would not be of interest to the other teams. Ideally, a code review involves only a few people at a time, perhaps the lead programmer and a team working on a specific module. The idea of a code review is for each programmer to outline her current tasks and discuss approaches to structuring the code. Not only can problems be brought to light and solved as a group, the review also gives other programmers the opportunity to understand how other code modules work. If for some reason a programmer leaves the team, someone else on the team will have at least a basic understanding of the code structure, making it much easier for another programmer to take over responsibility for the code modules and get up to speed more quickly.

Equipment and Software

Another task that takes up a programmer's time is updating hardware and software. Work stations continue to improve at a fairly constant rate—what is top-of-the-line today will be tomorrow's low-end test machine and then finally a doorstop. Likewise, publishers of commercial software regularly release updates to existing programs and bring out new products that a team might find useful. Updating equipment and installing new programs can take a significant amount of time, especially in smaller companies that lack an information technology (IT) department. Frequently, when new equipment or software is installed, problems arise and everyone turns to the programmers to help resolve the technical issues.

FYI *Upgrading Equipment*

12

The programming and art teams need the most up-to-date equipment a company can afford. As a rough rule of thumb, a company should expect to replace programmers' and artists' workstations about every eighteen months to two years, and these costs should be included in the overall budget. The designers' workstations can be replaced every two-and-a-half to three years. There is often a system of handing down equipment, especially at smaller developers who have limited budgets.

CONTINUED ON NEXT PAGE

» CONTINUED

Artists and programmers get the new equipment, the producer and designers get the first-generation hand-me-downs, and the testers and other staff get the second-generation hand-me-downs. If a developer is creating PC games, it is important also to have testing equipment available to serve as the benchmark for the minimum system requirements.

Another technological issue on which the programming team (and art team as well) must decide is when to freeze the technology that will be used for the game. This is more a problem for computer games than video games because computers continually improve, whereas video consoles improve only when a new-generation machine comes along. The development team always gets the newest, best, and most powerful equipment, but if they build a computer game to play only on high-end machines, they can miss a significant share of computer users who replace their equipment less frequently.

The team leaders must also decide when to freeze the technology of the tools being used to make the game. It can be tempting to use every upgraded version of their middleware program or development package, especially if the company is paying for licenses. However, an upgrade is sometimes so revolutionary that it outdates everything done on the project and forces the team to rebuild the game almost from scratch. The team must evaluate how much an upgrade will set back their schedule, and if it would cause a significant delay, they might have to make do with their current version—no matter how much team members whine.

Interviewing

It is almost inevitable that someone will be hired during the production process, either as a new hire or as a replacement for a team member who leaves. The more hires there are during production, the more time the programming team (and other teams, of course) must devote to interviewing. Ideally, the interview process takes more managerial time than productive worker time, but in most game companies, everyone on the team spends some time with potential candidates in head-to-head interviews. Although a human resources department can review the résumés and screen the applicants, it is up to each programming team to meet the candidates, talk to them, and even test their skills; and this process takes time because there will likely be multiple candidates for each position.

When a new hire joins the team, there is a period of adjustment until the person comes up-to-speed on the project. Many companies assign a senior programmer to be a mentor—someone who is available to answer questions and to offer encouragement. Being a mentor takes that person's time away from coding, so both interviewing and mentoring should be taken into account when developing the project timeline and milestone schedule.

Demos, Trade Shows, and Conferences

Demos are smaller versions of the game that can be given away on CDs, on Web sites, or via magazines to help raise the excitement level of the release version. Making a demo is always an issue for programmers because it is often forgotten when the schedule is set up, or in the worst case, someone in marketing or sales determines a sudden need for a demo when none had been planned.

The demo should be designed to be a part of the actual game—often, it comprises the first several missions or levels. Making a demo can be as simple as switching a few statements in the code when compiling a build. On the other hand, it could end up being a completely separate project that pulls team members off their work on the real game. If at all possible, the programmers should avoid making a completely new version of the game that is used only for demo purposes. If a demo is needed, it should be included in the overall schedule; otherwise, the schedule can fall apart when someone asks for a demo version and the team has to scramble to meet the request.

Programmers also are sometimes asked to actually demonstrate the product for management, investors, and/or the public. Programmers are the most technically skilled people on the team and are often the most familiar with playing the product, so they are often tapped to do demos, whether they want to or not. Of course, demonstrating the game takes the programmer away from coding it, but giving a good presentation might be absolutely vital, say, for a team that is showing off a shaky milestone to a dubious publisher.

There are three major industry gatherings a programmer may attend either voluntarily or at the behest of management. The Game Developers Conference, or GDC (**www.gdconf.com**), is a show for and about the industry that is held each March in California. Many seasoned programmers give lectures, participate in roundtables, check out the expo where game production products are shown, and renew old friendships with fellow industry professionals. Similar to GDC is the annual Association for Computing Machinery's Special Interest Group on Graphics and Interactive Techniques (ACM SIGGRAPH; **www.siggraph.org**) conference that focuses on computer graphics and interactive techniques. It also offers lectures and seminars that programmers find useful. The host city changes each year. The third major show is E3, the Electronic Entertainment Expo (**www.e3expo.com**), which is also held in California each May. Publishers and manufacturers show off their future releases at this show and get significant feedback from the gaming public about which products are likely to sell. Programmers are sometimes dragooned into presenting products at the expo. In both cases, work on projects can slow down as the team produces working versions of their games. A wise producer makes sure that time is added to the schedule for these important trade shows.

12

Company Web Site

In larger companies, the corporate Web site is maintained by the IT department and is often created by the marketing and sales department (sometimes using external Web development teams). But in smaller companies, one of the programmers might be assigned this task. Whatever their size, the company will almost certainly have an Internet site so they can tell the world what they are up to.

Companies use their Web sites to talk about the products they are developing (assuming they receive permission from their publishers), to offer demos, updates, and downloads, and to post job openings and contact information. In some larger companies, or in companies where an online presence is critical, a huge amount of time and effort are devoted to making a Web site. Not only does the site perform the traditional functions discussed above, but it also acts as a portal into the game world and must reflect that image. These sites might include fan forums, newsletters, company news, and minigames. Game Web sites, such as MSNZone and WildTangent, are specifically designed as such and operate as a business by selling online the games that they have made or purchased.

On the other hand, the intranet on the company's LAN is usually restricted to internal use only. This is where the game directory is located. The intranet also handles e-mail distribution, Internet access, and sometimes hosts an FTP (file transfer protocol) site to handle uploads and downloads from outside the company. If a small developer's offices are not prewired, someone on the team—usually a programmer—might be required to string the cable and deal with setting up work stations for new hires. New team members also need to be given access to the game materials as they come onboard.

Summary

The programmers can be considered the workhorses of the whole development team. Not only do they write the code that makes the game work, but they also provide valuable technical services to the rest of the team and even to the rest of the company. The designers and artists often get praised by players and reviewers because the gameplay and artwork are what everyone sees. No one sees the code that makes it all possible, but without it there would be no game.

One of the biggest challenges facing game programmers is that they are usually working at the leading (or bleeding) edge of technology. They are often the first coders to tackle new technologies while they are still tasked with making their code as bug-free as possible. In addition, they have to complete their work on the schedule that they developed, or the team will face the very real danger of seeing their project cancelled. Meanwhile, the software tools they use and the workstations on which they work quickly become dated, so they must constantly upgrade their work environment—all of this, and they are expected to assist other team members who also are dealing with updated tools. Despite all the daily pressures, most programmers delight in the challenge of creating something new and pushing the envelope of gaming technology. No other type of programming offers the same challenges and rewards as working on games.

Test Your Skills

MULTIPLE CHOICE QUESTIONS

1. What is currently the most popular language for making video games?

   A. C.

   B. C#.

   C. C++.

   D. Java.

2. Why is a high-level language desirable?

   A. It's easy to write and understand.

   B. It is faster to interpret.

   C. It's easier for the programmer to comprehend *1*s and *0*s.

   D. It compiles assembly code quickly.

3. What is OOP?

   A. Object-oriented programming.

   B. Objects of programming.

   C. Official object programming.

   D. Oriented operational programming.

4. True or False: Assembly languages are machine independent.

   A. True.

   B. False.

5. Which of the following are application programming interfaces (APIs)? (Select all that apply.)

   A. OpenGL.

   B. Open AL.

   C. DirectX.

   D. Sony Playstation.

12

6. True or False: The game engine for a 2D platform game such as *Sonic* is virtually identical to the game engine for a top-down isometric view game such as *Zelda?*

   A. True.

   B. False.

7. What is page flipping?

   A. The method of animation used in traditional cel-animated movies.

   B. A way to quickly move data in memory.

   C. Using a buffer to predraw the image on the screen and then flip to it.

   D. A means to give the illusion of movement to sprites.

8. What is a graphics primitive?

   A. A game made during the 1960s.

   B. A simple, low-level polygon building block that is combined with other polygons to make complex models.

   C. A code module that communicates directly with video hardware.

   D. A wire-frame mesh.

9. What is level of detail?

   A. A technique used to save computations when rendering smaller versions of an image.

   B. The amount video RAM required to run the game.

   C. The difficulty in a puzzle game.

   D. The ability to create more textured surfaces within a model.

10. Why is it a problem to have too many polygons on the screen at once?

   A. Everything goes slower.

   B. It is too busy, and the screen is crowded.

   C. It's impossible to tell what is closer and what is farther away.

   D. The computer will crash.

11. What is HSR?

   A. A method of using fog to obscure far away objects.

   B. The technique of not drawing what is hidden.

   C. The technique of drawing only what is directly in front of the player.

   D. A method of drawing the scene and then removing things that are obscured.

12. Which of the following is the correct order in which a 3D renderer should process the following tasks?

    A. Light all surfaces, apply fog, apply textures, draw to buffer.

    B. Draw to buffer, apply textures, light all surfaces, apply fog.

    C. Apply fog, apply textures, light all surfaces, draw to buffer.

    D. Apply textures, apply fog, light all surfaces, draw to buffer.

13. What is collision detection?

    A. Using bounding boxes to determine the intersection of two points.

    B. The detection in a virtual world of collisions between multiple objects or the world.

    C. The reaction of an object bouncing off a wall.

    D. The algorithms that are used to determine what direction and at what speed a ball will travel when hit with a bat.

14. What is collision reaction?

    A. Using bounding boxes to determine when a collision occurred.

    B. The algorithms that are used to determine what happens after a collision has been detected.

    C. The amount of gravity that should be applied during a game.

    D. Determining whether or not a collision has occurred.

15. Which of the following is an example of collision reaction? (Select all that apply.)

    A. How high a ball will bounce when dropped.

    B. How far a bullet will travel before gravity makes it drop to the ground.

    C. How much a character will bounce back if it runs into a wall.

    D. How much blood will be drawn when a character is shot by a bullet.

    E. How far a projectile will travel once it's off the viewable area of the level.

    F. How much a car will spin when traveling too fast on an icy surface.

16. Which of the following is handled by the physics engine? (Select all that apply.)

    A. Speed of a vehicle on a dry surface.

    B. Deceleration of a vehicle by the player.

    C. Rendering blood after an enemy collides with a bullet.

    D. A computer-controlled player sneaking around the back way to defend an outpost.

    E. Page flipping.

12

EXERCISES

Exercise 12.1: Game Engine Research

Research the various game engines listed in this chapter. Create a table listing their various costs, capabilities, and what they seem best suited to do.

Exercise 12.2: Design a Level Editing Tool

Write a concept document for a level editing tool that you would make for an FPS. Ideally, what would the interface look like? What sort of training would you expect someone to need before he could use the tool?

Exercise 12.3: Installed Game Structure

Examine one of the games installed on your own PC. What directory structure does it use when the game is installed? List out the structure. How much space is required? How are the various elements distributed or are all of the game elements in one directory?

Exercise 12.4: Bug Reporting

Bugzilla is a bug reporting application that is freely available on the Internet. Download a copy and explore its uses and functionality. What would you want to add? What seems to you to be unimportant and why?

Exercise 12.5: Level Editor Research

Download the level editor from one of the games you own. How simple is it for you to create a new level and import it into the game? How easy did the programmers make the interface for you to use? Did you have to spend a lot of time reading the manual or online help, and if so, was it useful?

DISCUSSION TOPICS

1. From the list of engines in Exercise 12.1, discuss the following: If you were designing an FPS, which would be your first choice and why? If you were designing an RTS, would you use the same engine?

2. Discuss with your classmates the options of using middleware or licensing an engine as compared to building your own. What are the pros and cons of each? When would you decide to build your own?

3. Many companies now require programming tests when interviewing potential programmers. Discuss why this is a good or bad thing.

4. New consoles are released about every five years, sometimes several at a time. Because each new platform is a significant improvement over the last, much of the skill already gained from developing on the earlier platform can be lost. What would you consider doing to alleviate this problem for developers? Discuss any reasons you would have to *not* to make it easier for the development teams.

5. Meetings and code reviews can drag on without good leadership. Discuss the tools, techniques, or methods you would use to keep a meeting with your programming team on track. If you were attending a meeting being led by another person and it was not staying on track or on time, what might you consider doing to help control the time commitment?

12

Chapter | 13

Visualizing the Game

Chapter Objectives

After reading this chapter and doing the exercises, you will be able to do the following:

- Understand the basics of 2D and 3D computer graphics.
- Explain how animation is done in 2D games.
- Understand how 2D graphics appear on the screen.
- Explain how 3D graphics are rendered to the screen.
- Appreciate other nongraphics tasks for which artists are responsible.

Introduction

Game graphics have come a long way since the slow-moving, square "ball" of Atari's *Pong* (1972). The current and next generation graphics for computer and console games feature high-resolution, elegantly lighted and shaded graphics unthinkable just a generation ago. Yet despite all the technological advances in graphics, creating the art for a video game still boils down to one basic mandate that has held true since the beginning—put the right color dot on the screen in the right place at the right time.

For many years, computer graphics were two-dimensional. Starting with monochromatic ASCII characters moving across the screen, 2D graphics improved as screens began to display more colors and ASCII characters became animated sprites moving against flat backgrounds. In the mid-1990s, 3D graphic cards became available for the PC and eventually for video consoles, and the graphics became much more detailed and realistic. In the next few years, game graphics are likely to become even more realistic as graphics cards continue to improve.

During the technical review phase, while the technical team is planning out the programming tasks, the art team is also hard at work determining the art tasks for the game and assigning staff members to complete them. The lead artist works with the producer and other team leads to set up a project timeline and create the milestone schedule. If the art team spends time creating an art design document (as discussed in Chapter 11, "Technical Review"), they know the style they want for the game as well as the look and feel for all the characters, locations, and items. When the review is complete, the team begins creating the assets that will go into the product. Unlike the programming team, however, the art team usually has few supplemental tasks aside from generating the artwork. They also have fewer technical issues to disrupt the process of creating art assets.

Basics of Computer Graphics

The art for all electronic games is created on computers by artists using commercial software packages to make 2D sprites and 3D models. Some of the initial artwork is created by artists using traditional, noncomputer tools. Ultimately, however, all artwork must be digitized and saved in a format that can be manipulated by the game engine. The following sections discuss several basic concepts and terms that pop up when discussing computer graphics.

Pixels and Texels

The *pixel* (a term derived from "picture element") is the smallest element of a CRT monitor that can be assigned a color; in other words, the smallest spot of phosphor that can be lit up on the screen. The more pixels that are used to represent an image, the more realistic it appears.

The size of a pixel is relative and is based on the dimension of the image in relation to the resolution of the screen. Suppose an artist creates an image that is 640 pixels wide by 480 pixels high. If the screen resolution is 640 × 480, then each pixel will be the size of an individual dot on the screen. If the screen resolution is higher—say, 1280 × 1024—then one of two things will happen: the image will take up 640 × 480 pixels on the screen, or the programmer can code the graphics engine to stretch the image to fit all 1280–1024 pixels. In this case, the resampled image will use 4 pixels for every one pixel of the original image.

A *texel* (for "texture element") is the basic unit of a 2D image that is applied to a polygon (through a process called texture mapping or wallpapering). In other words, it is an individual pixel in a texture, which is spread over the 3D object like a decal. The clarity of the texture depends on the viewer's relation to the surface. When the player is close to the texture, it might cover a number of pixels, and the pattern of the texture map will be evident. At a distance, such as when the texel is smaller than a pixel, adjacent texture maps are blended (or averaged), and the pattern of the map is no longer apparent.

13

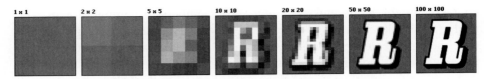

FIGURE 13.1 This figure shows how much clearer an image becomes as the resolution increases.

Resolution

Resolution refers to the number of pixels displayed on the monitor. It is defined by the number of pixels that appear horizontally and vertically. Thus, a resolution of 640 × 480 means that the screen has 640 pixels horizontally and 480 pixels vertically (a total of 307,200 pixels are drawn each frame). The higher the resolution, the more pixels there are and, therefore, the sharper the image (Figure 13.1). However, higher resolutions require more processing power to draw the larger image (a 1280 × 1024 image has to draw over 1.3 million pixels per frame). Computer games usually include multiple resolutions, so players can select the one that provides the best compromise between speed and detail.

Video games can also include multiple resolutions, but the user has less control over television screen resolution. A typical television has a resolution of around 640 × 480 pixels. Console games can be played at higher resolutions on more powerful TVs, such as high definition television (HDTV), but the player often has to buy special adapters for current consoles to make a game play at that resolution. This situation will change as the new generation of consoles appears. The Xbox 360, for example, supports HDTV natively for all games.

Colors and Bit-Depth

In the early days of personal computers, there were severe physical limitations on computer processing power as well as monitor display. As a result, games were initially limited to monochrome (one color on a black background), then expanded to four colors with *color graphics adapter (CGA)* hardware, then 16 colors with *enhanced graphics adapter (EGA)* hardware, then 256 colors with *video graphics array (VGA)* hardware, until the current technology was developed that enables computer screens to show over 16.7 million colors. Meanwhile, video cards have supported this growth with more computing power and memory. Obviously, the more colors the artist has available, the more realistic the art can be.

The human eye can discern somewhere around 10 million colors, so trying to assign more than 24 bits for colors per pixel is a waste of effort. However, assigning 32 bits of information per pixel (and higher) can be useful if the extra 8 bits are assigned to an alpha channel, which is reserved for transparency information. The transparency value is used to determine what percentage of each color (red, green, and blue) is used when a given pixel is blended with a pixel from the background that the image is being drawn over.

Graphic File Formats

There are two major types of 2D graphic formats: bitmap images and vector images. A *bitmap* image is made up of a number of pixels (bits) laid out in a two-dimensional grid. A sprite is an example of a bitmap. An artist can change the bitmap pixel by pixel as desired. Bitmap images are resolution dependent, meaning that the image is attached to its grid at a particular size. If the bitmap is resized, the look of it can change. When a bitmap is enlarged, the software adds more pixels and estimates their color values (this process is called *interpolation*). When the image is reduced, the software removes pixels.

There are many different formats for bitmap files. As with other types of computer files, the file extension defines what type of format is being used. Common bitmap file formats include BMP (Windows bitmap), GIF (graphic interchange format), JPEG (Joint Photographic Experts Group), PICT (picture), PNG (portable network graphics), and TIFF (tagged image file format).

Each bitmap format is best for different uses, depending on the image. For example, the GIF format is good for images that have sharp edges and minimal color gradations (such as text, line art, and cartoons). It is commonly used on the Internet because it supports animations. The BMP format is used by the Windows operating system to display an image on any type of display. However, the image is not compressed, so the file can be very large. The JPEG format works best with artwork and photographs and compresses well but at the cost of losing some image data. The PNG format is a replacement for GIF that supports true color (16 million colors) versus 256 colors for GIF. The PICT format was developed by Apple Computers and supports both bitmap and vector images, but it is being phased out.

Vector images are made up of multiple objects (curves, lines, and other shapes) and colors that are defined by mathematical equations instead of pixels. Vector images are *resolution independent,* meaning that no grid delimits the image when it is enlarged or shrunk. The format always renders an image at the highest quality at any resolution. Its drawback is that images cannot be reproduced photo-realistically. Vector images are not used much in games; however, they can be imported into 3D graphic programs for modeling. Popular vector image file formats include AI (Adobe Illustrator), SWF (Adobe Shockwave Flash), and WMF (Windows metafile).

In a 2D game, the images are flashed onto the screen one after another, and the eye blends them together into animated objects. On the other hand, the art for 3D games is not produced by image files. Images are flashed onto the screen one after another, but each of those images is created on the fly for every frame using 3D models and textures through a process called *rasterization* (described in more detail later in this chapter). The models are saved in the formats of the 3D graphics program in which they were created, such as 3DS (3D Studio Max), LW (Lightwave), and MA (Maya). The textures applied to the 3D meshes are saved as 2D bitmap files. Images created in most of these

13

FIGURE 13.2 The buildings in EA's *Command & Conquer: Red Alert 2* (2000) were modeled in a 3D graphics program and then saved in a 2D format. This helps give the illusion of depth, although they are really flat.

packages can also be saved as 2D bitmap files, which allows artists to create 3D objects that can be rotated in three dimensions within the tool but used in a 2D game or film. For example, the buildings in Westwood Studios' *Command & Conquer: Red Alert 2* (published by EA in 2000) were created in a 3D program and then saved as 2D art (Figure 13.2).

Sprites

A *sprite* is a 2D image or animation such as a character, monster, or power-up that is incorporated into the whole scene on the screen. The simplest way to understand sprites in video games is to consider the various actors hired to play roles in a play or a movie. Sometimes those actors portray more than one role, though not at the same time. Each time the actor appears on the stage, he wears a costume. Sprites are the equivalent of the costume that an actor wears on the video screen. A game actor (also called a *game entity*) can wear more than one sprite (costume), though again not usually at the same time. The one discrepancy in this analogy for video games is that a game actor can be put on the screen more than once. At any given time, you might have hundreds of copies of one actor on the screen. This is simple programming cloning, where each instance of the copy is unique and behaves individually as defined by the programmer.

Animation Cycles and Animation Sets

Animation cycles are sets of frames that, when displayed one at a time and looped repeatedly, animate a character performing some action. Walk cycles are the most common form of animation cycle within the game industry. Depending on the game type, there can also be run cycles, climbing cycles, and more.

Several other animations are not played as a looping cycle within a game. For example, jumping, shooting, crouching, and dying are considered *animation sets*. Animation sets play once and then stop. They can be repeated to allow the player to fire a weapon repeatedly or jump continuously, for example, although the death animation set usually triggers an end of level or end of game sequence.

2D Art Tasks

Even though most games are created using 3D graphics nowadays, game companies still need good 2D artists. Many companies still create games in 2D (games for Nintendo's Game Boy Advance and for online consumers, for example) and 2-1/2D (isometric projection). In 3D games, menus and head-up displays are often done in 2D. Therefore, most companies continue to maintain a small group of 2D artists. Although the sprites in a 2D game can be modeled in a 3D graphic program and saved as bitmaps, they still have to be animated, which is often done manually. Additionally, background and foreground art is often drawn by hand. Although it is possible to scan photographs into an art program to create a background, photo-realistic art might clash in style with the hand-generated art. It is difficult to generate fantastic environments using scanned photographs, so artists who can paint such settings, either with traditional art tools or in a computer, will find their talents sought after.

Even if the 2D artwork does not appear directly in the game, it might be needed to create the final 3D art. Many game companies actually prefer to hire artists who are trained in traditional art techniques as well as in 3D graphics programs. The tasks for 2D artists at a game company include the following:

- Storyboards: Storyboards are used to work out how a sequence of actions will look before trying to create them. In games, storyboards can be used to help visualize part of a story (such as a cinematic sequence) or to determine how a complex puzzle or other gameplay sequence (such as a racetrack layout) should be set up. A storyboard for a game might include information such as the image area, art notes, programming notes, audio notes, and production notes. The image

13

might be a quick sketch showing a direction of movement, a character's reaction, a close-up of an important item, and so on. The art is usually not too realistic at first, although it might become more detailed in later iterations as the particulars of the sequence are worked out.

- Concept Sketches: Starting with the game proposal, the designer might want a staff artist to provide sketches of important characters, locations, and items in the game to include in the document. The artist might turn out dozens of sketches per object as the team tries to reach an agreement on what it will look like in the game and how it will behave. The most recent sketches should be included with each updated version of the game design document. Management—marketing in particular—can have strong opinions about the look of characters because they are important intellectual properties for the company.

- Model Sheets (Templates): After the final look of the characters has been decided, a 2D artist can create a model sheet for each one. This sheet shows the model from the front, back, and side. These shapes can be imported into the 3D graphics program to serve as a guide when building the 3D model (Figure 13.3). The textures appearing on the model sheets can be scanned into a computer and imported into an art program to speed the creation of the skin to be applied to the character.

- Textures: In 3D games, textures are 2D bitmaps that are wrapped around 3D models (Figure 13.4). Just as X, Y, and Z coordinates are used to build a model in space, U and V coordinates are used to position the texture on the model. As discussed later in this chapter, texture maps store U and V coordinates in the vertices of polygons for the surfaces they are applied to. Most 3D graphics programs automatically

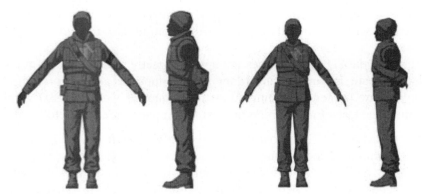

FIGURE 13.3 Model sheets for male and female resistance fighters appearing in Valve's *Half-Life 2*. They show the side and front views of the characters.

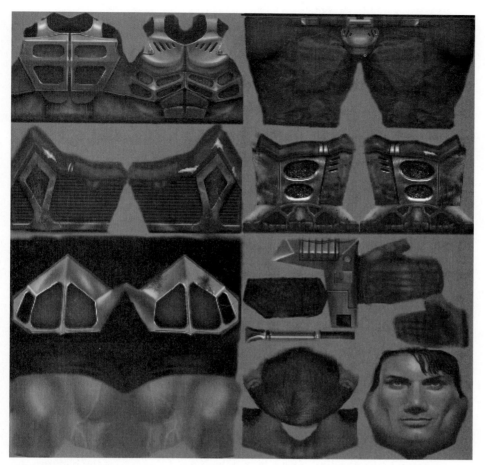

FIGURE 13.4 This is the texture for a soldier model used in Epic Games' *Unreal Tournament* (published by GT Interactive Software in 1999). The skin looks distorted in 2D because it wraps around the 3D model based on the UV coordinates created in the 3D graphics program.

assign the UV coordinates to the models as the artist massages their placement to get the desired look. Textures are applied to world objects in the same way. 2D artists spend a lot of time making the textures for the character and world models look correct so the game will have a consistent art style throughout.

■ Graphic User Interface (GUI): One artist might be assigned the task of creating the in-game head-up display (HUD) as well as the menu system and pop-up windows. Depending on the art style of the game, these interfaces can be two- or three-dimensional. The job of the artist is to make the information as intuitive as possible for the player (see Chapter 15,

13

"Interface Design," for more about interfaces). Work on the GUI can span the entire production cycle of the game because the layout for the interface screens might change a number of times during production as testers and focus groups give feedback about what works and what causes problems.

- Marketing Materials: The marketing group in a publishing company is responsible for promoting a game and getting the packaging together. The art for the front and back of the packaging is created by an in-house or freelance 2D artist. In addition to the packaging, the marketing team might ask for artwork to illustrate the manual and auxiliary materials (reference card, maps, and so on) that will be packaged with the game. Both the publisher and the developer might have Web sites displaying materials from the game. This is a good place to display a gallery of concept artwork. In addition, the sites might need additional 2D art in a style similar to the product being displayed.

Art in a 2D Game

After the team settles on an overall look for the game, the artists start building the artwork for the playfield and for objects moving around on the screen. The amount of art required for a 2D game can be relatively small or enormous depending on type of game, the target platform, and whether or not a brand or license is associated with the game. If the game contains numerous different characters, each of which moves freely in many directions and has many different animations, the number of art files can be huge. Likewise, if the background or playfield art is made up of large bitmaps, as opposed to small tiles put together in a map editor, the artwork can be massive. Two-dimensional games that are licensed-based often require more art work to meet the license holder's requirements. Conversely, games for handheld platforms such as cell phones require minimal artwork due to the platforms' memory limitations. However, this situation is changing as newer handheld devices increase the amount of available memory.

FYI *Photoshop*

Two-dimensional art can be created in a variety of ways, but the most common tool used is Adobe Photoshop. Other drawing and illustration tools are also used, but with its strong layering and art tools, Photoshop remains the current industry standard for generating 2D art.

Character Art

In a 2D game, every frame of every animation for a character is created separately, and the entire sequence is saved to be played back during the game. This process is time consuming because the artists must draw each frame. A large amount of storage can be required to accommodate all the animations for even a single 2D character, depending on the size of the image, the color-depth, and the amount of detail.

Each action performed by a character—walking, running, using a weapon, throwing something, jumping, ducking, falling down—requires its own animation set (Figure 13.5). There might even be a set for when the character is not moving at all (also called *idling*). For example, the character might tap her toe impatiently, breath heavily, or sway back and forth while waiting for the player to do something. Many animations require additional sets based on the number of directions in which the character can move. Other animations require only one set because the

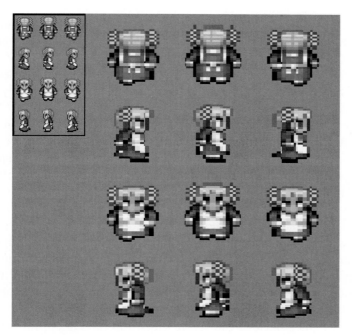

FIGURE 13.5 Three-frame walk animation for a townsperson used in RPG Maker 2, available from Kamains World (**www.Kamain.com**). There are four versions of the set to animate the character walking right, left, up, and down. The larger version to the right is an enlargement of the small version used in the product.

13

character does not turn around; for example, the idling animation usually has the character facing forward and a death animation generally shows the character lying prone on the ground in one direction.

Most animations consist of a number of individual frames similar to cells used to make cartoon figures animate. The specific number of frames required for an animation depends on its type and the smoothness desired. A dead-character animation just shows the character lying prone (one frame), a breathing animation shows the character inhaling and exhaling (two frames), and a walk needs a minimum of three frames (legs outstretched, legs together, and legs outstretched in the opposite direction). These are the minimums required; if an animation does not have enough frames, it can look jerky, so additional frames are frequently added. For example, the three-frame walk might look better if two additional frames are added with the legs halfway between being outstretched and together in both directions.

It might look odd to interrupt one animation sequence and go directly into another, so additional frames might be created to blend animations to transition smoothly from one to the next. Another option might be to include the required frame in an existing animation to act as a "between" animation. For example, to transition from running to performing a leg kick, the animation sequence might complete the current leg movement, go to the first frame of the idle animation, and then begin the first frame of the kick animation set.

Another factor that increases the number of art files for a character is the number of directions it can move in the game. As discussed previously, there are several kinds of 2D games: side-scrollers, top-down, and isometric (3/4-view). Each of these requires a different view of the characters. The side-scroller gives a side perspective of the game and character. It normally has left and right directions and can include a crouch and crouch walk, some form of range and melee weapons, jumping, and some type of death or end-of-play animation. If the game also includes ladders, ropes, or other methods to move up and down, the character will often faces away from the player to climb up or down. Although the number of animation sets might vary, the animator has to make only one version of each animation set that faces in one direction as defined in the GDD. The programmer then simply flips each frame of the animation when the character heads in the opposite direction. This trick is used to save space, although it can look odd when the character carries an item in one hand and then, when moving in the other direction, carries the item in the other hand.

Isometric, or 3/4-view, games, in which the camera appears at an angle above the playfield, normally allows a minimum of four directions for motion: up, down, left, and right. Although left and right motions can be flipped in the same manner as a side-scroller, up and down cannot because the down direction faces the player and the up direction faces away. Therefore, the animator must create a minimum of three sets per animation. Many games allow a character to move in eight directions: up, down, left, right, and four directions diagonally. In this case, the character needs a minimum of five sets per animation including the previous three sets as well as northeast/northwest and southeast/southwest (as with side movement, the diagonal movement can be flipped).

Top-down games usually require the least animation. The complete degrees of freedom the player can have in a game such as a top-down space shooter are commonly created by the program code, which rotates one set of frames for each animation to any direction. DirectX, one of the most common graphics APIs, can handle this rotation extremely well, and the artist needs to create only one image for most game objects.

The programmers might provide the art team with a tool called a *sprite editor* to preview animations as they will appear in the game. Using this tool, the artists can determine if an animation set has enough frames to run smoothly or if they can assign between frames to blend animations. Depending on the design outlined by the artist, designer, and programmer, the tool can also allow the artist to set the collision box, the *hot spot* of the animation set, and other information used in the game.

FYI   *The Hot Spot*

Two-dimensional animation techniques rely on the ability to build the motion of each frame based on the position of the character in the previous frame. An example of this is a flip book, which has an image on each page of the book. As you flip the pages, the character image appears to move. Yet for each page, or frame, of animation, only a part of the image might be different from the previous page. This page-flipping technique is essential for the artist to make the movements seem natural and continuous. For example, if the belly of the character doesn't grow larger as the arm moves; the artist simply redraws the same belly.

This technique requires that each frame of the animation be centered at one point, which is called a *hot spot.* The hot spot is the one point that, if moved the same distance with each frame, would change a walk-cycle animation so that instead of walking in place, the animation would look as though the character were actually moving. The hot spot is important to the artist creating the animation set because it allows them to make sure the weight and shift of the character are natural. It is also important to the programmer, who moves the hot spot of every animation to make the character move across the screen.

13

Another factor that determines the number and size of art files in a 2D game is the **level of detail (LOD).** Because they are resolution dependent, the bitmaps used to animate characters in a game cannot be enlarged or reduced without adding pixels to or subtracting pixels from the original bitmaps. Therefore, if the game allows the player to move toward and away from characters, the artists might need to create several animation sets for each character in the game, each being a different size. As the player moves away from a character, the game engine can shrink the bitmap by throwing away pixels and then, at a certain point, swap out the large sprites for the handcrafted smaller sprites.

Background and Playfield Art

Background art can be thought of as the scenery in a play or the backdrop of a movie. It adds ambience and setting and is occasionally part of the actual gameplay. In a side-scrolling game (including platform and fighting games), the background might be the countryside, a cityscape, or a building interior that the player strolls through as he works his way about the world. In a top-down game, the background is the ground over which the player moves. In an isometric game, the background might be in forced perspective that can appear almost three-dimensional, with a viewpoint looking down at an angle at the ground and buildings.

Playfield art is the art that the game entities appear to play on. In art and programming terms, playfield art is generally designated as stationary, unchanging objects on which the game entities can walk or climb. For example, in a side-scrolling game, playfield art consists of the ground, platforms, slides, ladders, overhead vines, and so on that the characters use to traverse each level. In top-down shooters and isometric games, playfield art and background art are usually the same. In these games, the objects that appear on the screen are usually sprites rather than background images.

A critical factor in all background art, regardless of the viewpoint, is the art style. Games targeting younger children are often based on an art style that consists of simple shapes, bright colors, and sunny skies. The art style of games targeting an older audience is generally dependent on the game's genre. Fast-paced games usually have simple backgrounds so the player can focus on the actual gameplay. Games in which the designer wants the player to experience fear might be shaded in grays, blacks, and whites with heavy shadows. Games that require that the player becomes immersed in a historical setting generally have either realistic imagery or an art style from that historical era.

Regardless of the art style, artists and programmers use standard methods to display the background art within the game. One approach for generating the background art is to create the background as one large bitmap that is loaded into memory at the start of the level. For a scrolling game, the background can get to be quite large, depending on the scale of objects on the playfield.

An artist might decide to paint the landscape on a canvas with ink or other traditional art supplies and then scan it into a computer (Figure 13.6). He can then fiddle around with the size of the art until he is satisfied with its scale. This approach can be much quicker than creating a bitmap pixel by pixel.

There are several drawbacks to using a single bitmap for the background. First, the file can be large. If the background is an 800 × 600 bitmap in 24-bit

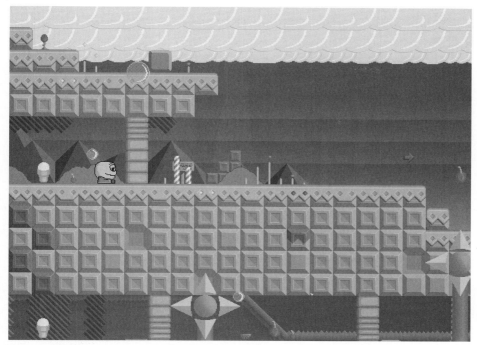

FIGURE 13.6 To obtain a pastel cartoon look, Bill Tiller, Maria Bowen, and Kathy Hsieh created this background art for LucasArts' *Monkey Island 3* by hand and then scanned it into the computer.

color with an 8-bit alpha channel, the resulting file is over 1.9 megabytes (800 × 600 = 480,000 pixels × 4 bytes per pixel = 1,920,000 bytes). Depending on the platform's processing power, it can take quite a while for the file to be loaded into memory. Another drawback is the difficulty of making changes to the artwork. If the designer needs to make changes to the background, the artist must either redo the art, rescan it, and resize it or try to make the changes to the existing bitmap. Such changes can be time-consuming. In the case of a background scene that must line up exactly with the foreground platform elements (or other elements for other styles of games), this can be very challenging. Still, if the background needs to be one large, unbroken piece of art, making a large bitmap file might be the only way to go.

A more efficient approach is to make the background out of tiles that are assembled into a background of the desired size (Figure 13.7). The tiles are usually individual, square bitmaps with dimensions that are a power of 2 (16 × 16, 64 × 64, 256 × 256 and so on). Whatever their size, the tiles are designed so that the artwork along the edges matches that of the adjacent tiles; the tiles might match along the horizontal edges, vertical edges, or both. The tiles are assembled with a map editor to form the complete background (see Chapter 18, "Prototyping and Building Playfields," for more about map editors).

13

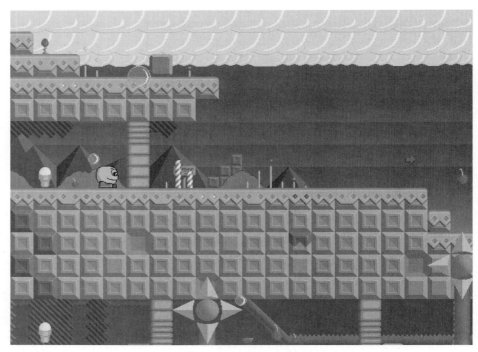

FIGURE 13.7 A playfield using the Super Happy Fun Land tile set for the Scrolling Game Development Kit (available at **gamedev.sourceforge.net**). Note the duplication of the square tiles, which greatly reduces the size of the art file.

There are several advantages in using tiles instead of a single bitmap to build the background. First, the tiles are usually repeatable, which means that several can be placed in a row without any discernable seam appearing between them. As a result, many different layouts can be created with the same tile set. Second, because the tiles are repeated, the overall memory required for the tile set is much smaller than for the single bitmap. Third, it is often easier to change the art for individual tiles than to change the art for a large bitmap. An artist might be able to create multiple tile sets quickly by changing some colors in the tiles but keeping the same design. For example, if some missions in a game are set in the summer, the predominant tile color might be green. If the greens are changed to white, the same tile art might work for missions set in the winter. The final advantage is that a tile image needs to appear in memory only once, but it can be repeated endlessly on the display. The 1.9 MB bitmap image described earlier might be cut down to only a few kilobytes, depending on the amount of detail and the number of repeating tiles. This is less critical on today's computers but is still important on machines with less RAM.

One special effect frequently seen in 2D games is **parallax scrolling,** which is a technique that gives a feeling of three-dimensionality to a game. This effect is achieved by creating several graphics layers in the game, each of which is animated at a different speed. The art for the distant background moves slowly to give the appearance that the terrain features are at a distance; the middle ground with the player moves normally; and foreground art moves more quickly than the player to give the appearance that those features are in front of the player. These varied speeds give an illusion of depth. Artists who make these planes need to think about how they overlap. The art will likely be fainter or foggier in the background and larger and clearer in the foreground. This technique is also used to create fog, clouds, rain, or other atmospheric conditions that can add ambience and challenge to the game.

Drawing 2D Art to the Screen

Although an artist is primarily concerned with making the game look good, she needs to understand how the drawing's mechanics work within the game. Others, including the producer and programmers, should also have a high level of comprehension of the mechanics because it affects how the art is made, stored, and ultimately appears on the monitor.

Scanning and Apparent Motion

When a graphic is drawn on a screen, an electron gun inside the monitor starts at the upper left corner and paints the image (also called *raster graphics*) from the top to the bottom. The faster the image is drawn on the screen, the more it looks like one continuous image. The electron gun draws the image in the same way as a standard television, although it takes two passes to create a complete frame on a standard television (LCD displays are different).

The human eye can perceive movement when still images are flashed on a screen at a rate as low as 10 frames per second (fps), but the motion is choppy and the image flickers. At a rate of 50 fps, the flickering goes away and the motion is smooth. Thus, to ensure smooth computer animations, a game should maintain a frame rate of 50 fps or faster.

FYI *Progressive versus Interlaced Scanning*

Television monitors work differently than computer monitors. Computer monitors use ***progressive scanning,*** which means that every line of the image is drawn in a single scan of the screen. Televisions

▶▶ CONTINUED ON NEXT PAGE

13

▶▶ CONTINUED

use *interlaced scanning,* which means that the electron gun makes two scans per image, drawing every other line per scan. Not including high-definition televisions (HDTVs), computer images also tend to be much sharper than television images because the resolution for computer screens can be set to higher values than a standard television (which is set at 525 scan lines in the United States).

LCD Monitors

Liquid-crystal display (LCD) monitors have become quite popular among computer manufacturers and will likely replace cathode-ray tube (CRT) monitors at some point in the future. LCD monitors are currently more expensive than CRT monitors, but they are lighter and take up less room than CRT monitors. LCD displays have a solution of liquid crystals between two sheets of polarizing material and a light bulb. When an electric current passes through the liquid, the crystals line up in order and act like shutters to either let light through at a point or block it. Each pixel consists of three cells (or subpixels) colored red, blue, or green that can be controlled individually.

Page Swapping

An artist could continually draw each frame of an animating image directly to the screen, but that would overdraw different frames on top of each other because the graphics updates would not be synced with the refresh rate of the monitor. The result looks like the animation has jagged or torn edges. To avoid this, most games use the video memory to create a hidden page, where the image is composed before it is actually displayed. Instead of writing directly to the screen, the game writes to this off-screen page in video memory and then displays that page to the screen (called *page flipping* or *swapping*) when the monitor is ready for it.

A small amount of time passes after the electron gun finishes its scan of the screen and travels back to the upper left corner to start the next scan. This time gap (called *vertical blanking*) is usually not long enough to compose an entire new frame, but it is sufficient to flip the off-screen, hidden page to become the onscreen image. The old onscreen image then becomes the new off-screen page, and a new frame is composed while the current onscreen image is being drawn. This double-buffering can be performed either by the hardware or the software.

Layers and Compositing

The next step in drawing images to the screen is to determine the order in which the objects will appear. The game engine might use layers and assign each layer a depth that determines how close it is to the viewer. For example, a layer of 0 could be used for the player's character as well as game objects appearing on the same plane. Layer –1 would indicate those objects behind Layer 0, and layer +1 would indicate those objects closer to the viewer. Any number of layers can be created.

When the picture is composited on the hidden page, the farthest layer is drawn first. The next layer is laid over the farthest layer and blocks anything on the farthest image that is located behind it. Then comes the next layer, blocking whatever is behind it, and then the next layer, and the next until the top layer is reached. This becomes the final composite image that will appear on the screen.

Transparency and Alpha Blending

A critical art technique for electronic games is the use of transparency. *Transparency* is the method used to overlay art over a background in such a way that the art looks as if it belongs in the image. This is an obvious requirement for any animation; otherwise, the artist would have to create every set of animations against every set of backgrounds, which would be both time consuming and a waste of memory and storage. Instead, artists and programmers coordinate to designate a particular RGB color as being "transparent." Although the color appears in the artist's drawing tools, the graphics engine will ignore every instance of that color for that animation set (similar to the green screen used for special effects in television and films). The result is that the animation set will overlay the background properly.

Ideally, the same transparency color is used for all animations, objects, and backgrounds. The art team usually selects the transparency color during technical review. It is important to select a color that will not be used to create art for the game. If someone accidentally incorporates the transparency color in a bitmap, holes will appear when the image appears on the screen.

Transparency does not have to be "all or nothing." If the graphics file format includes an 8-bit alpha channel (such as BMP, PNG, or TIFF formats), those bits can be used to create up to 256 levels of transparency (actually, *translucency* is the better term) within the graphics engine. At the extremes, game programmers can set the alpha channel to complete transparency or complete opacity. *Alpha blending* covers everything between these two extremes. In this process, increasing the transparency of the alpha channel allows more and more of the underlying pixels to appear. This technique is often used to make head-up displays for in-game interfaces appear to "float" above the playfield. It can also be used on the layers described in the previous section, for example, to make fog appear denser or thinner. It can even change color if the programmers set the game code to modify the amount of alpha blending of a particular art object.

13

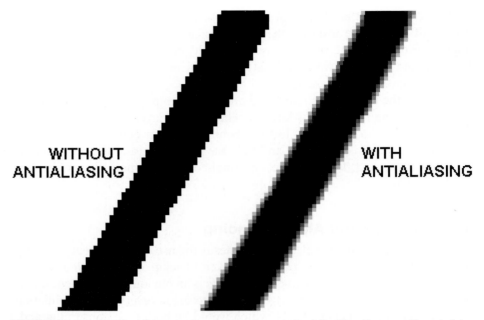

WITHOUT
ANTIALIASING

WITH
ANTIALIASING

FIGURE 13.8 The line on the left is jagged while the line on the right looks smoother when reduced because the antialiasing makes the "jaggies" disappear.

Translucency comes in handy with another graphic trick to make the edges of round objects look smooth. Depending on the resolution, an image might appear to have jagged edges where the bright pixels contrast sharply with darker background pixels. To get around this problem, an artist can add extra pixels to the edge of the image that are halfway in value between the two pixels to make the jaggedness disappear and edges look smooth. This technique is called ***antialiasing*** (Figure 13.8).

3D Art Tasks

Three-dimensional graphics are an important component of modern games, so companies today primarily hire people with 3D art skills. As described in Chapter 6, "The Production Team," there are many roles for 3D artists: modeler, animator, background artist, and level or environmental artist. Learning to use a 3D graphics program such as 3D Studio Max, Maya, or Lightwave is one way to get a job in the industry. However, these programs are very complex, so learning one and becoming highly proficient with it can take years. In addition to technical skills, many companies prefer to hire artists with traditional art skills such as painting, sculpting, architecture, and so on.

IN THE TRENCHES: Outsourcing Art Tasks

There is some concern among game professionals about jobs being outsourced to overseas labor. Many developing countries now promote computer literacy as a way of improving their economy, and a number of art houses that have popped up in India, Russia, China, and elsewhere offer to create 3D art at a cheaper rate than in developed countries.

The effects of a global economy are beginning to be felt in the game industry. However, there are some drawbacks to having artwork done at a distance. First, there is the problem of communication between companies in different time zones; one company might just be starting work when the other is ready to shut down for the night. Second, it takes additional time to make changes because of the time differences; if a problem is spotted with a model, an in-house art team can make the necessary change in a matter of hours, whereas an art house halfway across the world might not be able to get to the problem for a day or longer. So while some jobs might be sent overseas, most game companies will continue to retain a significant in-house art team.

Because the process of creating 3D art is so complicated, some companies have developed an assembly line approach to generating artwork. Using this approach, an artist is assigned to one specific task—such as building the model, animating it, or texturing it—for the entire project. The idea is to let artists concentrate on their best skill set. For example, an artist who can build terrific character models might have difficulty or be slow at animating them, so the completed models are given to another artist to animate.

3D Art Tasks

The 3D artists' four primary types of tasks are model creation, model animation, environmental art, and lighting.

Model Creation   Artists use 3D graphics tools to create a model of every object within the game. They usually build from a sketch of the character or object. They start with either a primitive shape (not to be confused with a graphics primitive as described in the previous chapter) such as a sphere, cube, or cylinder or from a basic character that is similar to what they want to create. Then they mold, sculpt, and modify the 3D *mesh* (skin surface) of the model to get their desired result. The mesh created during the modeling phase can be compared to a dress on a dressmaker's dummy. It might look perfect, but if you try to make it walk, nothing happens because it's only fabric.

Basic character forms are often included as part of the 3D tool (for example, 3ds Max provides a "biped" as the basis of a humanoid, bipedal form), or artists

13

can start with a character they have previously created and modify it. In the case of objects, model creation can be relatively fast and simple. In the case of animated characters, the process can be extremely time consuming.

Model Animation   In this step, the model is animated to perform all the necessary animation cycles or sets defined in the GDD. For 3D models, an intermediary step called *rigging* is also required. In rigging, the mesh created during the modeling phase is given some underlying structure. A common method of rigging is to create a skeletonlike structure for the mesh. This skeleton is very simple and is in no way as complex as a human skeleton needs to be. It consists of the major joints—ankle, knee, hip, some midwaist joint, and so on—needed to make the mesh become more of a puppet.

In model animation, the animator begins with the mesh/puppet construct and creates a series of *key frames.* These key frames are positions the model needs to appear in to look correct as it moves. Thus, a walking animation doesn't consist of each frame of animation as a 2D walk cycle requires. Instead, it consists of a key frame of the proper knee position as well as the proper ankle and foot position for all legs during a walk cycle. The graphics engine program will interpolate (figure out the moves) that translate each joint of the puppet (and the attached mesh) from one key frame to the next.

FYI   *Inverse Kinematics*

Inverse kinematics (IK) is a method of creating animation in which parts of the model are linked together so that they can be animated. In this case, the joints of the model are interconnected, with each joint linking to one or more parts of the body. IK affords the artist and programmer more freedom. Rather than requiring the animator to move all joints to simulate an animation, the mesh and skeleton act like a puppet on many strings. If the finger is moved to touch something, the finger also pulls the hand it is attached to. The hand in turn pulls the wrist, which pulls the elbow and the shoulder. All of these body parts move with the finger toward the target item.

Although IK allows a greater freedom of movement for the programmer, it is much more difficult to code properly. In traditional keyframing, the artist ensures that the elbow bends the correct direction when the hand is raised. In IK, joint constraints must be applied and mathematically added to make the elbow or shoulder move as humanly as possible.

▶▶ CONTINUED ON NEXT PAGE

>> CONTINUED

Only the starting and stopping positions of the limb are considered. It is easier mathematically to work backward than to start from the shoulder and work down the arm to the finger (***forward kinematics***). An advantage of inverse kinematics is that animations can be determined on the fly at runtime rather than always having to be precanned; thus, a figure can react realistically to gravity and other physical forces. This is especially helpful for realistically moving an IK character upstairs, along steep hills, or in other ways that historically have been a challenge for real-time animation. The movement of feet in a model is usually handled with inverse kinematics to keep them from shuffling or moonwalking.

Environmental Art   The creation of the 3D world is handled separately from the creation of the objects, characters, and their associated animations. Part level design and part art, the creation of these spaces requires an artistic eye as well as an eye for level design and a feel for gameplay. The artists will often create an environment and hand it off to a level designer to turn into a truly playable level. Some companies use standard commercial 3D graphics programs to build game levels, whereas others create their own specialized tools (such as the Valve Hammer Editor for *Half Life* shown in Figure 13.9). There are also companies that offer level creation tools for multiple games such as Radiant (**www.qeradiant.com**) and Delgine (**www.delgine.com**).

Lighting   Having lights within a scene that show the characters walking through light and shadow can add a great visual and emotional impact to the game. The art team also lights all the environments for the programmers, who then replicate this lighting in their graphics engine. Ideally, of course, the programmers and artists workout the details of this step so that a simple export of the artist's creation can be imported into the game and the lights will appear in the correct locations.

13

Drawing 3D Art to the Screen

The process for drawing 3D graphics to the screen is completely different from the process for drawing 2D graphics. Recall that in 2D graphics, the bitmaps are loaded into the graphic memory in layers, with higher-level layers overlaying the lower levels to create the final composite image that appears onscreen each frame. In 3D graphics, the renderer goes through a number of steps to determine

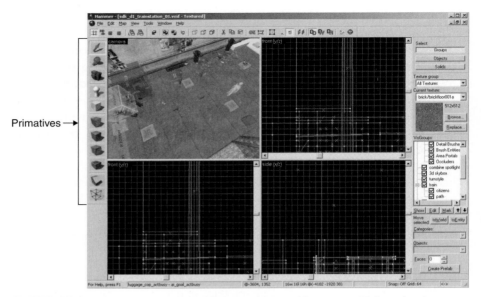

Primatives →

FIGURE 13.9 The interface for the Valve Hammer Editor looks similar to 3ds Max and Maya because the levels are built in three dimensions. Note the pregenerated primitives along the left side of the screen that speed the creation and placement of objects in the world.

what should be shown on the screen and how it should appear. Each of these discrete steps requires a certain number of cycles to complete before you can move onto the next step.

The 3D art objects created for a game are simply a group of points (*vertices*) that are stored in memory. The information that determines the relationships among the points in each object, how they relate to the 3D world, what texture is to be applied, and how they are lighted is stored along with the points. It is up to the renderer to display the objects in their correct orientation on the screen so that texture and appropriate lighting can be applied to surfaces. The surface of a 3D mesh is subdivided into smaller, more manageable shapes through a transforming process called *tessellation.* The shapes are polygons, which are in turn broken into triangles that are easy to manipulate mathematically. The number of polygons in all the 3D objects appearing in the world can be enormous, and trying to render them all can drag the frame rate down to an unacceptable level.

Hidden Surface Removal and Culling

As discussed in the previous chapter, the renderer does not have to show all the polygons in the world. The backs of objects can be ignored as well as objects or parts of objects that are blocked by objects in front of them. The process of removing the unseen polygons is called *hidden surface removal (HSR)* and the technique used to do so is called *culling.* The first step of hidden surface removal is to determine which objects currently appear in the world, where they are in the world, what textures are being used, and what frame of animation each moving object is at. The game engine then checks to see what is visible to the viewer.

The next step is to determine where the game camera is looking—that is, what part of the world can currently be seen on the screen—and deal only with it. One approach is to divide the world along its coordinates into small sections that are linked like a tree and then show only those sections currently visible to the viewer. Another method is to physically break the world model into small sections that are joined by portals; when the viewer moves through a portal, the next section appears, and the unseen sections are dropped from video memory. The goal is to wind up displaying only the minimum number of objects that have to be shown.

After determining which objects will not be shown, the next step is to pass the polygons for objects that will be seen through to the renderer for further handling. The renderer determines if the polygon has been moved; in other words, if it has been *transformed.* Each polygon is checked to see where it is on the model (for example, to see if the model has been twisted or taken a step) and where it is in the world (that is, if it has moved from its last location in the 3D world). The polygon can transform in four primary ways:

- Translation: movement along any of the three axes

- Rotation: movement around an axis

- Scaling: a change to the size of the object

- Skewing: a change to the model shape along several axes

After the transformations have been calculated, the renderer checks if the polygon is still visible. If it is now facing away from the camera, it can be culled.

Lighting

After culling the hidden surfaces, the renderer lights the objects and the world. Currently, lighting in most 3D games is performed by limiting light sources to include only direct sources of light and ignore reflected or refracted light. This is primarily due to the memory and time constraints of the game; in time, this will likely change.

Direct light is either *global* (throughout the world), *local* (near the object being rendered), or a combination of global and local. The three types of direct light to consider are:

- Directional: Global light from a great distance that illuminates everything equally, such as the sun

- Point: Local light from one source that illuminates in all directions, such as a streetlamp

13

- Spot: Local light from one source that illuminates in one direction, such as a headlight

As described previously, these light sources are often predetermined by the artist who creates the environment and then implemented by the programmer. Lights can be any color and any degree of brightness, as defined by either the artist or the programmer coding the level. The renderer determines the combined strength of all lights hitting an object.

One final modifier for the light value on the surface of an object is based on the following material properties of the surface:

- The *ambient* property is the diffused light on the underside of an object that is not directly illuminated (the shadowy side).

- The *specular* property is the bright point of reflected light from the source of illumination.

- The *diffuse* property is the color that changes from the darkness of the ambient property to the brightness of the specular property.

- The *shininess* property determines the smoothness of the surface and the tightness of the specular highlight.

- The *emissive* property is used if the object is emitting the light (for example, a light bulb).

- The *reflective* property is usually ignored as noted previously.

Figure 13.10 shows an example of light value based on a material's surface properties.

Clipping

After the renderer removes the triangles that do not appear in the scene, it deals with those that are in the scene but do not appear in full. There are several methods for *clipping* the triangles and recalculating them so that only the triangles appearing on the screen in a frame are shown.

After the renderer determines which triangles (and their associated vertices) to display in the frame and how they should be lit, it can convert them from their 3D representation into the flat X, Y coordinate representation that appears on the screen. This process is called *rasterizing.*

Rendering and Shading

The final step of the process is *rendering,* which is the process that determines the final color for each pixel appearing on the screen. The data for textures and color depth are stored with each triangle's vertices and are now applied (skinned) across each polygon.

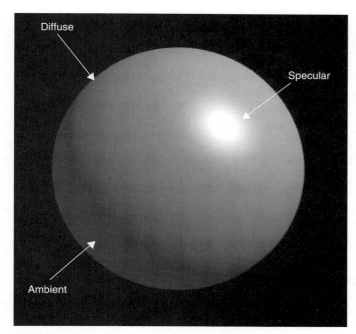

FIGURE 13.10 This figure shows how the surface properties affect the light.

A *shader routine* takes into account such things as light absorption and diffusion, reflection and refraction, texture mapping, and shadowing to determine the final surface properties of an object. There are several ways to shade a triangle:

- *Flat shading* is the simplest. The renderer evaluates the color values of the three vertices (corners) of a triangle and averages the values to determine a single color shade that is applied to the whole triangle. Although this is inexpensive in terms of processing power, it makes the edges more visible, makes the shapes simpler, and gives objects a blocky appearance.

- *Gouraud shading* (named for computer scientist Henri Gouraud) offers better graphics at a slightly higher cost in processing power. It produces a smoother surface by determining the light value at each vertex and then interpolating between the vertices of a given triangle to determine each pixel's color. The process' drawbacks are that it works less well on surfaces with few polygons and sometimes misses highlight details.

- *Phong shading* (named for computer graphics researcher Bui Tuong Phong) is an improvement upon Gouraud shading. It performs Gouraud

13

shading for each pixel within a triangle, not just the vertices, which gives much more realistic lighting effects but at a higher cost in processing power.

■ *Vertex* and *pixel shading* are two processes that are gaining popularity as graphics cards become more powerful. A vertex shader applies lighting effects to the vertices, or corners, of the triangles, which are then applied to the whole surface of the polygon. On the other hand, a pixel shader applies lighting effects to each specific pixel forming the polygon surface. The effects developed for vertex shaders include faking motion blur (the apparent "streaking" of fast-moving objects), a fisheye lens effect, and realistic shadows using "shadow volumes." The effects developed for pixel shaders include per-pixel lighting using Phong shading, simulating multilayer metallic paint, *toon shading* (imitating the shading of cartoons), and simulating smoke and air turbulence.

Texturing

Texturing is the final skinning of the mesh created by the modeler and rigged during the animation process. Although a game can use the shading techniques described in the previous section to "skin" each polygon of the model, it's more realistic to put something that looks like clothes on the characters.

An artist can just apply a standard texture—metal, glass, bricks, and so on—to a polygon in a 3D graphics program such as 3D Studio Max or Maya. However, when creating characters or unusual surfaces, it is often better to create textures by hand to apply to the 3D models' surfaces. An artist might photograph interesting real-world textures and scan them into a computer as a bitmap or create the textures pixel by pixel in an art program.

As explained previously, texture maps store U and V coordinates in the vertices of polygons for the surfaces they are applied to. The 3D graphics software uses the U and V coordinates to align the texture to the polygon correctly. The artist creates the texture map directly on the 3D model, and the graphics program automatically transforms the texture map into the 2D version using the U and V coordinates. The graphics engine maps the texture space (U, V coordinates) onto the three-dimensional object space (X, Y, Z coordinates of the object) and then prepares the combined image to be shown on the two-dimensional screen space (X, Y coordinates of the screen). Figure 13.11 shows the 2D map of a face mapped to the UV coordinates of the 3D model.

Each pixel already has a basic color value and shading value that were calculated earlier in the process. The texture color from the texture map is combined with the existing texture color value to produce a final color value for the pixel that reflects the lighting, shading, and texture.

Several tricks can be used when applying a texture to a triangle surface. As mentioned earlier, textures can look odd if the player is close to an object or a great distance away. If the player is too close, he might see multiple copies of

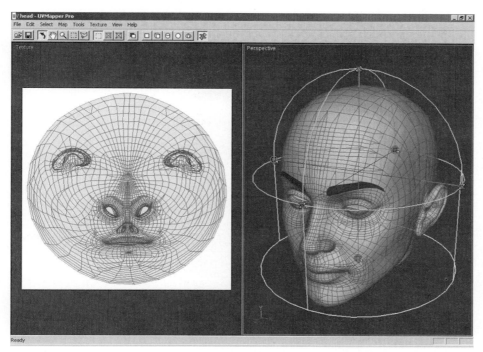

FIGURE 13.11 The 2D face is mapped to the 3D head model using UVMapper Professional for Windows (**www.uvmapper.com**), created by Stephen L. Cox.

a *texel* (a texture element), resulting in a certain blockiness because the texels do not directly correlate to pixels on a one-to-one basis. At a distance, multiple texels might be assigned to a single pixel, and the result can be blurry. Compounding this problem is that as the player approaches a distant object the missing texels suddenly appear as if by magic, possibly breaking the player's immersion in the game. This problem, called *pixel popping* or *texture swamping,* should be avoided.

The quickest fix for pixel popping is to program the graphics engine renderer to average the value of several textures adjacent to each pixel before displaying the final pixel (this is called *point sampling*). This method has problems and is not necessarily the best solution, though it can work. Most graphics cards use a slightly different approach called *bilinear filtering,* which compares four neighboring textures and uses their average for the final texture. Obviously, both of these solutions add to the processing time for displaying an image.

Another approach to solving the pixel popping problem is *MIP-mapping* (from the Latin *multum in parvo,* which translates as "many in a small space"). In this case, the graphics engine makes multiple copies of a texture whenever the texture is first loaded, with each copy being one-half the size of its

13

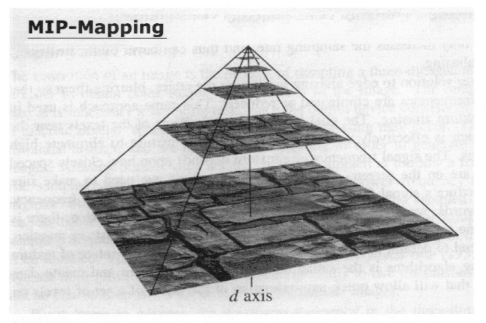

FIGURE 13.12 This figure shows how a MIP-map is laid out. The base image is reduced in half at each step.

predecessor. As the player moves away from a surface, the renderer swaps the current texture map for the next smaller one at a specified distance, and so on and so on, to the smallest map (Figures 13.12 and Figure 13.13). MIP-mapping is generally not a memory-saving feature. It is used for speed so you don't have to shrink large textures to fit into small polygons, and it actually takes up additional memory (approximately an extra 33 percent).

A third approach is **multitexturing,** which maps several different textures to the same polygon. In this case, the initial pixel color (produced by shading) is mixed with the multiple textures to come up with the final color that is rendered to the screen. Newer graphics cards can make multiple passes of this process per GPU cycle to apply several textures per pixel simultaneously. It is possible to use multitexturing to simulate the bumps and cracks in a surface without having to model them directly. This method, called **bump mapping,** allows surfaces and textures to crack or deform during gameplay.

Fog and Opacity

The next step in the rendering process is to apply **fogging.** This effect is used if the scene is set in an area where fog might appear, such as on an English moor, near a waterfall, or when rain is falling. The renderer determines how far the fog is from the viewer and then blends the fog color with the pixel's other color values for

FIGURE 13.13 In this screenshot, the left side uses MIP-mapping and the right side doesn't. Notice that the distant ground looks smoother with MIP-mapping on.

lighting, shading, and texturing. The fog does not always have to be at a distance, either. It can be an actual object made up of particles that the player passes through; this type of fog is composed using a process called *volumetric fogging*.

Fog serves another practical purpose. It can be used to mask how far the viewer camera can see into the distance as a means for culling world geometry and objects (Figure 13.14). As the fog reaches a certain density, everything from that point on is removed, which speeds up the processing.

Shadows

Shadows are as important as lighting in making objects look real in a 3D environment. Shadows are created in a separate, later step after lighting using some of the same data as the lighting system. The source of the light strikes the object casting a shadow (called the *occluder*), and then the shadow is seen on some surface. A shadow consists of two parts: the darker inner part, called the *umbra,* and the lighter outer part, called the *penumbra* (Figure 13.15). A poor-quality shadowing system casts only hard shadows, where everything is in the umbra. In real life, light is diffused by reflective surfaces and particles in the air, so even a dark shadow has a penumbra.

> ### Caution
> **Beware of Shadows**
>
> Rendering a realistic shadow is not a trivial matter. Whereas lighting disregards reflective surfaces, shadowing does not.

13

FIGURE 13.14 This screenshot from Surreal Software's *Drakan: The Ancient Gates* (published by Sony in 2002) uses fog in the background to cull objects in the far distance.

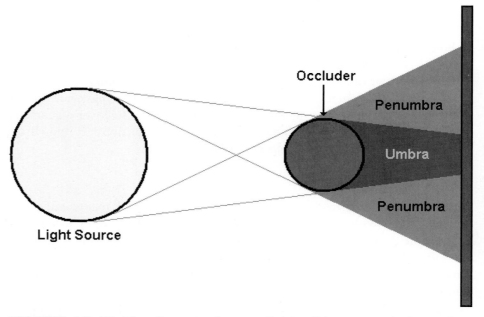

FIGURE 13.15 The diagram shows a light striking an occluder and casting a shadow.

FIGURE 13.16 This figure shows a light casting hard shadows against the wall, which makes them look odd. The light source is the bright ball on the floor in the front.

One approach to casting shadows uses the light source as a projector. The light cone hits the occluder and then projects the shadow onto a flat surface. The result is a hard shadow, as shown in Figure 13.16.

A variation uses several light sources at different angles, some of which create the penumbra for a softer shadow (Figure 13.17). The problem with this approach is that it works well only when the shadow falls onto a flat surface.

A better approach is called ***shadow volumes.*** This method creates a shadow cone beyond the occluding object and any object that falls into this cone is in the shadow. Using this approach allows a shadow to be cast on any surface—not just a flat surface (Figure 13.18).

Depth Testing

By this stage, the renderer has determined how the frame will be drawn on the screen in two dimensions, and it has made a number of rendering passes to get each pixel the right color (called ***overdraw***) and luminosity (brightness). By rendering the pixels in the nearest objects first (called ***Z-buffering***), the pixels in objects farther behind that are occluded by the front object do not need to be rendered. Basically, the renderer ignores all pixels that can't be seen. This process, called ***depth testing,*** is a way for keeping up the frame rate when numerous polygons are on the screen at one time.

13

FIGURE 13.17 This figure shows a light casting soft shadows, which look more realistic.

FIGURE 13.18 The figure is casting a shadow using shadow volume. Note how the shadow of the shield falls across the different angles of the body.

Antialiasing

The last step is to apply antialiasing to eliminate jagged edges. There are two ways to do this. The first is to render all the polygons in view from back to front so that each one can blend correctly with what is behind it. The second, more processor-intensive method, is to render the view initially at a resolution higher than will actually be shown and then to shrink it to the correct size. The jagged edges disappear when the view is scaled down.

Displaying the Frame

The finished frame is now ready to be copied from the buffer to the screen. Using the page-flipping technique, the current frame becomes the back buffer and is overwritten by the next frame. The entire process begins again as the next frame is prepared. If the game is running at 60 frames per second, each frame appears for about 17 milliseconds. Therefore, the processes discussed in this section must all be executed in less than 17 milliseconds—and executed correctly. To run through so many processes in such an amazingly short time is staggering. Modern CPUs can perform over 3 billion operations per second, however, and they receive assistance from the graphics card's GPU. So there seems to be all the time in the world to make each animation frame as beautiful and rich as it can possibly be.

Caution

Synchronize

The lead artist should check occasionally during production to make sure that all the art workstations are synchronized to time and date (a necessity for version control) and that all artists are using the same scale when building assets.

Additional Tasks for the Art Team

In addition to creating the art for the game, the art team has other responsibilities. The most important task is determining the art process pipeline during the technical review phase. During the production phase, additional tasks take the artists away from their primary duty of art creation. The producer should make sure to consider these extra tasks when creating the project timeline and setting up the milestone schedule.

Art Process Pipeline

The art process pipeline defines how the work will go from the artists' workstations into the game. The art and programming leads should work together to build the directory structure where the artwork will be stored. The number of art files can become gargantuan because there will be multiple versions of each object. Using a good version control system is vitally important to completing the project on time. The steps involved in the art process pipeline include:

- Define Art Assets Creation: All artists should use the same version of the same graphics software. Variations between versions of an application that the artists use to build objects or store them in memory can lead to unnecessary bugs. In addition, the artists should agree on how they will build their models, as well as animate and texture them. These standards should be defined in the art design document (see Chapter 11, "Technical Review").

■ Define the Directory Structure: The art assets are usually the largest percentage of files that make up a game, so the directory structure for storing their files should be worked out in as much detail as possible before production begins. Having to change the directory structure can be a major chore, especially deep into production. It is important that the artists understand where they should keep their working files versus the files that go into the official build. As with the coding files, the art files should be thoroughly tested before they are checked into the official build directory.

■ Test the Art Assets: The 3D art team might ask the programmers for a tool that will enable them to see their finished models as they appear in the game without having to start up the game directly. Much of the fine detail work in modeling involves tweaking polygons and making sure that textures are aligned correctly. Having to start up the game each time to check a fix takes too much time. The preview tool should use the same process pipeline as the current game renderer; otherwise, what was a perfectly fine model might suddenly fall to pieces if the preview tool is no longer in sync with the renderer. Indeed, the art team might want to make sure the renderer is close to completion before finalizing their artwork, lest any changes force them to redo what they have so painstakingly completed. During testing and debugging, the artists should be required to play the game to see how their models work in the game engine. They might detect subtle problems that the playtesters miss.

■ Review the Art: It is important that a system be set up to continually review the artwork for the game. Each artist's work should be reviewed every two to three weeks. The art director, the lead artist, the artists doing similar work, and a designer should go from workstation to workstation to see what is being done. The art review has several important outcomes. First, if an artist is having trouble with something, especially technical problems, the review committee can offer suggestions and alternatives to resolve the issue. Second, if an artist is not getting his work done, the review process will find this problem early in the schedule. Third, if the designer is involved throughout the process, he cannot complain later that the final art did not meet his expectations. Finally, most publishers conduct quarterly reviews of projects, and continually reviewing the art can prepare the team to handle any questions or suggestions from the publisher.

Project Support

Similar to the programming team, the art staff is involved in other mundane chores during production that take them away from their primary tasks. During the interview process, the producer should make sure that each new artist knows what is expected, both on the project and in support.

As with the other teams, the art team is involved in regular meetings and interviews, submits weekly reports and requests for software and hardware updates, attends trade shows, and takes part in demos.

Summary

Creating the artwork in a game is a complex process, and getting it to appear correctly on the screen is even more complex. However, players expect the art in the games to look professional and to complement the gameplay. Every screen in the game should look like it is part of an organic whole. It can take an art team several months to nail down the correct style for the game.

The art in games is all handcrafted, and few shortcuts are available to the artists. Creating a richly detailed game world requires that artists be trained in classical art techniques and have a mastery of the 2D and 3D software programs used to build games. Whether the game is 2D or 3D, the artists have to spend considerable time creating the original sprites and models, animating them to look realistic, and finally making sure that all the graphic glitches are removed. It takes time to become a game artist, but the personal rewards are great—seeing your art on the screen and hearing gamers "ooh" and "aah" at your work. And the financial rewards aren't bad, either.

Test Your Skills

MULTIPLE CHOICE QUESTIONS

1. What is a pixel?
   A. A color.
   B. A tiny computer.
   C. The smallest unit that can be displayed on a monitor.
   D. The number of colors that can be displayed on a monitor.

2. What is a texel?
   A. A texture element.
   B. A way to draw triangles.
   C. A drawing primitive.
   D. A texture after it is applied to a triangle.

13

3. What are common uses for 2D art today? (Select all that apply.)

    A. Menus and HUDs.

    B. Games for handheld platforms such as the Game Boy Advance.

    C. Online gaming.

    D. Mesh creation.

    E. Textures.

4. What is antialiasing?

    A. Averaging pixel colors across the edge of an image to smooth the outline.

    B. Adding more color depth to an edge to smooth the outline.

    C. Making an image so that it can appear on any background.

    D. Removing a color so that it is transparent.

5. How is depth testing used in the rendering process?

    A. It checks the color depth of all objects on screen and makes them match.

    B. It renders things farthest way from the front of the screen first, so backgrounds are not left out.

    C. It renders things closest to the front of the screen first, thereby not rendering those things that would be hidden by other objects.

    D. It is a method of antialiasing edges.

6. The *occluder* is a term used in which of the following processes?

    A. MIP-mapping.

    B. Lighting.

    C. Shadowing.

    D. Coloring.

7. What does the occluder refer to?

    A. An object blocking the way.

    B. An object that causes a shadow.

    C. A shadow created by reflected light.

    D. The normal to a plane.

8. On a screen with resolution 1024 × 1024 how many pixels are there?

    A. 1 million.

    B. 1 MB.

    C. 1,048,576.

    D. 640.

9. Which of these processes is used when rendering a 3D scene? (Select all that apply.)

   A. Clipping.

   B. Antialiasing.

   C. Parallaxing.

   D. Shading.

10. What are sprites?

    A. Two dimensional images drawn into the scene.

    B. Animation sets.

    C. Textures applied to a mesh.

    D. Images of power-ups.

11. What is meant by rendering?

    A. The act of drawing on screen.

    B. The process of generating an image from a model.

    C. The process of using lighting to create shadows.

    D. The process of making the image appear on the monitor.

12. What is the main benefit of tiling a background in a 2D game? (Select all that apply.)

    A. The game data can be smaller.

    B. The game data is easier to change or update.

    C. The game is faster.

    D. The image is easier to create.

13. Why does a 3D rendering process perform the task of lighting the scene after removing hidden surfaces?

    A. To help with the lighting of the game.

    B. To make shadows darker.

    C. To speed the process by running the lighting algorithm only on polygons the player can see.

    D. To more accurately light the surfaces.

14. How does shading differ from shadowing?

    A. Shading creates the color tone, whereas shadowing creates the reflected shadows.

    B. Shading determines the final surface properties of an object, whereas shadowing creates the shadows on those surfaces.

    C. Shading determines the color depth of a polygon, whereas shadowing determines the brightness.

    D. Shading creates the textures on an object, whereas shadowing darkens those objects that are within shadows.

13

15. True or False: When applying textures to a polygon, shading is not important.
    A. True.
    B. False.

16. True or False: A modeler usually creates the model and mesh and then rigs the final 3D model.
    A. True.
    B. False.

17. True or False: Page flipping is used only by 2D graphic programs.
    A. True.
    B. False.

18. True or False: Key frames are used by any 2D or 3D graphic system that can interpolate between positions for creating animations.
    A. True.
    B. False.

EXERCISES

Exercise 13.1: Tiling Exercise

Select your favorite 2D platform game for console or PC. Consider the background and foreground of the first level. Determine if the game uses tiling and count the number of unique tiles within the foreground/playfield.

Exercise 13.2: 3D Model Manipulation

Draw a cube on a piece of paper. Count the vertices. Now add a midpoint to every line. Redraw the cube with that point pulled away from the original line. Do this four times. What shape do you end up with?

Exercise 13.3: Handheld Game Research

Review the top games released for Game Boy Advance this year. How many of them use sprites? Did any of these games release on any other platform, and if so, how different did the art look?

DISCUSSION TOPICS

1. Making 3D models look good in both high- and low-polygon-count versions requires time and effort. Discuss whether it would be easier to make only the low-resolution version.

2. Consider an FPS that involves science fiction or fantasy elements. How could transparency and alpha-blending be used in the game? How could you incorporate these effects into gameplay?

3. Consider a tile-based platform game. How could you reuse a tile set over several levels yet make the levels look distinctly different? What minor art modifications could you use to accomplish this?

13

Chapter | 14

Hearing the Game

Chapter Objectives

**After reading this chapter and doing the exercises,
you will be able to do the following:**

- Discuss how music, sound effects, and voiceovers are used in games.
- Understand the basics of audio technology.
- Understand how audio helps set the mood of the game.
- Explain how audio gives the player clues and feedback during play.
- Discuss how poor audio breaks a player's immersion in a game.
- Understand how voiceovers are created for games.

Introduction

Audio is one of the things that human beings know a lot about, even without technical information. We are surrounded by ambient noise, spoken words, and music all the time, and we have developed an appreciation for audio that is different from our appreciation of visual input. We can hear sounds without paying any attention to them—yet when we hear something out of the ordinary, it immediately attracts our attention. This is a double-edged sword for game audio designers and engineers. It means that audio needs to be subtle and unobtrusive—that is, unless it needs to attract the player's attention. It also means audio that doesn't sound as expected, such as birds that sound artificial or metal sounds in an all-wood environment, will distract the player.

The audio in a game consists of the music, sound effects, and voiceovers (spoken information or dialogue). Until the mid-1990s, game audio was rather poor because the technology involved was primitive. For many players, game audio was something to be turned off rather than turned up. But advances in sound technology have made both computer and video-game audio feel much more realistic and exciting. Today, the audio in a game is as important as the audio in movies.

Audio is sometimes considered—wrongly—as a simple add-on to the game, so development teams might not implement it until late in the production phase. Because audio is such an integral part of gameplay, however, ignoring it can lead to last-minute crunches to get sounds into the game—whether they work or not. If the team wants to experiment with the modern capabilities of sound chips and cards such as Dolby 5.1 or interactive music, they must give themselves enough time to program the audio and create the appropriate sound effects and music.

The Functions of Audio in Games

The audio in a game serves several important functions. First and foremost, it helps set the mood of the game. A slow-paced, atonal piece of music combined with the melancholy drip of a broken faucet can give the player a perfect sense of walking through a deserted house where ghosts may be lurking. An adrenaline-pumping heavy-metal bass line can underscore the excitement of roaring, over-revved engines and screeching tires in a racing game. The distinctive thunk of a well-hit ball going over the wall for a home run can fill a player's heart with joy as the crowd roars its delight, the stadium speakers blare out Queen's "We Are the Champions," and the excited announcer shouts, "It's outta here!" In all of these examples, the audio works with the graphics to define the game world's *ambience*—the unique atmosphere of the player's current surroundings. Second, audio can give clues as to what is happening around the player. Many modern games literally surround the player with sounds and music (assuming she has invested in the correct surround sound audio equipment). Sound effects can provide clues to the player such as soft footsteps of an enemy creeping up from behind or the sudden roar of a Messerschmitt Bf-109 as it zooms down to strafe your position in a foxhole. Music, too, can provide clues. As a player inches forward through a dark forest, the foreboding music that has been playing since he first entered the woods might suddenly change to the heroic strands of combat music as several thugs drop out of the trees to attack him.

Third, audio gives the player feedback about what she is doing right and what she is doing wrong in a game. It can be as simple as hearing a click when an option button is pressed versus an angry buzz when trying to make a wrong selection, or it can be as complex as a compliment by an enemy for pulling off a particularly difficult combat combination or a verbal dressing-down by an angry drill sergeant when the player accidentally targets a fellow soldier during a mission. Every action in the game should involve some kind of feedback to let the player know that he has indeed done something, and the audio should work together with the graphics to provide useful feedback to the player everywhere in the game.

14

IN THE TRENCHES: Terraformers

Audio feedback is especially important to players with visual disabilities. A Swedish team, Pin Interactive, created a 3D game called *Terraformers* for both sighted and sight disabled players. In the game, players are guided through the world by an auditory feedback system. The player dons a power suit that provides such accessibility features as a sound compass, sonar, voiced global positioning system, and a voiced menu system. The game won the Innovation in Audio Award at the Independent Game Festival 2003 (**www.indiegames.com**).

How Game Audio Works

The music and sounds for a game can be created in a number of ways including an orchestra playing the score for the game, actors reading their dialogue, and audio technicians banging physical objects together for sound effects. All of these *analog* sounds must be encoded and stored in a digital format to be used by the computer or game console. Of course, music and sound effects can also be created synthetically directly to a digital format. However they are created, the files are stored with the rest of the game files on the CD, DVD, cartridge, or other storage medium. During gameplay, the audio files can be loaded into memory on the game machine (an easier task for computers than consoles) or streamed directly from the disk.

Sampling

The first step of creating game audio is to use a microphone to capture physical sound waves and convert them to analog audio signals. All sound waves have both an *amplitude* (the height), which corresponds to the volume of the sound, and a *frequency* (the length), which corresponds to the pitch. Amplitude is measured in *decibels (dB),* a relative scale that effectively equates to a doubling of sound volume for every increase of 10 dBs. Each wave cycle actually has two amplitude peaks on either side of a single point in the wave where the amplitude is zero. Frequency is measured in *Hertz (Hz),* which equals the number of wave cycles that pass a point in one second. The human ear can hear sounds in the range of about 20 Hz to 20,000 Hz (20 kHz). Every sound has its own unique pattern of amplitude and frequency changes. The goal of capturing sound is to ensure that enough of the sound's unique amplitude and frequency pattern is recorded that the audio sounds natural when played back.

The analog audio signal is converted to digital data (binary numbers) through a process called *sampling.* During the sampling process, the analog

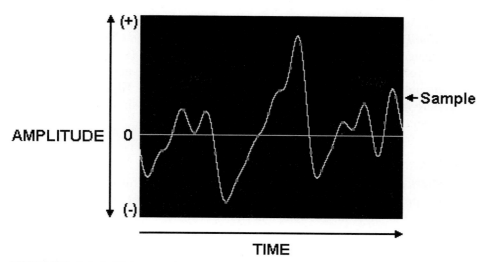

FIGURE 14.1 This graph shows an example of a sound recording. The amplitude of the analog sound wave is sampled at discrete points over time (the red dots) to create the digital audio signal.

signal is captured, or digitized, by measuring the amplitude at regular intervals and storing the measurement as a value (Figure 14.1). The quality of the sampling depends on two factors: how often the measurements are taken and how many bits are used to store each measurement.

The *sampling frequency* (not to be confused with the audio frequency) determines how often the sound wave is measured per second. By it's nature, the sampling measurement is imprecise because the analog wave cannot be recorded in its entirety, much as a movie does not capture visual information in one continuous motion but as a series of still photographs. Each time the wave is sampled, the software measures the amplitude of the wave at that point in time. The typical sampling frequency is between 4,000 to 96,000 samples per second.

The *bit depth* refers to the number of bits used to store the amplitude information for each sample. Generally, the more bits that are available, the more accurate and true-to-life the output from the data is. A bit depth of 1 would store only two states—sound or no sound. Each addition of a bit doubles the number of states that can be recorded: 2 bits allow 4 states, 8 bits allow 256 states, 16 bits allow 65,536 states, and 24 bits allow 16,777,216 states. This translates to greater dynamic range and higher fidelity in much the same way that increasing the number of bits used to store an RGB value translates to higher numbers of recordable color variations. The typical range is 8 to 32 bits per sample.

As you might guess, the more often the signal is measured and the more bits that are used to record the information, the better the quality, but there is a point where the average human ear can no longer distinguish differences between an analog wave and its corresponding digital version. This resolution is

14

44,100 samples per second (44.1 kHz) and 16 bits per sample, which is known as *Redbook Audio.* This is the standard used for music on CDs. However, this audio standard is a hog for disk space because it requires 10 megabytes of storage for every minute of stereo audio. Although computers nowadays have more than enough hard drive space to handle large CD-quality files, console games face more memory constraints and typically use compression to make the files smaller and more manageable.

MIDI

The *MIDI (Musical Instrument Digital Interface)* file format (.MID) uses a different process to create digital audio. MIDI files do not record actual audio data, but rather store instructions that can be read by the computer (similar to a musical score) to create the music in real-time through a synthesizer that is built into the sound card. To be able to reproduce MIDI music, the synthesizer on every sound card uses standard groups of instrument sounds; however, the quality of the cards varies widely, so the composer loses some control over the how the music will actually sound as the game is being played.

To generate a MIDI score, the composer connects electronic instruments such as keyboards, synthesizers, and so on directly to the computer and plays the music. The computer system translates the played music into a set of text-based representations of the sounds. When the music is played back, the instructions are read directly by the sound card to produce the instruments' notes. Because this format already stores a minimal amount of information, trying to compress it further saves no additional space.

Storing Audio Data

Sound files are often the largest data files in a video game, and compression is almost always used to reduce the amount of space required for storage and playback. However, as discussed in the previous section, some information is already is lost when an analog wave is converted to a digital wave, and compressing the data can lead to further loss. It's a tradeoff that the programmer, audio engineer, and designer must discuss in detail.

The basic idea of compression is to throw out data that the human ear might not notice in order to make the audio file smaller. For example, some of the original sound frequencies can be beyond the range of human hearing, or a very loud sound might simply drown out weaker effects. In both cases, the unheard data is removed to make the data files smaller.

Another approach to saving space is not to compress the recorded audio data files but to use a lower sampling frequency or smaller bit depth when recording. Depending on the selected frequency, the recorded audio can sound very good or very bad. Common sampling frequencies used in games are 22 kHz, which has the sound quality of an FM radio, and 11 kHz, which has the sound quality a telephone or an AM radio (depending on whether the bit depth is 8-bit or 16-bit). When using this technique, it's often helpful to use a higher bit depth for music and a lower bit depth for sound effects because sound effects are usually short and have less dynamic range than music between the loudest and softest sounds.

Another factor that affects the size of an audio file is whether it is sampled in **monaural (mono)** or **stereo** format. Mono format uses only one channel to deliver the sound, whereas stereo format uses two channels (left and right). The stereo data delivers two different waveforms that play together from two different speakers, which gives a sense of three-dimensional placement of the listener in respect to the sound sources. However, it also doubles the amount of storage required for the audio. Most games use mono sounds for sound effects and voiceovers (and sometimes the music) and then play them back in stereo or surround sound, which involves using more than two speakers.

File Format and Compression

The audio for a game can be stored in a number of different formats. The **Waveform Audio** file format (.WAV) was developed for Windows platforms and is one of the oldest and most popular. For programmers, the benefit is that the audio will play the same on almost any audio card because the recording is very similar to analog playback.

Several formats support compression of audio files while providing good sound quality on computers and consoles. One of the most popular is the MP3 format (.MP3), which allows up to 10-to-1 compression for files yet retains almost CD sound quality. Although MP3 uses **lossy** data compression, the quality of the playback is indistinguishable to the average listener. Another popular lossy format is the Ogg Vorbis format (.OGG), which provides greater compression than MP3 and also has the advantage of being open-source, so the user does not have to obtain a license to use it.

FYI   *Codecs, Lossy, and Lossless*

The software or hardware used to compress and decompress audio data to save storage space is called a **codec** (compressor/decompressor). Speech codecs and audio codecs designed for the special characteristics of voices and music are available. Codec algorithms also are available to do the compression completely via software (no hardware is involved). Most codecs are **lossy**—that is, they toss out some data in order to improve compression. One of the problems with lossy compression is that when the file is opened and then resaved, the compression algorithm is run again, which tosses out more data. Eventually, the file becomes too degraded to use. On the other hand, **lossless** compression methods throw no data away.

14

Playing the Audio

Audio files can either be played directly from the game storage medium (CD or DVD) or from the hard drive (computer or Xbox). Like all computer data, audio data is stored in binary code. The task of playing the audio is handled by a sound chip on the sound card or motherboard. The chip usually has a ***digital-to-analog converter (DAC)*** that converts the binary code into an analog signal. The analog signal then travels via a connector cable to an amplifier or other sound destination that sends the signal out to be played through the speaker(s).

Though computers and the Xbox have large enough hard drives to handle the storage requirements of large audio files, the developer might prefer to compress the files and decompress them at runtime because compressed files take less time to load onto the hard drive and take up less space. The files are then decompressed at runtime. The tradeoff is that the quality of the audio might be reduced slightly using this method. Other platforms such as the PlayStation 2, GameCube, and the new handheld platforms, generally stream all the audio directly off the game CD/DVD.

Surround Sound Audio

Realistic surround sound and 3D audio has become the standard. In the late 1980s, QSound Labs (**www.qsound.com**) became one of the first companies to develop 3D sound. Most computers have only two speakers (just as humans have only two ears), so the first efforts used just the two speakers and some clever algorithms (***Head Relative Transfer Functions,*** or ***HRTF***) to trick the brain into believing the sounds were coming from someplace other than the speakers. But there were problems with this approach; most notably, if the speakers were not positioned in the best places relative to each other and the listener, there could be ***crosstalk,*** where sounds meant for one ear were also heard by the other.

The best way to have true 3D audio is to surround the player with speakers and have software and hardware that can play the correct sound in the correct speaker. There might be several speakers in the front and several on the sides or behind the player. Setting up the speakers correctly so that the player is always in the ***sweet spot*** (the place where the 3D audio will sound best) can take time. However, after they are properly arranged, the player will have a true surround sound experience from games that take advantage of the technology.

The current standard is Dolby Digital 5.1, which Dolby Technologies (**www.dolby.com**) developed for movie theaters. This system uses five speakers (left-front, center-front, right-front, left-back, right-back) for mid- and high-frequency sounds and a subwoofer (also known as the ***low-frequency effects channel,*** or ***LFE***) for low-frequency sound (Figure 14.2 for an example of how the Dolby Pro Logic II system is set up). This setup is more likely to be found in the family entertainment room where television, stereo, and video game platforms are linked. However, a growing number of Dolby 5.1 speaker systems are available for computers as well.

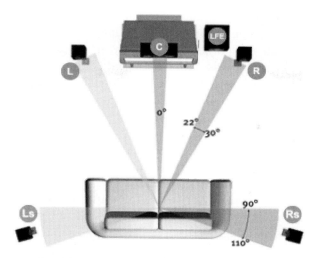

FIGURE 14.2 Dolby Pro Logic II system. The front left (L) and right (R) speakers are set up in front of the sound focus point (the couch), preferably at the angles shown. The center (C) speaker is positioned directly in front of the focus point, and the low-frequency effects channel (LFE, the .1 in Dolby 5.1) is a subwoofer. The side right (Rs) and side left (Ls) speakers are behind the focal point at the indicated angles.

Music in Games

The music in movies and television shows is carefully orchestrated to emphasize and reinforce the images appearing on the screen. The audience might not even be aware that the music is playing in a quiet scene until it builds in intensity during a particularly emotional sequence. Tying the music to the graphics is difficult to achieve in a game. There are often long stretches in a game where the player is simply moving about the playfield or dealing with minutia such as inventory or resource management. To hear the same music playing in a continuous loop can become annoying, which is why many players eventually turn the music down.

Many players regularly crank up the volume for the sound effects because they feel that they contribute directly to the play experience but turn off the music because they feel it adds little. There is some historical justification for their judgment. The audio playback of computers and consoles was so limited for so long that players learned to ignore the musical aspects of

14

games. Additionally, the constant repetition of looping music was quickly annoying for most players, and instead of adding to the ambience of a setting, it often would break the players' immersion in the game. Fortunately, the advent of modern sound cards, more advanced compression technology, and an increased interest in the audio aspects of immersion have improved matters. Of course, some limitations of the computer and consoles remain to be worked around.

Music in games continues to be greatly underappreciated. The music in games is very different from the music in movies or television. It is not currently possible to orchestrate a game the same way as a movie—where music is timed to specific events. On the one hand, a movie shows each incident only once, and a movie composer can tweak the music to perfectly enhance the emotion of the moment. On the other hand, in a game, the player can revisit an area multiple times and might get bored hearing the same musical motif over and over again.

A movie runs for only 2 hours or so, whereas a game often takes 20 to 100 hours to complete. Creating enough unique music to fill all of that time would require an enormous amount of storage space. At 10 megabytes per minute for Redbook quality music, 20 hours of music would require 12 gigabytes of disk space (20 hours × 60 minutes/hour = 1,200 minutes × 10 MB/minute = 12,000 megabytes). Even using 10-to-1 compression, the music would take 1.2 gigabytes of disk space (enough to fill two CDs). That does not include the game itself or the art for the game.

Instead, game companies usually resort to a number of methods to keep the music fresh and interesting while not wasting storage space. But the problem persists: when a player tires of a song, the natural inclination is to tune it out.

Innovation in Composition

Game companies have developed several approaches to get around this player indifference. These include making the music more interesting to the player through the choice of the performers, making the music seem more interactive during gameplay, and letting players select their own music at any time during the game.

The first technique involves hiring well-known rock bands, popular rap artists, or even traditional symphony orchestras to write and perform the game music. This can be an expensive endeavor for the publisher because well-known rap and rock stars make and expect a lot of money for their performances. The marketing of the product, of course, benefits from the publicity surrounding the famous performers, and sales to new fans can increase. The company might be able to recoup some of these expenses by releasing the game music as a commercial CD. For example, Square Enix has released several albums of music from their *Final Fantasy* series, including the recent *Final Fantasy XI: Music from the Other Side of Vana'diel: The Star Onions.*

A variation on this technique is to use up-and-coming bands or musicians for the game music. Although it does not help marketing or bring an established consumer base to the game, game audiophiles might appreciate being exposed to unknown, cutting edge artists. This assumes, of course, that the music is good and fits the genre of the gameplay.

IN THE TRENCHES: Game Music Symphony Concert

The Prague Filmharmonic Orchestra performs a yearly Game Music Symphony Concert in Leipzig, Germany, that features music from computer and console games. A number of other symphony orchestras such as the Seattle Symphony and Los Angeles Philharmonic have also included musical selections from games as part of their repertoire to attract younger audiences.

Another approach is to let the player select the music during play. Rockstar's *Grand Theft Auto 3* lets the player change songs by changing the "channels" on the radio while driving a hijacked car. In the computer and Xbox versions of the game, players can load and play their own MP3 files during the game. If the player is going to listen to the music she prefers anyway, this approach at least keeps her immersed in the game world, even if the music clashes with the game's mood.

The music can also be interactive (also called *adaptive music*) so that it continually changes as the game progresses. For example, one musical theme might play while the player is exploring the map, and a second warlike theme might be triggered when a combat encounter occurs. When the combat ends, the first theme would start playing again. The challenge with this method is that little subtlety is involved; at its most basic, the wandering theme and fighting theme can both become boring after a while. The music does not really interact with the game or with how the player performs different gameplay actions.

However, at its most complex, interactive music can involve an amazing interweaving of themes. To achieve this, the music programmer and designer divide the music into multiple threads, similar to leitmotifs in classical music. In this scenario, a musical passage or theme is associated with a character, setting, or situation. Through clever programming, the audio engine can make some of the musical threads interweave and overlap one another as the player performs one action (such as manipulating items in the inventory) and then launch new threads as another activity is started (for example, exploring the area). A number of musical themes might be associated with the different

14

gameplay actions, so the music could change continually as the player transitioned from one gameplay activity to another.

This approach lends itself to **_foreshadowing;_** for example, as the player approaches an area where a combat encounter is to occur, the first threads of a combat motif might appear and build in intensity as the player nears the trigger point. Konami's *Metal Gear Solid 2* uses such an approach to warn the player of imminent danger and to underscore changing events in the game. This approach is technically demanding and requires that the composer work closely with an audio programmer during production.

The use of music in games is still in the early stages of development. Composers and audio programmers will continue to experiment with new ways to make the music enhance the player's experience. The technological advances of the last decade have finally made digital game music sound as rich and full as its analog counterpart. Now it is up to the composers and audio programmers to experiment with the medium to make music a truly integral part of the gameplay experience, just as the soundtrack for a movie is integral to its enjoyment.

Legal Issues About Music

Most game companies use freelance composers to provide the music for their games. As discussed in the previous section, games sometimes use prerecorded songs by bands and other artists. When a company commissions the music from a composer, they can own all rights to it, whereas using prerecorded music might force the company to get a number of permissions before being able to use it. Music creators have a copyright on the music they create that allows them to perform, exhibit, copy, distribute, and create derivative works from it. Anyone else who wants to do the same must get a license and perhaps pay to use it.

If a game developer wants to use prerecorded music in a game, he must consider a number of different rights under the copyright laws:

- Performance Right: This right allows the music creators to collect royalties whenever a song is performed in public, including on radio or television, live onstage, or otherwise publicly performed. Even if the song is in the public domain (meaning that no one owns the copyright), the artist performing it is entitled to payment.

- Mechanical Right: This right allows the music creators to collect a royalty when a piece of copyrighted music is recorded for sale to the public.

- Graphic Right: This right lets the music creators collect a royalty whenever their copyrighted music is printed.

- Master Right: This right applies to using an audio recording in another medium, for example, using a movie or television theme in a game.

Caution

Consult an Attorney

In general, legal assistance is required to navigate the maze of licensing music and art content for games, whether procuring the rights to existing music or obtaining the rights for original music to be created for products. Because these rights are so convoluted, they are best left to the legal staff to fully arrange.

- Synchronization Right: This is the right needed to record the musical piece within another form of audio-visual media such as film, television, or commercials.

To obtain these rights, the game developer must contact a licensing organization such as ASCAP (**www.ascap.com**), BMI (**www.bmi.com**), SESAC (**www.sesac.com**), or the Harry Fox Agency (**www.harryfox.com**).

The rights listed above protect the music creators from exploitation, but they can be a headache for a game company that wants to use the music. Thus, most game companies usually hire freelance composers on a ***work for hire*** basis, where they pay a flat fee for the music and then own all the rights themselves.

Sound Effects in Games

Sounds not only add to the atmosphere of the game world, they also give clues about the player's surroundings. The growl of an angry animal, the snap of a twig, or the distant roar of an aircraft can all be harbingers of danger. Even if danger is not imminent, the game world is still alive with noise including the chirping of birds, the throbbing of subterranean engines, or an occasional rumble of distant thunder. These sounds help the player believe the world is real, although they are nothing more than the audio engineer's tricks.

It is generally more important for ***sound effects (SFX)*** to feel psychologically real to the player than to be accurate recordings of real-life sounds. A real sound effect such as the rat-a-tat of a machine gun might need to be enhanced to make it sound bigger than life and, therefore, more "real" to the player. The general public has been conditioned by sound effects heard in movies and television, and they expect similar quality from the sound effects in games. As a matter of fact, the player might get more of an emotional attachment to the character he controls if his character's gun sounds bigger and more dangerous than similar weapons wielded by the enemy.

Sound effects can be created by the music composer or by an audio engineer. The sounds can come from commercially available SFX CDs, although these sounds are often modified to make them feel more appropriate to the source. Often, there are no sources for fantastic sounds such as the roar of dinosaurs, the zaps of ray guns, or the shrieking of banshees, so audio engineers will mix different sounds together, overlaying one atop the next and adding effects until they come up with a sound that feels as though it is coming from creature or object on the screen.

Game audio engineers also have to create interface sounds, which movie sound designers do not have to worry about. Although both are concerned

14

with making sure the world in the film or game feels alive and that everything sounds exactly right, the audio engineer also has to worry about the sound effects for the menu system, HUD, inventory, and other interfaces. As explained in Chapter 15, "Interface Design," the player should get continual feedback while playing the game. Every time she clicks a button or otherwise interacts with the game, there should be either a visual or audio reaction or both to let her know that not only she did something but that she did it correctly or incorrectly. Therefore, the audio engineer has to go through the section of the game design document describing the interface screens with extreme care to make sure he finds all instances where audio feedback will be needed.

One of the biggest challenges facing an audio engineer is to make sure that the sound effects are synced with the graphics. As in a poorly dubbed movie, the player will notice any discernible gap between pressing a button and hearing the click or firing a weapon and hearing the bang. The best sound effects are those that the player does not even notice because they happen when they are supposed to.

The audio engineer also has to make sure the sounds match the environment, no matter what is happening in the game. For example, the sound of a car racing through a tunnel is completely different from the sound of speeding down an open highway, so the audio engineer must make sure both environments sound correct in the game. One option is to record different versions of the same sound, but this limits the game to predetermined conditions. Newer technology allows the programmer and audio engineer to apply filters or effects in real-time to the sound within the game. This enables the audio engineer to set up a series of trigger points in the map or model that will change or modify the sound effects so they still sound appropriate to changes in the game world.

Ambient noise, however, should not be predictable. If, for example, the chirp of a distant bird is set up in a loop of a fixed duration, the player will likely notice the repetitive call after a while and might lose his sense of immersion in the game world because the bird call is obviously artificial. The secret of ambient sound effects is to make them occur randomly so the player does not discern any obvious patterns.

The finishing touch to audio is to make sure that the sounds fit together and are acoustically similar. That is, if a scene takes place inside a large, empty warehouse with lots of reverberation, all sound effects for the location should have similar echoing effects.

Sound effects in games are most often stored in .WAV format (for PC and Xbox). For space considerations, sound effects are sometimes recorded at low sampling rates. However, because sound effects add a dimension of realism to a game and can be used for many things within the game, the audio engineer and programmer should consider accepting the increased space requirements in exchange for the higher quality.

Caution

Matching Sound to Graphics

Getting the sound effects to match the graphics correctly is a time-consuming task. Development teams should not make the mistake of putting off audio implementation until late in production.

Voices in Games

When the storage media for games was limited to floppy disks, there was less interest in including voiceovers for characters because the audio files were so large. Additionally, many sound cards could not reproduce quality voice recordings. Instead, games would use music and sound effects as much as possible and rely on players' reading the dialogue on the screen. Text, of course, requires little space to store, and there are no issues of actors, recording studios, or replicating voices correctly. However, as the processing power of game platforms has increased and 3D models used for game characters have become more highly detailed and realistic, there is an increased desire to make them interact verbally with the player and one another.

Nowadays, games use multiple CDs or a DVD that provides cheaper storage for large files. Also, the improvements in audio cards (and computer speakers) make it possible for voices to sound realistic—even movie like. As a result, even games that do not have a strong story element are using voiceovers for characters to make the game feel more realistic. For example, in a strategy game, a military officer might appear between missions to brief the player about the next assignment and then be available during the mission via radio or cell phone for further instructions. Many companies now hire professional actors and sports commentators to lend their voices to games—for a hefty fee, of course.

A final aspect of voice in games is discussed at the end of this chapter: the voices of the players themselves. For now, suffice it to say that a new trend in multiplayer games is for the player to be able to talk with other game players in real-time during the gameplay. This audio is not recorded or delivered by the game developers, so it is not discussed here. But interacting verbally with other players fulfills some of the same functions as other game audio: It enhances immersion in the game, lends a sense of realism, and in the case of action or FPS games, a sense of danger as well as camaraderie.

Preproduction for Voiceover Acting

During the preproduction phase, the team decides how to use voiceovers (VOX) in the game. It takes time and money to prepare for and record the voices, so the team should not decide to include voiceovers at the last minute. The following sections outline the steps involved in the process

Step 1: Identification of Needs   Prepare an outline of all possible uses of recorded voice in the game including everything from dialogue to grunts and groans to joyous exclamations to indications of "message received."

Step 2: Technical Considerations   The programmer, designer, and audio engineer working on the game need to determine the sample rate for the audio

14

playback during the game. However, this does not generally affect the quality of the audio recorded, because it should always be recorded at the highest quality possible and delivered on a digital medium that is easily imported into the development system. In general, voiceovers are recorded in professional studios for optimal audio engineering.

Step 3: Determine the Use of the VOX with the Art and Animation   If the voiceovers need to be synchronized to facial animation, the modelers and animators should be involved in determining how to do so. There are several options, ranging from motion capture of the actors faces to making several verbal basic shapes that the animator will use (such as for an "o" sound versus an "ooh" sound). This needs to be determined early on because the animation system written by the programmers must be capable of handling the technique used.

In addition, audio is generally used for cut-sequences or noninteractive storytelling. In this event, as well as in other dialogue events within the game, an artist or designer might be responsible for staging the movements and actions of the characters on screen as well as cutting or editing between different views or scenes. Again, the animation and graphics portions of the game engine need to be able to accommodate this feature, and it is likely that a tool (or two) will need to be created to enable the artist or designer to synchronize the audio to facial movements as well as to character animations or staging. In a final step, motion capture data might be used during the synchronizing to capture the movements or behaviors of the actor's actual performance. This approach is not currently used extensively in the industry, although it is expect to grow over the next few years.

Step 4: Draft of the Dialogue   The senior designer is responsible for determining the content of the dialogue in the game. If the dialogue is interactive—that is, based on the player's actions and dialogue choices—each computer-controlled character might have multiple responses. The designer should prepare a first draft of all the branching dialogue in the game. To make sure every possible dialogue branch has been covered, the designer should start testing the character interactions as soon the game engine is up and running.

This draft outlines all possible situations that the designer can conceive of. With a variety of responses possible based on the game's state, the designer needs to provide enough information to the audio engineer or audio director to get the correct emotional response from the actors for all situations.

Ideally the design and programming teams use this script to check for all possible permutations of events. The script needs to identify which character is speaking, the situation in which the line might be spoken, and the various permutations of emotions that might occur (angry, happy, relieved, scared, or others), so that the cast and director can record the required audio.

Step 5: Final Dialogue Script   The final draft of the dialogue can be given to a professional screenwriter, who can polish the prose and sharpen the personality traits of each character. Screenwriters can also help reduce the size of the dialogue because they are trained to minimize verbiage and let the action speak for itself in a movie. However, hiring a screenwriter can be costly, so the designer should make sure that the final draft of the dialogue is as complete as possible before handing it off. The designer should also be aware that the dialogue will inevitably need to be revised or updated based on testing, so the screenwriter's contract should call for some work on revising the materials.

An issue with using screenwriters is that they generally are not trained in nonlinear storytelling. Although it's relatively simple to see how dialogue can be based on previous situations and dialogue, it's often difficult to track which situation has occurred or has not yet occurred in a game, especially one that allows the player to solve puzzles in any order. This is especially challenging for story-driven games. Games that use audio simply to make the characters seem more realistic are often easier to record and create.

The final script must include a lot of information for the programmers to use during coding, information for the actors and directors to use during recording, and information for animators and artists to use for simulating mouth movements and synchronizing the audio to the animations.

Recording the Voices

During production, the designer and audio engineer or programmer generally hire several people to assist with the actual recording, including a director to help the actors create the correct emotional response, a casting director, and a studio engineer. In addition, they might need to hire the services of a recording studio. To accomplish all of this, the team needs to do the following tasks.

Casting   Although it might be possible to find people in the company whose voices match the characters in a game, the likelihood of these employees' being able to deliver the lines like a professional actor is limited. It is much wiser to use trained actors for voiceover work than employees, even though the expense is greater. To find the right voices for the game, the company can contact talent agents to line up the talent and then hold auditions.

Using an agent and professional actors can involve additional expenses, but these costs are often offset by the extra studio time required to get nonprofessionals to give life to the dialogue. Professional actors, especially professional voiceover actors, require little or no rehearsal for most games. Most can deliver the lines with a script they've read in advance and the director's assistance. Rehearsal generally isn't necessary because many takes can be made of each line.

Hiring a Director   Many people think directing is an easy task that anyone can do, but for the most efficient results, a company should hire an experienced audio

14

director for the recording sessions. The director reviews the script and asks questions of the designers, artists, and programmers about the setting and scenes. She asks whether a player should like or not like a character and inquires about the character's backstory. An experienced director uses all of this information to help determine the correct cast, the correct performance, and the correct microphone and room to use to create a voiceover that ends up the way the designer wants.

FYI | *Hierarchy During Recording*

In any recording session, a strict hierarchy must be followed because there can be only one person to whom the actors listen for direction. That person is the director. Only the director should speak with the actors about the performance, setting, situation, or other topic. The studio engineer is on an almost equal footing as the director, though she is rarely interested in the emotional performance. Instead, she makes sure the audio is recorded properly and at the same volume as other audio. She also makes sure the actor is close enough to the microphone and moves the mike around to provide the correct sound that the director wants.

All other participants at a recording session can talk to the director only when he is not working with the actors or actively recording. Generally, distracting the director or otherwise interrupting him will lead to the person's being expelled from the studio. Instead, designers, audio engineers, and others who might attend a performance should withhold comments until the end of a performance and provide feedback or new information only to the director.

Recording Sessions   The voice actors are brought into a recording studio either one at a time or in groups to record the dialogue (Figure 14.3). An actual recording studio is used to provide an environment free of unwanted external noise. Recording studios usually have several types of rooms available (though a small studio might have only one. These rooms are either acoustically "dead" or "hard." These terms refer to the quality of the sound that is created in the room. An acoustically dead room has virtually no echo, and it sounds and consequently feels oppressive. A hard room has an echo and sounds larger, though it also usually sounds empty. The director, sound engineer, and studio recording engineer will decide on the best type of room based on the script, the setting of any scene or line of dialogue, the emotional situation, and even whether a line of dialogue might be repeated in various locations.

It is generally easiest and best to record all dialogue in one room using one type of microphone. Just as with the acoustic quality of a room, the type and

FIGURE 14.3 Veteran actor Charles Napier provides the voice of General Harper in id Software's *Quake 4* (2005).

quality of a microphone affects the sound. If two different microphones and/or two different rooms are used for characters who are involved in a game scene that takes place in one room, the dialogue can end up sounding odd. The audio programmer can use tricks to apply effects or equalization during the gameplay, but these often sound artificial. Sometimes, however, significant changes in room settings should be reflected in the audio, and lines that are repeated elsewhere within the game should be recorded a second (or third, or thirteenth) time in the new room environment for that particular instance to maintain the acoustic integrity of the scene.

The audio engineer, designer, and director will benefit from adding scene information to the recording. They should keep track of the tape used for each scene and maintain a running dialogue chart to mark which take they feel is best. They can also mark dialogue that is incorrect and should not be used. The audio engineer will thus ensure that all audio is recorded and nothing has been skipped. It also provides a quick way to locate any particular line of dialogue from among the many recording tapes delivered or the hundreds of audio lines stored in the game assets folder.

The recording studio should deliver a series of *dry* (processed) audio recordings, preferably on a digital medium such as *digital audio tape (DAT)*.

14

> ## Caution
>
> ### Keep a Dry Copy
>
> If processing (such as ambient room effects) is added during recording through the use of audio equipment, it is ideal if the studio can make two recordings simultaneously: one with the processing and one without.

CDs and DVDs use compression, so only raw data should be delivered on those media. The delivery should also include a copy of the recording scripts, information about the recording equipment used, any additional processing performed on the audio, and names and dates of everyone involved in the recording sessions. Generally, the producer should ask for two copies of the tapes: one to be kept at the studio and the other to be used by the game developers. All processing performed on the audio should be performed during postproduction, not during recording. This method allows the audio engineer to revert to an unaltered recording if necessary.

Script Revisions and Pickup Sessions   As all the elements of the game come together, the team might discover places in the game where extra dialogue is needed. The team might also discover that some of the recorded voices included extraneous noises or find technical problems with a file or two. It is almost inevitable that the script will be modified and additional recording sessions will be needed in pickup sessions. During the hiring process, the producer should make sure that the screenwriter and/or voice actors will be available for this work late in production. Additionally, although this work might not require the original director, the producer or designer should make sure to use the same recording studio and the same equipment for the pickup recording. This extra step might not seem necessary, but a simple trip to the video store to watch and listen to a badly dubbed foreign film strongly demonstrates the need for consistency.

In the Trenches: Screen Actors Guild (SAG)

The Screen Actors Guild (SAG) has recently been at odds with the game industry over royalties for voice performers in games. The union felt actors were being underpaid for their work on games and broke off negotiations in mid-2005 with a demand that actors receive royalties. To bolster their argument, they pointed out that games outgross the film industry. However, the game industry so far is unwilling to grant royalties. It will be interesting to see if other unions start making similar demands of game companies.

Most game companies agree to use either all Screen Actors Guild (SAG) actors or none at all. This becomes an issue when a company wants to use a name actor for a performance because union rules require that all other actors, no matter how small their role, must also be members of SAG. Although no game developer wants to take advantage of an actor, it is difficult to pay for a full day of recording when an actor is only used for 5 lines of dialogue that requires only 30 minutes in the studio.

Some large companies set up recording studios on their own premises to generate and record game audio. Smaller companies either rely on their publishers for studio time and technical assistance or rent a recording studio and then hire trained technicians. It is expensive to rent a studio, so the team should have every detail nailed down before starting the recording sessions.

There is a delicate balance between waiting to record the dialogue until the designer is assured that the script is complete and rushing to get the voiceovers recorded to meet a shipping date. If the game artists are trying to match the mouth movements of the models to voiceover recordings, they need lots of time to tweak the meshes and make the animations look right. Therefore, the recording sessions should be scheduled as early as possible. If there are no plans to synchronize the models with the speech, the team can bring the musicians or voiceover actors back in for a pickup session after the designers have had a chance to thoroughly test the game and determine what changes are needed.

> **Caution**
>
> **Silence is Golden**
>
> When setting up a recording studio, it is important that it be made soundproof so that no outside sounds from the rest of the company get recorded by accident.

Getting Voiceover Audio into the Game

The final step is to get the audio into the game assets and into the game. Generally, an audio engineer is responsible for locating the best version of each dialogue line, editing out any dead space at the beginning or end of the line, converting it to the proper game format and delivering it to the asset folder.

Editing involves using the dialogue charts from the recording session as well as notes from the director, audio engineer, designer, and other recording participants to locate the lines required. As the editor assembles the various lines, he will probably want a way to get immediate feedback on how the audio works in the game. A tool from the programmers that allows a scene to play with audio can help the engineer make sure the performances achieve the desired goal, are the right length, and match in terms of volume and acoustic quality.

Localization and Player Chat

The market for games is international, and many successful games are sold in retail outlets worldwide. Game companies often make changes such as changing the voiceovers and text and altering the artwork of the game to fit local languages and standards of overseas markets. This process, called *localization,* requires considerable effort. If the amount of dialogue and art that must change in a game is limited, it might be possible to include several versions on the same CD or DVD, which helps reduce production costs. Publishers might make all the localization changes themselves, but there are companies that specialize in the process of taking products from foreign markets (say, the United States) and localizing them for their home market (for example, Japan, Germany, or other large overseas game markets).

14

Localizing audio requires delivery of the final script, final game, and final audio assets used in the game to the company doing the localization. The company then translates the text and records the vocal performances by actors proficient in the language. Extra work by the original artists might be required to synchronize the voiceovers with the facial animations. Because the final audio that appears in the game might not match the final script (due to pick-up recordings or changes in gameplay), copies of all notes should also be provided.

A Final Word

No matter how good the voiceovers are, players often treat them with the same lack of respect they show to the music—by turning them off. Although giving real voices to characters makes them feel more lifelike, there is a drawback. Most players can read the dialogue faster than the actors can say it. So, players might want to zip through the spoken dialogue rather than savor it. It's a good idea to let the player zip through the dialogue by pressing a button, especially if she has to view a scene more than once after loading a saved game. Many games include both text-only and voiceover versions and allow players to select the version they prefer.

Summary

The audio capabilities in games have kept pace with advances in graphics. The sound in modern games is as realistic as the 3D graphics that gamers are accustomed to. The audio helps players become immersed in the game world, gives clues and hints about the gameplay, and provides feedback to the player. If a player is willing to invest in a good sound system for his computer or console, he will be surrounded by mind-blowing sound effects and top-quality music as he plays.

The process of creating audio for games is becoming ever more sophisticated and challenging to implement. Teams can no longer postpone working on the audio in their games until the last minute. They must decide on their audio requirements during the design process and include all the tasks in the project timeline and milestone schedule. Creating the music and sound effects, recording the voices, and then incorporating the assets into the game are tasks that require considerable effort and patience to be done correctly. The point of all this work is to heighten the realism and excitement of the game without drawing attention to itself. The best game audio is often the audio that the players don't consciously notice. Players might not say much if the audio works as it is supposed to, but they will be quick to voice their criticisms if the timing is off or other problems arise. The audio may not be as obvious to the players, but it is just as important as any other element in making a game succeed.

Test Your Skills

MULTIPLE CHOICE QUESTIONS

1. Why is compression used? (Select all that apply.)
   A. To save space.
   B. To improve quality.
   C. To add ambiance.
   D. To load faster.

2. The .WAV format is (Select all that apply.)
   A. Used for sound effects.
   B. Lossy.
   C. Uncompressed.
   D. Compressed.

3. When should voiceover recording be done?
   A. During preproduction.
   B. During production, near the end of the development.
   C. During production, at the beginning of development.
   D. During postproduction, to make localization easier.

4. A DAC is used
   A. By the sound card to convert binary audio data to analog.
   B. By the computer CPU to convert digital to analog.
   C. By the audio engineer to compress audio files.
   D. By the voiceover recording as part of the audio equalization.

5. Who synchronizes the audio to animation?
   A. The audio engineer only.
   B. The animator only.
   C. Both the audio engineer and the animator.
   D. Either the audio engineer or the animator.

6. True or False: Ambient noise should be unpredictable.
   A. True.
   B. False.

14

7. The performance rights for music or audio is the copyright that applies to which of the following situations?

    A. The use of the music or audio in a performance.

    B. The using of a specific performance of some music or audio.

    C. The right to select the performer of some music or audio.

    D. The right to use a musical composition.

8. What is the sampling rate?

    A. The frequency at which audio is recorded.

    B. The number of audio samples recorded per second.

    C. The quality of the audio.

    D. The size of the audio file.

9. Interface sounds include which of the following? (Select all that apply.)

    A. Engine revving in a racing game.

    B. Mouse clicks.

    C. Door openings.

    D. Button presses.

    E. Key presses.

    F. Successful key presses.

    G. Unsuccessful key presses.

10. Audio is used primarily (Select all that apply.)

    A. To set the mood of the game.

    B. To get information to the user.

    C. As a means of storytelling.

    D. As a marketing tool to sell games.

11. If you want to create interactive audio in a game, you should use which of the following formats?

    A. WAV.

    B. MP3.

    C. Create your own format.

    D. MIDI.

12. How should the voiceover recording be delivered to the developer?

    A. In an analog format.

    B. On CD.

    C. In a digital format, preferably a DAT or other uncompressed medium.

    D. In WAV format.

13. What issues are involved in localizing a game with audio? (Select all that apply.)

    A. Correctly translating slang and idioms.

    B. Matching the tenor and quality of the voice actors with the original actors.

    C. Synchronizing mouth movements between languages.

    D. Streaming the audio off a CD.

EXERCISES

Exercise 14.1: Audio as a Secret Weapon

Select a game that you own or rent a game that is considered scary or suspenseful. Play the first level with the audio turned off—including all music, sound effects, and voiceover audio. How scary was the level? Play the next level with all the audio turned on again. How different was your experience?

Exercise 14.2: Subtitles versus Audio

Rent a foreign movie that has subtitles and watch it with the audio muted. Assuming the movie is one that would normally hold your interest, how difficult was it to watch without any music, sound effects, or voices? What does this tell you about audio?

Exercise 14.3: Research Current Games

Find a list of the current week's top 10 games (either PC or console) at a site such as **www.biz.gamedaily.com/charts.** How many have voiceover audio? How many use a recognizable named actor or have the name of an actor on the front or back cover of the box?

Exercise 14.4: Sound Effects Research

Use the same game from Exercise 14.2 or select new game for any platform. Play the first level and write down every sound effect you hear. How many do you end up with? How many are used by multiple game entities? How many player-specific sound effects are there, as compared to sounds from other objects in the game? This exercise is easier on a slower paced game or one with pause capabilities.

14

Exercise 14.5: Thematic and Ambient Music

Consider a game design for a first-person shooter in space. Select an ambient type of music that you would like to hear for the game music. List three themes for the game and list how they relate to game state (location, character, time of day, and so on). Write a description of how you could make the music interactive based on the player actions.

DISCUSSION TOPICS

1. If you were making a story-based game and had to chose between using only voiceover recordings or only 3D animations, which would you chose and why?

2. If you were making a shooter or action game and had to chose between using only voiceover recordings or only 3D animations, which would you choose and why?

3. Most game players can easily recognize the music from *Sonic* or *Mario* Bros. What games do you know the music from? Is there any game music that you have started to hum along with as the game begins?

4. List your top five favorite bands. Compare this list with a friend's list. What music on your friend's list would you immediately reject hearing repeatedly in a game? What music from your list would your friend reject? Discuss why you wouldn't want to hear the music repeatedly, specifically as it pertains to playing a game.

5. Consider the change that MP3 has brought to the music industry. What are those changes? Given that audio in games has progressed from sound card beeps to MIDI to .WAV format and now to MP3 and that the level of audio has significantly changed with each new format, what audio techniques can you imagine games will be capable of in the future? How could you use these techniques in actual gameplay?

Part Five

Elements of Game Design Implementation

During the production phase, the assets of the game are created, tested, and modified by the various teams. The programmers write the code that makes everything happen in the game. The artists build the characters, objects, and game world. The composer and audio team create the music and sound effects. Rather than sitting back and simply watching the other teams work, the designer takes an active part in bringing their design to life.

Now that they have defined what the product should be like in the game design document, the designer has the opportunity to turn their vision into reality. They work with the programming and art teams to determine how the user interface will work and what it will look like. They also help generate the maps and levels for a game, if not directly in an art program, then by creating paper prototypes and working with the artists who build the models. Additionally, the designer might use a specially designed scripting language to create the level scripts that trigger events in the game. They are also responsible for maintaining the charts and tables that are used to resolve various game actions such as combat or buying and selling items. Finally, if the game includes a story, the designers modify the plot and create the dialogue (at least the first draft).

Throughout the production phase, everyone working on the team has the chance to play the game and offer feedback on what works and what needs to be changed. When all the game assets have been created, the team works to polish the gameplay balance and remove the last bugs and inconsistencies. Then, finally, the game is finished, and the gold master disk is sent to the manufacturer for mass reproduction. The components of the final product are assembled, packaged, boxed, and sent to retailers. The idea has finally become "flesh," and the production team can glory in having done their job and created, as all hope, a great game.

■ **Chapter 15:** Interface Design
■ **Chapter 16:** Mathematics and Artificial Intelligence in Games
■ **Chapter 17:** Storytelling in Games
■ **Chapter 18:** Prototyping and Building Playfields
■ **Chapter 19:** Completing the Game

Interface Design

Chapter Objectives

After reading this chapter and doing the exercises, you will be able to do the following:

- Describe the elements of the user interface.
- Explain the differences between console and computer interfaces.
- Describe the importance of feedback in user interface design.
- Analyze how the control inputs influence interface design.
- Explain the difference between shell and in-game interfaces.

Introduction

The user interface makes or breaks a game. A poorly organized menu system, for example, can make a game difficult to play because players might have to hunt through endless menus to find the action they want to perform. Likewise, the controls can be so complex that players feel as if they are fighting them during play rather than mastering them. In addition, the information displayed on the screen can draw players' eyes away from the action at just the wrong moment, resulting in a loss or sudden demise.

One of the worst things a game developer can do is wait until late in the production phase to design the details of the interface. Although they might feel that the interface is likely to change several times during development based on playtester feedback, they will find that working out the details of the entire interface early on will actually save time toward the end of the production phase when everyone is scrambling to complete the project. Otherwise, they might wind up making the user interface unnecessarily complex and frustrating to use. Creating a user-friendly interface is an important requirement for making a successful game.

User Interface Elements

In the broadest sense, an *interface* is how the user connects or interacts with the game platform. There is a reciprocal action between the player's doing something and the machine's responding and then the machine's doing something and the player's responding. The code that drives the interface might be part of the machine's operating system or part of the game application. Nowadays, most people are accustomed to using a *graphical user interface* (*GUI,* pronounced "gooey"), which means that they interact with the graphics on the screen (such as icons and menus) to make something happen instead of with text commands. The interaction can be done with the keyboard, mouse, control pad, or a peripheral device.

A more general term, *user interface (UI),* covers all forms of user-computer connection including the visual interface (nowadays almost always graphical), the input devices, and the feedback to the player. It includes the combination of menus, screen design, keyboard commands, command language, and online help, that creates the way a user interacts with a computer. It includes input devices other than a keyboard and mouse. In the future, natural language recognition and voice recognition will become standard components of a user interface.

FYI *Development of the GUI*

The graphical user interface was pioneered at Xerox PARC (Palo Alto Research Center) in the early 1970s, where they came up with the WIMP (windows, icons, menus, pointers) concept. The first successful commercial version of a GUI was on the Apple Macintosh in 1984. Microsoft started using a GUI on their Windows 1.0 operating system in 1985.

The feedback that players receive from the game is as important as the game controls they use to input commands. Feedback can be visual or aural or both. The visual element is more important; if a player pushes a key or button or moves a thumbstick, something on the screen should move (or change color). If a player moves a character on the map, the movement should happen immediately, and it should happen as the player expects it to. If the game's reaction is counterintuitive to players' expectations, they might give up on it—unless the game includes an option to change the configuration of the controls. Even if the player is only clicking on a button or selecting an option menu, there should be some sort of visual feedback; the button should indent when pushed, change color, change shape, or otherwise have a graphical response.

The game provides other visual feedback through the ***head-up display (HUD),*** which is another important element of the game. The HUD is the visual framework that surrounds the main playfield screen and contains a number of feedback mechanisms such as numbers, meters, counters, scores, and so on. Players usually do not interact directly with the HUD elements (there are exceptions, for example, a strategic map that players can use to scroll around the playfield). Instead, the HUD elements give information about a player's current game status such as current health, magic points, ammo, time remaining, and rank or position, and they might include incoming text messages. HUD elements need to be positioned around the edges of the screen so that they are easy to grasp at a glance without interfering with what players see on the playfield.

Aural feedback can be just as important as visual feedback. Obviously, not every player input needs a sound effect. It would drive players crazy to hear a sound each time they use a control to move a character across the screen. But aural feedback can happen as a result of using a control; for example, footsteps might be heard as the character walks across a hard surface. In other cases, the aural feedback should sync with the visual. If the player pushes a button, for example, she should hear a click as the graphic changes. When describing the functionality of each element on an interface screen, the designer should point out where both aural and visual feedback will be needed.

Designing the Interface

Work on the user interface begins with the creation of the concept game design document (GDD). As the designer works out the gameplay mechanics, she should determine how these mechanics will be implemented by answering such questions as:

- What do players do to make an action happen?

- What do they see on the screen?

- What kind of feedback do they get?

- What input device will they use during the game?

- How many buttons or keys will they need to press to do an action?

It is important to define the ***functionality*** of the interface in the GDD, which consists of the controls (input devices), the screen visuals (the UI or GUI, if it is a graphical user interface), and the feedback.

Input Devices

It is important for the interface designer to consider the type of controller or input devices the player will use. For example, if a racing game is designed to be played with a peripheral steering wheel, the way the controls work might change to make playing the game with the wheel more natural. If the game should also be able to support a user playing with the keyboard, the keyboard commands required to play the game need to feel as fulfilling as the steering wheel. The designer needs to consider which key or combination of keys will feel the most intuitive to the player when performing actions such as accelerating, braking, or turning.

User Interface (UI or GUI)

The designer should not focus just on the in-game interface—the main playfield windows, menus, HUD elements, control inputs, and so on—but should also take into account every interface screen the user will see from installing the game to exiting it. An important facet of the UI and GUI is to make the interface always feel like it's part of the game. If the goal is to try to retain the player's immersion in the game, a gray dialogue box popping up during the middle of a gothic vampire game will not work. Instead, that dialog box should look and read as if it, too, were part of the gothic vampire world. Ideally, this consistency begins as soon as the player removes the game from the box or downloads it: the CD should look cool and the installer should set the creepy, gothic, spooky feel of the game itself.

Feedback

Computer games provide two kinds of feedback. First, as discussed previously, feedback is a response from the game that lets the player know that the computer recognizes that he did something. In the best case, this means that the game reacts as the player expects, such as when moving the cursor forward moves the character ahead a few steps. There is always an issue with what to do if the player does not use the interface as expected. Ideally, the game will let the player know that what he tried didn't work, by either some sound effect or visual signal. The worst case is for the game to do nothing, in which case the player might wonder if the computer just didn't get the input and try it again. The feedback from the game has to inform the player that it has recognized his input.

The second form of feedback occurs when the game gives the player information about events within the game that aren't necessarily related to actions he is currently performing. For example, if the player's car is running out of gas, the game might simply show that the gauge is running down; it might start a flash animation; or it might use some other means to inform the player. If the player is in fourth place in a race, or if there is a sharp turn coming up, this type of feedback helps the player know what's going on in the game, even though it's not direct feedback to his input.

Interface Design

Large companies often employ specialists who work primarily on interfaces. These specialists are generally teams that consist of a programmer to write the interface code modules and a 2D (or 3D) artist to generate the artwork. The senior designer should hold meetings with these specialists both during the preproduction phase and early in the production phase to brainstorm the look and feel of the final interface layout.

The interface will likely go through a number of changes as the game begins to gel and testers give feedback on how easy the controls are to use and how useful the feedback is. When all the functionality has been nailed down, the programmer can start creating the final code. The locations where things appear on the screen might change during the later stages of production, but the basic functionality should remain the same. A description of the final interface functionality (added to the production GDD) should be given to the quality assurance (QA) lead as soon as possible to help create the test suite for the game.

Meanwhile, the interface artist can start generating sketches for the menu systems and HUD elements. When enough of the final in-game art assets have been generated, the artist can finalize the graphic style of the user interface screens to match the in-game style.

FYI   *Widgets*

Widgets are graphical user interface elements with which the user interacts. They include such elements as buttons, check boxes, icons, menus, scrollbars, toolbars, and windows and often provide some sort of visual information or clue as to their purpose. The word may have come from the combination of *window* and *gadget,* but one legend has it the word refers to the whip holders on horse-drawn buggies.

Interfaces and Game Genre

Over time, the user interfaces for a number of game genres have become standardized. For example, first-person shooters (FPSs) for the computer generally use the keyboard as the input device for movement while aiming and firing with the mouse. Most console FPS games with dual control sticks use one stick to move the character and the other to aim the weapon. In addition, because aiming is still difficult, console FPS games use an auto-aim feature, which lets players automatically hit an enemy in the general vicinity of where the weapon is pointing. The HUD for FPS games has also become standardized (more or less) to show as much of the playfield as possible. In addition, the player's remaining health, armor, and ammo for the weapon being carried are shown as icons or meters around the perimeter of the screen. In multiplayer versions, text messages from other players might appear on the outer edges of the screen in addition to the player's current score and, perhaps, a timer. The idea is to keep the field of vision wide open in such a fast-paced game because seeing enemies at a distance can mean the difference between fragging and being fragged.

Racing games use a similar approach to the HUD layout as FPS games. These are adrenaline-filled, fast-paced games, so the player needs to see as much of the track as possible. Thus, the main HUD elements for a racing game consist of the timer, the player's position in the race, and the number of laps remaining. A minimap of the track can show players at a glance where they are on the track, and usually a speedometer/tachometer shows the current speed and vehicle performance (these elements also contribute to the player's feeling of racing rapidly). These HUD elements usually stand out more vividly—larger and in brighter colors—in a racing game than similar elements in a FPS game because players need to be able to glean information regarding their position in the race while maintaining their focus on the track.

The interfaces for other game genres are not always as well defined. Because there are so many game actions for players to perform, the interfaces for role-playing, strategy, and simulation games on the computer can become cluttered with lots of feedback for the player, lots of menus, and an overly busy HUD. Interfaces for sports games also vary because the amount of information and options available to the player differ from sport to sport, although different games for each particular sport tend to have similar interfaces. Likewise, each new puzzle game tends to have a unique interface and HUD.

It is important for the interface designer to watch how others play the game and pay attention to where the players focus while playing. The interface should not distract from the play but should be designed to help keep the player continually informed of the state of the game world during play.

Interfaces and Game Platforms

There are several important differences between computer-game and video-game visual interfaces and input controls. When writing the GDD's section on the interface, the inputs, and the HUD, the designer should determine whether the game will go onto multiple platforms, and if so, the interface functionality should be designed so that it can be played as easily on a game console as on a computer.

A computer offers the advantage of being able to assign many actions to individual keys. Computer keyboards give players quick access to complex menus via shortcut keys, whereas a console has to use many pop-up windows and/or menus for these functions. Moreover, the computer mouse gives players the ability to make rapid selections all across the screen, whereas a console requires the player to scroll the cursor across the screen using a thumbstick or the direction pad and then to make a selection with a button.

Another obvious advantage of the computer over the console is that the player can use the keyboard to input text (such as a character's name) or to type messages in multiplayer games. Console games usually have to rely on a virtual keyboard, where the player scrolls the cursor over letters, numbers, or symbols and then presses a button to select each one. As a result, sending messages via virtual keyboard is much slower and more tedious. Some console games include pregenerated chat messages to help players quickly respond to one another. The drawback to this is that the number of text strings is limited, so a player might have to slowly type out a message using the virtual keyboard anyway to describe a situation not covered by the text strings.

The great advantage of console games over computer games is that the control pad has fewer input controls, making it easier for players to memorize what each control does in the game. The first NES controller had four buttons (A, B, start, select) and the direction pad. Modern consoles have added more controls, and a typical controller has four *action buttons* (A, B, C, D), four *shoulder buttons* (L, R, X, Y) found on the front of the controller, the start/select buttons, and an on/off button if the controller has a vibration ability. In addition, they usually have several thumbsticks and a direction pad to control character and camera movement. Of course, just because there are fewer controls does not mean that all console game interfaces are simplistic. Many fighting games and other action games use combinations of multiple button pushes (*combos*) for special attacks or actions, and part of the player's enjoyment is in learning how to master these special button combinations.

Otherwise, games that let the player perform many different actions usually use a system of menus that group actions by function. In a typical console role-playing game where combat is turn-based, the combat interface usually includes a number of different menus; the first menu is used to select the primary action for the next turn, which then brings up other menus where the player can select a weapon to use, a magic spell to cast, or an item in inventory to use. The trick is to keep the number of menus to a minimum so players don't get bogged down or lost in the menu system.

As mentioned in Chapter 4, "Overview of Game Platforms," most console games are played on television sets that have a low resolution of 640×480 pixels. The text for console games has to be large enough to be seen at a distance and empty margins must be used on all sides to keep the text from being lost in the *over-scanning.* Thus, a simple text description that requires only one screen on a computer can require multiple pages in the console version. Likewise, because of overscanning problems, the game action tends to occur in the center of the screen in a console game, whereas a computer game can have actions taking place close to the edge of the screen. As high-resolution televisions become the standard, console games will be able to utilize the higher resolutions and spread the text and actions all across the screen. Of course, until HDTV is standard in most homes, console games will still have to include a low-resolution version as well, which adds another game option that players have to deal with.

15

Shell Interface

The *shell interface* consists of screens outside the game itself. It includes the installation program, main game start menu, option menus, and pause menu. Because computers have so many possible configurations compared to consoles, computer games have many more shell interface screens than console games.

Installing the Program

Computer games copy most of the data from the storage medium (CD or DVD) onto the computer hard drive for easier access during play. This process is handled by the *installation program.* Most such programs automatically detect when a CD/DVD is inserted into a drive and begin the installation process. A number of standard installation programs are available including Microsoft's Windows Installer, Macrovision's InstallShield, and the open-source InnoSetup. These programs let programmers decide which features to include as part of the installation. Some of the most common features are:

- Adding an option to uninstall the program when the user wishes to remove it.

- Putting an icon on the Windows desktop.

- Opening a readme.txt file that contains the latest updates on the program.

- Registering the product over the Internet.

- Updating the current version of DirectX.

- Checking the user's computer configuration to determine the optimal audio and graphics settings.

- Launching the game when the installation is complete.

The idea is to make the whole process as painless to the player as possible, which is a daunting task because of all the different sound cards, graphics cards, central processor speeds, microprocessor architectures (such as Pentium or AMD), and other components found in different manufacturers' computers. Many of the bugs found after a computer game ships arise from unexpected combinations of hardware and software on the users' machines.

During the installation process, the player might be called upon to perform certain actions. Changing the disks for a game with multiple CDs or DVDs is the most common action, but the player might also have to read and agree to a usage-agreement form, choose how much of the game data to install on the hard drive as well as which directory to put it in, or select options for the audio and graphics setups. Simply getting through the installation process for a computer game can be tedious.

From a design perspective, unless the company writes its own installer, the interface designer can only create bitmap images to be inserted in the installer dialogue boxes. The designer can also write the text for the installer, though it's not recommended to use archaic English or a cursive font to explain to the player how much hard drive space is required. Instead, it is best to keep the installer as simple as possible and to let the game itself set the mood.

Many games today do not copy key information onto the computer hard drive. There is often some form of copy protection in the game software that forces the player to keep the game CD/DVD in the disk drive to run the game. The idea is to cut down on the amount of piracy, although no antipiracy scheme has proven to be one hundred percent effective.

Console games do not have the same kind of installation programs because they are played directly from the CD or DVD, and the game already knows the hardware configuration. Instead, console software includes an initialization program that is loaded into ROM when the machine is rebooted. If the console has a flash memory card to store game data, the program can use this information when loading the appropriate sections of game code and level graphics. Otherwise, the player has to restart the game from the beginning. As a result, getting a console game up and running is much easier than starting a computer game.

Title Screens and the Main Menu

When a game is initialized and loaded into memory, the next step is to launch the title screen. The first screens are usually the logos of the companies that created or published the game. Then an animated introduction to the game might play; the player might be able to cut the animation short by pressing a controller button or hitting the Escape (ESC) key. Finally, the title screen appears with the game's title and copyright statement. It often contains the game's main menu or a start option that leads to the main menu.

The opening sequence gives the game designer and interface designer their first shot at setting the mood and ambience of the game. Whether it is an animated sequence of the title dripping blood or a sequence in which Pac-Man is chased by ghosts, this is where the tone is established.

The main menu has options for starting a new game, loading a saved game, changing the machine settings, and exiting the game. It might also contain options for viewing cinematic sequences as they are unlocked (that is, after the player has seen them once during play), credits of the people who worked on the game, high scores, a tutorial, and a final option for exiting the game. Each of these options can lead to other screens with more options. For example, a settings button could lead to several screens that allow the player to make changes to the audio and graphics setups in the game or to the configuration of the controls.

Console games usually have the same initial sequence as computer games—company logos, an introductory sequence, and the main menu. The main menu can offer a similar number of options as a computer game. However, console games have far fewer additional interface screens because the player has to make fewer changes.

Tutorial

Many complicated games have a tutorial that is available from the main menu. The tutorial might consist of a number of additional screens with text explaining how things work in the game (Figure 15.1), or there might be a number of small scenarios that demonstrate a few game actions at a time.

Many gamers prefer to jump right into the game instead of playing through the tutorial, but they often get frustrated if they hit snags or can't figure out how to do something on their own. To get around this problem, game developers have started to incorporate the tutorial materials directly into the game. They might include some type of basic training courses the player must go through before getting into the game (as in id Software's *Return to Castle Wolfenstein,* published by Activision in 2001), or the tutorials might be spread

> ### Caution
>
> **Three-Clicks**
>
> For all interface designs, it's best to consider a *three-click* approach. Users normally want to perform tasks on an interface or menu screen as quickly as possible, so it's best if they don't have to search far for the options. They should only have to select three buttons at most to accomplish their goal from the start of the menu system.

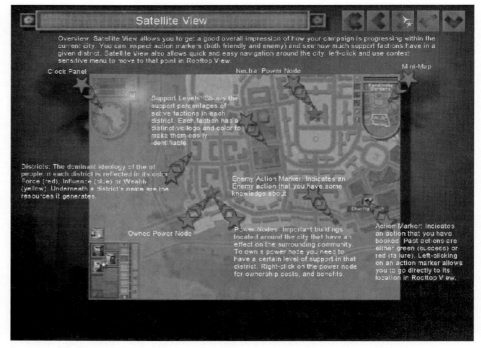

FIGURE 15.1 Tutorial screen from Nicely Crafted Entertainment's *Republic Dawn: Chronicles of the Seven* (in development), a sequel to *Republic: The Revolution* (published by Eidos in 2003). Note that it uses static screens with text callouts to explain parts of the game interface.

across the first several hours of play so the player encounters them piecemeal, as in Square-Enix's *Final Fantasy X* (2001) or Bungie's *Halo 2* (2004).

For console games in particular, it is important to get the player comfortable with the controls for all the different gameplay elements as quickly as possible. The more information the player needs to absorb, the more interesting the challenge for the designer to come up with clever ways to spoon-feed it in user-friendly doses.

FYI   *Context-Driven Help*

A context-driven help system can be used in place of or to supplement tutorials. To do this, the interface and game designer work out how to help someone who is lost in the game without making it look too obvious. One option could be to have a nonplaying character (NPC) arrive and offer a sequence of helpful clues. The clues can become more and more explicit until they culminate with a final "Go to the store and buy the briquette of eternal fire." In other instances, the F1 key is often configured as an in-game help button. If the help screens are context driven, pressing this button will activate a help text that is specific to the player's current goal.

Pause Menu and Saving Games

It is always a good idea to include some kind of a pause game feature that allows the player to break away from the game at any time and then resume play at the point where the action was paused. In many games, pausing the game also brings up a menu similar to the main menu; this menu enables the player to make changes to the graphics, sounds, control configuration, and other options without leaving the game. In most computer games, the player is given the chance to save a game at this time (or to reload a saved game). In many console games, on the other hand, the ability to save games is limited to the player's advancing to a *checkpoint* or sometimes using a save game token that is earned during play. In puzzle or arcade-style games, it's common to have the pause menu pop up and cover the playfield while displaying the actual game controls. The player then gets a chance to look at the input controls while obscuring the puzzle to prevent the player from using pause to strategize a solution.

Depending on the game genre, a saved game file can be relatively small or quite large. If the game allows saves only between missions or after completing a level, the save file can simply record where the player is in the game world in addition to other relevant information such as the current score, money, inventory items, and so on. In more complex games, the saved game file needs to be a snapshot of player's current position in the world as well as everything that has

15

changed, so the amount of stored information can be significant. If the player has left items strewn around the playfield, the saved game has to record their locations. If the player has completed parts of a story, the current set of variables has to be saved as well (see Chapter 16, "Mathematics and Artificial Intelligence in Games," for more details). In addition, everything in the player's inventory and his current game statistics need to be recorded, as well as every active character's facing and position in the world.

Having to save a large amount of information can lead to another problem—slow load time. Some games reload the entire level each time and then reset the playfield to the last saved position. It takes time to load the 3D graphics for the level and the creatures on the level and then make the changes to reflect the status as of the save position. Players can get frustrated waiting for the game to reload. The interface and game designers should work with the technical programmer in charge of level loading to make sure that this loading time is minimized, perhaps with a quick data check of what must be loaded versus what can be loaded after the game restarts.

Computer games can have many large save files because modern hard drives have lots of room to store big files. Often, the player can save the game whenever and wherever she wishes. On the other hand, console games use flash memory cards, which have a limited amount of space, to store saved game files. Therefore, console games often restrict where and when the player can save during the game and limit the number of saved game files so as not to fill up the memory card too quickly.

Interface Consistency

The shell interface should look the same, sound the same, and work the same as the in-game interface. The artist responsible for creating the shell interface should try to match the overall visual style of the game itself. Thus, when players pause the game or bring up the main menu, they should feel that they are still in the game world. Using dissimilar visual styles for the shell and in-game interfaces breaks the players' immersion in the game and makes them question the aesthetic sensibilities of the art staff.

There should also be a consistency in how the input controls work in the shell and in-game interfaces. If, for example, the Enter key or the X button is always used to perform an action during the game, then the same key/button should be used in the shell interface to select options. The sound effects should also be consistent in both style and volume through all interface screens.

The use of inputs in the game should also be consistent. If the player must use the mouse in the game but the keyboard arrows in the shell interface, her immersion in the game might be broken. The designer should keep input consistent in both the shell and in the game. Additionally, there should be a consistency in terminology or button locations. Option buttons such as Back, Done, OK, and cancel should be thoroughly thought out and used consistently throughout the

---

Caution

Design the Interface Early

Waiting until late in the production phase to nail down the details of the shell interface can lead to inconsistencies between the shell and the game. The goal of the team should be to present the player with an artistic whole—the shell and game interfaces are two parts of a whole, not two factions at war.

game. For example, if the Back button is in the lower right corner and takes the user back to the previous menu, it should be at the same location and perform the same action in all screens where it appears. If the player must use a Done button to designate the completion of a task on an interface screen, it should somehow indicate that the change was made successfully (or not) before returning the player either to the game or the previous menu.

In-Game Interface

The *in-game interface* consists of all the screens, windows, and menus the player uses to perform game actions. Depending on the game genre and the number of gameplay elements, there might be just one in-game screen (say, for a puzzle game such as *Tetris*) or a whole series of screens, windows, and menus (say, for a role-playing game).

Because this is the interface the player will spend the most time using, it should receive the most attention from the production team. It is important for the senior designer to work out the functionality of each interface screen while writing the concept GDD. As discussed in Chapter 10, "The Game Design Document," creating a simple schematic of each screen, window, and menu at this time will help the designer determine where there is too much clutter on a particular screen or where functions on several screens can be combined onto one. The designer should not overlook the shell interface while working on the in-game interface, and the final GDD should include a flowchart of all the screens, windows, and menus in the game.

The layout of the screen elements and the configuration of the controls can change several times during the production phase. When the basic gameplay and the initial interface are ready, the team should have focus groups test the configuration to find out how users feel about the controls, the number of screens, and the layout of the HUD elements. The team should observe the focus groups as they play the game and take notes about what they see. They are likely to find that the group's comments do not always jibe with what the team observes. The focus group members themselves might not be aware of the problems they encountered while playing the game.

If the game has unique gameplay, its interface often goes through many iterations until the team settles on a primary scheme for the final version. Even if the game is similar to others in the same genre, it can still contain subtle differences in how the controls respond and how information is displayed. In addition, even if the team comes up with the "perfect" configuration of game controls, some players are likely to find the configuration cumbersome, so it is always a good idea to let players reconfigure the controls as they wish.

15

Main Playfield Screen

There is always one screen in the game that the player views most. It is the screen where most of the game activity takes place, and it contains the HUD with the information the player needs while playing. This ***main playfield screen*** might be used for only one activity or several, depending on the game genre and the complexity of the design.

For example, Spectrum Holobyte's 1987 version of *Tetris* (Figure 15.2) has only one in-game screen with very limited functionality:

- Background Art: The art serves no purpose in the game other than as *eye candy* —something attractive for the player to look at while playing.

- Interactive Area: The player uses the controls to interact with the geometric shapes (made of colored tiles) falling from top to bottom in the center space. The player can rotate the falling geometric shapes, move them left and right, and drop them.

- Head-Up Display: The HUD contains three pieces of information: score, number of lines completed, and next piece.

- Controls: The computer version uses two keys to move a piece left and right, one key to rotate the current piece, a key to speed the movement of a piece (useful early in the game), and another key to drop the piece in place on the grid. Other keys are available to the player as well, but they handle such nongame functions as toggling displays on and off, changing monitor types, and pausing the game.

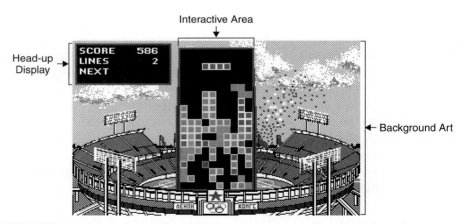

FIGURE 15.2 The GUI for *Tetris* is very simple, consisting of the background art, an interactive area where the game is played, and the information displays of the head-up display (HUD).

The game could have included many more functions (and eventually did in later versions), but the simplicity of the original design is what helped to make it so addictive to so many players. The interactive area of the main playfield is where the player manipulates objects either directly (for example, clicking on an object with the mouse to select it and then clicking on a spot where it is to move) or indirectly (for example, using thumbsticks to guide a character around the map). The player focuses on the interactive area, glancing at the HUD only occasionally. The controls are incredibly easy to learn and to master—but mastering the game takes a long, long time.

When planning how the game will play, the designer needs to consider how the player interacts with playfield objects. When production begins, the designer and programming team should decide as quickly as possible what scale the objects on the playfield will be. The farther away the player needs to see an object to be able to react to it in a timely manner, the smaller the scale of objects on the playfield. For example, in a fighting game where combat is hand-to-hand, the figures can be large because combat won't begin until the characters are almost adjacent to one another. However, if enemy troops are wielding long-range rifles and bazookas, the player will want to see them at a distance so he can act before being blown away in the first salvo. When the designer creates a working prototype of the game early in production (see Chapter 18, "Prototyping and Building Playfields," for more details), she should experiment with scale to make sure that players are comfortable with seeing and interacting with objects they don't control on the playfield.

In large-scale games where the playfield extends far beyond the initial viewport, the designer might need to include some kind of strategic map (also called an inset map) to help the player track enemies at a distance. The player will probably want to check out different areas of the playfield, so the designer needs to include some method for scrolling the viewport or jumping to different parts of the map. For a computer game, the player might use one set of controls to move the viewport (for example, the arrow keys) while using another set to manipulate playfield objects (for example, the mouse). For a console game, one thumbstick might move the viewport while the other manipulates objects, or a "move viewport" mode might be activated when one of the buttons is held down.

Head-Up Display (HUD)

The HUD is one of the most important sources of feedback for the player during the game. The HUD consists of various displays (meters, timers, counters, and so on) that are either set around the edge of the screen or overlay the interactive area of the playfield map.

15

> ### FYI | *Origin of the Head-Up Display*
>
> The term *head-up display* comes from military aviation and refers to the technique of projecting data over a pilot's forward field of view. As the pace of modern air combat increased after World War II, it became apparent that pilots could not look down at their instrument panels and then look back up to track enemy aircraft. So engineers designed displays to project the most important information directly into the pilots' view so they didn't need to look down so often (hence, they were flying "head-up"). The term was later applied to the information displays in games.

There is a balance between giving the player enough information to know what is happening to the character or unit she controls and flooding the player with too much information. As a rough rule of thumb, too much information displayed all over the screen can distract the player from the central game action. On the other hand, too little information can result in the player's losing the game frequently and therefore disliking it. Determining the best layout for the HUD elements can take time, and the team often has to try a number of designs before settling on one that the players like best.

For example, the HUD in Valve's *Half-Life* (1998) is minimal. The lower left corner displays the player's current health (small cross with a number) and armor (small diving suit with a number). The lower right corner shows the ammo for the weapon being carried (the number to the left of the slash is the remaining rounds loaded in the weapon, the number to the right of the slash is the number of rounds in inventory, and the picture shows the ammunition type). A small flashlight is in the upper right corner; when the player turns the flashlight on, the flashlight icon acts as a meter to show how much battery power remains. The final HUD elements are the barrel of the weapon the player carries that shows up along the bottom of the screen and the target reticule that moves with the mouse. In the screenshot in Figure 15.3, notice that the HUD elements are all orange so they stand out from the background; also notice that they are transparent so the player can see through them and has a wide-open view of the playfield.

The screenshots from Ensemble Studios' *Age of Empires* (1997; Figure 15.4) and Electronic Arts' *Need for Speed Underground 2* (2004; Figure 15.5) show two other approaches to HUD design. In *Age of Empires,* the information displays are divided between the top and bottom areas of the screen and appear inside framing bars. The interactive area is uncluttered, allowing the player to manipulate the figures easily so they can gather resources, erect buildings, and march units off to war. The designer decided to sacrifice part of the view of the playfield to make it easier for the player to check and interact with the information displays. In *Need for Speed Underground 2,* on the other hand, the information displays are very large

Flashlight

Aiming
Reticule

Health/
Armor Values

Loaded Ammo/
Maximum Ammo

FIGURE 15.3 The HUD for Valve's *Half-Life* is minimalist. The information displays are in orange to stand out from the playfield elements.

Resources

Available Menus

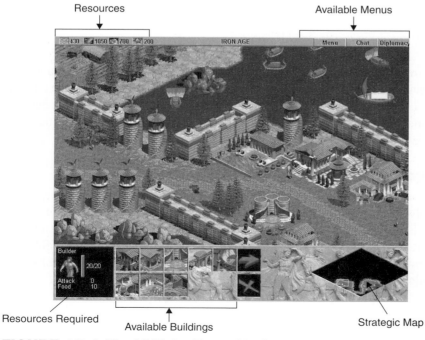

Resources Required

Available Buildings

Strategic Map

FIGURE 15.4 The HUD for Ensemble Studios' *Age of Empires* appears like a frame around the active playfield area.

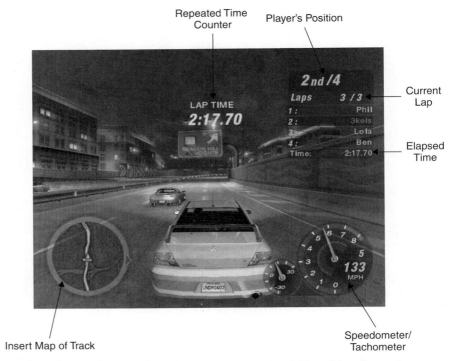

Repeated Time Counter

Player's Position

Current Lap

Elapsed Time

Speedometer/ Tachometer

Insert Map of Track

FIGURE 15.5 The HUD for Electronic Arts' *Need for Speed Underground 2* is a racing game, so players want to see as much of the playfield area as possible.

and overlay the interactive area. In a racing game, it is important for players to be constantly aware of their positions on the track and to know where the other racers are. The displays are transparent so they do not completely block out what is behind them. During the stretches of straight road, players can glance at these displays and then turn their attention back to driving.

Secondary Full-Scale Screens

The inherent complexity of a game and the number of gameplay elements involved can require additional interface screens during the game. A simple puzzle game might not need any screens other than the main playfield screen, whereas a complex role-playing game might have several other full screens for inventory, combat, strategic movement, and so on, plus additional pop-up windows and menus for handling special gameplay elements.

If the player performs a number of gameplay actions on one interface, it might be best to devote an entire screen to it. Inventories in role-playing games often are full-screen interfaces, as seen in the inventory screen from Black Isle Studios' *Baldur's Gate* (published by Virgin Interactive Entertainment in 1998) shown in Figure 15.6. There are 20 boxes for items that can be worn by a character

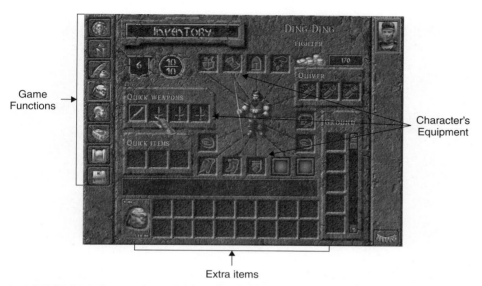

Game Functions

Character's Equipment

Extra items

FIGURE 15.6 The inventory screen from Black Isle Studios' *Baldur's Gate.*

(armor, weapons, quivers, charms, and so on) plus additional spaces for other items that the character carries or that appear on the ground where the character is standing. A player can spend considerable time moving items around and trying different combinations, so using a full screen gives enough space to display the items large enough to be easily distinguishable from one another. Of course, while this screen is open, the player cannot see what is happening on the main playfield screen, so he might be killed by monsters while dithering with his character's inventory. The designer should decide early in the production phase whether to stop the action or let it keep going when another interface screen is open.

Because of the complexity of combat in role-playing games, a full-screen interface often is devoted to this gameplay element. The combat interface typically includes menus where players can select weapons, magic, or items to use during the fight, as well as a HUD that shows health, remaining mana (magic points), and special conditions (poison, sleep, and so on) for both the player's party and the enemies.

If there is a large world to traverse and several modes of transportation are available, the game often includes a full-screen map to let the player select the next location to visit. The player might also be able to purchase various items either during the game (for example, role-playing games) or between missions or races.

Pop-Up Windows and Menus

A pop-up window can be useful if a particular gameplay element doesn't take much time for the player to deal with or presents information that isn't accessed frequently enough to appear as a HUD element. The window takes up only part

15

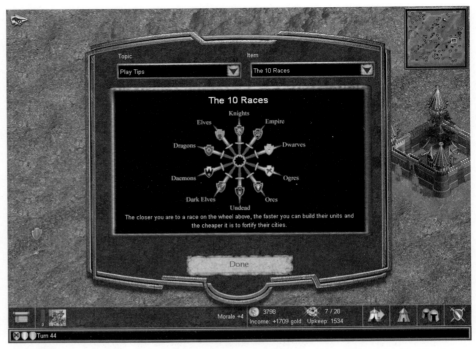

FIGURE 15.7 A pop-up information window in Ubisoft's *Warloads 4: Heroes of Etheria* gives a play tip about the races in the game and how their relationships affect the speed of building units and guarding cities. The player can change windows by selecting from the Topic/Item menus.

of the screen, and the player can quickly refer to it and close it. Again, the designer should determine if the game action stops while this window is open. Figure 15.7 shows a pop-up information window from Ubisoft Entertainment's *Warlords 4: Heroes of Etheria* (2003). The two pull-down options at the top let the player check out many different pieces of information without having to close the window and then open a new one.

When a lot of action is going on in the game and many options are available, it is usually better to design the menu system to speed up the player's decision-making. Figure 15.8 shows some of the menus used during combat in Square-Enix's *Final Fantasy X* (2001).

Menu systems can have many layers, depending on what actions are available to the player at each level. For example, during combat, there might be a main menu with options to attack (with a weapon), cast a magic spell, use an inventory item, retreat, pass, and so on. Generally, it is a good design principle to limit the number of options in each menu to six or less. Each option can bring up one or more other menus, depending again on what options are available. For example, selecting Cast Magic on the main combat menu can bring up a secondary menu with options for Attack, Defense, Creature, and Modify. Selecting

FIGURE 15.8 The combat system in Square Enix's *Final Fantasy X* includes a menu that the player uses to select combat actions in each round. In this case, the player has selected an attack action for Tidus in the next round. The small portraits on the right are another menu the player uses to bring up information about the characters.

one of these options might bring up another menu of available spells per type. However, the designer should also be careful not to have too many nested menu layers, or the player might get frustrated paging through them (especially if the action is nonstop).

Ease of Use

Designing an easy-to-use interface is a primary goal of the team, but it's a task that is often easier to talk about than to implement. Defining the functionality of the interface is up to the designer, and it can be quite easy to let functionality get out of hand (this is one type of feature creep, as discussed in Chapter 10, "The Game Design Document"). Defining the functionality takes time and should not be glossed over lightly. It requires the designer to imagine the player in the midst of the game trying to perform various game actions.

Take, for example, item manipulation. Suppose a character is traversing the map and runs across an object. The designer must consider what happens next. Does the item go directly into the player's inventory when he enters the

15

item's space or does the player somehow have to manipulate it (for example, pick it up, examine it, and then store it in an inventory space)? In a fast-paced action game, it is usually better to store the item in the player's inventory automatically so he can keep his focus on the playfield action.

Then what happens if the player's inventory is full? Does the item stay on the playfield or disappear? What if the supply of items is limited and the player needs every item he can find (for example, a limited supply of ammunition)? The player might want to examine the object and decide whether to pick it up or not. If the item goes into the inventory automatically, does the game determine the most space effective way to store it (assuming the item takes up multiple spaces), or does the player have to stop and rearrange inventory manually before he can pick up the item? Even the simplest game functions can have many variations, so the designer should study other games to see how they handle the same functions.

Even when designing a game in a well-known genre, the designer should describe the gameplay elements and their underlying mechanics as thoroughly as possible in the concept GDD. The more precise the designer is at this time, the easier the interface will be to implement—at least initially. Testing often shows that the designer's initial assumptions were flawed, which forces the team to rethink how the interface will work. Thus, creating a working prototype of the game early in the production phase can help the designer nail down the final implementation issues and save the team considerable time and effort later.

Interface Design

It is important to define the functionality of the interface early on because the team also needs to plan how the graphics for each screen will be laid out and how the controls will work. The screen should be organized so that similar functions are grouped together, and the most important groups should be the easiest to get to. Psychologist Paul Fitts studied human movement; in 1954 he described a model that applies to interface design. Fitts' law says, "The time required to acquire a target is a function of distance to the target and its size." This law indicates that a larger target is easier to select than a smaller one and that a distant target takes longer to reach. Hence, the easiest targets to reach are along the edges of a computer screen (especially the four corners), whereas reaching those in the middle takes longer.

Another approach that computer games often use is to have pop-up captions display an icon's title when a player holds the cursor over the icon for a second or so. This approach is especially helpful if the game has many icons. A similar approach is to show only the interface information that is relevant at the time. For example, menu options that can't be used by a character can either be grayed out or not even appear on the menu.

Yet another approach that computer games use is to make a right mouse-button click bring up dynamic context menus or activate a pop-up window with information. A dynamic context menu offers only the options appropriate to the current situation. The options change when another interface screen appears.

Video games can be even more challenging to design than computer games because of the graphics restrictions and the limitations of the controller. Complex games (for example, a role-playing game such as *Final Fantasy X*) use more secondary full-screen interfaces and menu systems to handle the different gameplay elements and the options available on each. They usually do not rely on many selectable on-screen icons because using the directional pad or thumb-sticks to move a cursor is slower than using a mouse.

One of the biggest challenges to a development team can be the task of porting a game from one platform to another. The originally designed interface might work well on the release game platform, but it might not work at all on other platforms. Action games tend to translate well because there are fewer gameplay elements to begin with, and therefore, it is easier to map the controls and interface design between platforms. Role-playing games are much more difficult and can require extensive redesign. For example, Figure 15.9 shows the main playfield screen where combat occurs from Snowblind Studios'

FIGURE 15.9 The combat screen for *Baldur's Gate: Dark Alliance* lacks the frame found in the PC versions of the game. The onscreen HUD elements are transparent, so the player can see the action happening in the background.

15

FIGURE 15.10 The combat screen for *Baldur's Gate: Tales of the Sword Coast* (for the PC) is enclosed by a frame with many icons that give the player more direct control of the characters in his party during combat.

Baldur's Gate: Dark Alliance (2001) for the PlayStation2, and Figure 15.10 shows the main playfield screens from *Baldur's Gate: Tales of the Sword Coast* (1999) for the computer. (The *Baldur's Gate* series is published by Interplay Entertainment.) Note that fewer on-screen options are available in the PS2 platform than in the computer version. The inventory screen for the PS2 uses a nested menu system with multiple screens to show all the different items, while the PC version uses only one screen.

Summary

Designing a game interface can be challenging. Not only does the designer have to consider how information will be provided to players, but she also has to determine how players will use the controls to manipulate objects in the game. Too much information can overwhelm or distract players; too little information can frustrate them. Correctly placing the information elements on full-size screens, pop-up windows, menus, or the HUD keeps players engrossed in the game and able to perform game actions without thinking about them.

The designer should describe the functionality of the user interface while creating the GDD. Early in the production phase, the interface programmer should create a prototype to test the design assumptions so that changes can be made as early as possible. After the final art style of the game has been settled, the interface artist can create the art and layouts for the various screens, windows, menus, and HUD. Player feedback is vitally important in determining what works and what needs to be changed. By the time the game finally ships, the customer should feel immediately at home with the interface—to the point where he might even believe that creating a usable interface is a piece of cake.

Test Your Skills

MULTIPLE CHOICE QUESTIONS

1. *Interface* refers to which of the following? (Select all that apply.)

   A. HUD.

   B. Installer.

   C. Input devices.

   D. Inventory screens.

2. A well done user interface does which of the following?

   A. Provides good control of the player avatar.

   B. Provides good feedback to the player.

   C. Looks good.

   D. Is obvious to the player.

3. What does visual interface design describe? (Select all that apply.)

   A. The shell interface.

   B. The installer.

   C. The game entities.

   D. The inventory screen.

4. Aural feedback is good for which of the following? (Select all that apply.)

   A. Warning the player he made an error.

   B. Warning the player of impending doom.

   C. Attracting the player's attention.

   D. Distracting the player when the frame rate drops.

15

5. What information is critical in fast paced games? (Select all that apply.)

   A. Current health.

   B. Number of lives.

   C. Location of enemies.

   D. Player chat.

6. Information about armor is important in which of the following game types? (Select all that apply.)

   A. Space shooters.

   B. FPSs.

   C. Racing games.

   D. RPGs.

   E. Adventure games.

7. User interface is a term that includes which of the following elements?

   A. The input devices.

   B. Visual interface.

   C. Program feedback.

   D. Music and audio.

EXERCISES

Exercise 15.1: Flowchart Game Interface

Sketch the flow of an interface from shell start to game end. What menu choices are available at the start of the game? Sketch how each menu choice flows down and then back up. Within the game, limit yourself to a basic in-game interface; if a button press goes to a map, what key press does it use? What key press returns the user to the game? Is there a pause screen?

Exercise 15.2: Design Inventory Screen

Write the design for an in-game interface where the player can buy and sell inventory items. What critical information could be represented with graphic images? What information requires some form of text or dialogue?

Exercise 15.3: Design a Racing Interface

Make a list of all the information you feel the player requires in a racing game. Make a list of all the information you have available in your car when you drive.

Compare the two. What additional information do you garner as you drive that is left out of a car driving game? Make a list of everything you can see, everything you can smell, everything you can hear, and everything you can touch. What does the game interface designer do to compensate for the lack of tactile interface? For the lack of audio?

Exercise 15.4: Design an Advanced Interface HUD

Consider a game design for a 3D, multiplayer game where the player uses the ability to manipulate gravity as differently shaped boxes, spheres, and cylinders enter the playfield from different locations. Sketch a HUD that shows the player the current gravity, some form of power/gravity ability that must be recharged before she can modify the gravity, and her health status. What other items would you add to the HUD?

DISCUSSION TOPICS

1. Select one of your favorite games. How well did the designer set the mood of the game from the shell start up? Were they able to maintain consistency throughout all the menus and interface screens?

2. From the game in Discussion Topic 1, what was the one thing you liked the most about the interface? What did you like the least?

3. Consider an in-game store interface where the player can upgrade his game vehicle by selling other items or using cash on account. What items do you feel are necessary for this interface to work? Discuss what type of game requires a dialogue with a store clerk for this type of interface.

4. If you were to make an interface for an FPS game that takes place mostly in the dark, would you consider using aural clues instead of visual? What information is critical to the player to know in a shooter? How would you get this information across? (Consider a situation in which spoken dialogue is not allowed.)

5. User interface doesn't have to include only the HUD, menu screens, or input devices. Discuss how a game designer might use lighting, music, or NPC behavior to provide the player with feedback from the game.

15

Chapter | 16

Mathematics and Artificial Intelligence in Games

Chapter Objectives

After reading this chapter and doing the exercises, you will be able to do the following:

- List what areas of mathematics programmers must know.
- Realize that the math used for a game database is relatively simple.
- Understand how lookup tables and algorithms are used in games.
- Explain how the rock-scissors-paper model is used to balance units.
- List the different approaches to AI for games.

Introduction

An appreciation of mathematics is vital for anyone planning to make a career in games. Many branches of mathematics are used in computer games, especially in 3D games—from the binary code used to speak directly to the computer, to the mathematics of physics, to the architecture of the 3D models themselves.

Of the team members working on a game, programmers must have the best understanding of how math works because they are forever dealing with quantities, spaces, structures, and changes. Audio engineers need a good grasp of physics because they deal with the variables of sound waves such as frequency, wavelength, amplitude, and so on. Artists need a basic understanding of mathematical proportions when they create two- and three-dimensional art, and now they must understand the Cartesian coordinate system to use complex 3D graphics programs. Designers should understand probability and statistics and also have an appreciation of how tables are created and used in databases. Everyone on a production team should have a solid knowledge of basic mathematics and physics. This allows them to knowledgeably address complex issues that arise during production, such as how the artificial intelligence (AI) will work and whether to use algorithms or lookup tables to resolve game actions.

The Mathematics of Games

Game mathematics are used to include animated objects on the screen, to make objects look as though they undergo the effects of gravity and other physics, and to make the gameplay balanced and fun. Movement in every game is simulated on two-dimensional and three-dimensional axes. For example, in a side-scrolling game, when the player presses a button to make an object move forward across the screen, the program increments the value of the object's location along the horizontal (X) axis. If the player presses the backward button, the program decrements the value on the same axis. When the player presses the appropriate button to make a character to jump, the button press is interpreted by the program to increment the vertical (Y) axis value. In the case of a 3D or pseudo-3D game, when the object moves toward or away from the player, the appropriate value is affected on the third (Z) axis. Figure 16.1 depicts a graph showing the coordinate system used to represent three-dimensional graphics in games.

Math is used for all objects that move in the game, not just the ones controlled by the player's button presses. For example, bullets flying across the screen must have their positions mathematically increased by the program, which then informs the graphics engine to draw the bullets in the new locations.

Physics extends to more than just motion, however. The program also has to determine whether the bullet collides with the target and, in some games, must actually determine what part of the target was hit. When a projectile hits the target, the program might look up the value of health points that are removed from the target, or it might generate a random number to use with a formula to determine how many points are removed from the target's remaining health. Each of these steps involves mathematical formulas.

Math in 2D Games

The math in 2D games is generally less complex than that in 3D games because there are only two dimensions to deal with. Still, to program such a game, a programmer has to be familiar with algebra, geometry, trigonometry, vector operations, matrices, and transformations—in addition to having a solid basis in physics.

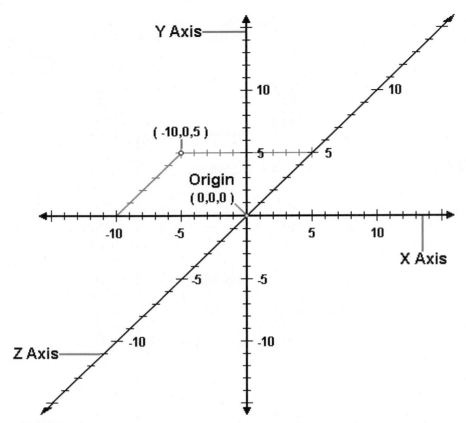

FIGURE 16.1 In this diagram, movement along the X axis appears on the screen as an object moving to the left or right. Movement along the Y axis is up and down. The Z axis represents movement toward and away from the player.

Consider the classic game of *Pong* as an example of what a programmer must deal with when coding (Figure 16.2). In *Pong*, two players control onscreen paddles with a rotating knob that moves the paddles up and down in place on each side of the screen. A small ball moves back and forth across the screen each time it strikes a paddle. If the ball goes past a paddle, it appears to go off the edge of the screen and scores a point for the other player.

First consider the paddle. It has maximum positions at the top and bottom of the screen, so the programmer has to set up the program to understand that when the rotating knob is turned all the way in one direction the paddle is at the top, and when the knob is turned all the way in the other direction the paddle is at the bottom. The program has to interpolate the position of the paddle between those two extremes as the player turns the knob.

Then the programmer has to determine when the ball hits a paddle. The paddle itself has a fixed size that does not change—say, for example, 4 pixels

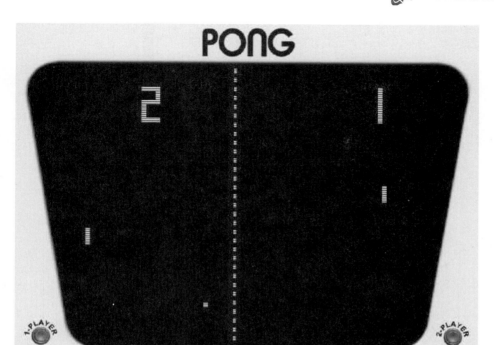

FIGURE 16.2 The main interface screen from the arcade version of Atari's *Pong* (1972). This is an extremely simple game, with two paddles, a square "ball," a net (used only for decoration), and the players' scores.

wide (X axis) by 32 pixels tall (Y axis). As a paddle moves up and down the screen, the value of the Y axis coordinate is continually incremented or decremented, but the X axis coordinate value never changes. The program checks when the ball (which might be 2 × 2 pixels in size) reaches the X axis coordinate of the paddle's front face. If the ball is within the Y axis range of the paddle at that instant, it ricochets off the paddle and a sound effect of a bouncing ball is played. Otherwise, it misses the paddle and continues to the edge of the screen, where it disappears and the program increments the score of the other player.

The ball itself travels in straight lines as it bounces off the top and bottom of the playfield as well as the players' paddles. The program must determine the direction that the ball will travel after it collides with a surface. If it hits a paddle straight on, it bounces or is reflected straight backward. If it hits at an angle, it bounces back at an angle equal to the incoming angle—or to put in mathematical terms, the **angle of incidence** (coming in) is equal to the **angle of reflection** (going out), as shown in Figure 16.3. The program has to calculate these angles as well as the velocity **vector** (the direction and speed of the object).

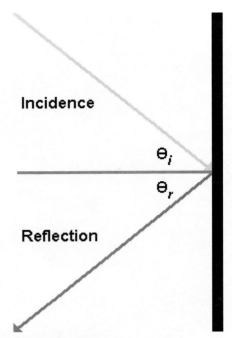

FIGURE 16.3 The angles of incidence and reflection of the ball striking the paddle and rebounding in a game of *Pong*.

Of course, the game involves more than simply determining whether the ball hits a solid object and the angle at which it bounces. A player can also impart momentum to the ball by hitting it when the paddle is moving quickly. The speed of the ball increases and crosses the playfield area more quickly (or decreases if the paddle is moving in the opposite direction). Thus, the programmer also has to deal with *acceleration.*

As you can see, even a very simple 2D game can require complex mathematics to make things work they way we would expect them to work in the real world. The programmer has to figure out the step-by-step order in which things will be calculated because the more efficiently the code is written, the fewer cycles it will take to perform them. That leaves more cycles to handle the graphics processing, artificial intelligence (AI), sound effects, and gameplay routines.

Math in 3D Games

The math in 3D games is more involved than in 2D games, but it is based on the same principles. When creating a move function in 2D games, the programmer basically moves an image to a specific location on the screen based on underlying calculations of speed, inertia, collision reflection, gravity, and so on. In 3D games, all of these computations are more complex. Instead of dealing with flat objects moving against a flat background, the programmer must deal with 3D models that move through a three-dimensional playfield.

In addition, instead of simply moving the correct image (which is essentially treated as a single point) to the correct location, a programmer trying to move even the most simple 3D object, a cube, must move every corner of the cube, recalculate all the edge connections for each corner, properly light, color, and shade the surfaces based on the amount of light and shadow, and most likely, do this as the object rotates about one or more axes in space. Three-dimensional physics are closer to real world physics; consequently, more advanced algorithms are used. In very realistic simulations that include physical attributes such as drag, inertia, air resistance, and friction on every individual surface, the programming and mathematics is astounding.

For advanced game engine technology, the programmer might have to study lighting techniques and ray tracing (the interactions of light and optical surfaces), splines and NURBS (nonuniform rational B-spline) to define movement paths, quaternions to handle three-dimensional rotations, and quadtrees (Figure 16.4)

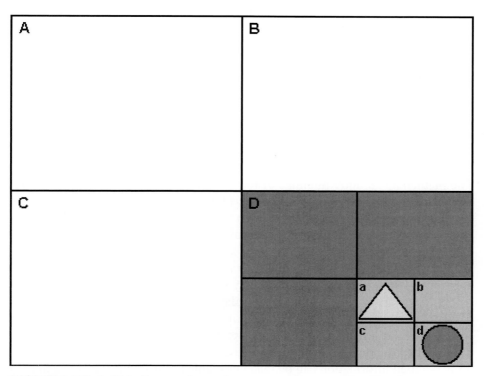

FIGURE 16.4 This figure shows how a quadtree works. The two-dimension screen space is partitioned recursively into four quadrants. The first division is into quadrants A–D, the second division into the four quadrants shaded gray, and the third division into quadrants a–d. Dividing the space in this manner makes computation much more efficient.

and octrees to partition 2D and 3D space. Many of the "game basic" math courses for programming in 3D are not available at colleges and universities until the master's level (or higher). Thus, more often than not, programmers have to teach themselves these advanced math subjects. There is no end to the learning curve in games.

Other areas of game programming also require high-level math skills. Some of the more interesting visual and audio effects require advanced physics classes in chaos theory, fluid dynamics, elasticity, waveforms, and acoustic engineering. Other uses of complicated mathematics include games that push the boundaries of unique gameplay, such as realistic wave motion in an ocean or the appropriate movement of a blob of gelatin that retains its mass but can change its shape to traverse the playfield. Online games also offer many mathematical branches to explore, such as data extrapolation to help smooth network irregularities, congestion control algorithms to improve data transfers via the Internet, and encryption/decryption of a user's private information.

There is no getting around the fact that a programmer needs to be comfortable with the advanced mathematics used in making 3D games. The reference section at the end of the book lists a number of books about mathematics and physics that game programmers might wish to read.

Math in Game Designs

Designers are not necessarily expected to have the same depth and breadth of knowledge as programmers, but they must still be functionally literate when it comes to mathematics because need to use some basic arithmetic when creating a game. What the player experiences when playing a game needs to be as simple as possible because games are not about the math but the gameplay. The mathematical underpinnings of the game can be complex, but any mathematics that players see—for example, *leveling up* or scoring points—should be simple additions and subtractions. Even fractions, multiplication, and division can be too complicated for players to easily grasp while they are immersed in the action of the game.

A good rule of thumb for designers is that if the values for game objects are visible to the player during play, they should remain small—in the order of 0 to 100. Conceptually, it's easier for players to grasp values under 100 at a glance than to sort out the significance of three or more digits as they fight for their lives against hordes of attacking enemies. Of course, when high scores are displayed or the detailed statistics are shown at the end of a level or mission, more detailed information can be made available because the player has time to study the numbers if she is interested—or she can quickly pass over the information and move on to more gameplay.

Players do enjoy dealing with large numbers but not necessarily during the game. As a rough rule of thumb, the faster the game action, the simpler the information that should be displayed to the player. Therefore, the math that supports the changing information should be easy for the player to understand without having to use a calculator.

Lookup Tables and Algorithms

Because all behaviors (AI, physics, and so on) are controlled by data that is, in turn, manipulated by the game mathematics, designers often create a master set of data about the objects that appear in a game in various states. This allows them to have complete control over gameplay tuning and balancing.

For example, assume the player is involved in combat with a giant warthog in an RPG. The combat is resolved using an algorithm (or formula) to determine if the attack succeeds, and then a combat resolution table is used to determine how much damage is involved. The basic combat statistics for the combatants are drawn from a character chart, and the program plugs those values into the combat algorithm (for example, "if attacker's strength is equal to or greater than the defender's strength, then the attack succeeds"). The amount of damage is determined by referring to the combat resolution table, and a specified number of hit points are then subtracted from the target's current total.

In a slightly more complicated example, a lookup table might be created for each game entity so that the game can have a beginner, a medium, and a difficult mode. This type of table lists all game statistics for an entity. It might include a second column with varied values to make the enemy easier to defeat and a third column with values that make the enemy more challenging. The designer might even create several columns for each game difficulty mode and then have the game randomly select which column to use, thereby making the game feel more dynamic.

The tables and charts created by the designer to list values for objects in a game forms the ***game database*** (discussed in detail later in the chapter). Early in the design, these values in the database are simply placeholders. The final values might not be determined until the game is halfway through the production phase. Testing these numbers as early as possible is a valuable exercise, so the designers might create a paper prototype and then ask for a simple working model from the programmers before they start their work on the game engine (see Chapter 18, "Prototyping and Building Playfields").

In some games where the computer must process lots of data as quickly as possible, it is often easier to use an algorithm to resolve an action rather than a lookup table. The advantage of a lookup table is that it can include any values, whereas an algorithm might require that the math values be simplified. For example, the designer might decide to use a lookup table containing the values 1, 2, 4, 5, 8, 11, 18, and so on. There is no obvious relationship between these values; therefore, the sequence cannot be represented as a mathematical formula (or algorithm). However, if the designer were to use values of 1, 5, 11, 19, 29, 41, and so on instead, the numbers could be put into a formula, $n + (n^2 - 1)$, which would be simple for a programmer to implement in the code and would help speed the processing during play.

An *algorithm* is a procedure that follows a sequence of well-defined steps to solve a problem. It can be a mathematical formula or instructions for a program. It can be likened to a cooking recipe in that steps are done in a certain order to reach the end product—say, a baked cake or bread loaf—although there might be times where some part of the process has to be repeated a number of times before the next step begins. The steps of the algorithm have to be correct or the final product will be flawed (for example, leaving the flour out of bread or a cake). Part of the testing process involves making sure that an algorithm gives the desired result every time.

> ## FYI   *Learning About Charts and Tables*
>
> A would-be designer who wants to get an appreciation of what goes into making the charts and tables for games is well advised to purchase the rules books for several role-playing games such as *Dungeons & Dragons* (published by Wizards of the Coast) or *GURPS* (generic universal role-playing games, published by Steve Jackson Games). Also, check out a number of strategic paperboard games such as *Settlers of Catan* (distributed by Mayfair Games, Inc.), *Napoleon at Bay* (Operational Studies Group), and *Axis & Allies* (distributed by Wizards of the Coast).

Caution

Separate the Data

The database information should be compiled into data files that are kept separate from the game engine code files. This arrangement enables the designers to manipulate and tweak the values without requiring the programmers to recompile the game engine code. It makes game balancing more efficient and frees the programmers for other tasks.

Charts and Tables (The Game Database)

While writing the concept game design document, the designers determine what values are needed and assign those values to the game objects. They can arrange the data into charts and tables to make it easier to look at all the values together to see if there are any imbalances. These charts are generally written during the game design phase and are used by the programming team during the production phase to drive the game actions. The initial values are relative and can (and often do) change as work on the game progresses and the designers see how all the gameplay elements actually work together. Designers continually return to these data tables throughout the development cycle, tweaking and modifying the values until the game plays as desired. Taken together, the charts and tables form the *game database.*

If the designer decides to create the charts and tables in a spreadsheet program such as Microsoft Excel, they will have to ask the programming team to create a tool that reads exported *comma-delimited data* (where each bit of data is separated by a comma), strips out the appropriate information from the spreadsheet and puts it into a data file the game program can read, or uses some other method so the game engine can read the data. The designers should work with the programmers early in the production phase to nail down all the information that goes into each table and chart. It is a good idea to include extra empty columns in case the team needs to add more data fields later during development. Adding extra data types late in production can invalidate all currently saved game files, adding to the testing time.

In addition to the charts and tables, the database often contains the text strings that make up the dialogue. Creating interactive dialogue can be daunting because of all the possible combinations of statements and responses (see Chapter 17, "Storytelling in Games," for more details). It is difficult to design multibranching interactive dialogue and keep all possible combinations in mind. The more complex the story, the more difficult the design task.

It can be helpful to use a spreadsheet to map out the dialogue branches, but it is difficult to read all the text when it is crammed into a single spreadsheet cell and even harder to edit the text when changes are needed. The alternatives include putting the text in data files and using a scripting language to trigger the text (discussed later in this chapter). However, a simple text file that lacks the in-game or situational references is almost impossible to translate or fix. The designer can use flow charts to represent the game paths for the dialogue or include extra columns in the spreadsheet that point to where the dialogue is used.

> ## Caution
> ### Keep the Text Separate
> As with the game data, it is important to keep the dialogue text separate from the game engine because the designers will likely make many changes during production.

Game Genres and Databases

Some game genres require multiple charts to define unit values and use many tables to resolve game actions, even if the player never sees them. Other games use only a few charts and tables, if any at all.

Role-Playing Games (RPGs)   Electronic RPGs have their roots in paper RPGs, which require dice to resolve almost every game action and which sport a large number of items with various statistics of which players must keep track. As a result, RPGs usually require an extensive database, including:

- Character Generation Charts: If the player is allowed to create a new character from scratch, the process usually includes *character generation charts* that list the starting statistics for the races in the game as well as their beginning weaponry, equipment, known spells/technology, and special abilities. Sometimes, the player generates the character statistics by "rolling dice" and receiving a variable number of points to assign to the starting values. In other games, the player begins with a set pool of points and assigns these points to the character's statistics as desired; the number of points is based on character class (knight, wizard, thief, and so on) and race (human, elf, dwarf, and so on).

- Item Chart: This is a large chart that includes all the different statistics and special abilities of all the weapons, armor, and inventory items (potions, spells, and so on).

- Magic/Technology Chart: This chart includes information about magic (if the genre is fantasy) or technology (if the genre is science fiction) in the game.

- Combat Resolution Table: A table is often used to determine the amount of damage applied to a target during combat. Depending on how the combat system works, the first step might be to determine whether the attacker's modified combat strength is greater than the defender's (the combat values are modified for such things as armor, powerful weapons, magic spells, and the like). The next step would be to generate a random value and consult the combat resolution table to determine how much damage is assessed against the target (that is, how many hit points are subtracted from the defender's total). In addition, the system might use another table to determine where the damage is applied to the defender's body. Note that there are many different approaches to combat resolution in role-playing games.

- Booty Table: This table determines the number of experience points, gold, and booty items that are obtained after defeating enemies. Some randomization is generally applied to the process so that the results will vary.

- Experience Chart: When characters earn enough experience points, they go up a level on the experience chart, and the player usually receives more points to assign to character statistics. The number of points needed to go up a level is often determined by the player's choice of the character's race and class.

- Dialogue Chart: Because there is so much dialogue in an RPG, the designer might decide to use a chart to keep track of character responses during play.

FYI | *Generating Random Numbers*

Many paper and board games use dice to generate random numbers to resolve game actions. Obviously, a computer doesn't roll dice to generate such numbers. There are several methods for generating random numbers in a game. One method is to use a large lookup table of random numbers and to have the game engine refer to this table when a number result is needed. A more efficient

CONTINUED ON NEXT PAGE

16

> **▶ CONTINUED**
>
> method is to use a mathematical formula to generate a random number between the minimum and maximum values involved (for example, between 1 and 6 to imitate a six-sided die). Whatever the process for determining the number, the most important thing is that the resulting value should be unpredictable, so that the player does not detect a pattern in the outcomes.

War Games   War games also have an extensive database. The ***unit chart*** in such a game lists the values for movement rates, attack strengths, defense strengths, hit points, and so on. Many units have values that reflect their special abilities—for example, the ranges and reload time for artillery, maximum air range and bombing capacity for air units, and command radius and morale rating for command units. The appropriate values are plugged into the combat resolution formula and then are modified for battlefield terrain, morale, supply status, and other factors. These games usually resolve combat via a ***combat results table (CRT),*** which is a matrix on which a die roll is cross-referenced with the appropriate combat differential column to determine what happens next in the game.

Figure 16.5 shows an example of a combat results table for a paper war game. The attacker's strength is compared to the defender's strength to come up with a ratio (for example, the 1:4 in column 2 means the attacker is attacking at one-quarter the strength of the defender). A six-sided die is rolled, and the result is cross-referenced with the appropriate column to determine the outcome of the battle. A result of "Ar/Dr" means the attacker or defender retreats. If there is a number after the *r*, the attacker/defender also takes losses. An "Ex" means that

COMBAT RESULTS TABLE

Die Roll	1:5+	1:4	1:3	1:2	1:1.5	1:1	1.5:1	2:1	3:1	4:1	5:1	6+:1	Die Roll
1	Ar	Ar	Dr	Dr	Dr	Dr2	Dr2	Dr2	Dr3	De	De	De	1
2	Ar2	Ar	Ar*	Dr	Dr	Dr	Dr	Dr2	Dr2	Dr4	De	De	2
3	Ae	Ar2	Ar	Sk	Sk	Dr	Dr	Dr	Dr2	Dr3	Dr3	De	3
4	Ae	Ar3	Ar2	Ar	Sk	Sk	Dr	Dr	Dr	Dr2	Dr2	Dr2	4
5	Ae	Ae	Ar3	Ar2	Ar*	Ar*	Sk	Sk	Dr	Dr	Ex	Ex	5
6	Ae	Ae	Ae	Ar3	Ar2	Ar2	Ar*	Ar*	Sk	Ex	Ex	Ex	6

The header reads: Probability Ratio (Odds) Attacker:Defender

Attacks at greater than 6:1 are treated as 6:1; Attacks at worse than 1:5 are treated as 1:5. "Ar*" may be Shock. If you obtain a "Sk" (Shock) Result, proceed to compare the Initiative Ratings of the best units on either side on the Shock Combat Table, and apply the Combat Result *(see 11.4)*

FIGURE 16.5 Combat Results Table used to resolve attacks in Operational Studies Group's Napoleonic war game *Four Lost Battles: Quadrigame of the Dresden Campaign, August–September, 1813.*

the attacker suffers the same number of losses as the defender. An asterisk or an "Sk" might result in a shock, which is resolved using another table.

Real-Time Strategy (RTS) Games   These games have a unit chart similar to the ones in a war game that shows the combat values of units. In addition, they include a *construction chart* that shows the resources needed to create buildings and new units as well as the time it takes for them to appear. Combat is usually much less complex in these games because the player usually does not directly command the units but instead simply points them toward the battle and lets them carry on. The units select which enemies to attack, and combat resolution is handled by a CRT similar to those found in war games.

Strategy Games   The charts and tables in other types of strategy games, including vehicle simulations with combat, are similar to those in war games and RTS games. If units are involved in conflict (which is not always combat), a chart lists their relative values, which are plugged into the algorithm to resolve game actions. There can also be a construction chart if the game deals with expending resources to create buildings and/or units.

Sports Games   If a game tries to realistically simulate a sport, it probably uses the statistics of real players when resolving game actions. Action-oriented sports games might not rely on real-world statistics, but they might include a *player chart* that lists each player's name, position, and whatever values are relevant to resolving game actions. The players' statistics are then used to determine if an event happens (for example, the ball is hit, a tight end catches a pass, a guard makes a three-pointer, and so on). They can also be used to determine the outcome of games in which the player is not involved if the sports game covers an entire season.

Racing/Flight Simulations   Games that simulate vehicles where no combat is involved occasionally use information charts. One chart might be used between races to determine the value of parts or modifications that can be bought and how they affect a vehicle's values. Another chart might be used during play that lists all the current statistics for each vehicle, which are then plugged into formulas to determine such characteristics as acceleration, braking ability, cornering, friction, and so on. There might also be a *random events table* to handle rare occurrences such as blown tires, air turbulence, or surface choppiness.

Action Games   Action games can include an item chart that lists the values for weapons, armor, and other items found on the playfield. The weapons and armor values can be plugged into the formula used to resolve combat, and the results can be compared to a combat results table that allows variability in damage.

Puzzle Games   Many puzzle games such as crossword puzzles, jigsaw puzzles, card games, and so on need no database. Others might have a simple

---

Caution

Sports Licenses

When developing a sports game that uses real player's statistics, the game company must get a license to use these statistics from the players' union.

16

list of the values that change from object to object such as a chart of the property and rental values in *Monopoly*.

Adventure Games   Adventure games often do not include a database of charts and tables. However, if there are many branches of interactive dialogue, the designer might want to use charts to keep track of characters' conversations and items in the game.

Balancing the Game

A major challenge facing a designer is balancing the game so that no unit dominates it while also making sure that the game remains intellectually stimulating. If players find a unit that is too powerful, they will always want to use it, and then by consistently winning, they become bored. If the game is too predictable, players will quickly move on to something new. Designers prefer that players experiment with the units to discover each one's strengths and weaknesses. They also introduce other, more powerful units or events during the course of the game to force players to modify or adapt their gameplay tactics. Making sure that gameplay is balanced is particularly important in online multiplayer games, where dominant strategies are quickly shared among the players almost overnight.

The Importance of Strategy

Designers often use the game of rock-paper-scissors as a model for balanced design. In that game, there is no dominant move (nor a dominant strategy). Paper beats rock but loses to scissors; rock beats scissors but loses to paper; scissors beats paper but loses to rock. However, a game where everything is too perfectly balanced can become boring if luck (that is, pure randomness) always determines the winner.

FYI   *Origins of Rock-Paper-Scissors*

It is likely that the game of rock-paper-scissors was invented by the Chinese. The first known mention of the game is in the book *Wuzazu* by Xie Zhaozhi (around 1600 CE), which refers to Han warlords playing a game called hand command. The game was introduced to the West in the nineteenth century through Japan. The World Rock Paper Scissors Society (WRPS) helped standardize the rules and holds yearly international world championships.

Players enjoy a game where some strategy is involved. Although that statement might scare off individuals who do not like the word *strategy,* all gameplay inherently involves making a choice that will result in some desired action. There is always a strategy involved in making the choice. In game design, this often means that some pieces will not be as strong as others so the game will not be fully balanced. This approach allows enough room in the game for players to experiment with strategies. In chess, for example, there are six different types of pieces (king, queen, bishop, knight, rook, pawn) that have different movement abilities. The queen is clearly a dominant piece because it can move long distances across the board in many directions. Yet, there is only one queen per side, so a player must defend the queen as well as using it offensively. The pawns in chess, weak and insubstantial as they seem, are used as a delaying or pressing tactic. A player moving the pawn might attempt to force an opponent into either taking the pawn and so putting the capturing piece in jeopardy or impelling a threatened chess piece to retreat, thus opening a hole in the opponent's defensive position that can be exploited.

On the other hand, when two players understand how tic-tac-toe is played, they almost always wind up in a tie (that is, winless) game unless one makes a mistake. The balance in tic-tac-toe is in position and the strategy of the players. In checkers, a game that is more complex than tic-tac-toe but simpler than chess, there is enough room on the board and a sufficient number of different starting moves for players to try different attack strategies, even though all the pieces are the same. As a result, the winner tends to be the better strategist.

Tools for Balancing

A designer has several tools available to help balance a game. First, there is *randomness* (or luck), which takes some control out of the players' hands. The designer might want to limit randomness to one important part of the game, rather than requiring everything to have a random result. Although players enjoy the challenge of overcoming an occasional bad result or string of results, having every game action determined randomly will make them feel powerless because any strategy they have can be undermined by random outcomes. Unless the game is all about pure luck, such as some forms of gambling, it's a good idea to limit randomness to one or two game elements (for example determining combat damage, hitting a baseball, setting up the number of monsters in a random encounter, and so on). A second balancing tool for designers is the use of compensating factors on powerful units. A *compensating factor* is a gameplay mechanic or value that offsets the dominating factors. For example, in a game of medieval warfare, the mounted knight is often the most powerful piece because it is armored, rides a horse, and carries a heavier weapon. Compared to infantry or bowmen, a mounted knight moves faster and farther, takes less damage because of its armor, and inflicts significant damage with its mace, sword, or lance. Compensating factors would be to make the mounted knight very expensive to create (buying the weapons, armor, and horse), to limit the pool of potential knights (such as to the aristocrats), and to take time to train the knight in combat (learning to use a weapon while riding). On the other hand, the designer might decide to let a player's game pieces become so powerful that they are dominant, and the compensating factor would be the length of time required to reach this level. If the player invests 60 to 100 hours in a game, perhaps it's time to let her game pieces be dominant (at least in solitaire games).

Artificial Intelligence

If a game is to be played solitaire and some kind of conflict drives the action, the player likely will face some kind of computer-controlled opponent. Even in games as simple as *Asteroids* and *Space Invaders,* the computer determines the movement around the playfield of those objects not controlled by the player. In more complex computer and video games such as Valve's *Half-Life 2* and Bungie's *Halo 2,* the enemies react to what the player does, and they seem to be aware of the dangers they face and respond accordingly. Now that game platforms have become more powerful, with multiple gigahertz of processing power, development teams are looking at ways to make the computer-controlled enemies behave even more like humans.

The code that controls the behavior of game objects not controlled by the player is referred to as the ***artificial intelligence (AI).*** This definition differs from the standard definition of AI as "the capability of a machine to imitate intelligent human behavior" (from Merriam Webster Online). The AI in games is currently often far less intelligent than humans. Game AI is usually associated with making enemies run around the playfield (***pathfinding***) and shoot weapons at the player (***target acquisition***), but AI can also handle subtler functions such as determining what types of buildings to create on a given terrain or determining which armies to send into battle and which to keep in reserve.

Considering the limitations of game platforms until relatively recently, such as the measly 640k of memory in the bad old days of MS-DOS, it is amazing that game teams were able to do such interesting things. Graphics have always been the biggest hog of processing power in game platforms, leaving relatively few cycles for interesting AI. To cut down on the amount of AI programming, many of these early games either used simple repetitive routines or let the computer enemies cheat. Still, programmers came up with a number of interesting AI routines that were used in games to make enemies seem at least somewhat intelligent.

The programmers make the game AI work. Although designers can describe how they see the AI working for various enemies in a game, they do not write the actual code to enable these behaviors. Nor should designers try to use a scripting language to create AI because the convoluted scripts needed for the AI would be too large and would slow down the game at runtime. The designers should work with the programmer responsible for writing the AI code module to make sure that the behavior they want in the game can actually be programmed, that it can be made to work efficiently without dragging down the game speed, and that it will be flexible enough so that the resultant behavior will not be predictable.

FYI | *The Father of Artificial Intelligence*

In 1956, John McCarthy of MIT coined the phrase *artificial intelligence* for the Dartmouth Conference on machine intelligence. In 1958, he invented the LISP (from **LIS**t **P**rocessing) language for symbolic processing, which was taken up by many AI researchers. He has been a professor at Stanford University since 1962.

Games that Need AI

Some games have a greater need for AI than others. Some need simple AI routines, whereas others need multifaceted AI. The game genre usually defines the demands placed upon the AI:

- Action Games: The AI has to determine how the enemies will react to the player, how they select movement paths, when they attack, what triggers them to react, and so on. Arcade games can include enemies whose behavior is simple and easy for the player to predict, so the challenge comes from dealing with many enemies at the same time or with different types of enemies appearing together. Shooter games (first-person and third-person) are primarily interested in moving the enemies around the map and engaging the player in combat, although recent games include less predictable AI, thus making the enemy seem more human.

- Role-Playing Games: The AI for these games primarily handles the enemy during combat. An enemy might be able to do several things in combat—shoot a weapon, use magic, heal, and so on—and will select from these options each turn or at a regular interval. Usually, little movement is involved except perhaps to dart in to attack the player and then dart back. Action role-playing games, such as Blizzard's *Diablo,* behave more like action games because the enemies are triggered, move toward the player, and then attack.

- Strategy Games: The AI requirements for these games can be fairly complex. War games need to evaluate the conditions in the midst of battle to determine where to move units, which units to attack, when to attack, and what to do after a battle if they succeed (or not). In real-time strategy games, AI routines might control the enemies as they gather resources and build new units.

- Simulation Games: Even if there is no enemy involved, the computer might still need to determine what the units not controlled by the player will do. In a game such as Maxis' *The Sims,* for example, the visiting sims are managed by the computer. The computer can also deal with changing conditions in the simulation world either independently or based on the player's actions.

- Sports Games: The game AI has to understand the rules of the game and use them toward winning the game. Both offensive and defensive AI routines might determine how an opposing team will select its plays while attempting to score or to keep the player's team from scoring. There can also be AI routines for individual positions on each team and even special "hotdog" routines that mimic real-world behavior by athletes.

- Vehicle Simulations: In a racing game, the computer-controlled vehicles have to select paths around the track—either by using invisible *splines* (a smooth curve that connects a series of points) that define their paths or by using waypoints and determining the fastest way to get to the next one. If combat is involved, the AI also has to handle target selection and perhaps determine the order in which the player's units will be engaged.

- Puzzle Games: In games that include a player-versus-computer mode, the AI demands can be great. Games such as chess, Go, and bridge have subtle strategies that require the computer to weigh the outcome of many possible moves each turn. Other puzzle games such as crossword puzzles, jigsaw puzzles, and trivia games require almost no AI.

- Adventure Games: These games generally need little AI except to control the random actions of characters. If some kind of combat is involved, the AI has to control the enemies' movement and target acquisition.

AI Behaviors in Games

A programmer can take a number of approaches toward creating the behavior for computer-controlled units in a game. Depending on the type of game and the desired complexity of behavior, the code for the AI can be relatively simple or very complex. Obviously, if a team is creating a simple arcade game similar to Atari's *Centipede,* it makes little sense to create complex behaviors, so a simple algorithm is sufficient to control an enemy's actions. On the other hand, creating an environment where creatures learn different things during play and begin acting independently, as in Peter Molyneux's *Black & White,* requires highly sophisticated AI behaviors that might involve the following techniques, which are listed in order from the simplest to the most complex:

- Deterministic Algorithms: These algorithms are a series of step-by-step procedures to drive simple behaviors such as a chase algorithm or pathfinding algorithm. The ***chase algorithm*** can check the player's coordinates in relation to the enemy and, if the player is within a set range, instruct the enemy to start the pursuit. The ***pathfinding algorithm*** determines the path the enemy will follow as it finds the optimal path around blocking obstacles. Figure 16.6 shows an example of A* pathfinding in which the green unit wants to move around the wall to reach the red square. The gray points indicate potential paths that the unit can take in adjacent spaces. A value of 10 is assigned to move horizontally or vertically into an adjacent space, and a value of 14 is assigned to move diagonally (the values appear in the lower left corner of each square). The algorithm calculates each possible path and determines the next move with the lowest cost. In this example, the lowest cost is 68 (14 + 10 + 10 + 10 + 14 + 10). Players will often figure out the inherent patterns of the algorithms and thus know how to beat the AI.

- Pattern List: To add variety to an enemy's behavior, the AI programmer can create a list of patterns that the enemy will follow. Each pattern

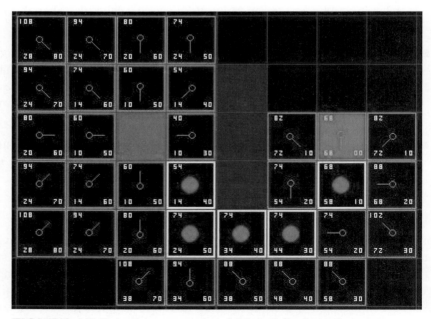

FIGURE 16.6 In this example of A* pathfinding, the green unit on the left wants to move around the blue wall to reach the red square.

consists of a list of steps to perform. For example, while patrolling near the entrance of a building, the enemy performs the following steps:

1. Move east four spaces.
2. Turn around and move west four spaces.
3. Turn south and move five spaces.
4. Turn east and move four spaces.
5. Turn north and move five spaces.
6. Turn west and walk four spaces.
7. Repeat the pattern until something triggers another pattern.

The AI programmer can create a number of such patterns with triggers that make it change patterns.

■ Random Behavior: To make an enemy seem less predictable, the AI programmer might decide to randomize the outcome of an algorithm or pattern. For example, instead of always selecting the most direct movement route to the player, the programmer can randomize the path selection every once in a while so the enemy takes unexpected paths toward the player. Another option is to use randomization to change the order in which patterns are selected or even to change variables within a pattern. For example, in a typical turn-based RPG, an enemy might be able to perform a number of possible actions in a turn, such as use a weapon, use a magic spell, or use an item. To make sure the enemy uses the weapon most of the time, the game can randomize the enemy's action in a turn by generating a random result between 1 and 10. If the result is 1 to 7, the enemy uses the weapon (70% chance); on a result of 8 or 9 (20% chance), it casts a magic spell; and on a result of 10 (10% chance), it uses the item.

■ Finite State Machines: A more complex AI method is to employ ***finite state machines,*** which are abstract models that have several predefined states. The enemy stays in one state until special conditions are met, and then it changes to another state until other conditions are met. For example, an enemy might be in a patrol state following a set path until the player moves within range, at which point the chase state is initiated and continues until the player is outside the pursuit range, at which point the enemy starts patrolling again. In effect, the enemy follows a script similar in structure to those created by a scripting language. It is possible to use a scripting language to create finite state machines, although they usually work more efficiently if they are coded in C++.

■ Environment Awareness: In a 3D game, a method of limiting the amount of information the computer enemy has—that is, to limit its ability to cheat—is to restrict its senses so they are the same as the player's. One way

FIGURE 16.7 Screenshot from Ion Storm's *Thief: Deadly Shadows* (published by Eidos in 2004). It is a "sneaker" game, in which the player tries to stay out of the sight of guards while infiltrating a castle.

to do this is to limit what the enemy can "see" by giving the model a *cone of vision* toward its front and limiting how far it can see. The enemy is not triggered to act unless the player enters the cone of vision. Another method is to use sound. If the player tiptoes around the playfield, the enemy does not sense him, but if he walks normally or runs within a specified distance, the enemy can "hear" the footsteps. Looking Glass's *Thief* series and other "sneaker" games use this approach (Figure 16.7).

- Fuzzy Logic: In binary code, everything is a *0* or a *1*. Fuzzy logic works between these extremes within a range of possibilities. Instead of using abrupt state changes, *fuzzy logic* uses ranges based on a set of rules; for example, an AI unit might determine the threat level of the player's units by applying a set of rules (closeness, size, armament, and so on) to evaluate the units and decide which ones present the greatest threat. It is quite useful in controlling what the enemy might do, such as offering a method for assessing the danger level of various threats. The enemy might have a set of overlapping objectives to consider, such as standing sentry duty at a base, tracking down noises, patrolling an area, or taking a cigarette break. Each of them has a percentage range, and the ranges might overlap. So, the enemy might wander off to have a cigarette, hear something (the player), pause to see if there is another sound, decide the cigarette is more important, and continue wandering.

- Neural Networks: The human mind has a tremendous ability to absorb knowledge and draw inferences from what it has learned. This same approach is being applied to computer AI. Instead of continually erasing what the player has done—that is, deleting the information that triggers a change in behavior—the AI can store the information in memory (or in a saved game file). As the player performs actions, the computer stores the information and can then use it to build a set of rules to start anticipating what the player will do next. Instead of just reacting, the computer behaves proactively. Likewise, instead of gathering resources it does not currently need, it stores the location of the resources until the need arises or until the player threatens to gather them herself.

- Genetic Algorithms: In a multiplayer game where the computer has to respond to many different players, each with a different style and combination of inventory items, weapons, and skills, it starts recording the best response to each combination as a *gene*. The genes that work best survive, and the computer uses them more frequently. When players figure out how to overcome those strategies, the computer stops using the dominant strategy and either pulls other successful genes (strategies) from its memory pool or tries new combinations until it finds one that succeeds.

These are just a few of the AI techniques being used in games today. By the time one reaches genetic algorithms, a goodly amount of processing has to be done before the computer acts. As game platforms grow more powerful and more cycles can be devoted to AI routines, computers will be able to present ever more interesting strategies to players. Like humans, they won't select the best strategies every time; instead, they will behave more human by making an occasional mistake or by changing methods of attack by learning from the player it faces.

Summary

Logic and mathematics go hand in hand in electronic games. The programmers create code, which is really just an extended series of logic statements to get the computer to do things in the correct order. The algorithms used in the code are step-by-step instructions for resolving different functions that range from putting the correct graphics on the screen to decompressing and playing the audio to creating the artificial intelligence that will challenge the players and keep them playing.

A top-notch programmer needs a solid understanding of logic and the many different branches of mathematics and physics used in different code modules. A designer does not need to know as much advanced math because the values used to drive gameplay are relatively simple. However, a designer should have a good grasp of logic if he wishes to have a hands-on experience building the game using a scripting language. It's all well and good for a designer to tell a programmer how to make things work, but it's a much more rewarding experience to get one's hands dirty developing code and crafting the logic for how things will happen in the game.

Test Your Skills

MULTIPLE CHOICE QUESTIONS

1. Math in games is limited to performing which of the following tasks?
   A. Moving objects around on the screen.
   B. Determining collision reaction.
   C. Statistics and data for gameplay.
   D. All of the above.

2. What are the charts and tables in games used for?
   A. Navigation.
   B. Menu and input.
   C. Inventory management.
   D. Storing and looking up data used by the game program.

3. Balancing a game is partly making
   A. All the game entities be equal.
   B. All the gameplay fair.
   C. The strengths and abilities of game entities fair.
   D. All teams have equal numbers of items to use.

4. True or False: Rock-paper-scissors is a good model for making gameplay balanced.
   A. True.
   B. False.

5. True or False: A game designer should always include air friction and drag when making decisions about physics in a game.
   A. True.
   B. False.

16

6. A unit chart in a war game should contain which of the following? (Select all that apply.)

   A. Weapons range.

   B. Health.

   C. Movement pattern.

   D. Dialogue.

   E. Resource requirements.

7. For an RTS, it's important to design which of the following?

   A. A balanced game for all sides.

   B. An AI that can win.

   C. Troops that you can earn that allow you to always win.

   D. Weaker and stronger opponents so the player can be satisfied.

8. In games, a physics programmer uses mathematics for which of the following? (Select all that apply.)

   A. Collision detection.

   B. Acceleration.

   C. Gravity.

   D. Speed of light.

   E. Weapons range.

9. Random behavior is a good way to do which of the following?

   A. Simulate realistic responses.

   B. Make the game seems more like gambling.

   C. Make the game feels more unpredictable.

   D. Help the AI cheat.

10. Lookup tables for gameplay are

    A. A means to help the AI cheat.

    B. A shortcut to performing complex computations.

    C. A means for the designer to have fine control of gameplay.

    D. More time consuming than writing formulas.

11. If an elf has a strength of 5 and a speed of 9 but can use ranged weapons (weapon attack value $+5$), which of the following orc types would be the most similar in balance?

    A. Orc 1 with strength 10, speed 2, ranged weapons -2.

    B. Orc 2 with strength 5, speed 5, ranged weapons $+3$.

    C. Orc 2 with strength 7, speed 5, ranged weapons $+3$.

    D. Orc 3 with strength 3, speed 8, ranged weapons $+9$.

12. If the elf described above were in an unmodified battle with a centaur that has strength 11, speed 9, and ranged weapons +6, who would win?

    A. Elf.

    B. Centaur.

    C. It would depend on the random number generator.

    D. The gazebo.

13. One enemy in an RTS has the following units (HP = health points, AP = attack points):

    soldier, 10 HP, 5 AP, speed 4

    general, 25 HP, 20 AP, speed 0

    commander, 15 HP, 10 AP, speed 4

    How would you make the game balanced?:

    A. Make the general be available only after all the soldiers are used.

    B. Make the soldiers take longer to train.

    C. Make the commander take the longest to train.

    D. Make the general take the longest to train and cost the most.

EXERCISES

Exercise 16.1: Build an RPG Balance Chart

Consider an RPG that has three types of species battling for dominance of a planet. Limiting the number of weapons to two melees and two ranged for each species (it's a small planet), build a chart to show this information. Make one species really good with distance weapons but poor with melee. Make another the opposite. What would you do to the third to make playing each species seem unique?

Exercise 16.2: Balancing Weapons

Add two additional columns for each species to the chart you created in Exercise 16.1. Make one of the columns the weakest of the three species and make one the strongest.

DISCUSSION TOPICS

1. Consider an FPS game in which your character needs to infiltrate a building, gather something, and leave, preferably without alerting the enemy agents that are patrolling the building. What different actions would you want the enemy agents to do as they idle?

16

2. For the game in Discussion Topic 1, how would you like the enemy agents to behave if the player had to shoot one of them? Would you want them to respond differently if they were in the next room or if they were several floors away?

3. To continue the discussion, what motivations would you consider including in your AI design so that a guard might be unwilling to ever leave his post due to orders, personal issues, health, fear, or any others you can think of? What would make him leave? How would you make this feel as natural as possible?

4. Consider the chart you made in Exercises 16.1 and 16.2. What do you feel you could do now to balance the three species better? Consider quantity, weapon power-ups, technology, AI, sneakiness, or your own ideas to make the game more balanced.

Chapter | 17

Storytelling in Games

Chapter Objectives

After reading this chapter and doing the exercises, you will be able to do the following:

- Understand how games use nonlinear stories.
- Describe the five elements of a story.
- Understand the importance of creating compelling characters in games.
- Understand why violence is found in so many games.
- Gain an appreciation for how dialogue is created for games.

Introduction

As electronic games have developed and matured over the years, some genres have proven well suited for telling stories. The early arcade games—from Atari's *Pong* in 1972 to *Pac-Man* in 1980—had no stories. Even the first generation of commercial adventure games, such as Infocom's *Zork* and Sierra On-Line's *Mystery House* in 1980 and their successors, had no stories per se, although they used text to describe locations and give a sense of purpose to the game's events. Moreover, the first electronic role-playing games, such as Sir-Tech's *Wizardry* and California Pacific Computer's *Ultima* in 1981, were less about characters living out a story than they were about raiding dungeons in search of treasure. These early games had little room to devote to character development, exposition, dialogue, or other elements commonly associated with storytelling.

In the mid- to late-1980s, adventure and role-playing games began to focus more on the adventures of characters from a third-person point of view. Up to then, most games were presented from a first-person point of view as seen through the eyes of the protagonist (main character)—that is, the player. During that time, a number of interesting characters began to appear in storytelling games, such as Sir Graham in Sierra On-Line's *King's Quest I: Quest for the Crown* (1984), Link in Nintendo's *The Legend of Zelda* (1986), and Dave Miller in LucasArts' *Maniac Mansion* (1987). Nowadays, many game genres include interesting characters participating in stories in one form or another.

Narrative Structure in Games

Stories in Western cultures traditionally have five elements, which collectively are often referred to as the ***narrative structure:***

- Setting
- Characters
- Plot
- Conflict
- Resolution

These elements can also be found in many games. The setting, of course, is the game world. The characters include object(s) controlled by the player (the central protagonist, a party of adventurers, giant robots, armies, and so on) as well as those controlled by the computer. The plot is the narrative of the story, or the tale that has been told by the end of the game. The problem, conflict, is the central struggle between the objects controlled by the player and those controlled by opponents. The resolution is the final mission, the last level, or the final encounter with the boss monster that concludes the action.

Although games are similar to stories, they differ in one major respect. Traditional stories are ***linear;*** they start at the beginning, go through a series of plot points, and reach a conclusion. A reader cannot just pick up a book and start hopping from page to page (although there are gamelike books, such as TSR Hobbies' *Pick a Path to Adventure* books, that let readers make choices about how to get through the story). Similarly, movies, theater, and television shows tell stories in linear fashion.

In all of these formats, the consumer makes no decisions about what will happen next. Each section of the plot is carefully constructed to rise to a point of tension or a turning point in events, followed by a release of tension, and then to build to the next tension point/turn of events. This pattern continues until the ultimate tension point—the climax—is reached and resolved. A bit of dénouement then follows to wrap up the various plot elements before concluding the tale.

> ## **FYI** *Terms that Apply to Storytelling*
>
> **Exposition:** This is the information at the beginning of the story that provides background information about the characters as well as their situations and motives. It explains what has happened up to the point where the story starts (the backstory), how the characters relate to one another, and how the central conflict arises.
>
> **Conflict:** This is the struggle between the main characters (the antagonist and protagonist) that is based on their sharing the same basic desire and trying to thwart one another in fulfilling it.
>
> **Rising Action:** This is the part of the story where complications arise for the protagonist and create conflict. The conflict often develops in stages, building to a point of tension followed by a period of relief. The subsequent stages continue to build in intensity until the climax is reached.
>
> **Climax:** This is the point of greatest tension in the story and is often where the protagonist confronts the antagonist. It is also called the **turning point.**
>
> **Resolution:** After the climax has been reached, the resolution resolves the story's plots and complications. It is also referred to as the **falling action** or dénouement.
>
> **Dénouement:** This is the final outcome of the story's main complication. It might include some last-minute exposition (such as the villain's motives) or, in games, the final animated sequence.

Games, on the other hand, are generally considered *nonlinear* because they are interactive. Each time a player works his way through a game from start to finish, he creates his own story. The game might include an element of randomness involving the decisions the player makes in a turn, as well as a randomly generated outcome determined by the game engine when resolving game actions. The randomness can be as minor as deciding which checker to move in a turn or as major as ordering a depleted tank regiment to attack the enemy's exposed flank before the front line breaks. This element of randomness allows the player to create a unique and individual story with each play.

On the other hand, if no randomness is involved, the game can be replayed in exactly the same way (such as a crossword or jigsaw puzzle), and the result will turn out exactly the same. In such a case, the game's story would be like a movie, where the player's choices don't affect the play of the game. However, this is not usually the case with electronic games. Due to this nonlinearity, which is inherent with the interaction of the player with the world, the narrative structure of games is somewhat different from linear storytelling.

FYI | *Rail versus Open Narrative Structures*

17

Some games put players on a *rail* that forces them to follow a preset path through the game world. The player makes only a limited number of choices while moving through the world. This approach is useful in a complex game where the player needs to understand all the game-play mechanics before moving on. Other games restrict the area the player can explore and slowly open the world. Still, other games (such as Black Isle Studios' *Baldur's Gate* [1998]) allow players to explore the game world in any way they wish. If there is an overarching narrative plot to discover, the players get to unlock the plot in whatever order they wish. If the game world is too large, however, the player might soon get lost and not know what to do next. The more *open* the game world is from the start, the more nonlinear the game's story is, and the more restrictive the world, the more linear the story.

Settings in Games

Setting refers to the place and time in which the story is set. The setting provides a backdrop for the action and can instantly put the player in the right frame of mind to know exactly what to expect from the characters. However, a good plot can often be set in any setting and feel right. For example, the plot of Akira Kurosawa's film, *Seven Samurai* (1954), in which a small band of Japanese warriors helps defend a poor village from bandits, was reincarnated in the nineteenth-century American West in *The Magnificent Seven* (1960) and even in outer space in *Battle Beyond the Stars* (1980). In games such as racing games, historical war games, and simulations, the settings are realistic, but most storytelling games are set in some fantastic world—science fiction, fantasy, horror, or supernatural—and include fantastic elements such as superheroes, invading aliens, ghosts, or talking animals. There are several reasons why storytelling games are usually set in fantastic worlds. One of the major gameplay elements in a storytelling game is exploration, and it is far more interesting to explore the unknown than to retread the same old familiar grounds of tired old Earth. Fantastic settings are filled with the unknown and simply beg to be explored. There can be monsters no one has ever seen before or landscapes that simply take one's breath away. When these worlds are well developed and richly detailed, they give players a sense of touching something akin to the divine.

Second, the rules in a fantastic world can be whatever the designer wishes them to be. Gravity might not always work as we expect it and can be more cartoonish and bouncy. Magic, superpowers, and psychic powers can all exist in fantastic worlds. Fantastic worlds give mere humans the chance to become mighty heroes, powerful wizards, and neo-Captain Cooks exploring strange new planets. Players are willing to invest the time to learn the rules of the game universe and then apply them to their advantage as they explore these brave new worlds.

Third, fantastic worlds, while seeming to be very dangerous, are really quite safe because players know they are not real. Players can tell the difference between the real world and the game world, and they know that they are temporarily visiting the fantastic world by willingly suspending their disbelief in the impossible. Whatever monsters they encounter, whatever evils they face—or perform themselves, such as robbing banks or otherwise unleashing mayhem—players know that it is all make-believe and that when they shut off the game they will be back in the mundane world.

Finally, fantastic worlds are stylish. Designers and artists tap their creative juices when dreaming up the wonderful geographies and bizarre monsters that inhabit the game world and defining the abilities and limitations of special powers and abilities unique to the universe. These worlds can be as visually stunning and enjoyable to view as a Hieronymus Bosch or a Salvador Dali painting. Certainly, games have specific art styles, such as the film noire atmosphere of 3D Realms' *Max Payne* (2001) or the art-deco–meets–Mexican-mythology's land of the dead in LucasArts' *Grim Fandango* (1998; Figure 17.1) or the 1,001 Arabian Nights setting of Ubisoft's *Prince of Persia: The Sands of Time* (2003).

Overall, it is relatively cheap to produce the stunning visual worlds in games. Fantastic movies and television programs are more expensive to make than games (so far). Although computers are used to generate the visual effects for films, television, and games, the graphics for movies and television have to look as realistic as possible because human actors interact with them, and it is expensive to make fantastic 3D graphics look natural. Game graphics, on the other hand, can get away with being more abstract as long as everything in the world shares a consistent style. Whereas films and television present fantastic worlds in toto to passive viewers sitting in the theater or at home, games demand that players become active participants in the fictional worlds and, in effect, give legitimacy to these worlds by voyaging through them.

Characters in Games

Designers have so far done a terrible job of creating fully rounded, emotionally complex characters for games. Of course, until recently, most characters in games were tiny sprites that lacked subtlety and personality with limited sets of animations and virtually no characteristics other than physical capabilities

FIGURE 17.1 The characters in LucasArts' *Grim Fandango* are based on the art style seen in Mexican Day-of-the-Dead festivals, whereas the settings feature an art-deco appearance.

or appearance. The arrival of 3D graphics has offered designers the chance to create more interesting looking characters, but the preponderance of characters in storytelling games remain stereotypes and caricatures.

Character, of course, refers to the personality, traits, behaviors, and responses of an individual. Because most games are based upon the actions of the user who assigns himself the role of the protagonist, character is left largely undefined, and development is almost nil. There can be more depth in story games where the player is encouraged to take on the persona of the lead character. In LucasArts' *Full Throttle* (2002), for example, the character of Ben as created by Tim Schafer is a well-defined antihero. Though stereotypical, Ben is also interesting to identify with as the player advances in the game. He does and says things that most players would not do or say, which allows them to act out or to go along with a friend on their adventure.

There are several reasons why characters in games tend to be bland. For one thing, many of the emotions that appear in a game are shown through cut-scenes, not directly by the player—the actor—doing something. Games don't usually include feel, weep, or laugh options. Interactive dialogue (which is described later in this chapter) allows some depth of character to be shown during gameplay.

However, the player is kept at a distance from whatever emotions her character is scripted to feel.

In narrative storytelling, the character of the protagonist is revealed to the reader by his reactions to the setting, situations, and the reactions of other characters in the story. If a protagonist in a movie acts cruelly, the people around him might respond negatively. Movie audiences respond as the on-screen characters do; although we might relate to the main character, when she does bad things to characters we care about, we don't like her.

In games, NPCs are often used to help define and reveal the motivations of the main character. For example, an NPC who doesn't like the protagonist but gives no reason for it might make the player wonder about the backstory between the two or suspect that the NPC has information he won't share. When the NPCs are nice, we believe they like the main character, and because the main character (that is, the player) is likable, we in turn like them. Unfortunately, many games don't take advantage of this technique, instead turning out minimal or repetitive dialogue with NPCs. In an ideal game, the player–character that performs a remarkable and popular feat would be treated differently by the NPCs than a character who has performed some heinous action. One example of a game where NPCs do change their reactions to the main character is LucasArts' *Star Wars: Knights of the Old Republic* (2003), in which the NPCs react according to whether the player chooses to follow the light or dark side of the Force.

Another reason that characters have been difficult to create in games is the point-of-view. The point-of-view in a game is important in identifying with characters and forming an emotional attachment to them. In an FPS game, the world is seen through the eyes of the player's character. This view can seem the most realistic, but it separates the player from the character: although the player is looking through the eyes of his character, he never feels he *is* his character. The player doesn't watch the character perform the actions on screen, so it makes the player tend to maintain his own frame of reference in the game rather than act the part of the character. Thus, when other characters approach and tell the player–character how to think or feel, the player is often irritated and distanced emotionally from the on-screen persona.

Other games might show the character at a distance in a third-person point-of-view—similar to a movie or theater stage set. This view is much more cinematic and makes it easier for the player to become emotionally attached to characters. The player can see the expressions, quirks, and personality tics of each character and come to like or dislike them. But there is still a certain detachment if the player views the character as in a movie rather than actually becoming him or her. Good movies are able to involve the audience with the onscreen characters because the director has continual control of the action, pacing, storytelling, dialogue, and emotional response of the actors. In a game, the designer and programmer are at the whim of the player, who might or might not perform the actions planned or in the order anticipated.

FYI *Marketing and Intellectual Properties*

The marketing department at a game company might strongly support the development of games with stories and strong, interesting characters. The advantage of such games is that they present more opportunities for character merchandising, where the rights to use the characters are licensed to other companies. The characters might then appear on books, comics, coffee mugs, movies, and television shows. These are all areas where considerable amounts of money can be made on intellectual property (potentially even more money than through the game sales), which is why companies are willing to go to great lengths to protect these rights.

Characters seen at a distance are defined by the actions they perform, by their appearance as they act, and by what they say. Thus, Sonic the Hedgehog (Figure 17.2) is defined by his ability to run like a rocket through the game world, roll up into a ball, and then leap high into the air. His spiky hair, sly smile, crossed legs and sneakers, right hand akimbo on his hip, and left finger giving the "I'm Number One" sign all work together to give him a roguish look and certain insouciance of manner. He has many physical personality traits with

FIGURE 17.2 Sega created a well-defined character in Sonic the Hedgehog, who has become the company mascot and appeared in numerous games as well as a syndicated cartoon show.

which players can identify, although there is no dialogue to reveal what kind of character he truly is. Instead, the player infers from these physical traits alone that Sonic is a likable character.

Game characters' actions have to be greatly exaggerated so they can be easily understood by the player. It is much easier to give a character big, splashy, he-man-like actions rather than subtle, delicate, graceful actions because the larger-than-life animations are both easier to create and easier for the player to comprehend when a lot of activity surrounds the character. Although game graphics have improved and can show more detail, characters' actions still tend to require overstatement to be seen during the game's fast pace. Current 3D graphics suffer from a lack of emotional subtlety in facial or other physical expressions because faces are drawn onto flat polygons that cannot simulate all the minute changes humans identify with and react to. Close-ups showing emotions are reserved for the high-resolution cut-scene sequences, which still tend to be relatively crude and unsubtle.

Female characters have certainly been given short shrift in games. On the one hand, they are often treated as objects of desire whom the male player–character must rescue from the main villain. The poor, forever endangered Zelda is a perfect example. Such women are weak, overly emotional, defenseless, and sometimes shrewish. On the other hand, games that do feature strong women such as Lara Croft in *Tomb Raider* and Samus Aron in *Metroid Prime* present these women as forceful, stoic, exceedingly capable of defending themselves, often domineering—and with overendowed figures that pander to the wish-fulfillment needs of teenage boys. As a result, neither portrait of women is flattering or realistic. Of course, one can also argue that the males in games are unrealistic as well, and they are more like comic-book wish-fulfillment figures than true humans. Games still have a long way to go toward presenting interesting and well-rounded women and men in leading roles.

Plots in Games

The plots in games can be relatively short (action games) or can run on and on (adventure and role-playing games). Game plots generally follow traditional narrative stories. They start with an introductory section where the player first meets the character she will control for the rest of the game. A scene that demonstrates the villainy of the antagonist usually follows—for example, the love interest is kidnapped, the protagonist's family is destroyed, and so on. This gives the player a goal to spend the rest of the game trying to achieve—revenge, recovery of an object, obliteration of the antagonist. The player is then launched on a journey of discovery, experiencing a number of plot points (locating a mentor, suffering reversals of fortune, acquiring allies, undertaking subquests, surviving battles with the antagonist's minions) and picking up plot coupons (weapons, armor, technologies or spells, keys). Finally, the protagonist is prepared for the final confrontation with the antagonist and—assuming the player survives the final battle—everything is resolved quickly.

> ## FYI *Plot Coupons*
>
> In a story-based game, **plot coupons** are tasks that must be completed or items that must be collected before the final confrontation, or climax, will take place. Collecting the coupons is one method to propel the protagonist through a world to the places where the coupons' items are found. This plotting device is particularly useful in fantasy and science fiction stories because the items give the protagonist the power to defeat the enemy either directly or together with some mystical force.

Games frequently use the trappings of epic fiction to define the plot, often drawing on Joseph Campbell's analysis of the hero's journey as a way to structure plot events. The journey is one way to structure the story for a game, but there are others as well. Another place to look for basic structures upon which to hang a story is Georges Polti's book *The Thirty-Six Dramatic Situations*.

> ## FYI *Joseph Campbell and Games*
>
> Joseph Campbell (1904–1987) was an outstanding scholar of comparative mythology and comparative religion. He wrote a number of books on world mythology that might be considered textbooks for game designers. Perhaps his best known work is *The Hero with a Thousand Faces* (1948), which describes the similarities behind the "hero's journey" in mythology from all cultures and provides a useful framework for telling a heroic story. George Lucas has said that this book influenced him during the development of the original *Star Wars* trilogy.

It is difficult to create a coherent plot for a game following the standard structure for a novel or drama. One solution to make this structure simpler is to restrict the player's actions and travels throughout the game world. Another choice is to use a *frame story.* This technique narrates events in a standard linear structure before and after the central game action. However, players might feel restricted in such a game, and the game structure itself will likely be very linear.

When creating a coherent plot for an interactive story in which players are allowed to wander unfettered around the world, the designer must be careful about the order in which the plot elements are discovered. He must account for situations where NPCs could give conflicting or incorrect advice. Usually, the responses are all carefully orchestrated and scripted based on variables that are incremented as the player performs actions that enable new sets of dialogue from NPCs. It can take extensive testing to make sure that all loose ends are wrapped up correctly.

Another common problem in open-ended worlds is that players might forget what they are supposed to be doing as they travel across the vast gamescape, meet many NPCs, and deal with many plot elements. Players can get frustrated when they get lost or confused about their goals in the game world.

To resolve this problem, the designer might decide to limit players' movements to certain areas of the world until all the plot elements within that area have been revealed and all tasks have been resolved. Characters are then transported to a new area for exploration and new plot elements are initiated. In addition, continuing plot elements often cross into the new area to tie the entire game together into a cohesive whole. This approach is akin to a reader's completing one chapter in a large tome before going on to the next, and it is easier to structure and to debug. If implemented correctly, players are not even aware that their movements have been restricted. This method is sometimes called *gating* because the designer keeps a "gate" shut until the player completes everything in one area before opening it to let the player move on.

Problems and Solutions in Games

The problem in a game is the central conflict between the protagonist and the antagonist. As in most fiction, the protagonist and antagonist in a game generally want the same thing—though not necessarily for the same reason—whether it be the princess or a kingdom or a world ordered according to their philosophies. Because they want the same thing, conflict arises, and the events that follow show the rising and falling of fortune for each side as they strive to achieve their mutually exclusive goal. Only one of them can reach this goal; the other must, therefore, fail.

The conflict between protagonist and antagonist leads to tension, and the matter is not resolved until the climax, when one side wins. In games, the winning side is almost always the protagonist because that is whom the player controls. Players would be very unhappy if, after over 40 hours of hard work, they discovered that their failure was inevitable because the antagonist was just too powerful. Completing the game means winning, and the player wants to win. Players are willing to replay the final battle as often as necessary to bring the antagonist to his or her knees.

However, problems and solutions in games are not only about the final conflict between the protagonist and the antagonist. Whether it is finding the correct puzzle piece in a jigsaw puzzle or acquiring the correct semiautomatic weapon in an FPS, the player is confronted with a problem or series of problems that he must solve to stay alive and win.

The solution in a game frequently takes the form of conflict or battle of some kind. While they strive toward their mutually exclusive goal, the protagonist and antagonist (and his minions) come into conflict. Text and graphic adventure games usually have a conflict rooted in puzzle solving, sometimes against a time limit. These types of games seldom include combat because they focus on solving puzzles. Action-adventure games sometimes include combat as one method of resolving problems. Role-playing games include combat, as do most real-time strategy games, war games, and military vehicle games. Sports games and racing games involve conflict because only one person or one side can win. Puzzle games and simulations, however, might not involve conflict at all.

Recently, there has been a strong reaction against video games being too violent and focusing too much on combat. Aside from sports games (which one could argue are a ritualized form of combat), all the early arcade games (Atari's *Asteroids* [1979], *Battlezone* [1980], and *Centipede* [1981]; Williams Electronics' *Defender* [1980]; and so on) included some kind of combat. Even cartoonish games such as Midway's *Pac-Man* (1980) and Nintendo's *Donkey Kong* (1981) had violence—chomping on ghosts or throwing barrels at poor Mario. One reason combat was so popular in these early games is that it is easier to program than complex dramatic interactions and certainly easier to create than a staged dialogue-based dénouement. (The success of Will Wright's *The Sims* [published by EA in 2000], however, proves that we're entering an era in which such a game can be artistically and financially successful.) In fact, one might argue that all games, including card games, board games, and electronic games, are about conflict, and the resolution is that one person comes out on top.

Games do not necessarily promote positive social values. They promote greed (*Monopoly,* gambling), warmongering (*Risk,* chess), violence (football, thumb-wrestling), one-upmanship (*Trivial Pursuit*), and other antisocial behaviors. They hearken back to the days when humans had to fight and kill to survive. But the violence in games is abstract. Gamers know they are not racing real cars, flying real airplanes, or engaging in real combat in games. They can imagine they are in the game situation, that they are immersed in the action, that they are the heroes and heroines in conflict with villainous hordes—all without losing their sense of who they are or what they are doing. There will always be a place for violence in games. Games are cathartic. They allow people to act out aggressive and negative thoughts in a setting where no one gets hurt.

Of course, the violence in some games, such as first-person shooters like Eidos *Hitman: Contracts* (2004) and Rockstar Games' *Manhunt* (2003), feels much more intense than in a game like *Asteroids*. Advances in 3D graphics make the game world look more realistic, and therefore, the bloodshed feels far gorier than in earlier games with their simpler graphics. Still, older players do not have a problem differentiating between the game world and the real world and know that the violence is simply make-believe. However, younger players are not as discerning, so it is important for parents to check the ESRB ratings of games before allowing their children to play the violent games that carry an M (for mature) rating.

Interactive Dialogue

One way that storytelling games differ significantly from other forms of fiction is their use of dialogue. In a novel, movie, or television show, the dialogue is fixed and unchanging. Characters say the same thing over and over again, no matter how many times you read a novel or view a film. In games, however, the designer and the programmer give characters the chance to change over time as events in the game change and characters react to the changes.

This is a challenging task, however, so many games still seem like novels where the NPCs say only one thing to the player and repeat that information at every opportunity until a major condition in the game changes (rather like rereading a chapter of a novel until you move to the next chapter of a novel where the fictional characters are given new dialogue). In games that use text for dialogue, this problem is easily fixed by providing various random responses for characters or varying their responses according to the changing world situation or the player's performance so far. Games with recorded dialogue can the use the storage capacity of CDs and DVDs for additional dialogue that will give the NPCs many different things to say to a player throughout the course of the game. Usually, the additional dialogue has little to do with the game plot per se and merely acts as verbal window dressing. But because it varies, the player feels that the game is not static and that she has an impact on the game world. This helps to deepen the player's engagement in the play.

Interactive dialogue in today's games usually involves the player's selecting from a series of responses during each step of a conversation. The player can chose between different questions, different attitudes, or even different behaviors. Often, the player's attitude toward NPCs influences how they will respond. If the player says nice things to an NPC, that NPC could react pleasantly in kind. If the player is nasty, then the character might act coolly or even angrily and might not even speak again until the player somehow appeases the NPC. This approach to dialogue makes a game feel more interactive because the NPCs seem a little more real. A good example of this kind of dialogue appears in LucasArts' *Star Wars: Knights of the Old Republic 2: The Sith Lords* (2004). The NPCs in this game react differently to the player's dialogue choices depending on whether the player moves to the light side or the dark side of the Force, as seen in Figure 17.3.

It is also through this interactive dialogue that players learn the most about the characters they are playing. In a game such as *Full Throttle,* Ben's written and spoken voice is dry, sarcastic, self-deprecating, and certainly aggressive. Even the nice things that the player can choose to have Ben say are always tilted toward the humorous or slyly humorous. The responses of the NPCs let the player know how acceptable Ben's behavior is or when he has crossed the line. In addition, the character's aggressiveness in combat also affects the dialogue choices available to the player at any time.

Of course, all the dialogue in a game is scripted. Nothing is really left to chance. There are no artificial intelligence (AI) programs in games at this

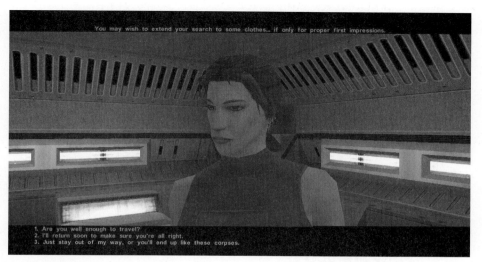

You may wish to extend your search to some clothes... if only for proper first impressions.

1. Are you well enough to travel?
2. I'll return soon to make sure you're all right.
3. Just stay out of my way, or you'll end up like these corpses.

FIGURE 17.3 In LucasArts' *Star Wars: Knights of the Old Republic 2, The Sith Lords* (2004), characters decide whether to follow the light side or the dark side of the Force. Depending on the player's dialogue choices when interacting with an NPC, the character's attitude can change, as will her responses.

time that allow NPCs to say truly random things, and a player's responses are always limited by what has been preselected for her. This situation will probably change as more time is devoted to developing AI routines for this functionality; however, programmers have been working on this problem, both in and out of games, for more than 40 years with limited success. Even games that let players select from multiple dialogue choices usually limit the NPC responses, so that an NPC often responds the same no matter what the player says.

NPC dialogue is usually restricted for several reasons. First, the player generally cares only about the responses that push the story forward. Idle responses that reflect an NPCs life story or comment on the player's actions are interesting once in a while, but it can be frustrating to wade through many responses in search of the few clues that relate to the game's plot. Second, writing interactive dialogue for a game can take a huge amount of time and can be very expensive. Each interactive dialogue can create many branches of possible responses, and the designer must be careful not to let the branching dialogue get out of control.

Assume for a moment that each NPC interaction offers the player two choices of dialogue and that the player interacts similarly with every character in the game. If there is only one character, then there are two dialogue strings to write. If there are four characters, then there are eight strings (Figure 17.4). If there are eight characters, there are sixteen strings. If, instead, there are four choices per interaction, the numbers of strings rises even more quickly. Eight

> **Caution**
>
> **Don't Waste Your (or the Player's) Time**
>
> Players can feel cheated if interactions with NPCs have no real effect on play. If the designers waste a lot of time and effort providing multiple choices that make no difference at all, they also waste the programmers' and the players' time in the game.

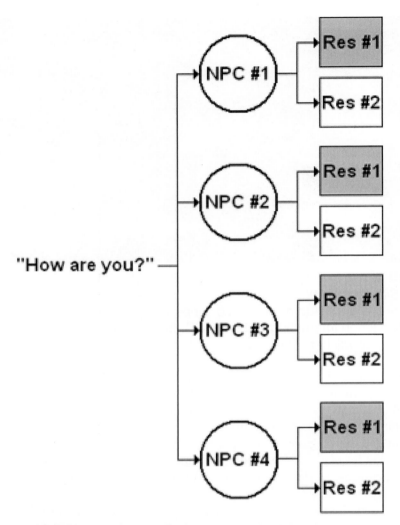

FIGURE 17.4 Branching dialogue can increase quickly. In this diagram, the player interacts with four NPCs, each of whom can give two responses, for a total of eight dialogue strings.

characters would require thirty-two text strings. If the dialogue per character changes with each major turning point in the plot, the number of test strings would quickly become astronomical as new locations opened up with more characters appearing in the world. It's no wonder that designers limit the number of responses each NPC gives.

Keeping track of the branching dialogue is another headache for the designer because no good commercial dialogue-writing tools are available. Tools are available to help screenwriters structure the dialogue for films, but these linearly based aids are not really useful to a game designer. It might be well worthwhile for the designers to ask the programmers to build a tool to help them test the interactive dialogue to make sure there are no holes or contradictions. Then the written dialogue needs to be added to the game (often using a scripting language) to test the logic and sequencing of the responses. Of course, having all the dialogue in a script file can slow the game, so the text is usually stripped out and put into a separate text-string file. Making changes to dialogue in the text-string file can be rather clumsy, and it might be difficult to ensure that the pointers in the scripting language point to the correct text strings (and that no typos creep in during debugging).

As a final step in creating the interactive dialogue, a designer might hire a professional writer to revise the text and make it sound better or tighter—especially if it is to be used in voiceovers. The ability to design interactive dialogue strings and the ability to write sparkling and clever dialogue are rarely found in the same person. In games using archaic language, such as fantasy games in a medieval setting, getting a professional to polish the language is almost a necessity. Many games have suffered from terrible dialogue (or bad voiceover acting).

Many designers seem to harbor a desire to be novelists. They load in lots of unnecessary dialogue or insert long passages where characters do nothing but spout at each other. Dialogue in games should be as sparse and direct as dialogue in modern movies. The player wants to play the game, not read a lot of dialogue—no matter how brilliant it is. As Shakespeare might have said if he had been a game designer: "Brevity is the soul of dialogue."

Caution

Check the Spelling

It is a good idea to write the dialogue in a word processing program that has a spellchecker tool, although the writer still needs to proof the text carefully for typos, missing words, and incorrect word choices.

IN THE TRENCHES: Insult Sword Fighting

In *The Secret of Monkey Island* (1990) by Ron Gilbert, published by LucasArts Entertainment (then LucasFilm Games), the pirate-wannabe hero, Guybrush Threepwood, has to fight the pirate antagonist at the end of the game but must become a skilled swordsman before the final conflict. To do this, he fights a number of pirates on the island where they are stranded, learning and improving his sword fighting skills.

Because this game was a graphic adventure that did not include a fighting simulation, however, Gilbert chose to incorporate the dialogues *as* the battle. During a sword fight, the pirate and the hero taunt each other with insults and witty responses. When the response is correct or successful, the person responding fights better. When the response is not successful, the person fights worse. The beauty of insult sword fighting is in the insults themselves; they are humorous and fun to read, and though they don't advance the story, they help players understand the world and characters better.

Summary

Although not all games need stories, a story can often add to a game and keep the player immersed in the game world. The primary genres that use stories are adventure games, role-playing games, and action games, although other genres sometimes use frame stories to tie the events of a game together.

Stories are linear, games are interactive. This interactivity allows players to create a new story each time they play the game. Stories are central to giving structure to a game, but they are secondary to good gameplay. Players often appreciate the artistic quality of animated sequences, but they can become impatient if play is continually interrupted by cut-scenes. Likewise, the dialogue in games is useful when it provides information for the player, but it can becomes unnecessary window dressing when NPCs discuss their private lives or opine about life in general. Gamers generally want to play the game, not watch the story.

Test Your Skills

MULTIPLE CHOICE QUESTIONS

1. When did games with stories become popular with gamers?

   A. In the 1980s, with graphic adventures.

   B. They've always been a popular part of game playing.

   C. In the 1960s, with the creation of the first text adventure game.

   D. Stories have not yet become important in video games.

2. True or False: The first text and graphic adventures required the user to type in commands on the keyboard?

   A. True.

   B. False.

3. What are the five elements of storytelling?

   A. Narrative, dialogue, conflict, resolution, protagonist.

   B. Setting, character, plot, problem, solution.

   C. Setting, protagonist, antagonist, problem, solution.

   D. Dialogue, character, exposition, setting, mentor.

4. What is exposition?

    A. The storytelling at the start of a narrative that sets up the situation.

    B. The description of the scenery within a narrative.

    C. The point of greatest tension in the story.

    D. The resolution of the action within the narrative.

5. Which of the following are common settings for video games? (Select all that apply.)

    A. Fantasy.

    B. Science fiction.

    C. Urban vampires.

    D. Gothic horror.

6. How do you define *character* in a story?

    A. How an individual acts.

    B. How an individual acts and what she says.

    C. How an individual looks.

    D. How an individual looks and speaks.

7. What is plot?

    A. The narrative structure.

    B. The story.

    C. The hero's journey.

    D. The problems and solutions the hero must overcome.

8. What is interactive dialogue primarily used for in a game? (Select all that apply.)

    A. Telling the backstory.

    B. Setting the player on the current goal.

    C. Confusing the player with other tasks.

    D. Helping the player solve the current task.

9. What does it mean to say a game is nonlinear?

    A. The narration within the story does not follow a traditional storytelling path.

    B. The game story is usually circular in that the player ends up back at the beginning of the story when he reaches the end.

    C. The interaction of the player affects the order in which the story is told.

    D. The game is usually built with multiple stories, and the player consciously selects the story she wants to hear.

10. What is a rail structure in video games?

    A. A video game that is open-ended, so that the player can go anywhere whenever he chooses.

    B. A video game that is constantly moving forward, so that the player must keep up with the story through constant action.

    C. A video game that is in third person, so that the game world is contained within a narrow chasm.

    D. A video game that allows the player limited access to the game world, constraining the player until she understands the game mechanic or the story well enough to progress to the next area.

11. How does dialogue with NPCs further the story in a video game? (Select all that apply.)

    A. The player gets a better understanding of the characters they portray.

    B. The player sees the world through the eyes of others.

    C. The player can learn more relevant information about his situation or objective.

    D. There is better player immersion into the game world.

12. What is one way to make the interaction with NPCs feel more realistic?

    A. Have them repeat important information until the player achieves his goal.

    B. Have them ignore the player if nothing new has happened.

    C. Have them interact with the player based on a series of responses that change as the player progresses or needs help.

    D. Animate them better.

EXERCISES

Exercise 17.1: Design a 3D Graphic Adventure

Assume you are designing a graphic adventure set in a 3D world. In this game, you need to communicate with many characters to gain knowledge or to learn answers to puzzles. Design the most simple interface or list of interactions that you would like to have in order to minimally interact with these characters.

Exercise 17.2: Improve Interaction with Characters

Based on Exercise 17.1, add to the list another five to ten options that you would like to have in order to fully interact with these characters.

17

Exercise 17.3: Use a Flow Chart to Structure a Story

Consider your favorite story or novel. Use a flow chart to plan structure of the story (either one or two chapters or a very high-level overview if it's a complex story) from the point of view of the protagonist. Because it's a story, the flow chart will likely be a series of events that happen one after another. Select three or four points and change the event into a puzzle or decision point for the protagonist.

Exercise 17.4: Use Branches to Change the Story

Based on Exercise 17.3, create your own branches to the narrative structure from the three or four decision points you added. Can you make the story change based on the choices or actions taken by the protagonist? Does the over-all story change or do the branches reconverge at another decision point or at the end of the narrative structure?

Exercise 17.5: Design an Action Game with a Story

Consider designing an action game with a story structure. How would you inte-grate the action, puzzles, or conflicts that the protagonist faces so that the player's choices affect the story?

DISCUSSION TOPICS

1. Discuss how you might be able to incorporate more tension in a graphic adventure game through dialogue.

2. Because FPS games are action packed and the player is usually tense, how important is the story of the FPS to the player? How could you make the story more important?

3. List any games you can think of that have a strong story element that is well integrated with the gameplay. How does the story fit into the game-play? How different would the game be without the story element? How similar would it be to other games?

4. If story isn't important to a game such as *Sonic the Hedgehog*, why did the designer create one? How might the player's experience have been different if there had not been any story?

5. If the character had not been Sonic but had been more like Mickey Mouse, how different would the game experience have been to the player?

Chapter 18

Prototyping and Building Playfields

Chapter Objectives

After reading this chapter and doing the exercises, you will be able to do the following:

- Understand how prototypes are used when designing a game.
- Explain how game playfields are created.
- Realize that level building is both an art and a science.
- Understand what goes into creating a 2D map editor.
- Understand what goes into creating a 3D level editor.

Introduction

Prototyping the game offers a means to play the game early in development to test the gameplay and the mechanics and otherwise determine if the play is fun. The game design document is an abstraction in which the designer attempts to put into words how the game will play. A prototype is a way to see how the game actually plays before too much time or money is spent developing the engine. Until there is something concrete for testers to play, the designer can't know whether or not the game idea will work as planned. By starting to test the design as early as possible, first through paper prototypes and then through a working prototype, changes to the game can be tested. The earlier that necessary changes can be determined, the easier it will be for the team to keep on schedule.

Prototyping can be applied to level, mission, or playfield design as well. A designer might want to work out many of the subtleties of a level's layout either by building a paper prototype or by working with an artist to create storyboards. What the team learns from prototyping a level, playing it, testing it, and then building the actual game level can provide great insight into how interesting the structures, puzzles, or events will be for all the levels. This process also helps orchestrate the pacing of the game; that is, how quickly things will be introduced to the player. Prototyping a level helps the designers see when it is too linear and restrictive or too sparsely populated and boring.

Thinking things through as thoroughly as possible during the preproduction phase before starting to implement them can help the team recognize problems they need to address. Prototyping is the final step that a designer can use before actual implementation to discover problems or resolve issues early in the production phase.

18

Prototypes

All designers, as well as programmers, reach a point in the design where they want to turn the abstract idea for the game into something real. Creating a prototype lets the designer test his assumptions about the gameplay before the team starts creating assets for the final product. For a programmer, prototyping is a means to test programming issues early in development. There are three kinds of prototypes the designer might want to use:

- Paper prototypes

- Storyboards and flowcharts

- Interactive prototypes

A fourth type of prototype, the fly-through of a level, is used as a marketing tool.

Of course, all four prototypes are not necessary to test every design, but one or two usually prove helpful. It is not necessary to prototype the whole design. The designer should concentrate on prototyping the most important gameplay elements, such as combat in a role-playing game or the availability of resources in a real-time strategy game. New and unique gameplay elements should also be tested in prototypes. Certainly, the shell interface screens can be ignored.

A secondary purpose for prototypes, which is equally as important as testing design concepts, is to familiarize team members (and management) with the product, especially if the game includes unusual gameplay elements.

Paper Prototype

During the initial design process, a designer might resort to his toolbox of physical props—grid paper, index cards, rulers, color markers, dice, and so on—as he works out the game mechanics. These physical tools are used in addition to the spreadsheet, word processor, and art programs on his computer. Part of the fun of being a designer is the chance to occasionally get one's hands dirty creating a paper prototype.

The process of creating a ***paper prototype*** encompasses several methods of making a playable version of the game using nonelectronic means such as creating a grid board and play pieces, making a deck of specialized cards, and modifying an existing board or card game. A paper prototype is a physical game that can be played either in small subsections or in its entirety.

Paper prototypes do have their drawbacks, however. Computer games tend to be continuous in action, and this is difficult to capture in a paper version. The paper version often requires many information markers to track what is happening to objects on the playfield. and the number of these markers can quickly become overwhelming. Finally, although the designer can get some sense of scale using a paper prototype, the final scale won't be determined until the team performs certain tests early in the production phase. Still, a paper prototype does give the designer a chance to examine the play mechanics and simplify them as necessary. It lets the designer play around with scale and experiment with values assigned to objects in the game.

Depending on the type of game, the paper prototype can be fairly simple or quite elaborate. A prototype that tests a small part of the design—combat, for example—might consist only of a small piece of grid paper, a few slips of paper, the combat tables, and some dice. The grid paper is useful for regulating movement, and the paper slips can represent objects and characters participating in the battle. For a larger game such as a role-playing game (RPG) the designer might want to create detailed maps of the world to test the time it takes a player to traverse the map and plan where the perils and adventures will occur. In addition, RPGs often include a separate interface for combat, which can be prototyped as the designer completes the character, item, weapon, and magic charts to make sure combat works out as anticipated. For a computer war game, the designer creates a map of the battlefield at the desired scale and uses cardboard counters to represent the combat units and information markers. When the war game is a representation of an actual historical battle, the designer uses actual military maps of the battle along with analyses of the strategies, unit placement (called the ***order of battle***), and their strengths and weaknesses. Simulation and strategy games are often good candidates for paper prototypes. Resource management systems often can be worked out in some detail. In many instances, the entire game can be simulated using paper units and a grid map, with each player taking alternating turns. Simulation games such as Maxis' *SimCity* (1989) and Take-Two Interactive's *Mall Tycoon* (2002) can easily be simulated as paper prototypes, as can strategy games such as *Sid Meier's Civilization* (1991) and Strategic Studies' *Warlords Battlecry* (2000), although modeling such large-scale games can result in complicated and difficult to make paper prototypes. Figure 18.1 shows how a paper map (created by this book's author) might have been created for *Mall Tycoon*. Figure 18.2 shows one of the actual interface screens from the game.

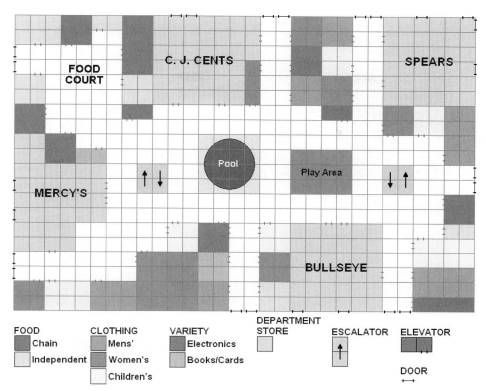

FIGURE 18.1 Paper map created by the author to show how a designer can create a paper prototype of a shopping mall interior similar to one in *Mall Tycoon.* The square grid is created in Microsoft Paint and can be filled in with the appropriate information and printed for testing.

Action games are more difficult to prototype using paper or cardboard because the movement and combat occur simultaneously. Imposing a turn-based structure (where players take turns moving objects on the playfield one at a time) on such an action game can be problematic because of scaling issues. Units often move at vastly different rates, and the weapons employed might fire at different rates. Moreover, if the game is 3D, it is difficult to create a paper version of a multistory level that won't collapse under its own weight. What can be designed on a paper grid are the game levels; this can help the designer decide where events will take place on the playfield. Still, when the 3D model is finally constructed and incorporated into the game, the designer might be disappointed with the results because what looks right on flat paper might not translate well into a 3D environment. In this case, the designer might find it worthwhile to use storyboards (discussed later in this chapter) to plan a level instead.

Puzzle games can sometimes be worked out directly as paper prototypes, depending on the subject matter. A designer might also find it helpful to use objects from other board and paper games such as dice, playing cards, dominoes,

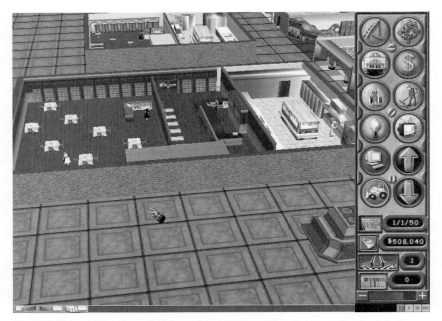

FIGURE 18.2 Screenshot from Take-Two Interactive's *Mall Tycoon* showing the shopping mall interior. Notice how the stores and hallways appear to be on a square grid, as shown in the floor pattern of the hallway.

chess pieces, mah-jongg tiles, and so on as a source of inspiration. As with action games, puzzle games that are dynamic (*Tetris,* for example), cannot be easily prototyped on paper. However, a ***static game***—that is, one that does not have a lot of dynamic, ongoing movement of play objects—can easily be prototyped on paper for early testing.

Sports games, vehicle games, and other games that represent real-world competition can be prototyped, but because the rules are well-known and established, there is little reason to do so. However, the designer might want to create storyboards and flowcharts for such games to help visualize the overarching competition, trading, or other play mechanics of the game.

FYI *Squares versus Hexagons*

There is a problem when using a square grid to control movement of objects in a game. To keep movement across the board consistent, each unit is given a movement rate based on how quickly it can move from space to space. Assuming a movement value of 1 between the

▶▶ CONTINUED ON NEXT PAGE

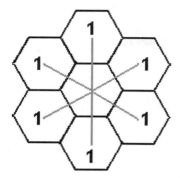

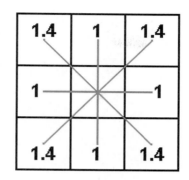

Hexagonal Grid   **Square Grid**

FIGURE 18.3 The movement value using a square grid varies compared to the constant value of a hexagonal grid.

centers of adjacent squares, it costs a unit 1 movement point to move horizontally or vertically from one square into the next. Moving diagonally into an adjacent square costs approximately 1.4 (the square root of 2). Thus, the cost to move into any adjacent square is not the same (Figure 18.3) and might lead to inconsistencies that players notice. Therefore, many military simulations use a hexagonal grid instead to regulate movement. The cost to move into any adjacent space on a hexagonal grid is 1 movement point (ignoring terrain effects), and therefore, objects moving across a map in any direction will always travel at the same rate.

Storyboard and Flowchart Prototypes

Another approach to creating a paper prototype is to use storyboards to help the team visualize what is happening at certain points in the game. In addition, the designer might find it useful to create a flowchart that shows how the disparate elements fit together as a whole. Flowcharts and storyboards complement each other as design tools and can help nail down the details of a game that is otherwise difficult to model.

Storyboards are useful in games with lots of action such as first-person shooters, platform games, racing games, flight games, and so on. Each *storyboard* shows one visual representation of the game in action. Arrows can be used to demonstrate the flow of the action (Figure 18.4). Thus, when designing a race track, especially one that contains unusual environments or terrain features that affect movement, storyboards can pinpoint the major visual and

FIGURE 18.4 Nolan Worthington created this storyboard of an action scene from Atari Interactive's *Pac-Man: Adventures in Time* (2000). Note the use of arrows to indicate the flow of action.

gameplay elements of the track. In addition, the art and design teams can add their comments to the storyboard to help make the game world come alive; for example, adding their notes about the music, sound effects, special visual effects, dialogue, and so on.

When creating storyboards, the designer can also create a flowchart of the game's action to show the team how everything ties together. A *flowchart* is a simple diagram that illustrates an activity step-by-step using a few simple symbols (Figure 18.5). As described in Chapter 10, "The Game Design Document," a flowchart is often included in the GDD to walk the reader through the menu system, and it is also useful in showing how the story in a game is structured. The designer can list the conditions that players must meet at each major decision point before the action moves on to the next section of the game. When used in conjunction with storyboards, the flowchart is a powerful tool that helps the designer walk the team (or management) through the structure of a complex game.

A good use of flowchart prototyping is for designing adventure games. Adventure games don't necessarily need prototypes created on grids, but the designer might still want to work out the details of the plot and puzzle designs on paper. Because adventure games usually have a number of control puzzles or gating puzzles that block forward progress until the player completes one or more tasks, flowcharting is a good way to help the designer visualize the game flow. Another way to work out these details is to use index cards and a pin board. Each major location is put on a large index card and pinned to the board. Puzzle items and characters can be put on smaller cards or even on

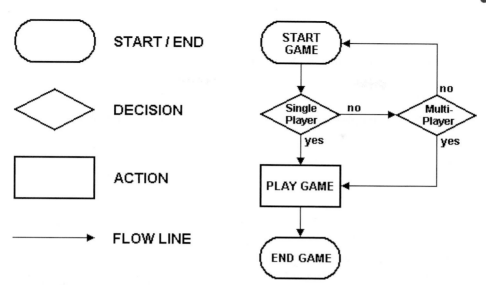

FIGURE 18.5 A few of the common flowchart symbols and how they can be used to create a flowchart, in this case illustrating the player's decision to play the game alone or with other players.

cards cut in half. Using a system of color-coded stripes along the top of the cards to differentiate one category from another is helpful. The designer can pin the small cards on the large cards and easily move them around as the story is worked out rather than drawing a new flowchart each time the design is changed.

Interactive Prototype

An *interactive prototype* (also called a *test bed model*) is created either at the end of the technical review phase or shortly thereafter as a final proof of concept. Although it is fundamentally a tool for the designers to test their design assumptions using a simple model of the main gameplay elements, it is also useful to the art and programming teams. The artists can use it to get a sense of scale for objects appearing on the playfield, and the programmers can get insights into how the game engine should be built. Additionally, the interactive prototype is usually used to demonstrate the gameplay to the corporate stakeholders who are not involved in the daily development of the project including company presidents, the publisher, and the marketing and sales teams.

The first iteration of the interactive prototype can be created using a commercially available program such as Macromedia's Director, which is a multimedia software program that can be used to create simple interactive game environments. This is a cost-effective solution because the programming team doesn't have to make any special version of the engine at an early stage, and the design team can use a program that they are familiar with and is easy to use.

This first type of prototype is helpful in resolving such issues as:

■ The relative sizes of characters, objects, levels

■ Basic gameplay, such as solving puzzles or collecting objects or play coupons

■ Layout of the HUD

■ Menus and transitions

■ Cut-scene or story sequences

■ Inventory screen layout

■ Secondary game screens, such as buying and selling of objects, modifying vehicles, character selection or equipping screens, and so on

■ Interactive dialogue and multiple storylines and branching

■ Basic AI response (usually as a simulation of the planned game response)

This kind of prototype is not useful for:

■ Testing complex gameplay mechanics, such as in an RTS

■ Developing input solutions, such as jump distance or height (though it can provide information for the designer)

■ Complicated interactions

Depending on the gameplay mechanics, a simple commercially available prototyping tool such as Director might not be able to model the gameplay elements as desired, so the team should schedule time to create a fully functional interactive prototype that can be used to test the gameplay as well as to demonstrate some of the game's technical issues. This second interactive prototype, the fully functional interactive prototype, is not a final version of the game. In this instance, it is focused merely on demonstrating gameplay. As such, it can be cobbled together from existing assets rather than having to be built from scratch. Art from other projects can be used; the code modules can be lifted from other company-created applications; and existing game databases can be modified to suit the new design applications.

Although the prototype coding doesn't have to be polished or elegant, it must support the needs of the designers. One programmer can be assigned to help the design staff in case the code needs to be reworked to provide the needed functionality. When the prototype is working, the design staff can play with values to see if everything works as they assumed. The designers should be able to easily make changes to the game database as well as to the values within the prototype. Moving the location of enemies or puzzles should be easy for a nontechnical designer. Ideally, other development teams on the project should test the game, not only to get feedback about gameplay but also to ensure that everyone working on the game gets a chance to see what they will be building. Adding some placeholder music, sound effects, and voiceovers can help to round out the play experience for testers.

This second form of interactive prototype is ideal for:

- Verifying movement and combat

- Testing character interactions

- Checking on the difficulty or ease in-game puzzles

- Playing with object manipulation

- Testing the placement of HUD objects on the screen to see what arrangement is most useful to players

- Verifying scripting language ease for the designers

The interactive prototype should in no way be considered a final product. It is a tool for the design staff to make sure their basic concept works in a computer environment and that the gameplay and the database can perform as envisioned. It helps identify possible problems in the design, art, and even code. It does not contain any of the final code—as a matter of fact, the code used in the prototype should be tossed and rewritten from scratch. The artwork is not final. The playfield design is probably not final. The music, sound effects, and voiceovers are not final. Nor does the prototype contain the full menu system. Although the team might demonstrate the prototype at a technical review to show that the game concept does work as described in the GDD, they should never give it to management or to magazine editors or other outsiders who might assume the prototype is the final product.

> **Caution**
>
> **A Prototype Is *Not* a Demo**
>
> Producers should be wary of using this prototype too much for demonstrations to management because the management team might misconstrue it as representing the current game status and demand copies to show off to outsiders. This should be avoided at all costs.

Fly-Through Prototype

The last type of prototype is a *fly-through* of a level, which is almost purely a marketing tool. This prototype uses finished artwork and audio to show a complete level as it will appear in the game. Fly-through is an appropriate description for this prototype; it is often just a short noninteractive movie in which a camera pans through a level or follows the main character as she performs a number of game actions. However, the fly-through can also be interactive, letting a player explore a level and experiment with the game activities. In both cases, the objective is to let the audience view some of the important characters, see what a level will look like, and play around with some of the gameplay elements.

A fly-through serves two purposes. First, an independent developer might want to create such a prototype to show to publishers as part of contract negotiations. Creating the fly-through shows the publisher that the product is compelling and that the team can pull off the project successfully. Indeed, many publishers now demand a working prototype of a level before signing up a developer. This version is usually interactive so the publisher can play around with it to find what works and what doesn't before committing to the contract. Moreover, the publisher requests this prototype to demonstrate the skill of the programming team, so the interactive version should be made by the team and should not use any commercially available products that will not also be used in the final game.

The second purpose of a fly-through is as a promotional piece the marketing department can show to retailers and customers to pique interest in the product. This version is usually noninteractive and is often created as a fully rendered movie in 3ds Max, Autodesk Maya, or another 3D graphics program. The marketing fly-through might be deceptive because the artwork in the short movie is likely to be of higher quality than what will appear in the actual game. The whole idea is to "sell the sizzle" and make the customers want to buy the final version because the product is so visually appealing and exciting. Ideally, this version is complete enough to be shown on TV or on Web sites—depending on the status of the prototype and overall game, of course.

In either case, it is important to remember that the fly-through is also a prototype that likely will not appear in the final release. The pacing of the fly-through is likely to be more hyperactive than the final product, and it might show off characters and objects that are scattered throughout the real game. At best, some of the level art and character models can be salvaged to use in the game, but the gameplay and actual code modules will be reworked before the final product is shipped.

Designing Playfields

Most games include multiple *playfields* (also called *maps* or *levels*) that can encompass a number of different environments. Some playfields might be completely open and not restrict the player's movement, in which case, they are little more than background art (Figure 18.6). Other playfields are more constricted and force the players to make choices relevant to gameplay. Most games restrict the player's movement across the playfield somehow either by incorporating dangerous or impassable terrain features or by keeping the player inside restricted areas (buildings, tunnels, and so on), possibly until some puzzle or task is successfully completed. In all these cases, someone on the team has to build the playfields using either a 2D map editor or a 3D level editor.

FIGURE 18.6 In Small Rocket's *Ultra Assault* (2003), the background is a painting over which the plane flies. The plane does not interact with the background as it moves across the map.

FYI Levels

For the purposes of this book, the term **level** refers to each distinct gameplay area within a game. For most games, the concept of a level is obvious; for example, a level in a side-scrolling action game is well-defined with start and end points. For other games, this concept might not seem so obvious. A real-time strategy (RTS) game, for example, has missions that correspond to the level concept. An FPS game frequently takes place in areas or maps that are loaded in and out of memory when the player crosses entry and exit thresholds. Adventure and storytelling games have major plot points that move the player to a new location or new situation and are not revealed to her until she solves some puzzle or trigger. Sports games are set within specific and well-defined sporting venues—arenas, stadiums, and ball fields—and each completed event, match, or game can be considered a level. RPGs, MUDs, and many online multiplayer games are more

CONTINUED ON NEXT PAGE

>> CONTINUED

open-ended and have less sense of individual levels, although they usually have different maps that appear when the player crosses thresholds or enters new sites within a location (for example, when entering a city).

The design team is responsible for what happens on the maps in the game and often builds them if they have the knowledge and skill to use the editor. In most current computer and video games, levels are built using either a 3D graphics program such as 3ds Max or Maya or a commercially available level editor such as Valve's Hammer Editor (previously called WorldCraft). The person building the level must have an artist's eye and be proficient in using such complicated tools. In some companies, the design staff actually builds the levels, whereas in other companies, an artist builds the level in combination with a designer. Many companies now have staff positions for level designers, who are proficient with 3D graphics tools and understand game design.

The Art of Level Design

There is an art to building an interesting level, whether it is in a two- or three-dimensional game. Level designers need an appreciation of architecture, not only for how buildings are constructed mechanically but also for how they reflect the society that creates them. They also have to understand ecosystems, whether they are realistic or fantastic, and how those systems interact within the game world. They must have a good grasp of topography so the outdoor scenes will look genuine.

To establish the visual look of a world or level, the art style of the game's various locations has to be a consistent. There are likely to be areas where architecture, the population, and even artistic styles differ from one another, just as an urban cityscape differs from a rural landscape. However, the contrast in styles throughout the game world should not be so glaring that players lose their sense of immersion. Players become accustomed to the art style after hours of play and might not even give it a second thought until they run into something bizarre or jarring that interrupts their reverie. The player should not start questioning why the designer decided to include a tanning salon in a medieval castle or why a desert world would have so many ice-crystal trees. There has to be a "rightness" about the look throughout the entire world. The visual look of a world extends beyond the objects and art style of those objects, buildings, costumes, hairstyles, or paintings. The way the world is lit and the ambient noises of the environment do much to make it seem alive and right. If the game is set in a desert world, the lighting should be sharp and hard-edged, and the winds should blow the sand around softly (or violently in a windstorm). If it is set in a spooky old mansion, the lights should be subdued with the unlit areas so dark that the shadows feel threatening, and the floorboards should creak as the player moves through the house. If everything is lit with flat, shadowless lighting and the audio track is silent, the world just does not feel right, and players might have difficulty suspending their disbelief and accepting the world as real.

The art director, along with the level designer, are normally responsible for the lighting aspects of level design. Ideally, they should have a tool powerful enough to place, move, and modify the light sources within any area. Sound effects, of course, are the realm of the sound engineer, but the game and level designers need to create complete lists of the effects and ambient noises they would like to include in the game. Ideally, the tool used to create a level enables the designer to include triggers for effects (sound effects, particle effects, fog or other environmental effects, and so on) within the level itself.

The Architecture of Level Design

Of course, a level must be functional as well as decorative, and that is as much a part of the art of level design as the visual and aural elements. This functionality encompasses the gameplay of the level, including the open areas, the gateways, the enemy placement or spawn points, and the position of power-ups or rewards. One might view a level as a chapter of a novel. In other words, it is part of the whole but still has its own story to tell. Players start at the beginning—the *entry point*—and go through a series of incidents such as encounters, puzzles, and combat before finally leaving through an exit. The player usually has a clear goal, such as finding a key that unlocks the door to the next area or clearing an area of enemies.

The following is one approach that a designer might take when initially laying out a level design:

1. Players start off in a safe area, unthreatened by any enemies.

2. They next begin moving around and exploring the level, perhaps encountering some of the easier enemies.

3. Somewhere during their progress through the level, they trigger an event and the action heats up.

4. After an area of intense action, they reach an area of relative safety, where they can relax, or they pass a checkpoint where they will reappear if their character dies.

5. This cycle repeats until players achieve the ultimate goal of the level and can exit to the next level.

Other gameplay elements the designer should consider when creating a level include the following:

- Creating ambushes where enemies lie in wait or having an enemy, especially a boss, waiting in the open and ready to confront the players

- Placing items to find along the way such as weapons, armor, ammo, heal potions, and so on

- Setting up a puzzle or two to resolve before players can leave the level

To mix things up, the designer might occasionally start players in the thick of battle or caught up in an emergency; for example, in a ship sinking with only minutes left to find an exit. Mixing up the tempo in a game is a good idea, but threatening players at the start of a level is a technique that should be practiced sparingly. Players, especially beginning ones, appreciate the chance to explore new environments in safety until they are ready to get things rolling.

A level can be either open-ended or linear. An ***open-ended*** layout means the player can go almost anywhere on the level without restriction. In a role-playing game, for example, a town might be open-ended, allowing the player to talk to any NPC and visit any of the shops or buildings whenever she wants in any order she wants. Certain areas might be off-limits until the player triggers some event, but generally, the player can explore anywhere.

If there are many places that the player can't get to, then the level starts feeling ***linear***. Sometimes levels are very restrictive, and players might be forced to resolve some plot point in one place to open the next place, where another plot point has to be resolved before moving on. The only places the players can visit freely are those they have already visited, and there is seldom anything new to find if the designer doesn't build in additional action or narrative to occur after the initial plot elements have all been exhausted. This kind of layout is very linear and can irritate players after a while.

Rather than exhaust the game's plot level by level in a linear fashion, the designer might want to break things up. One approach is to use open-ended levels as gateways to linear areas. That is, players can explore an open-ended level and then head off to an area that is linear in layout. The entrances to the linear areas can be shut until certain story conditions are met. This method can give players some sense of freedom that is otherwise lacking in a strictly linear approach to level layout.

Another approach is to tell only part of the story on a level and then move the players to another part of the game world that they must explore before they can return to explore a new section of the original level. If conditions on the original level have changed in the meantime, the player will be interested in exploring areas he previously visited to discover what has happened. This approach adds interest to those areas the player has already explored.

It is important to keep players interested enough in the game to keep them pushing onward. If they find themselves trekking over ground they've already visited where nothing has changed, they get bored. Likewise, if they feel they are being led around the world with no chance to explore on their own, they might resent the restrictions placed on them. In either case, the players will likely lose interest in the game world and might very well move on to another game.

Caution

Repeat Play within Levels

The level designer's biggest (and most common) error is to not consider what happens when players return to areas they have already visited. If the player must retrace her path through a cleared area and there is nothing to do along the way, she will be bored. Adding a shortcut or having additional enemies pop out of ambush makes the return trip more interesting.

The Science of Level Design

Designing a game level is as much a science as it is an art. If the finished level does not work within the limitations of the game engine, the designers and artists will have wasted their time. The designer might want to include huge landscapes and vast open areas, but the technical limitations of the level editor, the game engine, or even the target game platform can frustrate this desire. Designers might be waiting for technology to catch up with their vision, but they need to know what the current game technology is capable of and either push for improvements or work within those constraints.

When creating a 2D game, the designer has to understand the restrictions of the map editor and of the game engine. Specific issues in 2D design include the following:

- The file format of the art
- Whether the game is tile based
- The overall size of a level map
- How big the characters are relative to the level objects
- How high or far the characters can jump or perform other actions
- How many sprites or tiles can be displayed at one time on screen (this is particularly important in some consoles and handheld devices)
- The memory limitations on the number of AI objects that can operate at one time
- The length of time the player needs to complete a level
- Where to include checkpoints or save points

If the designer does not understand these restrictions, she might want to include more terrain features for a specific level than the map editor allows or ask the artists to make the level background one gigantic picture, only to find that the art file takes too long to load into memory. Working with a 2D map editor is a great way for a novice designer to learn the limitations of level building. A number of such editors are included with published games. Figure 18.7 shows the StarEdit map editor that is part of Blizzard Entertainment's *StarCraft* (1998).

As mentioned in Chapter 13, "Visualizing the Game," all art in a 3D game is based on drawing lines and creating polygons, usually triangles. A 3D level designer must be aware of restrictions on the number of polygons that can appear on the screen at any one time because having to render too many polygons can bog down the frame rate to the point where the game is unplayable. If the designer creates a level that is too large and detailed, it will have to be broken up into several sections or even be redesigned completely. If the game

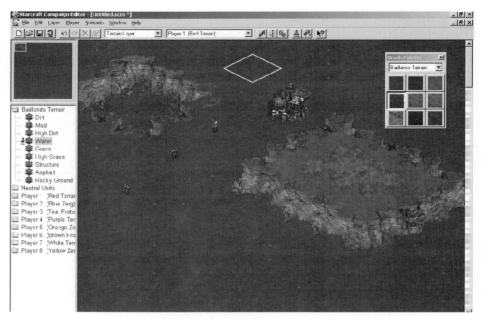

FIGURE 18.7 The StarEdit campaign/map editor that ships as part of Blizzard's *StarCraft* is very easy for a novice designer to use to create new levels.

engine uses a portal system (see Chapter 12, "Coding the Game"), the level designers should know the preferred maximum size of a sector. If a sector is designed too large, the level designer can work with the designer who thought up the level to find workarounds.

FYI *Loading Data During Play*

Streaming-loading is a method that programmers can use to load new information into a game as the player is actually playing in an effort to bypass the entire "loading screen" scenario. It is based on the designer and programmer identifying transition areas that lead into a new area. There is usually less gameplay or player interaction in these areas, so while the player traverses it, the game engine can concentrate on preloading new data and removing old data that the player will not use any more.

An example of this is Rockstar Games' *Grand Theft Auto: Vice City* (2003). As the player approaches a new city, she crosses a long

▶▶ CONTINUED ON NEXT PAGE

▶▶ CONTINUED

bridge. During this crossing, the game unloads the art and code for the level that was just completed and loads the next area. The coders also took the time to devise a means to slow the player down if the loading isn't fast enough: A "Welcome to. . ." sign appears and stays on the screen while the game finishes loading the new data.

18

Designers should also aware of other technical restrictions. For example, a level designer should know if the game renderer has limitations in terms of lighting. The senior designer might have dreams of a cityscape that is harshly lit by a large number of lights, each casting multiple shadows of varying depth and density. But if the game engine uses projectors to cast shadows instead of shadow volumes, the desired visual effect might not be available, and the level might be compromised by the limitations of the engine, which would require the engine to be redesigned.

There is also the matter of how the textures are applied and whether the engine supports MIP-mapping or multitexturing. The game engine's ability to create hills, valleys, and mountains also affects the design. Likewise, if the designer wants the game to have realistic wave action that moves boats in the water as well as wind effects that are highly refined, the game engine might have to be changed to accommodate these game- and level-design needs. In the long run, the more familiar the designers are with how the rendering engine works, the better they can design levels within its technical constraints.

It is important to realize, of course, that design can drive changes in the technology of the game, so designers should be aware not only of what the engine can do but also of what the programmers might be able to coax it to do. However, the tradeoffs of time, money, and impact to the gameplay need to be considered at this point, and certain desired game features might be better left for a sequel.

By using data-driven coding and scripting languages, designers can make quick changes to the game without requiring a programmer or needing to recompile the entire game. They will probably want to write scripts to trigger events in the game, so they should understand how the scripting language works. No debugging tools might be available for the scripting language, so the designers might wind up learning its limitations by being forced to go step-by-step through each line in a script to find out what is causing a problem. Ideally, the programmers who create the scripting language will include a tool that allows information to be written to log files during play or that outputs text to the screen to help in the debugging process. There can also be places where the scripting language doesn't work out as hoped, especially if a number of variables must be checked before an event is triggered. Therefore, complex scripting might be better handled by the programmers who are accustomed to working with real code.

The technical limitations of the game engine should not keep the design staff from trying to come up with the most ingenious levels ever seen in a game; however, the limitations are present and the lead programmer must occasionally bring the design staff down to earth and explain why certain things cannot be done. Still, as the poet Robert Browning wrote, "Ah, a man's reach should exceed his grasp, Or what's a heaven for?" Designers should be allowed to dream their wildest dreams, and the programmers should do their best to help mold those dreams into something that can be created within the constraints of the budget and schedule.

Designing a Level

Before starting to build a level, the designer should consider creating a checklist of features that need to be included. A sample checklist could include the following:

- The player's starting position relative to where all enemies start in the game

- The location of the exit point or the win condition for the level

- The enemies or opponents within the level

- What items the player must have to defeat particular enemies on the level and where they should be placed

- How far the player can progress in one level if he needs to find an important item in a previous level, as well as the possibility of finding a replacement item

- What the players earn or find by defeating various enemies on the level

- The locations of checkpoints

- The locations of health/recuperation points

- The locations of hidden caches or power-ups that are not necessarily required to complete the level

- The physical dexterity required of a player to complete the level (for example, the ability to double-jump, use combo attacks, balance on a wire, and so on)

- The skills the player must have to defeat the boss of the level and how they will be learned or acquired

If the game has a story arc, the designer should know how the levels fit together in terms of revealing plot elements as well as each one's approximate difficulty level (levels should become more difficult over time). If there is no story, the designer might still want to approach a level as a self-contained story.

During the preproduction phase, the design staff should work through the overall layout of each level, even if they expect to make significant changes after learning the capabilities of map/level editor and game engine. As discussed previously in this chapter, the designers should make paper prototypes or storyboards for each level, as appropriate for the game style, to plan the general structure per level, where items will be placed, and where encounters will be triggered.

Entrances and Exits   One of the first things to consider when designing a level is the number of entrances and exits. If the level is open-ended, there can be any number of entrances and exits to other maps or levels, but the designer should note the connections between levels carefully as well as the direction in which the player is facing. Unless there is a need for them (say, for an ambush at some point in the game), dead ends and culs-de-sac should be avoided if they force players to retrace their steps to get out. Sometimes the story demands that a level change significantly between visits—for example, if raiders have destroyed a town—and the designer should make sure that the layouts for both versions are exactly the same. Players will notice even small discrepancies.

If the level is linear, it might have only a single entrance and exit, and the exit won't open until the player finds a certain item or triggers the right condition. It is a good idea to allow the players to find the exit(s) during their exploration of the level, even if they cannot leave until they achieve the required task. Hidden exits should be used sparingly (except those leading to secret caches) because players will get frustrated if they can't find the exit. Also, it is a good idea to make the exit separate from the entrance so players never feel they are simply doubling back on their own tracks.

The designer should create a path through the level that keeps the player moving forward and limits the amount of backtracking. The path does not have to stay only on the one level. In a 3D game, the designer can make use of the third dimension (depth) by creating paths through a multitiered area using elevators, stairs, holes in the ground, ladders, and so on to transport the player to different heights that can overlap one another. In a 2D (or 3D) level, the designer can have the player explore one area of a level, go off to visit another level(s) and return later to explore the rest of the first level when some condition has been triggered. The most important thing is to minimize backtracking unless additional gameplay is included to make the area feel new to the player.

In racing games, however, the player goes around a given track repeatedly, so designers will often add graphic elements to the track to help the player remember the layout. Usually, these graphic flourishes do not affect gameplay and are often referred to as eye candy.

Hidden sections of the map can be fun to design but often turn out to be frustrating to players (at least until someone posts a walk-through on the Internet). Invisible doorways are the most maddening because players have to bump into every wall in the level to find them. This method adds to the overall time needed to finish the game but rarely adds to the enjoyment.

Caution

Give Some Feedback

The player should receive feedback of some kind if the item is not immediately useful; for example, if the doors to the hidden area are color-coded with matching keys, players will know that a red key is unlikely to open a nearby purple door.

One solution for the designer is to create the hidden section but to have a locked entrance in plain sight. Now the player must find a key or other trigger device to enter the cache, which adds more gameplay to the challenge. Sometimes the opening device is an object the player finds on the level or receives as a reward for solving a puzzle or defeating an enemy; at other times, a physical device (for example, an electronic eye) triggers the door to open and the player has to dash back to get through before it closes again. This latter approach can prove frustrating if the hidden area contains lots of goodies and the player repeatedly has to trigger the door and dash to get inside. It is a good idea to place the triggering item somewhere near the hidden area or along the path to the next hidden area so players associate one with the other. In later levels, of course, after introducing this device, the designer can add to the challenge by moving the trigger and door farther apart.

One way to alert players to a hidden area is through the use of a radar screen or overlay map that displays the player's path and known areas. A designer can let the player explore everywhere around the room except the area where the hidden cache is. An attentive player will notice that one area remains blank and hidden, thus piquing her interest to find a way in. Needless to say, if an area looks like it has something hidden in it, it actually should have something hidden it.

Distribution of Objects and Encounters The designer should also determine what objects are to be found, so they can be distributed across the level as the pace of the game demands. These objects include encounters, battles, puzzles, and collectables (power-ups, inventory items, ammo, weaponry, and so on). The objects do not have to perfectly distributed, but there should be enough of them to keep players from getting bored while walking around an empty playfield. It is odd, of course, to find things strewn around the level as though the inhabitants were thoughtless and careless of their valuables. Breakable crates are always a favorite place to store objects, as are cupboards, chests, closets, and so on. If the designer wants a story to maintain some semblance of reality, he might want to put items where they would logically be found; otherwise, if the fiction is just window dressing, the objects can appear wherever they are needed, with no reason for their placement.

Setting up encounters, especially combats, can be tricky. If there are too many enemies, players might feel picked upon; if there are too few, they might grow bored. An ambush can startle players and force them to react quickly. They usually enjoy the burst of adrenaline at being thrown into combat unexpectedly. Otherwise, if a particularly difficult fight is around the corner, the player should get some hint of what is to come (as well as a chance to save the game before the encounter).

One problem in many FPS games is that the number of enemy encounters is restricted by the size of the level and the number of models that must be loaded into memory. If the load takes too long, players get bored and irritable. The designers might be forced to cut back the number of enemy types on a level in order to speed up load time, thus making all the combats pretty much the same. Valve's *Half-Life* found a way around this problem by making each level small so the reload time was minimal. Even though each level had only a few enemy types, the levels' small size made players feel they were encountering many more enemies because they moved through the game world so quickly.

IN THE TRENCHES: Experiential Density

In his article "The Cabal: Valve's Design Process for Creating Half-Life" (**www.gamasutra.com**), Senior Software Development Engineer Ken Birdwell wrote about prototyping a level of the game early in development:

"The first theory we came up with was the theory of "experiential density"—the amount of "things" that happen to and are done by the player per unit of time and area of a map. Our goal was that, once active, the player never had to wait too long before the next stimulus, be it monster, special effect, plot point, action sequence, and so on. Since we couldn't really bring all these experiences to the player (a relentless series of them would just get tedious), all content is distance based, not time based, and no activities are started outside the player's control. If the players are in the mood for more action, all they need to do is move forward and within a few seconds something will happen."

This is a great summary of how best to make a game level fun and interesting.

Testing the Level   After the level has been built, it needs to be tested. Creating a level is a process of iteration as the designers set up the triggers for events, test them, make changes, test them again, make more changes, and so on. It is important to get new players to look at the revised levels. If the production team or a small group of playtesters tests the levels repeatedly, the designers will start to hear that the levels are too easy and should be made more difficult. Eventually, tweaking the levels to make them harder for experienced players will make them too hard for new players, who will quickly give up. It takes time and lots of feedback from different players to find the right balance for a level.

Map and Level Editors

The software applications used to build playfields are called map editors and level editors. The terms are often used interchangeably, but for purposes of this book, a *map editor* is a program used to create two-dimensional maps (and 2–1/2D isometric maps) for a game, whereas a *level editor* is a program used to create 3D maps. Map editors are usually proprietary tools created by the programmers for the designers to use to build the maps in the game, whereas level editors can either be proprietary tools created by a company (such as Valve's Hammer Editor) or commercially available graphics programs (such as 3ds Max and Maya) for building three-dimensional maps.

Level editors are much more complex to use than map editors because creating playfields in three dimensions is much more involved than building flat, 2D maps. Many map editors are readily usable for the design staff, and they might ship with the product because the general public also finds them relatively easy to use. Most level editors, on the other hand, require some training in a 3D graphics program and, therefore, usually do not ship with the final product (although they might be available by download from the developer or other Web site).

2D Map Editors   As discussed in Chapter 13, "Visualizing the Game," attempting to create one large bitmap for a playfield can create problems with memory and make it difficult to make changes. Therefore, rather than building one large map per game level, the production team generally uses a map editor to build the playfields. The major terrain features (lakes, mountains, buildings, and so on) are turned into a set of square tiles that can be used to build the map one square at a time. This approach might sound more time-intensive than simply painting a playfield, but it has several practical advantages:

- The same tile set can be used to create a number of maps with different layouts.

- If the tool is well-designed, a playfield can be built in a few hours.

- Making changes to the layout of a map requires the rearrangement of a few tiles and can be done in minutes rather than in the hours or days needed for repainting the map.

- Art changes to the tile set can radically change the look of a map without having to change the map itself; for example, a winter tile set with familiar features covered with snow can create a new level for when the hero returns to a village after several months away on adventure.

- Tile sets are relatively smaller, so the artwork for the maps can be loaded into memory more quickly.

The tile sets are created in an art program such as Adobe Illustrator or Photoshop and then divided into squares. Generally, the square tiles are 16×16, 32×32, or 64×64 pixels (they are grouped in powers of 2 for faster manipulation by the program as well as to comply with DirectX requirements). Terrain features do not have to fill the entire square. One fill color can be made transparent to let whatever is under that part of the square show through. Large terrain features might consist of a number of tiles. A lake, for example, often will consist of 9 tiles: 1 for the center, 4 for the edges (north, south, east, west), and 4 for corners (northeast, northwest, southeast, southwest). The artist might also create duplicates of each tile in a set so that the feature does not look the same every time it appears on a map.

The tiles might also be made to appear animated by having the game engine simply alternate the values of several colors on a tile; for example, a lake can appear to shimmer when several colors of blue alternate their values. This technique of palette shifting is simple for the programmer, but it forces the artists to limit colors in the tile set. For example, if the same blue is used in, say, a road, the road will also change color as the lake waters cycle through different colors.

When a tile set is loaded by the editor, it is usually displayed to one side of the map so the designer can select a tile and place it as though it was a piece of an actual map (Figure 18.8). A critical feature for 2D map editors (as well as 3D level editors) is a *snap-to-grid*. Especially in 2D maps, it's critical that tiles line up in exact in rows and columns with no space between them. Of course, the programmers should allow the designers to turn this function on or off as desired.

If the map editor creates overhead maps of a playfield, there is often a *fill* feature that generates an entire background by placing background tiles randomly on all spaces of the map. Using several different background tiles for filler avoids the problem of seeing a wavy moiré pattern as the player scrolls across the map (this pattern is seen when only one background tile is used).

After the background is generated, the map editor usually contains groups of tile sets to create large terrain features (lakes, mountains, and so on) that can be placed on the map as a group or drawn tile-by-tile. Tile sets might also be available for individual features (trees, rocks, ice pinnacles, and so on). If there

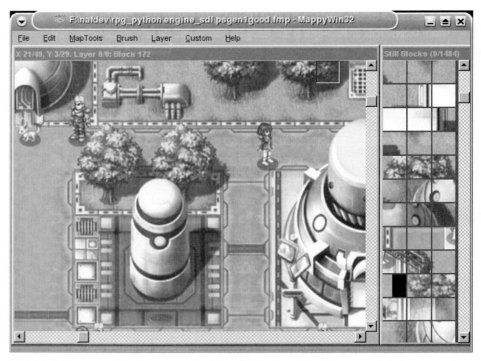

FIGURE 18.8 The map editor in the Iridium RPG, a toolkit for creating 2D RPG games. The tile set on the right is used to build the 2D map.

are multiple environments in the game, the major terrain features in each environment can use the shapes from other tile sets. For example, a grassland might include rivers and lakes while a desert might include dry gulches and dry washes. The artists can use the same shapes for the gulches as for the rivers and for the dry washes as for the lakes.

Another function that is useful to the designer is the ability to assign certain attributes to each tile. The programmers can set up the tile sets so that certain terrain features have permanent attributes on whichever map they appear. These attributes affect the movement ability of objects across the map and even their health. For example, a river tile in an RTS game can be made impassable, so that whenever an object moves adjacent to the river, it can no longer go forward unless there is a bridge to cross. A lava tile might not only bar movement but also cause damage if a character touches it. This terrain information is not saved with the level itself, but rather is stored with the tile information to make it easy for a designer to create more impassable rivers in other levels without having to reset that attribute.

If the game is a side-scroller, the terrain features in the map editor are viewed from the side, but the same principles of construction apply. For example, a temple might consist of a large roof supported by pillars, with one tile used to create a pillar of any height. Likewise, a tree trunk tile can be put together to create many trees of different heights. Walls in a side-scroller are generally impassible—that is, a character cannot walk through a cement wall. However, the character can probably walk behind a pillar. Thus, the attributes of the pillar and the wall tiles are preset and the designer can chose which tile to use for each instance of the game.

In a side-scrolling game, the programmers often set up the graphics rendering to give an illusion of depth (a technique called ***Z-buffering***). In this technique, the most distant feature might be the sky, which is created by repeating one tile or by using a color fill in an API such as DirectX. The next set of background tiles then overlaps the sky using a scale that makes their feature appear small because the object is so distant from the viewer (for example, faraway mountains or hills that appear hazy with the distance). The next set of tiles shows larger terrain features that create the immediate background against which the characters appear. Finally, a set of foreground tiles might appear over the characters to give the illusion that the characters are behind them.

The speed at which the different layers move also helps give an illusion of depth. the foreground tiles move by most quickly as the player scans across the screen; the middle tiles (and player character) move a bit slower; the distant features move very slowly; and finally, the sky does not move not at all. This effect is called ***parallax scrolling*** (it can also be used on overhead maps as well).

A complete map editor includes methods for the designer to set up trigger points; input enemy placements; hide or place power-ups, checkpoints, or other important game entities; and especially, to include the starting location of the player's character and the end point of the level. Ideally, the editor will also include access to a scripting language, so the designer or programmer can create scripted triggers or events without having to leave the editor and work in the game code. When a unit moves into a designated space, the corresponding event (combat, finding an object, meeting a character, switching maps) is triggered. Of course, players don't see this invisible layer while playing the game.

All of the information about the map or level is then saved into one or more files that the game engine loads when it is running to display the map and all objects. During production, this file is often a text file, though in shipped games it is usually encoded so players cannot easily modify the level without using the map editor. In fact, most shipped maps cannot be modified without serious hacking by a player. Game companies do this to maintain control of their intellectual property as well as to retain control of the gameplay that they have sold to the consumer.

However, many games now include map editors that allow players to create their own levels. Games that include map editors are Ubi Soft's *Warlord IV* (2003), Blizzard's *Warcraft III* (2002), Firaxis's *Alpha Centauri* (published by Electronic Arts in 1999), and Ensemble Studios' *Age of Mythology* (published by Microsoft in 2002; Figure 18.9). Many more map

FIGURE 18.9 The map editor for Ensemble Studios' *Age of Mythology* is simple to use and lets a player create a new level quickly. Compare this map editor with StarEdit in Figure 18.7.

editors are available as well. In general, these editors enable users to create their own levels or to create new levels based on an in-game level, but do not let them modify a level in the shipped version.

Level Editors

A 3D level editor is much more complex than a 2D map editor, and creating a level takes much longer. Although 3D level editors are similar in function to 2D map editors, they are complicated by the addition of 3D movement by the player in the game world. Not only does the level designer have to build the entire world, but she also has to texture it, animate things (flags, trees, and so on), and create scripts to trigger actions. The world must also be populated with enemies; lights must be placed; and special visual effects must be set up. In many ways, a level editor looks and acts like a commercial 3D graphics program, and most likely the models used in the level editor were probably created in one of these programs. Figure 18.10 shows Epic Games' Unreal Level Editor. Similar to 3ds Max, it has four viewports that show a model from the top, front, side, and in perspective (the one labeled "Dynamic Light"). As the artist or level designer builds a model, he can view what it looks like in all dimensions via these viewports.

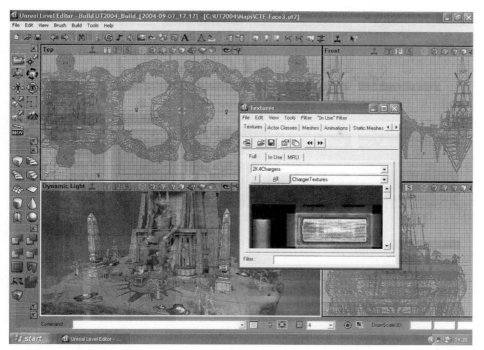

FIGURE 18.10 Epic Games' Unreal Level Editor uses the same four-window interface as graphics programs such as 3ds Max and Autodesk Maya.

A number of game developers use models imported directly from 3ds Max or Maya into the game and don't even bother with a level editor. But a level editor offers several advantages:

- Although it is more difficult to use than a 2D map editor, it is usually easier to use than 3ds Max or Maya and, therefore, someone with limited artistic or technical skills can create levels after a bit of coaching.

- The level editor might include a number of pregenerated models existing in the game world, so users don't have to create everything from scratch.

- If the level editor is made available to customers either as part of the product or through download over the Internet, users can create their own worlds (*mods*) and share them with others. Although the level editor might be too complex for most customers, those who do learn to use it can provide more play experiences for the game and help extend the shelf life of the product.

The first step in creating a level is shaping the geometry. The level designer can build the 3D geometry either by using the shaping tools to create a

Caution

Snap-to-Grid

As mentioned previously, a 3D level editor should have a snap-to-grid functionality similar to 2D map editors, so designers don't accidentally place stairs or boxes halfway inside walls.

static mesh or, if the editor allows, by selecting from a list of pregenerated primitives (cubes, cones, spheres, and perhaps a number of customized shapes such as staircases). The advantage of static meshes is that they speed the frame rate because the static mesh has to be rendered only once and then is stored in the video card's memory. Using the primitives might require the computer to check their intersections each time they are drawn to make sure they are being drawn correctly.

When the geometry is set, the level designer might want to play with the properties of the surfaces; for example, making a surface that is normally impassable passable so the player can walk through a waterfall. The designer then applies the correct textures to the surfaces. The surfaces often come bundled in packages that are drawn from different locations in the game, such as an alien planet surface, inside a temple, the corridor of a spaceship, and so on. The level editor automatically applies the correct textures to the appropriate surfaces and can often resize textures to fit areas of different sizes.

The next step might involve creating the lighting for the level. This function enables the designer to place individual lights throughout the level and move them around until he is happy with the result. The level designer might also include the ability to add ambient light from a distant source such as a sun. (The Unreal Level Editor includes a Sunlight actor to position the distant sun to light the world and cast shadows as the real sun would.)

The level editor might also enable the designer to add ambient sounds to the level in a way similar to adding the lights. It can have different sound packages for internal and external environments. The designer simply positions where sounds will be heard and how often they will be heard when moving across the level.

After the level is created, the designer will usually position objects (called *entities*) in it. The objects can include items such as weapons, ammo and health, enemies, allies, and the player's start position. The level editor generally includes an animation tool to enable the level designer to tie the animation of the 3D models to game events and see what they look like in-game. The artists can also use this tool to create the in-game animated sequences. The editor might even include a tool to sync character animations with conversation.

The level editor might also include a tool for creating the movement paths for the AI-controlled objects. The designer or artist can then either build the paths directly using invisible *splines* that the AI-controlled objects follow or by placing *nodes* to direct the objects along the splines' path as they move from one node to another. Using splines might limit the AI-controlled objects to following a repetitive path through the level, whereas using the node system allows objects to change movement routines based on the current situation (for example, if the player has been detected or if debris blocks a path).

FYI *Splines and Nodes*

In computer graphics, a **spline** is a smooth curve that connects two or more points. The term comes from the flexible metal or wood strip that was used in the days of mechanical drafting to create such curves. One type of spline is the **Bézier curve,** which is named after the French mathematician Pierre Bézier. It has two endpoints (called **anchor points**) and one or more center points (called **handles, nodes**, or **tangent points**) that define the shape of the curve. Each handle has two attached control points, which change the shape of the curve as they are moved (Figure 18.11).

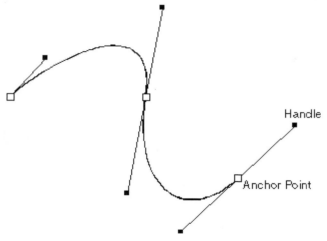

FIGURE 18.11 A Bézier curve (or spline) defined by the two endpoints and the central points, or nodes (with handles attached).

Many level editors use their own proprietary scripting languages to trigger events. As an option, they might allow a designer to use a language such as Lua or Python to build scripts (in which case the designer might need to work with a programmer to code the script correctly). Some scripting systems, such as Epic's UnrealKismet, have some interesting features such as the ability to lay out entire levels without having to touch the code, as well as the ability to tie simple behaviors together into a hierarchy of complex sequences.

To save time, the level editor should let the designer make changes to the game and immediately test them in-game without having to quit the editor and start the game. Another tool should keep track of the polygons in the level so that if the number gets too high, the designer can either split the model into several sectors and connect them with portals (assuming the game engine works this way) or determine where polygons can be removed.

Summary

Game level design is an iterative process. The designer starts with an idea that can be tested and refined through a series of paper and electronic prototypes. These prototypes not only enable the designer to study how the design works before committing to the creation of the assets for the final version but also help management understand what the design is about and might even become a promotional tool for the marketing department.

The iterative design process carries over into level design as well. The design staff's main task during the production phase is building enjoyable maps that are fun to explore and filled with activity. Rather than rushing in blindly and starting to build maps, the designers should plan what will happen on each map ahead of time using either a paper prototype or storyboards. Then each level is created in a 2D map editor or 3D level editor and tested repeatedly to make sure that the original idea for what would be fun turns out to be correct. Working out the details of a level ahead of time helps keep the project on schedule by limiting the number of iterations the team has to make to get everything right—and fun.

Test Your Skills

MULTIPLE CHOICE QUESTIONS

1. What is the purpose of a paper prototype?

   A. To demonstrate gameplay to marketing.

   B. To test gameplay ideas.

   C. To focus test the game with consumers.

   D. To determine the best location of the HUD objects.

2. How are RPGs best prototyped?

   A. Storyboards.

   B. Flow charts.

   C. Charts and grid paper.

   D. Cards and dice.

3. Which of the following statements applies to interactive prototypes made during preproduction?

   A. They should use the game engine.

   B. They should use a specialized engine made by the design team.

   C. They should use a commercially available engine.

   D. They should use HTML and be posted online.

4. RTS games should be

    A. Prototyped using paper to verify resource management, troop movement, and balancing.

    B. Prototyped using interactive storyboards to show story flow and plot.

    C. Tested only when the game engine is complete.

    D. Prototyped for enemy placement in the level.

5. Graphic adventures best benefit from prototyping using which of the following?

    A. An interactive model that can demonstrate the game flow.

    B. Flow charts and storyboards to show puzzle gateways and object interdependencies.

    C. Grid paper and charts to balance weights and experience.

    D. Cards and dice.

6. True or False: Puzzle games, such as *Tetris* or *Bejeweled,* will not benefit from prototyping.

    A. True.

    B. False.

7. Which of the following statements applies to prototypes that are submitted to publishers to demonstrate a development pitch?

    A. They should use an existing engine such as the Unreal Tournament Engine.

    B. They should demonstrate the game engine developed by the team.

    C. They should focus on the story.

    D. They should be a fly-through prototype with some interaction.

8. When is an interactive prototype ideal? (Select all that apply.)

    A. Helping work out the design of the HUD.

    B. Testing complex game mechanisms.

    C. Checking relative art sizes.

    D. Testing game ideas.

9. What are the aspects of making a level?

    A. Art, science, architecture.

    B. Art, music, dance.

    C. Architecture, design, structure.

    D. Organization, production, art.

18

10. What are some of the issues that a 3D level designer must consider? (Select all that apply.)

    A. Number of polygons on screen.

    B. Number of models to be loaded.

    C. Size and shape of the level.

    D. Loading time of the level.

11. Hidden areas in a level are

    A. A great way to deliberately frustrate the player.

    B. Good to use, but should be built as bonuses, not requirements.

    C. Difficult for playtesting because they are hidden.

    D. A good way to make the player explore every wall.

12. Because retracing your steps through an area already cleared can be boring, what should a good designer do? (Select all that apply.)

    A. Try not to require the player to retrace his steps.

    B. Always make the player find the key before locating the locked door.

    C. Respawn enemies so the player must duplicate the same battles.

    D. Change the enemies and NPCs to reflect other game states that have changed since the last time the player went through.

EXERCISES

Exercise 18.1: Beginning Paper Prototype

Using grid paper, draw a side view map for a side-scrolling game. First, create a character that is 2 grids tall, can jump 2 grids high, and can double jump 4 grids high. This character can run really fast. Make a marker to represent your character so that you can move it on the paper prototype. Assuming you're using a grid of 1/4" squares, your level map should fit on an 8.5 × 11" paper turned sideways (landscape mode). Start your character on the left side and make a level map where the exit is in the top right corner. Include enemies, objects, power-ups, mini-goals, checkpoints, and so on that you would like to see incorporated in your level.

Exercise 18.2: Analysis of Paper Prototype

List the gameplay mechanisms that were incorporated in the prototype you built for Exercise 12.1. List all physical dexterity in play (jumping, fighting, ducking, and so on) that you expect your game player to be able to perform in order to win the level. List all the game entities (power-ups, enemies, objects, checkpoints, and so on) that you included. List the game inventory that you expect the player–character to have (sword, gun, remote control, and so on). Given these lists, what do you assume the player will be able to do differently after she has completed your level?

Exercise 18.3: Advanced Paper Prototype

Using grid paper, four unique markers for play pieces, and dice, make a 10 × 10 grid square map of a top-down world with mountains, lakes, rivers, fields, and desert. To each marker, assign an attribute such as "can't swim" or "good climber" by filling in the following chart (you can replace the first two as you'd like):

Marker	Run?	Swim?	Climb?	Heat?	Cold?
"Swimmer"	Medium	Fast	Slow	Good	Bad
"Runner"	Fast	Slow	Medium	OK	OK

Given the game and the chart above, how would you use heat and cold in your game? From this chart and using your map, create some turn-based gameplay using the dice roll for the four characters. Where do they each start? What is their objective? How does someone win? If there is a conflict, how is it resolved?

Exercise 18.4: Modifying an Existing Card Game

Pick an existing card game such as *Magic: The Gathering, Pokemon, Munchkin,* or a basic deck of cards. Change some of the basic rules of the game. For example, instead of the player's selecting the attack in *Magic,* give the opponent the right to randomly select a card from the player's hand for herself. Or, in *Munchkin,* reverse the value of all strength modifiers so that a sword that would normally be +5 is now −5. If using a basic deck of cards, modify the game of hearts in some way, such as allowing the game to reverse order or letting the person currently playing the hand determine the next person to play.

- Play out the game you have selected for one complete game round (until someone wins).

- Make more modifications to the game so that it is even more different than the existing game.

Exercise 18.5: Modify an Existing Video Game

Select your favorite RPG, RTS, or FPS game. Using grid paper, design your own level for the game. You'll need a way to represent three dimensions for the

FPS game; the easy way is to use transparencies or translucent paper. For an RPG, what part of the game would be open-ended? What trigger event would launch a story segment, or would your level have only action? For an RTS, limit yourself to only two players and limit your ability to build to only five items. Which five would you chose? Recognize that certain items in the game require that the player already have other resources. Does this limit your design? (If you have an editor for the game selected, take your paper prototype and try to make it inside the game. How well does it work?)

DISCUSSION TOPICS

1. How are map editors and level editors similar? How are they different? Having reviewed what each can do, what kinds of user design would you want to see in either a 2D or a 3D editor?

2. Why would it be a bad idea to submit a paper prototype of your game idea to your publisher or marketing team? Can you think of a situation in which doing this would be a great idea?

3. Why is it important for a designer to maintain a consistent visual or artistic look throughout a level or game world?

4. If you were designing an RTS game, what would you want your level editor to be capable of doing? If you considered the user interface for the editor, what important features should be included?

5. If you had to use the same level editor described above for making an FPS game, what changes would be necessary? Why?

Chapter | 19

Completing the Game

Chapter Objectives

After reading this chapter and completing the exercises, you will be able to do the following:

- Understand what is involved in balancing a game.
- Describe how the last stages of the production phase can be the most difficult.
- Explain the steps involved in debugging a game.
- Explain what goes into creating the packaging for a game.
- Describe the importance of a thorough postmortem for a company.

Introduction

The production team spends month after month creating the assets of the game, testing them, making changes, and testing them again. This is part of the process of balancing the game. We have now reached the point where the development team switches from creating the game, whether from scratch or using purchased tools, to focusing on fixing bugs and final polishing. It is the point at which fun becomes one of the most important aspects of development as a variety of people work to tune, balance, and finish the game so it will be worth the purchase price.

It is also a risky time for the project because many on the team have likely grown tired of it after working on it so hard and for so long. The end of the production phase is often the hardest on the team, because everyone is exhausted by the crunch that happens trying to get the final product out the door. But at last that glorious moment occurs when the publisher accepts the final, finished version of the product—the gold release of the game—and the team's work is done (almost).

When the product goes gold, the burden switches to the publisher's production department to get the game burned onto CDs, assembled in the packages, boxed in cartons, and shipped to distributors and retailers. A few postproduction tasks remain for the original team, but generally there is a lull as the staff members rest and prepare for the next project.

Balancing the Game

After all the pieces have been put together, games, like any product, need time for the team to refine and polish what they have created. Movie directors frequently show completed movies to test audiences to gauge their reactions and make changes based on their feedback. Furniture makers take time to smooth and finish their woodworking, making the joints as seamless as possible and polishing the wood to a high shine. Games should be given the same treatment. Just because the coding is complete and the game no longer crashes does not mean it is necessarily ready to ship. Most companies plan a couple months at the end of the production phase to test the game thoroughly, get reactions from gamers, and make changes before releasing the gold version.

Balancing the game is an effort to make it as consistently fun, involving, engaging, and challenging to play as possible. The process involves balancing values, difficulty levels, and overall gameplay. The biggest issue for creating a balanced game is time. Due to the tight production schedules and the extreme exhaustion suffered by teams late in the production phase, many games wind up slipping in their overall schedule. The production is *finalized* (that is, shipped) as soon as all the major bugs have been fixed in order to get the product on the shelves as soon as possible. The result of this hurry-up-and-finish mode is an overabundance of unpolished, half-finished games reaching the market.

The development team should plan for several months of uninterrupted balancing and tuning to complete the game. It is a good idea to split the production team and have one group deal with balancing while the other deals with bug fixing and then have them alternate between the tasks. Allowing the programming and design teams to work on playability rather than just bug tracking and fixing can keep the team refreshed.

Balancing Values

As discussed in Chapter 16, "Mathematics and Artificial Intelligence in Games," part of the process of balancing a game is to make sure that the values assigned to units don't make any unit or opponent too powerful. *Balancing values* means carefully evaluating each unit in the game to make sure it isn't too strong, too fast, or too intelligent. If the design staff has tested the design in a paper prototype and then a working electronic prototype, they should be able to balance these values fairly easily when the real game is in production. Again, the primary concern when balancing values is taking the time required to test the values in all situations.

Real-time strategy games and war games are among the most complex games to balance. Powerful units should be given compensating factors that offset their major advantage; for example, an increased monetary cost or time required to build the unit. A role-playing game can take a long time to balance mathematically, simply because there are so many charts and tables to keep track of and to test. Sports games, of course, tend to have many built-in compensating factors including speed, health, cost, and endurance of the artificial intelligence (AI) players in comparison to the same physical attributes of the real players. Other real-world factors such as salary caps and the ability to draft new players can be used to help balance a sports game.

Adventure games generally require the least value balancing because combat is rarely a large part of the game. However, determining how difficult it is to solve puzzles in such games can require extensive input from new testers. Action games, on the other hand, have many values that need to be balanced. No weapon can be so overwhelmingly powerful that the game is simple to beat when the player finds it. There must be some compensating cost for the player using that weapon such as limited ammunition or a long time to reload between shots. Although many players might enjoy using a cheat mode to acquire a supreme weapon at no cost, the designer and the production team must remember that this should not be part of standard gameplay and must deal with it as a special case that can upset the pace and game balance.

19

FYI · "The Computer Is Cheating!"

If a game is rushed through production, its values might not be balanced, and players will soon notice the imbalance. In single-player games, this is less of a problem because it's the player versus the computer (and every gamer knows that the computer always cheats). Of course, when players find the imbalance, they will take advantage of it and eventually grow tired of the game. In multiplayer games, imbalance in the playing pieces is a major problem. One player might insist on playing only the side with the dominant pieces, causing rancor among the other players. Or if the problem has been posted on the Internet for everyone to see, all players might use the unbalanced pieces, making the game boring and predictable.

One way around this problem is to give players multiple choices and methods to tackle problems during play. For example, in games with puzzle elements, the designer might want to create several ways to complete a puzzle; if players can't figure out one way, they might figure out the other. To compensate, the designer can make the work-around solution more challenging or dangerous.

Balancing the Difficulty Level

Trying to find the right difficulty level for a game presents several challenges to designers. First, the general gaming population has many levels of skill at games, so what is easy for an experienced player can be almost impossible for a newcomer. Second, the designer wants to keep challenging players as they progress through the game, which frequently means making things more difficult. Third, as the team and playtesters test and retest the game to find bugs and smash them, they might tell the designer that the game is just too simple. The designer has to keep an open mind about these suggestions and listen to their recommendations, but she also has to weigh the feedback to find out where the real problems are.

One way around the first challenge is to include multiple difficulty levels in a game (such as easy, medium, hard, and impossible). There are several ways to make games more difficult based on the level the player selects:

- Change the number of enemies on the map: easier levels should have fewer enemies than tougher levels.

- Limit the number of items in a level so that fewer health potions and ammo reloads appear on the map as the difficulty rises.

- Create multiple databases with different values that correspond to the selected difficulty level so the number of hit points assigned to enemies, the damage they inflict, and their other statistics are not as good at easier levels.

- Tweak the AI routines so that tougher enemies are more aggressive and have better reactions to what the player does.

- For impossible levels, include a spawn function that keeps bringing new enemies into the level.

In great games, the designer and programmer work together to come up with a variety of solutions to use at each difficulty level.

 *Spawn Points*

Spawn points are places on a level or map where objects appear during play. The points might be where the player reappears after dying, where enemies continually generate, or where special items such as power-ups and weapons appear. **Spawn camping** refers to the practice of players hanging out near spawn points to kill opponents as soon as they appear on the map to collect booty or frag points.

The second challenge, making the game more difficult as the player progresses, usually involves making the enemies smarter and tougher. They can inflict more damage and absorb more punishment before being defeated. Also, as the game progresses, new units and weapons are introduced so the player continually finds new objects to experiment with. The trick is to make sure the new enemies are as balanced with the new items as those in the early sections of the game that have been played repeatedly.

Another way of making the game more interesting is to introduce new or modified gameplay mechanics. For example, where players have only been able to move on foot to a certain point in the game, they now find they can use vehicles. Or players might start running into puzzle-like elements that make them approach a level in a new way (for example, a level with no enemies but containing a maze that the player must get through to reach the exit). The designer can also take gameplay mechanics from earlier levels and modify or combine them in new ways; for example, where a player needed only to jump on platforms to get power-ups, now she must time her jumps between the swinging blades of a giant saw. Combining simple mechanics into more complex mechanics as the game progresses is a solid way to make a fulfilling game.

The danger at this point is making the new mechanics so difficult that players can't figure out how to use the controls or making them so alien to the genre that players lose their immersion in the game. Making the game continually challenging but not too hard takes considerable testing and balancing of unit values and map layouts.

The third challenge is keeping true to the original vision of the design. The team and testers will eventually get too good with the game (especially the first levels completed) and find it too simple. It is up to the designers to tweak the values to a certain point and then hold firm against further change requests. The designers and producers should ask for fresh testers on a continual basis, moving playtesters experienced with the game to more difficult levels or to other games entirely. This method ensures that the designers don't make the early levels too difficult as they continue working on later levels. It also helps to have testers take a break from the game so they can return with a fresh outlook.

Balancing Play Styles

Gamers have different play styles. Some charge headlong through an FPS level, blowing away everything in their path until they get to the exit. Others prefer inching along, saving frequently, and searching every nook and cranny for secret hiding places. Catering to multiple preferences is a challenge, but designers should attempt to make their games enjoyable for as many kinds of gamers as possible.

The designer can offer multiple ways to complete a level (or *paths,* which means not only new areas to explore but also different puzzles or NPC encounters within the original area), as well as allowing multiple solutions to puzzles.

19

> **Caution**
>
> **Time to Move On**
>
> The entire production team can help the designers understand when it is time to move on. Because it's a lot easier to continue polishing already refined levels than to start the process again on a new level, the production staff should impose freezes on level code and assets so programmers and designers can access only the unbalanced levels.

Each path can cater to a different play style; for example, a more dangerous path might be loaded with numerous enemies and lots of ambushes for aggressive players and another, more strategy-oriented path might require more planning and experimentation for thoughtful players. The more dangerous path might have fewer items to pick up or fewer NPCs to meet along the way, making it even harder, and the more strategic path might have lots of items and helpful NPCs the player won't necessarily require. When players reach the exit at the end of their selected path, they can continue onward to the next level or learn that there are still areas of the level they have not explored. Of course, building multiple paths requires the designers to think through the levels in advance and, hopefully, try them out in a paper prototype before building them.

During testing, the design staff should carefully note how testers approach different challenges in the game and observe the different ways they overcome them. As described in Chapter 20, "Marketing the Game," a game's product manager might set up a series of focus groups to get outsiders' reactions to the game. The designers should then talk with the testers to find out why they tried the approaches they used. They might discover flaws in the game design that should be fixed, or they might learn about new paths through the level they did not foresee. In either case, the testers can help point out weaknesses and unexpected rewards in a level.

Pushing Toward Completion

The later stages of the production phase, from the mid-alpha version on, are usually the most exhausting. The team has been working nonstop on the project for months (maybe years), and even though it is enjoyable to see the design come together, they are probably sick of it. They will likely have suffered through several crunch periods to meet their milestones or get builds ready for presentations and trade shows. The last six months (or longer) of the project sometimes demands extensive overtime from the team, but careful planning upfront and rigorous attention to the schedule throughout the production phase can alleviate some of the pressure.

The publisher at this point is usually in agreement with the development team about completing the project, or they might exert pressure to ship the mostly polished game as soon as possible. Obviously, rushing games to completion is not good corporate practice, yet it does happen all too frequently in the game industry. The primary reason is financial: Every day the game stays in production is another day requiring that more money be spent on salaries and other expenses, which may or may not be recouped in sales. For some games, this is an easy call. A few developers including id Software, Blizzard Entertainment, and Valve have developed reputations for refusing to ship games just to meet a schedule. These companies take the time to refine their products and

make them as good as they possibly can before releasing them to the public. Of course, these companies have successful track records and enough money in the bank to delay shipment until they are satisfied with the final product. Most independent developers rely on milestone payments and simply can't afford the extra time to polish their games, so their products can suffer as a result.

The secondary reason that games are rushed to completion is bad planning and management, which can lead to a crunch. There are many causes for this problem:

- The development and production teams underestimate the time needed to develop the game.

- Changes are allowed to happen in an uncontrolled way.

- Slips in production schedules are allowed to grow without restraint.

- Vacations, holidays, and other breaks aren't included in the schedule for the development team.

Any of these can cause leads to the tertiary issue of the development team's being worn to the point of no longer caring. There are serious dangers in pushing the team too hard. They might remain mostly productive during short crunch periods, but they will start becoming less and less productive the longer the crunch lasts. The worst that can happen is that the team ends up losing their passion for and interest in the title altogether. When a team reaches the point of no longer caring about the product, the product suffers. They will take short cuts. They will not focus on the big picture but on smaller, easily fixed issues. They will stop working intelligently to resolve the main issues. Even worse, a lack of caring can become endemic: When one person stops caring, this boredom can spread to all other members of the team, reaching both up and down the chain of management.

IN THE TRENCHES: Why Crunch Mode Doesn't Work

In his article, "Why Crunch Mode Doesn't Work: Six Lessons," Evan Robinson points out the following:

"When used long-term, Crunch Mode slows development and creates more bugs when compared with 40-hour weeks. More than a century of studies show that long-term useful worker output is maximized near a five-day, 40-hour workweek. Productivity drops immediately upon starting overtime and continues to drop until, at approximately eight 60-hour weeks, the total work done is the

▶▶ CONTINUED ON NEXT PAGE

▶▶ CONTINUED

same as what would have been done in eight 40-hour weeks. In the short term, working over 21 hours continuously is equivalent to being legally drunk. Longer periods of continuous work drastically reduce cognitive function and increase the chance of catastrophic error. In both the short- and long-term, reducing sleep hours as little as one hour nightly can result in a severe decrease in cognitive ability, sometimes without workers perceiving the decrease."

The complete article can be read on the International Game Developers Association (IGDA) Web site at **www.igda.org.** The IGDA is a nonprofit organization for professional gamers that promotes issues important to the game development community. Anyone can get a free IGDA user account, but there is a small fee to become a statutory member. Students who wish to join the organization are eligible for a discount to this fee.

Unfortunately, some in the game industry adopt the macho attitude that making games requires constant crunch time to the point that some companies pride themselves in always being in crunch mode. Management sometimes uses it as a method for sifting the weak from the strong, but it is very damaging to overall productivity and employee contentment. Moreover, it leads to burnout and the loss of talented, knowledgeable employees.

Unfortunately, the game industry is notorious for worker burnout. Burnout is a serious problem in the industry because there is so much stress. Part of the stress comes from worries about seeing the project get canceled if everyone doesn't work as hard as possible for as long as possible. Another cause of stress is perfectionism. Everyone who works on the team is an artisan in one way or another. They are very proud of the work they do and, thus, are willing to put in the extra time to make the final product as good as it can possibly be. This perfectionism can lead to stress. Yet another cause of stress for a team is a perception of management incompetence in the ranks of the leaders of the developer's company or the executives at the publisher. The game industry is notorious for canceling games and for companies that shut down suddenly because they run out of funds.

FYI | *Heard It Through the Grapevine*

The producer should listen carefully to what the team is saying about how the company is being run and see if anyone is spreading lies or rumors. Frequent meetings with the team to listen to their concerns and honestly answer their questions helps reduce this form of stress.

If someone burns out completely, it can take months for that person to regain his passion for making games. If the burnout is severe enough, the person might never recover, in which case it is probably better for him and the company to part ways so he can find something that rekindles his interest.

The average age of a game company production employee is generally in the mid-20s, with only one or two grizzled veterans who have survived a complete production cycle from first concept to gold release. After a while, most of the experienced professionals decide to leave the industry because they can get higher paid jobs elsewhere that don't demand as much crunch time. So a new crop of young team members gets to relive history all over again, making the same mistakes that those who left the company already made and learned from.

19

IN THE TRENCHES: Burnout

A survey commissioned by the IGDA (available at **www.igda.org/ newsroom/press_042904.php**) revealed, "34.3% of developers expect to leave the industry within 5 years, and 51.2% within 10 years." It also noted, "Crunch time is omnipresent, during which respondents work 65 to 80 hours a week (35.2%). The average crunch workweek exceeds 80 hours 13% of the time. Overtime is often uncompensated (46.8%)."

As discussed in Chapter 7, "Scheduling and Budgets," it is important for the producer to come up with as realistic a schedule as possible for completing a game. Games are not like other products where deadlines can be predicted easily; games are at the leading edge of technology, and technology changes rapidly. Because it is difficult to be absolutely certain when a game will ship, extra time should be added to the schedule to account for delays. If management asks for significant changes to a product, the producer should demand extra time to make the changes. If management refuses to change the ship date, the producer should be clear that either the changes can't be made, more staff will have to be added, or the product quality will have to suffer. (Good, fast, cheap— pick two.) Of course, adding extra staff means time has to be spent bringing them up to speed on the tasks they must accomplish, so the extra communication that must occur can actually slow down the project.

Although some crunch time is usually unavoidable, game company executives should do everything they can to minimize the damage it causes. It is important to keep the company's morale up during crunch time because lack of sleep can lead to frazzled nerves and lots of pent-up hostility. One way to improve morale is to set up shifts that give the staff occasional time off on a regular basis—and management must stick to this schedule. Another approach is to offer compensatory (comp) time off for those who put in more than 60 hours a week—and make sure that the staff members get this extra time off. Feeding the troops is another way to keep the staff content during their long hours at the computer. Many a pizza company owes its continued existence to local game companies during crunch time.

Testing the Game

The process of testing a game begins when there is something worthwhile to test. Toward the beginning of the production process, there can be paper and working prototypes to test, but these are useful only for making sure the design works as intended. It is not until the game engine is operational and some game assets have been generated that real testing can begin.

Testing is generally broken into two main areas: playtesting and quality assurance (QA). Playtesting usually covers the balancing and fun of a game, whereas QA testing confirms the proper operation of the program on all of the platforms it should run on. For massively multiplayer online games (MMOGs), both playtesting and QA are obviously enormous tasks due to the server issues as well as to the variety of consumer platforms and the number of different people playing the game.

Quality Assurance

Most medium and large game companies have a QA department that is tasked with testing the game throughout the production phase. Companies that do not have their own QA department either rely on their publisher to QA test the game or hire an external testing company to provide this assistance. A QA manager runs the entire department and assigns QA leads to projects. In some companies, the QA manager also hires and assigns playtesters for games.

A QA lead is usually a long-time staff member who not only understands the process of building a game but who can also manage a large and diverse group of testers. Ideally, the QA lead is assigned to a production team while the designers are still working out the details of the game design document (GDD). A good QA lead can analyze the GDD to understand how the interface works and suggest changes to the designers based on their testing and play experience. When the GDD is finalized, the QA lead starts building the *test plan,* which is a document that outlines every feature in the game and how those features should be tested. The test plan includes an overview of the hardware test suites that must be created to test the product completely.

During the first half of the alpha stage of the production phase, the QA testers might be asked to look at the new product, give feedback about its play mechanics, and evaluate the play. Any bugs found by the QA team are reported to the programming team, but it is not worthwhile to spend any real effort tracking down bugs at this time because the game engine and tools are still being worked on. The goal is to help the design staff by commenting on the fun factor in the game. Of course, this is also the time when the marketing team might consider starting focus groups to evaluate the gameplay mechanisms. These early focus groups rarely actually play the game but are more often asked to provide feedback on a verbal or visual presentation. Most in-depth playtesting doesn't begin until the beta milestone is reached.

The real work on QA testing does not begin until the second half of the alpha stage when the game engine is stable, the tools are finished, and the real game assets are being created. At this time, the QA lead often divides the test plan among the staff and has each member focus on several critical areas of the game. Although the QA staff can still contribute suggestions about gameplay, at this point in the schedule their focus is on testing the game engine, the interface, and all the gameplay elements. Whereas the rest of the production team is focused on completing the rest of the game assets, the QA team should concentrate on finding the bugs.

Bugs, of course, is the term used by software engineers to refer to coding or data errors within the software that cause the product to behave erroneously. The process of finding bugs and fixing them is long and arduous. Some bugs are relatively easy to find; others are almost impossible to track down. They can be something as simple as having a bad pointer in the programming language, hardware incompatibility with a video card, or loading data into the wrong memory location. For each bug discovered, the QA team must (ideally) repeat the error, write down the exact method used to repeat the error, and pass on the information the programmers need to determine the best fix for the error.

The team uses a bug-tracking system to help standardize the process. The system provides a means for the person who finds the bug to report all the necessary information to the programmer who will (try to) fix the bug. Several commercial bug-tracking software packages are available, such as Seapine Software's TestTrack Pro (Figure 19.1) and the open-source Bugzilla (**www.bugzilla.org/**), but many companies prefer to create their own database system.

When setting up a bug-tracking system, the programmer should ensure that each bug report indicates the individual who is reporting it, the kind of computer system the individual was using, where in the game the bug appears, how fatal it is, if it is reproducible, and who should be assigned to fix it (programming, art, design, or audio). The system commonly tracks the following information:

- Bug Number: This is usually auto generated by the bug tracking program.

- Tester Name: The person who discovered the bug.

- Date Found: This is usually auto generated by the program but can often be overwritten in the event of network problems.

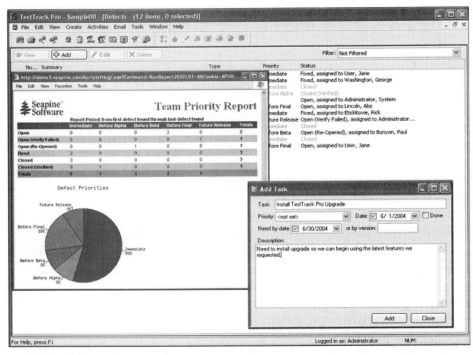

FIGURE 19.1 An interface screen from Seapine's debugging software package, TestTrack Pro.

- Software Version Number: The software should have a version number embedded in the game so that testers and programmers know which version is currently being tested.

- Bug Type: Crash, content, graphics, AI, input, other.

- Bug Priority: Explained later in this chapter.

- Bug Description: This is where the actions of the error are described; for example, "When picking up the blue potion in the store in Level 4, the game crashes."

- Bug Set Up: This is where the steps taken to produce (or reproduce) the bug are outlined; for example, "Load SAVE GAME3, stored on server. Go to the store and select TALK with the clerk. Select Dialog Choice 3, 'I'd like to buy that lovely blue potion.' Follow the steps to buy the potion. When the clerk places the potion on the counter, move the cursor over it and select 'Pick up blue potion.' The game will freeze; no cursor or keyboard input response. 'CTRL-ALT-DEL' does not work. Must hard-reboot the computer."

- Repeatable?: This is usually a pull-down menu or radio button with options such as: 100%, most of the time, not repeatable, and only seen once. This helps the programmer know more about how the bug occurs.

- Machine Information: This is usually a section of the report that breaks up information about the machine used for testing, such as CPU information, operating system, video card specifics, sound card specifics, versions of all DLL and API files, RAM space, hard disk space, network connections, and so on. This can be either automatically filled in by the database when given an assigned value for the machine being used (such as PC4) or the tester may be required to input all the information about the machine. Because hardware, software, and BIOS are often changed in a testing suite, the tester should fill out this information every time.

- Bug Status—Testing: This is where the testing team informs the programming team of the status of the bug. Selections such as open, fixed, not fixed, closed, duplicate, or ship with are usually provided via a pull-down menu.

- Bug Status—Programming: This is where the programming team lets the testing and production teams know if they have fixed or addressed the bug. The choices are usually open, fixed-to-check, duplicate (number), not to fix, or ship with. Until this status changes from open to fixed-to-check, the testers should not try to repeat the reported bug or see if it is fixed.

- Bug Status—Programming Version: This is where the programmer should input the version of the fixed-to-check file.

- Bug Status—Notes: In this section, both the testing and programming team should write short summaries of the bug status; for example, "JEN—bug found 5/1/04," "Rob—bug fixed version 1.1.3, 5/5/04," "JEN—bug replicated version 1.1.3, same machine, 5/6/04," "Rob—bug fixed better and verified, version 1.1.4, 5/6/04," "JEN—bug fix verified, version 1.1.4 5/6/04."

> **Caution**
>
> **Restrict Changes**
>
> The bug tracking software should be set up so that programmers cannot change the testing status of a bug and testers cannot change the programming status of a bug.

19

An associate producer might be responsible for collecting and collating the bug reports, making sure they are assigned to the correct team member, following up to make sure that the staff member has addressed the problem, and then reassigning the bug to a tester to verify that the problem has been resolved. Until a tester signs off on the bug, it is considered open and might prevent the product from shipping.

Game companies usually classify bugs into three categories:

- *A* bugs cause the system to crash and must be removed before the product can ship.

- *B* bugs are not fatal, but are noticeable and should be removed before shipping.

- *C* bugs are mostly cosmetic and should be removed if time allows.

After a computer game ships, the developer can create patches that fix any remaining bugs and make them available for download via the Internet. Console games, however, cannot be patched easily, so they must be as bug-free as possible when released for shipping. Although computer games are sometimes allowed to ship even if they still contain serious bugs, console game manufacturers thoroughly test each gold version of a product submitted by an internal or external team. If they find any serious bugs, they will send the product back to the development team for further work.

There are rarely more than a few bugs in video (console) games when they are shipped. Bugs do occur in video games, and some can be horrendous. Because it is almost impossible to patch any problems, publishers and developers work hard to minimize the problems within the game. Because the console hardware manufacturers have the final say on replicating and shipping all products, their approval cycle should be built into the development plan. The manufacturer has a large test department to check every submitted game and make sure that it is as bug-free as possible. Often, this cycle is a two-week bug-free period during which the game developer is not allowed to submit new changes to the game. If an external development group submits a buggy gold version to the manufacturer, they might find the product pulled from the shipping schedule, and their company can be in deep financial difficulty as a result, so it had better be as rock solid as possible.

One reason why computer games tend to be more buggy than console games is that video consoles are much simpler machines that use one hardware standard and don't run any software except the game. The hardware components in players' computers, on the other hand, often come from many different manufacturers and have widely different specifications. Even though the IBM-compatible personal computer is the standard, there are many variations among the numerous sound cards, video cards, motherboards, memory chips, and other components available—not to mention all the different software applications that might be resident on a PC.

Although most software applications do not cause problems with running the game, some applications do. An even more subtle problem stems from the fact that some software applications require different versions of drivers or other embedded software technology that conflicts with the requirements of the game product. Not having the correct driver or API installed can cause various problems in a game ranging from poor performance to crashing to actually damaging data on the computer.

During the design phase, the QA lead should look at the hardware required for the end user and create a list of test suites that will be used. Assembling a hardware test suite is rarely simple for most computer games; the various versions of operating systems, drivers, video cards, bus and speed requirements, networking cards, and even wireless connections can be almost overwhelming. As a result, many game publishers contract with companies that specialize in compatibility testing to run the game on as many different hardware combinations as possible. Whether the testing is contracted or performed in house, the goal is to try to recreate the most commonly available consumer systems. Still, it is likely that all possible combinations will not be tested, thereby resulting in crash bugs that irritate consumers.

When a game reaches its beta version, the company might send copies to outside testers (called ***blind testers***) to check for bugs and compatibility issues. Massively multiplayer online games in particular have long test runs to perform stress tests that make sure their hardware systems will stand up to the sudden onslaught of consumers when the game becomes available.

Because a typical game can have well over half a million lines of code, most products inevitably have some bugs when they ship. At the very end of the production cycle, the final approval process for most games to go gold requires a meeting of the production staff including the lead programmer, lead designer, and lead tester. This group reviews all open bugs to determine if the game can ship with the bugs or if there are too many to allow it to ship.

Publishers have customer service departments to handle problems and offer support for shipped products. Consumers sometimes think they can get better answers by contacting an independent developer that worked on the game, but small companies don't have the staff to answer questions or solve players' problems. E-mailing a problem to the developer might bring a resolution, but more than likely the response will be to contact the publisher for assistance.

Gold Release and Beyond

Going gold—shipping the product—is the goal of every game team. It is a long way from the original concept to the final version of the game, but there is a huge feeling of relief and victory when the publisher accepts the gold version. This is the end of the line for the team . . . almost.

Gold Master

Reaching the final stage of the process usually involves very little ceremony. There is a final sign-off of the delivery, as well as some form of agreement between the development team, the publisher, the lead tester, any license holders, and the producers. As mentioned previously, if the game went through a licensing test phase for a brand (such as *Batman)* or for a console, it has already been placed in code freeze. *Code freeze* is a point at which the source for the game is not to be changed or modified in any way by anyone. This means no code changes, no changes to data, not even writing a new installer or read-me file on the CD. At code freeze, a final version of the game is made and the version number 1.0 is assigned to the game. If this is a second or third submission into code freeze, the version number is usually incremented to reflect this. The game is tested for as long as possible, usually a minimum of two weeks, as it will appear once replicated. If the game passes this testing and no changes are required, the game goes *gold* and master copies of the game CD are delivered to the publisher, who then delivers a master to the replication house.

In addition, the game is also archived at this point. All source material that is used in the game—code, APIs, tools, data, art, voice, music, sound effects, text—is copied and stored on CDs, backup tape, or other format. The archive is often tested, usually by a junior programmer, by rebuilding the game executable and verifying that it is identical (preferably byte by byte) to the game master. If it is not identical, this must be reconciled, so that the game can be rebuilt in the event that anything happens to its gold master(s). In addition, this is the source that can be used for sequels.

If one of the outcomes of making the game is the creation of a reusable game engine, this process is most likely not complete. When the game goes gold, the engine used is also archived and assigned a version number. However, the work on the game engine will likely continue, albeit after a brief respite for the development team.

Bugs and Patches

If the team worked on a computer game, there is a good chance that there will still be some bugs to fix. When the game ships, the publisher's consumer service department will likely receive calls from consumers who are having problems getting the game to run. To help the staff who assist the end users, the testing and programmer group work together to write a frequently asked questions (FAQ) sheet (or sheets) that contains all known bugs with explanations on the status of patches, new versions, or work-arounds.

The consumer services group also keeps track of new bugs found by consumers. Part of the FAQ is used as a means to track the questions and errors found by the consumers. Usually, the problems arise from hardware/software incompatibility, and it can take a while to track down where the problem lies. The reports are sent to the development producer, who compiles the reported bugs and has the programming team try to come up with work-arounds for the more common problems after the error has been replicated. If the game is popular enough and the same problems are found repeatedly, it's more likely that a patch will be created to fix the problem. When enough significant problems have been found and have been fixed, the publisher (or the developer) will often post a patch on its Internet site for consumers to download to fix the problems. The patch often contains a read me file (readme.txt) that offers suggestions to consumers on changing settings in their hardware to overcome a problem or downloading the latest hardware or software drivers from a manufacturer's Web site.

R&R

The postproduction period is a chance for the exhausted team members to recharge their batteries. If they put in extensive crunch time completing the project, they might receive extra comp time from the company. If the team has to go immediately into crunch mode again—say, on another product the company is trying to ship—there is an excellent chance that some of the team members will suffer burnout and quit.

While the team is recuperating, they should consider writing a postmortem of the project that just shipped (discussed later in this chapter). They should also take the time to renew family ties, especially if a spouse and children are involved.

Ideally, after a product ships, a team should be allowed to each take vacations or minivacations away from each other and from the stress of the game. It might be difficult for a company to logistically plan to lose a portion of their workforce all at the same time, but losing that workforce for a short period is highly preferable to losing them altogether if they quit and move out of the industry.

The following ideas offer a few suggestions to alleviate the problem:

- Before crunch mode begins at alpha or beta, allow programmers to take 3-day weekends every other week. This helps them to build up a reserve of enthusiasm, which they will need during the actual crunch time

- Try to plan to not have a crunch mode: Build enough time into the cycle to get the game done without working 60 to 80 hour weeks, which don't tend to get the game done any faster. Use detailed milestone checklists throughout the development cycle so that everyone knows what their current tasks are. Build in at least a quarter of the overall length of the development for tuning, balancing, and bug fixing.

- As soon as a game goes into testing and most bugs are fixed, allow the programmers to again have 3-day weekends if possible. This might mean they have pagers or work at home, and it usually means they are not allowed to be farther than an hour away from the office if they are on a critical path.

- Employees who are considered critical to the final stages of the project should be the first to have a vacation.

- Recognize and acknowledge the work of all individuals on the product team. Offer plenty of verbal praise of their work and effort, especially for those who work *smarter* (not necessarily longer) and get the job done without working overtime.

FYI | *Work Smarter, Not Longer*

Recognize that people don't have to work long hours to get their work done and get other things done, too. Much too often, a company will congratulate staff who stay late after hours, figuring that they will do what it takes to make the game complete. What the company misses, however, is whether they are staying late because they procrastinated, because they are fixing work they did badly, or because they didn't predict their schedule well. Employees who get the work done on time and on budget are even more valuable—they probably did it all right the first time.

- When the game is being tested, reward the team with different engaging activities; for example, play a game, go to a shooting range, play paintball, go to a theme park, or go to an early screening of a new movie.

- When the game is being replicated, allow all the team members to go on minivacations. They shouldn't leave the country or be far away in the event that something unexpected happens, but they should be able to get away with family and friends and do something different.

- "Force" people to take vacations. It is all too common for programmers in the game industry to be too isolated or to not have family or friends nearby. A good producer and team leader will recognize that even though a person might continue to hang around the company after the game ships, she must be forced to get away and do something else to recharge her batteries.

New Projects

Some team members might be pulled from a project before it is completely finished to start work on a new design. Usually, the senior designer for the project starts working on the new design at least three to four months (or more) before the current product ships—as soon as the last major design bugs have been squashed. As work on the current project winds down, other team members often are pulled out to work either on the new project or on other projects—after getting some rest, of course.

Although designing a game is work, it is highly enjoyable work and can actually be quite restful and rejuvenating for a designer. The chance to sit around and contemplate a new project is very much like Zen meditation. Of course, the designer has to eventually get down to real work, writing up her ideas in a pitch paper to present to management. And then the whole process starts again . . .

Packaging the Game

Completing the gold version of the game is only one step in the process of getting the product onto retail shelves. There is also the matter of creating the packaging, which includes the box assembly for computer games or the plastic case for video games, the manual, other supplementary materials, the jewel case that holds the CD or DVD, and promotional materials. These services are handled by the publisher's creative services group, which is often part of the marketing department. The schedule for developing these items runs parallel with the development, usually starting about half-way through the production cycle. The actual production of the paper products (the box, manual, and inserts) is done no more than one month before the replication date for the CDs, DVDs, cartridges, or other distribution media. These materials are shipped either to the replication house to package together with the distribution media or to the location that will put the boxes together, shrink-wrap each box, fill the cartons, and then load palettes for shipping.

Game Manual

Depending on the type of game and its complexity, the game component that can take the longest to complete is the game manual. The manual for a complex strategy game or combat flight simulation can be over a hundred pages long, whereas a puzzle game manual might be only a few pages long.

The development team is usually responsible for writing the first draft of the manual because they are familiar with the controls and what the game includes. One of the designers might be assigned to this task. Sometimes, a playtester will be included because they often also know the game very well. The first draft is submitted to the publisher's creative services group or an external group hired for the product. This group often has a writer/graphic designer on staff who is assigned the task of writing and laying out the manual. More often than not, the company hires a freelance writer to complete the manual. The writer takes the first draft from the production team and expands on it.

For a time in the mid-1990s, manuals for PC games were quite large and gave the package extra weight. Even if the manuals were mostly fluff, publishers thought that the perceived value of the extra weight would convince consumers the product was well worth their money. Some games still have large manuals, but most have reduced the size as much as possible to reduce the cost of producing the package as well as to reduce shipping costs. Console games usually have small manuals that tuck inside the plastic DVD clamshell case. A number of computer games print only a "getting started" guide and include the manual as a PDF or HTML file on the game disc.

Players often complain that manuals have mistakes or don't cover information that is basic to playing the game. These problems arise if the manual is produced too early, before the game is finalized. Sometimes features don't get implemented until late in the production phase, so they aren't included in the original draft submitted by the team. A freelance writer might not even have an opportunity to play the game, especially if it is a console game, so he must write about the product in the abstract. Added to these issues is the lead time for printing, which takes much longer if the manual is printed in full color instead of simple black-and-white. All of these factors taken together mean that the manual is often completed many months before the gold version of the game is released.

The manual usually includes sections about installing the game, starting a new game, saving/reloading games, and other options. Computer game manuals frequently include a troubleshooting section because of compatibility conflicts. The manual might include game development credits if there is available space, although it's more common to find this information embedded in the game itself. Finally, the manuals also contain the warranty information and other important legalese including all copyright information.

Although many gamers never even bother to look at the manual, it is still important to include one with the product. It's common for many players to launch into the game first and then read the manual only if they're unfamiliar with some of the icons or can't figure out a gameplay mechanism. Even with a good in-game tutorial, the manual should discuss every gameplay element in enough detail to enable the player to understand how the game plays. It should include all the major interface screens with callouts to point out the various functions on each screen (Figure 19.2).

Game Packaging

New computer games usually come in a 5-1/4 $\times$ 7-1/2 $\times$ 1-1/4" cardboard box whereas video games ship in a 5-1/4 $\times$ 7-1/2 $\times$ 1/2" plastic case. Both boxes are about the same size. At one time, computer games came in larger boxes (around 7 to 8" wide by 10 to 12" tall), often varying greatly in size. Retailers complained about the changeable sizes and said the boxes were too big, taking up too much shelf space. The computer game publishers responded by reducing the size of the boxes, which allowed retailers to store more products in the limited shelf space devoted to games.

As the package size shrank, so did the space available on the back to describe what was in the game and show screenshots of gameplay. As a result, many computer game boxes now include a swing cover that opens out like the

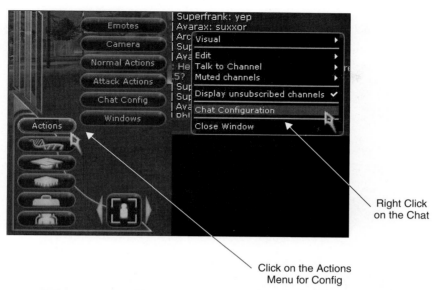

Right Click
on the Chat

Click on the Actions
Menu for Config

FIGURE 19.2 This screenshot of Funcom's *Anarchy Online* (2001) manual shows two callouts that are used to help a player configure the game's chat window.

cover of a book. The resulting area is almost as large as the back of an older box and allows more room for text and screenshots to promote the game (Figures 19.3 and 19.4). The spines of the box are also important for grabbing the consumer's eye as she walks down the aisle. The computer game title should be printed as large and clearly as possible along both side spines. The system requirements for computer games often appear on the bottom spine in tiny type.

The game CD or DVD is usually included in a jewel case (similar to an audio CD case) that is molded to allow the CD or DVD to snap securely onto a center post. This post keeps the disc from sliding around and scratching its surfaces. A double-size jewel box can hold up to four disks. For a simple game, a small manual often slides into slots on the inside cover of the jewel box. The final jewel-box assembly is sometimes shrink-wrapped and then inserted into a stiff cardboard holder that slides into the box. The game manual, game maps, charts, marketing materials, or other inserts might also be put into the box, which is then sealed with a plastic sticker to prevent someone from stealing the game CD.

Although computer game boxes have become smaller in recent years, there is still considerable wastage in the packaging. The main components—the jewel box with game CD/DVD and manual—could be sold in a package half the size of the entire box. Of course, there would not be much room on the package for promotional text and screenshots.

Video game packages have traditionally been smaller than computer game packages. Before CDs and DVDs, video games came on cartridges, and their

FIGURE 19.3 The left side of the swing cover for Sierra On-Line's *Empire Earth* (2001). The swing cover gives the publisher more room for promotional copy and screenshots to sell the game.

costs were quite high—much higher than the cost of floppy disks used for computer games. Additionally, video game manufacturers required developers to pay both a licensing fee and the cost for making the cartridge. To keep costs down, publishers used smaller packages for video games (the same size as movie DVD packages), and the tradition has continued even though the production cost for a CD or DVD is much lower than for a cartridge.

The front and back of video game cases have recessed areas in which the printed cover and back copy are sealed. There is much less space on the back of the case for promotional text and screenshots. The game logo usually appears only on one spine, which faces out when the games are stacked on a shelf.

The game CD/DVD is attached to the central post on the inside back cover (there can be a second post on the front cover if two disks are included).

FIGURE 19.4 Right side of the swing cover for *Empire Earth*.

The four-color manual and whatever other printed materials the publisher provides are then put into the plastic case. An adhesive plastic strip is usually attached to the top and side of the plastic case to prevent theft, and the product is shrink-wrapped.

Shipping the Finished Game

After the publisher accepts the gold release, it is sent to a CD or DVD manufacturer. A *glass master* of the release version is made with a *laser beam recorder (LBR),* which records a thin groove in a continuous spiral. The spiral supplies timing and tracking information for the recording laser to make sure the information is recorded at a steady rate. The recording laser follows the groove as it etches the data as a series of pits onto the glass master.

After the glass master has been tested, the disk is silvered to allow it to conduct electricity for the next step, *electroplating.* It is placed in a chemical bath containing nickel, and an electrical current is applied. After about two hours, a metal surface forms. This *metal father* is removed from the glass disk so it can be used to stamp replicas of the CD. If the order is large, the father undergoes the electroplating process again to create a reverse-image *mother* and then *sons* that are all identical to the father. A hole is punched in the center of the glass master and the back is polished smooth.

Heated polycarbonate is used to create the duplicated disks. The hot material is injected into a mold containing the stamper, which forms its impression on the hot polycarbonate under extreme pressure. The impression is then water cooled and hardened. The plastic impression is removed from the mold, coated with a special dye and allowed to dry. A metal layer is added because the disc must reflect laser light. Aluminum is most commonly used, although gold and silver are sometimes employed because they reflect light better. One or more layers of acrylic plastic are applied and allowed to dry to keep the metal from being scratched. The final step is to apply the label by using an ink that adheres to the acrylic surface.

FYI *DVD Storage*

Although a DVD is the same physical size as a CD, it has about four times as many pits per surface area because the recording laser makes smaller pits along a tighter spiral. A DVD can hold more than 26 times as much data as a CD: from 4.7 gigabytes for a single-sided, single-layer DVD up to 17.0 gigabytes for double-sided, dual-layer DVD.

The final CD or DVD is sent to the company that will assemble the components into the retail package. The components are carefully put together in an assembly line fashion, and the final products are shrink-wrapped and put into cartons for delivery. They are then sent to distributors, who might repackage the games and send them on to retailers. The retailers add UPC stickers (universal product code), decals, and other promotional materials (or they might have it done by another company) before the final goods are put on the shelves for consumers to purchase.

Conducting a Postmortem

After team members have had the chance to recoup their energy, they should try to hold a postmortem on the game that just shipped (or was cancelled). A *postmortem* is an analysis by the team of what happened during the production process including what went wrong and what went right. Many companies do not bother with a postmortem, but in doing so they miss the opportunity to improve their production methods, learn where the process can be improved, and identify where bottlenecks might occur on future products.

Ideally, the entire original team should take part in the postmortem, and some of the executive staff might want to sit in as listeners. Holding the postmortem a few weeks after the product has shipped, should allow any bad feelings or heated emotions that might have existed among team members to have dissipated. The overall atmosphere for the postmortem should be friendly but serious.

Programmers should bring notes they took during the development, including lists of items they had to cut to meet the schedule. Producers should prepare by reviewing all important milestones and considering the state of the game and team at each one. Testers should be included to get their feedback on gameplay and the development pipeline. Artists should try to recall the process and pipeline used for development of the art and consider ways it might have been improved. Finally, everyone should come prepared with the top three things they think went right with the development process (or game) as well as three things that went wrong and be ready to discuss them. When the team has talked the matter over, they should decide on the five most important things that went right and the five most important things that went wrong to include in their written report. All or none of this material might be used during the review: The objective is to have the tools in the room.

The postmortem should be run by the producer or, if there was a large problem with the management of the game, by the lead designer or lead programmer. In any case, the person leading the postmortem should be someone whom everyone respects, regardless of the outcome of the final product. This person should have a list of all the milestones and all change requests made for the game. She should review and bring copies of the GDD, TDD, ADD, and overall schedules.

One person should be appointed secretary to keep notes during the session so the team can write up their findings. Either the producer or the designer can write up the final report, although artists and programmers have done them as well. When the report is finished, it should be circulated to the team and posted on the company intranet. Management might want the team to submit the postmortem for publication by *Game Developer Magazine* or to be posted online at Gamasutra (both are owned by CMP Game Group). Hard lessons learned at one company can certainly be shared with others to keep them from making the same mistakes without giving away proprietary information.

Structure of a Postmortem

The postmortem normally consists of an overview of the production process and the team's goals, followed by a discussion of five things that went right and five things that went wrong. The team should indicate how close they came to meeting their initial goals and where they had to change their goals, either voluntarily or under duress.

One of the biggest concerns of running postmortem sessions is the emotions that can be raised, so the leader should try to avoid this as much as possible. The leader should start by presenting his list of top things that went right and then ask for everyone else to summarize their own lists. The team might have discovered a better way to handle the assets in the game—for example, a better bug-tracking system—or created an excellent set of tools that sped the development. Outstanding contributions by individual team members can be included, but it is more important to look at the overall methodology and processes of development than to focus primarily on individual achievements. It's always better to start with what went right and then progress into the more emotionally charged lists of things that went wrong.

When discussing the things that went wrong, the team should not point fingers directly at any team members, but if there were personnel problems, they should explain where things started going wrong. The people who create games are artisans and usually have strong egos, so clashes between egos often causes serious problems for the rest of the team.

If a confrontation occurs during a postmortem, the leader needs to step in and remind everyone that the goal is to identify and fix the problem so it will not be repeated, not to place blame. It is not a time for personal attacks, which can often happen if the game development went far astray. It's a time to think about the underlying development process and improve on it for the future.

One problem continually mentioned in many postmortems is that lack of planning at the beginning came back to haunt the team later. The lack of planning can involve not specifying the game design in enough detail or not holding a technical review to decide how the product would be built. Another problem that frequently arises is that the team underestimated the time required to complete the game and then was forced into extensive crunch mode to ship the project on time. These lessons reinforce the importance of planning the design in as much detail as possible early in production, allowing for changes as required.

The team should try to find ways to address the problems they faced to make sure they are not repeated. The discussion of each problem should conclude with one or two proposed solutions for the next project. Any problems that are raised without proposed solutions should be flagged for management to look at.

The last section of the postmortem can include a short list of recommendations for changes to the company's production process. If the list is too long, nothing will be changed, and the same problems will likely arise down the road. The recommendations should be concrete, not wishes or idle hopes. For example, "less crunch time" or "more appreciation of problems by management" are vague suggestions at best. "Create a better bug-tracking database" or "add more time to schedule for publisher's marketing requirements" are more realistic.

Summary

Completing the game can be the most tedious portion of the production process. The main game assets have been completed, and the team now focuses on getting the balance correct and smashing bugs. The fun part of creating materials gives way to the detail-oriented process of polishing the product before it can be shipped. Although computer games can get away with being buggy when they are shipped, console games must be as bug free as possible or the manufacturer will reject the submitted gold version and demand a better one.

After the team completes the game, they can get some rest, although they should schedule a postmortem to analyze how they can improve the way their company produces games before the group completely loses touch and forgets the lessons learned during the production process. Because games require ever longer production schedules, any recommendations a team can offer management to streamline the process and make it more efficient are vital for the company to remain a successful competitor in a very competitive industry.

Test Your Skills

MULTIPLE CHOICE QUESTIONS

1. How might a designer balance a puzzle in a game?
   A. Give the player multiple ways to solve the puzzle.
   B. Playtest, tune, playtest, tune until the puzzle is neither too easy nor too hard.
   C. Use the puzzle repeatedly in the game so the player has to solve it multiple times.
   D. Punish the player who cannot solve the puzzle by killing her game character.

2. Offering multiple difficulty levels is a good way to do which of the following?
   A. Balance values.
   B. Balance play styles.
   C. Balance for player skill.
   D. Offset playtester's skill.

3. Why would a designer create multiple paths and multiple methods for solving game element gates?

   A. To accommodate players with different styles.

   B. To accommodate players with different skill levels.

   C. To teach the player to always find the easiest solution.

   D. To make her own life simpler.

4. Why should games increase in difficulty as the player progresses?

   A. The player expects things to get easier.

   B. The player has acquired the skills necessary to face more challenging gameplay.

   C. More enemies should appear in the game.

   D. It's easier for the playtesters to evaluate.

5. True or False: Crunch mode is a necessary evil.

   A. True.

   B. False.

6. Which of the following is one of the surest ways to resort to a crunch mode?

   A. Spend too much time planning and designing.

   B. Meet once a week with the team to keep abreast of the game status.

   C. Complete every milestone early and surpass it.

   D. Allow people to make changes to the game without discussion.

7. A bug tracking system will help

   A. The producer keep track of what is left to do in the game.

   B. The programmer keep track of what is broken in the game.

   C. The playtesting team focus on the same general issue in the game.

   D. The art department find and fix code errors.

8. Bug status should be set by the playtester and

   A. Updated by the programmer.

   B. Updated by the producer.

   C. Updated by the playtester based on checking the programmers' fix list.

   D. Never changed until the bug is closed.

9. It's important to know which of the following pieces of information about a bug?

    A. Can it be repeated?

    B. What steps are taken to repeat the bug?

    C. What machine does the bug happen on?

    D. Does the bug happen on more than one type of machine?

    E. What version of the product was being tested?

    F. What operating system was in use?

    G. All of the above.

10. After the product ships, it's good for the team to do which of the following?

    A. Immediately hold a postmortem before going on vacation.

    B. Write up the bug list for consumer services.

    C. Change their phone and pager numbers.

    D. All of the above.

11. When is it best to write the game manual?

    A. As earlier as possible, to get it out of the way.

    B. After the game is at gold master, so the manual will be up-to-date.

    C. As late as possible to accommodate gameplay changes.

    D. By the engine proof milestone.

12. How can a postmortem help the development team?

    A. Refine their development process for future games.

    B. Hash out any individual grievances before its too late.

    C. Fix all bugs before shipping.

    D. Restructure the management hierarchy before starting the next project.

13. What is a gold master made of?

    A. Polycarbonate and nickel.

    B. Polycarbonate and silver.

    C. Glass and nickel.

    D. Polycarbonate and aluminum.

14. True or False: The father stamp master is made as the reverse image of the CD to replicate.

    A. True.

    B. False.

EXERCISES

Exercise 19.1: Game Balancing

Select a board game such as chess, checkers, or *Scrabble.* Play the game with a friend (or with several friends). Modify one of the elements of the gameplay by increasing its power. For example, in *Scrabble,* you could increase the number of triple word score squares on the board itself, or you could increase the value of the letter E to 10. For a game such as chess, consider giving the king more power, giving the pawns more power, or giving the rook the ability to move diagonally if it takes the queen. How does the game change? Try changing the elements so that only one opponent has more power. For example, if the first player in *Scrabble* to play the letter Q gets 25 points, how does the game change?

Exercise 19.2: Playtesting

Break into groups of five to seven students. Each group should select two games already owned by individuals in the group. Half of the group should play one of the games, and the other half should watch. Note how people play; do they focus on only one aspect of the game, or do they try many different types of solutions for puzzles? Do the people squirm in their chairs as they play or are they very still and focused on the game? If the game has long cut-scenes, do the playtesters watch them or skip through them? Throughout the playtesting, the observers should not speak with the players. The observers should try to find five things to consider about the play. At the end, the team playing should give a brief summary of the gameplay as well as what they liked and didn't like. Each team should then swap roles, but with a new game.

Exercise 19.3: Game Packaging

Using a box from a game you already own as an example, create a concept package for a game you're interested in making. Design a logo for the game title and consider how you would display it on a box. Create a box that is 5-1/4" wide × 7-1/2" tall × 1-1/4" deep using paper, scissors, glue, and tape. Put the recommended ESRB rating on the front of the box. What image would you select for the cover? Would it be a simple black box or feature some colorful character? What four key features would you want to have on the back of the box?

Exercise 19.4: Postmortem Review

Go online to **www.gamasutra.com** and read three of the postmortems on that Web site. Create a chart or list of the three to five things in each postmortem that were described as going right or going wrong, summarizing each very briefly. Compare the items in the lists. What are the similarities? What are the differences? Did any teams make the same mistakes or compliment themselves on the same positive action?

DISCUSSION TOPICS

1. Consider a puzzle game such as *Tetris* or *Bedazzled*. What are several balancing issues to consider when making a puzzle game feel "finished?" Does the designer need to consider all balancing issues (play styles, values, difficulty levels) when polishing a puzzle game?

2. Discuss the issues that seem to cause a game to be unfinished or to ship without going through a balancing phase. From the other chapters in this book, what have you learned about managing the project to minimize these issues?

3. Given the forms of testing for games for a console platform (playtesting and QA testing), which do you consider more important and why? If you were considering this question for a computer game, would your answer change and why?

4. Imagine that you are working on a game project—perhaps an RPG that features a band of flying monkeys who must work together to save a princess—that has a team of 10 full-time programmers and 10 full-time artists. The game is nearing completion, and the team is starting to burn out and run out of interesting gameplay ideas. With a partner, discuss five team activities you can think of to renew the teams' interest in the game. Discuss five additional ways you can renew each individuals' interest in the game—ideally without spending any cash.

5. Consider a project that you have worked on with friends or schoolmates. Review what you think went right on the project, including your own work and the work of your friends. Then review what went wrong. Consider how you would want to change the outcome of the project, whether it's the project itself or your feelings about the people you worked with. What would you do differently? How would you handle the same situations now?

19

Part Six

The Business Side of Games

The work of a production team is complete (mostly) when they finally release the gold master of the game. As the team works on building, testing, and polishing the game assets during the production phase, a product manager from the marketing department is assigned to develop a marketing plan to promote the game and the marketing department begins its work of preparing the game audience for the product's release. The marketing begins by issuing occasional press releases to various media. As the game nears completion, the campaign builds until finally, just as the product is about to hit the shelves, a full advertising campaign aimed at magazines and television announces the game's release. If all works as planned, gamers will be lining up to buy the game as soon as it hits retail shelves.

Over the past twenty years, the game industry has shown remarkable growth as it has developed from a hobby for the technically literate into a broad-based entertainment medium played on many different devices. As computer technology continues to advance, new game platforms will continue to appear, and new kinds of gaming experiences will offer players ever-increasing challenges.

Games appeal to all cultures around the world, and people everywhere want to get into the industry but don't know quite what to do to get started. Developing skills that the industry needs, such as programming or 3D graphics, is the best way to get a job at a game company, but the industry is open to everyone who has the dream, the ambition, and the stamina to make great games.

- **Chapter 20:** Marketing the Game
- **Chapter 21:** Economics of the Game Industry
- **Chapter 22:** Breaking into the Game Industry

Chapter | 20

Marketing the Game

Chapter Objectives

After reading this chapter and completing the exercises, you will be able to do the following:

- List the responsibilities of a marketing department in a game company.
- Explain what goes into preselling a game.
- List the elements of a marketing campaign for a new game.
- List where games are advertised.
- Describe the other responsibilities of a marketing department.

Introduction

A production team can spend years producing the best game ever made, so they want to make sure that the public is ready to buy it when it ships. The marketing department at a publisher is responsible for promoting new games and preparing the audience to run out and buy them at release. Unfortunately, a rift can sometimes develop in a company between those who create the games and those who promote them, and misunderstandings can arise when one group fails to appreciate the other's efforts. However, both groups are necessary to the success of a game. Whereas production teams are responsible for creating exciting games with massive appeal to many players, the marketing department is responsible for promoting those games by getting the word out about how wonderful they are.

Marketing Department Responsibilities

Marketing departments are typically found only in large game publishers. Smaller publishers often work with independent marketing companies rather than bearing the expense of maintaining an entire marketing department. Independent developers leave marketing to their publisher. Whether internal or external, the marketing department contains people who are interested in promoting a product and making it as profitable as possible. They are not necessarily interested in the artistic merits of a game, and they might not even play the game, but they are interested in trying to get as many consumers as possible to purchase the product.

The marketing department should be involved in a new game from the first pitch until well after the complete product ships to retailers. Most publishers include someone from marketing in meetings where designers and independent developers pitch their ideas for new games to give feedback to management on which projects are likely to sell best. During the preproduction phase, a designer might ask for assistance from the marketing department when creating the marketing analysis for the game design document (see Chapter 9, "Committing Ideas to Paper"). Getting the marketing department interested in a new game is particularly helpful when selling the idea to management. Additionally, the marketing department might include evaluators whose primary responsibility is to test competitors' products and write up reports about the good and bad points of each product.

When a new game title has been approved and enters production, a *product manager* from marketing is assigned to the project. The product manager is responsible for creating and managing the product marketing strategies for the game. When the game reaches the alpha version, the product manager's job really begins. After alpha, the real game assets are available, and the product manager now has something to show off. As the game nears the beta version, the product manager's involvement kicks into high gear. He oversees the creation of promotional materials for the product, creates presentations for trade shows, helps develop the packaging, and sets up the advertising campaign. In addition, he holds a series of focus groups to get feedback on various parts of the game, such as the interface design, fun factor, consumer interest in the subject, and so on (see the section on focus groups later in the chapter for more information). The product manager works closely with the producer and the sales department throughout this time to prepare for the release of the game.

After the product ships, there is likely to be additional promotional work. There are trade shows (such as the Electronic Entertainment Expo [E3]) and industry shows (such as the Game Developers Conference [GDC]) to attend, promotional tours, and cross-promotions with partners and licensors. One of the product manager's most important jobs is to keep the product on retailers' shelves as long as possible so it can be as profitable as possible.

Preselling a Game

As a game takes shape and begins playing the way the designer imagined and looking the way the team has agreed upon, there is a natural desire to start showing it off to people. A development team inside a publisher can use the company's resources to promote the game. An independent developer under contract to a publisher is restricted as to what they can do to promote the product, for example, setting up a dedicated Web site or revealing art assets to the industry press. The publisher's marketing department determines when materials from a game will be revealed as part of the overall marketing campaign.

The Lead-Up to Product Ship

Depending on the product, the marketing of the game can start as early as when the contracts are signed, especially if the game is based upon a well-known license. For example, a game based on a blockbuster movie is likely to draw heavy media attention and will probably be scheduled to ship at about the same time the movie is released. If the game and movie are released close together and the game captures the essence of the movie, the resulting publicity might result in better sales for both products. Of course, it helps if the game is fun, too.

More likely, the marketing of a game will not begin until about halfway through production. There are several reasons for this, not the least of which is that the schedule of the game is likely to be set at this point, with (one hopes) most of the major technical issues resolved and a firm release date established. It's also the first time when the team can provide screenshots of the game that are close to the final artwork.

As described later in this chapter, there are a number of ways to get the audience's attention and to keep them interested in the game until it actually ships. The whole point is to whet players' appetites and get them to ask their local game stores when the game will be available. The retailer might even have empty game boxes on hand to let players know what the package will look like when the game ships.

The main challenge for marketing is to make a new game stand out from the rest. A new game has a limited time to find its market, and if gamers don't start buying as soon as the game hits the shelf, it will disappear within a matter of weeks (if not days, especially around the Christmas selling season). Every month, dozens of new games appear on shelves, and the competition for retail shelf space is fierce. If the public isn't primed to buy the game when it ships, the publisher stands to lose millions of dollars.

> ## FYI *Christmas Selling Season*
>
> The Christmas season (from mid-November to mid-January) is the hottest time for retail sales, and games are no exception. The *International Herald Tribune* has reported that 50 percent of video game sales occur during this season (others place the figure as high as 90 percent). To cash in on these sales, many publishers set up their schedules so that new releases appear primarily in October and November. Retail stores are so flooded by new game titles that many never get onto shelves and either sit in boxes until the rush is over or get shipped back unopened. A product that slips a Christmas season ship date takes much longer to recoup its expenses.

Overselling and Underselling the Game

There is always a tension between overselling and underselling a game before it is ready to ship. Overselling comes from showing off the product too early in the production phase or promising too much. If the product is promoted long before its actual release date, the audience can grow tired of hearing about how great it is and relegate it to *vaporware* (a product that is promoted but never ships). Even if they are anxious to play the game, they might grow frustrated and angry if it has to slip for any length of time. There is also a serious threat that another company will release a similar product before the game is finished, diluting its audience.

Underselling comes from not promoting the game enough before it ships. If the product misses its milestones several times, the publisher might not feel comfortable promoting it until just before it goes gold. In this case, if many other games are shipping at the same time, the new game might not get the notice that the competitors do. Another reason for underselling the game is that the publisher has lost interest in it, for whatever reason. In this case, the publisher will generally write off the product as a loss and will not be willing to spend the money to promote it . . . unless it happens to find an audience. Rather than spending a huge amount of money promoting the game, the publisher simply ships it with minimal fanfare to see if word-of-mouth will make any difference. Even if the publisher does promote it, the game can suffer if the industry press does not think it is cutting-edge enough, so they ignore it or give it bad reviews. Finally, even if the product is well promoted and praised by critics, the gaming audience might not be interested in it because the field is already too crowded with similar products, another big title is released at the same time, or the target game platform has lost its appeal.

IN THE TRENCHES: Game Industry Press

The people who write game reviews are usually dedicated gamers who have a thorough understanding of the industry and are up-to-date on the latest technological advances. They usually have the finest equipment and are considered "hard core" gamers. They write for readers who have similar tastes in games. Because most game industry writers are relatively young and lack journalistic training, they have strong opinions about what is right and wrong with games and aren't afraid to share their opinions with their readers. They often praise games for being technologically advanced and leading edge even if the gameplay is poor, and they often ignore games with middling graphics but good gameplay.

20

Marketing Campaign

A marketing department has many different "weapons of mass information" at its disposal to inform the gaming public about products as they get close to shipping. However, none of these weapons comes cheap. The marketing budget for triple-A games has grown substantially, almost in tandem with the production budget. So if a production team spends $3 to $4 million to create the game, the marketing department might spend another $3 to $4+ million promoting it. That budget includes the cost to develop and purchase print ads, promotional demos (distributed CDs or diskettes), sell-sheets (explained later in the chapter), and other promotional items. The cost of the package is also included in the marketing budget. A marketing budget can actually be greater than the production budget if the publisher plans to include television ads as part of the campaign. Of course, the game must sell a few hundred thousand extra copies just to pay off these marketing expenses.

A game has to be sold not only to the public but also to retailers. If major retailers don't know a product is coming out, there might be no shelf space available when it appears. Even if the shelf space is available, the retailer might have to be convinced to stock the game, especially if the publisher is small and doesn't have a steady stream of new titles. Publishers often have to promise to buy back unsold inventory and pay for the delivery. Moreover, in exchange for shelf space, the publisher is expected to offer *marketing development funds (MDF)* to the retailer to help pay for the newspaper ads where the publisher's game cover appears. The publisher might also have to pay extra for desirable eye-level shelf space or for an end-cap display. It can seem like extortion, but retailers have limited shelf space to devote to games, and because some 1,500 titles can be published in a year, they have to try to select those that will make the most profit for them.

FYI *End-Cap Displays*

An **end-cap display** is a special display set-up placed at the end of a tier of shelves in a retail store. It is a prime location for displaying featured goods or items because customers pass by and see the display even if they don't go down the aisle. Frequently, a manufacturer will create a special display for this area to show off the company's products, especially new releases. The manufacturer often has to pay the retailer to use this space.

One of the critical steps for developing a marketing strategy is the establishment of the *unique selling points (USPs)* of the product. USPs might be as simple as "fun, compelling gameplay," but they are more likely to be along the lines of "from the same team that brought you the million-seller game XYZ" or "ideal for the gamer with the newest game hardware" or "includes music from rap master ZYX." These USPs are established as early as possible in the development of the game and form the basis of the key features listed on the back of the game box when the game ships. Beyond that, however, the USPs are the fundamental reasons why a company decides to invest several million dollars into the development of a new title. They also should give *store buyers* (the people at each chain or retail outlet who decide what the store should purchase and sell on their store shelves throughout the year) reasons to decide to purchase a particular game.

Marketing Tools

To prepare retailers and the public for a new game, the product manager uses a number of promotional tools to keep them aware of its progress and to whet consumers' appetites. The following sections discuss a few of the tools used for marketing games.

Press Releases   One of the oldest marketing tools is the *press release,* which is a one- or two-page document about a product that is submitted to the media. Newspapers, magazines, and news programs are always hungry for interesting stories, and if a press release is more than simple promotional copy for the product and talks about a legitimate topic of interest (such as an emerging technology or item of particular local interest), it might lead to a news story or article about the game. In many cases, the press release is quoted in part or in whole as the news story.

Press releases are sent out a number of times throughout a game's development process whenever a newsworthy event occurs. Early in development, the release might talk about a license or perhaps some well-known artist's or musician's becoming associated with the product. Later on, releases might be sent out when the game enters alpha or beta or goes gold. The goal of each press release is to lure game magazines or Web sites into doing articles on the game at each major phase of development. A great advantage of press releases is that they are fairly cheap to produce and distribute, and if they interest someone in the media enough to write a story, the free exposure can more than pay for the expenses involved in producing them.

FYI | *Good and Bad Press*

There is an old adage that there is no such thing as bad press—any information that is published about your product is good. It is true that the more people hear about an idea or product, the more comfortable they are with that idea. With that in mind, marketing is never as unhappy as the public might think when bad press comes out.

One of the most important elements of a press release is an exciting headline that mentions the publisher, the game title, and some piece of information that grabs the reader's attention. The next important element is the lead sentence, which captures the essence of the entire release (similar to the way the high concept captures the essence of a pitch paper). In addition, each press release should explain the basic concept of the game, point out one or two interesting facts, mention the target game platform(s) and ESRB rating, and then end with the scheduled ship date and suggested retail price. The press release should be written so that the reader (or viewer) becomes as excited about the product as the writer. The writer also needs to include such information as the source of the press release, the contact who sent the release (for more information), and the desired release date for when the information is to be made public.

Sell Sheets   A *sell sheet* is similar to a press release in many respects in that it contains considerable information about the game, explaining why it is so good that customers should buy it. Unlike press releases, which are aimed at the general public (albeit through media outlets), sell sheets are targeted primarily at distributors and retailers (Figure 20.1). A sell sheet is usually printed in four colors on slick paper and is more expensive to produce than a press release. The front often uses the same artwork that appears on the front of the game package, and the back of the sheet includes copy that describes the major features of gameplay, several screenshots of the game action, and product release information. These sheets are created primarily to be handed out at a publisher's booth at trade shows. They are sometimes mailed in bulk to retailers and distributors to make available to customers.

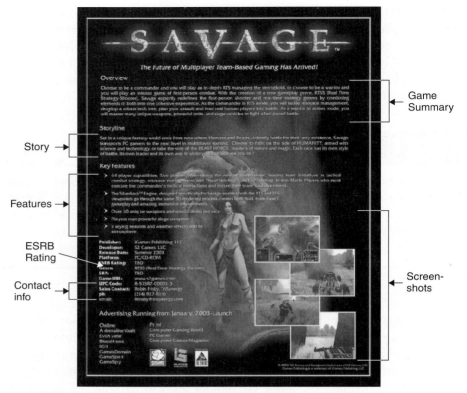

Game
Summary

Story

Features

ESRB
Rating

Contact
info

Screen-
shots

FIGURE 20.1 Sell sheet for S2Games' *Savage: The Battle of Newerth* (2003), a massively multiplayer online role-playing game.

Advertising One of the biggest promotional expenses for a publisher is the advertising campaign. Print ads are scheduled for game industry magazines such as *Electronic Gaming Monthly, PC Gamer,* and other magazines that appeal to the target audience of young males aged 13 to 35. Pop-up ads are created for Internet sites that cover the game industry. In-store cardboard displays are placed in retail outlets that specialize in games. Television ads, while expensive to make and show, can reach both nationwide and game-oriented audiences. Ads for games even appear in such unusual places as on or with DVDs of movies (especially if the game ties in with a film) and in movie theaters before feature attractions. The marketing department develops the concept for the advertising campaigns as part of the overall marketing strategy, although an advertising department or consultant actually creates the ads (see the next section of this chapter for more details about advertising campaigns).

Trade Shows The most important U.S. trade show is the Electronic Entertainment Exposition (E3) that is held every May at the Los Angeles Convention Center. The major publishers all have huge booths that cost thousands of dollars to build and take up considerable floor space in the exposition area. The European Computer Trade Show (ECTS) is analogous to E3 and is held in September. The Tokyo Game Show (TGS) is held in the spring and primarily promotes Japanese game developers and hardware manufacturers.

Promotional Stints   Players enjoy meeting the people who work on games, so some members of the development team might be asked to take part in various promotional junkets. They might take part in online chat sessions hosted on a gaming site to answer gamers' questions about the game. The G4 cable channel, which is dedicated to games, often airs programs on upcoming and new releases. There are also local conventions such as QuakeFest in Dallas that are attended by local industry professionals and game players. A number of major corporations have started to sponsor game tournaments including Intel, Samsung Electronics, and Razer Group (they make computer mice). Additionally, some game companies send promoters to colleges and universities to run gaming nights in dormitories or student unions.

Product Placement   A relatively new way to promote games is product placement, where a game appears in a different medium (usually a movie or television show). The idea is that if the mass audience sees the fictional characters enjoying the game, they might become interested in checking it out too. A related trend in product placement is for nongame products to appear in games, either as objects on the playfield or on billboards.

Electronic Arts has used product placements in several of their games. Not only do they show actual car models in some of their race games like *Need for Speed;* they also include products and services such as Burger King, Best Buy, and Cingular Wireless (in *Need for Speed Underground 2*). Games offer companies an audience that is focused on the game action yet is attentive to details such as ads on billboards or labels of real products on game objects—as long as they are not distracting (for example, a cola ad in a fantasy setting). BBC News reported that studies have shown that 30 percent of such ads are remembered shortly after they are seen and 15 percent are recalled after five months or more. Although the money made from product placement is small compared to sales of the game itself, it does contribute to a company's profit margin. Certainly, the target audience is one that advertisers are very interested in reaching, and this trend is likely to grow.

Other Marketing Tools   Other marketing tools are occasionally used to sell games. Some companies produce videos about the creation of a game to run on television (for example, MTV or G4) or to appear as a special feature on a movie DVD if the game is a tie-in to the movie (for example, a video about the making of the *Matrix Online* MMORPG appears on the *Matrix: Revolutions* DVD). Bungie produced a movie about the creation of *Halo 2* that is included on the second DVD of the special gold version of the game. Another approach is creating fake blogs (Web logs) purportedly by gamers discussing the merits of a game.

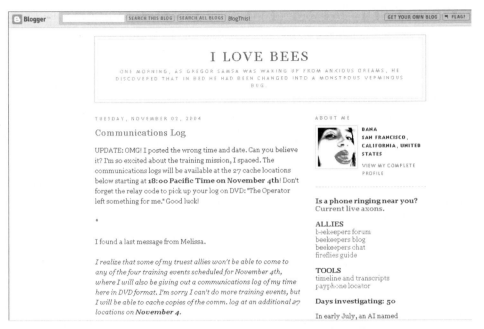

FIGURE 20.2 The "I Love Bees" blog site (**ilovebees.blogspot.com/**) was a clever marketing campaign by Microsoft to promote the release of *Halo 2*.

Or, a company might create a blog to promote a game, such as the "I Love Bees" blog (Figure 20.2) that was created to promote Bungie's *Halo 2* (published by Microsoft); it appeared to be a personal diary created by characters living in the Halo universe. Its goal was to get players interested in the backstory of the game.

Strategic Marketing Plans

When setting up marketing campaigns for new products, a publisher must think strategically about the long-term goals of the company and how each new product contributes to them. When the goals have been agreed upon, the marketing department can create a strategic marketing plan to promote new products as well as support existing ones. Otherwise, each new game release might be treated as a unique event happening in a vacuum, and existing products might be forgotten and die off before their time.

A *strategic marketing plan* takes into account not only when new products will appear but also what resources will be available over a long time period—primarily, money, and manpower. A large publisher can have considerable funds and a large marketing department that can take advantage of opportunities whenever they arise. A small publisher often has less money and a small marketing staff (or marketing consultants), so they must be very clever about what opportunities they pursue. A publisher should help the marketing department develop definite goals; for example, increasing the company's marketing share by a specific percentage, improving the corporate image in the public's eye, achieving greater penetration in more outlets, and so on. These goals should be realistic and achievable given the company's resources and the current market conditions.

By coordinating its efforts under a long-term plan, the marketing department can save a company money. For example, instead of submitting print ads to game magazines one at a time as each new game is released, the product manager might decide to group the ads to get a better price from the magazine's publisher and possibly get better placement in the publication. Rather than creating one ad per game, they might create a composite ad or brochure that promotes several similar games that share a similar look and feel (such as a line of sports games that feature a common layout for all covers).

Advertising Games

The advertising department is usually either part of the marketing department or an independent consultant. It is tasked with the responsibility of creating and placing advertisements for a publisher's products in coordination with the overall marketing strategy. The whole point of advertising is to let potential customers know that a game is going to ship soon, so the advertising department's goal is to create a campaign to show the new product to as many potential buyers as possible by targeting as many different media outlets as the budget affords. This department is also responsible for providing camera-ready artwork to retailers for use in their advertisements.

FYI | *Camera-Ready Artwork*

Camera-ready artwork for a print ad refers to art and text laid out on a board or mat in such a way that it can be photographed to produce black-and-white or four-color negatives. Some companies are willing to pay extra money to have the magazine art staff prepare the ad for them rather than go to the expense of providing camera-ready art themselves.

The primary outlets for ads are magazines, the Internet, and television. As part of a marketing campaign, the product manager determines how much money will be spent on advertising and how much on other promotional activities. Television ads are the most expensive to produce and place, followed by magazine ads, then Internet ads.

Magazine Ads

For many years, the most popular forum for advertising a new game was in hobby magazines. As the industry developed, a number of new magazines launched every year. With the advent of the Internet, the number of magazines began to dwindle as online game sites started to provide the same kind of reviews and articles as print magazines but for free. However, a number of game magazines continue to be published including *Computer Games, Computer Gaming World, Electronic Gaming Monthly, Game Pro, Nintendo Power, Official Xbox, PC Gamer, PSM: 100% Independent PlayStation,* and *Tips & Tricks.* Gamers still enjoy buying these magazines; one reason why is that the ads that let them know what new products will soon appear in stores (Figure 20.3).

Because the magazines are read primarily by young males between the ages of 18 and 30, the ads are targeted at this group. As a result, they usually take up a full page or two pages to best draw the reader's attention, and they are often edgy and can be rather crude, sexist, and violent. Indeed, it can sometimes be difficult to tell at first glance what is an ad and what is an article or even what kind of game is being touted in an ad.

One danger of using magazines to promote a game is the long lead time that most magazines demand. It can take three to four months for an ad to appear (especially a four-color ad that requires extra processing time), and during that

FIGURE 20.3 A typical example of the type of ads that appear in most game magazines. In this case, a two-page ad for Sega's *Phantasy Star Online* for the Dreamcast is obviously aimed at a male audience.

time the product might slip its schedule (or be cancelled). Also, because the most popular time to advertise new games is during the Christmas season when most sales occur, everyone wants to run ads at that time. Therefore, a magazine might be overstuffed with full-page game ads, thus diluting the effectiveness of a given ad. A smaller publisher with fewer funds to spend on promoting their games can find their smaller ads getting lost in a sea of similar titles.

Magazine ad rates are determined by the number of readers (the *circulation*) and by the subject of the magazine. The rates are based on the number of issues sold and are measured using a *cost-per-thousand* (*CPM,* with *M* being the Roman numeral for one thousand) ratio—that is, the cost of reaching a thousand people. Nationwide magazines such as *Time* and *People* have huge circulations and can charge high fees for ads. On the other hand, smaller magazines targeted to specific audiences can also charge high fees because they provide a target consumer that is already more interested in the topic of the ad than the general public. A publisher that wants to appeal to a wider audience by placing ads in a nationwide magazine might decide to target a limited number of areas with thriving gaming communities, or they might ask for remnant space in the magazine.

20

FYI   *Remnant Space*

A magazine typically devotes a certain number of pages in an issue to ads. If all these pages do not fill up, the unused pages are referred to as **remnant space** and usually sell at a lower rate. The ad buyer has to accept wherever the ad is placed, which can be buried in an undesirable location in the magazine.

Advertisements in game industry magazines are cheap compared to nationwide magazines, but even their costs can add up. Full-color ads are more expensive that black-and-white ads. Inside covers also incur an extra cost as well as ad pages opposite a popular feature or column in the magazine. A game publisher can usually get a cheaper rate by buying a certain number of ads per year (for example, six per year), which might also result in more say-so over exactly where the ads appear in the magazine.

Internet Ads

Advertising on the Internet has grown substantially in the past decade, reaching about $10 billion in 2004, and it is expected to grow another 21 percent in 2005 according to an article on Gwinnett Daily Online (**www.gwinnettdaily online.com**). Dedicated online game sites, such as GameSpot, AdrenalineVault, GameSpy, and HappyPuppy, among many others, are perfect places for publishers to advertise their new games. Publishers often place media-rich ads on these sites to let players know the product is available in stores. These online sites depend upon ads as their primary source of income, thus allowing them to offer their services for free or for a small subscription price.

There are a number of different types of Internet ads a publisher can use:

- Banner Ads: This is the best-known and most popular type of ad. Banners feature a graphic image that runs in the margins or across a Web page, and most of them include some kind of animation to attract the customer's attention and get more people to click on the ad. The size of such ads is usually limited. The Interactive Advertising Bureau (**www.iab.net**) has released a set of size specifications for such ads to standardize the "interactive marketing units," as they refer to the ads.

- Interstitial Ads: These are pages or pop-up ads that appear between the time a user clicks a link and the time she reaches the selected site. They can also appear while the user is downloading something. They are often animated to keep the user's attention until the connection is made or the download is complete. Because they tend to stay on the screen longer than banner ads and are harder for the user to ignore, they are usually more expensive to place.

- Floating Ads: These ads combine the features of pop-up and banner ads. The ad appears on the screen and seems to hover over the background until the user closes it. It usually contains a link to the advertiser's Web site.

- Infomercials: On television, infomercials are program-length promotions for specific merchandise like beauty products, cooking utensils, or exercise equipment. On the Internet, these are interactive ads that use Flash animations. They are often referred to as *rich media.*

- Splash Pages: This is a form of interstitial ad that appears before the regular home page on a site (Figure 20.4) and that promotes either a feature on the site or an outside product. Users interested in the service or product can wait for a timer that automatically forwards them to the home page, or they can click on a button or ad itself to go straight to the site.

Just as each magazine has its own price structure for advertisement placement, there are several ways an Internet site can set up its payment structure for ads.

- Pay-per-View: A simple weekly or monthly fee based on the number of Internet users that visit the site.

- Cost-per-Click: The fee is based on how often Internet users actually click on the ad to go to the client's Web site.

FIGURE 20.4 Splash page Internet ad for Buena Vista Games' *The Chronicles of Narnia: The Lion, the Witch and the Wardrobe* action game (published by Walt Disney) that appeared on GameSpot before the game and movie were released in 2005.

■ Cost-per-Action: The fee is based on the user's performing an additional activity over and above just visiting the client's site; for example, clicking on an offer for a free brochure.

■ Cost-per-Lead: The fee is based on the number of visitors to the client's Web site that provide enough information (usually through a media-rich ad) to become an active sales lead.

Because they can lead to instant sales, Internet advertising for games is particularly useful at the time a game ships. Although pop-up and floating ads can be annoying, Internet advertisements are an effective way to reach the right demographic, and creators continue to try to figure out the best way to put new products before users' eyes without upsetting them too much.

Television Ads

Television ads are expensive to make and very expensive to air, but they do reach the largest potential audience of all forms of media, so the expense can be worth it. Whereas a magazine ad might be seen by a few hundred thousand potential customers, a television ad can be seen by tens of millions of viewers. A television ad is similar to a minimovie, and if it is to be released nationally, requires top-notch audio-visual quality. Many expenses are involved in using a professional advertising company to create a television ad, including actors and crew salaries, location expenses, script writing, equipment rental, transportation, and other production costs. It can cost anywhere from $250,000 or up to create an ad. Although a 30-second ad costs less to create than a 60-second ad, there is a cost benefit in producing a 60-second ad because it usually can be edited down to 30 seconds relatively easily and cheaply to allow more flexibility when buying ad time.

Television ad rates are established on a CPM basis similar to magazines. The cost of running an ad varies dramatically based on the popularity of the program and the number of households that can view it. A 30-second ad running prime time on a major television network costs hundreds of thousands of dollars. The *New York Times* reported in September 2004 that a 30-second ad run during *American Idol* cost $658,333. The Fox network charged advertisers $2.4 million to run a single 30-second spot during the 2006 Super Bowl.

On the other hand, running ads on cable channels is cheaper, but the audience is smaller. According to Video Age International (**www.videoageinternational. com**), a major U.S. network often averages an 8 rating (17 million viewers) during prime time, whereas the average rating for a cable channel remains below 2 (around 4 million viewers). Still, if the channel appeals to the primary audience for the product, it can be more cost effective on a per-viewer basis. Thus, publishers often run game ads on MTV, Sci-Fi, Comedy Central, Spike, and other channels that are watched by the primary game-playing audience (males 18 to 35). Local channels that provide service to individual cities or areas are even cheaper, and publishers might decide to advertise on these channels if they broadcast specific shows the publishers know their audience is likely to watch either in reruns or in syndication.

As with magazines, most television ads for games appear around Christmas. When a manufacturer releases a new game console, it will advertise around the time the new machine appears during whatever part of the year that happens. However, the desired target audience for games has been cutting back on television viewing significantly. In August 2005, Ziff Davis Media (**www.ziffdavis.com**) released their annual *Digital Gaming in America* study, in which they reported that 24 percent of gamers interviewed had cut back their television watching during the previous year, watching an average of 16 hours of television weekly in 2005, down from 18 hours weekly in 2004.

Television ads will continue be an important source of information for gamers about new products and new game platforms, but it is unlikely that game ads will be as prevalent on nationwide broadcast television as cars, laundry soap, and other consumer products.

Other Advertising Outlets

A product manager tries to find every possible way to advertise a new product without going over the marketing budget. Some of the additional outlets for advertising are:

- Promotional Art and Displays: These include other printed materials that are not included in the box, such as in-store point-of-purchase display units, posters for store displays, company and game logos in the correct format for use in shared advertising campaigns, and other artwork that is provided to retailers, chain stores, reviewers, and press.

- Radio: Although radio ads are much cheaper to produce and run than television ads, they are not often used because they can't show the visual richness of a game's graphics. Local groups, however, often use the radio to run ads for events such as a convention.

- Billboards: Publishers might put ads on billboards at sports stadiums and arenas to promote their electronic versions of the sport. The billboards at race tracks are great for promoting racing games. Otherwise, publishers usually do not use billboards to promote games.

- Movie and DVD Ads: If a game is based on a license, there might be other places the publisher can advertise the game. Some ads for games have appeared in movie theaters as trailers before a main feature. These ads can be expensive because they are minimovies and must have good production values. (They might be more cost effective if they are also used as television ads.) When a movie is released on DVD, the publisher will sometimes include a short feature about the game as one of the extra features on the disk.

20

Other Marketing Tasks

In addition to promoting and advertising new games, the marketing department performs a number of other critical functions for a publisher.

Game Packaging

The marketing department is responsible for creating the packaging for the game. The artwork used for the package is often featured prominently in the promotional materials. A publisher often has an internal creative services department that is responsible for designing the package and creating or commissioning the artwork and manual. Some publishers use independent marketing companies for these services.

The *package designer* is brought on the project about six months before the game is scheduled to ship. She usually meets with the producer, lead artist, and senior designer to discuss the overall look and feel of the artwork and design concept for the packaging. She then works up a number of concept pieces for the others to review, and eventually a design is agreed upon. An artist is commissioned to create the artwork, and copywriters generate the box copy. A dummy package is put together to show what the final product will look like, and when all the stakeholders sign off on the final design, the product is prepared for the printer.

Meanwhile, the production team writes up a first draft of the manual, which is frequently handed off to a freelance writer to finish. If secondary printed materials such as a map of the game world, a technology tree poster, or other game paraphernalia are to be included, the marketing department lines up an artist, if necessary, to work with the senior designer on the layout. The marketing department also deals with other minutia of the game packaging such as ads to promote other products, a feedback card, a registration form, the CD/DVD labels, and perhaps an installation manual.

FYI *Shovelware*

Shovelware refers to the practice of bundling several old games together in the same package, often at a steep discount. It is one method of squeezing as much money as possible out of the product, but the publisher usually makes very little on each copy, and the developer makes almost nothing.

As discussed in Chapter 19, "Completing the Game," all the packaging materials are printed several weeks or months before the gold version of the game is released. The printed covers and backs are attached to the game box or plastic case and sent to the assembler. After the product manager signs off on all the components, the assembly and packaging of the final product can begin.

Research

A large publisher might set up a group in the marketing department to research the industry. Although a number of independent market research companies specialize in the game industry, a publisher might still find it useful to perform its own research. This group performs several kinds of research:

- Evaluating Competitive Products: The group might include a number of avid gamers whose sole responsibility is to play games by other publishers and analyze their strengths and weaknesses. The group's written reports are made available to management to help them make strategic decisions about which new products to fund for development.

- Collating Market Research Data: Large publishers subscribe to the many newsletters and white papers put out by market research companies. There is a huge amount of data to sift through each year, so the publisher might have a small group analyze the data to determine what trends are occurring. Because it can take several years to bring a triple-A game to market, publishers want to make sure that there will still be an audience for the product when it ships. Analyzing trends in the industry is important for helping to make strategic decisions about which new games to support and which projects to stop developing.

- Collating Feedback Data: Many companies ship feedback cards with games or have online sites where gamers can give their comments about the game. This data has to be collated and analyzed to make sure that the broad customer base is satisfied with the company's products and customer service.

- Marketing Analysis for Game Proposals: Game proposals usually include a section on market analysis to show why a new idea for a game will sell. The designers work with someone in the marketing department who is familiar with competitive products and can find the data on how well they sold. The marketing team can provide management with hard data such as sales figures, sell-in and sell-through numbers, length of time on retail shelves, and similar information about competitive products to convince them that a new game will sell well and persuade them to approve the game proposal.

20

FYI Sell-In and Sell-Through

Sell-in refers to the number of copies of a product that are delivered to retailers for delivery, whereas **sell-through** refers to the number actually are sold. A publisher might ship a large number of games to a retailer, but if the game doesn't sell, the games get shipped back, in which case the sell-in number far exceeds the sell-through number. Some publishers or developers use the sell-in number to give an inaccurate estimate of a title's success and make it look more popular than it actually was.

Focus Groups

It is important to get feedback from gamers during the later stages of the production phase to make sure that the game is fun to play, that the controls are easy to use, and that the packaging is attractive and on target. The marketing department uses focus groups to get this feedback. A *focus group* consists of a small number of people from the general public who are brought in to the company (usually by the product manager) to play the game at various stages of development after the main gameplay elements are in place and working as desired. After the group plays the game for a while, the product manager talks to them to get direct individual feedback. They might also be asked to fill out a questionnaire. In addition to having the chance to play a game well before it ships, the participants are frequently rewarded with a token of appreciation such as a t-shirt or a free game. Each focus group should concentrate on a specific feature such as how useful the layout of the HUD is or how easy the game controls are to learn and use during play. Focus group feedback is particularly useful in games that have new and unusual control configurations. The team might assume the controls are intuitive, but outsiders can flounder when they try to direct the game action. Other focus groups are also asked to give feedback about the game packaging and marketing campaigns.

Focus groups are vital to a game company because they help determine which things in the game need to be changed before the product can ship. However, although focus groups can help locate problems in games, their suggestions should be taken with a grain of salt. The team should make sure that suggested changes to their game are really needed and not simply the whims of a small group of people who might never buy the game anyway.

Corporate Communications

The marketing department is also responsible for handling corporate communications. Some of these duties might include publishing a regular company newsletter for employees. They also write press releases about the company for events such as new hires, changes in personnel, and other newsworthy corporate happenings. If the company is publicly held, the marketing department is often responsible for producing the annual report. The marketing group is also usually responsible for other corporate materials, such as the company logo, company letterheads, business cards, brochures, and other promotional or corporate materials. Although these tasks have nothing to do with games, they do play an important part in creating and maintaining the image of the company as a whole.

Summary

The marketing department is responsible for creating a promotional campaign for new games to let customers know when they will ship. A product manager is usually assigned to each new game and is responsible for working with the game producer to set up the marketing plan and determine how the promotional budget will be spent. Many marketing tools are available to the product manager including press releases, advertisements, and promotional tours.

In addition to promoting new games, the marketing department usually has other corporate responsibilities such as holding focus groups, doing market research, and supervising the company's communications with the rest of the world. Overall, the marketing department at a game publisher has many different responsibilities and duties, but the most important is to make sure that each production team's efforts are supported by a strong marketing campaign in order to get each game to the widest possible audience and give it the best chance for success.

Test Your Skills

MULTIPLE CHOICE QUESTIONS

1. Which of the following are responsibilities of a product manager? (Select all that apply.)

    A. Maintaining the schedule.

    B. Creating a budget.

    C. Creating marketing strategies.

    D. Developing an advertising campaign.

2. Which of the following is included as part of marketing a game? (Select all that apply.)

    A. Creating the box art.

    B. Making sell-sheets.

    C. Writing press releases about the game.

    D. Developing promotional activities.

3. What issues should a company consider before creating a TV marketing campaign for a game? (Select all that apply.)

    A. Time slot.

    B. Target market.

    C. Purchasing trends.

    D. Branding.

4. When is the best time to start collecting game screen shots of the game?

    A. During preproduction.

    B. During technical review.

    C. About half-way through the development cycle.

    D. During beta.

20

5. How do retailers deal with limited shelf space?
   A. By only stocking games they know.
   B. By rotating products so that they all get an equal share of the shelf space.
   C. First come, first put on the shelves.
   D. Publishers pay for premium shelf space and end caps.

6. True or False: The number of gaming magazines has decreased due to increases in TV advertising for games.
   A. True.
   B. False.

7. Making your announced in-store date is most critical for which of the following types of games?
   A. Unknown games.
   B. All games.
   C. Popular games.
   D. Brand games associated with movies.

8. Why is analyzing consumer purchasing trends important?
   A. That information is used to help create the TV advertising campaign.
   B. That information is used to help determine the strategic marketing plan.
   C. It helps the marketing team know the proper time of year to release the game.
   D. Marketing teams don't play games and need assistance knowing the best kinds of games to make.

9. Which of the following applies to marketing development funds?
   A. They are provided by the publisher to help a retailer pay for local newspaper advertising.
   B. They are built into the development budget for marketing research and analysis.
   C. They are refunded to the retailer if the product does not sell all the units in inventory.
   D. They are used by marketing to design, develop, and manufacture the manual and box.

10. Which of the following conferences in the game industry is most focused on selling and marketing games?

   A. E3.

   B. SIGGRAPH.

   C. GDC.

   D. CES.

11. Which of the following does a marketing person usually do during a press tour? (Select all that apply.)

   A. Does not participate in the actual interviews.

   B. Schedules and arranges all travel and interviews.

   C. Distributes demos, t-shirts, or other material.

   D. Works to get the best reviews possible for the product.

12. What is a focus group useful for?

   A. Finding bugs.

   B. Testing new game designs before coding begins.

   C. Gauging market reaction to a product.

   D. Evaluating the intelligence of the market.

20

EXERCISES

Exercise 20.1: Make a Sell-Sheet

Select one of the games you own and create a two-sided sell-sheet for it. Remember that this sell-sheet goes to the retail stores to help them decide how many copies of the game to purchase.

Exercise 20.2: Market a Product

For this exercise, choose a common household item (such as paper towels or milk) and create a marketing plan for it. Write out three to five unique selling points for the product. Make sure the USP can establish the differences between your product and competing products in the minds of your market. Create a PowerPoint presentation to market your product to a focus group of your target market and be prepared to present it. The end goal of the presentation is that the people watching will want to purchase your item.

Exercise 20.3: Develop an Advertising Campaign

Assume that you have $500,000 for an advertising campaign. Select either the game used in Exercise 20.1 or another game and draft an advertising plan for it. How would you spend the money? Explain your choices and include a rough schedule based on the development milestones discussed in earlier chapters.

Exercise 20.4: Research a Game Company

Select a well-established game company that has it's own Web site and is mentioned at least once in a game-reporting news medium such as Gamasutra.com, *Game Daily,* or another game magazine. Determine how many games this company has shipped to consumers in the past 12 months. List where you found the information about the shipped games (the company Web site, press releases, news Web sites, or other). Determine the genre of each game, when it was scheduled to ship, and when it actually shipped (you won't be able to do this for all games). Can you establish a trend in the types of games the company makes or when they tend to ship games?

Exercise 20.5: Write a Press Release

Draft a press release for a fictional company. This company is announcing the start of development of a new game. Include USPs, information on the publishing company, information on the development company, and quotes from fictional people in the companies. (Suggestion: Review online press releases from other companies to get ideas on what is important to the reader, what should be included, and how to format the information.)

Exercise 20.6: Take a Field Trip to a Video-Game Store

In a group of three or four, go to a store that sells video games. Analyze how the games are displayed. Do many of them face outward, or are they mostly spine out? Are there any end caps? If there are, do they feature games that you previously knew about? Discuss which games most catch your eyes. Do they get your attention based on your desire for a sequel, the marketing plan, your knowledge of the brand or company, or something else? Can you convince the other people in your group that they should consider purchasing the game you are most interested in?

DISCUSSION TOPICS

1. Why is it important not to oversell a game before it is released? Discuss three games that you know didn't make the original scheduled release date in the past. Based on the prerelease marketing, how did you feel

about the games by the time they were released? Were the games over-sold or undersold?

2. In a group of three or four, select one or two game companies and write down their names. All the individuals in your group should now think of all the descriptive words they can associate with each of the companies listed. Include not only genres of games or game names but also the connotations associated with the company name. At the end, rank the companies in order of those with the most popular descriptors within the group.

3. Discuss the relevance of TV as a medium for advertising games. How is it good or bad? Can using this medium increase the sales of a game? How could it decrease the sales? Can those sales outweigh the costs of making and airing a commercial?

4. What about other forms of advertising such as radio, newspapers, direct-mail, and telemarketing? How could they be used to sell games. What are the pros and cons of each?

20

Chapter 21

Economics of the Game Industry

Chapter Objectives

After reading this chapter and completing the exercises, you will be able to do the following:

- Describe how the game industry has grown financially over the past decade.
- List the expenses a publisher bears in addition to funding development.
- Explain the differences between console and computer game income.
- Realize that online, handheld, and mobile games are a growing part of the industry.
- Describe how small developers make money and what rights they need to protect during contract negotiations.

Introduction

The game industry has grown into a major economic powerhouse over the past decade, and this growth will likely continue as the new generation of game consoles hits the market. Games now compete directly with movies, television, music, and books for the consumer's money. However, although the industry is making billions of dollars each year, serious problems of instability continue to plague it.

Each year a number of small developers go out of business, and even some big publishers have difficulty struggling along. New developers continue to come into existence, and small companies start publishing, but the financial and staffing resources needed to start up a successful company have grown, and it will be increasingly difficult for newcomers to compete. Still, the film and television industries have faced (and continue to face) the same kinds of challenges, and the studios, distribution channels, theaters, actors, and others are still making money. Game companies will have to face these same challenges if they are to survive and prosper as well.

Game Industry Economics 101

The game industry has seen remarkable growth over the past decade. Figure 21.1 shows the growth of game sales in the United States since 1996 based on figures provided by the Electronic Software Association (ESA). In 1996, the industry generated about $3.7 billion ($1.7 billion in computer games and $2 billion in video games) in the United States just in games. By 2004, that number had grown to $9.9 billion ($1.08 billion in computer games and $8.82 billion in video games). According to the ESA, over 248 million computer and video games sold in the United States in 2004. This works out to two games per household. Note, however, that this growth has been almost entirely due to video game sales because computer game sales have been sliding steadily since 1999, when they reached a high of $1.9 billion. JupiterResearch projects that computer and video game software will pass the $14 billion dollar mark by 2007.

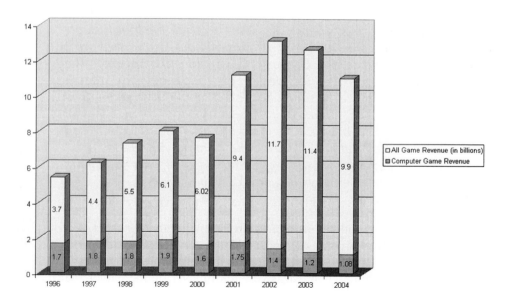

FIGURE 21.1 Sales of computer and video games in the United States from 1996 to 2004. The figures are based on data provided by the Electronic Software Association (ESA) and the NPD Group.

It seems that everyone is playing games nowadays. According to a survey conducted by the ESA, 75 percent of the heads of households in American play console and computer games (2004). The popularity of games in other markets across the world is also growing. In their "Video Game Industry" report of 2004–2005, RocSearch Ltd. (**www.rocsearch.com**) projected, "The worldwide market for video games, computer games and interactive entertainment hardware and software would grow from 20.7 billion dollars in 2002 to 30 billion in 2007." DFC Intelligence (**www.dfcint.com**) likewise forecasts that the worldwide market for game hardware and software will be around $28.4 to $30.1 billion in 2007. Although not all games translate well from one culture to another, the international market for games helps publishers and developers offset the rising costs of game production.

IN THE TRENCHES: Projecting the Future

In response to a message from the author about determining accurate figures for the worldwide game industry, David Riley of the research company NPD Group wrote:

"There is no hard figure for total worldwide sales, but I can give you an idea of how to calculate it. This year, we're expecting sales to reach a record high. Now . . . with the XBox360 and the new portables already in the market (and the fact that half of industry sales occur in the fourth quarter of the calendar year), it goes without saying that we'll see U.S. sales rise above $10.3 billion (the record). The general industry understanding of worldwide retail sales is to double the U.S. sales. So, for example, last year's $10 billion in U.S. sales indicates worldwide retail sales of approx. $20 billion. This does not take into account used game sales, online sales, mobile gaming downloads, etc., etc. If you take all of these into account, you're talking worldwide sales of well over $23 billion."

Internet games and mobile games have a smaller market share. A report by International Data Corp. (IDC) indicated that revenues for computer-based Internet games in 2003 were $450 million and are projected to grow to $1.5 billion in 2007 (Figure 21.2). Massively multiplayer online games (MMOGs) are also predicted to keep growing according to IDC, tripling in size from $656 million in 2004 to $2 billion in 2008 (Figure 21.3). Another report by Informa Telecoms and Media projected revenues for mobile games in 2005 at $2.6 billion and to grow to $11.2 billion by 2010 (Figure 21.4). Most of the income for mobile phone games came from downloading the games, but MMO games

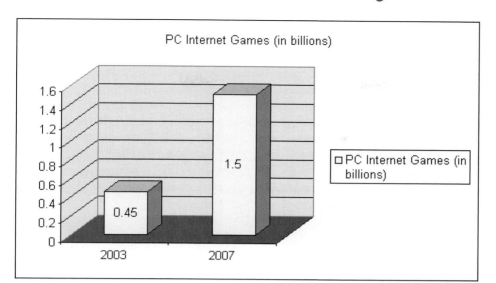

FIGURE 21.2 Projected growth in computer Internet game revenues from 2003 to 2007, based on a report by IDC.

for mobile phones are expected to earn significant revenues, with projections of generating 20.5 percent of total global revenues by 2010.

Thus, barring unforeseen global economic changes, the market for electronic games appears likely to continue growing and will continue to challenge other traditional forms of entertainment (movies, books, music, television) for consumer

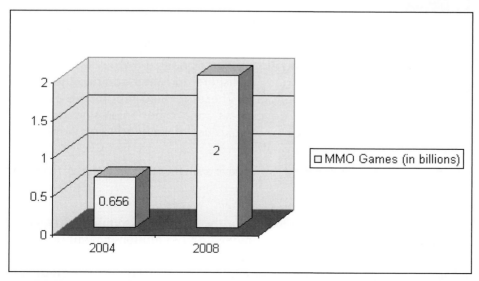

FIGURE 21.3 Projected growth of massively multiplayer online game revenues between 2004 and 2008, based on a report by IDC.

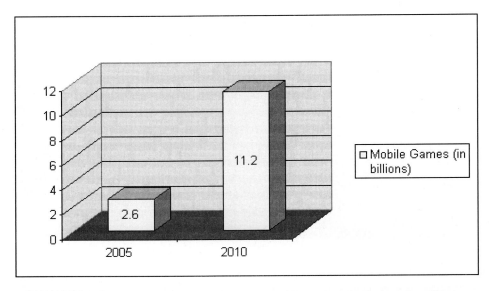

FIGURE 21.4 Projected growth of mobile game revenues between 2005 and 2010, based on a report by Informa Telecoms and Media.

dollars. Of course, no one can predict the future with 100 percent accuracy, so all predictions should be taken with a grain of salt.

> ## FYI Gathering Information about the Game Industry
>
> A number of companies such as ESA, IDC, Informa Telecom and Media, Jupiter Research, NPD Group, RocSearch, and others gather information about the game industry and analyze it. They obtain their information from retailers and publishers and then compile the data and write reports on their findings. These detailed reports are usually sold to game publishers, developers, and other interested parties. However, these companies also make useful summaries available on their Web sites for no charge.

Publisher Expenses

When Bungie's *Halo 2* was released for the Xbox in November 2004, about 2.4 million units sold the first day, ringing up $125 million in retail sales. The game is still available through retail outlets and continues to sell, so obviously it has been a huge success for the publisher, Microsoft. But Microsoft did not get to pocket the entire $125 million dollars earned on that first day of sales. As mentioned in Chapter 7, "Scheduling and Budgets," the publisher makes roughly 65 percent of the retail price of a game, after reductions of the whole-sale price for ***market development funds (MDF)*** and other retailer contributions. So, for a game that sells for $50.00, the publisher makes about $32.50 per copy. The other $17.50 goes to the retailer and distributor. So of the $125 million dollars in retail sales, Microsoft's share was about $82 million, which is spectacular. But the $82 million is not pure profit for Microsoft because they incurred other expenses as a publisher.

Publishers bear a number of overhead expenses to run the company, finance product development, finance inventories, finance receivables, cover general overhead expenses, pay royalties, market the finished product, and distribute it to retailers. These expenses take chunks out of the $32.50 dollars received by the publisher:

- Overhead expenses for running the publishing company vary depending on the number of games being published at one time, the cost of rental space, utilities, phone, computers, and so on. Usually, a company sets an average amount that is applied across the board for all games being released. This number can add up to about $2 to $3 per copy.

- When the game is finished and is being manufactured for release, the publisher must replicate the delivery media (CDs, DVDs, and so on) and print the boxes, manuals, and other components shipped as part of the product. The ***cost of goods (COG)*** for the physical components that make up the game comes to about $4 to $6 per copy.

- The company might have licensing fees and royalties (separate from those paid to independent developers) if they use middleware or another company's game engine or if they base their product on someone else's intellectual property (movie, book, television show, and so on). This cost can vary greatly, but for now, let's assume a cost of $4 per copy. (As noted in the following section, an additional licensing fee is also paid to the console manufacturer for video games.)

- The commissions for the salesmen, costs for distribution and inventory management, and other expenses related to getting the product to the retailers can tack on another $2 to $3 to each copy.

- The marketing cost can also vary based on the expected unit sales and the actual marketing expenditures, but $3 to $5 per copy is a reasonable estimate. For example, if the publisher spends $4 million on marketing and anticipates selling a million copies, the marketing cost is $4 per copy sold.

All these extra costs bring the publisher's share down to about $11.50 to $17.50 dollars per copy (Figures 21.5 and 21.6).

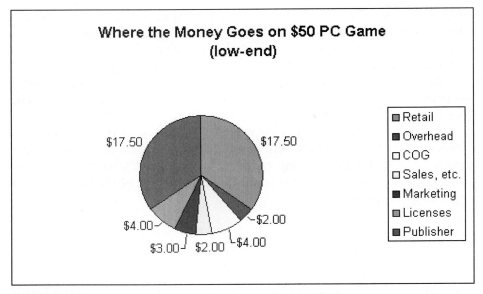

FIGURE 21.5 Distribution of revenues from a $50 game assuming minimum expenditures for cost of goods, overhead, and so on, leaving the publisher $17.50 dollars per copy.

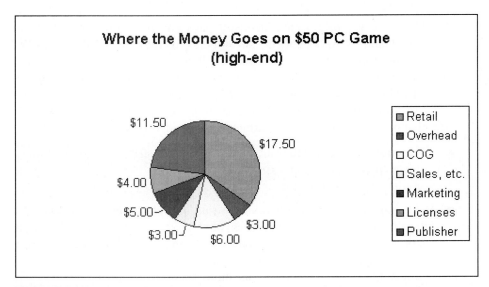

FIGURE 21.6 Distribution of revenues from a $50 game assuming maximum expenditures for cost of goods, overhead, and so on, leaving the publisher $11.50 dollars per copy.

Console Licenses

Three types of licensing fees are typically associated with games: intellectual property, middleware, and console licensing. Game companies that acquire a license to create a game based on an intellectual property such as a movie or television show pay a fee no matter what platform the game appears on. Likewise, if the developer uses middleware such as Renderware or Gamebryo to create the game, a licensing fee is paid for all copies of the game. However, companies that create games for personal computers don't incur the additional fees that console game makers do. A publisher has to pay an $8 to $10 licensing fee to the console manufacturer, which includes the cost of manufacturing the CD/DVD.

These extra costs are offset by the fact that a console game normally sells many more copies than a computer game. But it still means that a console game makes less money per copy than a computer game—about $11 to $13 per copy versus $11.50 to $17.50.

Console manufacturers do not have to pay licensing fees to themselves, so creating games for their own platforms brings in more money. They make about $15 to $19 dollars per copy (if they license a property, however, they still have to pay royalties to the licensor).

21

Development Costs

None of the costs described so far in this chapter include the actual cost of making the game. The publisher still has to pay for the development of the product. If the game is developed in-house, the publisher simply pays for the salaries and benefits of the team producing the finished game as well as their overhead. In addition, the in-house team might get bonuses for meeting their milestones on time and finishing the product on schedule, but in-house teams seldom receive money (that is, royalties) after the product ships.

On the other hand, if the game is created by an outside developer, the publisher usually pays them to create the game in the form of ***advances against royalties.*** These payments are normally tied to the developer's meeting the milestones that the two companies have agreed upon. These advances generally cover the cost of the salaries and benefits for the development staff, as well as some margin for overhead and a certain amount of built-in profit. But these payments are called advances against royalties for a reason: An external developer is entitled to a ***royalty,*** which is a percentage of the wholesale price of the game for all copies sold. If the royalty rate is 15 percent, the developer gets about $5 per copy for a computer game and about $3.40 per copy for a console game. However, the developer must first pay off the advances that the publisher paid during development before starting to receive royalties. If the developer is paid $3.4 million in advances to create a console game (as indicated by the budget presented in Chapter 7, Scheduling and Budgets), the game would have to sell over a million copies (receiving $3.40 per copy) before the advances from the publisher are paid off. When that happens, the developer starts receiving royalties for every copy sold. However, few games sell this well, so many developers must plan to survive only on advances, anticipating royalties only if they have done their job very well.

FYI | *Cross-Platform Development*

One way to make more money on a product, especially for an independent developer, is to develop the game so that it plays on multiple platforms. After all, few gamers own all three video consoles and a computer. Developing a game to play on as many platforms as possible means a larger audience and more revenue. Developing a game for the Xbox is almost the same as developing on a computer because the Xbox uses the Windows operating system.

Developing for the Xbox *and* the PlayStation 2 *and* the Game-Cube is different, however, because each has a unique operating system. The new generation of video consoles presents even more difficult problems because the architectures of their central processing units are radically different from one another. Although the art and game design elements can transfer easily from one platform to another, the same cannot be said for the code. Thus, significant portions of the game-engine code have to be rewritten to make the game run on each platform. Making these changes takes time and money and, therefore, reduces the profitability of developing a game to run on multiple platforms. The publisher has to consider the costs involved in making multiple versions of a game against the expected increase in sales revenue before making a final decision.

The Lifetime of Games

An old adage in the game industry, called the **90–10 rule**, says that 90 percent of the money each year is made by 10 percent of the products. As a matter of fact, it is estimated that only 15 percent of the games published each year are actually profitable. A comparison between the game industry and the movie industry can be made. A few major blockbusters each year earn most of the money, while the rest of the movies (or games) either just break even, show a small profit, or never recoup their initial expenses. Therefore, publishers and developers have to reinvest the profits earned from a smash hit such as *Halo 2* into the development of other games.

As it turns out, a lot of money is invested in games that are either cancelled during production or don't sell well after they reach retail outlets. The retailers also try to predict game sales, and in an effort to maximize their profits, they allot shelf space for products that they know the consumer is interested in purchasing and quickly remove those that consumers ignore. With approximately 1,500 CD/DVD-based entertainment products appearing every year, the competition for shelf space is intense, so if a game doesn't sell as soon as it appears, it might get pulled and returned to the publisher within days. As discussed in Chapter 20, "Marketing the Game," sales teams spend considerable time and money to convince retailers to put their game boxes in end-caps or in other prominently displayed areas. During the Christmas season, when most products are released, games from small publishers can sit unopened in the back rooms; there is no shelf room for them because larger publishers often have the financial clout to get their products on the shelf first.

Like movies, games normally have a limited lifetime in their initial release. Although movies get a second life on DVDs and in rental stores, even if a game is a success, it often stays on retail shelves for only a few months. The average shelf-life of a game is about six weeks. Only a very few of the best sellers, often well-known brands, stay on shelves for six months or more. Games that don't sell well are pulled from the shelves and dumped in the remainder bins or sent back to the publisher, who bears the costs of manufacturing, distribution, and—finally—destruction.

When a movie ends its run in theaters, it usually comes out on DVD and video, then pay-on per-view channels a few months later, then on premium cable channels, and eventually on broadcast television. Each of these incarnations makes money, which can help eventually to recoup the production and marketing costs of the movie. On rare occasions, a very popular game such as *Tetris* will reincarnate in modified form on a new game platform and continue to make a profit for many years. Another source of income for older games is ***OEM (original equipment manufacturer)*** deals, where a few games are included as part of a hardware purchase; for example, either installed on a new computer or as part of a bonus for buying a new sound card. Some games get extra shelf life by being repackaged and repriced—for example, the lower-priced Greatest Hits games (priced at $20) for Sony's PlayStation 2. Older games also get packaged in bundles with other products (called ***shovelware***) and continue to sell after the individually packaged version is off the shelf. There also have been unsuccessful attempts to reincarnate older games such as when Electronic Arts brought out a commemorative edition of Dan and Bill Bunten's *The Seven Cities of Gold* in 1993 (the original was published in 1984), which met with mediocre sales.

However, most games don't get those second and third chances, partly due to the continual changes in technology that antiquate them. Although many older games are remembered fondly by aging gamers, they eventually go away not only because the technology continues to change to the point where they can no longer run on new machines but also because the taste of the gaming audience changes over time. What was fun once can be boring to a younger audience that demands high-definition 3D graphics and surround-sound audio.

Console Platform Costs

Although it appears that the console manufacturers should be making money hand over fist, this is not always the case. True, they manufacture the video platforms customers must own to play the games. They also publish games developed by in-house teams to run on their platforms. Furthermore, they receive licensing fees from other publishers to create games that run on their machines and production fees to manufacture the game CDs/DVDs. However, the expense of producing a new game platform is enormous. According to *Forbes* magazine (**www.forbes.com**), Microsoft lost about $4 billion over four years in launching and promoting the Xbox.

To create a new game platform, a company must invest heavily in technological research because the platform has to be as technologically advanced as possible when it finally ships. Due to the ***closed architecture*** of a console, there can be no significant changes to its architecture after it hits the market until the next generation appears. The company has to set up strategic alliances with developers to make sure that games will be available when the platform ships and that additional products are in the pipeline to keep gamers happy over time.

Because the technology is cutting edge, the manufacturer has to provide developers with a ***software development kit (SDK)*** that helps them understand the technical specifications of the platform and how best to make the programming and art assets show off the console's new features. The SDK might be reworked several times if the manufacturer makes changes to the machine's architecture as the system approaches launch, and it can be a race to the finish to see which products will actually ship when the platform appears. The worst thing that can happen is to have a new platform launch and have only a few games available, as happened to the Sega Saturn system when it was released in 1995. Sega advanced the Saturn's release date from September to May and developers were still working on release products when the system was released.

The new game platform has to be promoted as well. Although a devoted fan base will keep up-to-date on the platform's development, the general gaming audience might not know much about the product until it ships. So, the manufacturer has to launch a massive marketing campaign to promote the platform and the launch titles. Reaching a wide, general audience means investing in expensive television advertisements. Still, the manufacturer might spend many millions of dollars to get the audience prepared to rush out and buy the new machine.

Merrill Lynch Japan estimated that Sony will spend $494 to manufacture a single PlayStation 3 unit for the American market. The expected retail price for the machine is $399, so Sony stands to lose almost $100 per unit. Moreover, the marketing campaign is likely to bump up the per-unit loss by several hundred dollars. So how can Sony make any money if it's losing $300 to $500 dollars per unit? (Merrill Lynch predicts Sony will lose over a billion dollars on the PS3 hardware sales.)

The answer lies in the long-term sales of the software. The machine manufacturers have a monopoly on their machines as well as on the games sold and played on those machines. Only PlayStation games can play on Sony's machines; only GameCube games can play on Nintendo's machines; and only Xbox games can play on Microsoft's machines. Any computer game, on the other hand, can

---

Caution

Buying in Bulk

It's always cheaper to buy components in larger bulk quantities, but a company should not spend that money if they aren't sure about the actual sales. When a product has become established, however, bulk component purchases become easier and more reasonable.

play on any manufacturer's PC as long as it meets the technical requirements. The console manufacturers are following the "razor and blade" model: they are willing to lose money on the "razor" (the game platform) because in the long run they will make money on the "blades" (games). In retail sales terms, the hardware can be also be referred to as a ***loss leader;*** the item itself will lose money but will lead the consumer to buy other products that will make money.

In addition, the cost of producing hardware units almost always decreases as manufacturing methods improve and the components get cheaper. Moreover, the initial marketing campaign to publicize the platform will change to focus primarily on new game releases as the machine reaches a certain level of penetration among consumers. So after a few years, the per-unit cost of the game platform is reduced to the point where the manufacturer can actually make a small profit on the machine itself.

There is a catch, however. If a company decides to release a new generation game console ahead of its competitors, it runs the risk of not paying off the initial development costs for its currently available machine. The other manufacturers will also be forced to accelerate their plans to release their next-generation machine to avoid losing significant market share. This has happened several times in the game industry. In 1993, for example, Sega and Nintendo were jockeying for dominance in the video game market when Panasonic released the 32-bit 3DO console and Atari launched the 64-bit Jaguar. To keep up with their rivals, both Sega and Nintendo quickly announced plans to launch new competitive machines. The Sega Saturn and Nintendo64 were both released in 1995, the same year Sony entered the picture with the release of the PlayStation in America. More recently, Microsoft decided to release the Xbox 360 in an attempt to gain significant market share before Sony's PlayStation 3 and Nintendo Wii were released.

21

Mobile and Handheld Games

There are markets for games over and above traditional computer and video games. These include Internet games (either playing games online or downloading games), games for mobile electronic devices such as cell phones and personal digital assistants (PDAs), and handheld games. The finances of investment and profit for these kinds of games differ from traditional retail outlet finances. These markets currently make up a small share of the industry, but the income they generate continues to grow as more competitors vie for a share.

Electronic Software Distribution (ESD)

There is a way for independent developers who create computer games to skip the middlemen (publishers and retailers) and sell games directly to customers: the Internet. A number of small game companies have Web sites where consumers can order games directly from the developer (referred as **B2C** or **business-to-customer**). The profit margin is much greater for these direct sales, but the sales are small compared to retail sales of packaged games. The publishers, of course, are not happy to be cut out of the pipeline because they don't get a share of the money.

Valve Corporation has directly challenged the retail stranglehold with their Steam network. Steam was originally used to set up multiplayer games of *Half-Life,* which Valve developed, but it also lets customers buy *Half-Life* products directly through downloads. The game's publisher, Sierra Entertainment (a subsidiary of Vivendi Universal), did not approve of this means of selling the game, and Valve sued them over distribution rights in 2002. The companies settled their disagreement in April 2005, and Valve is now allowed to distribute their *Half-Life* games by retail as well as by download. However, Valve's customers need a broadband connection to download the game, and they then have to register it through Steam to play either solitaire or online. Several other games are now offered exclusively through Steam including Flying Lab Software's MMORPG *Pirates of the Burning Sea* and Mark Healey's *Rag Doll Kung Fu.* If Valve's Steam content delivery system succeeds, it could be the start of a revolution in the way consumers buy games.

IN THE TRENCHES: *Doom* Shareware

One of the first companies to successfully sell a game directly to customers via the Internet was id Software. When they released *Doom* as shareware in 1993, they let players download the first third of the game free via the Internet. Customers could then order the rest of the game from them directly. Eventually, they contracted with Activision to distribute the game and their later works through retail outlets.

There are several problems with selling games directly online. First, because most full-price games are so large, only customers with broadband connections can reasonably purchase them this way. According to Internet World Stats News (**www.internetworldstats.com**), around 43 percent of Internet households in the United States had broadband connections as of 2004. Jupiter Research predicts that by 2010, about 69 million homes (78 percent of Internet households) will have broadband connections. However, until broadband is more pervasive, games will continue to be available primarily through retail outlets.

Second, marketing online games will be difficult for small independent developers and publishers because many sites will likely be offering games, and it will be difficult for small companies with limited marketing funds to gain customers' attention. Finally, many customers enjoy browsing through a store, holding the game box in hand, reading the back copy and seeing the screenshots, comparing one game against others in the same genre, and talking to a knowl-edgeable staff about why a game is good or bad. Therefore, ESD won't replace in-store shopping—at least for the time being.

FYI *Piracy and Steam*

Two other important issues are facing online distribution of games. The first is the developers' concern over piracy, and the second is the consumers' concern about being able to reinstall a game in the event of a computer failure. ESD channels look to solve both of these using a variety of methods. In particular, Steam maintains a database of what each consumer owns (or has leased through Steam) and acts as a centralized library for all those games. The consumers never have the entire game stored on their computer. Instead, the game system knows where the player is and, during off times, downloads upcoming portions of the game to the player. It also then removes other portions of the game, to make the installed footprint of the game smaller on the consumer's machine. This protects the developer from having the game stolen at any time while also allowing the Steam system to provide updates or patches automatically as they become available.

21

Online Games

Online games are a growing market worldwide. A 2004 report by ESA found that 42 percent of active gamers in the United States indicated they played games online for one or more hours per week. According to DFC Intelligence, online games worldwide made $1.9 billion in 2003, and they estimate earnings will grow to $9.8 billion by 2009. According to CNET News.com (**www.news.com.com**), revenues from online games amounted to $670 million in the United States in 2004. These sales are small compared to console games, but they represent a significant share of the computer game market. The next generation of game consoles offers customers the ability to purchase a hard drive that will allow console gamers to download games from the Internet.

Online gaming can be broken into four primary categories: game hosting sites, subscription sites, casual game sites, and game download sites.

Game Hosting Sites   The first and simplest type of online game is the free hosting sites. Here, gamers who have bought a copy of a game can go online to link up with others who own the same product and engage in online cooperative or competitive games. No products are generally sold at these sites, and they simply offer the means for game players to connect with other players. They often include player-to-player chat, bulletin boards, and discussion forums. Gamers can play FPS or action games, such as Epic Games *Unreal Tournament 2004,* id Software's *Doom 3,* and Blizzard's *Diablo 2,* without having to pay extra money. Console games are also tapping into this market as the console manufacturers either host or support game sites that allow online multiplayer versions of popular console games. These sites include XboxLive.com, PlayStation.com and Battle.net. Their economics is such that game developers and publishers do not directly make any money from a site itself. They might earn money from banner ads and other merchandising opportunities, and they might see a slight increase in unit sales based on site activity, but because a gamer must already own the game to participate in this "match-making" forum, this amount is negligible. However, such a site offers minimal interaction other than helping players locate other people to play a game, so it is the least expensive to set up and maintain, sometimes requiring minimal security because little critical information about the consumers is stored online.

Subscription Sites   A second category of online play includes subscription sites where players pay a monthly fee to play a game. The consumers usually buy a retail copy of the game (such as a massively multiplayer online RPG), which often does not include a single-player (solitaire) mode. Instead, they have to go to the company's Web site and register to play. Subscription-based games usually include a trial period with the retail purchase of the game, which means that for a limited time buyers can play for free. After the trial period is over, they have to start paying for a subscription to continue playing. Over four million customers currently subscribe to massively multiplayer online (MMO) games. If each is paying an average of $10 a month, then these games are generating $480 million a year ($120 per year times 4 million customers). Most MMO games, such as Blizzard's *World of Warcraft,* Sony's *EverQuest,* and LucasArts' *Star Wars: Galaxies,* use this model. The current generation of game consoles supports a limited number of MMO games, such as Sony's *EverQuest Online Adventures* (2003) and Square Enix's *Final Fantasy XI* (2002), which are available in both PC and PlayStation 2 versions. As the new generation of consoles becomes available, online gaming in persistent universes will likely continue to grow in popularity (Figure 21.7). To keep their customers loyal, the game publishers regularly offer expansion packs that open up new portions of the game universe to explore.

Casual Game Sites   A third category includes online sites where players go to play simple puzzle games. These sites might be subscription based, such as Pogo.com and AOL Games, or they might let gamers play their products freely such as MSN.Games (**zone.msn.com**) and Playsite (**www.playsite.iwin.com**).

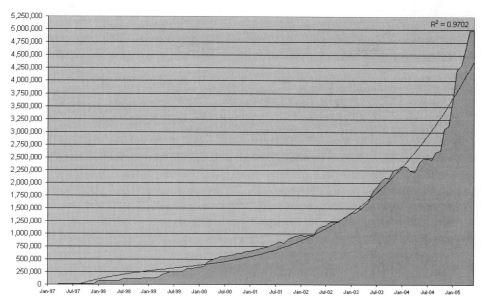

Total MMOG Active Subscriptions (Excluding Lineage, Lineage II, and Ragnarok Online)

FIGURE 21.7 The continuing growth of massively multiplayer online subscribers from 1997 to 2005.

Source: Woodcock, Bruce Sterling. "Total MMOG Active Subscriptions (Excluding Lineage, Lineage II, and Ragnarok Online)". 2006. www mmogchart.com.

In the latter case, the sites rely upon advertising to generate income. In other cases, players might be able to pay for the games and download them to play later, following a shareware model. The games on these sites are often referred to as *casual games* because they are small and can be played in a short amount of time. Many are created in Flash or are small Java applets that get downloaded onto the player's computer. They are perfect, for example, for someone who wants to spend a few minutes during her lunch break doing a crossword puzzle or playing a simple card game against online opponents.

Game Download Sites   The fourth category is similar to the previous one and includes those online sites that only offer downloadable computer games for which customers must pay before they can play (the Xbox also has this ability). In this instance, the customer pays once for the game and does not have to pay a monthly subscription fee to join the Web site or play the games online directly. Examples include Garage Games (**www.garagegames.com**) and Handheld Games (**www.handheldgames.com**). At the moment, the downloadable games tend to be casual games, but as more households get broadband Internet access, the games might become as large as the current computer and console games.

FYI *Most Popular Online Games*

In their 2004 white paper, the ESA reported that the most popular online games were:

1. Puzzles/board/game show/trivia/card: 56.8 percent
2. Action/sports/strategy/role-play: 19.0 percent
3. Shockwave/Flash/browser-based minigames: 9.5 percent
4. Persistent multiplayer universe: 9.1 percent
5. Other: 8.5 percent

Mobile Games

The market for mobile games (those played on cell phones and PDAs) in the United States is also small compared to computer and console games, but it is growing. In their 2004 white paper, the ESA said that 34 percent of heads of households played games on mobile devices (including phones and PDA). In-Stat, meanwhile, estimated that mobile game sales in the United States accounted for $204 million in 2004 and forecast that this figure could grow to $1.79 billion by 2009.

Compared to the United States, the worldwide sales figures for mobile games are much more impressive. Many countries have only one predominant cell phone system, so almost everyone uses it. In-Stat estimated that internationally mobile games made $1.1 billion in 2003, and various projections by In-Stat and others indicate that the worldwide market for mobile games could be between $4.2 and $8.4 billion by 2008. Although the mobile gaming market is only now developing in the United States, it is strong in the rest of the world and could eventually challenge the dominance of consoles as the preferred game platform.

The economics of developing, marketing, and distributing mobile games is still relatively new. In general, the standard distribution arrangement is that a company Web site, usually the cell-phone service's site, sells the games and performs the transactions. The games themselves are either downloaded via the Internet connection of the mobile device or first downloaded to a computer and then transferred to the phone.

The costs of making mobile games are much lower than the costs of developing full-scale games, console games, or even casual games. The limited memory and display capabilities of modern phones and PDAs, which are the primary markets, mean that developers have to create fewer assets. Although the technology used in these mobile devices continues to advance, the current generation of games is often similar to games made in the 1980s for computers (for example, 16-bit color 2D graphics). Although the devices' limitations pose some technical problems, they can be overcome without spending a lot of time, resources, or money. The game art is simple, large enough to see on the screen, and bright enough to be displayed well. The programming, therefore, is usually simpler because the lack of storage on the mobile devices means that the gameplay must be fairly simple and not as time-consuming to code. From a financial aspect, making games for mobile devices is relatively inexpensive, and the profits made on selling single games are pretty good. Depending on the type of game and the platform, the cost of developing a game for this kind of platform can run from approximately $20,000 for a simple game to $300,000 (or more) for a high-end game. Without the additional costs of packaging or replicating, the only other costs the developer/distributor has to factor in are for the servers and the bandwidth that must be purchased for distribution. Because the games average less than 10K in size, these costs are very small.

Several problems face game developers in the mobile game market in the United States. First, several major cell-phone systems compete with one another, so trying to build a game that works on all of them means making significant changes for each port. Second, the cell-phone service companies usually offer only limited advances to independent developers, so product development can be more expensive. Third, the technology of cell phones is changing rapidly, so it is difficult to create one version of the game that will work on both the current generation of cell phones and older phones. Finally, the customers are often confused about how to purchase the games and download the software to their phones. They might be able to download a free demo of the game as shareware, but then they are expected to go to the game site, purchase the full version of the game, and download it.

Handheld Games

By September 2005, Nintendo claimed they had sold over 6.6 million units of the Nintendo DS worldwide. Sony has claimed similar numbers for their PSP. The two systems seem to be in a neck-and-neck race for dominance, although in the end the two systems might appeal to different demographics, appealing to both older and younger audiences. Nintendo has long dominated handheld platforms with the Game Boy (over 177 million units sold worldwide since it was released in 1989), but Sony is challenging this dominance.

For several reasons, the advantage might ultimately go to Sony. First, the PSP can do more things: the Nintendo DS is only a game platform, whereas the PSP can play UMD movies (Sony's mini-CD format), play videos and songs, and display photos. Second, although the initial round of games for the Sony PSP was limited, in the long run more independent developers are working with Sony than with Nintendo. It can be inferred that eventually there will be more games for the PSP than the Nintendo DS. However, Nintendo has a number of strong intellectual properties with the Mario Bros., Donkey Kong, and Link, so consumers might decide to opt for the platform that supports their favorite characters and gameplay.

> ### FYI *Small versus Full-Size Games*
>
> *Small games* and *full-size,* or *full-scale, games* are terms used in the industry to distinguish smaller games with shorter gameplay time from larger games with longer gameplay times. **Full-size** usually refers to games that are delivered on one or more CDs/DVDs, take 20 or more hours to complete, and have a distinct goal with a beginning and an end. **Small** or **casual** games might not have a distinct goal or ending, such as *Tetris*, poker, and other games that can be played for a few minutes and then left.

Developing Small Games

It is difficult, but not impossible, to make a living developing small games. Developers can make a living creating casual games if they keep their companies small (no more than a few programmers and artists). These games are much easier and quicker to produce than full-size computer or console games, but they earn far less money per unit sold. In many cases, developers survive by turning out many casual games per year in hopes that one or two will gain widespread acceptance.

> ### FYI *IGDA on Small Game Finances*
>
> The International Game Developers Association (IGDA) issued a white paper on casual games in 2005 that discusses their finances in more detail. The paper is available on the association's Web site (**www.igda.org**).

In general, the cost to develop a small game that takes from three to four programmers/artists four months to complete might total only $50,000 to $150,000. If the game is sold as a casual game, it usually includes a demo version with limited play or limited time. The full version of the game is usually sold for around $20 per unit. If the developer sells the game on their own site, they get that entire $20. If the developer sells the game on someone else's game site, they are usually paid a percentage. Sometimes this percentage is on a sliding scale, starting at something like 25 percent for all copies sold up to 1,000 copies, then 30 percent up to 1,500 copies, then 35 percent up to 2000 copies, and so on.

After getting a few releases under their belt, some small developers might decide to transition from casual games to handheld games. A typical game for the GBA might sell retail for $30, whereas a PSP or Nintendo DS game might sell for $40, which is in the same price league as full-size computer and console games. The royalty rate for handheld games tends to be lower than for console or computer games, but developing a handheld game takes much less time. A major hit for the GBA can sell over 5 million units. Assuming an average retail price of $25, a title could generate $125 million retail. The developer might make only one dollar per copy, but that could still add up to $5 million for a major hit. If a developer has several hits in the handheld market, the owners might then consider expanding into full-size games.

Financial Drains

The game industry has experienced huge growth over the past decade, but it would have been even bigger except for several major drains on retail sales. The worst threat to the financial health of the industry is piracy, which steals a huge amount of money from publishers and developers. Another drain to sales is the rental and resale market for video games, which allows customers to play games without paying the publisher for them.

Piracy

Piracy is the illegal theft of intellectual property, and there are no reasons to excuse it. It has reached a point where it is significantly affecting the very existence of small game developers. Piracy is devastating to the game industry. Games are ephemeral, and when the initial sales are over, the developer has almost no means to make more money. If half the people who play pirated versions of a game paid for it instead, smaller developers would be getting a significant increase in royalties and might actually make a profit instead of barely surviving on advances against royalties. As development costs continue to rise, the survival of many small developers is in doubt, and piracy is a leading reason why many small companies have to shut their doors. Every user who offhandedly makes a copy of a game for a friend contributes to the piracy problem and threatens the continuing existence of the game industry.

Piracy is not new, and publishers have tried many forms of copy protection over the years to cut down on their losses. No matter what protection tricks and gadgets publishers have tried, the pirates have always managed to find a way around them. Some forms of protection that have been tried so far involve the user's typing in a word found on a certain line on a certain page in the manual, or some physical object might be required such as a red cellophane viewer to find the correct word hidden in a multicolored scramble of squiggly lines. The Internet makes such approaches obsolete, because anyone can post online the work-around to a copy protection scheme.

For a time, it was assumed that the size of a CD or DVD made it too difficult to make copies, but now CD and DVD burners make perfect replicas of the original media. Most games still require that the user have the CD/DVD in the disk drive in order to play, although there are work-arounds even for this protection. Valve requires that owners of *Half-Life 2* register their products online through Steam to enable play of the single-player version of the game. Massively multiplayer online game companies are solving this problem by keeping the player's saved games and character information on their sites and downloading the information to players only when they sign on.

A recent report by the Business Software Alliance indicated that worldwide the level of computer software piracy has been falling but still causes significant losses to publishers and developers. The ESA estimates that piracy worldwide cost the U.S. entertainment software industry about $3 billion in 2004. For 2004, the piracy rate for computer software was 35 percent, a slight decrease from the 36 percent rate in 2003. Assuming a similar rate for piracy of computer games, that means that about one of every three copies of PC games is pirated.

In early 2005, Macrovision did a survey of console gamers and found that about 21 percent of video game software was pirated (mostly from peer-to-peer networks). Moreover, some customers have incorporated mod-chips in their consoles to get around the manufacturers' copyright protection. These chips enable players to play bootleg copies of games that have been burned onto CDs or DVDs, but they are illegal in the United States because of copyright infringement. The legal situation elsewhere is unclear because courts in Spain, Italy, and Australia have ruled that such chips are legal, whereas a court in England has ruled that the chips are illegal.

Renting and Reselling Games

Another drain on the income of game publishers is retail stores such as Blockbuster and Hollywood Video that rent video games. According to the Video Software Dealers Association, video game rentals in the United States accounted for $700 million in 2004 for the renters (they still have to buy the copies they rent). On the one hand, renting a game lets users test the product and determine if it really is the kind of game they want to buy before spending their money. On the other hand, a publisher makes only a pittance from rental fees compared to the lost sales of a title, so rentals can lower the total income for a game.

Computer games cannot be rented because it is too easy to copy the software illegally and distribute it to others. Instead, these games include an end user's license agreement (EULA) that basically says the customer is leasing the software and not buying it outright. The publisher is the copyright owner and, under United States copyright law, can prevent the rental, leasing, or lending of a copy of the game that has been sold. As a result, a retail outlet is restricted from renting the software to other users because doing so would break the copyright law. Video games, however, can be rented due to an exemption. In 1990, the Video Software

Dealers of America argued that they should be exempted from part of the copyright law. At the time the copyright law was passed, it was almost impossible to make copies of the cassettes on which video games appeared, so this exemption was granted. Thus, retailers can rent video games to customers.

In addition, stores such as Gamestop and EB Games resell both computer and video games. According to Money.CNN, the market for resold games was about $800 million in 2004. Although this is small compared to direct sales of games, some larger companies such as Best Buy are considering entering this market. The resold games typically sell for 50–75 percent of the original retail price, so the potential lost revenue for the publishers exceeds $800 million.

Although the combination of revenue lost from rentals and resold games remains relatively small compared to the overall income from games each year, it is still significant. In combination with losses from piracy, it means that publishers make less money each year and, therefore, can fund fewer projects. Independent developers lose significant income from these lost sales, which can be particularly difficult for a company surviving primarily on milestone advances.

21

Surviving as an Independent Developer

As can be seen from the economics discussed thus far, it is becoming increasingly difficult for independent developers to survive in the game industry. There is little room for error when developing a title. As discussed in Chapter 7, "Scheduling and Budgets," a developer can spend several million dollars developing a major release. The developer sets up a schedule with the publisher to receive payments during the development process, but these payments are advances against royalties, which means that when the product ships the advances have to be paid off first. Although the advance payments usually cover all overhead costs for the developer plus a small profit, it is only after the advances are paid that the developer starts receiving royalties and seeing any true profit from the game.

As discussed earlier, royalties are paid on the money the publisher receives from the retail store, not on the game's cover price (that is, the wholesale cost and not the retail cost). In addition, the publisher holds some money aside to cover the cost of returns and other expenses, so the final royalty is paid upon the publisher's net sales (wholesale minus expenses). Very few computer games sell well enough to start paying royalties to the developer. In 2004, according to the ESA, only eighteen PC titles in the United States sold a quarter million units, and just two made it to a half million units.

The situation is even worse for console games. According to the ESA, only twelve video games in the United States broke the one million mark (and this was a record) in 2004. Fifty video games sold more than half a million

Caution

Read the Fine Print

Developers should read their contracts carefully, and it is best to hire an agent or attorney who knows the industry to review the payment schedules and make sure developers understand how much they will receive. This caution also holds true for any OEM, bundles, packs, or other means of distribution that the publisher might use.

units, and 197 passed the quarter million mark. Although these numbers are much larger than those for PC games, developers' royalty rates for console games are about half of those for PC games. It is almost impossible for independent developers to turn out expensive triple-A titles and make back their development costs. However, the top games receive international distribution, which is where a lot of cost recovery occurs for a publisher.

The developer must consider other factors as well. If the publisher sells the game internationally, it might not actually distribute the game in the foreign countries itself but use another publisher or distributor instead. That additional middleman will now also take a cut of the wholesale price, and the original publishers will receive only a portion of the money from foreign sales. The developer's share, still based on a percentage of the original publisher's income, would then be significantly reduced as well.

FYI   *Game Industry Agents*

Just as most entertainment industry professionals rely on agents to represent them in negotiations and offer sage advice about their career choices, so the game industry has a growing number of agents. For example, senior agent Paul Kohler of Digital Entertainment Agency offers independent developers insights into growing their companies and making prudent business decisions and helps them develop contracts with publishers. Gamasutra offers a list of game industry agents under Companies >Business & Legal >Agents.

Some publishers are willing to reward developers who turn out good products. Instead of just a flat royalty fee, the developer might be able to negotiate an escalating royalty that triggers rate increases whenever the game reaches predetermined sales figures. In this way, the developer can make more money if the product sells more units. There is usually a cap on the maximum royalty rate, but this approach rewards the developer for creating a game that sells well.

In addition, some publishers offer on-time completion bonuses that reward a developer with extra income for meeting milestones when scheduled. There might also be a bonus for a developer based on the final quality rating a game receives; for example, if the game is given a score of 70 or better on a game site such as metacritic.com.

Intellectual Properties

When negotiating a contract with a publisher, an independent developer must be aware of the various intellectual properties involved in the transaction and should strive to keep as many rights as possible. Most of the time, this is not an issue because the intellectual property belongs to the publisher. If this is not the case, the publisher will, of course, try to get as many rights as possible as well, and it can take some hard bargaining to arrive at mutually satisfactory terms.

If the idea for a game originates with the publisher, the matter is simple: The intellectual property belongs to the group that originated the idea. A publisher might also lease an intellectual property (IP) from elsewhere (for example, a movie, comic book, or television show) and have a third party develop the title. In this case, the original licensor owns the intellectual property and the publisher or developer pays for the rights to use the IP in a game. However, they do not then own the rights to any derivative works based on the original IP.

When negotiating the contracts, the developer or publisher should determine who owns the rights for locations or characters not found in the original work of ownership. Most likely, the original licensor will demand that the rights to any original characters be transferred to the licensor. There is little that the publisher or developer can do if they want to do a game based on the original IP.

In the case of a developer who comes up with an original concept, the publisher will probably demand the rights for the IP, which can be a serious bone of contention during contract negotiations because it usually deals not only with the original title but also with all derivative works (such as sequels and add-ons)—usually in perpetuity. A small developer, especially if new, has little negotiating power on this point. Then there is the question of who owns the IP rights if it the game is made into a movie, book, comic, board game, lunch box, or other commercial merchandise. These ancillary rights for derivative works can—although very rarely—wind up being much more valuable than the original video game.

Other ownership rights the developer must consider when negotiating with a publisher include:

- Game Engine: Who owns the rights to the game engine itself? This point involves not only who builds the different portions of the engine but also whether the developer created every code module from scratch or used commercial APIs or renderware when creating the engine. The developer can usually keep these rights. Retaining the IP of the game engine can ensure that the developer can make other games without having to start the code from scratch.

- Tools: The developer might create tools that the publisher finds useful and would like to have. There have been cases where publishers acquired developers primarily to get their hands on a tool set or game engine and cared less about the intellectual properties being created by the developer. Again, the developer can usually keep these rights.

- First Refusal: If the developer created the IP, they will want to retain the right of first refusal, meaning that the publisher has to negotiate the sequel with them first. The developer might keep these rights so they can develop the sequel themselves or, more rarely, have a different independent developer create the sequel while they work on another product. In the latter case, the original developer gets some money from the publisher even though the second developer does most of the work.

- Music: The composer might contract with the developer to provide the music for a game, but that does not mean she gives the publisher the right to use the music in any other way the publisher desires. The publisher might have to carry on separate negotiations with the composer (and possibly the musicians) to use the music in ports of the game to other platforms and especially when using the music to advertise the product or in ancillary works such as a compilation CD. Most music, however, is considered part of the game and goes with the IP.

Other issues besides ownership rights that developers should consider in their contracts include:

- Milestones: The developer should make sure that the contract covers the publisher's acceptance process so that both parties know when a milestone has been met and accepted. In addition, if the publisher demands changes, the process for making them should be spelled out in detail.

- Payments: The developer should make sure the contract covers the terms of payment by the publisher, for example, how long after acceptance of a milestone the payment will be made.

- Royalty: The terms of the royalty should also be specified in detail, including how the royalty will be determined and when payments (if any) will be made. The developer should make sure that any advances are not *recoupable,* meaning that the publisher can't ask for advances back if the game doesn't sell as well as predicted.

- Cancellation: The contract should stipulate what happens in case the publisher cancels the product. The process for canceling the project should be spelled out, as well as any related financial considerations. The contract should also explain how a project can be cancelled if the developer fails to fulfill the conditions stated in the document.

All told, there are many rights that developers should be aware of it, and it behooves a developer to hire a good agent, contract attorney, or both, who understands the nuances of the game industry. This expenditure might well pay for itself many times over by providing the developer extra sources of income and maintaining the rights to the code, tools, and assets the developer might have otherwise given freely to the publisher.

Summary

Although the electronic game industry has been growing steadily over the past decade, the prospects of long-term survival for smaller companies are becoming more problematic. An individual game can reap millions of dollars for a developer, but there are only a limited number of blockbuster hits each year. These hits must sustain not only the developers who create them but also the publishers who bear the financial responsibility of marketing and distributing them.

In addition to the traditional computer and console games, new markets for games have become available or have matured into steady sources of income. Online, mobile, and handheld games do not have the same kind of sales that console games offer, but they do provide enough money to support up-and-coming independent developers. These markets continue to grow and might someday challenge the traditional computer and video game markets.

It appears likely that the boom in the industry will continue for the foreseeable future as the next generation of game consoles appears. However, many of the companies that develop games might disappear even as the platforms succeed. The economics of the game industry are harsh, but for every small developer that disappears, a new one usually comes along to carry on making games.

Test Your Skills

MULTIPLE CHOICE QUESTIONS

1. How many video games sold more than 500,000 copies in 2004?

   A. 100.

   B. 50.

   C. 20.

   D. 75.

2. How many PC games sold more than 500,000 units in 2004?

   A. 100.

   B. 20.

   C. 2.

   D. 18.

3. The increase in sales of electronic games from 1996 to 2004 represents what percentage?

   A. 108.

   B. 51.

   C. 73.4.

   D. 97.

4. What is the projected increase of Internet game sales from 2003 to 2007?

   A. <150 percent.

   B. >200 percent.

   C. 175 percent.

   D. >250 percent.

5. If a PC game is priced at $59.95 retail, which of the following would be closest to its wholesale cost?

   A. $32.50.

   B. $42.50.

   C. $50.95.

   D. $38.95.

6. What additional costs does a publisher have to account for with a console title? (Select all that apply.)

   A. Bandwidth costs.

   B. Hardware licensing fees.

   C. IP licensing fees.

   D. Packaging costs.

7. Currently, what is the largest retail sales time for new console hardware?

   A. Year round.

   B. Christmas time.

   C. Summer time.

   D. Just after the release of a new movie.

8. Traditionally, when do U.S. video game sales reach a peak?

   A. Year round.

   B. Christmas time.

   C. Summer time.

   D. With the release of new console hardware.

9. If the development costs for a game total $1.3 million dollars and the developer has a 15 percent royalty rate against a $38 wholesale price, how many copies will have to be sold before the developer starts earning a profit?

    A. 392,000.

    B. 195,000.

    C. 1,000,000.

    D. 578,000.

10. How do console manufacturers recoup their development and manufacturing costs?

    A. By loss-leading the consoles and raising prices on peripherals.

    B. Through the sale of software.

    C. Via online subscription fees.

    D. Through price reductions and OEM.

11. What can gamers do at a subscription site?

    A. Purchase their game online.

    B. Pay a monthly fee to play their game.

    C. Get connected with other players for free.

    D. Download patches for their game for a fee.

12. Approximately what percentage of gamers play pirated software?

    A. 20.

    B. 30.

    C. 45.

    D. 35.

13. If the estimated U.S. sales for mobile games in 2004 is $204 million, what percentage of overall games sales in the United States does the mobile market represent?

    A. 2.8.

    B. 25.

    C. 5.

    D. 12.3.

21

14. Which of the following constitute intellectual property? (Select all that apply.)
    A. Game engine.
    B. Characters and environment.
    C. Stories.
    D. Tools.

15. What is the estimated market of resold games?
    A. $1.6 billion.
    B. $204 million.
    C. $2 billion.
    D. $800 million.

EXERCISES

Exercise 21.1: Online Game Comparison

Research three online subscription games. Chart the retail price of the game and the monthly subscription cost. Compare what each game offers for the retail price. If possible, determine how many consumers participate in the subscription. What differences account for the disparities in subscription rates?

Exercise 21.2: Price Comparison

Select ten games currently on the market—five for console and five for PCs. Establish the retail price of the same games at three different stores. Averaging the retail price, extrapolate the wholesale cost. From this, determine how many units any of the games would have to sell if their average development cost was $1 million per game. Given that development cost, how much would have been spent on marketing?

Exercise 21.3: Casual Games Research

Visit at least two of the casual game sites mentioned in the chapter or any other site that has multiple games available. Determine which online model each site follows. What appears to be the most popular game in terms of online players? If you can, determine which game on each site has been downloaded most often? Compare the two sites and the most popular games. Are the same games popular on each site? Given the look and content on the sites, do you think they cater to different target markets? Are their pricing strategies significantly different?

Exercise 21.4: Game Rental Research

Contact a store that rents video games. Gather information on how many games they stock, how many games they rent on average each week, how much they charge per rental on average, and how long renters can keep the game. From this information, do you think that each rented game could have been a game sale instead? If those individuals renting the games were all convinced to purchase a game instead, how much additional income would the game earn?

Exercise 21.5: Game Hardware

Research the top hardware platforms released since 1995. Create a table showing the initial cost of each unit and subsequent price drops. Include the cost of software for the console at release, the cost of software at the midpoint for the console, and the current costs of software, most likely resold or unopened software on auction sites. How many different types of hardware consoles have there been? (Restrict your research to console only, handheld only, or mobile only.) How many of these platforms have spawned sequels, and how many of those sequels support the software from the initial hardware devices?

DISCUSSION TOPICS

1. Piracy is an issue in all forms of entertainment, software, books, or just about any form of intellectual property. Discuss three copy protection methods you would consider incorporating in your game or business to make your game less likely to be pirated.

2. Given the economics described in this chapter, it seems unlikely that game companies can survive. Yet they do. Discuss how you think they are able to stay afloat and make new games each year.

3. Express a pro or con position on video game rentals. Support your opinion with as much factual evidence as you can.

4. Consider a game company that has an established base with an existing console. Given that the current standard of recouping hardware costs is 5 years based on software sales, how often should a company realistically consider releasing new hardware? What impact does a new hardware release have on existing hardware or software sales? What could you consider doing to ameliorate the impact?

5. Discuss which of the following types of games you would be interested in making: casual, handheld, online, consoles, and computer games. Consider your personal interests and make a case for your choice. Defend how you would deal with the economics of the type of game platform you would develop games for.

21

Chapter | **22**

Breaking into the Game Industry

Chapter Objectives

After reading this chapter and completing the exercises, you will be able to do the following:

- List the skills that game companies look for in applicants.
- List schools that offer game-related degrees and training.
- Explain why game companies want candidates with "soft skills" as well as technical skills.
- Describe how to apply for a job in the game industry.
- Be successful when you get a job.

Introduction

As discussed in the previous chapter, the game industry has been growing steadily for the past decade and appears likely to keep expanding for the foreseeable future. Because it is a growth industry, many people want to get in, not only because they love games but also because they hope to make a good living. But developing games is not the same as playing games. Anyone who wants to get into the industry should be aware that it can be demanding, both professionally and personally, just like the movie and television industry.

There are two ways to get into the industry: one is to get an entry-level position as a tester and work one's way up; the other is to learn a specialized skill that developers need. (Chapter 6, "The Production Team," discusses the various positions in a company that require these specialized skills.) The first approach—getting a testing position—requires a certain amount of serendipity; basically it's a matter of being in the right place at the right time. The second approach—learning a relevant skill—provides a better opportunity for getting into a company, but it requires considerable education and training. Both methods require continuous self-education after landing a job.

Getting a Testing Position

Getting a testing position and working your way up through a game company remains one way to get into the industry, but it is much more difficult nowadays than it was in the past. At one time, a knowledgeable tester could start at a company in the quality assurance (QA) department or playtest a game externally and impress a development team with cogent comments about the design, programming, or art. A job on the team might then be in the offing. Today, however, this quick promotion is less likely to occur because companies usually demand some formal education from testers.

The process of getting a testing position in a game company starts with submitting your résumé to a game company, placement company, or testing house. After you're accepted, you can work your way into a full-time position by proving you're an excellent tester who turns in superior bug or playtest reports and who doesn't overly bother the development team. One of the hardest things for a playtester or QA tester to remember is that the development team is often hard-pressed to stay on schedule and, therefore, doesn't usually have time to listen to suggestions from someone who wasn't involved in the overall game design from the start. When making suggestions, a tester should not only be intelligent and well-informed but also humble and respectful of the development team who have already spent so much time on the project.

Education and Relevant Skills

A number of game companies require that full-time employees have at least a bachelor's degree. Although companies are willing to consider people without a college degree or who have only an associate's degree, you will be up against many other individuals who have either a bachelor of science (BS) or bachelor of arts (BA) degree. Finishing college demonstrates to potential employers that you have been able to stay with a program and to see an important undertaking through to completion. That kind of stick-to-it-iveness is an essential requirement for any employee on a development team. Moreover, requiring that an applicant have a degree is one way to cut down on the number of résumés a company has to review. So a college degree—associate's or bachelor's or higher—is a minimum prerequisite demanded by most companies. Starting salaries for people entering the industry with a bachelor's degree are usually higher than for those with an associate's degree or high-school education.

FYI *Master's Degree and Higher*

As the technology involved in producing games grows more complex, the basic knowledge base for understanding and manipulating the information also increases. Manipulating objects in three-dimensional space requires advanced math such as quaternions and computational algebra, as well as computer science courses such as 3D graphics and advanced AI algorithms. These subjects often are not taught until graduate school. An increasing number of game companies are interested in hiring applicants with a master's or doctoral degree in computer science or mathematics for their programming teams. Candidates with postgraduate degrees have usually focused in one particular area of expertise for their graduate work, and this knowledge can be very useful to game companies. Moreover, having an advanced degree is almost always a requirement for teaching at the college or university level, and teaching is a wonderful way for game professionals to pass on hard-earned knowledge to a new generation of game developers.

Caution

Learning a Programming Language

Many BS programs in computer science do not emphasize one programming language over another. However, the video game industry has been using C/C++ or variants of these languages for many years. Anyone wanting to work in the game industry should make sure to get plenty of experience in the C/C++/C# and .NET languages during his college years.

Most colleges and universities offer one or more degrees in computer science that teach the basics of programming, database structure and maintenance, networking, and artificial intelligence. As part of your class work, you might work on small teams to complete a project. At most schools, these projects are not related to games, but the lessons learned from working together as a team are invaluable. The focus of many schools is to give students a theoretical understanding of the subject and promote research into new areas rather than simply teaching work skills. In addition, college-level programs usually require that you take some general education classes in addition to advanced math and physics classes to round out your skills and knowledge base. If you earn a bachelor of science (BS) in computer science, you stand a reasonable chance of getting a job in a game company—if your C/C++ skills are good and you have a presentable portfolio of code samples. The more you work on projects that exercise your programming skills, either alone or on teams, the better your portfolio will be.

Many higher education institutes offer associate of arts (AA), bachelor of arts (BA), and bachelor of fine arts (BFA, considered a professional degree) degrees as well. Some schools emphasize both fine arts and computer arts skills, whereas others, especially community colleges, focus on specific skill sets such as using 3ds Max or Maya. If you're an artist with such a degree and exhibit excellent art skills, you also have a good chance of finding a job in the game industry. You should assemble as good a portfolio as possible to show off your 2D and 3D art projects. As mentioned in Chapter 6, "The Production Team," game companies tend to hire more 3D artists than 2D artists, so you should know at least one 3D graphics program as well as being skilled in traditional art methods. The more you can demonstrate mastery of 2D or 3D skills, the more interested a game company will be in hiring you.

There are also technical colleges (sometimes called polytechnic institutes) that provide both four-year training programs in specific engineering and physical science fields, as well as art colleges and institutes that offer programs in many different fields of design (graphic design, industrial design, Web design) and fine arts (painting, sculpture, photography). In these institutions, there is less emphasis on theory and research than acquiring hands-on skills.

Although these schools offer computer and art courses, they are sometimes only tangentially relevant to game production. For example, computer courses might cover computer hardware, information technology, networking, and circuitry, whereas art courses might cover Web page design, filmmaking, and color theory. If you attend such a school and can put together an impressive portfolio that shows a broad range of skills as well as an in-depth knowledge of a few skills relevant to the game industry, you might be interesting to game companies. You should also try to create some small games or mods of commercial games, not only to demonstrate your skill as a programmer or artist, but also to go through the experience of creating a game from the ground up.

A number of colleges and universities now offer classes in games—either in design, art, or programming—and more are considering adding similar classes. These courses tend to be overviews that describe the processes involved in creating games (such as creating game documentation, working with existing game engines, using middleware, and so on), but some actually teach students specific skills (such as C/C++ programming, 3ds Max/Maya, and Photoshop). However, most schools offer only a handful of such classes and concentrate instead on a well-known course of study (for example, an English major for game designers, a computer science major for programmers, and a graphic arts major for artists).

About 100 schools in the United States offer in-depth studies in fields specifically related to game production. The more established programs currently available include those at the following institutions:

- Carnegie Mellon in Pittsburgh, Pennsylvania (**www.cmu.edu**): Offers academic and professional BS, MS, and PhD degrees in various areas of computer science as well as a two-year masters of entertainment technology degree that combines fine arts and technology.

- De Vry University in various U.S. locations (**www.devry.edu**): Offers a BS in game and simulation programming.

- DigiPen Institute of Technology in Redmond, Washington (**www.digipen.edu**): On the technical side, they offer a BS in real-time interactive simulation (equivalent to a CS degree with a focus on game programming), a BS in computer engineering, and an MS in computer science. On the art side, they offer an AA in 3D computer animations and a BFA in production animation. They also offer a degree in computer engineering (CE).

22

- Full Sail in Winter Park, Florida (**www.fullsail.com**): Offers game-related degree programs in computer animation (AS and BS), digital arts and design (AS and BS), entertainment business (BS), game design and development (BS), and recording arts (AS).

- Guildhall at Southern Methodist University in Dallas, Texas (**guild-hall.smu.edu**): Offers 21-month postgraduate certificate programs in art creation specialization, level design specialization, and software development specialization.

- University of Southern California in Los Angeles, California (**interactive.usc.edu**): Offers a BA in interactive entertainment and an MFA in interactive media.

Gamasutra (**www.gamasutra.com**) has a list of schools that offer college-level courses related to the game industry. Their associated magazine, *Game Developer,* also offers a yearly summary of schools and the programs they offer.

Relevant Skills

The most important thing someone interested in the game industry can do is to develop needed skills. The most basic skill that the industry needs is the ability to use a computer because everything is done on computers. Most of the work—coding, art, database, scheduling, and so on—is done on IBM-compatible systems, but artists frequently prefer to use iMac systems by Apple Computer. In any case, you should feel comfortable with such basic computer tasks as creating a document, working on a spreadsheet, performing searches on the Internet, and sending and receiving email. Surprisingly, many young people who are experts with console game systems have a limited understanding of how computers work.

If you're interested in programming, there are many different software programs and tools you could learn. It is not necessary to know all of them, but the more you know, the easier it is to understand everything that goes into making a game. In terms of computer languages, the C/C++ language is still predominant in games, although C# and Java are both useful. It is important not only to learn the basics of the language but also to use it in projects and become intimately familiar with its structure and abilities. It would also be a good idea to read books that discuss programming as it applies to games.

A number of specific programming skills and subjects that game companies look for are listed below. Note that it is not a complete list of all the languages, middleware, or other commercially available tools currently used in the industry (a comprehensive list could be its own book):

- Compiled Computer Languages: C/C++, C#, Java, assembly, HTML

Caution

Must Know Computers

It is important to emphasize that knowing how to use a personal computer is a prerequisite for getting any job in the game industry because all electronic games are created on computers.

- Interpreted Computer Languages (commonly referred to as *scripting languages*): Lua, Python, Perl, Ruby, JavaScript

- Development Platforms: Microsoft Visual Studio 6.0, Visual Studio .NET, Borland C++, Linux.

- Handheld Development: BREW, J2ME, J2EE

- APIs and Libraries: Windows API, DirectX 9.0, OpenGL and OpenAL, Glide, FMOD, Winsock

- Middleware: RenderWare, GameBryo

- Commercial Applications: Unreal engine, Torque engine, Reality engine, open dynamics engine (ODE), Havok SDK

- Level Creation Utility: Valve's Hammer

- Version Control: Visual SourceSafe, CVS, SVN, Doxygen

- Networking: UPD, TCP/IP, client/server architecture, socket, multithreading

- Graphics: Ray tracing, ray casting, software rasterization, Phong lighting, Gourard shading, 3D graphics pipeline, BSP trees, pixel/vertex shading, polygons and models, lighting, occlusion and shading

- Special Visual Effects: Billboarding, environment mapping, fog, lens flares, level of detail (LOD), MIP-mapping, motion blur, particle systems

- 3D Animation: Inverse kinematics, forward kinematics, rag-doll physics, 3ds Max Plug-ins and exporters

- User Interface Design: GUI design, creations and tools, including UML and XML

- Audio: DirectSound, DirectMusic, Java Media API, FMOD, OpenAL, sound creation, sound theory, music editing, music and sound file formats

- Math: Linear algebra, calculus, analytical geometry, quaternions, number theory, cryptology, graph theory, probabilities and statistics, Bezier curves, B-splines

- Physics: Collision detection, motion dynamics, waves and optics, rigid-body simulations, spring simulations, particle systems

- Artificial Intelligence: A* (A-star), finite state machines, fuzzy logic, machine learning techniques, neural networks, flocking, genetic algorithms, LISP programming language

- Security: Encryption and compression, streaming media, network security issues

22

- Database: Database design, relational databases, SQL, SQL server
- Software: Microsoft Word, Microsoft Excel, Microsoft Project, Microsoft PowerPoint, Visio, Adobe Photoshop, Autodesk 3ds Max, Autodesk Maya, Macromedia Flash (including ActionScript), Macromedia Director (including Lingo script)

Following are some of the specific skills, software applications, and studies pertaining to art that game companies are interested in:

- Basic Art Skills: Art history, color theory, composition, proportion and perspective, life drawing, character design, animation theory and techniques, storyboards, cel painting, mechanical drawing
- 2D Computer Graphics: 2D raster graphics, vector graphics and animations, environment and level design
- 2D Software: Adobe Illustrator, Adobe Photoshop, CorelDRAW Graphics Suite 12, Corel Painter IX, Pixologic ZBrush 2, Right Hemisphere Deep Paint 3D, Maxon Bodypaint 3D
- 3D Computer Graphics: 3D modeling, rigging, animation, texturing, lighting, 3D camera techniques, audio for animation, special effects, environment and level design
- 3D Software: Autodesk 3ds Max 7.0, Alias Maya 7.0, NewTek LightWave 8.0, SoftImage|XSI 5.0
- Commercial editors: Valve Hammer editor 3.4, GtkRadiant
- Other Software: Macromedia Director, Macromedia Dreamweaver 8, Macromedia Flash Professional 8, Macromedia Fireworks 8, PowerProduction Software Storyboard Artist 4, k XPress 6.5
- Associated Skills: Sculpture, stop-motion animation, motion capture, architecture, photography, typography, preprint production and publication, packaging design, video production, scriptwriting, Web design, streaming media, programming for artists
- Animation: Keyframe animations, animation blending, inverse kinematics, forward kinematics, rag-doll physics, morphing
- Special effects: Billboarding, environment mapping, fog, lens flares, level of detail (LOD), MIP-mapping, motion blur, particle systems

The skill sets required of a game designer are less precise because part of being a good designer is having many different life experiences and sources of information to draw upon. However, the author recommends these skills as a minimum:

- Programming language: Visual Basic, C/C++, *or* Java

- Software: Microsoft Office, Microsoft Project, Microsoft PowerPoint, Visio, Adobe Photoshop, Autodesk 3ds Max *or* Alias Maya

- Commercial editors: Valve Hammer editor 3.4 *or* GtkRadiant

- Math: Probabilities and statistics, calculus, matrix/linear algebra

- English: Technical writing, creative writing, mythology, world literature, poetry, playwriting, screenwriting

- Science: Astronomy, biology, chemistry, physics

- General Education: World history, military histories, sociology, anthropology, world religions, archaeology, psychology, economics, art history, introduction to theater, film history, comparative religions, interpersonal communications, public speaking, at least one secondary language

Of course, no game company expects you to learn all these areas, but the skills you know well and can talk about at length should be listed on your résumé. Ideally, you should have examples that show your expertise in these skills either on a Web site or a demo CD.

Soft Skills

In addition to the technical skills (or **hard skills**) indicated in the previous section, game companies are also interested in what are called **soft skills**—your ability to interact well with other people. Companies check for these skills during phone interviews and personal interviews. If you speak well and have a pleasant personality, you might be preferred over someone who is technically brilliant, but lacks social tact or graces. The soft skills that game companies look for include:

- Love of Games: Anyone applying at a game company should love games— not only playing them but also analyzing them for what is good and bad. It is important to show this passion in your résumé and during interviews.

- Writing: Designers should be experts in writing, and everyone else on a production team can also be required to turn in written reports about new software, new hardware, new work methods, and weekly production reports. Knowing how to put together intelligible sentences is a basic requirement.

- Communication: Employees can be called upon to give presentations, speak at conferences, chat with gamers, and otherwise engage in public speaking. Potential employees do not have to be great orators, but they should be able to speak up, talk clearly, and think on their feet. Additionally, employees should know how to listen to others and ask for help if they are stuck on a problem.

22

- Research: Everyone on the team should know how to research information via the Internet and libraries. Team members are often assigned to research rival products or read up on new hardware, software, and work methods.

- Work Ethic: Game companies want people who get things done correctly, so it is important to let them know that you are willing to put in the long hours to get projects done. Potential employees should demonstrate self-confidence in their knowledge of the industry and their skills and self-discipline in setting schedules and carrying through on assignments.

- Time and Task Management: The game industry wants and needs people who know how to work *smart*. They appreciate people who can break tasks into manageable chunks, reasonably estimate the time to complete each one, and maintain priority lists and work schedules. On-time delivery of milestones is critical, so the estimates provided by team members are taken very seriously.

- Teamwork: The days of the lone maverick off in a corner coding independently are gone. Games are created by teams, so companies look for people who can work easily on teams. They are interested in people who help one another, offer suggestions and positive criticisms, and honor their commitments. People must know how to critique the work of others without hurting feelings as well as how to accept criticism without feeling hurt or getting upset. Often, when it comes down to selecting someone to hire from a group with identical skills and experience, it's a question of who has demonstrated the best teamwork skills in the past and who is most likely to work well in the current team.

- Courtesy: Workers have to rub shoulders with one another for hours on end, so companies look for people who are polite ("please," "thank you," "excuse me," and so on) not only with management but also with fellow team members. In addition, personal hygiene falls under this heading. Nowadays, unless someone is at the end of a long crunch period, everyone on the team should shower and change clothes regularly.

- Positive Attitude: It is important to have a positive attitude toward life and to show potential employers that one is comfortable with oneself. Having a "can-do" outlook on life is refreshing and can help keep a team vitalized during crunch periods.

Getting a Job

The game industry goes through regular periods of growth as new companies start up and of contraction as companies merge or go out of business. Starting in late 2003, a hiring boom followed the announcement of the next generation of video consoles. The manufacturers need a number of releases to appear at the same time their new platforms debut. The current boom will likely die down a bit after the machines ship and as developers wait to see who the eventual winners will be. But the job market in games looks healthy at least for the next few years.

Part of getting a job is pure luck, part is knowing someone who knows someone in the industry, and part is presenting yourself as a professional to other industry professionals.

Résumé

The résumé is the first step toward applying for a job. Countless books and a number of sites on the Internet show you how to create a presentable résumé. You should take advantage of their advice to make your résumé as professional as possible.

There is no one format for a résumé; the key is to present the information as clearly as possible. In general, if you're already working in the industry, you'll want to create a *chronological résumé,* which lists your industry jobs from the most recent backward. If you're trying to get into the industry for the first time, consider creating a *functional résumé,* which highlights your skill sets that are most closely related to the industry and particularly to the job you're applying for.

In either case, the human resources (HR) department of a game company is the first group to see your résumé. Most likely, they are not skilled programmers or artists, so you need to make it clear immediately to them which job you're applying for. This is done either as a stated objective or as a title attached to your name.

22

FYI   *Objective or Title?*

An *objective* is a single line on your résumé that should summarize the specific job you're applying for or the general area you're interested in. Some companies, such as Microsoft, require you to have an objective. Other companies don't care. It is a personal choice for the individual writing the résumé. It's a good idea to keep the objective short and to the point and to include the company as part of your objective (for example, "To be an entry-level programmer at Microsoft" or "To join the networking programming team at Sony Online").

If you decide not to state an objective, then you should at the least include a title after your name at the top of the page; for example, "John Smith, Game AI Programmer" or "Jayne Doe, 3D Modeler and Animator." Either the objective or the title is necessary and makes it easier for the HR department to forward your résumé to the correct person for review. Moreover, if you don't have an objective on your résumé, you should include the information as part of your cover letter.

As mentioned earlier, most game companies require an applicant to have at least a bachelor's degree in some field, so your educational information should appear near the top of the résumé. Then you should list the skills sets that relate to the industry, starting with those that match a job opening on the company's Web site.

Cover Letters

Always include a cover letter when applying for a job and submitting a résumé and portfolio. Whereas a résumé can appear to be very dry and formulaic, a cover letter is an opportunity for your personality to come out. As with the résumé, many Web sites and books describe in great detail how to write cover letters.

In the first paragraph, you can introduce yourself and indicate which job you're applying for and where you heard about it. This is the first opportunity to make an impression on the company, so your cover letter should explain why you want to work for this company. The letter can also draw attention to the specifics of the résumé that meet or exceed the requirements listed with the job description. In addition, you should include your personal goals and why you feel you're the right person for the job. Finally, make sure you include your contact information (phone number and e-mail address) in the last paragraph, and thank the reader for taking the time to review your résumé and portfolio.

Portfolios

Anyone looking to enter the game industry should consider creating a portfolio of work that demonstrates her abilities as a programmer, artist, designer, or producer. This portfolio can be a Web site or a CD/DVD to showcase your projects in such a way that will impress employers. If you have published titles to your credit, list them prominently with links to downloadable demos. If you're just trying to get into the industry, include your school or hobby projects that relate to the industry. Additionally, you should continue to add new projects to show that you are keeping your programming skills up-to-date and to show off your impressive individual work.

Your Web site or CD/DVD should also include the most current version of your résumé. You might want to include printable versions of your résumé in different formats—.DOC (Microsoft Word), .PDF (Portable Document Format for Adobe Reader), .RTF (most word processing programs), .TXT (plain text), and HTML are the most common.

Caution

Never Lie on Your Résumé

Never lie on a résumé because anything on it is subject to verification and discussion during an interview. If you say you have a certificate, be prepared to produce the supporting documentation. Make sure that everything you've written can be proved either by your references or previous employers.

| **FYI** | *Art Portfolio Advice* |

Portfolios should not focus exclusively on the type of art that the individual enjoys the most or on the type of art that the game company most often uses in their games. Instead, art portfolios should show a broad range of skills, focusing, of course, on the specialized skill of the individual. However, showing a breadth of ability in a variety of media (computer, paint, charcoal, 3D models, hand sketches, storyboards, and so on) demonstrates that the individual can work in different styles. You should have your portfolio reviewed by other artists and listen to their feedback. Often a company will review a portfolio without the artist's being present, which means the art must stand on its own.

If you're an artist, put together both a physical portfolio and a CD/DVD of work that can be presented during an interview. The artwork should be put in a folder that is easy to carry and includes a variety of 2D and 3D work. The best work should appear in the front because first impressions are important. If the portfolio starts with weaker work, the employer might never get beyond it. Also, have photocopies or reproductions available to leave at the company, along with a CD containing the same materials and animations. If you worked on team projects as an artist, you should define exactly which parts of the project you were responsible for. The portfolio should include your résumé and explanations of the work including discussions of the media, when the work was done, and, in the case of 3D models, polygon counts, examples of textures, or other technical information.

Most companies also ask artists to submit a ***demo reel*** of their work on a CD/DVD. As with the portfolio, it should start with the strongest work and include a variety of art skills. An artist should be able to create work in many different styles, so make sure that you include a wide assortment. Also, include a copy of the résumé and a ReadMe file that explains each submission on the CD/DVD.

Looking for Jobs

One of the best ways to get a job in the industry is to check out the company's Web site. Most company sites have a jobs or employment page that lists current openings. Depending on the company, this information could be either up-to-date or outdated, so even if no jobs are listed, jobs might still be available. The company might require a waiting period before jobs are posted openly so that current employees can apply for openings before the general public. Also, the human resources (HR) department might find it too time consuming to deal with the large number of résumés they receive each week, so they might prefer to use recruiters to find the most promising candidates. Moreover, even if no jobs are available, a company might be so impressed with your résumé that it decides to create a job to get you on staff.

> ## FYI Internships and Cooperative Work Experience
>
> Many game companies set up arrangements with local colleges to offer internships and cooperative work experience programs. An internship allows a student to earn college credits for hands-on work experience at a company for a quarter or semester. The student works a set number of hours per week and usually does not get paid. A cooperative work experience involves a student's working part-time or full-time and getting paid by the company. Someone at the company has to supervise the student and monitor the workload. Both approaches allow students the experience of doing actual work at a game company, networking with game industry professionals, and perhaps getting their names on published games, which is a valuable addition to their résumé.

Another way to find out about jobs is to check Internet sites where jobs in the industry are regularly posted. Some of the better online sites for game jobs include:

- Gamasutra (**www.gamasutra.com**)

- Game Developer (**www.gamedev.net**)

- Game Industry (**www.gameindustrybiz.com**)

- GameJOBS (**www.gamejobs.com**)

- Hot Jobs (**www.hotjobs.com**)

- Monster (**www.monster.com**)

- Dice (**www.dice.com**)

Even if you do not meet the requirements listed for a job opening on one of these sites, it might still be worthwhile to submit your résumé. A company might advertise only those positions that it is having difficulty filling, and there might still be other openings that you qualify for that they don't post anywhere.

Some schools have placement counselors who help students find jobs in companies. If a school offers a number of courses in game development, it is worthwhile to check to see if they know of any openings.

FYI — Recruiters and Placement Companies

A common way for experienced individuals to find a new job is to use a recruiter or placement company. There are a number of well-respected companies, but candidates should do some research before using one. Employers use placement companies and recruiters to find the best candidates to fill positions, and usually the employer pays for those candidates who are referred by a placement company or recruiter and subsequently hired. Recruiters and placement companies are less likely to accept recent college graduates as candidates because they have no practical work experience.

Networking

At times it seems like getting into the game industry has its own catch-22: You can't get a job in the game industry unless you already have a job in the game industry. Although there is a certain amount of truth to this, the industry does need new talent and hard workers, so lack of practical experience should not keep you from applying for a job. A certain amount of luck is also involved in getting a game job (for example, living in an area where a game company has an office or knowing someone who knows someone in the industry), but getting a job in the industry also requires determination and effort on your part.

To get a job, you have to do continuous research on companies and try to make contacts in the industry (also known as networking). The idea is not for you to make contacts so you can bug them continually about jobs at their companies but instead to develop and maintain real relationships and friendships with people who could wind up being your coworkers. No one likes being used, so you should never approach an industry professional just to milk them for information. But people who make games are more than happy to discuss their work, so they are approachable. They might even give you a business card (it helps if you offer them one of yours first) so you can correspond with them.

There are several ways to meet the professionals. First, there are trade shows and conferences such as E3 and GDC where the game industry gathers. Also, the IGDA has chapters across the country, and most have regular meetings where you can meet industry professionals. It is important to emphasize that you should never pester industry professionals for jobs, but you should instead try to open a line of communication with them at your first meeting. For example, a programming student might ask for advice on how to code a certain part of a project, whereas an art student might ask about the preferred methods for rigging models. Keeping the conversation on a professional level earns the respect of the people you talk to. Eventually, you might become friends. Often speakers will post their names and email addresses and ask people to contact them with questions about their talk. This is an ideal way to establish yourself as a legitimate individual by asking reasonable questions, thus creating a solid line of communication.

If it is difficult to meet people in person, see if you can find Web sites and forums where industry professionals come online to talk about their projects. They don't necessarily care for flattery or enjoy dealing with flame-mails, but they are usually willing to discuss topics about the industry and how they do things. Forums such as those hosted by the IGDA are an excellent place to network, usually in your own area, with people who have the same interests in gaming that you have. Professionals participate in these as well. Another source of information is local game clubs or game stores, where you might meet people who know people in the industry.

Interviewing

The interview process at a game company usually involves two steps: a telephone interview and then an in-person interview. For technical positions, a third step is often included: a programming test or programming aptitude test.

The phone interview might be done by someone in the HR department or someone in a management position (producer, lead artist, lead programmer, senior designer). Its purpose is to go over your skills and background and make sure you're right for the position. During the conversation, the interviewer checks not only your technical skills but also your soft skills (or interpersonal skills)—that is, your ability to communicate, your attitude, and your friendliness. The company wants to make sure they are hiring talented people, but they also look for people who fit in with the company culture. Depending on the position, you might have to go through several telephone interviews before you're invited in for a personal interview. Telephone interviews save a company considerable time and money; for they are usually short (30 minutes or so) and involve only a few people at the company. There might be many candidates for a job, and the company will want to cut down on the number it will finally invite for personal interviews.

For technical positions, a company will often require that candidates take a programming or technical test at this point. The test can be electronic, timed, take-home, or if the candidate is local to the company's offices, can happen onsite. Programming tests are designed to demonstrate that the candidate actually knows something of use to the company. No two tests are the same, but it's likely that no one could easily complete all of the questions on the test. For recent graduates, the important thing is to demonstrate that you either know the information or that you can think about possible solutions.

Bringing candidates in to interview at the company is a major investment, for it means that team members will be pulled off their projects to take part in interviews. Moreover, if you live out of state, the company will have to fly you in and perhaps get you a hotel room for a night or two. By the time you're

called for an in-person interview, you're likely to be on the short list of those being considered, so you should approach the interview with a positive, "can-do" attitude. Depending on the company and the position, a personal interview might last an hour or so or take the whole day. Some companies want everyone on the team to talk to each candidate before they decide, or they might use a round-robin approach, handing you off to team members one at a time and ending the process as soon as someone decides you're not right for the position. If you live near the company, you might have to come in several times to interview with different employees as they are available, so the process can stretch out for weeks.

Make sure you have your references ready. You'll need references from at least three people. They should know that you are interviewing at a company, that you're using them as references, and what position you're applying for so they are prepared to give relevant information about your skills. It's a good idea to provide your references with the same résumé you sent the company. Have them contact you after they talk to the company so that you can see how it went and to ask what was discussed.

Accepting a Job

When a company offers you a job, make sure you get the offer in writing. Until you have an actual offer letter signed by a company representative, you really cannot assume that you have a job to go to and you might precipitously leave another job or turn down another position. The offer letter should include the job position, your responsibilities, the salary you agreed upon, the start date, and any special benefits (stock options, bonuses, moving expenses, and so on). The offer isn't official until you sign and return the letter to the company. If you're leaving another job, you should make sure that you have enough time to give them two weeks notice. You never want to burn your bridges, because the industry is small and you'll keep bumping into the same people over the years.

Don't be surprised if the company hires you on a probationary basis for three to six months. During the probation, either you or the company can decide that things are not working out and they can let you go with no legal ramifications. This procedure ensures that both sides are happy with your work and that you fit into the company as desired. Companies sometimes pay a lower salary during the probationary period and then raise it after you demonstrate that you are working out as expected as a new employee. In addition, you might not receive company benefits until the probationary period is over.

Make sure to thank anyone who helped you get the job, be it the contact who helped you find the job, the references who gave you quality recommendations, or your parents and friends who supported you through college and the application process. Sending thank you notes to these people not only shows you are polite, but also reinforces your communication skills. After you have a job at a company, you'll want to maintain and expand your network. Contact friends and acquaintances, especially those in the industry, and give them your new contact information. It is now your turn to offer support to others and help them when you can.

Working at a Game Company

Although working at a game company often requires long hours and great perseverance, the process of making a game is incredibly enjoyable and rewarding in itself. Moreover, the people who work at such companies are highly talented and share a desire to turn out the best product possible. There are occasional stretches where things can get a bit dull and routine, but most days bring new challenges and opportunities to shine.

The following are a few tips about working at a game company for the first time:

- Teamwork: It's a good idea in the first months to keep your ears open and your mouth closed unless you have something relevant to suggest. Also, teams are supportive of one another, so maintain a good sense of humor and be ready to lend a hand at any time.

- Mentor: Many companies assign a long-time staff member to act as a mentor to new hires, especially those who are new to the industry. If this is your first job in the industry and the company doesn't assign someone to be your mentor, ask for one. Listen to your mentor and learn as much as you can as quickly as you can.

- Bulldogging: One mistake newcomers make is "bulldogging" a problem—grabbing it, worrying it, shaking it, and trying to make it work. Although trying to resolve a problem on your own is admirable, it can cause problems. It's much better to admit, after trying your best, that you can't solve the problem on your own and talk to your teammates. If they can't help, talk to management and ask for help. If your dogged insistence causes a slip in the schedule, a ripple effect can delay others who depend on you to finish your part. Asking for help is a critical skill for any game developer.

- Long Hours: There's no getting around the fact that many game companies demand that employees put in long hours. There are many reasons for this demand. In the worst case, the people running the company or the team are poorly organized and simply don't know how to schedule a product. But there are other reasons for long hours—the team needs to meet a deadline and there is a stubborn bug that can't be tracked down; the marketing department makes an unexpected demand for a working version of the latest build; the programmers are tackling a new technology and encounter unforseen difficulties in implementing the code. If working standard hours at a company is a requirement for you, the game industry is likely not your best choice. At some point, you might find that the long hours cause your personal life to suffer, so you'll have to decide whether to stay with games or go into another line of work.

- Burnout: As a corollary to the previous point, long hours can lead to burnout, another major reason why people leave the industry. Burnout doesn't happen immediately but is a slow process. Some of the symptoms to watch for are chronic fatigue, irritation at little things, cynicism and negativity, sleeplessness, weight loss, increased risk taking, and a feeling of being helpless. If you find yourself suffering some of these symptoms, you should talk to your superior at the company and also consider talking to a doctor. It takes a long time to recover from burnout, and no job is so important that it should make you sick. If you can't take it anymore, consider leaving the industry.

- Get Published: It is important to get your name on shipped products, so plan to stay at a new company until your project ships. Many people jump from company to company in search of higher salaries and better opportunities, but this constant change looks bad on your résumé. Because it takes so long to go from initial game idea to shipped product, many people in the industry have never experienced a complete production cycle. As the industry continues to change and evolve, it might turn out that fewer people are actually involved in any project from start to finish; the game industry could become more like the movie industry, where people are hired to complete a few select tasks and only a handful are involved in a project all the way from start to finish. Still, having a number of shipped titles to your credit greatly enhances your reputation in the industry as someone who gets things done.

- Learning Curve: Unlike many other jobs, where you learn a certain set of skills and then use them repeatedly for years on end, the game industry is always evolving as new technologies are developed. Anyone getting into the game industry should be prepared to spend a lifetime learning new things, be they new software packages used to develop games, new platforms on which games are played, or new methods of coding, designing, composing, or creating art. When you land a job in a company, be prepared to continuously expand your skills and knowledge base. The inexorable advance of technology means that anything learned today will likely be obsolete in a couple of years. There is always a tremendous learning curve. If you don't enjoy teaching yourself new things, you will soon become obsolete. Of course, if you enjoy learning new things, the game industry is the perfect place to spend a lifetime.

22

Rewards of the Job

There are real rewards in working in the game industry, over and above the fact that making games, although work, is one of the most enjoyable activities on earth. The process of bringing an interactive experience into being is breathtaking. There are endless meetings to discuss the best way to implement an idea, the progress reviews where you see an original idea become real, and lots of late hours where you hunker over pizzas and share life stories. The following are some of the most enjoyable things about working on games:

- Learning New Things: As mentioned earlier, there is always something new and different happening in the game industry, so you can always pick up new techniques and learn new methods to do things. Designers often have to study fields they never considered studying in school; programmers have to learn new languages and figure out more efficient algorithms; and artists learn new techniques to improve their creations as well as subtle variations in the graphics programs they use. Because games are always at the cutting edge of technology, the people working on them are usually the most technologically savvy about new techniques. It is possible to leave the industry and find a job in another industry that is just starting to implement some of the techniques that would be considered old hat in games.

- Avid Consumers: The people who play games are vociferous, always ready to express their pleasure or displeasure at a product. Meeting fans (and critics) is always a pleasure, for this is one way to get feedback about your performance. One of the best places to get feedback is in MMOG games, where you can talk online to people directly about the product and get immediate feedback about their feelings as to what works well or not. The customers are often as intelligent and passionate as the people who make games, and it can be eye-opening to hear from them.

- Top-Notch Talent: Some of the smartest and most talented people in the world are in the game industry. These are dedicated people who are willing to put in the extra effort to turn out as good a product as they possibly can. They are intelligent and insightful and many of them enjoy partying with their peers at game conferences and trade shows. Although there are occasional egomaniacs to deal with, most industry professionals tend to be modest and self-effacing and a joy to meet.

- Shipping a Product: Perhaps the ultimate thrill of being in games is seeing a product that you worked on and that has your name in the credits finally ship. You can proudly hold up the product and say, "I made this." Of course, after spending years on it, you will probably never willingly play the game again. Nonetheless, just having finished a game is an achievement and everyone on the team should be filled with pride at their accomplishment.

Summary

The best way to get a job in the game industry is to develop a skill that game companies need. Many schools teach programming and 3D graphics courses. Students with these skills should create a number of projects to show companies they are employable. Getting a job as a designer is more problematic because a good designer has a wide range of knowledge and excellent communication skills that can take years to develop. Getting into a company as a producer often means starting off as a playtester and working your way up into management. Earning a master's in business administration (MBA) can help an individual learn the business and team management skills that are sorely needed in the industry.

Working in the game industry is challenging. There is always a learning curve to face because game technology continues to advance. Still, the rewards of working in a game company are extraordinary. The process of creating games is challenging and can be tiresome at times, but nothing compares with the feeling of holding in your hands a finished product that you helped to create and bring to fruition.

Test Your Skills

MULTIPLE CHOICE QUESTIONS

1. Which of the following basic art skills is required in the industry? (Select all that apply.)
   A. Color theory.
   B. Composition.
   C. Anatomy.
   D. Animation theory.
   E. Storyboards.

2. Which of the following computer languages is currently used most often in the game industry?
   A. C++.
   B. Java.
   C. COBOL.
   D. HTML.

3. Visual SourceSafe is a type of
   A. Archiving.
   B. Version-control software.
   C. 3D modeling software.
   D. Project scheduling.

22

4. True or False: Sculpture is a required skill that all artists should have.
   A. True.
   B. False.

5. An artist looking for a job in the video game industry should have experience in which of the following?
   A. Collision detection.
   B. 3D rendering software.
   C. Texturing.
   D. Flocking.

6. True or False: All programmers should be able to write networking code.
   A. True.
   B. False.

7. A* is a type of
   A. Learning technique.
   B. MIP-mapping .
   C. Artificial intelligence.
   D. Stop-motion animation.

8. True or False: Only designers need to be concerned with writing skills.
   A. True.
   B. False.

9. Communication at a game company includes which of the following? (Select all that apply.)
   A. Presentations.
   B. Weekly production reports.
   C. Packet structure.
   D. TCP/IP.

10. If you're an artist, you should have which of the following?
    A. A CD portfolio.
    B. A printed portfolio.
    C. Both A and B.
    D. Either A or B.

11. True or False: Anything on your résumé is fair game during an interview.

   A. True.

   B. False.

12. Having a strong love of games is important for which of the following positions? (Select all that apply.)

   A. Game designers.

   B. Programmers.

   C. Artists.

   D. Producers.

13. Which of the following is one of the best ways to find a job right after graduation?

   A. Hire a headhunter.

   B. Read company press releases.

   C. Network with local game developers.

   D. Attend industry conventions.

22

EXERCISES

Exercise 22.1: Company Research

One of the best ways to get a job in the industry is to check out the company's Web site. Select a company and visit their Web site. List the jobs that are currently posted, including all the requirements for each. How many jobs are posted? How many jobs require a bachelor's or associate's degree? Review the press releases on the site. How many games have they released in the past year or do they expect to release within the next 12 months? What feeling do you get about the company from the jobs posted and the games they have previously released?

Exercise 22.2: Write a Résumé

Write a one-page résumé as if you were applying for one of the jobs in Exercise 22.1. Be honest, but see if you can match at least 50 percent of the requirements for the job. If you are new to the industry, write a functional résumé listing your job skills, your education, and your experience making games or other software.

Exercise 22.3: Research Game Jobs

Visit two of the job sites listed in the chapter. Select a type of job in the industry or a region of the country and locate all jobs that fit that category on each site. How many jobs are there? Create a chart of all the jobs, their locations, and requirements. How different are the job requirements?

Exercise 22.4: Social Aspects of Games

In a group of three or four other students, friends, or family, play a board game of your choice. Then play a card game, and then play a video game, preferably one that is multiplayer, although a single-player game can also be interesting. Do people maintain their interest? How is the social aspect of the game different when you play at the same table and can see each other?

Exercise 22.5: Interview Preparation

From the chapter, copy the list of technical skills and soft skills that are relevant to your area of interest in game development. Using a job from Exercise 22.1 or 22.3, circle all the skills called for in the job description. Highlight those skills that you currently possess. Write down how or where you would gain the missing skills that the job requires.

DISCUSSION TOPICS

1. Think about a time when you bulldogged a problem. Were you able to solve it alone or did you get help? Consider how much time you spent working on the problem and compare that to how you could have better spent your time.

2. Love of games is important for everyone working in a game company. Consider your favorite game or game genre. What is it about that particular game or genre that you truly care about? Is it the game element, the cinematics, the feeling of success when you win? Attempt to explain it to someone who doesn't play that kind of game so they will be inspired to try the game.

3. Burnout is a significant factor in game development. How would you maintain a healthy balance of work, life, and play if you worked in the industry? Consider what your long-term goals are and how you want to achieve them.

4. A game designer's job does not have any fully defined set of requirements; however, it's easy to recognize someone who has design skills. How would you determine if someone would be a good game designer?

What tests or questions might you ask him? Consider your favorite game and think about how you would evaluate someone to work on the sequel.

5. Look around at a classroom or room of people whom you don't know very well. How would you meet one of these people if you knew they were a hiring manager at your favorite game company? What would you say to them to get their attention and not seem bothersome?

22

Index

2-1/2D perspective games, 397, 433, 438
2D artists, 207–209
2D games, 523–526, 583
2D graphics, 372, 396–399, 433–436, 443–446
2D map editor, 171, 590–594
3/4 perspective games, 397, 438
3D animator, 210–211
3D appearance with parallax scrolling, 442
3D environment modelers, 212
3D game engine, 200
3D games, 171, 526–528, 587
3D graphics, 207–208, 371, 396, 446–461
3D graphics renderer, 399–402
3D graphics software, level designer
   knowledge of, 197
3D level editor, 594
3D modeler, 209–210, 240
3D models, 431, 447–448
3D Studio Max, 446
3D texture artist, 211–212, 240
3DO Company, 45, 47, 126
3ds Max, 171, 208, 210, 369, 371, 580
8-bit, 42
8-bit alpha channel, for transparency, 445
90-10 rule, 670
1942, 67

A
A-10 Tank Killer, 96
A* (A-Star) pathfinding method, 369, 406, 540
A titles, 187
AAA (triple-A) titles, 14, 187
abstract items, 348
abstracted modes of movement, 330
abstraction, 7–8, 22
acceleration, 526
accepting job, 707–708
Acidfonts, 384
acoustically dead studio room, 484
action-adventure games, 69, 74–78
action buttons, on console controller, 501
action games, 62–73, 82, 101, 103–105, 176, 605
Activision, 38, 45
actors, for motion capture, 162, 163
Adams, Alexis, 75
Adams, Scott, 75
adaptive music, 477
add-ons, for *The Sims*, 91
addressable resolution, 143
Adkison, Peter, 29
Adobe Illustrator, 591
Adobe Photoshop, 209, 436, 591
advance against royalties, 236, 669
Adventure (Colossal Cave), 35
adventure games, 74–78, 195, 341, 351, 539,
   548, 574, 605

Adventure International, 75
Adventureland, 75
advertising, 180, 635, 644, 647–653
Age of Empires, 88, 510
Age of Mythology, 593
Age of Sail, 98
AGEIA, 403
agents, in game industry, 684
AI. *See* artificial intelligence (AI)
AI (Adobe Illustrator) file format, 431
air vehicles, 95–97
Air Warrior, 96, 137
Akbar I (Mogul Emperor), 24
Alcorn, Al, 35
algorithms, 530
Allen, Paul G., 36
allies of protagonist, 344
Alone in the Dark, 78
alpha blending, transparency and, 445–446
Alpha Centauri, 593
alpha channel, 430
Alpha milestone, 231
alquerque, 23
Altered Beast, 43
amateur sports, 107, 109–111
Amazin' Software, 41
ambience, 265, 469
ambient noise, randomization, 480
ambient property of surface material, 452
ambush, 589
American Challenge: A Sailing Simulation, 98
American Civil War: Gettysburg, 325
amplitude, 470
analog sound, conversion to digital format, 470
Anarchy Online, 623
anchor points, of Bézier curve, 597
angle of incidence, 525
angle of reflection, 525
Animal Crossing, 91
animation, 162, 163, 343, 349, 371, 373, 382–383,
   399, 448, 480
animation cycles, 433
animation editor, 411
animation frames, 366
animation sets, 433, 437
antagonist, 291, 345
antialiasing, 446, 461
antipiracy scheme, 503
APIs (application programming interfaces), 48
appendices in GDD, 349–354
Apple II personal computer, 36, 122
Apple Macintosh, 123
application programming interfaces (APIs), 48, 395
approval process, for game proposal, 303–304
Arakawa, Minoru, 37
arcade games, 35, 36, 62–73, 122

Arcade Volleyball, 106
Arcanum: Of Steamworks & Magick Obscura, 328
archive of game, 618
armament, game design document
   description of, 333
Arneson, Dave, 29
art design document, 15, 168, 206, 354,
   377–378, 429
art design document structure, 378–384
art director, 191, 581
art portfolio, 694
art process pipeline, 461–462
art specification, 168, 296, 298
art staff, 206–213
art style, for background art, 440
artificial intelligence (AI), 8, 63, 202, 368–370,
   405–407, 537–543
artists, 163, 167
ASCAP, 479
Asheron's Call, 83
assembler, 394
assembly languages, 394
assistant (associate) producer, 193
assistant designer, 197
associate's degree, 693
Association for Computing Machinery, Special
   Interest Group on Graphics and Interactive
   Techniques, 421
Asteroids, 36, 62
Atari, 35, 36, 38, 40–42, 45, 70, 122–123, 126
Athens 2004, 111
athletic games, first recorded, 20
attack value, in war games, 86
attainments section, in production report, 231
attributes of game objects, 324
audio, 44, 118, 125, 136–137, 145, 298, 342–343,
   375–376, 409–410, 468–488, 596
audio and visual director, 217
audio staff, 163, 204–205, 213–214
Avalon Hill, 29
Avalon, the Legend Lives, 83
Axim X50v Pocket PC (Dell), 149
Axis & Allies, 530

B
B-17 Flying Fortress, 96
B titles, 187
B2C (business-to-customer), 674
bachelor's degree, 693
backgammon, 24–25
background art, 440–443, 508
background artists, 209
backstory, 166–167, 291, 318, 350
backtracking, 587
backups of files, 414
Backyard Hockey, 109

Baer, Ralph, 34
balance in game play, 8, 176, 266–267, 536–537, 604–608
Balance of Power, 89
Baldur's Gate, 79, 80
Baldur's Gate: Dark Alliance, 518
Baldur's Gate II: Shadows of Amn, 331
Baldur's Gate: Tales of the Sword Coast, 518
Bales, Kevin, 4
Bally Corporation, 32
Ballyhoo, 32
Banking, 27
banner Internet ads, 650
Bard's Tale, 82
BASIC (programming language), 36
batch file, for game build, 416
Bates, Bob, 75
Battlefield 2, 130
Battles of Bull Run, 87
Battlezone, 70
beat 'em ups, 65
behaviors, technical design document on, 370
beta, 177, 231
between animation, 438
Bézier curve, 597
bible, 354
bilinear filtering, 455
billboards, 653
binary code, 394
binary space partitioning, 401
Bink Video (RAD GameTools), 411
BioGraphic Technologies, A.I Implant API, 369
Biped (3ds Max plug-in), 210
Birdwell, Ken, 589
bit depth, 430, 471
bit rate, for game consoles, 142
bitmap images, 431, 440–441
Black & White, 539
Blade Runner, 78, 265
Blank, Mark, 75
blinder testers, 617
Blizzard Entertainment, 205
Blockbuster, 682
blogs, creating fake for marketing, 645
Blood Bowl, 107
BMI, 479
BMP (Windows bitmap), 431
board game industry, 26–31
board games, 21–26, 60, 105–106, 119
board of directors, 189
Boggle, 102
Bolo, 137
Bomber, 129
Boolean logic, 173
booty table, 532
boredom, by production team, 609
boss, 345
bots, 72, 406
bounding box, 403
Bowen, Maria, 441
Bradley, Mr., 27
Brainburst!, 102
brainstorming, 279–282, 283, 310
branching dialogue, 561
break-even point, 349
Breakout, 126
BREW (Binary Runtime Environment for Wireless), 198
broadband connections, 674
Brøderbund, 77
Brookhaven National Laboratories, 33

budget, 15, 168, 235–243, 299, 320, 349, 641
buffer, 397, 410
bug reports, 216, 226, 232, 613–615
bug-tracking database, 417
bugs, 205, 231, 502, 604, 613, 616, 618. *See also* debugging
Bugzilla, 613
builds of game, 414, 416
bulk purchases, 672
bulldogging, 708
bump mapping, 456
burn rate, 243
Burnout 2: Point of Impact, 258
burnout of employees, 610–611, 619, 709
Bushnell, Nolan, 35
Business Software Alliance, 682
business-to-customer (B2C), 674
buying in bulk, 672

c
C titles, 187
C# programming language, 394
C++ programming language, 198, 394, 696
Caffrey, Matthew, 87
CakeWalk Pro, 410
Call of Duty: Finest Hour, 169
cameras, 332, 372, 554
Campbell, Joseph, 557
cancellation of product, developer contract and, 686
Candyland, 27
capture the flag, 72
card games, 7, 106
Card, Orson Scott, 77
career in game industry, 693–699, 700–710. *See also* art staff; design staff; management positions; programming staff
Carnegie Mellon, 695
Carter, Howard, 21
cartridges, 135, 623
casting for voiceovers, 483
Castle Adventure, 4
Castlevania, 66
casual game sites, 676–677
CDs, 625, 702
cell phones. *See* mobile phones
Centipede, 9, 62, 539
central processing unit (CPU). *See* microprocessor
CEO (chief executive officer), 189
CFO (chief financial officer), 189–190
CGA (color graphics adapter), 42, 430
challenge, 6, 263–265
Championship Manager, 106
changes, 270, 314
character generation charts, 531
character sketch, 209
characters, 74, 78, 79, 298, 327–329, 344–345, 368, 379–380, 434, 549, 552–556
charts and tables. *See* database
chase algorithm, 540
chat, 374, 409, 487–488
chaturanga, 23
chaupar, 24
cheap, fast, good, 225, 611
Checkered Game of Life (Bradley), 27
checkers (draughts), 23, 536
checkpoints, 230, 505
chess, 8, 23, 536
chief executive officer (CEO), 189
chief financial officer (CFO), 189–190
chief information officer (CIO), 190
chief operating officer (COO), 190

children, 27, 126, 139, 175, 259
Chinese Book of Mencius, 23
choice, challenge of, 7
Christmas selling season, 640, 671
chronological résumé, 701
Chutes and Ladders, 27
cinematics, 410–411
CIO (chief information officer), 190
City of Heroes, 80
civilian aircraft simulations, 95, 96–97
Civilization, 85, 251, 570
clean machine, 416
client-server network architecture, 408
clients, for networked game, 373
clipping, for 3D graphics, 452
close combat, 332
closed architecture, 672
Clue (Milton Bradley), 8, 27
clues, 505
CNET News.com, 675
code. *See* program code
code freeze, 618
Code Name: Sector, 37
codecs, 473
Codex Exoniensis, 25
coding standards, technical design document on, 376
Colayco, Bob, 266
Coleco Industries, 31
ColecoVision, 121
collectibles, in game design document, 336
colleges, 695, 704
collision box, 439
collision detection, 403
collision reaction, 404
color, for transparency, 445
color graphics adapter (CGA), 430
color graphics array (CGA), 132
colors, and bit-depth, 430
Colossal Cave (Adventure), 35, 75
combat, 252, 260, 332–335, 337, 513
combat resolution table, 532
combat results table (CRT), 333, 533
combat simulations, with air vehicles, 95–96
combinatorial solutions, 74
combos, 501
comma-delimited data, 530
Command & Conquer, 88
Command & Conquer: Red Alert 2, 432
Command: Aces of the Deep, 98
Command HQ, 88
Commodore Amiga 1000, 123
Commodore Business Machines, 41, 123
communication skills, 195, 699
communications, corporate, 656
community colleges, 694
compact discs (CDs), 135, 144
company logos, art design document on, 383
company startup, in game industry, 188
company web site, programming staff responsibility, 422
Compaq Computer Corporation, 123, 124
compatibility tester, 218
compensating factor, 536
compensatory (comp) time, 611
competitive mode for multiplayer game, 374
competitors, marketing analysis on, 302
compiler, 394
completing the game, 558
complexity in game development, 157, 159
composer, 213–214
compositing, 444–445

compression/decompression of audio files, 375, 472–473
computer games, 34, 616, 682, 683
Computer Graphics Adaptor (CGA), 42
Computer Othello, 36
computer science degrees, 694
Computer Space, 35
computers, 12, 45, 88, 125, 131, 419–420, 500
Computing-Tabulating-Recording Company, 33
concept art, 377, 434
concept game design document, 166, 311–315, 354, 361, 516
cone of vision, 542
conferences, programming staff attendance at, 421
confidential disclosure agreement, 166, 284
conflict, 550, 559
Conquests of Camelot: The Search for the Grail, 336
console development kits, 120–121
console games. *See* video console games
construction, 255, 261
construction chart, for real-time strategy games, 534
context-driven help, 505
continuous level of detail, 212
contracts, for independent developers, 684–686
contrast, 382
controller, for video game consoles, 143
COO (chief operating officer), 190
cooperative mode for multiplayer game, 374
cooperative work experience, 704
coordinate system for 3D graphics, 523
copy protection, in game software, 503
copyright, 317, 478, 682
Cornerstone, 75
corporate communications, 656
Corporate Machine, 89
cost of goods for physical game components, 667
country, game design document description, 347
cover letters, in job search, 702
CPU (central processing unit), 155
crash, 616
Crawford, Chris, 178
Cray-1 (supercomputer), vs. Nintendo64, 47
Crazy Taxi, 61
creative director, 191, 198
creatures, magic and, 339
Cricket 2000, 108
Criterion, RenderWare, 169, 362
critical path, 227
cross-platform games, 119, 670
crosstalk, 474
Crowther, William, 35, 75
crunch time, 241, 609–610, 611, 619
Crusade in Europe, 85
culling, 401, 450–451
customer service departments, 617
customers, feedback from, 710
cut-scene animation, 349
cut-scene sequences, 212
CVS (Concurrent Versions System), 414
Cyan Worlds, Inc., 77

D

D-pad, 143
Dabney, Ted, 35
dance arcade games, 64
Dance Dance Revolution, 64
Dark Age of Camelot, 83
Darrow, Charles B., 27

Dartmouth Conference on machine intelligence, 538
Das Boot: German U-Boat Simulation, 98
data structures, 394
database, 173–175, 232, 351, 417, 529–535
Day of the Tentacle, 76
de Coubertin, Pierre, 20
dead-character animation, 438
deathmatches, 72
debug version of game, 414
debugging, 176–177, 416–418
decibels (dB), 470
dedicated server, for networked game, 373
Deer Hunter, 111
defense value, in war games, 86
delays in schedule, identifying potential, 232
Delgine, 449
Dell, Axim X50v Pocket PC, 149
demo reel, 703
demos, 421, 577
dénouement, 550
dependencies, in project timeline, 226
depth, 459, 593
descriptions in GDD, 344–349
derivative works, ancillary rights for, 685
design goals, 263–268
design process, documentation in, 277
design staff, 194–198
designers, 163, 278–283, 304, 309–310, 495, 528–529, 654, 698
Destroyer Command, 98
Destruction, 256, 261
deterministic algorithms, 540
Deus Ex, 71, 80
development costs, 669–670
development phase, of movie production, 160
Devil May Cry, 73
DeVry University, 695
DFC Intelligence, 300, 664, 675
Diablo, 82
Diablo 2, 676
diagonal scroller, 68
dialogue, 350–351, 483, 531, 532, 560–563
dialogue writer, 217, 351, 563
Dickens, Charles, 27
diffuse property of surface material, 452
Dig, 77
Digimation, SpeedTree 3, 412
DigiPen Institute of Technology, 695
digital audio tape (DAT), 485
Digital Gaming in America study, 652
digital-to-analog converter (DAC), for audio, 474
DirectDraw, 396
DirectInput, 396
directional light, 451
DirectMusic, 410
director, 194, 483–484
directory structure, 413–414, 462
DirectPlay, 396
DirectSound, 396, 410
DirectX, 396, 410
DirectX APIs, 48
display manager, technical design document on, 372
distribution phase, of movie production, 162
divination, dice for, 25
documentation, 179, 247, 269, 310–311, 621–622. *See also* game design document; game proposal; pitch paper
Dolby Digital 5.1, 474
dominoes, 26
Donkey Kong, 39, 42, 67

Donkey Kong Country, 46
Doom, 46, 68, 70, 72, 137, 408, 674
Doom 3, 130, 266, 676
Double Dragon, 65
Douglas, A. S., 33
download sites for online games, 677
Dr. J and Larry Bird Go One-on-One, 41, 110
Dragon Quest, 80
Drakan: The Ancient Gates, 458
draughts (checkers), 23
driving. *See* vehicle games
dry audio recordings, 485
Dune II, 88
dungeon crawls, 82
Dungeon Siege, 82
Dungeons & Dragons, 10, 29, 530
DVD (digital versatile disc), 135, 144, 625, 626, 702
dynamic bots, 406
dynamic context menu, 517
dynamic sound, 410

E

Easter eggs, 336
economic/political strategy games, 88–89
economics. *See* game industry economics
Economist Global Agenda, 138
ecosystem, game design document description, 347
EDSAC computer, 33
education, 694–699
EGA (Enhanced Graphics Adapter), 42, 430
Elder Scrolls, 80
Electronic Arts, 41, 45, 48, 50, 71, 108, 169, 189, 204, 645
Electronic Entertainment Expo (E3), 178, 234, 235, 421, 644
electronic game industry, 3, 11, 12, 13
electronic games, 3, 5, 8–12, 19–52, 60–61. *See also* platforms
Electronic Gaming Monthly, 644
Electronic Software Association, 663
Electronic Software Distribution (ESD), 673–675
Electronics Software Ratings Board (ESRB), 11
Elite Force, 71
emergent behavior, 407
Emergent Game Technology, Gamebryo, 242
emissive property of surface material, 452
emotion, 482, 553, 628
employee benefits, 241, 620
emulators, 145, 395
encounters, 589
Ender's Game, 77
enemy characters, 345–346, 407
engine proof, as milestone, 230
Enhanced Graphics Adapter (EGA), 42, 430
Entertainment Software Rating Board (ESRB), 45, 66, 319
entities, 596. *See also* objects
entry point for level, 581, 587–588
environment awareness, 541
environment of game. *See* locations
Epic Games, Unreal Engine, 169, 172, 201, 362
ergonomics, video game consoles and, 139
Eric the Unready, 75
ESPN NBA Basketball, 108
ESRB (Electronics Software Ratings Board), 11
Eureka effect, 101
European Computer Trade Show, 644
EverQuest, 49, 83, 137, 409, 676
executive management, 187, 189–190
executive producer, 191
executive summary, for game design document, 318

exits for levels, 587–588
expansion packs, 676
experience chart, 532
experience level, 79
experience points, 327
experiential density, 589
exploitation, 252–253, 260
exploration, 252, 260
exposition, 550
extended graphics array (EGA), 132
eye candy, 508

F

F-15 Strike Eagle II, 96
F-16 Combat Pilot, 96
facial animation, voiceovers synched to, 482
falling action, 550
Fallout, 80
fantastic world as story setting, 553
fantasy role-playing games, 29, 80, 347
FAQ (frequently asked questions), 618
Far Cry, 334
fast, good, cheap, 225, 611
Fast Lanes Bowling, 110
feature creep, 269, 311
feedback, 178, 269, 469, 480, 496–497, 655–656,
    710. *See also* head-up display (HUD)
feel of game, 265
fees for licensing, 667
female characters, 556
Fertile Crescent, 21
FIFA Soccer 95, 108
fighting games, 65
Fighting Steel, 98
fighting the parser, 75
files, 413–414, 431–432, 473
fill feature, in map editor, 591
films. *See* movie industry
filters for sound effects, 480
Final Fantasy, 80, 144, 476
Final Fantasy IX, 330
Final Fantasy X, 268, 333, 505, 515
Final Fantasy X-2, 338
finalized product, 604
finances, and production pressure, 608
financial analysis, in game proposal, 165
finite state machines, 541
first-person shooter games, 68–73, 80,
    258–259, 499
first playable milestone, 230
first refusal rights, 685
Fitts, Paul, 516
Flash animations, 650
flash memory cards, for saving games, 506
flat shading, 453
flickering, 443
Flight Unlimited, 97
floating Internet ads, 650
floppy disks, 135
flowchart, 324, 351, 573–575
fly-through prototype, 577–578
focus groups, 178, 507, 655–656
fog and opacity for 3D graphics, 456–457
fog of war, 86, 329, 370
fonts, art design document on, 383–384
foreshadowing, 478
forward kinematics, 449
frame rate, 366, 400, 443
frame story, 557
frames, 437, 461
Freedom Force vs. the Third Reich, 364

freelancers, 216–218
freezing code, 618
freezing technology for game, 420
frequency, 470
frequently asked questions (FAQ), 618
Frogger, 104
front matter, in game design document, 317
full-motion video (FMV), 349
full-motion video (FMV) artists, 212–213
Full Sail, 696
full-size games, 680
Full Swing! Golf, 151
Full Throttle, 553, 560
fully functional interactive prototype, 576
fun factor, 249–259, 260–261, 292
functional management, 188, 191–192
functional résumé, 701
functionality, 350, 497
functions, 394
fuzzy logic, 202, 542

G

G-4 cable channel, 645
Gabriel Knight, 75
Galactic Pinball, 111
Galapagos: Mendel's Escape, 104
Gamasutra Web site, 268, 299, 684
Game Boy Advance (Nintendo), 51, 146–147
Game Boy (Nintendo), 13, 42–43, 146–147
game concept, 364, 379
game consoles. *See* video game consoles
game database. *See* database
game design dangers, 268–271
game design document, 14, 163, 166, 229, 262,
    304, 309–311, 354–355, 497, 507, 568
game design document structure, 315–316, 344–354
game design specification, 166
Game Developers Conference (GDC), 178, 421
game development cycle, trends, 157
Game Editor, 172
game engine, 168–170, 200, 585
game engine modules, 530, 685
game engine programmer, 200–201
game entity, 432
game flow, in game design document, 323–324
game idea development, 278–283
game industry, 159, 178, 188, 249, 447, 641, 664,
    666, 684. *See also* career in game industry;
    electronic game industry; production cycle
    for games
game industry economics, 663–687
Game of Life, 27
game-pad, 143
game plot, 292
game production, in-depth studies in fields
    related to, 695
game proposal, 14, 164, 289–304, 311
game specification, 309. *See also* game
    design document
game teams, 186
game titles, classification, 187
game tournaments, 645
Gamebryo, 242, 362
Gamebryo (NDL), 201
GameCube (Nintendo), 50, 120, 139, 140, 144, 670
gameplay, 249, 319, 322–343, 536–537, 558
gameplay elements, 79, 80, 247, 259–262, 264,
    285, 290, 292–293, 569
games, 1, 6–8, 11, 19–26, 101, 259, 295
The Games: Summer Challenge, 111
Gamestats, 299

Gangsters: Organized Crime, 89
Gantt, Henry Laurence, 228
Gantt chart, 228, 277
Garage Games, 677
Gates, Bill, 36
Gateway, 75
gating, 558
GDC Mobile, 178
GDD. *See* game design document
GEnie network, 137
genres of games, 1, 9, 60–73, 74–78,
    79–89, 90–91, 93–99, 100–106, 106–111,
    533–534
geometry editor, 412
geometry, for level creation, 595
Gettysburg!, 85
Ghost Recon, 71
GIF (graphic interchange format), 431
GIGNews, 165
Gilbert, Ron, 76, 563
glass master, 625
global light, 451
Go (wei-qi; I-go), 23–24
Goals, 16, 90, 179, 292, 365, 617–618
gold master, 231
Golden Voyage, 75
golf games, 110
good, cheap, fast, 225, 611
Gosling, James, 198
Gouraud shading, 453
graduate work, 694
Grand Theft Auto 3, 51
Grand Theft Auto: San Andreas, 139, 169
Grand Theft Auto: Vice City, 584
graphic adventure games, 74, 75–78
graphic rights for music, 478
graphical user interface (GUI), 124, 203, 496.
    See also user interface
graphics, 132–133, 142–143, 428–436, 462.
    See also 2D graphics; 3D graphics
graphics APIs, 395
graphics card, program communication with, 396
graphics engine, technical design document on,
    370–373
graphics processing unit, 130
Greece, 20
green light, 167
Grim Fandango, 76, 552
Guild War, 52, 130
Guildhall, 696
Guinness Book of Records, 67
Gunship, 96
GURPS, 530
Gwinnett Daily Online, 649
Gygax, E. Gary, 29

H

H2Overdrive, 97
Half-Life, 49, 71, 449, 510, 589, 674
Half-Life 2, 130
Half-Life: Counter-Strike, 415
Halo, 50, 71
Halo 2, 139, 416, 505, 645, 666
Hamill, Mark, 100
Hammer Editor, 580
Hanafuda, 28
handheld games, 13, 128–129, 149–150, 680
handles of Bézier curve, 597
hard drive, 131, 136
hard room, 484
hard skills, 699
hardware, 419–420, 617

hardware requirements, in game design document, 322
Harpoon, 85
Harry Fox Agency, 479
Harry Potter and the Goblet of Fire, 294
Hasbro, 31, 48, 51
Havok physics machine, 362, 403
Hawkins, Trip, 41, 45
Hawks, Tony, 111
HDTV, resolution, 143
Head Relative Transfer Functions (HRTF), 474
head-up display (HUD), 209, 269, 435, 497, 499, 509–512
header (high concept) in pitch paper, 285
helicopter combat simulations, 96
help for users, context-driven, 505
The Hero with a Thousand Faces (Campbell), 557
Herodotus, 25
hertz (Hz), 470
hexagons, vs. square grid, 572–573
Hidden Agenda, 89
hidden exits, 587
hidden surface removal, 401, 450–451
high concept (header), 285, 317–318
high concept paper, 283. *See also* pitch paper
high definition television (HDTV), resolution, 430
high-density floppy disks, 135
high-level languages, 394
Higinbotham, Willy, 33
HIND: The Russian Combat Helicopter Simulation, 96
hiring, director for voiceovers, 483–484
history/backstory, in game design document, 350
Hitchhiker's Guide to the Galaxy, 75
Hitman: Contracts, 559
Hodj 'n' Podj, 105
Hollywood Video, 682
home computers. *See* computers
hosting sites for online games, 675–676
hot seat, 342
hot spot, 439
hourly wages, 241
hours of work, 708
House of the Dead, 62
Hoyle, Edmond, *Short Treatise on the Game of Back-Gammon*, 25
Hsieh, Kathy, 441
human resources (HR) department, 701
hunting skills, 20
Hydro Thunder, 97

I
I-go (wei-qi; Go;), 23–24
"I Love Bees" blog site, 646
IBM (International Business Machines), 33, 44, 123–124
Ibuka, Masaru, 32
Icons, 348, 516
id Software, 46, 70, 125
IDC, 300
ideas. *See* game idea development
idling, 437
"if-then" statements, 173
image puzzles, 103
ImagiNation Network, 137
improvisational theater, 280
in-game interface, 324, 350, 507–518
in-game sequences, 213
in-person interview, 707
In-Stat, 678
Incredible Machine, 104

Independence War: The Starship Simulator, 99
independent characters, 345, 346
independent developers. *See* third-party developers
Independent Games Festival, 178
Indiana Jones and the Infernal Machine, 78
industry research, 654–655
Infocom, 36, 45, 75
Infogrames, 31, 51
infomercials on Internet, 650
Informa Telecoms and Media, 664
information, 278, 313
Innocents Abroad, 27
InnoSetup, 502
input devices, 133–135, 143–144, 497–498
inset map, 509
installation, 418, 502–503
InstallShield, 418, 502
insult sword fighting, 563
integrated development environment (IDE), 395
Intel, 25 MHz 486 microprocessor, 124
intellectual properties, 555, 681–682, 684–687
Intellivision, 37, 41
Interactive Advertising Bureau, 650
interactive area, in main playfield screen, 508
interactive dialogue, 560–563
interactive fun, 251–259
interactive prototype, 163, 170–171, 575–577
interactivity, 8
interface. *See* shell interface; user interface
interface artist, 209
interface programmer, 202–203
interim checkpoints in milestone schedule, 230
interlace method for television, 142
interlaced scanning, vs. progressive, 443–444
International Business Machines (IBM), 33, 44
International Game Developers Association, 610, 680
International Herald Tribune, 640
international sales, language translation for, 218
Internet, 10, 48, 61, 137–138, 145, 203–204, 408, 588, 644, 650–651, 664. *See also* networks
Internet sites for job postings, 704
Internet World Stats News, 674
internships, 704
interpolation, 431, 448
interstitial Internet ads, 650
interviewing, 420–421, 706–707
intranet, 190, 354, 422
introduction in GDD, 316–322
inventory system, for collected items, 336, 515
inverse kinematics (IK), 448
invisible doorways, 587
Iridium RPG, map editor, 592
isometric (3/4-view) games, 433, 438
isomorphic view, 397
items, 348, 382, 515, 532

J
J2ME (Java 2 Platform, Micro Edition), 199
Jagged Alliance, 85
Jagged Alliance 2, 398
jaggies, 133, 142, 446, 461
Japan, war game preparations for Battle of Midway, 87
Java, 198, 394
Jeopardy!, 103
jigsaw puzzles, 27
job search, 700–708
job titles, 187, 701
Jobs, Steve, 36
joystick, 63, 134, 396

JPEG (Joint Photographic Experts Group), 431
junior programmers, 201–202
Jupiter Lander, 99

K
Katamari Damacy, 104
Kenya, 20
key frames, 448
keyboard, 134
kill fee, 271
King, 129
King's Quest, 75
King's Quest I: Quest for the Crown, 549
Kinook Software, Visual Build Professional, 416
KISS Principle (Keep It Simple, Stupid), 268
Knights of the Sky, 96
Knockout Kings, 110
Kohl, Herbert, 45, 66
Kotick, Robert, 45

L
Lander, 99
language, translation for international market, 218
laser beam recorder, 625
latency for networked game, 375
layers, 444–445
LCD (liquid-crystal display) monitors, 444
lead artist, 206–207
lead programmer, 199–200, 342, 361
lead-up to product ship, 639
leadership ability, of game character, 327
Leakey, Richard, 20
learning curve, 709
learning, games and, 259
Leather Goddesses of Phobos, 75
Lebling, David, 75
legal issues, in music, 478–479
Legend Entertainment, 75
Legend of Zelda, 69
Legend of Zelda: Ocarina of Time, 48
Legend of Zelda: Quest for the Crown, 549
Leisure Suit Larry, 75
Lemmings, 61, 104
letterboxing, 143
level designer, 197
level editor, 590, 594–597
level of detail, 402, 439
level up, 74
levels, 264, 368, 506, 568, 578–590, 593. *See also* map editor
Levine, Ken, 266
Lexicon Word Challenge, 102
LHX: Attack Chopper, 96
library, for research, 283
licensing, 169, 294–295, 362, 384, 534, 667, 669
Lieberman, Joseph, 45, 66
lifetime of game, 670–671
lighting, 373, 401, 449, 451–452
Lightspeed, 99
Lightwave, 208, 446
line producers, 193
linear level, 582
linear stories, 10
linear storyline, 549
LISP programming language, 538
literacy, and board games, 27
"Little Wars" (Wells), 28
loading data during play, 584–585
local area networks (LAN), 407
local light, 451
localization, 487–488

localization staff, 218
locations, 346–348, 380–381
locked entrance, hidden key for, 588
logic puzzles, 101, 102–103
lookup tables, 324, 529–530
Loom, 76, 77
looping music, 476
Lord of the Rings, 29
Lord of the Rings: The Return of the King, 294
loss leader, 673
lossless data compression of audio files, 473
lossy data compression, 473
Lost Vikings, 104
low-frequency effects (LFE) channel, 474
Lua, 395
Lucas, George, 557
Lucasfilm Games, 77
Ludus Duodecim Scriptorum (twelve-lined game), 24–25
Luigi's Mansion, 50
Lunar Lander (Moonlander), 99
Lydians, 25

M

machine language, 394
Macromedia Director, 289, 575
Macrovision, 502, 682
Madden NFL, 107, 119
Madden NFL 2004, 139
magazines, advertising in, 648–649
magic, 337–340, 532
Magic: The Gathering, 29
Magnavox, Odyssey, 34
mahjong, 106
main game loop, 365–366
main menu, design, 503–504
Mall Tycoon, 570
Maloney, Raymond, 32
mammals, play behavior, 20
mana, 337
management, 164, 316, 361
management positions, 187–194
management skills, 700
management tools for scheduling, 225–232
mancala, 20, 22
Manhunt, 559
Maniac Mansion, 76, 549
manual for game, 197, 621–622
manual writer, 217–218, 622
map editor, 171, 396, 441, 590–597
maps, 331–332, 509. *See also* levels
market development funds, 667
marketing, 16, 177–179, 234, 287, 319, 436, 555, 637, 639–640, 667. *See also* packaging
marketing analysis, 290, 299–303
marketing campaign, 641–647
marketing department, 641, 638–639, 653–656
marketing development funds, 641
marketing information companies, 299
Marufuku Company, 28
massively multiplayer online role-playing games (MMORPGs), 83, 137, 409, 617, 664, 676
Master of Magic, 85
Master of Orion, 85
master rights for music, 478
master timeline, 226
master's degree, 694
mathematics, 523–537. *See also* artificial intelligence (AI)
Matrix Online, 645
Mattel, 31, 37, 41

Max Payne, 552
Maya, 171, 208, 369, 446, 580
McCarthy, John, 538
MDK, 73
mechanical rights for music, 478
meetings and code reviews, by programmers, 418–419
Mega Man, 66
Meiers, Sid, 7
melee combat, 332
memory, for personal computers, 131
memory games, 102–103
memory manager, for video memory, 396
mental exercise, games as, 101
mentoring, 421, 708
menu display, 143, 203, 480, 503–504, 513–515
Meridian59, 48, 137
Merlin (Parker Brothers), 37
meshes, 209, 411, 447, 450
metal father, 626
Metal Gear Solid 2, 478
Metroid Prime, 71, 556
microphone, for voiceovers, 485
microprocessor, 1, 130–131, 140–141
MicroProse, 31, 49
Microsoft, 36, 39, 48, 50, 51, 124, 126, 227, 395, 411, 414, 502. *See also* Windows (Microsoft)
Microsoft Disk Operating System (MS-DOS), 39, 45, 131
Microsoft Flight Simulator, 97
Microsoft Space Simulator, 99
Microvision, 148–149
middle class, board games and, 26
middleware, 168, 169
MIDI (Musical Instrument Digital Interface), 472
Midway, 36
Might & Magic, 80
Miles sound system, 362, 410
milestone schedule, 226, 228–232, 241, 363, 365, 379, 619, 686
milestones, 15, 226, 320
military simulation games, 84. *See also* war games
Milton Bradley, 27, 31, 37, 148–149
Mind Forever Voyaging, 75
Minesweeper, 102
miniatures for war games, 28
minibosses, 345
minimum hardware requirements, listing for game, 364
MIP-mapping, 455
Mirrorworld, 83
mission statement for team, 321–322
Mitchell, Billy, 62
MITS Altair, 122, 129
Miyamoto, Shigeru, 39
MMORPGs (massively multiplayer online role-playing games), 83, 137
mobile games, 77
mobile phones, 10, 13, 129, 150–151, 199, 664, 678
mod-chips, 682
model in 3D game, 399, 411
model sheets (templates), for characters, 434
moderator, for brainstorming session, 280
modifiers of magic spells, 338
mods, user creation of, 595
modules of code, 394
Monarch Publishing, 29
monaural format for audio, 473
monitors, 430, 441, 443–444
Monkey Island 3, 441
Monopoly, 27, 31, 48

Monsters Inc.: Wreck Room Arcade: Bowling for Screams, 107
monsters, 345
mood of game, audio and, 469
Moon Lander (Lunar Lander), 99
moon landing games, 99
Moore, Gordon E., 125
Moore's Law, 125
morale, 611
Morita, Akio, 32
Morris, 25
Mortal Kombat, 45, 65
motion capture, 162, 163, 213, 482
motion capture technicians, 216–217
mouse, 134
movement of objects, 329–330, 369
movement rate, in war games, 86
movie and DVD ads, advertising on, 653
movie industry, 160–162, 294–295
MP3 file format, 473
MS-DOS (Microsoft Disk Operating System), 39, 45, 131
MSN.Games, 676
MSNZone, 422
MUD (multi-user dungeon), 36, 82, 137
M.U.L.E., 88
multiplayer versions, 72, 118, 203–204, 267, 341–342, 605
multiple versions, in game design document, 353
multitexturing, 456
music, 342, 475–479, 686. *See also* audio
Musical Instrument Digital Interface (MIDI), 472
MVP Baseball, 108
Myst, 77
Myst V: End of Ages, concept art, 165
Mystery House, 38, 75, 548

N

N-Gage (Nokia), 51–52, 128, 147
Namco, 38, 207
Napoleon at Bay, 530
narrative structure, 549–559, 563
native resolution, 143
NBA Street, 109
NDAs (nondisclosure agreements), 166, 284
Need for Speed Underground, 510
Neolithic Period, 20
NES (Nintendo Entertainment System), 41
net sales revenue, 236
networking for job opportunities, 705–706
networking programmer, 203–204
networks, 136, 373–375, 396, 407–409
neural networks, 543
new hires, interviewing, 420–421
new ideas, risks in, 249
new projects, employees shifted to, 620–621
NHL Hockey 1994, 108
Nintendo, 13, 42–43, 45, 47, 50–51, 126, 128–129, 139, 140, 146–147, 679
Nintendo DS, 52, 129
Nintendo Entertainment System (NES), 41, 42, 126, 139, 140
Nintendo of America, 37
Nintendo of Japan, 36
Nintendo Playing Card Company, 28
nodal pathing, 406
nodes, 597
Noguchi, Matthew, 416
Nokia, N-Gage, 13, 51–52, 128, 147
nondisclosure agreements (NDAs), 166, 284

nonlinear stories, 10, 550
nonplayer characters, 11, 79, 346, 554, 557–558, 560–562
NoodeX, 403
NPCs. *See* nonplayer characters
NPD Funworld, 299
Nutting Associates, 35
NXN Software, Alienbrain Studio, 414

O

object manager, 367
object-oriented programming, 394
objective of game, in game proposal, 292
objective on résumé, 701
objectives section, in production report, 231
objects, 344–345, 366, 381, 588–589, 596. *See* physics processing unit
obstacle avoidance, 405
occluder, 457
Oddworld: Abe's Oddysey, 104, 195
Odyssey (Magnavox), 34, 121
OEM (original equipment manufacturer), 180, 671
office expenses, 241–242
Ogg Vorbis file format, 473
Olympic Games, 20, 111
On-Line Systems, 38
on-rails gun shooters, 62
online 3D models, limitations, 212
online chat, for networked game, 374, 409
online gambling, 137
online games, 411–412, 675–677
online service for games, 409
opacity for 3D graphics, 456–457
open-ended level, 582
open-ended role-playing games, 79
open narrative structure, vs. rail structure, 551
OpenAL (Open Audio Library), 410
OpenGL (Open Graphics Library), 396
operational-level war games, 85
operational management, 188, 192–194
order of battle, 569
original equipment manufacturer (OEM), 180, 671
Othello, 31, 36
outdoor terrain editor, 412
outsourcing jobs overseas, 447
overdesign, problems from, 269
overdraw, 459
overhead expenses, 667
overhead scroller, 67
overlay textures, 402
overscanning, 501
overselling, 640
overwriting files, 414
Oxford History of Board Games (Parlett), 20
OXO, 33

P

P & L (profit and loss) analysis, 235
Pac-Man, 40, 62
package designer, 654
packaging, 621–626, 653–654
packets, 374, 408
padding in schedule, 233, 299
page flipping, 397, 444
page swapping, 444
Pajitnov, Alex, 42
Palamedes (Greek warrior), 25
palette shifting, 591
Panasonic, 45
Panzer General, 85
paper and design proposal, 164–165

paper prototype, 168, 569–572
paper war games, 84
parallax scrolling, 396, 442–443, 593
Parcheesi, 8, 24, 27
Parker Brothers, 27, 37
Parker, George S., 27
Parlett, David, *Oxford History of Board Games* , 20
particles, technical design document on, 372
patches, 418, 616, 618–619
pathfinding, 369, 405, 537
pathfinding algorithm, 540
paths, 597, 607
pattern list, 540–541
pause game feature, 505–506
pay-per-view for Internet ads, 650
payment schedule, in contract, 686
PC clones, 124
PC Gamer, 644
PDAs (personal digital assistants), 129, 149–150
peer-to-peer network architecture, 408
penumbra, 457
perfectionism, 610
Perforce, 414
performance rights for music, 478
performance speed, of computers, 130
Perl, 395
persistence of vision, 133
persistent worlds, 83
Phantasy Star, 80
Phong shading, 453–454
physical dexterity, 253, 261
physics processing unit, 131, 368, 403–405
physics, role in games, 522–523
PhysX (dedicated physics chip), 131
pickup sessions, 486–487
PICT (picture) format, 431
pin board, 574
pinball, 32, 104
piracy, 503, 675, 681–682
pitch paper, 164, 259, 283–289, 311
Pitfall, 38, 66
Pitfall: The Lost Expedition, 254
pixel popping, 455
pixel shading, 454
pixels, 429
placeholder art, 171
placement companies, 705
plagiarism, 282
Planescape: Torment, 80
Planetfall, 75
planning, importance of, 168, 628
platform dependent games, 119
platform games, 66
platform independent games, 119
platforms, 118, 119–145, 146–150, 500–501, 517, 671–673
PLATO Network, 70
play behavior of mammals, 20
player chart, for sports games, 534
players, voices of, 481–488
playfield, 329–332, 351–352, 440–443. *See also* levels
playfield objects, user interaction with, 509
Playsite, 676
PlayStation, 46, 47
PlayStation 2, 120, 670
PlayStation Portable (Sony), 13, 52, 129, 147
playtesters, 231, 241, 265
plot, 350, 549, 556–558
plot coupons, 557
PNG (portable network graphics), 431

point light, 451
point of view for game. *See* cameras
point sampling, 455
Pokémon, 29
Police Quest, 75
Political Machine, 89
Polti, Georges, *The Thirty-Six Dramatic Situations*, 557
polycarbonate, 626
polygons, count on playfield, 399
polytechnic institutes, 695
Pong, 9, 35, 62, 121, 122
pop-up windows and menus, 513–515
portfolio, for job search, 702–703
positive attitude, 700
postmortems, 626–629
postproduction phase for games, 179–180
postproduction phase of movie production, 162
Powell, Jay, 165
Power Game Factory (Sawblade Software), 397
power politics, 271
power-ups, 68, 336
PowerPoint presentation, 288
Prague Filmharmonic Orchestra, 477
pre-rendered cut scenes, 213
preproduction phase for games, 164–170, 249
preproduction phase of movie production, 160
prerecorded music, permissions, 478
preselling game, 639–640
presentation, 288–289, 421
president, 189
press releases, 642–643
primary controls, 268
Prince of Persia, 66
Prince of Persia: Sands of Time, 73, 552
Pro Powerboat Simulator, 97
probationary hiring, 707
problem conflict in story, 549, 558
problems section in production report, 231
producers, 192–194, 627
product manager, 194, 638
product placement, 645
product ship, 639, 709, 710
production coordinator, 193
production cycle for games, 158–159, 160–180, 393
production game design document, 311, 354–355
production houses, external, 216–218
production phase of movie production, 160–161
production reports, 226, 231–232
production schedule, development, 15
productivity, overtime and, 609
professional sports, 107–108, 110
profit, from games, 670
program code, 376, 394–412, 418, 618
programmers, 163
programming languages, 198–199, 694
programming staff, 198–205, 393, 537–538
progressive scanning, 142, 443–444
project manager, 194
project timeline, 226–228
project triangle, 225
projectiles, 368, 403
prologue, 318
promotional stints, 645
proprietary scripting language, 173
protagonist, 291, 344
protocol, for networked game, 374–375
prototype code, avoiding in final version, 170
prototyping, 569–578
publisher, income from game sale, 235
Puck Man, 38

Punisher, 73
Puyo Pop Fever, 254
puzzle genre, 61, 100–106, 534–535
puzzles, 74, 261
Python, 395

Q

QDOS (Quick and Dirty Operating System), 39
QSound Labs, 474
quadtrees, 527
Quake, 137
Quake 4 (id Software), 5
Quake III Arena, 72
QuakeWorld, 137
Qualcomm, 198
quality assurance, 176, 612–617
quality assurance staff, 205, 215–216, 417, 612

R

racing game. *See* vehicle games
RAD Game Tools, Bink Video, 411
Radiant, 449
radio, advertising on, 653
Radio Shack TRS-80, 123
rag-doll physics, 404–405
Raiden, 67
rail structure, vs. open narrative, 551
Railroad Game, 27
Railroad Tycoon, 89, 90
random access memory (RAM), 131, 140
random events table, for racing games, 534
randomizing factor, 8, 101, 251, 256, 532–533, 536, 541, 550
range, in war games, 87
ranged combat, 332
raster graphics, 443
rasterization, 431, 452
real-time strategy games, 87–88, 534, 605
recommendations, 364, 628
recording sessions, for voiceovers, 484–486
recording studio, 482
recoupable advances, 686
recruiters, 705
Red Baron, 96
Redbook Audio, 472
references of job applicant, 707
reflective property of surface material, 452
refresh rate for computer display, 132
regression testing, 232
relative scale, for object attributes, 324
release candidate, 179
release version of game, target files for, 414
remnant space in magazine, 649
rendering, 370–371, 372, 452–454
RenderWare (Criterion), 169, 201, 362, 403
renting games, 682–683
repetition of music, 476
replayability, and randomizing factor, 251
Republic Dawn: Chronicles of the Seven, 504
research, 283, 312–313, 654–655, 700
research companies, 299–300
reselling games, 682–683
resolution, 142, 430, 431
resolution of story, 549, 550
resource loading, 227
resources, 88, 91, 336
response to collision, 404
retailers, 61, 180, 641–643
return on investment (ROI), 190, 236
Return to Castle Wolfenstein, 504
reviews of games, 641

rewards of game industry job, 710
rich media, 650
rigging, 448
Riley, David, 664
rising action, 550
Risk, 8, 27
Risks, 365, 379
Roberts, Charles, 28, 84
Robinson, Evan, 609
rock-paper-scissors game, 535
RocSearch Ltd, 664
Rogue: The Adventure, 132
ROI (return on investment), 190, 236
role-playing games, 9, 29, 79–83, 166, 174–175, 195, 309, 326, 351, 501, 513, 531–532, 548–549, 605
RollerCoaster Tycoon, 253
Rome: Total War - Barbarian Invasion, 252
Rosen, David, 33
rotating 2D graphics, 398–399
royal game of Ur, 21
royalties, 236, 667, 669, 686
rules of games, 7
run-time sequences, 213
Russell, Steve, 33

S

S&M (sales and marketing), demands from, 234
sales department, 290, 667
sampling, 470–472
sampling frequency, 471–472
Sanger, George A., 214
saving games, 505–506
Sawblade Software, Power Game Factory, 397
scale of game, 329, 402, 509
scanning, progressive vs. interlaced, 443–444
Schafer, Tim, 553
Schedule, 320, 349, 365, 379
schedule development, 168, 225, 232–235, 298–299, 611
science fiction role-playing games, 80
Scrabble, 27, 31
screen, 203. *See also* user interface
Screen Actors Guild (SAG), 486
screenplay, game design document and, 314
screenwriters, 217, 483
Script Creation Utility for Maniac Mansion (SCUMM), 76
script for dialogue, 483, 486–487
scripter, 198
scripting language, 173, 394, 411, 585, 597
Scrolling Game Development Kit, 442
scrolling games, 65–68
SCUMM (Script Creation Utility for Maniac Mansion), 76
Sea Dogs, 80
Seapine Software, TestTrack Pro, 613
Seattle Computer Products, 39
secondary controls, 268
Secret of Monkey Island, 76, 563
Secret Weapons of the Luftwaffe, 96
SEGA (SErvice GAmes), 33, 42, 43, 45–48, 50, 68, 126, 672
Segali, Mario, 40
Selchow and Righter company, 27, 31
sell-in, 655
sell sheets, 643
sell-through, 655
selling game to management, 320–321
senet (senat), 21
senior designer, 195–197

sequels, first refusal rights, 685
servers, for networked game, 373, 374
Service Games company, 33
SESAC, 479
setting for story, 549, 551–552
Settlers of Catan, 530
The Seven Cities of Gold, 671
shading, for 3D graphics, 452–454
shadow volumes, 459
shadows, 373, 457–459
Shanghai, 61, 103
Sharkey's 3D Pool, 111
shaturanga (chaturanga), 23
shelf life of electronic game, 180, 670–671
shelf space for games, 639, 641, 642, 670
shell interface, 323, 350, 502–507
shininess property of surface material, 452
shooters, 68
Short Treatise on the Game of Back-Gammon (Hoyle), 25
shortcut keys, 500
shoulder buttons, on console controller, 501
shovelware, 654, 671
Shun (Chinese emperor), 23–24
Sid Meier's Civilization III, 339
Sid Meier's Railroad Tycoon, 255
side-scrollers, 65, 438, 592
Sierra Entertainment, 49
Sierra Interactive, 75
Sierra On-Line, 38, 75, 137
Sikora, Drew, 270
Silent Service, 98
Silicon Graphics, Inc., 207
SimCity, 91, 255, 569
SimCity 2000, 256
SimCopter, 97
Simon (Milton Bradley), 37
Sims, 90, 130
simulation games, 84, 89–91, 95, 98, 104, 106–111
simulators, 145
simultaneous multiplayer games, 341
skeletal animation system, 412, 448
skin, for 3D model, 211, 454
small developers, 190–191, 270, 283
small games, 680
Smash Court Tennis Pro Tournament, 110
snap-to-grid, 591, 595
Snoopy's Silly Sports Spectacular, 106
social values, games and, 559
software, 362, 379, 411–412, 419–420, 462, 694
software development kit (SDK), 395, 672
solitaire card games, 106
Sonic Heroes, 169
Sonic the Hedgehog, 43, 66, 555
Sony, 2, 3, 13, 32, 46–49, 51, 52, 126, 129, 140, 144, 147, 679
Sony Online Entertainment, 49
Sophocles, 25
Sorry!, 27
Sound Blaster Live! sound card, 136
sound effects, 214, 343, 479–480
sound manager, technical design document on, 375
soundproofing, for recording studio, 487
Space Invaders, 9, 36
Space Quest, 75
spaceship simulations, 98–99
Spacewar, 33
spaghetti code, 363
Spasim, 70
spawn, 72
spawn camping, 606

spawn points, 606
special abilities, of objects, 326–327
specialists, external, 216–218, 483, 563
Spectrum Holobyte, 31
specular property of surface material, 452
speed, action games and, 60
Spellcasting 101: Sorcerors Get All the Girls, 75
spellchecker, 563
Spider-Man 2, 294
splash page, 650
Splashdown, 97
splines, 539, 597
Spolin, Viola, 280
Spolin Center, 280
sports games, 106–111, 195, 534, 539, 309, 605
spot light, 452
spreadsheet, 324, 530
spreadsheet program (*VisiCalc*), 36
sprite editor, 439
sprites, 431, 432–433, 440
Squad Battles: Vietnam, 85
square grid, vs. hexagons, 572–573
staffing, 240, 270, 310, 317, 321–322, 447.
  See also art staff; design staff; management
  positions; programming staff
stakeholders, 192, 235
Star Trek: Bridge Commander, 99
Star Trek Voyager, 71
*Star Wars: Galactic Battlegrounds: Clone
  Campaigns*, 378
Star Wars: Galaxies, 80, 676
Star Wars: Knights of the Old Republic, 80,
  257, 554
*Star Wars: Knights of the Old Republic 2:
  The Sith Lords*, 560
Star Wars trilogy, 557
Star Wars: X-Wing, 99
StarCraft, 88, 583
StarEdit map editor, 583
StarForce: Alpha Centauri, 87
starting company, in game industry, 188
starting salaries, 693
Startrek, 129
static bots, 406
static game, paper prototype, 572
static mesh, 596
Steam network, 674, 675
steering wheel, as computer input device, 134
stereo format for audio, 473
Stern Pinball, 32
Storage, 135–136, 144
store buyers, 642
stories, 10, 250, 257, 313–314, 351
storyboards, 208–209, 320, 381, 433–434, 573–575
storytelling, 256, 261, 549–559, 560–563
strategic marketing plans, 646–647
strategy, 84, 535–536
strategy games, 60, 84–89, 90
stream-loading, 584–585
streaming multimedia, 411
Street Fighter II (Capcom), 4
structure of games, 7
styles of play, balance for, 607–608
Sub Battle Simulator, 98
sub-bosses, 345
Submarine, 132
submarine simulations, 98
subscription sites for online games, 676
subwoofer, 474
Sudoku, 102
Suikoden, 80

Sumer, 21
Summer Heat Beach Volleyball, 109
Super Mario 3, 43
Super Mario Bros., 42, 66, 67, 126
Super Metroid, 46
Super NES, 43
Super VGA (SVGA), 44
surfaces, properties of, 596
surround sound, 474
SWAG ("silly wild-a** guess"), 228
sweet spot, for surround sound, 474
SWF (Adobe Shockwave Flash) file format, 431
swing cover of game package, 622
synchronization rights for music, 479
synthesizer, for MIDI, 472
System Shock II, 71, 80, 267
Syzygy Engineering company, 35

T
table of contents, for game design document,
  316, 317
tables. *See* database
tables (Codex Exoniensis), 25
tactical-level war games, 85
tactics, 84
Tactics (war game), 28
Take-Out Weight Curling, 108
tangent points, of Bézier curve, 597
Tapwave Zodiac, 52, 129, 147
target acquisition, 537
target market, in marketing analysis, 300
target selection, technical design document on, 370
targets, in pitch paper, 285–286
tasks, subdividing, 233
TCP/IP (Transmission Control Protocol/Internet
  Protocol), 373–374
team members for game development. *See* staffing
team mission statement, in game design
  document, 321–322
team summary, in game design document, 354
teamwork as job skill, 700, 708
technical analysis, game design document and, 314
technical colleges, 694
technical design document, 15, 167, 354, 361–363
technical design document structure, 363–377
technical director, 191–192, 361
technical review, 14, 167–168, 229, 361
technical specification, 167. *See also* technical
  design document
technology, 225, 339–340, 532
technology tree, 339
telephone. *See* mobile phones
television, 34, 142, 143, 430, 443, 651–652
Tennis for Two, 33
Terraformers, 470
terrain, 330, 368, 591
terrain editor, 412
tesselation, 450
test bed model, 574
test plan, 612
testers, 163, 627, 693, 700. *See also* career in
  game industry
testing, 16, 414, 416–420, 462, 590, 606, 607,
  612–617
testing for job applicants, 706
Tetris, 7, 43, 61, 104
texels (texture element), 429, 455
text, 372, 383–384, 481, 531
text-based adventures, 74–75
texture mapping, 429
texture swamping, 455

textures, 211, 372, 402, 434–435, 454–456
theme games, 22
Theodosius (Roman emperor), 20
Thief, 73, 542
third-party developers, 38, 40–41, 193, 229, 236,
  578, 609, 669, 683–687
third-person shooter games, 68, 73
The Thirty-Six Dramatic Situations (Polti), 557
three-click approach, in interface design, 504
three-dimensional. *See* 3D . . .
Tiberian Sun, 88
tic-tac-toe, 25, 536
TIFF (tagged image file format), 431
Tiger Gizmondo, 52, 129, 147
Tiger Wood's PGA Tour 2000, 110
tile editor, 396
tile sets, 171, 441, 442, 590–591, 592
time, 461, 608–609
Time Crisis, 62
time management, 609, 700
time wasters, 102
time zones, and schedule, 216
title page, for game design document, 316, 317
title screen, 383, 503–504
Toastmasters International, 288–289
Tokamak, 362, 403
Tokyo Engineering Company, 32
Tokyo Game Show, 645
Tolkien, J. R. R., 29
Tomb Raider, 73, 556
Tony Hawk's Pro Skater, 111
Tony Hawk's skateboarding series, 144
tools programmer, 201–202
toon shading, 454
Top Angler: Real Bass Fishing, 111
top-down games, 438, 440
top performing games, in marketing analysis, 300
Total Annihilation, 88
total conversion, 415
track role-playing games, 80
trackball, 63
tracking, technical design document on, 370
trade shows, 644–645
Tramiel, Jack, 41
transformed polygon, 450
transition, between animation sets, 438
translucency, 445
Transmission Control Protocol/Internet Protocol
  (TCP/IP), 373–374, 408
Transparency, 430, 445–446
triple-A game, 14
Trivial Pursuit, 27, 31, 102, 103
Trubshaw, Roy, 36
TSR Hobbies, 29
TurboGrafx-16, 43
turn-based games, 341
turnaround, 380
turning point, 550
Tutankhamen, game in tomb of, 21
tutorial, 267, 504–505
twelve-lined game (*Ludus Duodecim Scriptorum*),
  24–25
two-dimensional. *See* 2D . . .

U
U and V coordinates, 434–435, 454
UDP/IP (User Datagram Protocol/Internet
  Protocol), 373–374
Ukagi Matome, 87
Ultima, 80, 548
Ultima Online, 48, 83, 137

Ultima Underworld, 82
Ultra Assault, 579
umbra, 457
underdesign, problems from, 269
underselling, 640
unique selling points (USPs), 642
unit chart, for war games, 533
University of Southern California, 696
Uno, 31
Unreal Engine (Epic Games), 169, 172, 201, 362
Unreal Level Editor, 594
Unreal Tournament, 72, 435, 676
updates, 418
Ur (Sumerian city), 21
User Datagram Protocol/Internet Protocol
    (UDP/IP), 373–374, 408
user interface, 175–176, 196, 267–268, 295–296,
    323, 350, 376, 383, 435–436, 479–480, 495,
    497–501, 515–518. *See also* in-game interface;
    shell interface

V

values, balance in, 604–605
Valve Corporation, Steam network, 674, 675
Valve Hammer Editor, 449
Vampire: The Masquerade-Bloodline, 80
vaporware, 640
vector, 525
vector images, 431
vehicle games, 84, 93–99, 257–258, 262, 286,
    500, 534, 539, 587
Verdu, Mike, 75
version control, 414
vertex shading, 454
vertical blanking, 444
vertical scroller, 67
vertices, 399, 450
VGA (Video Graphics Array), 44, 132, 430
vice presidents, 190
Video Age International, 652
video cards, 430
Video Computer System (VCS) from Atari, 36
video console games, 395, 503, 622
video game consoles, 5, 12, 51, 63, 68, 121,
    126–127, 138–145, 430, 500–501, 616, 669
Video Graphics Array (VGA), 44, 132, 430
video RAM, 131, 396
Video Software Dealers Association, 682
Video Software Dealers of America, 683
view-port, controls for, 509

villian, 345, 346
violence in games, 11, 45, 51, 139, 559
Virtua Fighter, 65
Virtual Fighter 3, 48
virtual memory, 45
virtual reality, 135
Virtual Sailor, 98
VisiCalc (spreadsheet program), 36
Visual Build Professional (Kinook Software), 416
visual disabilities, game for player with, 470
Vodafone KK, 151
voiceovers, 298, 343, 481–486, 487–488
voices of players, 481–488
volatility of RAM, 131
volumetric fogging, 457
Voodoo Castle, 75
VR Powerboat Racing, 97

W

walk cycles, 433, 438, 448
wallpapering, 429
war games, 84–87, 312, 533–534, 605
Warcraft, 88
Warcraft III, 593
Warhol, Dave, 214
Warlord IV, 593
Warlords 4: Heroes of Etheria, 514
Warlords Battlecry, 570
warm-up exercises, for brainstorming, 281–282
Warner Communications, 35, 40, 41
warping, 375
Wasteland, 80
water movement, 397
Watson, Thomas, Jr., 33
Wave Race, 97
Waveform Audio (WAV) file format, 473, 480
WCW Nitro, 110
weapons, in technical design document, 368
web sites, 102, 422, 702. *See also* Internet; intranet
wei-qi (Go; I-go), 23–24
Wells, H. G., "Little Wars", 28
Westwood Studio, *Blade Runner*, 78
Who Wants to Be a Millionaire, 103
wholesale price, 235
widgets, 499
Wii (Nintendo), 51
WildTangent, 422
Williams, Ken, 38, 75
Williams, Roberta, 38, 75
Wilmunder, Aric, 76

WIMP (windows, icons, menus, pointers)
    concept, 496
window, 203, 513–515
Windows (Microsoft), 45, 48, 395
Windows XP (Microsoft), 51
Wing Commander, 99
Wing Commander III: Heart of the Tiger, 100
Wing Commander IV: The Price of Freedom, 100
Wing Commander: Prophecy, 100
Winter Olympics: Lillehammer '94, 111
wire-frame, 70
Wizardry, 80, 548
Wizards of the Coast, 29, 31
WMF (Windows metafile) file format, 431
Wolfenstein, 70
Woolley, Sir Leonard, 21
word games, 102
Word Search Mania, 102
word size, 142
work ethic, 700
work for hire, 479
workstations, synchronization of time
    and date, 461
world geometry editor, 412
World of Warcraft, 52, 83, 130, 205, 409, 676
worlds, game design document description, 347
Wozniak, Steve, 36, 126
writing habit, 278
writing skills, 699

X

X-COM UFO Defense, 85
Xbox, 120, 122, 140, 144, 670, 672
Xbox 360, 140
Xerox PARC (Palo Alto Research Center), 496
Xevious, 67
Xie Zhaozhi, *Wazazu*, 535

Y

Yahtzee, 27
Yamauchi, Fusajiro, 28
You Don't Know Jack, 61, 103
Yu-Gi-Oh! (Konami), 29

Z

Z-buffering, 459, 593
Zaxxon, 68
Ziff Davis Media, 652
Zoo Tycoon 2, 170
Zork I, 36, 75, 548